10

LEFT BACK
RAB BUTLER

CENTRE HALF-BACK
SELWYN LLOYD

LEFT HALF-BACK
REG MAUDLING

CENTRE FORWARD
ERNIE MARPLES

INSIDE LEFT
R.A BUTLER

OUTSIDE LEFT
IAIN MACLEOD

AS USUAL READY FOR ALL EVENTUALITIES

THE MACMILLAN YEARS
1957–1963

THE MACMILLAN YEARS

1957–1963

The Emerging Truth

RICHARD LAMB

JOHN MURRAY
Albemarle Street, London

First published in 1995
by John Murray (Publishers) Ltd,
50 Albemarle Street, London W1X 4BD

The moral right of the author has been asserted

A catalogue record for this book is available from the British Library

ISBN 0-7195-5392 X

Typeset in 12/12½ pt Bembo by Colset Private Ltd, Singapore

Printed and bound in Great Britain by The University Press, Cambridge

Contents

Illustrations		vii
Acknowledgements		ix
	Introduction	1
1.	Mending Bridges with Ike	17
2.	Vote-winning Budgets	45
3.	The 1959 General Election	58
4.	Economic Policy 1960	64
5.	Selwyn Lloyd as Chancellor	69
6.	Macmillan's Last Chancellor	87
7.	EFTA of the Seventeen	102
8.	EFTA of the Seven	126
9.	EEC Negotiations	158
10.	After the Veto	204
11.	Kenya	221
12.	Wind of Change	231
13.	The End of Federation	266
14.	Defence	282
15.	Khrushchev and the West	322
16.	The Far East	377
17.	Home Affairs	407
18.	A Bad Year	443
	Notes	502
	Bibliography	516
	Appendix: The Macmillan Cabinets	519
	Index	525

Illustrations

(*between pages 244 and 245*)

1. Macmillan campaigning in the 1959 General Election
2. With Eisenhower in 1958
3. With Khrushchev in the same year
4. Peter Thorneycroft, Chancellor of the Exchequer 1957–8
5. Derick Heathcoat Amory, Chancellor 1958–60
6. Selwyn Lloyd, Chancellor 1960–2
7. Reginald Maudling, Macmillan's last Chancellor
8. Edward Heath, in the course of EEC negotiations
9. Macmillan with de Gaulle before the 1963 French veto
10. Duncan Sandys, Commonwealth Relations Secretary during the 'wind of change'
11. Iain Macleod and Reginald Maudling, successive Colonial Secretaries
12. Roy Welensky, Prime Minister of the Central African Federation
13. Lord Devlin, who reported on the Nyasaland disturbances
14. Dr Hastings Banda, Nyasaland nationalist leader
15. Jomo Kenyatta, Kenyan leader
16. Rab Butler, who disentangled the problems of Africanization
17. Khrushchev at the time of the Berlin and Cuban crises
18. Macmillan with Kennedy
19. Jack Profumo, Secretary of State for War
20. Christine Keeler, whose affair with Profumo led to his resignation
21. Lord Denning, who reported on the security aspects of the Profumo case
22. Alec Home, Macmillan's successor as Prime Minister
23. Reginald Maudling, Quintin Hailsham and Rab Butler, Home's unsuccessful rivals

Endpapers: Cartoon by Vicky, 'Whitehall blacklegs united – as usual ready for all eventualities', *Evening Standard*, 19 January 1961 (Centre for the Study of Cartoons and Caricature, University of Kent, Canterbury)

The author and publishers are grateful to Lady Butler for permission to reproduce Plate 16; to the Hulton Picture Library for Plates 1, 2, 3, 7, 8, 10, 11, 17, 18, 19, 22 and 23; to Topham Picture Source for Plates 4, 5, 6, 9, 12, 13, 14, 15, 20 and 21; and to John Appleton, Solo Syndication and Literary Agency, for the endpapers.

Acknowledgements

THIS BOOK IS based largely upon government archives recently released in the Public Record Office; many are hitherto unknown and may cause accepted views to be revised. I give my warm thanks to the staff of the Public Record Office for their unfailing help and courtesy.

Under the Waldegrave initiative a considerable number of closed documents in the PRO have been released to me, and I thank for their help in this field in particular Pat Andrews and Richard Ponman of the Cabinet Office Historical and Records Section; Barbara Bagden of the Treasury Departmental Records Office; Irene Cummings, Foreign and Colonial Office Records Branch, and Patricia West, Department of Trade Records Office.

I am most grateful to the Librarian and staff of the London Library; Chatham House Library; the Royal United Services Institute Library; the City of Westminster Library, and the Wiltshire County Library. In the USA I give thanks to the staff of the Kennedy Centre, Boston, Massachusetts, and the Eisenhower Library, Abilene, Kansas. I am indebted to Clare Brown, Rhodes House archivist, for valuable help over previously closed documents about the Devlin Commission which were made available to me on the authority of my old friend Sir Edgar Williams, former Warden of Rhodes House and the only surviving member of the Devlin Commission.

I am deeply grateful to the historian Dr Elizabeth Evans for her work on my behalf in the Public Record Office; without her research and help I could not have covered anything like so wide a field in the time available. Fortunately I was well informed on all that had gone before from writing *The Failure of the Eden Government*, published in 1987 and also based on the official archives.

I am most grateful to Alistair Horne, Harold Macmillan's official biographer, for his co-operation and encouragement and for allowing me to read the original Macmillan diaries for 1957–63 which are in his possession. Harold Macmillan warned Alistair Horne that his diary entries should be treated with caution because, 'written in the heat of the moment', they were not always 'factually accurate nor fair'. I have borne this much in mind in using them as historical evidence; it is clear to me that Macmillan often selected for his memoirs sections supporting the view of his conduct of the nation's affairs which he wanted to be accepted as correct history by future generations.

Sir Alec Cairncross, Sir Patrick Reilly, Sir Michael Butler, Sir David Hunt, John Pinder, Tom Sharpe QC and Dr Judith Wale have kindly read parts of the manuscript. I am deeply grateful for their valuable advice and corrections. Lord Denning has been generous with his help and hospitality and I thank him also for offering me privileged access to his closed archive on the Denning Report in the Hampshire Record Office. Piers Dixon kindly allowed me to see the papers of his father, Sir Pierson Dixon, and also some concerning his father-in-law Duncan Sandys whose biography he is writing. I thank him warmly for his help.

Sir Edward Heath, the key British statesman in the long, unsuccessful 1961–3 negotiations for British entry into the European Economic Community, has been most helpful, giving me two hours of his time to explain the background to the whole affair; I am very grateful to him. Sir Michael Franklin lent me the illuminating diary he kept during the 1961–3 EEC negotiations when he was private secretary to Christopher Soames, Minister of Agriculture; Edmund Neville-Rolfe has lent me his unpublished history of the l961–3 negotiations which he was commissioned by the Ministry of Agriculture in 1987 to write from the Ministry documents. I am very grateful to them both.

In addition I have been fortunate in that many people have generously given me the benefit of their important recollections or research about the Macmillan Government, and I particularly thank: Julian Amery; John Barnes; Harold Beeley; John Boyd-Carpenter; the late Russell Bretherton; the late Roger Bullen; McGeorge Bundy; Mollie Butler; the late Harold Caccia; Brian Cathcart; Peter Catterall; Ian Clarke; William Deedes; Lord Gladwyn; Quintin Hailsham; Nicholas Henderson; Alec Home; Richard Hornby; Donald Logan; Brian MacDermot; David Newman; Alastair Parker; Edwin Plowden; Peter Ramsbotham; Eric Roll; the late George Selkirk; Roger Sherfield; Mary Soames; the late Peter Thorneycroft; Edgar Williams; Roy Wright.

I thank the following for allowing me to quote material for which they hold the copyright: Macmillan London Limited for extracts from the Macmillan Memoirs, and Alistair Horne's *Macmillan 1957–1986*; Sidgwick & Jackson for extracts from Reginald Maudling's *Memoirs* and John Boyd-Carpenter's *Way of Life*; Jonathan Cape for extracts from *Selwyn Lloyd* by D. R. Thorpe; Unwin Hyman for extracts from *The Robert Hall Diaries* edited by Alec Cairncross; Oxford University Press for extracts from Ian Clarke's *Nuclear Diplomacy and the Special Relationship*; the *Sunday Telegraph* for an extract from an article by Lord Deedes on 2 January 1994; Andrew Roth for extracts from his *Westminster Confidential* newsletter.

Transcripts of copyright material in the Public Record Office appear by kind permission of the Controller of Her Majesty's Stationery Office.

I give warm thanks to all at John Murray for their kindness and encouragement and especially to the editors Grant McIntyre, Gail Pirkis and Howard Davies.

Finally I thank Joan Moore and John Mark for secretarial help, and also my wife for her constant support.

Broadchalke
December 1994

Introduction

THE RELEASE BY the Public Record Office on 1 January 1994 under the thirty-year rule of the final official archives relating to the Macmillan Government enables historians to write the truth. Harold Macmillan in his own memoirs put a gloss over many facets of his premiership, and he also told the tale as he wanted it to be accepted to his biographer, Alistair Horne, for the latter's highly readable official biography.

The archives show that even more than generally believed Macmillan ran his Government on the lines of an American President rather than a traditional British Prime Minister. In this he was considerably influenced by Winston Churchill's methods during the Second World War. Like American presidents Macmillan favoured the use of personal policy advisers; as a result his Principal Private Secretaries, Tim Bligh and Philip de Zulueta, played important roles in deciding government policy. Macmillan consulted Bligh on Treasury matters and de Zulueta on foreign affairs, often in preference to the Ministers responsible and their Departments; Burke Trend of the Treasury and Cabinet Offices was frequently asked for his personal view, chiefly on colonial and economic affairs. The practice must have been galling for Ministers.

Intellectually Macmillan towered head and shoulders above his Cabinet colleagues and, often mistrustful of their judgement, he insisted on full control. He worked prodigiously hard, probably partly as a means of coping with bitterness at his wife's well-known liaison with his friend Robert Boothby. There is a surprising weight of minutes and memoranda in the archives written by Macmillan himself; they show not only that he fussed greatly sometimes over small matters, and interfered continuously with his colleagues' conduct of their departmental affairs, but that he had a great command of detail and an impressive capacity to absorb at once the implications of any problems facing the Government. One fascinating comment after another by Macmillan turns up in the Prime Minister's files.

Macmillan tried hard to live up to his reputation of being 'unflappable'. Indeed in 1957 he took the resignation of his friend Lord Salisbury in his stride, and the year after was little perturbed when Peter Thorneycroft and his Treasury Ministers Nigel Birch and Enoch Powell resigned. Later however, when his Government had run into smoother waters and had a long expectation of life, and especially after his increased majority in the 1959 General Election, he showed nervousness at any likelihood of Ministerial resignations and tended to give way when Ministers took a firm stand, in sharp contrast to his attitude to Salisbury and Thorneycroft. Some of his surviving colleagues have commented to me that the strain of running the country for so many years had told on his worrying nature so that he was more temperamental in his last years in Downing Street than at the start. Probably the answer is that, philosophical at first, knowing that his administration might not last – he remarked to the Queen on kissing hands in 1957 that he could not answer for his Government lasting six weeks – he came later to think that the continuation of his premiership was essential for the well-being of the nation.

When Macmillan became Prime Minister in January 1957 Anglo-American relations were at a post-war low, with President Eisenhower and his colleagues indignant at the Suez invasion and the international uproar it had created during the crucial final days of the presidential election. Macmillan claims to have been almost immediately successful in restoring the sunny Anglo-American special relationship of the past. The archives do not support him. However within nine weeks of Macmillan attaining office Eisenhower invited Macmillan and Selwyn Lloyd, the Foreign Secretary, to a conference in Bermuda. According to Macmillan Eisenhower recalled with nostalgia their wartime days together in Algiers, but the rift over Suez was far from healed and there was tension over the British independent nuclear deterrent. The Americans were strongly opposed to Britain continuing with nuclear research while the British V bombers which would carry atom bombs were becoming obsolete, so that Britain would shortly have no means of delivering them. With reluctance the Americans allowed Britain the Thor ballistic missile without warheads, but to which British atom bombs could be attached: Thor was little use to America since its range was too restricted to reach Russia across the Atlantic. Thor was despised by the British Defence Chiefs as 'part of an inferior generation system which would soon have to be replaced', and it was already clear that the American submarine Polaris was the nuclear weapon of the future. At Bermuda the Americans had no intention of letting Britain have Polaris, although three years later at another Eisenhower–Macmillan meeting at Camp David in March 1960 America, with as much reluctance, agreed to let Britain have Skybolt (without warheads), then considered an up-to-date delivery system, as part of a bargain in which the Americans were given a Polaris base on the Clyde.

In common with other British post-war governments, including Attlee's Labour Government, the Macmillan Government believed it was important for Britain to possess an up-to-date nuclear deterrent independent of America. Their argument was that it gave Britain more influence at international conferences *vis-à-vis* the Americans and other powers. Whether it was worth while continuing with nuclear research at a crippling cost to the economy is likely to be challenged more fiercely by future generations of historians than it is currently. Even after the Clyde Polaris base had been agreed there was a bitter wrangle between the British and American governments about whether America should have the right to launch nuclear warheads from British territorial waters without the consent of the British.

In Macmillan's second year (1958) there was a degree of Anglo-US military co-operation in the Middle East – in sharp contrast to Suez in 1956 – when the overthrow of the pro-Western Government in Iraq posed a Communist threat to Lebanon and Jordan. Macmillan, although he does not disclose this in his memoirs, overplayed his hand by trying to push the Americans into adopting a large-scale military presence in Lebanon and Jordan as a shield against the spread of Communism through the Middle East. The archives disclose that Selwyn Lloyd, as Foreign Secretary, then made a startling gaffe by telling Dag Hammarskjöld, Secretary-General of the United Nations, that the British Government was eager to involve America in a military adventure in the Middle East to prove that Britain 'had been right over Suez and America wrong'. This was repeated to the American State Department and did harm. No mention is made of this in either Macmillan's memoirs or Lloyd's diaries. In personal letters to Eisenhower Macmillan emphasized the danger of the Communist threat to oil pipelines and installations and the immense economic harm that would result if they fell into Communist hands. The Americans rejected out of hand a large-scale Anglo-US military operation in the Middle East which would be tantamount to a second Suez, and only permitted a limited military presence in Lebanon, adamantly refusing to send troops into Jordan.

Throughout the period of the Macmillan Government there were running and sometimes acrimonious disputes with the USA over Far Eastern policy. During the Churchill Government, when Anthony Eden was Foreign Secretary, there had been a fierce wrangle about the Chinese offshore islands of Quemoy and Matsos which were held by Chiang Kai-shek's troops and under bombardment from Chou En-lai Communists from the nearby Chinese mainland. Eden told John Foster Dulles, the American Secretary of State, in no uncertain terms that he thought

Chiang Kai-shek should be ordered to evacuate the offshore islands, these being of no value in the defence of Formosa (Taiwan) which was eighty-five miles to the east. Eden's attitude was much resented by the Americans, but fortunately this Anglo-American quarrel dissolved temporarily in 1955 when the Chinese Communists ceased shelling the islands. However it reasserted itself in August 1958 when the Communists started shelling again: Eisenhower had declared in 1955 that the islands would be defended by US troops, and his declaration held good in 1958 (as it does today).

Macmillan was as opposed as Eden to Chiang Kai-shek maintaining a garrison in the offshore islands but he was more statesmanlike in his dealings with the Americans. In September 1958, to the horror of the British Government, Dulles escalated the crisis by giving a public warning that the USA might use atom bombs against Communist China if Quemoy or Matsos was attacked. This led to a heated correspondence between the Prime Minister and Dulles; worried at the same time by Chinese threats against Hong Kong, Macmillan succeeded in alerting the Americans to the fact that they would not have the support of either Britain or the outside world in using nuclear weapons against China. Fortunately the Anglo-American rift over the offshore islands never reached breaking point because suddenly the Chinese ceased their bombardment, and Quemoy and Matsos remain garrisoned by American and Chinese Nationalist troops to this day.

Even more serious than the rift over the offshore islands was the long-standing Anglo-American dispute over Laos. At the Geneva Conference in 1954 inspired statesmanship by Anthony Eden produced peace in Vietnam after the French had been defeated by the North Vietnamese at Dien Bien Phu; partition of Vietnam between the Communist North Vietnamese and the pro-Western South Vietnamese governments was agreed. The Americans and British then hoped that Laos and Cambodia would become buffer states on Vietnam's western frontier. However, against British wishes the Americans tried to convert Laos into a pro-Western and anti-Communist military bastion. This proved impossible, and the Chinese and North Vietnamese used Laotian territory to infiltrate large quantities of military supplies and considerable numbers of guerrilla fighters into South Vietnam. When President Eisenhower left office in March 1961 he handed on to President Kennedy what Eisenhower described as 'a dangerous mess' in Laos.

Kennedy at once sought Macmillan's help and urged the British Prime Minister to send British and Commonwealth troops to support the Americans in Laos. The British Government were opposed to this policy and did everything they could to resist it. With Dulles's departure diplomatic relations became easier but the British policy of encouraging

US military intervention in the Middle East in 1958 was now reversed in the Far East in 1961, with the Macmillan Government trying to curb rather than encourage US military action. Laos was a running sore between the Americans and British, and when Macmillan left office the dispute had not only embittered Anglo-US relations but also set the stage for the ten-year war which the Americans were to fight against the Communists in Vietnam.

In February 1959 Macmillan visited Moscow hoping to play the role of mediator between East and West. In spite of some hiccups his visit was a breakthrough in the Cold War and paved the way for an eventual détente between East and West. After Moscow Macmillan travelled to Washington where he tried to persuade Eisenhower to agree to a Summit meeting with Khrushchev. Eisenhower was unenthusiastic but invited Khrushchev to America; the visit was a partial success. Berlin was now an acute problem, and eventually Eisenhower agreed to arrange a Summit with Khrushchev in Paris in May 1960 to discuss Berlin and disarmament. Alas, this meeting proved a disaster and undid Macmillan's good work; his ambitions for world peace turned to ashes in his mouth. With strange naïvety the Americans had allowed their spy planes to fly over Russia regardless of the imminence of the Summit, and one was shot down a few days before the meeting. Macmillan recorded ruefully in his diary: 'The Summit on which I had set high hopes and for which I worked for over two years was blown up like a volcano. It was ignominious.'

When President Kennedy succeeded Eisenhower in 1961 it was difficult for Macmillan to get on terms with a younger man. Although Macmillan had visited him a few weeks previously Kennedy did not inform Macmillan in advance of his plans for a CIA landing in the Bay of Pigs in Cuba in April 1961. However in Vienna that summer Khrushchev treated Kennedy so badly that the American President was genuinely grateful for Macmillan's sympathy in London on his way home.

A further setback to Macmillan's plans for a détente with Khrushchev occurred when the Russians erected the Berlin Wall on 13 August 1961 to seal off the two halves of the city, causing monstrous damage to the interests of the citizens. In addition Russia resumed H-bomb testing and exploded one in the atmosphere on 19 August. Macmillan asked Kennedy for a fourth meeting in a year, so anxious was he for a test ban.

A Macmillan–Kennedy conference was held in Bermuda in December 1961. This produced another disappointment for Macmillan; Kennedy firmly rejected the Prime Minister's pleas not to resume American atmospheric tests and to invite Khrushchev to another Summit for the purposes of discussing disarmament and a solution to the Berlin crisis.

Kennedy discountenanced both suggestions and on 25 April 1962 the US resumed testing again in the atmosphere.

On 21 October 1962 Kennedy informed Macmillan personally that Russia was planting medium-range atomic weapon launching sites on Cuba; this put all America at risk. At this stage Macmillan had begun to doubt the existence of the special relationship, and had sent a questionnaire to the Foreign Office asking them to define it. During the week of crisis over the Russian missiles in Cuba Kennedy spoke to Macmillan each day by phone, but the records show that US policy was in no way influenced by the need for British support.

Macmillan has described the Cuba crisis as 'one of the great turning points of history'; this is correct, and when Macmillan and Kennedy met in Nassau in December 1962 Khrushchev took the opportunity to send the promising message that 'the time had come to end once and for all nuclear tests.' At last Macmillan's efforts for bans on tests were about to produce results.

In June 1963, amid great publicity, Kennedy stayed at Macmillan's private country house, Birch Grove. They agreed that there would be 'Full steam ahead with Moscow talks – Test ban to be No. 1 priority.' However Kennedy made it clear that he would not allow his visit to be used for electoral advantage as Macmillan had used Eisenhower's visit prior to the 1959 General Election. It was their seventh and last meeting.

Macmillan in his memoirs claims that the Birch Grove talks were a meeting of two statesmen's minds; this is fiction. The documents show that the US Ambassador in London had informed Kennedy in advance that Macmillan's days as Prime Minister were numbered because the Profumo scandal was bound to bring him down, and Kennedy thought that Macmillan was on his last legs. Although Kennedy appreciated the sterling work Macmillan had done in paving the way for a test ban treaty he and his advisers thought Macmillan and his Foreign Secretary, Alec Home, were 'fuddy duddy'. The archives show that the American delegation were so derogatory afterwards about the British leaders at Birch Grove that de Zulueta complained to Kennedy's adviser on foreign affairs. The Birch Grove meeting lasted barely one full day, and during that time Kennedy insisted that two sessions should be devoted, not to world affairs as Macmillan wanted, but to British Guiana where the President feared the Communist Government in this British colony close to US territory might allow the Russians to plant missile sites as on Cuba – a situation that would create grave electoral difficulties for him.

Eden as Prime Minister had been adamantly opposed to British participation in the Messina powers' plan for a united Europe of Six, which resulted in the Treaty of Rome. Macmillan had no such prejudice against the designs of the Six, but believing that the rest of Europe was still grateful for the way in which Britain had saved them from Nazi domination, he and his Cabinet never thought the Six would go entirely their own way without including Britain. This was a misjudgement. In 1957 when Macmillan entered Downing Street he could have led Britain into the Europe of the Six and been received with open arms. He and his Cabinet would not consider doing so, and the Six proceeded with their plans for a customs union and integration regardless of Britain. In retaliation the British Government embarked on protracted negotiations for a European Free Trade Area (EFTA) of Seventeen to include the block of Six. This aroused hostility against Britain from the Six, and when de Gaulle came to power in France in November 1958 he vetoed the plan. In vain Britain tried for a *modus vivendi* with the Six to prevent their customs union damaging British exports in the rapidly growing European market.

As a riposte to the EEC, EFTA of the Seven was formed in Stockholm in the summer of 1959; this provided for import tariffs to be lowered between the UK, Sweden, Norway, Austria, Switzerland, Denmark and Portugal. The motive behind Britain's participation in this plan was the search for a strong bargaining position from which to prevent the Six's discriminating further against Britain by lowering internal import tariffs. British efforts to enlist US support for an agreement between the Seven and the Six were unsuccessful. The Americans instead wanted Britain to join the Six.

During 1959 and 1960 the Macmillan Government became increasingly alarmed at being excluded by tariffs from the EEC. Tentative approaches were made to the Six about the possibility of the UK acceding to the Treaty of Rome; these aroused strong opposition from the Empire wing of the Conservative Party. Eventually in July 1961 Britain applied to accede to the Treaty of Rome and complicated negotiations followed.

All was not plain sailing with de Gaulle ruling France. He was jealous of Britain's position as a nuclear power holding an independent deterrent while France did not possess one. Only if Britain shared her nuclear know-how with France would he welcome her into the Europe of the Six. As Lord Privy Seal in charge of the entry negotiations Edward Heath became aware of de Gaulle's attitude to the nuclear deterrent, and in March 1962 wrote a key minute pointing out that the consent of France to Britain joining the Common Market would depend on whether France was allowed to become a nuclear power, and that he was alarmed that we were trying to negotiate entry into the EEC 'with all too few cards to play'. Heath must have felt then that unless de Gaulle was bribed with the promise of nuclear know-how, the negotiations would fail. Macmillan and his Foreign Secretary, Home, paid no attention to Heath's warning about the need to bribe de Gaulle. Britain could only give France nuclear know-how arising from pure British research, and in pursuance of the Americans' non-dissemination policy had promised not to give France nuclear secrets passed to Britain by the Americans. On this rock the British attempts to enter the EEC between 1961 and 1963 foundered.

In the earlier stages of these negotiations de Gaulle was probably not in a strong enough political position in France to veto British entry unilaterally, but in October and November 1962 in the French referendum and General Election the electorate rallied to him strongly and he achieved an impregnable personal ascendancy from which he could impose a personal veto regardless of the views of the other Five. Sir Pierson Dixon, British Ambassador in Paris, and also head of the delegation in Brussels which was conducting negotiations with the Six, was of the view that Britain should have accepted all the consequences of the Treaty of Rome and signed on the dotted line before the autumn elections in France made de Gaulle so powerful.

During the Brussels negotiations Britain tried for the best of both worlds by retaining cheap imports of food from the Commonwealth while gaining tariff-free access for British goods into the markets of the Six. The Six particularly resented the British effort to retain cheap food imports from the Commonwealth whilst they were formulating an agricultural policy designed to protect their own farmers but which would put up food prices in the shops.

Heath overcame many difficulties in protracted negotiations in Brussels and has told me that it is his firm view that, had it not been for de Gaulle's reservations about France being forced to remain a non-nuclear power, he could have reached final agreement at a marathon session of the Ministerial Negotiating Committee in Brussels in January 1963. However in December 1962 at Nassau President Kennedy made an offer to Macmillan to provide Britain with the latest atom bomb delivery system, the Polaris submarine; the two agreed that France should also be offered Polaris but only on condition that it was kept as part of a NATO force and that France would only be allowed to launch nuclear weapons with American consent. This was unacceptable to de Gaulle, and according to Heath Nassau so upset de Gaulle that he decided on impulse to impose a veto on Britain joining the EEC before the marathon session took place.

This was not the view of the late Sir Pierson Dixon, who has recorded that he felt by the summer of 1962 that de Gaulle had already decided to ban Britain and was seeking excuses to do so without antagonizing the other Five. Sir Patrick Reilly, who was in charge of the negotiations at the Foreign Office end, told me that in his view there was too much 'unfinished business' for Heath to have been successful in one session, and that it would have taken at least until Easter. Sir Patrick Reilly does not accept Heath's view that Nassau was the reason for de Gaulle's veto and he agrees with Dixon that de Gaulle had beforehand decided to keep Britain out. He recalls in support of his argument the way in which de Gaulle adamantly opposed any new approach when the Wilson Government tried to reopen entry negotiations in 1967.

Failure was the Government's fault. They had rejected the EEC out of hand in 1957 and should have swept Britain into Europe before de Gaulle was strong enough to prevent them. With the veto of January 1963 Britain's European policy lay in tatters; it was a blow to the prestige of the Macmillan Government from which the Conservatives did not fully recover.

Macmillan had four Chancellors of the Exchequer. The first was Peter Thorneycroft. Macmillan, who had himself been Chancellor of the Exchequer before becoming Prime Minister, wanted expansion and a give-away Budget in advance of the General Election. Thorneycroft, strongly influenced by Enoch Powell, a convinced monetarist, was too cautious for Macmillan. When with Enoch Powell and Nigel Birch, his junior Treasury Ministers, Thorneycroft resigned in January 1958 during a sterling crisis during which the Chancellor had insisted on freezing government expenditure, Macmillan skilfully covered up the dispute by claiming that Thorneycroft had resigned on a very narrow point – £50 million of economies or one per cent of national expenditure.

Heathcoat Amory, Macmillan's second Chancellor, reluctantly introduced a vote-winning pre-election Budget in April 1959, giving away £370 million in tax relief including a reduction of 9d in income tax which was the largest tax relief ever given in any Budget. With the economy buoyant and the sterling crisis out of the way Macmillan sailed to victory in the 1959 General Election.

In 1960 Amory retired and was succeeded by Selwyn Lloyd, a lawyer. Lloyd showed no enthusiasm for management of the economy, only for tax reforms; he found it difficult to cope with Macmillan's barrage of memoranda and minutes advocating alternative courses for safeguarding Britain's prosperity. Advised by the unorthodox Oxford economist Roy Harrod, Macmillan urged expansion; Lloyd with few views of his own relied on his Treasury advisers Robert Hall and Alec Cairncross, who insisted on the need for higher taxes and higher interest rates to keep inflation at bay and the pound strong. This resulted during 1960 and 1961 in lower home demand and stagnation in production, so that Macmillan, shocked also by the Conservative showing in by-elections, sacked Lloyd and one third of his Cabinet in July 1962, during the 'night of long knives'.

Reginald Maudling, the last of Macmillan's Chancellors, was the most intelligent and Macmillan enjoyed long discussions with him on the management of the economy. The archives reveal that the two had decided to float the pound, sell off the dollar portfolio and impose import controls so as to help the balance of payments and produce an election-winning Budget in 1964. The contents of these archives only released on 1 January 1994 were until now unknown.

But after Macmillan's resignation in October 1963 Maudling was so complacent that he failed to pursue the plans agreed with Macmillan, while the incoming Prime Minister, Alec Home, took little interest in the economy. Thus Macmillan's carefully laid scheme to win the 1964 General Election with a buoyant economy went astray when a balance of payments crisis hit the country in the closing week of the election campaign.

Other surprising archives show that in a desperate search for an alternative economic policy after de Gaulle's veto on EEC entry in January 1963 Macmillan insisted that the Cabinet Economic Policy Committee consider unilateral import tariff cuts (in advance of the Kennedy GATT round), and fierce action against monopolies and price rings which were raising industrial prices against the public interest. Had Macmillan continued as Prime Minister beyond October 1963 it is likely that strong action would have resulted, but when he was succeeded by Home these plans for greater price competition, like the measures to protect the balance of payments, withered on the vine.

The documents indicate that Macmillan personally spent an unexpected amount of time over colonial problems and followed the negotiations for independence extremely closely.

Cyprus, a thorn in the flesh of previous governments, was partly solved by releasing the dissident Archbishop Makarios from detention, and granting independence with provision for Turkish participation in the government of the island while retaining important British bases such as the airfield of Limassol. However it did not bring peace to this troubled island. A considerable number of the official files on Cyprus during the period of the Macmillan Government remain closed until the next century in the Public Record Office, and I have not attempted to cover the tortuous and often contradictory course of British policy towards Cyprus between 1957 and 1963.

Kenya in 1963 became the first independent member of the Commonwealth under her President Kenyatta, a charismatic figure who, like Makarios, had been kept in gaol because of his participation in terrorist activities.

The most difficult problem for the Macmillan Government was the Central African Federation (Southern and Northern Rhodesia and Nyasaland) which was obviously in great trouble and whose continued existence was in doubt. Quite astonishing are the official documents about the Devlin Enquiry into the conduct of the police during the 1959 Nyasaland state of emergency; Macmillan asked his Minister of State for the Colonies, Lord Perth, to try to persuade Lord Devlin to rewrite parts of his official report. Devlin would make little change, and in the face of his devastating criticisms the report was not accepted.

Deciding that his first Colonial Secretary, Alan Lennox-Boyd, was proceeding too slowly with Africanization, Macmillan replaced him after the 1959 General Election with the more radical Iain Macleod. Unfortunately for the Prime Minister Macleod wanted to move faster than his master. Although Macmillan rang the bell for advance with his famous 'Wind of Change' speech, he wanted full African rule to be delayed for some years mainly to pacify the strong pro-settler lobby within the Conservative Party. However after the chaos and blood bath in the Congo, the granting of independence to Tunisia by the French, and the bloodshed in Algeria, the clock could not be held back. Following a short honeymoon period Macleod and Macmillan clashed. Macleod threatened to resign three times – over the February 1961 White Paper on the future of Nyasaland, the release of Dr Hastings Banda and over the release of Kenyatta. On each occasion Macmillan yielded to his Colonial Secretary even though he had strong support for his alternative policy from senior members of the Cabinet – the Lord Chancellor Lord Kilmuir, the Foreign Secretary Alec Home and the Commonwealth Secretary Duncan Sandys – evidence of how influential Macleod was in the Conservative Party. Weakly Macmillan refused to have a showdown with his difficult Colonial Secretary and preferred to shift him sideways, but he had an equally unhappy experience with his next Colonial Secretary, Reginald Maudling, who also threatened resignation and would have brought Lord Perth, and his under-secretary, as well as Macleod out in sympathy. With difficulty Macmillan skated over these cracks in his Cabinet.

Finally Macmillan, having worried himself to distraction over Roy Welensky and his British Tory supporters, decided to entrust the resolution of the problem of the Central African Federation to Rab Butler. Once in his capable hands the smack of firm government was felt, and Butler achieved the orderly dissolution of the Federation and the creation of the two new states of Malawi and Zambia out of Northern

Rhodesia and Nyasaland. However, the intractable problem of Southern Rhodesia was left to succeeding governments to resolve since the divided Macmillan Cabinet did not give Butler a firm mandate to deal with it.

The release of official documents in the Public Record Office relating to the Profumo scandal in 1963 (some documents have been withheld) has enabled me to write the first complete account of the affair. I am much struck by the naïvety with which Martin Redmayne, the Chief Whip, John Hobson the Attorney-General, and Peter Rawlinson, Solicitor-General, accepted in January 1963 Profumo's denial that he had been intimate with Christine Keeler. Anyone knowing Jack Profumo should have found it difficult to believe that he would spend time with such a girl, let alone write her a letter beginning 'Darling', if there was no sexual relationship. Lord Denning told me that he was horrified at the way in which, late on the night of 21/22 March, Profumo was harried into rushing out a statement denying intimacy with Keeler within a few hours of allegations being made in the Commons. Lord Deedes, after the official archives were released on 1 January 1994, wrote in the *Sunday Telegraph* that he 'deplored' this hurry and the insistence by himself, the three named above and Iain Macleod, Chairman of the Conservative Party, on a rushed and immediate denial. In his autobiography Rab Butler also deplores it and records his shock and surprise that Profumo had not been given at least the weekend to consider his position and his personal statement. The clue to Profumo's strange behaviour must be his later admission to Lord Denning that he was concentrating on the security allegations, which he knew to be baseless, and this caused him to look on his adultery as a minor issue.

It was unfortunate for Macmillan that these Ministers blithely accepted Profumo's improbable denial as gospel truth. A minute on Macmillan's file on 1 February by his political secretary, John Wyndham, very much a man of the London world, should have alerted the Prime Minister at an early stage, but it did not. His Principal Private Secretary, Tim Bligh, was the first to express doubts in writing, minuting to Redmayne that he was 'disturbed' by the suggestion that Profumo had written more than one letter to Miss Keeler: 'Like the clock that strikes thirteen it is not only unsettling but casts a doubt on all that has gone before.'

It would have been much better for the Prime Minister if Bligh had then emphasized his doubts about Profumo's veracity to his master. As it was, Macmillan was caught unawares when on 4 June Profumo came clean and admitted that he had told a lie to the House of Commons. In the debate which followed it became clear that Macmillan had ignored the rumours, and he damaged his reputation by admitting he was the last to hear. This debate put Macmillan's premiership in jeopardy, and for a few days it was widely expected that he would fall and be succeeded by Reginald Maudling. Conservative MPs' resolve that it was time for him to go was expected to crystallize at a meeting of the 1922 Committee. However Derek Walker-Smith defused the situation by stating plausibly and confidently that if Macmillan resigned the Queen might not ask another Conservative to form a Government, and there would be a dissolution. The argument was nonsense but it did the trick. All depended then on the Denning Report. It was widely rumoured that Denning would name as security risks other Ministers whose sexual peccadilloes laid them open to blackmail.

In the official biography Alistair Horne discloses that Macmillan wrote in his diary that he feared Lord Denning's report would condemn 'one important Minister and one unimportant Minister', which would make his position impossible. Lord Denning in his wisdom omitted any reference to these Ministers in his published report. Had he not, it is likely the Government would have been toppled. Lord Denning told me that their conduct was 'discreditable' but did not in the event constitute 'a security risk'. His decision to omit their names can be criticized since it opened the door to blackmail. But as regards Profumo the Denning Report found that there had been no security risk as a result of his association with Keeler.

Profumo had been a friend of Stephen Ward who had introduced the Minister to Keeler and also to Captain Yevgeny Ivanov, the military attaché at the Soviet Embassy. The archives show that Macmillan came close to interfering with the course of justice when on 30 May 1963 he was informed that Stephen Ward was likely to be arrested and charged with living on immoral earnings. As he left for Scotland Macmillan instructed Bligh to suggest to Sir Joseph Simpson, the Metropolitan Police Commissioner, that the arrest of Ward might be postponed for a few days. This was an attempt to gain time for a cover-up, as Ward on arrest was likely to disclose the triangular association between Profumo, Keeler and Ivanov.

Once the Denning Report had exculpated the Government and the test ban treaty had been well received Macmillan recovered popularity, and opinion polls showed a swing back to the Conservatives in the early autumn of 1963. Suddenly on 8 October Macmillan was struck by prostate trouble. His doctor has told me that this was not serious and that Macmillan could have been well within a fortnight and able to carry on. Instead, believing he had a malignant condition, he panicked and resigned. If he had continued as Prime Minister there is every reason to believe he would have won the coming General Election for the Conservatives.

As Macmillan lay in hospital he intrigued incessantly to prevent Rab

Butler taking his place. This is inexplicable. Rather than Butler, Macmillan wanted Alec Home to be Prime Minister and his manoeuvring was successful. For the Conservatives this was a disaster. Home was well liked and had charm and sincerity, but he had not given the impression as Foreign Secretary that he understood the economic scene which was bound to be the key election issue. Nor as Prime Minister did this impression change. Butler was also popular and, unlike Home, widely acknowledged to have complete command of all the political issues. Few can doubt that with Butler as Prime Minister the Conservatives would have won the 1964 General Election which under Home they lost by only four seats.

How should Harold Macmillan be rated among Prime Ministers? He was the most interesting and intelligent of the post-war holders of that office. Future historians will probably criticize him for allowing African independence to proceed too hastily. This would be unfair. It is true that British withdrawal from Africa has in many instances led to chaos and great poverty. This was not his fault; it was the responsibility of previous British governments who shamefully neglected secondary education so that at the time of independence there were few Africans sufficiently educated to pick up the reins of government when British colonial officers left. In the early 1960s it needed another generation to produce the necessary civil servants and entrepreneurs, but the wind of change was blowing so strongly that it was impossible to halt independence.

Acceptance of the Beeching Plan for the massacre of the British railway system in 1963 has been a social and economic disaster for the British people. Yet it was also accepted as necessary by the Labour Government in 1964. Macmillan, unlike his pedestrian Transport Minister, Ernest Marples, perceived the flaws in the Beeching Plan, and in the days before he was stricken by his prostate trouble he was consulting with his favourite civil servant, Burke Trend, on how to create a complementary new plan for roads which he correctly foresaw the Beeching proposals made essential. Recently released documents contain evidence that Macmillan almost alone among Cabinet Ministers at the time saw through Beeching, and if he had continued in office he would probably have been able to mitigate some of the harmful consequences of the Beeching Plan.

I believe future generations of historians will claim that Macmillan's biggest error was his slavish devotion to the British independent nuclear deterrent despite the crippling burden on the economy, and even after it had become clear that, unless Britain defied America over the non-dissemination of nuclear know-how and shared nuclear technology with

France, there was no possibility of de Gaulle allowing Britain into the EEC.

Macmillan's attitude to the economy makes me certain that if he had had a third term as Prime Minister he would have prevented the galloping inflation of the late 1960s and 1970s and would never have acquiesced in the later Conservative monetarist policy that led to the wholesale erosion of Britain's industrial base and sky-high unemployment.

A book such as this inevitably concentrates on the problems and errors of the Government. Therefore I must record that in my view Harold Macmillan was by far the best of Britain's post-war Prime Ministers, and his administration performed considerably better than any of their successors.

CHAPTER 1

Mending Bridges with Ike

IN JULY 1956 the British and American governments made a sudden and impromptu decision to refuse finance for the Egyptian project of the Aswan Dam on the Nile. Generous funding had been promised by both governments but when the Egyptians purchased arms from the Russians and appeared likely to fall under Russian domination the financing was abruptly cancelled, to the surprise and mortification of the Egyptians.

On 26 July 1956, in retaliation for this humiliation, the Egyptian dictator Gamal Abdel Nasser announced before a huge crowd in Alexandria that he would nationalize the Suez Canal, and use Canal revenues to pay for building the Aswan Dam. Furious, the Prime Minister Anthony Eden decided that Egypt must immediately be forced by military action to give up the Canal, but his plans were checked when the Chiefs of Staff told him it would take weeks or months before such an operation would be feasible.

The Foreign Secretary Selwyn Lloyd and other government spokesmen claimed that nationalization – and the closure of the Canal that would ensue, since the Egyptians were incapable of operating it – was a grave threat to British standards of living. Such arguments were gross exaggeration and the frenzied government response was unjustified. Nevertheless public reaction in Britain persuaded Eden that the use of force to recover the Canal would not only be tolerated by the nation but would make him personally popular. However the last thing President Eisenhower wanted was a war in the Middle East during the forthcoming presidential election, and in the absence of American encouragement Eden's ardour for war waned and he began instead to look for a negotiated solution.

At the same time the British Cabinet continued to draw up contingency plans for an invasion and the installation of an alternative Egyptian Government in Cairo. In an attempt to defuse the situation, the US Secretary of State John Foster Dulles suggested to Britain on 4 September the formation of the Suez Canal Users Association (SCUA). Under this scheme shipowners using the Canal would employ their own pilots, paying their dues to SCUA, who would manage the Canal in co-operation with the Egyptian Government.

Harold Macmillan, Chancellor of the Exchequer at the time, was averse to the scheme, advising the Cabinet that a long delay in reopening the Canal would 'undermine our financial position': this despite warnings from the Treasury that the pound would be in danger if military action was taken against Egypt. In mid-September the Cabinet gave Eden a mandate for a military attack on Egypt if negotiations to form SCUA failed.

On 14 August, on Dulles's initiative, eighteen nations – users of the Canal – assembled at Lancaster House in London, and Dulles pressed Egypt to accept his plan. Nasser refused. Faced with Nasser's attempts to stir up Pan-Arabism in French Algeria and Morocco France declared itself in favour of a military assault on Suez. With the failure of the SCUA project the question was remitted to the United Nations. In New York the Foreign Secretary Selwyn Lloyd began direct talks with Dr Mohamed Fawzi, the Egyptian Foreign Secretary. With Nasser's agree-ment Fawzi indicated that Egypt would accept a compromise solution and allow a combined Egyptian and Users Association board to manage the Canal and collect the dues. This diplomatic solution was close to success in the first days of October.

Then on 13 October there was a dramatic development. Guy Mollet, the French Prime Minister, sent an urgent message to Eden saying that he wanted Albert Gazier, acting Foreign Minister (the Foreign Minister, Christian Pineau, was in New York), and General Maurice Challe, Deputy Chief of the French Air Force, to go to Chequers to talk to the Prime Minister. At Chequers the following day Gazier unfolded a plan which provided for Israel, in collusion with France and Britain, to attack Egypt. The plan was involved: the French suggested that Israel should be 'invited' to invade Egypt across the Sinai Peninsula with a promise that if it did so Britain and France would order both Israel and Egypt to withdraw their troops from the Suez Canal. Then an Anglo-French force would separate the combatants and occupy the Canal on the nominal grounds that they were saving it from the damage which would be caused by war. Faced with the possibility of the British and French obtaining possession of the Canal and thus being able to operate it regardless of Nasser, Eden immediately became enthusiastic for this secret plan and decided thereupon to settle the Suez affair by war, not diplomacy, despite the fact that Selwyn Lloyd was on the brink of agreement with Fawzi in New York.

Summoned back abruptly from New York Lloyd was sent to Sèvres near Paris to talk to the French and Israelis. At first Ben-Gurion, the Israeli leader, demurred on the grounds that Israel would be 'accepting the opprobrium of aggression followed by the ignominy of accepting an ultimatum'. However, on 24 October at Sèvres agreement was reached between the British, French and Israelis and the secret Treaty of Sèvres was signed. Israel would invade Egypt, and on the next day Britain and France would issue appeals to the Egyptian and Israeli governments to 'cease fire' and in the event of either rejecting the appeal, Anglo-French forces would occupy the Canal on 31 October. This agreement was kept secret by Eden from his main Cabinet.[1]

The Sèvres plan was duly put into operation. On 29 October Israel attacked the Canal Zone of Egypt. The Anglo-French ultimatum was issued. Israel but not Egypt accepted the ultimatum, and on 5 November Anglo-French forces landed at Port Said and overcoming slight Egyptian opposition pushed fast down the Canal.

Eden decided not to inform the Americans in advance of the planned attack on Egypt. This was to say the least tactless. His telegram announcing it arrived at the White House later than expected, so that the news first reached Eisenhower via a Press Association tape. He was shocked; engaged in the last crucial stages of his presidential campaign, he feared that the British attack on Egypt would jeopardize his chances. Although this did not turn out to be the case, the President seethed with resentment against Eden and the British Government – a feeling shared by his colleagues. Overnight the American Government became intensely anti-British. At the moment when a peaceful solution of the Canal dispute was within reach, so Foster Dulles told the British Embassy in Washington, there had been deliberate concealment by the British and the attack on Egypt 'just as the Soviet orbit was crumbling was one of the greatest tragedies for our trust in each other'. Anglo-American relations dropped to an all-time low.[2]

Then came Nemesis. In the face of what was accounted unprovoked aggression against Egypt – so Pierson Dixon, the British Ambassador to the United Nations, reported – world opinion had turned against France and Britain, and unless the invasion was halted, the Arab/Asians and the Soviet bloc in the Assembly of the United Nations would rush through an emergency motion urging collective measures against the two European powers. There was no chance, Dixon added, of Britain being able to move towards her objectives without alienating the whole world including the United States.[3]

The next day, 6 November, little over twenty-four hours after the landing, Eden and his Cabinet panicked. According to Macmillan the Americans were selling sterling viciously and there was a deadly danger of a panic devaluation of the pound, British reserves not being adequate to prop the pound up against such heavy American selling. A forced devaluation, so Macmillan reported, would mean the collapse of the sterling area with unforeseeable consequences for world trade. He was adamant that the fighting must stop; for Eden the threat of an adverse resolution by the United Nations Assembly was the key factor. The Cabinet also feared a Soviet invasion of Syria or some other part of the Middle East.

Without consulting with the French the Cabinet decided to abandon the campaign. Prime Minister Mollet was furious when Eden telephoned the news to him, but so enthusiastic were Pineau and other members of the French cabinet to overthrow Nasser and stop his encouragement of rebellion in Algeria that they wanted to continue the attack without Britain. A stormy second French cabinet meeting agreed to the cease-fire but Anglo-French friendship had been shattered.[4]

On 7 November the General Assembly of the United Nations passed a resolution calling for the immediate withdrawal of British, French and Israeli troops from Egyptian soil. Eden refused to comply; he insisted that British salvage ships should clear the Canal speedily,* and wanted to use British and French possession of twenty-three miles of the Canal as a bargaining counter with Nasser so as to obtain better terms from him for the future operation of the Canal. Nasser however refused categorically to discuss the future of the Canal until Britain and France had withdrawn.

Meanwhile the Americans, in revenge for Britain risking a Middle East war at a crucial moment in Eisenhower's presidential election campaign, continued to attack the pound and refused to sell oil to Britain. Incredible to relate, the Americans not only refused to support sterling, but they deliberately drove it down by selling pounds regardless of the effect of this action on the stability of world trade. The much prized special relationship between Britain and the United States had ceased to exist. With the Suez Canal closed and several Middle East oil pipelines out of action the Americans' refusal to sell oil to Britain was a deadly blow, aimed deliberately at embarrassing the British economy so as to force Britain to withdraw from Port Said.

On doctor's orders Eden left for a long convalescence in Jamaica to recuperate from the strain of the Suez war which together with recurrent high fevers had put him in a bad way. Rab Butler, Deputy Prime Minister, took over what he described as 'the odious duty of with-drawing the troops, re-establishing the pound, salvaging our relations with the US and the UN', besides bearing the brunt of the general criticism from Conservative MPs and the general public over the Suez fiasco. He came in for much public criticism as acting head of government.[5]

---

* The Egyptians had sunk block ships in the Canal at the start of the Anglo-French invasion to prevent it being used without their co-operation.

However it was Macmillan, not Butler, who became the key figure in London during Eden's absence. According to Eden's official biographer many thought he was making a deliberate bid for the leadership. At a crucial Cabinet meeting on 21 November, held in Eden's absence, Macmillan solemnly warned his colleagues that they had to face the grave choice of deciding 'whether to mobilize all our financial resources to defend the pound, including the compulsory purchase of privately owned foreign stocks or floating the pound'. According to Macmillan if the pound floated it might cease to be an international currency, and this would lead to the dissolution of the sterling area. (He omitted to say that such consequences were far from certain and a matter of controversy.) He clinched his argument with the assertion that to float 'would be a severe blow to the prestige of the United Kingdom and a major victory for the Soviet Union and must entail almost as great a demand on our reserves as the maintenance of a fixed rate'; assistance from the US could not be expected until the situation in Egypt had been resolved.[6]

In charge of the US Treasury was Senator George Humphrey whom Macmillan considered a personal friend. Humphrey however did not behave like a friend. In response to an emotional letter from Macmillan pointing out that sterling was being undermined and begging for US support, Humphrey was unhelpful. Seldom can Anglo-American exchanges between two heads of Treasury have been so prickly. Humphrey told Sir Harold Caccia, British Ambassador in Washington:

> In the eyes of the world Egypt had been invaded by us, and as long as she remained occupied she would have world sympathy and United States support. If the United Kingdom by remaining in Port Said appeared to exert force over negotiations in clearing the Canal or the settlement of the future regime for the Canal the world would never believe that these negotiations were not held at gun point.

More than once, so Caccia reported, Humphrey had compared the United Kingdom to an armed burglar who had climbed in through the window while Nasser was the householder in his nightshirt appealing for protection. According to another message from Caccia:

> Evidence is accumulating that Mr Humphrey is the most intransigent member of the Administration about our actions at Suez, and he is most vindictive. This may stem in a large part from his belief that we went into Suez without due thought for the economic consequences of our action and that these consequences will almost certainly lead to demands on the United States which will seriously affect his already precariously balanced budget. This, as you know, is an absolute fetish with him.

As a final ignominy for the Eden Government, on 24 November the

General Assembly passed a resolution censuring Britain and France. For the British Lloyd promised to withdraw within four weeks, as did the French, but neither agreed to 'unconditional withdrawal'. Headlines announcing the censure motion and the promise to withdraw were splashed across the British national newspapers, and Conservative popularity plummeted. From New York Lloyd reported:

> The hard core of [American] policy makers, some of whom have been strongly pro-British in the past, are now against us. This will continue until we have made what they would regard as the *amende honorable* by rapid withdrawal. Their feeling is that we have to purge our contempt of the President in some way ... If we are going to have a difficulty with the [Conservative] Party over announcing withdrawal I think we may have to tell selected individuals that the Americans have no intention of lifting a finger to preserve us from financial disaster until they are certain that we are removing ourselves from Port Said quickly ... They are temporarily beyond the bounds of reason.

Caccia and Dixon endorsed Lloyd's view. Caccia commented: 'We have passed the point where we are talking to friends,' while Dixon wrote: 'The past weeks have shown that those directing United States policy are impervious to arguments and appeals to sentimental ties.' The US still refused to sell oil to the UK. With trade in Middle Eastern oil disrupted by the Suez war this was a serious blow.[7]

On 29 November Macmillan, armed with devastating Treasury warnings about the danger of a forced devaluation of the pound, precipitated the Cabinet into acceptance of 'unconditional withdrawal' – to the consternation of some of his colleagues who feared this would split the Conservative Party. It was decided that Lloyd, not Butler or Macmillan, should announce this to the Commons, and a formula was concocted in an effort to appease dissident Conservative MPs. This formula included the words that the Suez operation had been so successful that British and French troops could now be withdrawn because 'we were satisfied with the size of the UN force'. This could not be sustained; during the debate on 3 December, Aneurin Bevan for the Opposition summarized the Conservative humiliation by saying: 'We sympathize with the Right Hon. and learned gentleman in having to sound the bugle of advance to cover his retreat.'

Following the Cabinet decision Butler telephoned Humphrey to advise him that Britain would capitulate. Almost incredibly Humphrey refused to accept Butler's promise at its face value, and demanded a firm date for total evacuation. However after Lloyd's statement in the Commons on 3 December Humphrey's doubts were overcome and the US supported an application from Britain for a large drawing from the International Monetary Fund to support the pound.

From Jamaica Eden objected strongly to withdrawal. Macmillan and Butler ignored his objections, treating him, so Eden's official biographer writes, 'as a retired Prime Minister'. Clearance of the Canal was put in the hands of the UN who refused Anglo-French co-operation when Nasser objected to the presence of their salvage ships. Nasser was triumphant, claiming total victory for his army over Israeli, French and British forces who had been forced to an ignominious retreat, while the UN force and salvage fleet were present in the Canal Zone only thanks to Egyptian goodwill towards the rest of the world.

Had Butler and Macmillan kept Eden properly informed of events the Prime Minister would probably have returned to London earlier. On 3 December he asked Butler if the Cabinet wished him to come home, but this was the last thing Macmillan and Butler wanted while they were busy tearing up his policy. Butler replied: 'We conclude you should not interrupt your rest.' Both Butler and Macmillan wanted Eden out of the way until the Commons had approved surrender; once home they feared the Prime Minister might dig his toes in and refuse to capitulate to the Americans over withdrawal.

On 14 December Eden flew into London looking well. He believed he was completely cured and fully intended to continue as Prime Minister. But in his absence strange telephone calls had taken place between Macmillan, Butler and Eisenhower which indicated that the Americans would be far more co-operative in supporting sterling if Eden was replaced by one of the other two. Macmillan recorded in his diary that there was 'a general acceptance that the Government could not go on. As soon as Parliament met it would be in trouble, in a few weeks it would fall.'

When Eden had left London on 22 November the Suez action had been popular and the Conservatives had increased their support in the opinion polls since the outbreak of war. By mid-December, as Eden set up shop again in Downing Street, the nation had come to realize that the Suez operation, mounted at vast expense and costing the lives of British servicemen, had been a gigantic failure with no compensating gain; rather it had aroused much ill-will abroad. Rumours too had gained currency of the secret Treaty of Sèvres and of collusion with Israel – about which Eden had prevaricated.

Conscious of his popularity when he had left for Bermuda, Eden was appalled at his cold reception on his return. Lord Salisbury, President of the Council and influential member of the Conservative Party, and Butler, the acting Premier, told him that unless his health was restored by Easter they felt a new head of government was required: they and the rest of the Cabinet intended to make Eden the scapegoat for Suez and the unpopularity of the Conservative Party.

On 18 and 20 December Eden spoke in the Commons and to the Conservative 1922 back-benchers Committee. He misjudged the feeling of disappointment over unconditional withdrawal from the Canal, and continued to maintain falsely before the 1922 Committee that there had been no collusion with Israel. (Of course if he had told the truth it might have imperilled the lives of British servicemen still in Egypt.)

On 23 December a telegram came from Dixon saying that Egypt was preparing claims for damage to the Canal and Egyptian property arising out of the war, and was drawing up a draft resolution for the UN Assembly requiring an 'investigator' to be appointed who was mutually acceptable to Britain, France and Egypt, to assess claims. Britain, of course, had a large counter-claim against Egypt for sequestration of British property in Egypt, and Dixon proposed 'a mutual waiver of claims ... If the value of British property in Egypt is as great as I understand, the balance might be in our favour.'

The head of the Foreign Office, Ivone Kirkpatrick, reported to Eden that he feared the UN Assembly might pass a resolution requiring Britain to pay £300 million. Eden minuted plaintively: 'Surely we are not going to pay the Egyptians on top of all.' It was a low moment for the Prime Minister, and probably even worse for him was the news that despite an understanding between Fawzi and the UN Secretary-General Dag Hammarskjöld to the contrary, Nasser would still not allow British salvage ships to help to clear the Canal south of Port Said 'under any circumstances'. At a weekend meeting at Chequers Eden and his Ministers agreed they could not run the risk 'of losing our salvage fleet to the Egyptians, nor of being compelled to withdraw it by force'. They decided to order out the salvage fleet. This, coupled with the threat of having to pay damages, was a final humiliation for Eden.[8]

Convinced now that Butler and Macmillan were disloyal and unlikely to co-operate with him in the future, Eden felt his authority at risk. This, combined with renewed concern over his health, made him decide to resign on 9 January 1957. The newspapers forecast Butler to succeed. They were wrong. Lord Salisbury and Lord Kilmuir polled the Conservative MPs and there was a substantial majority for Macmillan.

Harold Macmillan's promotion from Chancellor of the Exchequer to Prime Minister in January 1957 was unexpected. Rab Butler had acted as Deputy Prime Minister during Eden's convalescence in Bermuda and was considered the natural successor. Macmillan was also known to have been an enthusiast for military action against Egypt over the nationalization of the Suez Canal – an action which by January 1957 had made Eden very unpopular. Having pushed Eden into starting the war, Macmillan within a few hours had insisted on stopping hostilities.

He deserved Harold Wilson's often-quoted criticism of being 'first in and first out'.

Macmillan prevailed over Butler not so much because of his positive support amongst Conservative MPs but because there was more opposition within the Party to Butler. Older peers and MPs remembered Butler as one of the chief appeasers of Hitler right up to the outbreak of war in 1939, when he held a key position as Under-Secretary for Foreign Affairs with the Foreign Secretary, Lord Halifax, unable to speak in the Commons. After Dunkirk in 1940 too, so Winston Churchill had let it be known, Butler had toyed with negotiating with Ribbentrop through the Swedes to end the war, and these tales were assiduously fanned by the influential Randolph Churchill who bore a dislike for Butler and did everything he could to discredit him. Randolph also alleged that Butler had been weak over Suez, disapproving of the use of force but never pressing his argument.[9]*

As one who had pushed Eden into the Suez venture Macmillan was an unworthy benefactor of the disaster. But there is never fairness or gratitude in politics. As First Lord of the Admiralty Winston Churchill was to blame for the fiasco of the Norway campaign in 1940 which was the consequence of his impetuosity and lack of judgement; yet when Chamberlain was forced to resign because of its failure, it was Churchill who became Prime Minister. Macmillan's destiny followed a similar course to Churchill's. One might have thought Macmillan's overnight switch from being the foremost protagonist of intervention at Suez to being the leading proponent of disengagement would have damaged his reputation. However he had cleverly passed the buck to Butler while the latter was deputizing for Eden.

As soon as Macmillan arrived in 10 Downing Street he instructed Guy Millard in the Foreign Office to write a report for the Cabinet on relations between the UK, France and the USA in the months following nationalization of the Canal. There was no comfort in Millard's report which stated that 'Suez had severely shaken the basis of Anglo-American relations,' and 'exposed the limitations of our strength . . . on the face of it Britain and France had nothing to compensate for political defeat of the first magnitude.'[10]

Macmillan's first priority as Prime Minister was to mend the bridges with America; those with France were temporarily past repair. He was greatly relieved when on 22 January Eisenhower suggested in a friendly manner a conference in Bermuda in March. Macmillan accepted eagerly.

Meanwhile America was proving unco-operative in the Middle East;

---

*Lord Home has written to the author: 'Rab was constantly asking us all what we thought but in the end he always supported the Prime Minister's decisions with the rest of the Cabinet.'

the United Nations were threatening sanctions against Israel if they did not evacuate the Gaza Strip and Sinai which they had occupied during the Suez war. Britain could not back Israel without enflaming the USA. In his diary Macmillan wrote: 'The Americans are behaving very weakly ... with idealism and pedantry.' Fortunately this running sore was healed when the Israelis yielded to pressure from Washington and withdrew from Gaza and their positions on the Gulf of Aqaba and allowed the UN peace-keeping force to move in.

When Macmillan with his Foreign Secretary, Selwyn Lloyd, flew to Bermuda on 20 March 1957 he was determined to revive the special relationship with America and to exploit his wartime friendship with Eisenhower to the hilt. He would not admit that the Suez failure was a turning point, and that Britain was no longer a great power in the world; nor that the refusal the previous year to send a representative to the Messina Conference of the Six which launched the Common Market meant that Britain's influence in Europe was enormously reduced while her Achilles heel had been revealed – her perpetual problem of lack of currency reserves to support the pound and the sterling area.

By far the most important proposal discussed at Bermuda was the American offer to supply Britain with a ballistic missile designed in the US with a range of 1,500 miles and equipped with nuclear warheads. This was Thor. Unaccountably Macmillan plays this down in his memoirs. To be of military use to the United States, Thor would have to be based either in the UK or in Western Europe, otherwise it would not be within striking distance of targets in the Soviet Union. The offer, although it had defects, was accepted. Agreement was also reached on the deployment of Corporal, an intermediate range ballistic missile. In a secret note signed by officials at Bermuda it was further agreed that 'We [Britain and the United States] should not assist the French plans for an atomic programme, and should keep in close touch with each other about it through diplomatic channels.' Basically the Americans did not at all like the French plans and would have liked to stop them, but they did not know how to do this effectively.

Over the subject of nuclear weapons the personal relationship between Macmillan and Eisenhower had been restored at Bermuda. But although there was closeness at the top there was antagonism within the US State and Defence Departments which did not augur well for the future. The idea of exclusivity between America and Britain over nuclear matters caused grave problems with France and, because of the hostility of US civil servants, was eventually to bring to an end Britain's special nuclear status in Washington under Eisenhower's successor, President Kennedy.[11]

At Bermuda Macmillan appealed to Eisenhower for help over the Suez

Canal: 'I hope you will do everything you possibly can . . . to get a Canal settlement, short and long – especially regarding dues – which we can claim as reasonable, if not quite what we would like . . . I hope you will denounce Nasser and all his works in the strongest terms. Bring every pressure – political and economic – upon him.' But Eisenhower was unsympathetic and recorded in his memoirs that he found it difficult to talk to Macmillan and Lloyd about Suez 'because of the blinding bitterness they felt towards Nasser'. However although Dulles told the British that he wanted Canal dues paid to an international authority, not the Egyptian Government, he took no action. In his memoirs Macmillan claims the Bermuda Conference went swimmingly and restored Anglo-American relations to their former strength. The archives do not support him.

Macmillan insisted querulously to the Americans that Nasser's proposals for reopening the Canal were 'unsatisfactory' because Egypt intended to collect the dues from the passing ships direct instead of paying them to an international body, as the United Nations Security Council had suggested in their six principles of October 1956. Although Hammarskjöld, the UN Secretary-General, was in Cairo for talks with the Egyptian Government during the Bermuda Conference, neither Eisenhower nor his Secretary of State, Foster Dulles, would put pressure on Nasser or the Security Council to ensure that SCUA or an alternative international body should collect the dues.[12]

The Suez Canal Users Association (SCUA) had been set up with US help in October of the previous year after Egypt had nationalized the Canal; it included all the nations using the Canal and, as has been seen, in November 1956 the Egyptians had been on the brink of agreeing that all dues should be paid to it by ships entering the Canal. Selwyn Lloyd had been negotiating over SCUA with Mohamed Fawzi, the Egyptian Foreign Minister, during the October 1956 session of the United Nations in New York and there is every reason to believe that the Fawzi–Lloyd talks would have solved the Suez crisis peacefully if the British Government had not impulsively decided on war. Now in 1957 only Egyptian agreement to allow SCUA to function stood between Britain and final humiliation over the Suez war.[13]

The Egyptians were in a strong position and refused to compromise over SCUA. As it became clear in March 1957 that the Canal would soon be reopened to shipping, the British Government decided to authorize British shipowners to pay in transferable sterling direct to Egypt but only 'under protest and without prejudice'. They hoped in vain that Egypt would agree to pay the dues into a suspense account for SCUA. Unfortunately in spite of US support SCUA was a dead duck.

Macmillan and Lloyd went to Paris on 9 March 1957 to discuss the imminent reopening of the Canal with the French Prime Minister, Guy Mollet, and his Foreign Minister Christian Pineau. Pineau declared that France would not pay dues to Nasser, French public opinion would not stand for it. Mollet pressed for a boycott of the Canal. Macmillan was cautious and replied that 'we would have to calculate the additional dollar cost per month of oil imports if they did not come through the Canal.' To Pineau's insistence that dues should be paid to a neutral account rather than to Egypt direct, Macmillan urged a compromise, suggesting that half the dues should be paid to Egypt.

Confirming the British refusal to take the strong line against Nasser demanded by the French, Lloyd stated that a policy of boycott by Britain and France alone would 'do us no good', while Macmillan finished the meeting by stressing that it was essential to know what the dollar cost would be of a boycott, and the worst course of all would be to start a boycott which subsequently failed. In the end the British made it clear to the French that they were in full retreat, and would have nothing to do with a boycott or a concerted effort not to pay the dues to Nasser.[14]

In a declaration issued on 15 April 1957 Egypt announced that the Canal would be open as normal, subject to the terms that the Canal would be operated and managed by the Egyptian state-owned autonomous Suez Canal Authority established in July 1956 immediately after nationalization. The declaration was only a partial acceptance by Egypt of the Suez Canal Convention of 1888. Egypt promised that tolls should not be increased by more than one per cent per annum, and that 25 per cent of all revenue would be put aside for development and capital expenditure. However, the declaration was a clear breach of the 1888 Convention in that it gave Egypt 'unfettered control' of the Canal which that convention forbade. There was also no mention of the Canal profits being taken to finance the Aswan Dam project as Nasser had originally proposed in August 1956.

The declaration made it clear that Egypt was contemplating no institutional arrangements for official co-operation with user nations, and no special provisions by which she could be made to conform to the obligations affirmed in the declaration. The arbitration tribunal for disposing of disputes was to be Egyptian and not international. However these omissions aroused no opposition from the Americans, and the declaration was accepted world-wide. The Nasser Government was thus stamped as fit to manage the Canal on its own, and this made it impossible for Britain and France to hold out.

For Britain the acceptance by America and other nations of the Egyptian declaration meant total defeat. However once Nasser had allowed the Israelis to use the Canal, the Suez issue could be buried as the Canal returned to normality. In his diary on 8 April Macmillan wrote: 'Our real problem is how to use the Canal with minimum short-term loss of face.' With Dulles's announcement that American ships would pay the dues 'on the drumhead' direct to Egypt, the British Government bowed to the inevitable. A secret meeting was held at the Ministry of Transport with Lord Simon and Colin Anderson of the inner circle of British shipowners;* they were told the British Government would withdraw their advice that British ships should not use the Canal, and that the Bank of England had come to an agreement with the Egyptians about paying in sterling. *The Times* wrote on 25 April that as the US was content 'just to let the matter slide', Britain, France and other users had to make 'the best of a bad job'. The Foreign Office comment was 'A hands down victory for Nasser of a very undesirable nature.'

A Suez debate was arranged in the Commons for 15 and 16 May. Macmillan was apprehensive, and even envisaged defeat and the collapse of his Government. He wrote to Peter Thorneycroft, Chancellor of the Exchequer, that he 'feared a large number of abstentions from our own Party on whom the fate of the Government will depend'.[15] In the debate Hugh Gaitskell, leader of the Opposition, pointed out that the terms of the Egyptian declaration were substantially worse than those offered before the war broke out; Denis Healey said that Egypt had bypassed SCUA and it was 'capitulation'. The most telling blow came from the Labour MP Emrys Hughes who declared that 'the Government was trying to gloss over the most spectacular retreat from Egypt since Moses.' There were only fourteen Conservative abstentions – all from the hard-line Suez Group (including Julian Amery and Fitzroy Maclean) who had opposed the treaty with Egypt in 1953 under which Britain had given up her large military base in the Canal Zone.

At the end of the two-day debate the Government had a poor press, but Suez slid gently out of the news, much to the relief of the Government and the benefit of the Conservative Party in the opinion polls. There were no British Cabinet resignations after the crisis although Lloyd has recorded that he wanted to go.

Guy Mollet, the French Prime Minister, showed more conscience. On 11 May 1957 he told the British Ambassador, Gladwyn Jebb, that he and Sir Anthony Eden in 1956 had declared publicly that 'they would never accept complete control by Nasser of the Canal'; he therefore felt

---

*Lord Simon was Deputy Chairman of P. & O.; Colin Anderson was Chairman of the International Chamber of Shipping.

obliged to resign in face of Nasser's complete victory although he appreciated 'the realism which inspired our present attitude'. Mollet was gentlemanly and made no criticism of Britain in his resignation speech.[16]

Happily the Eisenhower Government now considered 'stability' in the Middle East vital to US security, and under the new doctrine formulated by the State Department, American troops were to be used to defend Middle East nations against aggression whether from Egyptian Pan-Arabists or Communists. The British, much to American annoyance, tried to take this as condonation by the Americans of the Suez war.

First, in the summer of 1957 a rebellion against the rule of the Sultan of Muscat and Oman produced a fresh Anglo-US divide. Since the Eisenhower doctrine regarding the use of armed force did not apply to internal troubles, the Sultan appealed to Britain for help. The RAF carried out rocket attacks against the rebel military positions and three infantry companies were sent in, who with government troops forced the rebels back into the mountains. In the Commons the Labour Party sided with the Government, but the Americans disapproved, and in Macmillan's words 'behaved outrageously' by refusing support. The Arab League complained about this British military action to the United Nations; fortunately the Americans softened their hostility and abstained, so that the Arab motion for a UN investigation into British aggression was lost, despite Russian backing.

It took great courage on the part of the British Government to intervene in support of their Omani ally after the world-wide denigration of the Suez war and it did much to restore British prestige in the Middle East. By successfully defying charges of 'colonialism' and 'imperialism' over Oman, Britain put herself in a stronger position to protect her other allies in the Middle East, Jordan and Kuwait, by military means.

A few weeks later, Britain had overwhelming US support over the next Middle East incident, in face of a Russian effort to launch a Communist take-over of Syria. The oil pipelines from Saudi Arabia and Iraq, both of whose governments were friendly to Britain and America, flow through Syria. In this instance, unlike the Omani episode which they viewed as an internal revolt, the Americans saw the Russian threat to interfere in the internal affairs of an independent oil-exporting country as a *prima facie* case for implementing the Eisenhower doctrine. On 22 August Dulles sent a letter to London stating that if Syrian developments carried a threat to Syria's Muslim neighbours 'they would have our moral support in any defensive measure they take'. Dulles asked for Lloyd or Macmillan to come to Washington to discuss Syria. Instead Freddie Bishop, Macmillan's personal private secretary, who was friendly with

Dulles, went and found the US State Department in accord with Britain.

Lebanon warned the USA that they could not hold out against Syria without help from outside, and in September 1957 the situation was menacing and there were fears it would lead to war between America and Russia. When Selwyn Lloyd followed Bishop to Washington he and Dulles quickly reached an understanding. The US sent a large supply of arms to Jordan, arranging for the delivery to be given great publicity. Military 'contingency' planning against an escalation of the crisis began in London and Washington.

On 16 October Syria made a formal appeal to the United Nations claiming, without any real grounds, that they were under threat of an imminent Turkish attack. Dulles replied that if Russia attacked Turkey the US would not confine themselves to 'purely defensive operations'. King Ibn Saud of Saudi Arabia then offered to mediate in the Turkish-Syrian dispute. Both Syria and Turkey accepted his offer, but Russia insisted that Syria withdraw her consent. Lebanon, Iraq and Saudi Arabia declared their solidarity against Russian infiltration. Suddenly Nikita Khrushchev, the Russian leader, dissolved the crisis by stating in a speech in Russia that there was no 'threat' and the whole affair had been 'misunderstood'. Syria then withdrew her complaint from the agenda of the United Nations.

Thus Britain and America in harmony achieved a notable diplomatic success in the Middle East, and the Russian infiltration of Syria, more than the Bermuda Conference in March, was the turning point in Anglo-American relations post-Suez.

Events in the Middle East during the next year, 1958, did much to restore the special relationship. In 1955, after a tour of the Middle East, Dulles had decided that Middle Eastern countries were paying too little attention to the 'menace of Communism'; accordingly he had encouraged Anthony Eden, the British Prime Minister, to form the Baghdad Pact with a view to encircling the Russian borders with countries placed in a military alliance. As Foreign Secretary Macmillan had successfully negotiated such alliances with Turkey, Iran, Iraq and Pakistan, the countries around the Soviet southern frontiers, with the avowed intention of keeping Communism at bay. However, the Americans themselves shilly-shallied and would not join the Pact.

Macmillan was anxious that all signatories should receive weapons from Britain and America and tried hard, but in vain, to persuade America to join. From the start Nasser viewed it as a continuation of colonialism and a threat to his leadership of the Arab world and of those states now tenuously grouped together in his Arab League whose unity it threatened to split. In 1955 it appeared to be a plausible *cordon sanitaire* to restrain the Kremlin, but Macmillan in his memoirs wrote that it was arguable how far the Pact was a 'prudent move' or how far a 'hazardous adventure'. It turned out to be neither.[17]

Having declared war on Germany in 1943, Iraq remained on friendly terms with Britain after 1945 and allowed British troops to be stationed there. In following years Britain agreed with Iraq to evacuate her military bases and to leave only staging posts for the RAF, but continued to guarantee the country's defence. Iraq was governed by the young King Feisal and the veteran Prime Minister Nuri-es-Said; they were well-disposed towards Britain, although the friendship had been strained during the Suez war. In early 1958 they had formed the Hashemite Union of Iraq and Jordan in opposition to Egypt, both Jordan and Iraq being strongly opposed to Soviet infiltration and Communism, and to President Nasser's attempt to place Egypt at the head of a new supranational Arab Middle East Republic with as many Arab countries adhering as possible.

On 14 July 1958 revolutionaries led by General Qasim and a group of officers overthrew the Iraqi Government, assassinating Nuri-es-Said and the King in Baghdad. There is no evidence that the *coup* was inspired directly by Egypt. Britain and America were taken completely by surprise, but there was no question of reinstating the old anglophile regime since the revolution was the work of the Iraqi army. On 14 July the British Ambassador, Sir Michael Wright, who had narrowly escaped with his life when the Embassy was looted and burnt, asked for the British Parachute Brigade stationed in Cyprus to be sent in to protect the British and other foreign nationals in Baghdad and to safeguard the RAF staging post at the aerodrome of Habbaniya where 1,200 personnel were in danger. This request was sensibly refused. No government established with the help of British arms could have survived, although some of the Iraqi generals wedded to the old regime might have welcomed it.

For a short time Baghdad was full of emblems and photographs of Nasser. On 16 July Russia recognized the revolutionary Iraqi Government, and on 18 July Wright and the US Ambassador changed their minds and, in confirmation of London's decision not to send troops, cabled that Allied landings in Iraq would cause indiscriminate killing of British and Americans.[18]

Prior to the 14 July revolution in Iraq, Jordan and Lebanon had sought promises of military aid from Britain and America, and immediately on hearing of the *coup* President Chamoun of Lebanon and King Hussein of Jordan asked Britain and America to send troops to their countries, fearing Russian-backed attacks by the Iraqi army. On the evening of 14 July Macmillan saw Gaitskell and told him the Government were considering the request for military aid from Lebanon and Jordan. Gaitskell was co-operative.

In the spring of that year the Lebanon had found itself in turmoil and in the first weeks of May the crisis deepened. Muslims and Christians were deeply divided, as were the pro-Western and the pro-Nasser sections of the population. Although the President, Camille Chamoun, was a Maronite Christian, and his Prime Minister Sami es Solh a Sunni Muslim, they were powerless to stop fighting between government and anti-government forces. Nasser had been fomenting the trouble since the Suez war and was hoping to make Lebanon as well as Jordan part of his United Arab Republic.

Sir George Middleton, the British Ambassador in Beirut, reported that there were an estimated 6,000 to 9,000 armed rebels operating in the Lebanon and that Lebanese government troops had captured heavy mortars, sub-machine-guns and anti-tank ammunition; he thought the rebels were probably being controlled from Syria, while an extra 1,000 volunteer rebels were expected to cross into Lebanon from Syria. Unless the Lebanese Government released the army from security duties in urban areas Middleton feared that the country would be overrun by the rebels.

Requests for military assistance had been made by Chamoun to both London and Washington on 14 May. The atmosphere between the British and American governments was so improved, compared with the situation at the time of the Suez crisis two years before, that there was immediate Anglo-US co-operation. At a meeting of Ministers with the Defence Chiefs on 14 May Macmillan informed them that telegrams had been received from Washington intimating that the US Government were about to announce their support for Chamoun, offering the use of military force if necessary to preserve the independence of the Lebanon. Sir George Middleton in Beirut had been authorized to give similar British assurances. The US 6th Fleet (which had been a threat to the Franco-British invasion forces at the time of Suez) was in the Mediterranean, as were several Royal Navy ships, including one aircraft-carrier; there were British troops in Cyprus. Although for logistic reasons the British contribution must at first be the larger, Macmillan stressed that the British contribution to the whole operation was to be kept as small as possible – certainly under half the total operation. After the disaster of Suez the British Government did not want to be seen as taking the lead in military operations in the Arab world. The Prime Minister also emphasized that he wanted the task force to be under the command of the US Admiral James Holloway and not a British commander.[19]

On 11 June Nasser told the United States Ambassador in Cairo that although there was 'no truth' in allegations that Egypt had been stirring up trouble in the Lebanon he would be willing to use his influence with the rebels to bring an end to the fighting, provided that Chamoun, when his term of office as President expired, would stand down in favour of General Fuad Chebab, commander-in-chief of the Lebanese army. At first Middleton described Chebab as 'a completely broken reed', both with regard to taking active steps against the rebels and any pro-Western action, and the Ambassador even feared that Chebab might head a *coup d'état* against Chamoun. However Chebab, although he had a personal feud with Chamoun, was ardent for Lebanese independence and he reacted well after the Iraqi revolution. As President later in succession to Chamoun he carried out a reasonably pro-Western policy.[20]

Dulles told Caccia in Washington on 11 June that Nasser wanted a bargain which would include cessation on his side of propaganda against the Lebanese Government, and suspension of aid to the insurgents across the Syrian border, in return for an amnesty for the rebels. However Dulles was worried at the danger of the US being associated with any initiative by Nasser to restore peace in the Middle East since it would discourage the pro-Western regime in Iraq, and other pro-Western elements in the area. Caccia suggested that Nasser was afraid Chamoun might call on Britain and America for military assistance in accordance with our 14 May assurances, and that the Russians might have told Nasser not to allow the trouble in the Lebanon to become so serious as to lead to Anglo-American intervention 'because at all costs they wanted at present to avoid the chance of a third world war'. Joining the talk between Dulles and Caccia, President Eisenhower said he would not allow 'the United States Government to become Nasser's lackey in this matter', and they should only inform Chamoun of Nasser's approach without making any recommendation, and reiterate the American assurances of military help if required.

Selwyn Lloyd, British Foreign Secretary, then made a gaffe in conversation in London with Dag Hammarskjöld, the UN Secretary-General. Lloyd told him, so Hammarskjöld reported, that he was eager to involve America in an adventure in the Middle East to prove that he (Lloyd) had been 'right about Suez and the United States wrong'. This impression, Lloyd later assured him, was a 'grievous misunderstanding of their conversation', although 'some malicious people' had attributed this motive to him. There can be little doubt, however, that Hammarskjöld was correct: Macmillan's subsequent communications to Eisenhower show that he was hoping for a large-scale Anglo-US military operation which would amount to a second Suez. Macmillan had formed the view that if there was to be military intervention it must be on a massive scale or not at all. This was not Eisenhower's view.[21]

On the evening of the day, 14 July, when news of the revolution in Iraq was received Macmillan and Eisenhower had a long telephone conversation about the situation in Lebanon and Jordan. Macmillan urged that if the US 'did this thing in the Lebanon it might be part of a much larger operation'. Eisenhower cautiously replied: 'So far as we are concerned we cannot undertake anything beyond the Lebanon. The situation elsewhere is going to be much more complicated.' Macmillan countered:

> We have to think of the danger to the pipelines and losses we shall suffer. There is no point in running these risks unless we are going to do the whole thing together. They are all tied up together now, and if this thing is done (which I think is very noble of you) in the Lebanon – all the same it will set off a whole series of things throughout the whole area. The operation once started will have to be carried through to the end.

Eisenhower then asked if Macmillan believed that 'unless we had made up our minds to carry this thing through to the Persian Gulf we had better not start'. Macmillan replied:

> It is no good being left in that place and sitting there for a few months and the whole of the rest of this area being in flames. We have got to face it that we shall have to do the whole thing.

If it was planned to initiate a big operation that would run all the way through Syria and Iraq, Eisenhower said, 'we are thinking of decisions which are beyond anything which I have the power to do constitutionally'. Macmillan went on:

> I feel only this, my dear friend, that if you set off this great show which I think is the right course, you cannot confine it to one place. It is likely that the trouble will destroy the oilfields and the pipeline and all the rest of it, and will blaze right through. We shall have to go through with it. We may well be ruined. It is not much fun getting nothing back. But I am all for it if we are determined to see it through.*

Macmillan followed up his provocative telephone call with a letter to Eisenhower the next day. Not surprisingly his memoirs fudge the bellicosity of both the phone call and the letter; the tone of the letter

---

* In his memoirs Macmillan claims that during this conversation he told Eisenhower, 'You are doing a Suez on me,' and Eisenhower was 'amused'. This is not mentioned in the official record of the conversation and it is unlikely that Eisenhower would have been amused if Macmillan actually made this remark.

makes it clear that Lloyd was echoing what was in Macmillan's mind when he spoke to Hammarskjöld of Britain being eager to get America into 'a major adventure in the Middle East'.

> What I was trying to say on the telephone was that the action you contemplate must necessarily have great repercussions. It will set off a lot of trouble. The installations at Tripoli [the Lebanese port] cannot be immediately protected and will probably be destroyed, and all the pipelines through Syria will be cut. There may also be attacks on other oil installations throughout the whole area all of which will inflict great loss upon the international companies and particularly upon us who depend on sterling oil. I have talked this over with my colleagues who are quite prepared to face these risks if it is part of a determination between us both to face the issues and be prepared to protect Jordan with the hope of restoring the situation in Iraq. Now Lebanon is only part of a much wider crisis. But if you decide to go into the Lebanon realizing all that is involved we will give you every support.

Later that evening a telegram came from the King of Jordan specifically asking for an assurance from Britain and America that 'we will come to his assistance militarily if he thinks this necessary to preserve the integrity and independence of Jordan.' The Prime Minister cabled to Eisenhower: 'I very much hope that you will agree we both ought to give this assistance at once,' adding, 'If we are asked to send British forces we should use for this purpose the forces now earmarked for the Lebanon.' Eisenhower at once sent US troops into Lebanon but not into Jordan.

The next evening (15/16 July) Lord Hood, British Chargé d'Affaires in Washington, telephoned the Prime Minister saying that Mr Dulles had sent King Hussein a holding reply and wanted the British Foreign Secretary to go to Washington urgently to discuss matters.* Macmillan asked Hood what he thought would be the American reaction to a British holding operation in Jordan because while they were discussing 'the larger matter [a combined US-UK task force in the Middle East] Jordan might fall, and then it would be impossible to do anything about Iraq'. Hood told the Prime Minister that the Americans were very satisfied with their landing in Lebanon which had gone well. Were the Americans friendly, Macmillan then asked, and had they minded his 'frankness' in putting his problems and difficulties in his phone call and cable to the President? They were 'very friendly', Hood replied.

---

* Dulles told Hood that King Hussein's request was new and unexpected; he had no idea what US forces could be made available, and wondered whether US-UK intervention would strengthen the King's position, since it might alienate his remaining support.

Macmillan then revealed his true feelings about the crisis, telling Hood on the telephone at midnight on 15 July, according to the record:

> There was a great burden on the UK. There was already pressure on the pound which meant a lot of money being spent to maintain its value. The pipelines had not yet been cut but they might be. The UK had more at stake than the US. He hoped the US Government understood this.

The Prime Minister's alarmist view was not shared by the Americans.

Following King Hussein's pleas to Britain and America for immediate military aid, Macmillan telephoned Dulles who would not promise troops for Jordan, but only 'moral and logistic support'. At a Cabinet meeting hastily called late in the evening of 15 July, Macmillan put it to his Ministers that immediate intervention in Jordan was advisable; the airfield at Amman might otherwise fall into the hands of insurgents, and with Hussein unable to resist, Jordan would drop into the orbit of Nasser's United Arab Republic. The Cabinet agreed unanimously, and 2 Parachute Brigade from Cyprus was flown immediately to Jordan. There was a minor hiccup because they had to overfly Israel and in the confusion of the hurried decision permission had not been obtained so that the usually friendly Israeli Prime Minister, Ben-Gurion, protested vigorously from Tel Aviv.[22]

In the debate in the Commons on 17 July the Opposition were divided over whether or not to approve the Jordan military operation. The Liberals voted against the Government but some Labour members, notably George Brown, abstained and Macmillan was loudly applauded as he left the Chamber by all the Conservative and some Labour MPs.

Eisenhower would have nothing to do with Macmillan's plan for a 'great show', a combined British-American operation based on the Lebanon with the aim of overrunning Syria and restoring a pro-Western government in Iraq. It must have appeared too like Suez for the Americans, and the world should be grateful to Eisenhower for snubbing Macmillan over this wild project which could have led to a third world war, and would certainly have produced a serious long-term breach with Nasser.

On 17 July Middleton from the Lebanon reported that

> The American build-up amounted to almost 20,000 troops, and at the same time [Robert] Murphy [US Middle East Adviser] and the American Ambassador are entirely without political directives and are in the dark as to whether this massive concentration is intended purely for psychological effect on the political front or presages an agreed plan for more extended military action ... We appear to be conducting two disconnected operations in Lebanon and Jordan and to have no conception of our ultimate objectives.[23]

The problem was that Macmillan wanted a permanent military presence in the Lebanon and Jordan but the Americans did not, and all the British efforts to push America into a Suez-type operation in these countries came to nothing. The US State Department was too wary of the dangers of a permanent military presence in the Middle East.

On Iraq Macmillan received a reassuring brief on 19 July from Sir Frederick Hoyer Millar, who had replaced Kirkpatrick as Permanent Under-Secretary at the Foreign Office and kept in close touch with the British Ambassadors in the Middle East:

> The rebels seem to be far from certain of themselves and anxious to be friends with us. They are probably apprehensive of an attack from Jordan. But they recognize some genuine community of interest. In conversation with a member of the Embassy the Finance Minister said their policy was friendly relations particularly with Arab States but including the West; respect for UN; continuation of the flow of oil without nationalization although seeking higher prices. No decision reached yet about the Baghdad Pact. He thought it unlikely that Iraq would remain a member until period of peace expired and then review the position. She would *not* join the United Arab Republic.
>
> We have to deal with a group of young enthusiasts who are all unsure of themselves and do not know where they are going. They are certainly inspired by raw nationalism and are probably admirers of Nasser ... Perhaps they offer us another chance of coming to terms with the youthful Arab nationalism which has so far been consistently on the other side. It may not be easy to recognize the new regime. It will certainly offend King Hussein and the Jordan Government and might well cause great bitterness among other friends in the Middle East.

Sir Michael Wright, the Ambassador in Baghdad, reported that the new Ministers were 'personally' very friendly and wanted to maintain the traditional good relations with Britain despite Baghdad's current cult of Nasser; 'they are sorry that Communist countries had recognized them and not Great Britain.' However, he added, their overwhelming fear 'is that Hussein may attack them with British support'. Wright advised recognition.[24]

Arrived in Washington at Dulles's request, Lloyd was soon agreeing that it was 'out of the question' to mount a military operation to unseat the rebel regime in Iraq. Macmillan reluctantly acquiesced and admitted defeat in his effort to persuade Eisenhower to 'do the whole thing' and mount a Suez-type operation in the Middle East. However on 19 July Macmillan sent a message to Lloyd in Washington: 'The essential thing is that the United States should not be jostled or pressurized out of Lebanon as we were out of Suez.'

Told by the Americans that the Turks intended to invade Iraq, Lloyd cabled to Macmillan that 'this would be folly because it would give the Soviet an excuse to send in troops following an invitation from the Iraq Government.' Macmillan minuted on this message: 'An attack on Iraq by Turkey would be criminal folly; we would lose our oil supplies. The first statements of the new Iraq junta [Qasim's Government] are not discouraging.' In a cable to Lloyd in Washington Macmillan wrote: 'Iraq may turn out to be more nationalist than Nasserite. They have made quite a good statement on oil. They might even wish to stay in the Baghdad Pact.' Why Macmillan thought an Anglo-US attack on Iraq would not also have been 'criminal folly' and might result in Qasim asking Russia for troops is unclear. Anyway faced with American intransigence Macmillan gave up all hope of toppling Qasim; the reassuring views of Hoyer Millar and Wright prevailed, and his panic prediction that the oil pipelines would be cut proved groundless.[25]

Eisenhower refused adamantly to allow US troops to go to Jordan. Within forty-eight hours of the Iraq revolution he had rushed out a statement to Congress emphasizing that his administration had no plans for US forces to go anywhere except Lebanon, and he felt that if he reneged on this he would lose prestige; he also doubted if Congress would approve further operations. Macmillan wrote to him:

> I only wish that a decision about Jordan had been deferred until the Foreign Secretary arrived in Washington. We ought to have made proper joint plans before embarking on any operation . . .
> I very much dislike from a military point of view the sort of operation to which we are now committed in Jordan where our troops have no port, no heavy arms, and no real mobility. If the gamble with the Jordan army does not come off our troops will be in a difficult position. We cannot withdraw until somehow we have restored stability and strength in at least some areas of the Middle East. I am sure Foster and Selwyn will be able to work out a joint plan for the future.

Macmillan was obviously annoyed by Eisenhower's precipitate refusal over Jordan, but Eisenhower paid no attention to his letter.

In Washington Lloyd urged US participation in Jordan without success. Dulles emphasized 'his complete solidarity with the UK' but said that he was inhibited by Eisenhower's statement to Congress. He did not exclude 'early military action to secure Kuwait' although his Under-Secretary William Rountree, a Middle East expert, demurred on account of 'the grave political consequences of such a move'. Dulles emphasized to Lloyd that US troops would remain in Lebanon indefinitely although the idea of even token forces for Jordan was not 'on', but when Lloyd pointed out the danger of a *coup* in Kuwait by Syria or Iraq Dulles eventually agreed that US forces might participate in the defence of Kuwait in order to forestall Nasser getting hold of the oilfields.

To Macmillan Eisenhower replied that US public opinion and Congress would be 'much against' use of US ground forces in Jordan but he would lend US Globemaster aeroplanes to fly supplies from Cyprus to Jordan. Fortunately once British ships had sailed through the Suez Canal to Aqaba the supply difficulties were solved.

Dulles came to London with Rountree for a meeting of the Baghdad Pact countries on 28 July. On the day before, 27 July, he and Macmillan came into face to face contact for the first time over the Middle East crisis. Their meeting showed a substantial divergence of views.

Revealing his opposition to any long-term US military presence in the Middle East, Dulles maintained that although there was still heavy fighting between the Lebanese government forces and the rebels around Beirut 'we must work for some kind of neutral Lebanon with a United Nations presence'. When Selwyn Lloyd expressed fears for the British troops in Jordan, should the Americans withdraw from the Lebanon while British forces were left there, Dulles admitted to worries of his own about the future of Jordan. In his view:

> the disintegration of Jordan would probably lead to the Israelis seizing the West Bank, and this in turn would mean an Arab-Israel war with a very dangerous chain-reaction. It was possible Khrushchev could be made aware of the dangers of such an upheaval and might agree to co-operate to prevent it. This, of course, was presupposing that Khrushchev was motivated by reason. But there were great dangers that both Khrushchev and Nasser were inclined to act spontaneously without any rational approach.

Both the Americans and British agreed that Ben-Gurion's tacit agreement to the British airlift to Jordan overflying Israel was building up 'a backlog of Russian and Arab resentment' against Israel, and that once American and British forces withdrew Israel would have no 'hard Western guarantees'.

Macmillan then stated that it was important to get 'real United Nations safeguards for the Lebanon and Jordan while our troops were still there. If as soon as we withdrew these countries fell into Nasser's lap our whole operation would have been a failure.' Dulles's reply showed his resentment at Macmillan's efforts to inveigle America into a large-scale military adventure in the Middle East:

> We had achieved our main objectives which were not so much to preserve Jordan and the Lebanon as to show that our friends did not call on us for help in vain, and to show Nasser that he could not always assume that his plots could succeed without a reaction by us. In fact our intervention might well have made the solution of the ultimate problems harder.

In a last effort Selwyn Lloyd pointed out the danger of a Nasserite *coup* in Jordan in the next few weeks, stating that much depended on how far the United States were prepared to show that they too were implicated in the Jordan situation. Dulles however would not be drawn over further US military commitments to Jordan, and replied that Nasser would be unlikely to cause internal trouble in Jordan while there was the possibility of high level meetings to discuss the Middle East.

'We broke up in good heart in spite of all the troubles and dangers,' wrote Macmillan in his diary on 29 July. In fact the Baghdad Pact was by now a broken reed. Suez had diminished the influence of Britain in the Middle East, and the Baghdad Pact countries now had to tread the path between Nasserism and Communism unaided. British hopes for the future of the Baghdad Pact were wishful thinking.[26]

On 27 July Chamoun had agreed that Chebab would be the best candidate to succeed him as President of Lebanon; the British and Americans concurred, albeit with misgivings, and on 31 July Chebab was elected President. He assured the Americans that he would not ask for their troops to be withdrawn until the security situation had improved. Chebab turned out to be a better national leader than expected, and after the elections the security situation improved rapidly.

As Lebanon and Jordan quietened down in August, fears of either a Turkish or a British-backed Jordanian invasion of Iraq were dispelled by the Anglo-American recognition of the new Iraqi regime under General Qasim. And at the General Assembly of the United Nations in the middle of August, through Nasser's intervention, a reasonable composite Arab resolution was passed unanimously, requesting the Secretary-General

> to make such practical arrangements as would adequately help in upholding the principles and purposes of the Charter in relation to Lebanon and Jordan, bearing in mind renewed assurances that Arab countries would respect each other's obligations not to interfere in each other's internal affairs.

Following this resolution Pierson Dixon, head of the British delegation to the United Nations, talked to Mohamed Fawzi, the Egyptian Foreign Minister, in the presence of Dag Hammarskjöld, the UN Secretary-General. Fawzi said that the Egyptian Government could not undertake to support Hussein, but they would stop attacking him and would do what they could to prevent internal trouble for him. However Fawzi did not think the King would continue for long and the best thing would be for him to leave the country; 'the worst thing for Egypt', he added, 'would be for Jordan to be placed in her lap,' because Egypt could not carry the financial burden and 'they had had enough trouble already over refugees'.

After more talk Dixon and Hammarskjöld persuaded Fawzi to agree that King Hussein should be maintained, and that Egypt would 'gradually turn off the tap' of propaganda against Hussein; this would be of the greatest value, Hammarskjöld said. Reporting on this talk to London, Dixon said that Hammarskjöld and he had gone 'some way towards convincing Fawzi that they must take some positive steps to maintain the *status quo* in Jordan if they really wanted to avoid a collapse'. His pleading with Fawzi was a turning point. Nasser accepted his Foreign Minister's advice and softened Egyptian propaganda against Hussein, and the threat to the Jordan regime soon evaporated.[27]

Dixon also talked to Dulles about the line some American diplomats were taking that Jordan could not survive. Dulles denied this and added that Britain had done an 'international service of the highest order in going in to Jordan to keep it alive'; he recognized that the continued existence of Jordan was necessary to prevent another Arab-Israel war. Dixon then urged Dulles to reconsider the American refusal to give financial help to Jordan to re-equip her army. The King was asking for far too much, Dulles replied, but he promised to reconsider the proposal in the light of Dixon's remarks, and admitted there might be something to be said for giving a modest sum. No American funds were at first provided but a substantially increased supply of weapons was made available to Jordan by America.

As Nasser implemented Fawzi's promises to Hammarskjöld and Dixon during August, and the situation in Lebanon and Jordan stabilized, the Americans decided to withdraw from Lebanon, and the British followed suit in Jordan. US troops left Lebanon on 25 October; British troops departed from Jordan on 2 November. A dangerous situation had been calmed by vigorous Anglo-American co-operation, but Macmillan's hopes for a major US military presence in the Middle East were in the end disappointed. The dismay caused to the British Government by America's decision to withdraw from Lebanon was summed up in a message from Lloyd to Macmillan on 11 August. Murphy, he said, had 'very unsound ideas' about Lebanon:

> He was in favour of no international arrangement about Lebanon's future, and the withdrawal of American troops fairly rapidly ... I think the Americans will look very silly if they withdraw from Lebanon without anything at all in exchange except Chebab's rather wobbly word.

Macmillan replied that he was concerned at Murphy's attitude towards the withdrawal of American troops from the Lebanon 'leaving us on the hook in Jordan. I know you will fight this hard with Dulles. If you want any help from me please let me know and I will weigh in behind you.'[28]

Nonetheless Macmillan was delighted by a message from Eisenhower in early November 1958:

> Now that the missions of the British forces in Jordan and the American forces in Lebanon have come to a close, I think that your country and mine

can take deep satisfaction in the successful accomplishment of undertakings
of wide and historical significance.

Without firing a shot in anger, and in close and friendly collaboration
with the local authorities our forces have achieved what they were sent to
Lebanon and Jordan to do . . . I consider this development of the highest
significance to the free world . . . We can take special satisfaction in the
complete understanding and splendid co-operation which was evident
between our two Governments in these undertakings.[29]

With this Macmillan felt he had restored Anglo-American relations to
the pre-Suez level. This was not entirely true, however. The two
countries were still far apart on Middle East policy.

On 20 December 1958 Rountree had a long interview with Sir Roger
Stevens, former Ambassador to Iran and now an Under-Secretary at the
Foreign Office, when Rountree stopped off at Heathrow during his
flight back to Washington from the Middle East. Over dinner Rountree
told the British diplomats he was convinced from his tour of the Middle
East that there was growing antagonism between the Communists and
Nasser; the Egyptian and Syrian press were branding Communism as 'the
enemy of Arab nationalism'. In Jordan he had found the King and the
leaders obsessed with fear 'both of Nasser and Communism'; however
he had been impressed by the popularity of King Hussein, although he
had told him that the United States could not continue their financial
support of Jordan indefinitely.

Rountree had been given a very hostile reception in Baghdad with
the mob obviously organized by the Government. When he met Qasim
he formed a 'horrible' impression of him and his entourage, and thought
Qasim had 'very little chance of following a middle of the road policy'.
The President and political leaders in Lebanon had received Rountree
very warmly, and he thought they all wished for good relations with
the United States within the context 'of the modern trends of relationship between Arabs and Western governments' (detachment; freedom
from alliances); the recent US aid there had been well received. Rountree
reported that he had sensed on his trip much more than before a very
real danger of Communism, especially in Syria and Iraq.

Philip de Zulueta, Macmillan's private secretary with responsibility for
foreign policy, was present and minuted to the Prime Minister on the
transcript of the interview:

This is rather what we had expected and shows again there is a real danger
of another disagreement between us and the US about policy in the Middle
East. Mr Rountree seems to forget that the Communist doctrine has always
been that 'semi-colonial countries' often need a bourgeois nationalist
revolution to prepare the way for Communism. Although the Jordanians'
idea about Syria (to obtain it) [*sic*] has obvious dangers, they may not be
so silly if we and the US are prepared to carry out an aggressive policy to

support a middle of the road policy for the Middle East. If we are not jointly ready to pursue such a policy we may well have to choose between Nasser and Communism in the short term; but either would be bad for us.[30]

Fortunately, despite the impression made by Qasim on Rountree, Iraq did not go down the road either to Communism or Nasserism. The honeymoon with Nasser soon ended, and was followed by a period of Russian influence. But though Russia supplied arms, aircraft and other military equipment, and technicians and capital for industrial development, Qasim wanted the best of both worlds and kept on good terms with the British.

There was a nasty incident in July 1961 when Qasim unleashed a plan to occupy Kuwait by force. Kuwait was guaranteed by the British who promptly despatched troops, the Commando carrier *Bulwark* arriving off Kuwait on 4 July. America made no move. Immediately Qasim backed down. The other Arab states supported the Sheik of Kuwait and relations between Iraq and Britain soon became friendly again.

Qasim justified Britain's faith in him up to a point, cleverly steering a middle course between Communism and Nasserism while preserving friendship with the West. But a vicious dictator who had his rivals executed usually without trial, he made many enemies by his brutal methods, and not surprisingly was assassinated in February 1963. After his death Iraq was governed by a succession of unstable rulers who continued to exercise power through military dictatorship.

CHAPTER 2

Vote-winning Budgets

WHEN MACMILLAN TOOK up the reins of government, Conservative popularity was at rock bottom following the Suez disaster, and from the opinion polls it seemed unlikely that they could win the next General Election. At his first interview with the Queen, Macmillan said realistically, 'I may only be Prime Minister for a few weeks.'

From the start Macmillan believed that rising prosperity would be the key to restoring Conservative popularity and he manoeuvred to put Britain into an economic position which would enable the Government to introduce a tax-cutting and vote-winning Budget in 1959 prior to the General Election. He chose Peter Thorneycroft as Chancellor. Sir Robert Hall, Economic Adviser to the Treasury, has described Thorneycroft as 'the best of the possibles; very pleasant, but also clear and firm'.[1] Enoch Powell, then little known, became Financial Secretary, and Nigel Birch, Economic Secretary. Thorneycroft was to introduce only one Budget and to resign within a year.

In his Budget speech in April 1956 Macmillan as Chancellor had been able to say with justification that the economy was running at a high level with more jobs than men to fill them; more orders than industry could meet; easy profits, but rising costs. However, Macmillan added, he was not happy about inflation running at 3 per cent. He considered this a threat to the pound whose value was important with Britain being 'banker to the sterling area – a large part of the world'. He therefore cut government spending by £100 million, a large sum for those days; it was mild deflation.

The new Cabinet were anxious to give the impression that Suez had done no harm to the economy. Actually, its effects on the home economy were small. Once the drawing from the IMF had been arranged and America had agreed to sell oil the situation stabilized, although it made nonsense of the warnings in August 1956 from Lloyd, Eden and Macmillan that Nasser's nationalization of the Canal was a dire blow to Britain's trade. Consumption of oil had been restricted first by a higher tax and then by rationing. But industrial output, except of cars, was hardly affected.

As a gesture of confidence bank rate was gingerly lowered from 5½ to 5 per cent on 6 February 1957: a sign that the crisis over the pound was over. However, in the immediate aftermath of the Suez crisis the economic situation had been alarming, and, although the outlook was improving fast, there was uneasiness in the Cabinet about the weakness of the pound, and an inclination to play safe by pursuing stringent financial measures. Against this background the 1957 Budget was harsh, giving tax concessions of only £100 million – minimal in view of the deflated state of the economy.

Surprisingly after Thorneycroft's moderate Budget a crisis over sterling and a run on the pound suddenly blew up out of a clear sky in September 1957. Contrary to the expectations of the Treasury economic advisers, and despite a substantial current account surplus and further deflationary measures by the Government following unacceptably high wage settlements, speculative pressure on the pound became acute in August 1957. Although the economic indicators had given no cause for alarm, with the balance of payments in surplus, the crisis was due to widespread rumours that the Government might let the pound float, in which case the exchange rate would have plunged temporarily downwards. It became known that Thorneycroft had discussed a floating rate with Professor Robbins of the London School of Economics who had advised strongly against it.[2] It was also leaked that Sir Robert Hall, the Government's Economic Adviser, with Sir Denis Rickett and other senior officials of the Bank of England, were studying the question of whether a floating rate for the pound would be in the interests of the British economy. Although their report was not finalized until March 1958, they had of necessity to canvass the opinion of leading economists, and such activities could not be carried on in secret.[3]

In his diary for 19 August 1957 Hall records that he had changed his mind and withdrawn his previous objections to a floating rate. He also wrote on the same day that Lord Cobbold, Governor of the Bank of England, favoured holding the value of the pound against the dollar but letting it float against European currencies. The devaluation of the French franc in August, coupled with strong rumours that the German mark was about to be revalued upwards, convinced speculators that sterling was likely to be depreciated as part of a general realignment. It had been weakened first by the Suez war and then by British operators selling sterling and buying dollar securities as investments through Kuwait; this market in Kuwait was a gaping hole in the Government's defence of sterling. By the time Thorneycroft closed it (against the objections of Cobbold) in July 1957 it had cost British reserves £70 million. The above factors were more important in the sterling crisis than fears about inflation.[4]

Macmillan toyed with the idea of floating rates in the hope that it would make a soft electioneering Budget easier since a popular income tax cut would not then produce a run on the pound. Amongst other serious papers *The Economist* discussed the case for a widening of the margin in which the sterling exchange rate was allowed to move, but on 19 September commented: 'the case has been rejected; the fact that the emergency measures were taken only on Thursday instead of last month suggests that there had been a swaying debate within the Treasury and the Bank before rejection.' The Treasury archives show *The Economist* to have been correct. This authoritative press comment triggered off a serious run on the pound.

Thorneycroft was convinced that the sterling crisis was due mainly to inflation at home; during this period he came strongly under the influence of Enoch Powell, his Financial Secretary, who convinced the Chancellor that wage push inflation could be held in check provided there were sufficient controls on the money supply. This was also the view of Professor Robbins whose advice Thorneycroft valued, and the two converted Thorneycroft into a thorough-going monetarist.

The Prime Minister did not approve and consulted Roy Harrod, an Oxford don whom he looked on as a greater economic expert although this view was not shared in Whitehall. On 7 September 1957, as the sterling crisis developed, Harrod wrote to the Prime Minister:

> The idea that you can reduce prices by limiting the quantity of money is pre-Keynsian. Hardly any economist under the age of 50 subscribes to it. If it were supposed the Conservatives were associated with any such idea, that might drive many middle of the way economists into the ranks of Labour and what is more, Gaitskell could probably succeed in galvanizing them all into lambasting and ridiculing this policy. I do sincerely hope that no government speaker would use words implying that the Government subscribes to such an antiquated doctrine.[5]

Macmillan always took the advice of his economic guru seriously. Nuffield Professor of International Economics at Oxford, Harrod however was originally a classicist, not an economist, and his views were looked on with scepticism by many leading economists. But every few weeks from 1956 until Macmillan's retirement in 1963 Harrod sent from Oxford letters replete with economic advice for the Prime Minister; he saw Macmillan frequently and made so many telephone calls to Downing Street asking for interviews that the private secretaries found him a nuisance. Macmillan usually passed Harrod's letters on to the Chancellor; this annoyed the Treasury economic advisers Sir Robert Hall and Sir Alec Cairncross who had to 'waste their time' preparing replies.[6]

There was considerable opposition to the Chancellor's measures from the Prime Minister and other members of the Cabinet, but Thorneycroft persuaded them that the crisis over sterling was so acute that they must agree to him announcing on 19 September 1957 a deflationary package which became notorious. It consisted of raising bank rate from 5 to 7 per cent, cutting public sector investment and putting a ceiling on bank advances, whilst the Capital Issues Committee* was instructed to be more restrictive over allowing new issues to be floated on the public.

The September measures were ill-received in the City and did not help Conservative popularity. The general reaction of the City editors was that the Government, faced with a continuing drain on the reserves, had decided on a 'kill or cure' remedy disregarding the heavy cost to certain sections of the City and believing that only a 'short sharp shock would do the trick'. This was not the interpretation the Government wanted. They would have preferred the measures to be looked on as a skilful use of the 'brake' to keep the economy on an even course, but with their prestige so damaged by Suez, criticism was harsh even in traditional Conservative circles. Macmillan helped to defuse the crisis by refusing to recall Parliament early, and by the end of September the pound was at its highest level since June, regaining its parity with the dollar of $2.80. Alas this recovery was not sustained.

When Parliament reassembled, the Chancellor's measures were debated in the Commons on 29 October 1957. Thorneycroft argued that, if the supply of money was limited, inflation would run up against 'an immovable obstacle'; rising prices would be prevented if necessary at the cost of ailing activity and falling employment. This was Thatcherism and Friedmanism with a vengeance. He continued:

> The Government are determined to maintain the internal and external value of the pound . . . There can be no remedy for inflation and the steadily rising prices which go with it which does not include and indeed is not founded upon a control of money supply. So long as it is generally believed that the Government are prepared to see the necessary finance produced to match the upward spiral of costs, inflation will continue and prices will go up.

He insisted that the value of the various monetary totals must be kept constant; in particular current government expenditure, public investment and bank advances.

Thorneycroft's measures were less drastic than the austerity implicit in the monetary theory behind them,[7] but he was attacked in the Commons by both Harold Wilson and Patrick Gordon Walker on the grounds that his measures were reactionary and based on faulty analysis.

---

* This had been set up by the Attlee Government to channel investment into useful projects, and was much resented by the City of London.

Wilson argued convincingly that merely to freeze the supply of money does not in itself freeze prices.

The impact on the public of the rise in bank rate was fudged, Harold Wilson accusing Oliver Poole, Chairman of the Conservative Party, of leaking the proposed rise in the bank rate so that substantial private gains had been made on the Stock Exchange by individuals and firms in the know selling gilts. The allegation caused a furore. A full-scale tribunal was set up under Lord Justice Parker, whose findings eventually exonerated the Cabinet and humiliated Wilson by exposing his 'gullibility'. However in his diaries Robert Hall noted that 'the City end seemed to be questionable', and he criticized the excessive number of members of City firms who were always consulted by the Governor about changes in bank rate; this obviously greatly increased the dangers of a leak.

It soon became evident that Thorneycroft's September crisis measures were not having the impact he expected; accordingly, spurred on by Powell, he urged even more cuts in state spending to which Macmillan and the spending Ministers were opposed.

In December Macmillan noted in his diary that he had had a long talk with Thorneycroft who was very worried about the rise in government spending for 1958/59 and wanted swingeing cuts in welfare expenditure – 'more, I fear, than is feasible politically' – whilst the rest of the Cabinet were 'bitterly opposed to his main proposal which is to abolish the children's allowances and thus save £65 million'.

Thorneycroft was in fact demanding a total cut of £153 million and in order to satisfy him the Cabinet had agreed, by the end of December, to economies amounting to £100 million. Spurred on by the convinced monetarist Powell, Thorneycroft dug his heels in over the remaining £50 million[8] and without any consultation with the Minister of Pensions decided to abolish the entitlement to family allowance for the second child in a family. (There was no right to family allowance for the first child.) On Wednesday, 1 January 1958, Treasury officials informed the Departments involved that the Chancellor was intending to abolish family allowances for the second child and increase NHS prescription charges; a paper was circulated giving the details.

The Cabinet met at 11 a.m. on Friday, 3 January; the atmosphere was tense. John Boyd-Carpenter, as Minister of Pensions and National Insurance, was asked to attend and was told by a colleague that at a meeting the previous day Thorneycroft had informed the Prime Minister, Butler, Hailsham and one or two others that he would resign if he could not get the estimates for 1958/59 down to the 1957/58 levels. Boyd-Carpenter has recorded that he was always 'a great believer in family allowances on their social merits' and had often expressed this belief in them publicly. Upset too that Thorneycroft had not consulted him on a matter that concerned his Department, he had accordingly decided to resign if the allowance for the second child was withdrawn. His letter of resignation was written out and remains in his archives.

After a repetitious discussion in which only Reginald Maudling, the Paymaster-General, came out in favour of abolishing the family allowance, the Cabinet adjourned until 4.30 p.m. Thorneycroft then threatened resignation until the Prime Minister asked him point-blank if he would stay if he got economies totalling £113 to £117 million. Thorneycroft said he was in a very difficult position and wanted time to consider, and the Cabinet again adjourned. At 6.30 it resumed.

A revealing account very different from the official Cabinet minutes and other records has been written by Boyd-Carpenter:

> At 6.30 we came back and took our seats at Cabinet table. Chancellor and Lord Chancellor were missing. At 6.40 they had not re-appeared, and someone commented that Home Secretary had better arrange for Lake in St James's Park to be dragged. At 6.42 Lord Chancellor [Kilmuir] appeared; it was realized that he had been reasoning with Chancellor. As he came in, Hailsham [Lord President] said, 'Will jury be out long?' Lord Chancellor without hesitating said, 'The foreman has come to ask a question.'
>
> Lord Chancellor then began to propound Chancellor's conditions for staying. It became clear, however, that figures and details didn't tally, and PM said Chancellor must really come back to discuss this himself. He was sent for, and came in looking rather flushed and puffy. PM then asked those concerned to '*constater leurs positions*', with particular reference to what they would do if all the others did their bit. 'Otherwise all bets off.'
>
> On civil side PM suggested £30m should be attempted, or indeed pruned 'from the Civil Estimates as a whole'.* Chancellor said he wanted £30 million certain from 'Welfare' and to be free to seek other economies on rest of civil side. Iain Macleod said this was like Hitler tactics. I said I didn't see why 'Welfare' should be specially singled out for a cut, as distinct from Civil Estimates generally.
>
> PM then said he would adjourn Cabinet and if on Monday agreement couldn't be reached, following discussions at weekend, he would have to consider question of placing resignation of Government in hands of the Queen. He would regret this very much after all we had been through. When he took over he told the Queen that his Government couldn't last six weeks. She often reminded him of this now. It seemed a tragedy in the present state of the world to break up the Government over about half of one per cent of national expenditure, or perhaps over about £10m. Similar appeals were made by Lord Chancellor and Lord President on behalf of Party. PM said some of them should meet at weekend. Iain Macleod should represent Social Service Ministers. Meeting then adjourned at about 7.40.[9]

---

*Civil estimates are the total state spending for each year.

Macmillan had no intention of resigning. He was being devious and bluffing his Cabinet into accepting Thorneycroft's departure.

On Monday, 6 January 1958, Thorneycroft resigned together with Powell and Birch. According to Macmillan's diary Thorneycroft's resignation letter was 'brutal' and 'calculated . . . to do the maximum injury to sterling. It sought to give the impression that he alone in the Cabinet stood against inflation.' Macmillan read out the letter to the Cabinet at 11 a.m. and thought it was received with indignation. After the Cabinet he offered Derick Heathcoat Amory, his Minister of Agriculture, the post of Chancellor of the Exchequer. Reviewing Macmillan's memoirs later in the *Spectator*, Powell wrote of the Thorneycroft resignation that Macmillan was intent on 'buying votes in 1959', though Powell admits he is 'an unsympathetic witness'.[10]

Macmillan had taken a gamble: Thorneycroft might have been able to engineer the overthrow of the Government. Skilfully underplaying the gravity of the crisis, Macmillan remarked the following day at the airport, as he set off on his Far East tour, that 'these were little local difficulties and all there was between him and Thorneycroft was £50 million, less than one per cent of total government expenditure'. Although noting in his diary that there was great danger of the Cabinet completely disintegrating, and of multiple resignations leading to the fall of the Government and dissolution, Macmillan dealt with the worrying situation with firmness and sang-froid. He had done the same a few months earlier when Lord Salisbury had resigned over the release of Makarios. This was to be a great contrast, as will be seen, to his later agitation and weakness in face of Macleod's several threats of resignation over the Central African Federation.

Derick Heathcoat Amory was a more malleable colleague and Macmillan in presidential fashion was able to exercise his own control over the Treasury. A bachelor with liberal ideas, Heathcoat Amory was popular in the Conservative Party. Though Macmillan described him in his diary as 'stupid and rigid', according to the Treasury Knights he was not stupid but very slow-working and conscientious; they found his habit of collecting Makins, Hall and other senior Treasury officials late in the day in his room and sitting on talking about the economy when they all wanted to go to dinner very trying. Sir Robert Hall describes him as 'very slow in business and making up his mind, likeable and the soul of politeness although he has a mind'. Sir Alec Cairncross thought him an able Chancellor with a 'good understanding of economic problems'.[11]

Despite Thorneycroft's precautionary increase of the bank rate to 7 per cent in September there was only a shallow recession in the next six months with a small rise in the number of unemployed to a peak of 467,000 or 2.1 per cent in November. Once Heathcoat Amory was in the saddle, the policy of money supply control was thrown out of the window; the Cabinet wanted expansion to be resumed although there were doubts about the resultant effect on inflation. One of Heathcoat Amory's first statements was 'We shall not keep the brakes on one day longer than we must. A steady expansion of the economy is wanted.' However he was still frightened of wage push inflation and a run on the pound if economic activity increased too rapidly.

A sharp world-wide fall in commodity prices occurred at the end of 1957 which reduced the incomes of Britain's overseas customers, and this fall was widely presumed to mean the beginning of a world slump. Alarming letters from Harrod forecasting a slump and stressing the urgent need to stimulate demand at home began to reach Macmillan in early 1958. However, as a Conservative candidate for a marginal seat in Norfolk, it is probable that some of Harrod's remarks were made in the belief that such measures might help him to win.

On 15 February 1958 he wrote to Macmillan: 'You can still revive the waning fortunes of the Party in two years by a skilful and well-advertised anti-slump policy.' Writing to Maudling in 1962 when the latter was Chancellor of the Exchequer, Macmillan commented: 'I regard him [Harrod] as a man of genius – considerable genius. He is often wrong, but then he is often right ... Do not pass this on to your Department who have a great dislike of Roy.' On another occasion Macmillan's private secretary, Tim Bligh, had difficulty in getting Harrod off the telephone, so insistent was he on having an interview with the Prime Minister. However Macmillan was not always pliant: he firmly rejected a suggestion by Harrod that he might come to Birch Grove during one recess to discuss the state of the economy.

Macmillan now had his mind firmly set on the next General Election which he hoped to hold in the autumn of 1959. With the votes in mind he minuted to Amory on 5 March 1958:

> The people need encouragement and I believe the view that high taxation is anti-inflationary has been pretty well exploded ... Will the cinema tax have to be halved? Would this have to be offset by another pound on TV? The things I would think about are remission of stamp duty on house purchase. Best of all, abolish Schedule A.*

---

* Schedule A was the unpopular tax on owner-occupied houses. It raised considerable revenue. Macmillan realized that Schedule A tax on owner-occupied homes was a vote loser besides being unfair. He was unable to convince Amory that it should be abolished in face of Treasury arguments in favour of keeping it. It was strange that Amory, a very fair man, did not appreciate how unjust the tax was because home owners who kept their receipts for repairs and made 'maintenance claims' recovered their tax, whilst others, mainly the less well educated, just paid the tax due.

> There is the possibility of a straight cut in income tax. I imagine you would not feel that a cut in the standard rate would be preferable to some of the other concessions but it might be worth considering, something to help the family man.

He wanted to merge wives' earnings with husbands', a scheme turned down by the Treasury as it would forfeit too much income tax. He also wanted cuts in purchase tax on luxury goods (90 per cent at that time on fur coats) and insisted on a relaxation in 'monetary policy', allowing the supply of money to expand by low interest rates so that consumers would spend more.

Amory replied to Macmillan's minute by sending him a long memorandum from Evan Maude of the Treasury which he then discussed with the Prime Minister at dinner. This paper shot down Harrod's calls for immediate expansion. Macmillan noted on the paper: 'The dinner was much better than the paper.'

On 16 March 1958 Macmillan was still prodding Amory into tax cuts, minuting to his private secretary: 'He has rather accepted the concept of considering the two Budgets as one and it might be better to make any remission now than in the second Budget. I am more and more convinced the slump is nearer to us than we know ... the Americans have made the same mistake.' Through all the Prime Minister's minutes runs the theme that the 1958 Budget must be designed to make possible a soft vote-winning Budget in 1959, and he was worried that if the brakes were not taken off in 1958 there would be insufficient time to get Britain out of slump before the votes were counted.[12]

In the event Amory took steps to fulfil Macmillan's design. Bank rate was reduced to 6 per cent on 20 March, and in the 1958 Budget on 7 April the Chancellor announced £50 million of tax cuts; various other expansionary measures were taken in the summer of 1958 as industrial production dipped by three points compared with the year before. The ceiling on bank advances was removed in July, and hire purchase restrictions reduced in September and removed altogether in October, while bank rate was brought down to 4 per cent in November.[13]

As early as 30 September 1958 Sir Robert Hall told the internal Treasury Budget Committee that there was

> a strong case for an easy Budget [in 1959] as the trend of the economy was still downward, investment and stocks were declining and unless there was a definite change round in the world economy it should be possible to consider substantial tax reductions. For example, 6d off income tax.

But he did not expect that any measures to stimulate the economy would be needed before the Budget and it was 'too early to say'.[14]

By 18 February 1959 Amory had caved in to the Prime Minister's

remorseless prodding, telling the Budget Committee on 9 March that
he wanted 9d off income tax and for the Budget of 1959 to be followed
by a no-change Budget in 1960. The Economic Secretary, Anthony
Barber, had argued for the reduction of a shilling in the pound, but
Sir Edward Boyle, the Financial Secretary, agreed with Amory. Lord
Hailsham, now Chairman of the Conservative Party, was organizing the
election campaign and he wrote to Heathcoat Amory strongly urging
a substantial reduction in income tax.

Macmillan in January 1959 thought the Treasury were putting brakes
on Amory and giving him bad advice 'as it has to every Chancellor in
turn'. In his diary he wrote that he had 'greater belief in Roy Harrod'
who in a letter in January reiterated that industrial production was still
falling, and who urged a programme of public investment especially
in housing and education.[15] Macmillan enjoyed challenging orthodox
Treasury thinking over money supply. In February 1959 he argued that
the Bank should now

> buy gilts instead of selling them* . . . the only reason for not pursuing this
> policy is anxiety about funding. I cannot accept this view. If the traditional
> policy is followed, even if it means some temporary change in funding
> policy, the recession will end; the Conservative Party will be re-elected;
> property will be sound, and funding in 1960 will be easier than ever. If it
> is not followed, the Old Lady of Threadneedle Street can take no consolation
> from the fact that she brought her ruin on herself as well as on wider
> interests, national and international.

The Prime Minister asked Amory to put these views, which were
Harrod's, to his experts; the corollary being lower interest rates. The
Treasury however replied that they considered this policy dangerous,
since it would involve too fast an increase in money supply and would
tend to produce balance of payments deficits because imports would rise
too steeply.[16]

When unemployment peaked at 621,000 in January 1959 Macmillan
became worried. So concerned was he about the electoral effect of high
unemployment that he personally chaired a Cabinet committee on the
subject which held nine meetings between November 1958 and March
1959. As a result, in February 1959 he exhorted his Ministers to phase
their spending 'to make the maximum contribution to the relief of

---

*The Treasury needed to sell gilts to raise the money to pay for state spending. This is known
as funding the Public Sector Borrowing Requirement (PSBR). If they were to buy gilts instead,
as Macmillan wanted, interest rates would fall and banks would have more money to lend, thus
making life more comfortable for the consumer.

unemployment'. In an election year Macmillan knew rising unemployment might spell disaster. In all this he was stimulated by Harrod.[17]

Harrod was a continual support to Macmillan in his pursuit of expansion. Macmillan wrote to Heathcoat Amory in October 1958: 'I do not always find Harrod convincing, but I have always found him interesting'; he was impressed by Harrod's letter of 28 October 1958 after the removal of hire purchase controls:

> I have an uncomfortable feeling that all the excellent things you have achieved in the last few months will still not add up enough to prevent a serious growth in unemployment in the time ahead. Why not give the consumer credits back in full right away?*

On 2 January 1959 Harrod urged the Prime Minister to have a 'thumping Budget deficit to stop recession'. He also thought that booming home demand was bad for exports, and that it would be easy to impose wage restraint. Wage restraint in the years ahead was to elude both Conservative and Labour governments.

In March 1959 Macmillan wrote to Harrod: 'I am preparing the way for expansion,' but Heathcoat Amory on Robert Hall's advice sent to the Prime Minister a strong warning that Harrod's main thesis that 'the battle against inflation is won' was wrong.

> At a moment when major [wage] claims covering a large proportion of the population are still to be settled how can he say inflation is no longer a threat? We must not throw away all the prizes we have won by assuming too quickly that the battle is won.

Burke Trend, a Principal Treasury Secretary much esteemed by Macmillan, had struck another warning note in a memorandum to the Prime Minister on 4 December 1958:

> The picture which emerges is one in which [there are] some signs of a recovery in demand, particularly *re* consumer expenditure and public investment, but production remains well below capacity and there is some risk of renewed pressure by prices on wage level. In other words we have reached a point when we have done all the Chancellor thinks that we can safely do to stimulate demand.[18]

Macmillan would not accept Trend's caution, and put all the pressure he could on Amory for more expansion before the General Election.

He had been angry when Amory on 27 October 1958 sent him a paper prepared in the Treasury which pointed out the limitations

---

*By this Harrod meant the abolition of all restrictions on bank lending and hire purchase.

on the use of public investment as an instrument for fostering reflation or checking inflation ... We feel the attempts to use public investment as a short-term equilibrator of the economy are at any rate at present in danger of leading to most damaging results.

As Macmillan was determined to use public investment to the full in creating expansion for the General Election this did not suit his book. He minuted: 'This is a very bad paper. Indeed a disgraceful paper. It might have been written by Mr Neville Chamberlain's Government.' Spurred on by Harrod, Macmillan continued to ply his Chancellor with a barrage of memoranda all calculated to overcome his natural caution and make him plump for expansion.[19]

Macmillan was well pleased when his Chancellor yielded in the face of this bombardment and agreed to a more expansionary Budget than either he or his Treasury advisers wanted. The Budget introduced by the Chancellor of the Exchequer on 7 April 1959 was an ideal pre-election package. Income tax was reduced by 9d from 8s 6d where it had stood for some years, with further reductions in the lower rates. Purchase tax was cut and 2d taken off the price of a pint of beer while investment allowances (the tax rebates on investment in new factories and machinery) were restored.

The results were dramatic, and were helped not by a world slump such as Harrod and the Treasury had been forecasting, but by an international boom. Production in Britain soared by 10 per cent in a year. Such a rate of growth was unsustainable. In his Budget speech the Chancellor had said: 'We must at all costs make it our business not to return to an overload on the economy which would make a resumption of inflation inevitable. At the present time however this is clearly not an immediate danger.' However, this was exactly what the Budget did, but fortunately for the Conservatives it did not become apparent until after the votes had been safely counted on 9 October 1959.

In a clever speech for the Opposition Harold Wilson reminded the House of Butler's 1955 Budget which had to be followed by slamming the brakes on the economy; he doubted whether after the September 1957 crisis the nation would be so gullible a second time. The Budget, he alleged, was no more than a preparation for the General Election, and the Government had deliberately held down production until now.

On 22 June 1959, in widely reported speeches, both the Prime Minister and the Chancellor of the Exchequer spotlighted the fact that retail prices had dropped by one point in May compared with twelve months before so that the retail price index stood at 109 against 110 the previous year (1955 = 100). The claim was echoed enthusiastically in the Conservative press, and it was entirely overlooked that the fall in prices was mainly due to the continuous fall in commodity prices during the previous eighteen months, not to skilful government.

On 1 July 1959 Macmillan was delighted to read in the *Daily Mail* spectacular confirmation by their lobby correspondent, Henry Fairlie, that the 1959 Budget was doing what he hoped. He kept the cutting in his private papers:

> What they [the people] see are all the gleaming evidence of a society which is out on a spree; a Stock Exchange behaving more like a Casino than ever; extravagant parties and expensive cars; refrigerators, washing machines and gadgets piling up in the kitchen. Luxuries become necessities, necessities being forgotten.[20]

Macmillan sensed he was on his way to an election victory.

However, sombre warnings of 'overheating' consumer spending were coming from the Treasury where Heathcoat Amory was having qualms of conscience about 'having too reflationary a Budget'. In his diary Macmillan noted:

> Unemployment figures showed a 50,000 decrease (4,000 above the estimate which I have been given). This is good. At the same time the cost of living has remained unchanged for a year. So we have really brought off the double.

On 8 September 1959 the election date was announced with the economic indicators showing Britain entering a rip-roaring boom which went so fast that it led to balance of payments crises and cast a cloud over the economy in the years to come. The following day, 9 September, *The Times* leader stated: 'People are prosperous; prices are steady; unemployment is low.' This was exactly what Macmillan wanted to read as he girded himself up to stump the country.

CHAPTER 3

The 1959 General Election

SUPPORT FOR THE Eden Government in by-elections had declined fast in 1956. In June 1956 in spite of a personable and experienced candidate in Richard Hornby, Tonbridge was nearly lost to Labour with the Conservative majority dropping from 10,196 to 1,602; had a Liberal stood Tonbridge would have gone Labour, because at the time the Liberals were staging a sudden revival after years in the wilderness, taking 23.8 per cent of the poll at the Torquay by-election, 36.4 at Hereford, and 21.6 at Gainsborough.

In December 1956 at Melton, where the sitting member Anthony Nutting had resigned his seat over his opposition to the Suez war, the Conservative majority was reduced from 10,780 to 2,362. Nutting had been Under-Secretary at the Foreign Office and refused to countenance the secret collusion with Israel and its subsequent denial.

By 1957 the Macmillan Government thus faced by-elections with apprehension. Marginal Lewisham was lost in February, and in Carmarthen where the deceased Liberal member Clement Davies had not been opposed by the Conservatives since 1931 Lady Megan Lloyd George (a former Liberal MP) stood as the Labour candidate and won the seat. At Warwick, where the vacancy was caused by the elevation to the Lords of the former Prime Minister Anthony Eden, there was a swing of 12.2 per cent against the Government although the Conservative candidate scraped home.

Early in 1958 the Conservatives sustained three nasty consecutive by-election losses: the result of the unpopularity of the penal 7 per cent bank rate together with harsh credit restrictions, while in 1957 twice as many working days had been lost through strikes as in any previous year since the war. Labour won Rochdale from the Conservatives mainly because of the intervention of the charismatic television personality Ludovic Kennedy with his glamorous wife Moira Shearer; Kennedy achieved a spectacularly high Liberal vote although his Party had not contested the seat since 1950. Kelvingrove in Glasgow also fell to Labour, while at Torrington in Devon Mark Bonham-Carter (grandson of the Liberal Prime Minister Herbert Asquith) achieved the first Liberal by-election gain for thirty years. This was an enormous surprise and a setback for the Government although Torrington had a strong Liberal tradition. Bonham-Carter's mother (Violet Bonham-Carter, later Lady Asquith) played an important part in his victory with her speeches and television appearances. She was a veteran of the hustings, having played a leading part in her father's campaign when he won the Paisley by-election in 1920.

However during the period from the spring of 1958 until the October 1959 General Election there was little swing against the Government at by-elections. According to Gallup polls the recovery in government popularity began in the summer of 1959, and from the answers to Gallup questions this was due to lower bank rate, increased consumer spending and the unpopularity of Labour over the seven-week London bus strike. Also popular was the strong government stand over Jordan where, unlike Suez, armed intervention was, with US help, a success;* while Macmillan's appearances on television were much liked with his show of 'unflappability' in face of setbacks. In Gallup poll samples during the fifteen-month run-up to the 1959 General Election Conservative support grew from 28 per cent to 41 per cent.

In these final nine months of the 1955 Parliament, as has been shown, the nation became more prosperous with tax cuts of £300 million in the 1959 Budget (including 2d a pint off beer). Foreign affairs dominated the political news and Macmillan skilfully exploited these, especially the suspension of the Russian ultimatum over Berlin and the beginning of the Foreign Ministers Conference at Geneva in May 1959, which he claimed as personal successes.†

As the Commons went into recess in August 1959 no date had been fixed for the General Election. Then came a notable political *coup* for Macmillan. He persuaded Eisenhower to pay a visit to London at a moment which coincided with intense speculation about the date of the election. It was an astute move. (President Kennedy firmly refused in 1963 to allow Macmillan to exploit his visit to Britain similarly.) Together Eisenhower and Macmillan issued grandiloquent phrases about the importance of the impending Summit meeting with Khrushchev; a joint presidential and prime ministerial television appearance was justifiably hailed by some lobby correspondents as 'the first General Election campaign broadcast'.[1]

After the spectacular ebb and flow of Party fortunes since 1955, the Conservatives in August 1959 appeared to be on a stable course for their third consecutive election victory. Macmillan was confident he had won

---

* See Chapter 1.   † See Chapter 15.

the election by the economic policy he had pursued prior to the dissolution. He was right. On 8 September, five days after the joint Eisenhower-Macmillan television appearance, Macmillan announced the election date as 8 October, saying from the point of view of home affairs there was no need for an autumn election but 'as important international negotiations lay ahead the people should decide who was to represent them'. He wrote several letters to Eden 'beseeching' him for a personal endorsement of the campaign. Eden offered to issue a statement supporting the Conservative Party but refused to give his imprimatur to Macmillan personally.[2]

The Prime Minister did not return to the theme of foreign policy until the last week of the campaign when he tried to capitalize on the usefulness of his trip to Moscow and the subsequent joint announcement with the President in Washington that the way had been opened for a 'full Summit meeting'. In the last week of the election campaign Macmillan stated that the date of the Summit meeting would be announced within 'a few days'; this produced a denial from the White House which was embarrassing to Macmillan. Gaitskell exploited the gaffe cleverly by taunting the Prime Minister with 'playing politics over a vital matter'.

As usual foreign affairs were only a minor issue in the 1959 election; the voters appeared indifferent to them and there was not a wide gulf between the attitudes of the parties. Many Labour candidates were reluctant to hit hard over Suez for fear of seeming unpatriotic, while the Conservatives preferred to ignore Suez because it aroused internal quarrels. The two other important overseas issues, the Hola Camp killings and the Devlin Report, which had caused such bad publicity and embarrassment for the Government only a few weeks previously,* were hardly mentioned.

The leader of the Opposition, Hugh Gaitskell, and the Labour Shadow Foreign Secretary, Aneurin Bevan, were in Moscow when the election date was announced, and they tried to exploit their presence there as an antidote to Eisenhower's visit to London. The *Daily Express* carried the headline 'Hugh and Nye defend the Empire', and the fact that Gaitskell and Bevan were travelling together after their long-standing and much publicized quarrel over unilateral disarmament, which had just been made up, was useful in emphasizing Labour's new-found unity. Simultaneously the Trades Union Council was in session at Blackpool where Frank Cousins's demand for unilateral British renunciation of the atom bomb was defeated by 2 to 1 although a protest against the proposed Polaris base in Scotland was carried.

Labour produced an effective propaganda leaflet entitled *The Tory*

---

* See Chapters 11 and 12.

Swindle which painted an accurate picture of the Government's misdeeds over Suez and an exaggerated account of growing hardships amongst the poor sections of the community. Randolph Churchill unsuccessfully sought an injunction to prevent publication of this pamphlet on the grounds that it breached the copyright of his recent book on Suez, *The Rise and Fall of Sir Anthony Eden*, published earlier that year – a book violently critical of Eden, Macmillan and the Cabinet over the Suez affair. In a series of articles in the *Daily Express* preceding publication Randolph had secured great publicity for the collusion between Israel, Britain and France which had been denied by Eden and Selwyn Lloyd. In December 1958 there had been an adjournment debate about Randolph's revelations, and Labour also asked at Question Time for a Select Committee on Suez. 'Leave it to the judgement of the country and electorate,' Macmillan had been content to reply. This row hardly rippled the surface during the election, which showed how far the Macmillan Government had ridden out the unpopularity of Suez.[3]

The Labour manifesto similarly painted a picture of the contrast between the Government's claim 'You never had it so good', and the plight of the old, the sick and the unemployed. It also attacked the Conservative Rent Act which had come into operation in October 1958 and was unpopular because it decontrolled many house rents and resulted in a great number of stiff rent increases; probably unwisely, Labour proposed to nationalize all tenanted houses with controlled rents over a long period by a complicated and little understood process.

The campaign took on the appearance of a mud-slinging match when a City of London scandal gave Harold Wilson the opportunity to describe the Stock Exchange as a 'spiv's paradise', and the Chairman of the Conservative Party, Lord Hailsham, and other Conservative leaders berated Labour for promising to spend extra state money which would make them unable to carry out their promises to reduce taxation – especially their promise to abolish purchase tax on all essential goods.

In the early days of the campaign opinion polls showed Labour gaining ground; they made it look like a closer run thing than it actually was. According to most lobby correspondents the turning point came ten days before the end when Conservative spokesmen skilfully exploited the contradiction between Labour's promises of tax cuts and higher government spending. The Conservatives made headway by alleging that Labour could not plausibly answer the question 'How will you pay for it?' Lord Hailsham had a telling phrase: they were trying to bribe the electorate, he said, 'with their own money'.

Certainly the well-being of the people was the vital issue, but the lobby correspondents' oft-repeated claim that the decisive factor was Gaitskell's contradictory call for reducing taxation and increasing public spending cannot be substantiated. The truth lies deeper.

The key factor in the Conservative victory was that average real pay for industrial workers had risen since Churchill's 1951 victory by over 20 per cent; this had created a new prosperity which was blunting the class divisions which had been so important in previous General Elections. The traditional working-class loyalty to the Labour Party had been severely weakened by wages of up to £30 per week. Many skilled manual workers now enjoyed the same standard of living as middle-class white-collar workers. Television sets, cars, vacuum cleaners and new furniture were now reaching the majority of working-class homes, and even where they were not possessed there was usually a prospect of obtaining them.

Although Labour throughout the election strongly questioned the soundness of Conservative economic policy they could not dent materially the Government's credibility, while the Conservatives succeeded in sowing the seeds of doubt about Labour's economic plans. Thus the Conservatives attracted sufficient trade unionists and factory workers from Labour to sway the balance. This was to be the pattern of Heath's and Thatcher's later Conservative victories, and only in the General Elections of 1964, 1966 and 1974 did Harold Wilson cleverly manage to discredit the Conservative management of the economy sufficiently to bring victory to Labour. The 1959 result in seats was: Conservative 365, Labour 258, Liberal 6, Independent 1. This gave the Macmillan Government a steam-roller majority of 107 over Labour, and 100 over all parties. (Their majority in 1955 had been 60.) Such a result would have seemed beyond the bounds of possibility when Macmillan had become Prime Minister two and a half years before. But his strategy of holding the election at a time of rising production and rapidly rising living standards had been so successful that Labour propaganda misfired, and Suez was forgotten.

The Conservatives were cock-a-hoop at the way in which their leader had brought their Party from its disastrous state at the time of Eden's resignation to a third election victory with a much increased majority. It is no wonder that he became known as 'super Mac'. His official biographer has written: 'Nobody doubted that Macmillan with his hundred-seat majority was now one of the most powerful Prime Ministers in British history, and nobody doubted that here was a man who revelled in power.'[4] Few historians will challenge this. However his next four years in Downing Street were not to be so easy or successful as his earlier term, and he admitted that he became known as 'Macblunder'.

An important factor in the Conservative 1959 win was that the Liberal recovery, which Macmillan himself much feared, did not materialize. Their star performer Jo Grimond, after one successful London rally, retired to his offshore constituency of Orkney and Shetland from where he made only one sortie – by helicopter – to the hopeful Liberal seats of Rochdale, Torrington, North Cornwall and North Devon. In his absence the Liberal Party, with no recent Cabinet Minister in its ranks, got poor press coverage; still Jo Grimond's solo television programme on 3 October was extremely successful. Ed Morrow, the leading US commentator, rated it 'in terms of communication as effective as anything in the campaign'. In the end the Liberals doubled their share of the vote but only from the negligible total of 2.7 per cent in 1955 to 5.9 per cent. Grimond's brother-in-law, Mark Bonham-Carter, lost Torrington which he had worked so hard to win in the 1958 by-election. However Jeremy Thorpe won the safe Tory seat of North Devon for the Liberals.

Thorpe was an outstanding campaigner and his 1959 General Election victory broke the cast-iron pattern of two-party politics which had prevailed since 1931. From 1959 onwards Liberals and Nationalists were seen as stimulating alternatives by the voters, and at by-elections neither Conservative nor Labour candidates could any longer count on automatic traditional support for their parties. However despite by-election wins the surge in the vote of the smaller parties has produced disproportionately poor results in the number of MPs elected in General Elections. This has been due to the first past the post voting system and the refusal of the electorate to indulge in preferential voting in General Elections where the emphasis is on electing a Government and not an individual MP.

CHAPTER 4

Economic Policy 1960

EVEN DURING THE 1959 General Election Heathcoat Amory was worried that the economy was overheating and disturbed at Conservative election promises of more spending. When he put it to his Treasury advisers that he needed a tough Budget in 1960 to counteract this overheating, they told him 'it would hardly look seemly to deflate so soon after the election'.[1] As usual deflation was anathema to Macmillan and his economic adviser Roy Harrod.

However as 1960 began it could not be disguised that the post-election boom was going too fast, with unemployment in the words of the Treasury 'nose-diving' towards one and a half per cent and unfilled vacancies rising. The Conservative victory had triggered a spectacular investment boom in factories and new machinery, and the country was obviously heading for a large trade deficit. However at first this was cloaked by a flood of hot money coming to London attracted by British interest rates but liable to be withdrawn quickly at the first signs of sterling weakness following bad trade figures.

By December 1959 the after-effects of the popular expansionary Budget of that year had become apparent. The trade gap between exports and imports for November jumped from £40 million to £50 million with imports up by a disturbing 7 per cent; *The Times* pointed out that these extra imports were 'consumer goods to a substantial extent'. A worried Amory made a widely reported speech on 8 December, appealing for price stability. He asked manufacturers to

> share the benefit of increases in efficiency and profitability with your customers ... I am not asking for a price freeze nor for all prices to be cut now. We have had practically stable prices for eighteen months and I do not want this lost. Increases in efficiency should be shared with consumers and not just go to wages and profits. Lower prices are needed to keep our exports profitable.[2]

According to Robert Hall, within a month of the 1959 election Amory was 'in an acute state of nerves over the loss of reserves and wanted to raise bank rate immediately'. Macmillan would not have it. Amory went to see the Prime Minister with Sir Roger Makins, Permanent Under-Secretary at the Treasury, but was told there was nothing to worry about.[3]

Throughout his premiership Macmillan was engaged in a running battle with the Treasury, as he repeatedly deployed Harrod's arguments in favour of continuous expansion. This controversy peaked during the run-up to the 1960 Budget. Amory and the Treasury had decided on a deflationary Budget but met such hostility from Macmillan that they were obliged to change course shortly before the Budget.

On 1 January 1960 Frank Lee had replaced Makins as Permanent Under-Secretary to the Treasury. Understanding the management of the economy much better than Makins, he became a powerful influence. He believed in the merits of price competition for keeping down inflation and wages, but had no success in persuading a Conservative Government to reduce import tariffs nor to take action against monopolies who formed price rings and overcharged.

By early 1960 national output in Britain was 14 per cent higher than in 1955, but in Europe growth was twice this rate. Used as a criticism of government policy, this made Macmillan even more resolved to oppose a tough Budget in 1960.

The crunch came with a strong memorandum from Lee to the Chancellor on 23 February 1960 which was passed on to the Prime Minister. If the boom was allowed to continue, Lee said, without putting some check on imports 'we cannot exclude the possibility of a payments crisis in the autumn'. At the same time Tim Bligh, Macmillan's private secretary – a former Treasury official – minuted that the soundings he had taken from top Treasury officials indicated that they were thinking in terms of a standstill Budget. Even though it was a late stage in the run-up to the 1960 Budget Macmillan expressed himself to Amory in a forthright fashion:

> Max Beerbohm once said that history does not repeat itself, it is the histor-ians who repeat one another. This is certainly true of the economists and professors ... The *Guardian* rightly says the economy is not yet working at full strength ... An additional £50–100 million of taxation in the Budget will have practically no effect.* It is purely marginal. After all the national income is of the order of £20,000 million. Do you mean that taking away 1/200th part of spending power is going to alter the result of this year's out-turn on the balance of payments or the overseas monetary position?

---

*Bligh had reported to Macmillan that this was the figure the Treasury were considering.

I just do not believe it. Moreover following the Budget of last year and the election of last autumn a deflationary Budget would either be very foolish or very dishonest. Unless it is supposed that we would be thought very modern and up to date, like those young ladies who oscillate daily between the stimulant and the tranquillizers, the new Progressive Conservatism will turn out to be a policy of alternation between Benzedrine and Relaxtabs. I do not like it at all.

For these reasons I still think that you should consider a *standstill Budget* ... It cannot be sensible to cheer the economy on vigorously one moment and then push it violently back the next. What is all this based upon? Not the certainty of a loss on the balance of payments; but only upon a very shadowy calculation that our overseas monetary position at the end of the year may be rather less good than it is now. My confidence in the accuracy of figures of this sort is just about as much as I have in Old Moore ... I have not much confidence in any of these figures, and certainly not enough to reverse what seems to me a sound policy of expansion, and start again the whole dreary cycle of squeeze and disinflation. It is the policy of Sisyphus and the Governor [Cobbold] is well cast for this part.

The cautious Amory was appalled by this memorandum; he thought it reckless. His Treasury advisers told him it was based on flimsy economic arguments, and with their help he sent the Prime Minister a strong reply on 29 February 1960:

the important differences between us on the state of the economy and what should be done concern the balance of payments. I regard the prospects – on the latest forecast – over the next year or two at least as so unsatisfactory as by itself to call for a checking of the present exuberance of the internal situation as a matter of urgency ... the best chance we have of making really extreme measures unnecessary in a few months time is to begin acting now – not at all ruling out the necessity for further measures during the summer. The correct Budget actions as a whole ought, I consider, to be recognized as being mildly deflationary and not merely standstill. They should be accompanied by some action – not very severe – against further sharp increases in bank advances and HP. The fiscal measures must, to my mind, make a positive contribution in the same direction.

The Chancellor continued that he would aim at an increase in taxation of £60 million in 1960/61 and £100 million in 1961/62, and that he believed the 'prospective measure of demand is going to prove dangerous both to the balance of payments and to continuing price stability'. He also stated that the use of special deposits* and a mild application of hire purchase controls would be helpful, and he had these in mind.

---

* These were forced loans by the clearing banks to the Bank of England imposed to cut down the balances the banks had available to lend to the public.

This paper contradicting the advice he had received from Harrod angered Macmillan. He minuted crossly on the same day:

> I think it is a very weak document and should be subject to very careful cross-examination. (a) It is so ill written as to be almost unintelligible; (b) I have very little confidence in the figures; (c) the conclusions it draws hardly seem to follow from the premises.
>
> I hardly dare show it as it stands to some outside critic for I suppose that would be a breach of the Official Secrets Act; but it could perhaps be summarized or a précis made of it and in that form I could show it to outside people.[4]

The archives do not reveal what outside advice Macmillan took, but he replied with a long tirade to Amory saying *inter alia* how devastating 'it would be to check economic activity just as it was getting started and what fools it would make the Conservatives look'.

Robert Hall thought Amory would resign when he received this rebuke, and he must have been close to it. But Macmillan forestalled the resignation with a long and affectionate talk with the Chancellor in which the Prime Minister used all his charm and force of personality to make Amory reconsider his departure. According to Hall they were 'more or less reconciled', except that Amory still wanted his Budget to 'give the country a bit of a shock' while the Prime Minister wanted it to look like 'a continuation of expansion'.[5]

Amory, who had decided to quit politics for reasons unconnected with his difficulties with Macmillan, produced a Budget very different from the deflationary one he and his advisers had first prepared. The 1960 Budget introduced 'no change' so far as consumers and individual taxpayers were concerned. Taxes were raised by £72 million in a full year, but this was almost entirely accounted for by an increase in profits tax (from 10 to 12½ per cent); bank rate had been raised from 4 to 5 per cent in January; hire purchase restrictions were reimposed at the end of April and simultaneously for the first time 'special deposits' were called for from the banks, while at the end of June bank rate was raised to 6 per cent. In his Budget speech Amory said: 'It is clear I cannot make any reduction in taxation in this Budget . . . the position calls for some modest increase in profits tax . . . the Budget releases no further spending powers. Its effect indeed is to withdraw some . . . [it promises] a buoyant level of activity.'

As Shadow Chancellor Harold Wilson made an effective and biting attack on the Budget. Just before the election, he said, Amory had let us in for a rip-roaring boom, and now there was a serious danger of balance of payments problems. In a radio broadcast Wilson added:

For three years it was Tory policy to hold production down even to the point of endangering full employment. This lurching from a semi-depression to boom and back again emphasizes the need for a steady year-to-year expansion big enough to maintain our place in the world and raise living standards but not such as to cause periodic threats of inflation and foreign exchange crises.

Labour propaganda over the contrasts between the 1959 election year Budget and the 1960 Budget damaged Tory popularity. Businessmen became more and more critical of Conservative economic policy.

Severe differences over economic policy with the Prime Minister may well have decided Amory to hasten his retirement from politics. He resigned on 1 July 1960. In his valedictory note to the Prime Minister on 27 June 1960 Amory wrote:

Economic judgements are difficult when one is dealing with such an erratic science. My conclusions have derived from two things – the paramount importance to the country and to our Party of sound balance of payments and price stability. This must, to my mind, take precedence over everything else. We must not drift into crisis. If we err on the side of doing too much we can let up and the people will like it. Added to these thoughts is a personal one; I do not want to leave it to my successor to have to do unpleasant things, the necessity for which was not his fault but mine. I know you will understand the feeling.

Given Macmillan's desire for continuous expansion there was no doubt Amory's successor faced 'unpleasant situations', and Amory told Macmillan's official biographer that his 1959 Budget 'went a little too far ... I was much more cautious than he was, I foresaw our paths would have diverged in one or two years' time.'[6] However Amory's final message was probably inspired by criticism from Harold Wilson in the Commons four days before: how, the Labour Shadow Chancellor asked him, could he say 'the economy is in a healthy state when the gilt market is at its lowest level almost within recorded memory'? 'Over-reliance on monetary policy', Wilson had argued in a final thrust, 'is inimical to public and private investment.'

CHAPTER 5

Selwyn Lloyd as Chancellor

WITH HEATHCOAT AMORY'S resignation in June 1960, Selwyn Lloyd, the Foreign Secretary, replaced him as Chancellor of the Exchequer, and Lord Home moved from the Commonwealth Relations Office to become Foreign Secretary.

Lloyd had no wish to leave the Foreign Office; he had no experience of economics and little interest in the management of the economy. He was not a success in his new post, but enjoyed using his legal talents to improve methods of taxation. Alec Cairncross describes him as having 'no knowledge of economic theory, shy and rather diffident in discussing matters with experts, and at the same time distrustful of would-be experts. He stuttered more than any other Minister I have known and was given to taking up the time of his officials in long meetings to draft speeches and memoranda.' According to Cairncross, the Government's Economic Adviser Robert Hall had 'no very high opinion of him, but there were no marked disagreements'. Samuel Brittan writes in his book *The Treasury under the Tories*: 'He did not have a large enough grasp to distinguish between big issues and minor points of detail, and he seemed to think about economic policy without the aid of any intellectual framework.' Brittan considers Amory to have been 'intellectually' the better Chancellor.[1]

Amory's gloom over the balance of payments was soon justified: the October 1960 trade figures proved alarming with the trade gap up from £76 million in September to £122 million, although part of the rise could be attributed to a strike of tally clerks in the London docks. Even so, Lloyd was able to bring bank rate down to 5 per cent. In March 1961 there was a serious balance of payments crisis following the revaluation of the German mark, and the intervention of the central banks was needed to put a 'safety net' under sterling. This provided a difficult scenario for Lloyd's first Budget in April 1961.

The week before the Budget Macmillan and Lloyd held a 'mini economic summit' at Chequers which led the press to speculate that the Prime Minister was running the Treasury. Macmillan would certainly have liked to do so and his flow of memoranda to the Chancellor never ceased; he found Lloyd more malleable than Amory.

On 3 February 1961 Sir Frank Lee had told Lloyd that a tough Budget was needed. Previously the internal Budget Committee had suggested the introduction of regulators to raise taxes between Budgets and deplored the lack of a capital gains tax as the 'largest defect'. Lloyd shied away from a capital gains tax but was attracted by the idea of regulators.

Two regulators were suggested by the Treasury and accepted by Lloyd. The first was the purchase tax regulator which gave the Chancellor the power to vary duty on tobacco, alcohol and petrol and all consumer goods by up to 10 per cent between Budgets. This became law and was a useful method of applying the accelerator or the brake to the economy. Lloyd's second regulator was a pay roll tax. This ran into difficulty and resulted in a little known threat of resignation from John Boyd-Carpenter, the Minister of Pensions.

A pay roll tax was a headage payment by all employers for every worker on their pay roll. It was the brainchild of Robert Hall, who first put forward the idea at a meeting of the Budget Committee on 15 June 1960 when Amory was still Chancellor. Lloyd was immediately attracted by it. Hall held a dinner discussion with Lord Robbins, the academic economist, and Lord Plowden, former Chairman of the Atomic Energy Commission, on 5 January 1961. Both approved of the plan and thought it ought to be operated 'by way of adjustment of the National Insurance employers' contribution to the National Insurance stamp'. The Treasury considered that it would be a valuable tool to prevent overheating of the economy, and it was decided in the draft Budget that it should be collected by taking powers to vary the National Insurance stamp charge.[2]

Boyd-Carpenter, who has told the author that he was not consulted in advance by Lloyd although as Minister of Pensions he should have been, wrote a strong protest to Lloyd:

> The stamp is the only effective discipline against irresponsible pressure for improvements in National Insurance benefits, particularly pensions. We shall be undermining this principle if we use the contribution or any part of it nakedly as a means of taxation unappropriated to the service.
>
> As I understand it the Chancellor's proposal has the intention that the surcharge shall be imposed in time of boom, and that it will be passed on to the consumer in the form of higher prices. Movement in the Retail Price Index is a main factor in determining amounts of benefits and National Insurance rates and the surcharge will in this way both further provoke pressure for increased benefit rates and seem to provide the means for financing them.

Lloyd wrote to the Prime Minister that Boyd-Carpenter would certainly resign if he proceeded with the proposed stamp charge and said that much as he would like the revenue he was prepared to drop the proposal, although he did not consider Boyd-Carpenter's arguments sufficient to outweigh the benefits of the regulator. 'However, the last thing I want to do is to inflict on you another resignation crisis. I myself would not die in the last ditch over this. I am afraid I can do no more with him.'[3]

As usual Macmillan asked Butler, the Home Secretary, to pour oil on troubled waters. After talking to Boyd-Carpenter Butler was convinced that the Minister of Pensions would press his opposition to the proposals to the utmost, and told Macmillan so, adding that he thought the Budget was already overcrowded – 'There is plenty in it without the proposal affecting the Minister of Pensions. The House may think one economic regulator is enough.' The plan, Butler concluded, should be dropped on general grounds.

The Prime Minister asked Boyd-Carpenter, who was not in the Cabinet, to attend the Cabinet on 1 April. Having been offered a drafting amendment in the Budget speech in the form 'I will consider other methods of levying such a surcharge', Boyd-Carpenter withdrew his objection. A political storm was avoided, but the second regulator was never operated although it became law.

Apart from the difficulties over the pay roll regulator Lloyd's first Budget proposals in 1961 were welcomed by the Cabinet. Heeding Lee's words that 'a tough Budget' was needed, Lloyd was persuaded by the Treasury to budget for a large surplus. He raised the limit for exemption on earned income for surtax from £2,000 to £5,000, to the delight of his supporters, and recovered the revenue lost by an increase in profits tax. To the relief of most Conservative MPs Lloyd refused to create a capital gains tax. However his refusal to do away with Schedule A tax was more controversial. The 1960 Conservative Party Conference at Scarborough had passed a motion calling for its abolition, and the Prime Minister had argued for this in talks with Lloyd in March 1961, asking the Chancellor to take into account that all houses which were owner-occupied including new ones had to be assessed for Schedule A on 1935 values, which was absurd, whilst the Inland Revenue feared that any increase in Schedule A assessments would lead to a rush of rating appeals which would overwhelm the system.

The failure to remove Schedule A led to a loss of many Conservative votes to the Liberals in by-elections because the Liberals campaigned for the immediate abolition of Schedule A and their candidates sent out leaflets to owner-occupiers explaining how to make maintenance claims based on the cost of their repairs so that they need not pay the tax. This became a powerful source of support for Liberals in residential areas which were traditionally Conservative.

Martin Redmayne, the Chief Conservative Whip, commented to the Prime Minister after the 1961 Budget statement: 'There is fairly strong objection to the pay roll tax. The Northern Irish members are writing to you and will put down an amendment unless they can receive some assurance that it will not apply to development areas there.' At this stage William Armstrong of the Treasury, soon to become Joint Treasury Permanent Secretary, recommended the Chancellor to drop the second regulator, the pay roll tax, but in his television broadcast following the Budget Lloyd said putting 4s (20p) on the National Insurance stamp by the pay roll tax would give him power to raise £2,000 million which was 'an important anti-inflationary measure'. Harold Wilson, who must have had wind of the Tory dispute, said prophetically that Lloyd would never use this regulator.[4] He was right.

The 1961 Budget was soon followed by a repeat of the sterling crisis of September 1957. The Treasury had forecast 'very slow growth in 1961'; instead, the first half of 1961 saw growth at a fast 4 per cent, with the labour market very tight and an alarming increase in wage settlements and bad balance of payments figures. As before 'hot' money in London had buoyed up the value of the pound, and when in his Mansion House speech in 1960 the Governor of the Bank of England, Lord Cobbold, in a much-quoted and misleading remark, had said: 'A good deal of what now looks like "hot" money may turn out to be more permanent investment,' he was being wildly over-optimistic.

When on 5 March 1961 the German mark was revalued upwards the 'hot' money poured out of London and many authoritative commentators said that sterling would be devalued as part of a general realignment of currencies. A more astute Chancellor than Lloyd would have appreciated this in time, and brought in an even tougher Budget as advocated by some of his Treasury advisers, although the Prime Minister would have been opposed. Reduction in demand in the 1961 Budget could have improved the balance of payments position substantially.

In April 1961 the Treasury prepared a memorandum on the balance of payments prospects. Bligh minuted to the Prime Minister that this paper showed the outlook to be 'very bad, and there does not seem to be any idea as to how to meet the situation. I suppose there are only three courses: (1) Devaluation. (2) Import controls. (3) Significant expansion in world trade in which our exports could play their part.' Bligh emphasized that because of the alarming balance of payments prospects remedial action must be taken in the very near future.

Faced with this daunting prospect Macmillan and Lloyd discussed the possibility of imposing import controls – which Lloyd turned down – and of raising the bank rate – which he again rejected 'because this would just attract hot money from overseas'; it was too late also, the Chancellor argued, to make further changes in initial deposits on hire purchase. Macmillan wanted to call for higher special deposits by banks, but Lloyd had been advised that these would not be effective, and that 'there would be some embarrassment picking yet again on the banks when we are unable to produce any viable means of comparable restraint on the finance houses.'*

The Prime Minister also wanted drastic cuts in public spending. Spending had been worrying him before the Budget and on 20 March 1961 he had sent a testy note to Lloyd about trends in public spending: 'You and your group have shown that this problem is virtually insoluble. It is therefore only fair that you should be charged with finding the solution.'[5] Lloyd proposed to form a small Ministerial group to produce a plan for controlling the public sector; but though Macmillan liked this idea, nothing came of it as with so many of the hares which the Prime Minister started in the financial field.

Evidence of Macmillan's frustration came when the Secretary to the Cabinet, Norman Brook, submitted a report on overseas aid and diplomatic spending abroad, reminding Macmillan that he had personally promised Kennedy that we would support the work of the United States in development assistance. The Prime Minister minuted: 'Yes, but what will happen? Pledges and agreements cannot be honoured if the dough is not there.'[6]

Alec Cairncross succeeded Robert Hall as Economic Adviser to the Government on 1 June 1961. He was immediately asked by Lloyd for his advice on how to deal with the balance of payments crisis. Lloyd was particularly worried by the failure of production to rise but did not, according to Cairncross, have 'a particular anxiety' over the pound.

On 6 June Cairncross submitted a paper pointing out that there was an urgent need to make room for a big expansion in exports: the reduction in domestic purchasing power needed to free resources for exports would be about £600 million a year. He proposed as a first step a cut of £300 million. The Budget Committee of the Treasury agreed and asked the Chancellor to use both regulators to bring in £300 million. Simultaneously the Bank of England warned the Chancellor that the reserves were being run down rapidly and a dangerous situation was looming.

---

*Merchant banks as opposed to the big five clearing banks were immune to the compulsory special deposit which the clearing banks were forced to make.

Cabinet Ministers had a nasty shock when Lloyd submitted a memorandum to them dated 28 June 1961 stating that 'the pressures on the economy both from without and within are becoming increasingly dangerous . . . the situation is more serious than at any time during the past ten years.' Lloyd pointed out that since the middle of 1959 the balance of payments had been heavily in deficit, and prospects until 1962 and beyond were bad; 'a succession of adverse balances of this duration is unprecedented in our post-war experience. This prospect is alarming.' Lloyd stated that he must reduce government expenditure and home demand and restrain the growth of wages and salaries; without wage restraint, he emphasized, we should be forced into devaluation of the pound.

The Prime Minister and his Cabinet colleagues much disliked the Chancellor's plans but could conceive of no viable alternative. They were debated at three acrimonious Cabinets. At the first on 30 June Lord Home, the Foreign Secretary, raised serious objections to cut-backs in spending on troops in Europe because it would weaken NATO. In the face of Soviet threats over Berlin* Macmillan agreed that no action could be taken which would in any way weaken the alliance. Surprisingly import controls were rejected by the Cabinet on the grounds that they would be too slow-acting, and Christopher Soames, Minister of Agriculture, supported by several other members of the Cabinet, stated categorically that he could not agree to any reduction in farm subsidies.

Several members thought that the long-term balance of payments could not be corrected without floating the pound. Lloyd did not comment. Now under grave attack, Lloyd weakly agreed to review his proposals in light of the Cabinet criticisms. He was unable to come up with alternatives.[7]

On 20 July the Cabinet resumed their discussion, Lloyd detailing the measures he would announce to the Commons on 25 July. Again he emphasized the need for wage restraint although he had no coherent plans to put this into effect. The President of the Board of Trade stressed that to secure wage restraint it was essential to impose a tax on short-term capital gains on investments and land. Lloyd promised to try to refer to this in his statement. He did not do so, although Macmillan emphasized in Cabinet that short-term capital gains should not be exempt from tax.[8] The success of the measures, the Cabinet agreed, depended on Lloyd being successful in finding a means of imposing wage restraint, although the Chancellor offered no plausible explanation of how he would do so. All this Cabinet achieved was to decide not to approve the latest increases in teachers' salaries which had recently been agreed.

---

*See Chapter 15.

At a final meeting on 24 July, after a weekend meeting at Chequers between Macmillan and Lloyd, the Cabinet reiterated their objection to a pay roll tax and emphasized their belief that success in achieving wage restraint 'would be decisive for the future of the economy'. Reluctantly they agreed to the harsh measures proposed by Lloyd. Lloyd stated that if necessary he would not hesitate to bring in further measures to damp down demand. The Cabinet were under no illusions; they knew that the mini-budget that Lloyd was to announce the next day would have ominous repercussions on Conservative popularity.[9]

The emergency or 'little Budget' which Lloyd introduced on 25 July 1961 raised the purchase tax regulator by the maximum 10 per cent, and put a fierce squeeze on government spending and bank advances, on top of raising the bank rate to 7 per cent. These measures were highly deflationary and gave a sharp shock to the economy. With⅞his 10 per cent rise in purchase tax Lloyd withdrew £210 million purchasing power; it was the biggest immediate cut in purchasing power in peacetime.

The Treasury and even more the Bank of England did not look on these measures as adequate to save sterling and had argued in favour of raising income tax. To raise income tax so soon after the April Budget would have been humiliating for the Government, and already it was crystal clear there was nothing in the little Budget which could not have been enacted with more dignity in the April Budget. On 25 July Lloyd also announced that the Government would review defence expenditure in Germany, cut overseas administrative expenditure and restrict overseas investment by holders of sterling.

On 28 July 1961 the Prime Minister wrote to all spending Ministers asking them to scrutinize their expenditure with utmost stringency both for the rest of the year and for 1962/63: 'Rigid economy is necessary both in current expenditure and capital expenditure. I do not want any temporary adjustments or shifts which secure immediate savings by piling up greater expenditure later. The aim must be to secure true and lasting savings.'[10] This note is evidence of how worried Macmillan was about the run on sterling and the danger it posed to the Government's credibility and popularity if the crisis ended in a panic devaluation of the pound. Sir David Eccles, Minister of Education, refused to make cuts in education spending; other spending Ministers tried to be more co-operative.

The Treasury had alarmed the Cabinet with warnings early in 1961 that, with the extreme shortage of labour, pay rises were getting out of hand: the most important part of Lloyd's 25 July statement therefore, so far as the Government was concerned, was the institution of a 'pay pause'. Unfortunately no effective machinery for imposing it was ever devised and it became a will-o'-the-wisp.

It is strange that Lloyd had not heeded the warnings of his Treasury advisers and accepted that wages were out of control before his April Budget. The *Economic Survey* pointed out that earnings per head in the second half of 1961 were forecast to be 6½ per cent higher than in the previous year which was far higher than productivity could possibly rise. In his Budget speech Lloyd mentioned the Treasury's fear 'that the cost inflationary process will speed up further. That I feel is the principal menace at present which it is impossible to exaggerate.'

Surtax concessions without any quid pro quo such as capital gains tax to redress the social balance created the worst possible scenario in which to introduce a pay standstill three months after the Budget. Almost incredibly Lloyd announced the pay pause without consultation with the trade unions.* His explanation was that he could not put them in the picture without mentioning his other measures including the 7 per cent bank rate which had to be kept confidential. He would have been wiser to have introduced his package in two stages – passing the fiscal measures first and then holding discussions with the unions.

In his 'little Budget' speech on 25 July Selwyn Lloyd pointed out to the Commons that in 1960 wages and salaries had increased by 8 per cent while national production had only risen by 3 per cent. This, he said, meant we were becoming uncompetitive and therefore a pay pause was essential. The trade unions reacted badly and immediately the Government were caught up in conflict with them. The July measures restored confidence in the pound but the Government failed miserably with their pay pause.

The Prime Minister's and Cabinet's view was that the pay pause was an appeal to the common sense and patriotism of both employers and employed. Unfortunately Lloyd and the Treasury had overlooked that in many industries there were automatic pay increases corresponding to rises in the Retail Price Index while compulsory arbitration was in force in others. Neither employers nor trade unions would agree to set these arrangements aside to oblige the Government. Also in the very tight labour market there was a widespread tendency among employers, when they needed to recruit or keep workers or attract them from other firms, to offer inducements by upgrading jobs into a superior category carrying automatically higher rates of pay. Industrialists showed little loyalty to the Government over the pay pause.

The Government had conceived the July 1961 pay pause as a temporary expedient to last only until 31 March 1962, and balked at taking

---

* Sir Alec Cairncross visited George Woodcock, the TUC General Secretary, and found him 'indignant' because he had not been consulted beforehand.

statutory powers to enforce it. A gaping hole in the pay pause was driven with the award of double what the Government expected to electricity workers in November. The Prime Minister was angry because the negotiator and the Minister of Power, Richard Wood, did not inform him or Lloyd before they made the agreement.[11] This breakdown shows how ill thought out was the procedure. Only in the public sector could the Government enforce the pay pause, and this led to grave resentment from civil servants and other state employees.

There is no satisfactory evidence that the pay pause was an important factor in slowing down pay rises between 25 July 1961 and April 1962. Treasury calculations designed to show the success of the pause cannot stand up to 'rigorous sceptical scrutiny'. The statistics show undeniably that wage push inflation had led to an increase of 1.6 points in the Retail Price Index between 13 March and 17 April 1962 – the largest rise for any month for six years – while the cost of living rose by 5½ points between the General Election in October 1959 and April 1962. The Government had been beating the air with their July to March pay pause. Rising unemployment was more important in keeping down wage settlements than government entreaties.[12]

With the introduction of the Chancellor's go-slow measures on 25 July 1961 the Government desperately needed to show that they had some long-term economic plan apart from 'stop-go' and adjusting the brake and accelerator according to the monthly balance of payments figures. In his 25 July statement Lloyd forecast the creation of a new institution for joint planning of the economy: after long consultation Macmillan and Lloyd had decided to invite both sides of industry to join a 'National Planning Council' (later entitled the National Economic Development Council: NEDC). The idea was not welcomed by some members of the Cabinet; Maudling, President of the Board of Trade, was the main opponent. However in spite of remonstrances, the Cabinet acquiesced. Frank Lee had been ill during the July crisis. As soon as he was well enough to work again, he did everything he could to bring into effect a planning body, and insisted with Lloyd that it must be outside the Treasury if it was to obtain the confidence of the unions.

At first leading trade unionists were diffident about serving, but with tact their objections were overcome so that the TUC gave a provisional agreement to participate on 20 November 1961, but withheld final agreement for two more months because of disagreement over the pay pause. However the TUC only agreed to join on the express understanding that their representatives would not be asked to preach wage restraint. Finally the Council met on 7 March 1962. It had six private industry employers, six trade unionists, two independent members (Lord Franks and Professor Phelps Brown) and three Cabinet Ministers (the Chancellor, the President of the Board of Trade and the Minister of Labour). It was given an office outside the Treasury on the Embankment.

Obviously there were considerable advantages to be derived from the contacts and discussions between the Government and leaders of industry and the trade unions about the economy, but the achievements of NEDC were infinitesimal and it never justified the Government's high-falutin claims for its role in guiding the economy. Harold Wilson claimed with justification that NEDC in its first phase made no contribution at all to solving our economic problems.

The NEDC's main report, *Growth of the United Kingdom Economy to 1966*, optimistically claimed that a 4 per cent growth rate between 1961 and 1966 should not prove 'impossible'. By the time this report was published in spring 1963 investment in new machinery and factories was so poor and unemployment so high that the country was already a long way behind the predicted target. NEDC stated frankly that if the target was to be reached British exports would have to be more competitively priced, although they made no suggestions as to how this could be accomplished. All illusions that Britain might have cheaper exports were shattered when, twelve weeks later, their first report was followed by a second, *Conditions Favourable to Faster Growth*, which showed that British export prices during 1962 had risen while those of her competitors had on average remained stable.[13]

The first NEDC report contained detailed estimates of the probable growth of seventeen of the most important national industries based on the assumption of entering the Common Market. The credibility of this survey was demolished by the amazing remark, 'The effect of non-entry [to the EEC] is negligible,' which made a nonsense of the Government's European policy. For the coal industry NEDC predicted that 236,000 miners were expected to leave between 1961 and 1966 whereas in the previous five years only 135,000 had left. They forecast that the dwindling coal mines would raise their output to 2,000 million tons, though stating that it was already clear that much of export manufacturing industry would have to switch to cheaper sources of energy if they were to survive. For steel in particular, they emphasized, cheap fuel was important in order to compete with Continental manufacturers who were obtaining cheaper supplies than British steel makers.

Neither report produced any fresh ideas how the Government might solve the recurrent balance of payments problem and encourage the expansion of the economy so that British standards of living might rise as fast as those in other industrial countries. Both NEDC reports turned out to be damp squibs and damaged the Government's credibility. Seldom can a Prime Minister and Chancellor have been so wrong in attributing such importance to the role of planning as Lloyd and Macmillan were over NEDC. During Macmillan's premiership NEDC did nothing to affect industrial practice and must be dismissed as a failure. Further efforts at economic planning by Labour also came to nothing.

On 18 and 25 October 1961 Roy Harrod, the Prime Minister's economic guru, wrote two long letters to Macmillan. The correspondence amounted to a repetition of his previous arguments in favour of continuous expansion and import controls; he said he was 'deeply distressed' at the brakes on growth imposed by Lloyd in his 25 July measures.[14] Harrod claimed that 'the embarrassment in the summer of 1961 was due to the wantonly precipitate de-restrictions on imports by that know-all Fred Erroll', then President of the Board of Trade; and that Lord Cromer, the new Governor of the Bank of England, and Selwyn Lloyd had let it be known in Washington that his (Macmillan's) view on international finance did not represent British thinking. Harrod wanted the Prime Minister to 'jolly well tell them of how you were sabotaged on your recent visit to Kennedy'. This was a wild statement, but Macmillan as usual took Harrod with grim seriousness, and asked him to lunch at Downing Street to meet William Armstrong of the Treasury.

Following this meeting Macmillan as usual made the Treasury draft a reply to Harrod. On 3 November 1961 Cairncross wrote to Macmillan stating first that Harrod covered 'so many different aspects of economic policy' that it would be difficult to deal adequately with all the points without trying the Prime Minister's patience'. Cairncross also pointed out that some of the points now raised by Harrod had been dealt with before in replies by his predecessor Robert Hall. Harrod had belittled the importance of a short-term wages policy while stressing the importance of a long-term one. Cairncross pointed out that the attempt at a pay pause had been received favourably abroad, and had produced greater confidence in the stability of sterling, and if we had tried to run the economy at an even higher pressure of demand than we had done we should have run into even bigger crises in our balance of payments.

To Harrod's suggestion of an annual expansion target of 5 or 6 per cent, Cairncross replied that this would land the country back in another foreign exchange crisis within a year.* Over import restrictions Cairncross thought Harrod 'wrong-headed' and, as the machinery had been dismantled, it would take some time to bring it into operation again and an anticipatory increase in imports would be likely, while it was 'not open to us to impose import restrictions at the same time as

---

* Sir Alec Cairncross told the author that Selwyn Lloyd also wanted a 5 per cent growth target, and he had to argue him out of it.

we still owe money to the IMF and it will be some years before it is repaid'. (The IMF debt arose from post-Suez drawings.)

On aid to undeveloped countries Harrod wanted to give India £1,000 million, plus large sums to other undeveloped countries so as to get the maximum opportunities to export to them. Cairncross commented:

> Not only would we have to raise the money in taxation but we should also be in some difficulty in our balance of payments . . . we simply do not have the spare capacity and manpower to produce the additional quantity of goods . . . and [it would mean] limiting our power to export to other countries.[15]

Macmillan does not mention any of this in his memoirs although it took up much of his time and that of his advisers. In spite of this crushing rebuff to Harrod from an authoritative source Macmillan continued to welcome his letters and to send notes to his Chancellor trying to point him in one direction or another – notes, so Cairncross records, that were always expansionist and 'sometimes remarkably naïve'.

A Treasury memorandum on economies in public spending was submitted to the Cabinet on 30 October but not discussed. This produced an outburst from Macleod, now Conservative Party Chairman;* in a minute to the Prime Minister he pointed out that 'major decisions would be needed' which were likely to boil down to questions of additional charges on children or health services – a position that had been reached at least four times in the last ten years. He in effect threatened resignation if major cuts were made. Macmillan sent Macleod's letter to Martin Redmayne, the Chief Whip, with a squiggle: 'Chief Whip, I do not think anything need be done on this message. Do you? Should I acknowledge it or not?' Redmayne replied 'No' to both questions, indicating that he had had enough of Macleod's resignation tactics over African affairs,† and no more was heard by way of protest from Macleod.[16]

As it became apparent that the pay pause with its appeal to patriotism was not producing results, Frank Lee headed a Treasury team to work out a set of guidelines designed to govern the movement of wages. Their conclusions appeared as a White Paper in February 1962 – *Incomes Policy – the Next Step*. In this the Government gave approval to a 'guiding light' of 2–2½ per cent annually for wage increases.

The official published Treasury forecast was 'No great likelihood of deep recession' and a slow recovery in the first half of 1962 gathering speed in the second half with rising exports.[17] They were wrong. In the

---

* The press at this stage were flattering Macleod, and predicting that he would replace Macmillan as Conservative leader.
† See Chapter 12.

first half of 1962 exports did well, increasing by 5 per cent, but in the second half they flattened out as a result of the expansion of internal trade in the Common Market while Britain's goods were penalized by higher import tariffs together with a depression in the USA.

In the Treasury Budget discussions a rise in gross domestic production of 4 per cent was forecast; this was far above the rate actually achieved. The Bank of England was worried that taxes would have to be raised because of the high borrowing requirement, while sterling was troubled by rumours that if Britain joined the Common Market the pound would be immediately devalued. In the end the Treasury under Cairncross's influence recommended a neutral Budget for 1962 although Macmillan as usual wanted tax cuts for expansion.

By early 1962, as a result of the pay pause and the economic slow-down following the July 1961 measures, the Government had become very unpopular. By-elections went badly, with the Liberals the chief beneficiaries, and the safe Tory seat of Orpington was lost to them by a large margin in March.

After the Orpington result Iain Macleod wrote to the Prime Minister:

One thing that emerges with absolute clarity is that the popular reasons such as pensions, Schedule A, nuclear disarmament and colonial policy had nothing whatever to do with the result.* Incomparably the leading factor was the dislike of the Government ... I am sure it is true as the pay pause begins to show results much of the dissatisfaction will be removed, but a great deal will hang both on the Budget and on the words that the Chancellor uses when he speaks.[18]

Macmillan agreed strongly that 'a great deal will hang on the Budget', and he was disappointed when it proved not to signal a new period of strong growth in the economy.

Instead Lloyd's second spring Budget was neutral and pleased nobody, least of all the Prime Minister. What was given with one hand was taken away with the other. Grotesquely, purchase tax was reduced on motor cars, television sets and washing machines but increased on soft drinks, sweets and ice cream. Lloyd ducked on Schedule A, though hard pressed to remove it by the Prime Minister. In an effort to conciliate the trade unions a short-term capital gains tax was introduced, paid only on profits arising from sales of shares on the Stock Exchange within six months of purchase, or land within three. This was quickly seen to be innocuous because speculators only had to wait for one day after the six-month period to cash their gains tax-free.

---

*Macleod was quite wrong about Schedule A, which was manna to Liberal candidates.

At the Cabinet meeting of 7 April 1962 at which the Budget proposals were discussed Lloyd faced severe criticism; he wrote in his diary: 'Hailsham said the Budget was unsaleable. Eccles said the economic balance was right but the methods were wrong, and others joined in. Not one of those whom I had consulted supported it.' Belatedly Lloyd included a promise to abolish Schedule A in a future Budget and made changes in his draft speech. He knew the Cabinet expected him to improve their election chances, and was depressed because he felt he could not do this without damage to his efforts to put the economy on a sound footing.

Macmillan was acutely aware of his colleagues' disenchantment with the Chancellor. However he managed to write after the Budget speech to Lloyd: 'Your colleagues were too apprehensive. The scale of reform was put across admirably. The last-minute change was right; I am sure of that. Well done! You must be tired, but happy.' Lloyd was not happy. Seldom has a Chancellor been forced to make last-minute changes because of criticism from his colleagues.[19] The popular newspapers spotlighted the unpopularity of taxes on sweets amongst the young whilst the broadsheets regretted that there were no export incentives nor any relaxation of credit controls.

Other journalists seized on Lloyd's admission in his Budget speech that Schedule A was an unfair tax, although he refused to abolish it until next year's Budget. This was a clumsy attempt to defuse criticism and journalists argued that if he thought it 'unfair' he should remove it immediately. Schedule A, Bernard Levin commented, was now Schedule 'Orpington'; the promise to remove it in 1963 was received as a gimmick to spike the Liberal guns.

There was a sigh of relief from the City of London over the details of the short-term capital gains tax. A swingeing tax on capital gains had been expected as a quid pro quo for trade union co-operation in a pay pause. However the cut-off period of six months was hailed by financial journalists as farcical. The much esteemed economic commentator Nicholas Davenport wrote in the *Spectator*: 'I cannot imagine anyone being fool enough to pay it.' He called it a 'mouse of a tax', an accusation repeated by other journalists. Davenport pointed out that although the tax would prevent dealings by a few private 'stags'* and professional short-term operators on the Stock Exchange, anyone could avoid it by running a six months Stock Exchange account or by waiting one day over the six-month period before cashing gains. He also declared that the yield would be minimal, which it was.[20]

---

*Professional Stock Exchange operators who subscribed to new issues solely for the purpose of drawing an immediate profit.

The trade unions had let it be known that they would only co-operate in economic planning and a pay pause in return for controls on prices, profits and dividends. Neither Lloyd nor Macmillan had ever contemplated such drastic steps. Although, prior to the Budget, they had discussed means of controlling prices in line with the brake on wage increases, they could agree on nothing practical.

Before the Budget Macmillan had had high hopes that Lloyd would come up with some innovations that would restore lagging Conservative electoral fortunes. They had had several cordial discussions but none of the many suggestions coming from Macmillan's fertile brain aroused any spark in Lloyd.

The poor reception of the Budget and the ineptness of the short-term capital gains tax exposed by the press, together with Conservative displeasure at the refusal to abolish Schedule A, sowed the seeds of dissatisfaction in Macmillan's mind at Lloyd's performance and doubts about his ability to save the Conservatives from electoral defeat. He decided to give Lloyd a last chance to redeem his lack-lustre Budget and to create a more imaginative economic policy. New economic tools were badly needed to keep the economy on an even keel, and make it possible to introduce a tax-cutting and vote-winning Budget in 1963 or 1964 before the General Election which had to be held at the latest in the autumn of 1964. On 11 April 1962 Macmillan wrote to him:

> I cannot see why you should take much part in the Finance Bill [Budget] debates. You have three Treasury Ministers. Cripps refused and got away with it. If you get immersed in the Finance Bill you will lose three vital months when you ought to be thinking about the future. We ought to be preparing right away possibilities for next year's Budget on the assumption that the economic situation allows an expansion Budget and substantial reductions in taxation. Do not leave it too late.
>
> It is as easy to study them now as at Christmas ... Should we make income tax changes particularly advantageous to the classes of the population who are now most squeezed – for married people in children's allowances – for old people in increased unearned income allowances – for all pensioners consideration to be given – as to other pensions should not they be regarded as earned income and so forth?
>
> These measures to be weighed against the psychological and political advantages of a straight reduction in income tax. I am very anxious that we should start work on all these immediately after Easter. As the summer progresses we shall be immersed in Common Market discussions and have time for little else.[21]

Lloyd was more interested in using his legal skill to simplify existing taxation and had neither flair nor enthusiasm for planning electioneering Budgets. He failed completely to respond to Macmillan's prodding, and this failure to produce any new ideas led to his early downfall.

An important Cabinet discussion of economic policy took place on 3 May 1962. The official Cabinet minutes reveal little, but Sir Norman Brook thought the discussion so important that he wrote a long account for the Prime Minister thinking it would be more 'illuminating' than the minutes: he did not consider it suitable for a full record in the printed Cabinet minutes (evidence of how misleading official Cabinet minutes can be to historians).

According to Brook, Lloyd stated naïvely that the policy of wage restraint was providing a sound base for economic expansion and if it could be accepted as a permanent feature there were 'grounds for sober confidence about the future'. In the ensuing discussion other Ministers agreed that the incomes policy was being a success but they recognized that it had not been well received and was one of the causes of the Government's unpopularity. A few Ministers felt that despite this unpopularity it was essential to maintain the White Paper policy 'for the immediate period'. The majority felt that it would not be possible to maintain the policy 'unless steps were taken to remedy before long some of the injustices to which it had given rise'. All agreed on the need for the early formation of a permanent incomes policy which would avoid anomalous treatment for categories such as nurses, probation officers and university teachers by providing a means of revaluing certain categories of workers without provoking demands 'for consequential increases from other classes'. (This was crying for the moon.) They considered it indefensible that 'wage differentials should be permanently petrified at the level at which they had happened to stand in July 1961; a permanent incomes policy, if it was to be acceptable, must be formulated in consultation with employers and trade unions.' When it was suggested that it should be evolved through NEDC the Ministers directly concerned thought it 'most unlikely' that the Council would endorse a permanent incomes policy. Summing up, Macmillan said they must dramatize 'the Government's approach to the country's problems by a speaking campaign'. The kindest comment one can make is that the Cabinet were confused.[22]

After reading Brook's account Macmillan produced a long memorandum for his colleagues instructing them to make a concerted effort in their public statements to forget their own preoccupations with particular issues and to concentrate on 'claiming success for our economic policies'. The main points which he wanted Ministers to stress 'whenever possible' were that

(1) Policies of restraint 'are the means to the end . . . of creating a firm base for expansion.

(2) The supreme task is to keep the pound strong; if we fail,

devaluation will follow causing grave damage; last spring we faced 'the most serious sustained attack on sterling since the war' which put a drain on our reserves, but after borrowing heavily from the IMF and Central Banks our reserves are now much higher than last July.

(3) The tough credit squeeze has prevented excess pressure on the economy from building up. It slowed expansion, but 'this could not be avoided if we were to build a firm base for future growth.'

(4) 'Our incomes policy, by slowing down increases in costs, has improved our competitive position. There is a good chance of getting through NEDC the national co-operation we need for sound growth.'

(5) The tough 1962 Budget must be explained by saying that if the 'economy had been stimulated in April by cuts in taxes, this would have ... led to real trouble as our exports grew'. The strong Budget has made possible reductions in bank rate and possible relaxation of credit restrictions.

(6) By next April personal consumption in real terms should be 4 per cent higher, and we are on the way to 'doubling our standard of living'.

Although this exercise failed to convince journalists and the public of the merits of Conservative economic policy, it reveals clearly Macmillan's intense worry about the state of the economy and his dissatisfaction with his Chancellor and the Treasury after the 1962 Budget, and also his wrong judgement of the mood of the country.[23]

Harrod suggested after the Budget that Macmillan ought to announce that he was aiming at a growth rate of 4.1 per cent per annum. The Prime Minister passed his letter on to the Treasury. Cairncross thought that such an announcement would prove 'very embarrassing' because the Prime Minister would then be asked what the implications were for government policy, and how the Government proposed to make productivity grow at least 50 per cent faster than in the past decade. Harrod had also asked for restrictions on machinery imports and a ban on the chartering of foreign tankers; Cairncross replied that we should aim at a larger total volume of trade rather than 'crash action' to help the balance of trade current account. Macmillan shied away from the import controls which Harrod was urging, and became enthusiastic for a formal incomes policy. He found the difficulties were as great as those of imposing a price freeze.[24]

The idea that a pay pause could be imposed solely by pressure of public opinion was a non-starter especially after George Woodcock, Secretary-General of the TUC, publicly stated that the intrusion of a third party into wage bargaining was an 'impertinence'. Macmillan became more and more anxious to set up formal machinery to make an incomes policy effective, when the nurses and dockers in May 1962 received an award far in excess of the norm set out in the February White Paper. The press described this as driving a coach and horses through the Government's incomes policy and maintained that the pay pause was not working. In vain Macmillan looked to Lloyd as Chancellor of the Exchequer to take the initiative. As Lloyd produced nothing, the Prime Minister took the matter into his own hands and called a meeting at Chequers on Sunday, 20 May. This was the start of discussions which led to the appointment in July of the National Incomes Commission whose remit was to pronounce judgement on wage settlements. With Lloyd lukewarm, Macmillan personally took charge of the plan. NIC did not come into being until after Selwyn Lloyd had been replaced by Reginald Maudling as Chancellor on 13 July, though the new Chancellor showed as little enthusiasm for the idea as had Lloyd.

NIC did not hear its first case until 1963; in all, it heard four cases, and was made impotent by the boycott of the trade unions. As a result NIC had no significance as a contribution to a long-term incomes policy,[25] and its failure must be accounted a humiliation for Macmillan whose personal initiative it was.

CHAPTER 6

Macmillan's Last Chancellor

THE 1959 BUDGET with its massive tax cuts had triggered off a spending spree which caused long-term balance of payments problems. Selwyn Lloyd's measures of July 1961 went too far the other way; they severely depressed the economy, and obscured the fact that the pound was over-valued.

The neutral Budget of 1962 was unpopular; the weakness of the pound made it difficult for the Government to give the tax concessions which the public wanted. Instead of facing up to the unpalatable fact that the pound was over-valued the Government believed that by planning with NEDC, and curbing wage increases through NIC, they could still have a pre-election boom without inflation or a crisis over the pound. They were wrong. Shortly before Macmillan resigned he had accepted that alternative measures such as floating the pound or import controls were needed if there was to be a pre-election boom. During the last months of his premiership he and his Chancellor of the Exchequer, Reginald Maudling, were agreed on what should be done. After Macmillan had resigned, these precautions were forgotten.

After the 1962 Budget Lloyd and Macmillan had several private discussions which focused on the shape of the 1963 Budget.[1] Macmillan had almost decided to hold the General Election in the autumn of 1963 and was determined on an expansionary 1963 spring Budget with tax lolly for the voters. He and Lloyd differed. The Chancellor with his nonconformist conscience feared that too rapid expansion in an election year would produce damaging inflation. Macmillan, still under Harrod's influence, did not agree and anyway was prepared to take risks to win the General Election. At the Treasury they joked that Macmillan's motto was 'When in doubt reflate.'[2]

Meanwhile Macmillan had taken preparations for the formation of the National Incomes Commission – to preside over a formal incomes policy – out of Lloyd's hands and into his own. More and more he was acting like a President over financial policy, and he expressed dissatisfaction with Selwyn Lloyd's February White Paper on Incomes Policy, claiming it was 'insufficiently flexible'. When the dockers got a 9 per cent increase on 12 May Macmillan made up his mind to take drastic action by way of a massive shake-up of his Cabinet.

The spring 1962 by-election results were, like Orpington, clear evidence of the continued unpopularity of the Macmillan Government. At Derby North on 17 April the Tory candidate dropped to third place with only half the 1959 vote. Middlesbrough, Stockton-on-Tees, Derby West and West Lothian all showed the Liberals making large inroads into the Tory vote.

Macmillan was convinced that the decline in Tory popularity was due to an over-austere economic policy. As usual he wanted expansion instead. On 22 June Macmillan sent Lloyd a significant minute saying that he was 'making too much of the danger of inflation'. Lloyd's reply spotlighted his disagreement and showed how reluctant he was, like his predecessor, to take risks with the economy to court electoral popularity.

> For the first time since the war there is in general an absence of inflation in the world today, and normal disciplines on prices through international competition have begun to assert themselves. We do not want to see the development of a general deflationary movement, nor would we wish to take action that would create a return to the inflationary conditions of the early post-war era.[3]

This was strictly in line with the orthodox views of the Treasury Knights who were advising Lloyd. They were afraid that reflation of the economy would produce inflation and balance of payments crises. Macmillan on the other hand was ready to take risks in order to start a reflationary boom which would be at full tilt during the General Election.

Macmillan consulted with Rab Butler, Iain Macleod, Chairman of the Party, and Martin Redmayne, the Chief Whip; they all pressed the Prime Minister to make a Cabinet reshuffle before the recess. On 8 July Macmillan gave Butler lunch, and asked him if he favoured Reginald Maudling as the replacement for Lloyd. Butler agreed, and Macmillan then told him he intended to make a number of further Cabinet changes.

On 11 July there was a bizarre incident. At a luncheon given by Lord Rothermere, proprietor of the *Daily Mail*, Butler committed one of the worst indiscretions of his career by leaking that Lloyd was about to go. This was spotlighted in the *Daily Mail* the next day and Whitehall buzzed with rumours. Macmillan had been hoping to ease out Lloyd and the others tactfully; the Butler bombshell convinced him that he must act at once, and on 12 July, in an episode known as 'The Night of Long Knives',* he sacked Lloyd and six other Cabinet Ministers abruptly.

It seemed inconceivable that Lloyd should be sacked summarily without any offer of another post. But the offence was compounded by another bizarre event the following day, when Tim Bligh, Macmillan's private secretary, telephoned Lloyd and said: 'In his distress last evening the Prime Minister forgot to offer you the CH. Would you like it?' Lloyd's biographer, Richard Thorpe, comments:

> The truth remains that whatever the political expedience, however urgent the necessity, Harold Macmillan treated Selwyn in a most shameful and personally wounding manner. The man who was privy to all his counsels was unceremoniously and ungratefully despatched to an intended political oblivion. It was the unworthiest moment of Macmillan's entire premiership.[4]

Few will disagree with this, but happily for Lloyd within fifteen months he returned to high office as soon as Alec Home replaced Macmillan as Prime Minister.

In Maudling Macmillan had the Chancellor of the Exchequer he wanted. Unlike Amory and Lloyd, Maudling, with his great intelligence, had a good understanding of the management of the economy and was ready to dispute and flout the warnings and orthodoxies of the Treasury. Unlike Lloyd he was prepared to reflate, and as will be seen, to plan in conjunction with the Prime Minister the unorthodox measures of floating the pound or imposing import controls if the balance of payments caused trouble before the election.

Reginald Maudling was 'delighted' when on 13 July 1962 Macmillan asked him to take over the Exchequer: he was well qualified and by far the most intelligent and able of the younger Conservative Ministers. Maudling has written that Macmillan's experiences of the shocking conditions of the out-of-work in Stockton in the thirties 'moulded his subsequent approach to economic affairs'. (He could well have written 'muddled' rather than 'moulded'.) Macmillan believed economic policy should always be 'expansionist', and considered that the economic 'orthodoxy' of the Treasury had held back progress and created unnecessary waste of resources.

Macmillan's first directive to Maudling was to break the stop-go cycle and impose an incomes policy which would ensure that an expansionary phase did not lead inevitably to a growth of incomes more rapid than the economy could stand, thus producing inflation and a strain on

---

*See Chapter 18 for a full discussion.

sterling. However both Maudling and Macmillan agreed that it was desirable to have at least a show of continuity with Lloyd's cautious policy and that there should be no untimely dash to a new expansionist policy. As *The Economist* wrote, Maudling's difficulty was 'to reverse the policy of his predecessors while all the time pretending that he was not doing so'.[5]

The real problem, Maudling admits, was how to achieve a steady and adequate rate of growth without inflation. Despite his brilliance and capacity to absorb new ideas and new economic theories rapidly, Maudling failed to solve this problem as abjectly as his predecessors and successors. After working for six months with Maudling, Cairncross noted in his diary: 'The Chancellor keeps his own counsel ... There is undoubtedly some coolness between him and the Department. They don't like his preference for gimmicks ... he has also been fairly free in rejecting advice ... or indicating distrust.'[6]

In the summer and autumn of 1962 the economy slowed down. At the end of August the new Chancellor introduced minor measures to remedy the situation, including a one per cent reduction in bank rate and a release of special deposits. On 5 November 1962 he announced a further package of measures to encourage expansion; the most important was a reduction of tax on motor cars from 45 per cent to 25 per cent. Further relaxations in purchase tax were announced on 13 December, and increases in unemployment pay and retirement pensions on 23 January 1963.

De Gaulle's veto on Britain entering the EEC in January 1963 produced intense speculation about Britain's future economic policy. *The Times* leader stated that, with the veto on Europe, another balance of payments crisis was inevitable unless the Government made a radical alteration of their policy in the form of a massive programme of new work and the abolition of restrictive practices. Graham Hutton, a well-known free market economist, commented in *The Times* correspondence column that the Government needed a 'vast Unity loan' to help them to reflate on the lines of Lloyd George's Yellow Book of 1929.* Macmillan was interested; he sent the cuttings to Maudling with the comment:

> We have got somehow to look as if we are doing Haleyish and Huttonish things. Please think this over for it is on this that the whole thing will

---

* In the 1929 Liberal Yellow Book the Liberals, in order to ease unemployment, had urged that there should be massive government loans to finance infrastructure on roads, railways, ports etc. This was also the basis of the famous Mosley plan of 1930. Both Sir William Haley, editor of *The Times*, and Graham Hutton, the Liberal free-marketeer, were advocating similar policies at the beginning of 1963, and obtaining great publicity for their ideas.

turn if Europe finally breaks down or has to be put off to a more distant future . . . we do not need £1,000 million Unity loan; all that Hutton and Haley urge is being done by Government spending on docks, schools, etc.[7]

Maudling replied that Hutton and Haley were 'positively mischievous' in suggesting that his measures would lead to a balance of payments crisis.

Meanwhile Harrod was sending his usual exhortations to the Prime Minister, writing on 14 December: 'We could well spend more than we do on defence . . . it would probably be a useful fillip to all-round growth. I am sure most people would gladly pay no small price for greater independence.' He followed this the next day with a wild suggestion conveyed by telegram: 'We can step it up by at least one third to name a lowish figure.'* In other letters Harrod argued as usual for import restrictions, and in one said there was no choice except devaluation or import restrictions because the balance of payments situation was so bad. Harrod saw Macmillan on 25 January 1963; they were both alarmist but the Treasury managed to convince the Prime Minister that the economy was not drifting irrevocably towards devaluation of the pound.[8]

On 11 February 1963 Harrod wrote again to the Prime Minister: 'The Treasury has just not equipped itself to present competent views . . . In recent years it has been proceeding without any understanding or even knowledge of the figures – witness the howlers that the Ministers are allowed to perpetrate with the consequence of a series of powerful economic blunders.' From the start Harrod 'regarded NIC as worthless. My view was formed independent of the TUC boycott. It should be condemned like the Cohen Committee[†] to complete oblivion. Let it fade out of existence.' That Harrod could dismiss NIC, into which Macmillan was putting so much effort, shows how confident he was of Macmillan's faith in his opinions.

The Prime Minister indeed took Harrod's letters of February 1963 very seriously, especially Harrod's assertion that the balance of payments situation was so desperate that we had no choice but devaluation of the pound or import restrictions. 'We can only get rid of our trade deficit by more protection,' Harrod wrote. 'Two years ago I pointed out that our balance of trade had gone down due to the excessive pace of import de-restriction . . . The Americans should be told at once that we shall certainly have to become more protectionist before we can embark on

---

*It was at this stage that Macmillan told Maudling that Harrod was a man of genius although often wrong.

† For the Cohen Committee (Council on Prices, Productivity and Incomes – COPPI) see below, Chapter 10.

any more moves towards freer trade.' Harrod hoped the Americans might reduce import tariffs unilaterally against Britain.[9]

Disappointed at Britain's being barred from the EEC, Macmillan pressed Maudling for action on import controls along the lines suggested by Harrod. Cairncross pointed out that America could not reciprocate, as Harrod expected, to cuts in tariffs because by the Kennedy Round they were prohibited from slashing reductions in tariffs and could give only 50 per cent reductions staged over five years, and 'it was also too soon to suppose that the balance of payments would lapse into severe deficit although there would be a case for emergency controls if this happened.' Maudling was blunter, telling the Prime Minister that 'Harrod did not seem fully conversant with facts', and Bligh minuted that Harrod was 'preaching bad economics'. But Macmillan continued to pester the Treasury with Harrod's views and to encourage the Oxford don to keep up his correspondence.

However as the 1963 Budget approached, Bligh managed to fob off the Prime Minister by pointing out that Harrod's mistaken policy of restricting imports would invite retaliation, and would be evidence of the Government's lack of confidence in their own economic policies and might lead to a weakening of sterling. This led to a suggestion by Macmillan that it would be 'fun' to get Harrod to meet Cairncross with the meeting treated lightly. Cairncross told the author that what Macmillan called an 'intellectual joust' took place at which Harrod argued for import quotas.[10]

As 1963 opened, Macmillan had been contemplating an autumn election that year. However the opinion polls and by-election results were so bad that he decided to keep his options open, with October 1963 and May 1964 in mind. He wanted Budgets in 1963 and 1964 which would ensure rising prosperity and greater spending money in the pockets of the electorate over both periods. Accordingly he advised Maudling to consider the two Budgets as one. Macmillan's fear was that if the 1963 Budget was too expansionary the brakes might have to be slammed on before an election was called in 1964.

Fortified by Harrod's belief that massive expansion was possible Macmillan egged Maudling on towards maximum tax cuts in his 1963 Budget although the Prime Minister was conscious that excessive tax reliefs, such as those of 1959, could put the Government into difficulties in 1964. How important the Budgets were in Macmillan's electoral plans is shown by a letter of 22 February from Macmillan to Maudling: 'The Budget should be a great national plan for expansion ... This would give local encouragement as well as the feeling of a national forward movement.' On 26 February Macmillan wrote again to the Chancellor:

The Budget and all that goes with the Budget will be the key to the success or failure of the Government, the Party, and in my view of the country's effort over the next period . . . This will be the moment to launch the post-Brussels policy on the home front . . . The whole country is waiting for what is called a lead. The lead cannot be given merely by exhortation. It must be accompanied by a fairly clear picture of a policy for the next period, say a three- or four-year plan which will command general approval. If this kind of lead is given there will be plenty of people ready to follow. If it is not given we shall merely drift, and the leadership may well pass to the Labour Party not necessarily as people think for two or three years, but perhaps for a long period.

The long *aide-mémoire* which accompanied this letter exhorted Maudling to bring in the maximum tax cuts:

The economy is running below capacity; there are perhaps 600,000 unemployed (not counting the bad weather figures). The balance of payments is ticking along; production is increasing slightly; on present rates of taxation there would be an above the line surplus.* There would probably be room for some minor tax concessions including the abolition of Schedule A without either exciting the economy or bringing about a deterioration in the balance of payments. In short we are in a Paish paradise. Are we going to continue to be Paishites?

Professor Paish's theory that with 2½ per cent out of work there could be no inflation was gaining ground in the City but was hotly disputed by many prominent economists. The *aide-mémoire* continued:

Is this to be the basis of our economic policy in 1963/64 – to expand the economy cautiously within modest limits and to keep the favourable balance of payments position? This is not necessarily an ignoble position . . . But though not ignoble it is not exhilarating. *Nor would it bring political rewards.* [Author's italics] The first question then, Paish or expansion?

An expansionary Budget, Macmillan continued, might be 'snookered before it had started to achieve its target by a balance of payments crisis, a run on the pound and all that'. If we have expansionary Budgets, he concluded, we must 'go on to a floating exchange rate and take all other possible steps to strengthen the reserves'. This meant mobilizing 'any loans we can' and drawing the maximum amount from IMF. He wanted 'a national campaign for expanding the economy' with great publicity to show that in the long run this would strengthen the pound, and an announcement of the steps taken to increase the reserves; this he thought should 'give us a breathing space of perhaps three years to break the

---

*That is, taxation and other government income would exceed state spending for the year in question.

vicious circle of stop-go', and 'Behind the national plan it should be possible to mobilize the nation.'

Over floating the pound the Prime Minister thought that the breakdown of negotiations in Brussels* should be 'pleaded' as the occasion for this radical change in British policy: 'With a floating rate we could make £400 million tax cuts in the Budget provided we abandoned the usual methods of defending sterling.'[11]

In further letters in March Macmillan told Maudling to consider 'liquefying our assets' (selling the Government's dollar portfolio), so as to be able to safeguard the pound after swingeing tax cuts, and on 22 March when the statistics showed output lagging he again urged more tax concessions. Macmillan had some justification for asking for £400 million tax cuts because this figure had been recommended by the National Institute of Economic and Social Research, a body which was rapidly gaining influence.[†] It had been rejected by the Treasury as far too high. Maudling records in his memoirs that he was prepared to take a risk with his 1963 Budget. However he was not prepared to gamble as heavily as the Prime Minister.[12]

The letter and *aide-mémoire* were not circulated in the Treasury. Maudling himself was probably shocked that the Prime Minister wanted excessive cuts in taxation which were likely to lead to a balance of payments crisis and was arguing for a floating pound solely on electoral grounds. Maudling thought a floating pound could be justified, but not as an electoral gimmick.

In reply Maudling forwarded to Macmillan a memorandum about the shape of the 1963 Budget written by Sir William Armstrong, then Joint Principal Secretary to the Treasury, for the Treasury's internal Budget Committee. Armstrong recommended tax concessions totalling from £200 million to £300 million which 'could be presented as fitting in with the policy of searching for a more efficient and faster growing economy with a reasonable chance of avoiding an adverse movement of confidence abroad'. A stimulus of £400 million suggested alike by the National Institute and Macmillan would, Armstrong thought, be 'unlikely to produce excessive pressure of demand during 1963/64 but might well do so in 1964/65'. Excessive pressure in 1964 was the one thing which Macmillan wished to avoid, because it would mean unpopular tax and interest rate increases in an election year.

---

*De Gaulle's veto on British entry into the EEC in January 1963 brought the Brussels negotiations to an abrupt end. See pages 195 ff.

[†] A semi-governmental economic forecasting body, set up in 1961 to check on economic forecasts from Government Departments.

Armstrong's memorandum was compelling and after reading it Macmillan made no more demands for £400 million tax cuts, accepting Maudling's more modest proposals without demur. Taking cognisance of the internal Treasury Budget Committee's recommendations of tax reductions of £200 to £300 million, Maudling chose a middle figure for his 1963 Budget and produced tax cuts of £260 million. Sensibly he concentrated on increasing personal allowances and tax reductions in the lower rate bands, firmly refusing City pressure for large reductions at the higher end. He also introduced free depreciation for investment on new machinery and factories in areas of high unemployment, together with increased state spending.[13]

The 1963 Budget, termed by the press 'a dash for growth', was not without its risks, but it provided a reasonable climate for a General Election with consumption rising fast and unemployment falling. The serious financial press recognized Maudling as an intelligent and resourceful Chancellor. The City thought his pump-priming was not quite enough but welcomed the first 'deficit' and therefore expansionary Budget for nine years. Unfortunately for the Government's economic plans, although the tax reductions were equivalent to a 2 per cent rise in wages, the trade unions refused to recognize this and adamantly refused to have anything to do with the National Incomes Commission, or to accept restraint in wage claims.

By now Macmillan had great confidence in Maudling, and much enjoyed discussing with him national economic problems. Maudling had a greater grasp of these than Amory or Lloyd who had been at a loss in the long talks with Macmillan unless they had their Treasury advisers with them. Macmillan and Maudling must have been pleased when in March 1963 Nicholas Davenport in a much-quoted article in the *Spectator* had written: 'The old Treasury idea that we help exports by restricting home demand is dead. I hope it never returns.' The Lloyd myth that home trade must be restricted to boost exports, he later wrote, had been exploded by Maudling, and he castigated Professor Paish for being 'the apostle of spare capacity': Thorneycroft, he said, had been spellbound by Professor Robbins's enthusiasm for controlling the money supply, while Lloyd had been spellbound by Paish, who held the theory that only with a certain amount of unemployment could wages and inflation be kept down.

In the summer of 1963, however, misfortune overtook the Conservative Party. Chiefly because of the Profumo scandal Gallup polls showed them 20 per cent behind Labour, which made an autumn election impossible despite the fact that unemployment had fallen and production risen with unexpected speed.

Once he had decided to postpone the General Election from the autumn of 1963 to 1964 Macmillan was assailed by fears that the mini-boom started by the 1963 Budget might lead to a sterling crisis. Pondering all means of bolstering up the reserves so as to avoid a balance of payments crisis in an election period, he plumped for three measures to shore up the reserves, so that the pound would not be under strain if the balance of payments went into sharp deficit the following year: these were (1) import controls; (2) a floating pound; (3) selling off the dollar portfolio.

Even before the Budget Macmillan had asked Maudling to be ready 'with various possibilities open to us if a balance of payments and sterling crisis should arise in the way we have become accustomed to'. He wanted the possibility of import controls examined again and added: 'I know you are considering a floating or devaluation of the pound.'

Rumours that the Government would float the pound rather than risk a balance of payments crisis during an election period had already leaked out in the Commons. On 8 March 1963, Andrew Roth wrote in his *Westminster Confidential*, the newsletter popular with MPs and lobby correspondents:

> the Government seems to be counting on its luck changing and the Chancellor's pulling a rabbit out of his hat. Mr Maudling is embarked on a programme in which the old cycle of expansion-and-contraction is avoided. The Government has, of course, already put a considerable amount of credit into the economy to 'reflate' it, as a way of mopping up unemployment. But once this unemployment has been mopped up, there is the danger of a balance of payments crisis, as has happened so often before since the war. In order to avoid it, a number of economists have suggested a slight devaluation. But in Britain devaluation has unfortunate connections in political mythology. So Chancellor Maudling has decided on a 'floating pound' which could rise or sink in value between 3 per cent and 8 per cent below its present value, thus cutting the cost of British manufactures in foreign markets.
>
> This is a gamble.

While Heathcoat Amory and Lloyd were Chancellors the Treasury advisers had firmly turned down import controls. In the summer of 1963, when Macmillan again proposed them, they were pressed by Maudling to change their minds. This they did, and at a meeting on 15 July with the Prime Minister Maudling explained 'the circumstances in which officials had ceased advising [that] such a scheme was impractical'. In a Treasury memorandum it was stated that £200 million could be saved annually by import tariff surcharges and quantitative restrictions, and by the autumn the Board of Trade could have a plan ready to impose them.

On this memorandum Macmillan minuted to Bligh: 'I simply cannot take this cold attitude lying down after my three years of agitation. Please prepare a blistering reply.' Bligh drafted:

> For the last four years I have been suggesting usually in mild terms that we should be prepared to consider the reimposition of what are called physical import controls. My suggestions have been turned down by the Treasury at every stage. I was told that any such scheme would be unworkable; that it would take a long time to recruit the staff; that one could never bring a scheme into operation in a short enough period to avoid forestalling and that this was the sort of action that would do us more harm than good because people to whom we export would retaliate. I am now told that such a scheme could be drawn up and put into operation within a month of the decision and that no serious forestalling could take place within that month.

To Bligh's draft Macmillan added, 'Even the walls of Jericho could put up a better show than this,' and sent it off to the Treasury and to the Chief Whip.[14]

In the event the Conservative Government did not impose import controls: when the time for them arrived, with the economy overheating in 1964, Macmillan had ceased to be Prime Minister. Instead the Wilson Government took advantage of the Treasury plan drawn up in July 1963 and imposed them within weeks of coming into office in October 1964.

In March 1963, in a minute to Maudling, Macmillan had first raised the possibility of strengthening British reserves by selling all government-held overseas investments including dollar securities and their shares in the Suez Canal Company and British Petroleum * Maudling's reply made it clear that his Treasury advisers did not approve, and Macmillan noted on the minute: 'A tendentious Treasury minute. Why should the Government be in this investment business anyway? It should surely be for merchant bankers (and not the old Bank of England or Lazards) to advise here.'

Macmillan returned to the attack in September after he had decided to postpone the General Election until 1964, and when there were ominous signs of the economy being on its way to overheating again. He discussed the proposal with Lord Cromer, Governor of the Bank of England, without Maudling being present. On 20 September Maudling warned him that it might be regarded as 'unfriendly' if we tried to sell the dollar portfolio (known also as the Treasury Portfolio) in New York. The Americans had their own balance of payments problems, and would

---

* In his old age Macmillan complained in a speech in the Lords about the Government selling off the family silver; selling off the dollar portfolio was doing exactly this.

have resented the large outflow of dollars to Britain following the sale of the shares. However a long Treasury memorandum pointed out that £850 million could be realized by selling British Petroleum and Suez Canal shares, and the whole dollar portfolio.

In a long letter to Maudling Cromer approved the idea, saying he understood the desire of the Prime Minister 'to put the situation on a more sensible footing, and that the ratio of reserves to overseas liability [debts] is far from satisfactory'.[15] He pointed out that we would be unlikely to improve this ratio by balance of payments surpluses and the only feasible way of adding to our existing reserves by a substantial amount would be to sell the Treasury dollar portfolio for foreign exchange. This would reinforce the official reserves by one million dollars, and 'with the steady accruals that the liquidations of the securities would provide ... I think that, although there may be an initial strain in the first year, we could well afford to implement these policies which I believe would benefit the economy and strengthen our reserves position over a period of time.'

Warburgs who were consulted were, not unnaturally, enthusiastic; they pointed out that they had carried out a similar operation recently for the Italian Government with shares in the Italian armament firm Breda and expected to raise £½ billion from outside the sterling area by selling the British portfolio to private capital markets in North America and Western Europe. They supported the Prime Minister in his view that the dollar portfolio was a third reserve in addition to the gold and foreign cash holdings of the Bank of England and IMF drawing rights.[16]

Macmillan had discovered a useful weapon to buttress the reserves if the pound came under strain before the General Election. In the event it was the Labour Government who benefited, and Harold Wilson gratefully sold the dollar portfolio when the pound came under pressure in 1965.

Macmillan continued to press for a floating pound. In principle Maudling favoured a floating rate. As he wrote in his autobiography: 'I had always been a supporter of flexible rates.'[17] The Suez war had put a great strain on both British reserves and sterling, and during its aftermath in 1957 and 1958 the Government had seriously considered floating the pound so as to relieve the strains which inhibited the expansionist Budgets sought by the Prime Minister.

In March 1958 Sir Robert Hall had produced a long memorandum based on papers by Sir Denis Rickett and the Bank of England. He concluded that if we allowed our balance of payments to go into deficit or if there was any really determined movement out of sterling 'we would probably prefer to float than to devalue'. (In 1964 the Labour

Government took a different view when its Chancellor, James Callaghan, preferred a straight devaluation to floating.) In his memorandum Hall commented that a floating rate had long been advocated (especially by Professor Meade)* because of its effect as an automatic regulator of the balance of payments:

> With fixed rates adjustments had to be made by inflations or deflations and if these are inadequate by periodic devaluations or revaluations. All of these, it is argued, involve or may involve unnecessarily violent internal adjustments. But if the rate is free to move exports can be stimulated and imports checked in a gradual way or vice versa. A country with a floating rate can concentrate on an internal policy of smooth development instead of having to take a series of crisis actions.
>
> Floating would threaten the destruction of sterling as a form of international liquidity and thus accentuate the present tendencies towards a world economic recession . . . It would be for us to demonstrate that we intended to keep sterling strong and stable.

In April 1958, when forwarding the Hall memorandum to Amory, Roger Makins had minuted: 'I have reluctantly been convinced by the arguments *against* moving to a flexible rate in the near future.' Makins was a career diplomat, a former Ambassador to Washingon, who in 1957, at Macmillan's special request, had been transferred from the Foreign Office to head the Treasury. As he admitted in an obituary of Sir Edmund Compton, published in the *Independent* on 14 March 1993, 'he had been imposed on the Treasury and did not know much about home finance.' He was not qualified to pass an opinion on Hall's memorandum, and was probably influenced against it because Hall had stated that floating would be regarded as a disruptive act 'on our part towards closer economic co-operation in Western Europe and certainly be a further obstacle towards negotiating a Free Trade Area'. In 1958 an arrangement with Europe was a top government priority. Makins seized upon this point, remarking, 'The only consideration which gives me pause is the effect of an immediate move on our European negotiations. The stronger countries of Europe would welcome it but it might upset the Scandinavian countries.'[18]

As de Gaulle had vetoed British entry into the EEC, and as EFTA – in which Scandinavia was involved – was proving a broken reed, the Makins arguments of 1958 against floating were no longer valid in September 1963. The Hall memorandum was taken out of the Treasury pigeon-holes and shown to Macmillan, who cited Hall's support for

---

*The much esteemed Professor of Economics at Cambridge who expressed robust free market views, and was opposed to any sort of import tariffs.

floating to Maudling, and pointed out that Makins had only opposed the plan on out-of-date arguments about Europe. Maudling acquiesced and agreed that a floating rate would be considered urgently if at any time before the election the balance of payments situation worsened, so that a slowdown in the economy could be avoided.*

Thus in September 1963, four weeks before he was stricken by prostate trouble and left office, Macmillan with the agreement of his Chancellor of the Exchequer had put in place three weapons to ensure that a balance of payments crisis did not damage Conservative electoral chances – import controls, sale of the dollar portfolio, and floating the pound.

When Macmillan was replaced as Prime Minister in October 1963 by Alec Home, the whole style of government changed. Macmillan had behaved like a President and treated Africa, European negotiations and the management of the economy as his own province, and in many ways was himself his own Chancellor of the Exchequer and Foreign Secretary. Under Home this presidential type of government was replaced by Cabinet government with the Prime Minister acting as a committee chairman. Home took little interest in the management of the economy, and understood less. He was content to leave it in the hands of Maudling. Thus the carefully laid plans made by Macmillan to neutralize the electoral damage of deficits on balance of payments were thrown out of the window.

On his own the easy-going and over-optimistic Maudling never implemented Macmillan's plans, preferring to believe all was well with the pound. Even when in 1964 there were clear signs of danger he refused to admit that the economy was overheating, believing that expanding production and exports must mean that the balance of payments position would improve. In fact exports were not rising as they should because British manufacturers, sheltered by high import tariffs, were not making cost-reducing innovations like their counterparts in other European industrial countries, while tax cuts and higher wages were sucking in a rising volume of unnecessary imports. The Maudling–Macmillan agreement to float the pound if necessary was kept secret and as a result there was talk in 1964 about a forced devaluation which damaged the Conservatives' image of being financially competent. By the beginning of 1964 it was clear that expectations of continuous growth on a sound basis were disappearing, and the press was full of prognostications of economic disaster.[19]

---

*It is worth noting that at a Cabinet meeting on 30 June 1961 it was recorded that several Ministers had 'argued for a floating rate as otherwise long-term balance of payments difficulties could not be countered'. During the EEC negotiations talk of floating the pound was postponed.

Maudling has recounted that he would have preferred not to have produced a Budget in 1964; in the event he introduced tax increases of £100 million (puny by today's standards, but considerable at 1964 prices). The Treasury advisers, albeit with qualifications, told Maudling that his Budget was unlikely to produce a deficit on balance of payments during 1964.

They were wrong. The deficit accelerated alarmingly immediately after the April Budget. Maudling advised Home, the new Prime Minister, to hold the election early in the summer. Home refused and insisted on an autumn election. On the last day of election campaigning in October 1964 an enormous deficit was revealed for September. This was given headline publicity in all the national papers and did the Conservatives grave damage. When Wilson arrived in Downing Street he declared the situation 'disastrous' and proceeded to impose the import controls designed by Macmillan, and shortly afterwards to devalue the pound.*

If Macmillan had stayed as Prime Minister until the General Election he would have insisted that Maudling took the steps they had designed to ward off a balance of payments crisis. The result was close. Labour had a majority of only four seats. The archives reveal how Macmillan planned to keep the economy on a buoyant course, and if his plan had been implemented it is highly probable on economic grounds that the Conservatives would have won the 1964 General Election.[20]

*In his memoirs Maudling writes that he and the Cabinet never contemplated 'devaluation'. He is less than frank over floating, hiding the fact that he and Macmillan had decided to embark on devaluation if the balance of payments ran into trouble between September 1963 and the 1964 General Election. But he is correct in saying that it was never discussed in Cabinet.

CHAPTER 7

EFTA of the Seventeen

WHEN THE MACMILLAN Government was formed in January 1957
Britain had already lost the chance to join the Common Market on
the ground floor. Eden, as Prime Minister, had shied away from any
European institution which envisaged supranationality and pooling
of sovereignty; his priorities were Britain's special relationship with
America and her position as head of the Commonwealth. Eden wanted
Britain to play a key role in Europe from the outside, not the inside.
His attitude was shared by his Cabinet.

The first decisive move towards a Common Market was the Schuman
Plan, launched on 9 May 1950 by the French Government. Named after
their Foreign Secretary it contained dramatic proposals for pooling the
coal, iron and steel resources of France and Germany, and of any other
European country willing to join, and putting them under the control
of an independent high authority.

The Attlee Government refused to have anything to do with the
Schuman Plan. A Committee of Ministers chaired by Attlee himself
turned it down out of hand, and the general view of Ministers was
that as British coal and steel had been nationalized they could not be
integrated into a Continental combine of private enterprise firms. Attlee
told the French Ambassador that 'because of the importance of steel to
Britain's economy this country could not consent to hand over to irresponsible persons such wide powers over essential matters.' This was
slamming the door on the promising European movement.

The Conservative Opposition tried to make Party propaganda out of
Labour's refusal to consider the Schuman Plan, and in a Commons debate
at the end of June 1950 Eden said that 'subject to safeguards' he would
accept the Schuman high authority for coal and steel, while Churchill
went even further, stating: 'Without hesitation we are prepared to consider and, if convinced, to accept the abrogation of national sovereignty
provided we are satisfied with the conditions and safeguards ... national
sovereignty is not inviolable.'

Thus when Churchill formed his post-war Government after winning the 1951 General Election there were high hopes in Europe that Britain would join other European countries in yielding economic power to supranational institutions which by now were popular with European politicians. Unfortunately Churchill and Eden quickly ate the words they had uttered in June 1950 when seeking the downfall of the Labour Government.

Eden soon defined the stand which he was to take consistently both as Foreign Secretary and as Prime Minister. Early in December 1951, in a memorandum to all overseas Embassies, he wrote: 'We want a united Europe . . . it is only when plans for uniting Europe take a federal form that we cannot ourselves take part.' Ten days later Churchill confirmed to Schuman that Britain's attitude to the Schuman Plan would be that we should be 'with it though not of it'.

This was a shattering blow to the European enthusiasts for an integrated Europe. Harold Macmillan, then Minister of Housing and Local Government, struck a chord of dissent. He wrote a letter to Eden urging that Britain should give a strong lead 'in the creation of a [European] confederation organized on the same lines as the Commonwealth with a common currency and a European customs preferential area interlocking with imperial preference'. Eden snubbed Macmillan over this letter, and when Macmillan brought the issue up in Cabinet he had almost no support. He got no satisfaction from Churchill when he wrote a letter pointing out the inconsistency of the Conservative attitude of favouring the Schuman Plan while in Opposition and then of shunning it once in office.

If Macmillan had persisted in advocating a single European currency and a preferential trading system the outcome might have been very different. Having found little support among his colleagues for his pro-Europe views he toed the Eden line, and as will be seen it was some years before he took a more positive attitude to European integration.

While leader of the Opposition after the war Churchill had been one of the chief promoters of the European movement. In 1947 at the Albert Hall, in high-falutin but impressive language, he had called for European unity, and he had launched the European movement at The Hague in May 1948. On both occasions he played down all the reservations which as Prime Minister he later expressed against Britain's integration. It was largely due to him that the Council of Europe began, and his inspired vision of a united Europe had great influence on the French, German, Italian, Belgian and Dutch politicians who conceived the European Community.

Typical of Churchill's contradictions was his call, in May 1950, as leader of the Opposition for 'the immediate creation of a European army under a united command'; as Prime Minister in 1951 he shocked his

European friends by refusing to take Britain into the very European army that was being proposed – a stance which caused Paul-Henri Spaak, the Belgian Foreign Minister, to resign in protest as President of the Council of Europe. Churchill may well have thought, during his years in opposition between 1945 and 1951, to achieve a political ascendancy over Attlee by re-evoking his role as the great wartime leader of Europe. Nonetheless he was definitely inspired by the ideal of a united Europe. Though carried away to a certain extent by his own oratory, and unable to discuss problems with civil servants, he doubtless thought he could accommodate the European ideal as well as Britain's Commonwealth commitments in his wide-ranging purpose, ignoring the contradictions. His ambivalence can be explained by the theory that once in office, and faced with Eden's opposition to any sort of integration with Europe, he decided it was not worth while having a clash with his popular Foreign Secretary, and instead, at the age of 70, he opted for a quiet life and the peaceful enjoyment of his last years in Downing Street, sacrificing his genuine desire to unite post-war Europe.

The Eden Government was ready to join a European free trade area but not a customs union, because the customs union envisaged by the architects of the Common Market entailed a common external tariff against all outside countries including the Commonwealth, and this meant the eventual abolition of preferences for colonial and Commonwealth imports coming into the United Kingdom and a corresponding downgrading of preference for United Kingdom exports to the former British colonies. With a free trade area imperial preference could continue side by side with the elimination of all tariffs on European industrial trade with Britain.

A great boost to Common Market aspirations came when the Faure Government in France replaced that of Mendès-France in February 1955. The new administration included several enthusiastic federalists, amongst them Schuman, and France, Italy, Germany and the Benelux countries (Holland, Belgium and Luxemburg) agreed to meet at Messina in June 1955 to discuss forming 'a Common Market'.

The Six countries wanted Britain to participate in the Messina talks, and were chagrined when the suggestion was turned down. Eden refused even to send an observer to Messina, and Macmillan as Foreign Secretary, despite his earlier enthusiasm for an integrated Europe, concurred. This was an appalling mistake which Churchill would never have made.*

---

*A myth has grown up, as a result of a well-publicized BBC programme, that Russell Bretherton, an Under-Secretary at the Board of Trade, went to Messina. This is completely untrue, as Bretherton has categorically confirmed to the author.

The Eden Cabinet's attitude was that, owing to her special relationship with America and her leadership of the Commonwealth, Britain could never accept equal status with the six Messina powers. Nothing would induce them to contemplate pooling sovereignty with other European countries or entering a customs union subject to supranational control. The barrier to British co-operation with the Six was the 'gut' feeling of Eden and Macmillan and their Cabinet colleagues that there were still 'three great powers in the world – USA, Russia and Britain'. As we shall see, only slowly did this concept crumble as Europe moved towards unity after Messina and the Common Market plans took firm shape.

The Six showed considerable goodwill to Britain. They had high hopes that even if she would not join she would form a close association with the Common Market. A warm invitation was sent to the United Kingdom in the summer of 1955 to join in the work of the Spaak Committee in Brussels which was translating the Messina initiative into a formal treaty to bring the Common Market or, as it was now called, the European Economic Community into being.

The British sent 'representatives' to the Spaak Committee – mainly so they could know what was going on there. The Government could still hardly believe that the Six would enter into a customs union without Britain, so confident were they of Europe's sense of gratitude to Britain for having saved them from Hitler during the war. Gradually the Treasury and Foreign Office convinced the Cabinet that the Six were in deadly earnest and were travelling fast down the road towards a formal treaty. Eden and Macmillan then set out to sabotage the Common Market.

The Organization for European Economic Co-operation had been set up in April 1949 with the aim of furthering European trade by reducing tariffs and quotas, and administering American aid for Europe under the Marshall Plan. The British Government now decided that the status of OEEC should be enhanced in order to try to meet the aspirations of the Common Market powers. This was a clumsy move which did not impress the Six. It was apparent that Britain only wanted to talk and delay, and had no intention of joining the new grouping. Both Johan Beyen, the Dutch Foreign Minister, and Paul-Henri Spaak, the Belgian Foreign Minister, came to London on fruitless missions of goodwill in an effort to induce Britain to participate in the Common Market.

When Beyen met Rab Butler, then Chancellor of the Exchequer, in November 1955, they failed to hit it off. Butler emphasized the importance of avoiding harm to the OEEC, the need for the Six to go slowly to avoid crossing wires, and above all to maintain contact with Britain and the OEEC. With his evasive style he gave the misleading impression to Beyen that Britain still might join the Six: had he been frank he would have told Beyen that the Prime Minister and the Cabinet were completely opposed to the Common Market concept.

Spaak saw Butler a fortnight later. This time Butler claimed that OEEC should be the vehicle for all the negotiations – a claim which Spaak dismissed, saying the OEEC was a 'boutique'. Even if Britain would not sign the treaty to form the Common Market, Spaak said, it might be possible for the Six to have a special association with the UK and he had no desire at all that the Six should put Britain 'in a difficulty with regard to her relations with her Commonwealth partners'. Robert Rothschild, Spaak's Chef de Cabinet, who accompanied the Minister, afterwards recorded: 'the warmer Spaak, the colder and colder Butler obviously became.'

Meanwhile on 11 November the Cabinet Economic Policy Committee had decided not only to tell the Six firmly that Britain could not join, but also to do everything possible to wreck the project: it decided 'to divert as far as possible the activities of the Brussels Conference into the wider framework [OEEC]'. Emphasis on the importance of OEEC annoyed Spaak and Beyen. Nonetheless Macmillan and Eden decided to push its claims and planned that a British *démarche* against the Common Market should be made in Paris on 7 December 1955 at a meeting of permanent delegates to OEEC. However the manoeuvre was counterproductive because Beyen and Spaak saw it clearly as a British effort to sabotage the Common Market.

The senior British official at OEEC was Sir Hugh Ellis-Rees. A man with no diplomatic experience, having spent his career in the Inland Revenue, he was prejudiced against supranationality. He handled the *démarche* badly. His instructions were to tell the Messina powers that Britain could not participate in the Common Market because of British links with the Commonwealth, and a Common Market could not be reconciled with a one-world system; it would also impede the workings of the OEEC. The full rage of the Messina powers at this statement had to be met by Macmillan as Foreign Secretary when in Paris on 14 December for the Western European Union Ministerial meeting. Asked by Beyen if Ellis-Rees's declaration constituted 'condemnation of the Messina Plan', Macmillan had difficulty in replying.

Macmillan went in for further sabotage by sending telegrams to his Ambassadors in Bonn and Washington instructing them to stress that in the British view 'the political cohesion of Europe [i.e. the adhesion of West Germany to the West] would be damaged by the Six, and it would be deplorable if all OEEC stands for were to be jeopardized for the shadow of the Common Market which either never came to anything or, if it did, proved harmful to the world-wide movement towards freer trade.' Roger Makins, then British Ambassador in Washington and later head of the Treasury, took Macmillan's cue and tried to sow seeds of doubt among American diplomats. His disparaging remarks were quickly leaked to the Spaak Committee in Brussels and fanned Spaak's anger and that of other Foreign Ministers of the Six against the British Government.

When the Foreign Office made it clear that the Six were on the brink of agreement, the Cabinet became concerned at the danger of British manufacturers being excluded by tariffs from this large new European market which was in prospect. Macmillan, now moved from the Foreign Office to the Treasury, asked his officials to study a plan 'for an alternative which might prevent the Messina proposals being implemented'. Macmillan told the Treasury Knights he would not join the Six but was seeking an initiative which would block the Messina powers' plan; although he was not opposed to their customs union, 'he wanted to join it with the Commonwealth but to have no part in any supranational or federal tendencies'. Given the enthusiasm of the Six for unity, he was crying for the moon.

As the archives show, an inter-departmental Treasury and Foreign Office working party beavered away at speed to find counter-proposals which might spike the Messina guns. However the Spaak Committee, now without a British representative, worked even faster, and in April 1956 produced a detailed plan for customs union and supranational institutions. It held out a friendly hand to Britain, inviting states which did not feel able to join to establish close relations.

The British Government was horrified by the declaration in the Spaak Report that all obstacles to trade in agricultural products within the Six must be 'eliminated'. This meant that if Britain were to join the EEC all preferential duties on food from the Commonwealth would have to be abandoned. Here was the sticking point on which future negotiations were to founder.

The Foreign Ministers of the Six met in Venice at the end of May for formal consideration of the Spaak Report. The British were not asked to send a representative although they hinted they would like an invitation. Sir Leslie Rowan of the Treasury commented on the eve of the conference:

> It is quite likely that the Six will not progress very much further in fact at Venice, and it may be thought the risk is negligible of our receiving an embarrassing invitation to join . . . it is not very likely there would be any very clear cut decisions to which we could possibly be asked to subscribe or show our sympathy.[1]

This was wishful thinking and he could not have been more wrong. It reveals how out of touch Whitehall was with the mood of the Six.

The Venice Conference went swimmingly and the Governments of the Six decided to draft a treaty based on the Spaak Report and to reconvene at Brussels for this purpose on 26 June 1956. The Six again showed friendship to Britain, by issuing invitations to all members of the OEEC to come to Brussels and stating that the treaty would provide for the adherence or accession of other states.

The British were in a cleft stick. Alarmed at the prospect of the Common Market coming into being without them, they were also afraid that if they accepted the invitation to Brussels they would have to accept the principles of the Spaak Report which envisaged the end of Commonwealth preference and tariff-free imports of cheap food.

In April Macmillan's Whitehall working party had produced their report – an unimpressive document putting forward six alternative propositions. Once the Venice Conference had closed Macmillan hastily convened a meeting of Ministers at the Treasury to consider the report. Present were Macmillan, Salisbury (Lord President), Lloyd (Foreign Secretary), Heathcoat Amory (Chancellor), Lennox-Boyd (Colonies) and Boyle (Under-Secretary, Education). They rejected all the alternative suggestions in the report except (e) which read:

(e) Partial Free Trade Area with Europe by which tariffs would be removed on imports from the Six to the UK on a list which excluded goods in which the Commonwealth was significantly interested and agricultural products.

This partial free trade area became known as 'Plan G'. The Ministers ordered a further study of (e) to try to make it more attractive to the Commonwealth, thus turning a blind eye to the evolution of the Common Market and the fact that a treaty to bring it into being was about to be signed. It became plain that if Britain was to keep down her labour costs by cheap food from the Commonwealth the Six would never allow her into their customs union. For the next three years the British Government spent abortively a vast amount of time in trying to reconcile these two incompatibles, and the problems became more difficult as the customs union of the Six diverged ever further from the direction taken by the rest of Europe.

A further report, *UK Initiatives in Europe* [*Plan G*], elaborated on (e); it ran to fifteen pages, and naïvely recorded:

We should expect the Plan [Plan G] to be enthusiastically received by some European countries particularly the more highly industrialized. The Plan would be a major encouragement to the European Movement and to the supporters of the Messina initiative who would see their hopes of tying Germany into Western Europe and creating a greater coherence in the Western European economy greatly strengthened.

Such thinking was misplaced. Plan G was a red rag to a bull as far as the Messina powers were concerned, and the Six immediately recognized it as a delaying tactic contrived as an attempt to wreck the Common Market. The Messina powers were determined not to abolish tariffs against Britain and face British industrial competition if Britain enjoyed low-priced Commonwealth food imports.

However there was one bonus from the plan. It induced Britain to accept change from being a high tariff country to being part of a free trade area, and this meant abolishing the high protective duties which had cushioned British manufactures against competition from abroad through the high duties of the 1932 Import Duties Act, and some even higher ones of 33 per cent dating back to the Key Industries Duties of the First World War.

Macmillan as Chancellor was authorized by the Cabinet to discuss Plan G with the Commonwealth Finance Ministers at their conference in Washington at the end of September 1956. He recorded: 'The younger Ministers seemed favourable; some of the older ones doubtful or hostile.' On 3 October he told the Cabinet: 'We must be satisfied before entering a Free Trade Area in Europe that agricultural products are excluded.' With these words he spelt the doom of Plan G since the Six had by now decided to include agriculture in their treaty.

In October Macmillan wrote to Spaak begging him to keep the Common Market negotiations as fluid as possible in the forthcoming Brussels negotiations 'so as to permit us and other countries to associate with the customs union in wider free trade if we can do so. Binding decisions at this stage might make this difficult.' Spaak was unmoved; he was not going to be diverted by the British spoiling tactics.

In Brussels that October the Six quickly concerted their plans for a Common Market treaty. They decided to incorporate a common farm policy which would sustain artificially high prices for farmers, and to extend their customs union to their overseas territories. The writing was on the wall for Britain; in retaliation, the Cabinet decided on 20 November to embark on negotiations with the Six and other European countries for agreement for adherence to Plan G. But Plan G was ill received by the Six and its main effect was to cause them to press on even faster with their draft treaty.

On 7 January 1957, two days after Macmillan had succeeded Eden as Prime Minister, Spaak came to London and talked to Macmillan and Thorneycroft (now Chancellor of the Exchequer). Spaak was met by the categorical statement that agriculture must be excluded if Britain was to take any part, with Macmillan stressing that this was 'non-negotiable'. It was the first and a typical example of the Macmillan Government overplaying their hand *vis-à-vis* the Six. Enforcement of a common agricultural policy was also the sticking point for Spaak and his visit to London was an abject failure. Spaak logically insisted if there was to be agreement with the Messina powers over Plan G British food imports must be subject to the common external tariff, and Britain could not have cheaper food than the rest of Europe if she was in a customs union.

Much to Macmillan's disappointment the OEEC meeting in February 1957 went badly, with Britain in a minority of one in arguing that agriculture must be excluded from any new customs arrangement. The Six refused to slow down ratification of the Treaty of Rome although they agreed that negotiations for a wider free trade area alongside the EEC could be continued. The Continental press was full of reports that Britain was trying to torpedo the Common Market – reports that were correct although British Government spokesmen continually denied them – and spurred on by fears of British proposals bringing negotiations to a halt, the Six went on to sign the Treaty of Rome on 27 March 1957.

The Cabinet minutes for 2 May 1957 show that the Government had become thoroughly alarmed at the fast progress already being made by the Six since the signing of the treaty; it was agreed that if the new alignment, or third force in Europe, went ahead without Britain being associated 'the consequences would be grave'. The Six had made it plain that the door was still open, but the Cabinet felt it would be difficult to offer any concession on agricultural products without alienating the Commonwealth 'and offending our supporters'. If the customs union felt unable to co-operate with Britain, Macmillan said, they must expect her to adopt measures of self-protection. The Chancellor of the Exchequer was asked urgently to examine inducements which might persuade the Six to accept a European Free Trade Area (EFTA), and steps which might mitigate the adverse effects on the UK of the customs union in the absence of a free trade area.

In August 1957 Reginald Maudling, Minister of Supply under Eden and now Paymaster-General, was given the full-time task of negotiating a successful conclusion to the EFTA negotiations. Intelligent, with a flair for mastering detail and a pleasant easy-going personality, he was an ideal choice. However, like Macmillan and the rest of the Cabinet, he had no enthusiasm for political unity in Europe and was only interested in any economic advantages which might flow from integration. On 8 October 1957 he submitted a memorandum to the Cabinet on EFTA negotiations, saying we could count on support from Germany, Belgium and the Netherlands, but not from France who in the Treaty of Rome had secured substantial concessions in her favour. He emphasized that Britain was committed to the exclusion of agriculture but could not rely on the Six failing to make the EEC effective.[2]

British efforts to create a European Free Trade Area had still come to nothing when, on 1 January 1958, the Governments of the Six ratified the Treaty of Rome in their national parliaments, with tariff reductions due to come into operation on 1 January 1959. In 1956, if Eden had been willing, Britain could have sailed into the Common Market at the beginning, and with the resultant goodwill obtained many concessions for the Commonwealth, although in the end cheap food imports would have had to go. Macmillan in his first few weeks as Prime Minister could have undone all the harm done by Eden.

From its formation in January 1957 until the summer of 1961 the Macmillan Government tried by all means in their power to sabotage the Messina powers and the planned evolution of the European Economic Community (Common Market). There were two stages. Until December 1958 when the proposition was vetoed by General de Gaulle, who had recently come to power, the British tried to persuade the Six to accommodate a surrounding free trade area consisting not only of the Six but also of the other eleven countries of Western Europe. This was to be EFTA of the Seventeen. With the collapse of this project in December 1958 the British Government aimed for the alternative of a free trade area of seven countries as a rival trading group to the Six. The seven countries were to be Britain, Switzerland, Portugal, Sweden, Denmark, Norway and Austria. The EFTA treaty of these Seven was signed at Stockholm on 19 November 1959, but it soon became plain to the British Government that the EEC was prospering and pushing ahead with their plans so fast that EFTA of the Seven could only be a second best. As a result, in the summer of 1961 after much heart-searching the Macmillan Government decided to apply for entry into the EEC community. Over four years of frantic diplomacy had come to nothing.

After the French Parliament had ratified the Treaty of Rome setting up the EEC in July 1957 (much to the disappointment of the British) the British Cabinet hoped as a counter to make rapid progress with the free trade area of the Seventeen, intending that the two should come into operation simultaneously and in harmony on 1 January 1959.

There was strong opposition from the French to any association between the free trade area and the EEC; they feared not only the competition from British manufactures but also that Germany and the Benelux countries might renege on concessions made to France in the Treaty of Rome. EFTA was 'objectionable', the French emphasized, because it would be far more advantageous to Britain than France as Britain would have a cost advantage both from cheap food and the low or nil tariffs on Commonwealth raw materials, while also retaining their favoured treatment for exports to the Commonwealth. The French claimed that Britain was trying to *'jouer gagnant sur deux tables'*. Two years of continuous negotiations ending in success had given the Six a sense of cohesion and common purpose and they were anxious to ensure the free trade area would not prejudice the evolution of the Common Market into a true economic union. Although the Common Market agricultural policy was still embryonic it appeared to many in the EEC that the British position with far cheaper food than the rest of the Continent was inconsistent with the request for EFTA of the Seventeen to replace the EEC as an economic union.

On 16 and 17 October 1957 key OEEC Ministerial meetings were held in Paris. Britain wanted to increase the importance of OEEC; the Six wanted to curtail its role. France and Britain took opposing sides: had the two been able to agree on an arrangement between the Six and the other OEEC countries, negotiations would have been easy. But they had fundamental disagreements on essentials which were incapable of being fused into a compromise settlement. However in general terms the Council declared its determination 'to secure the establishment of a European Free Trade Area ... which would associate on a multilateral basis with the EEC and other member countries ... and which would in practice take effect parallel with the Treaty of Rome'. At least this was an improvement on the February 1957 meeting of OEEC which had broken up in discord. An Intergovernmental Committee of Ministers was established, and Maudling was elected Chairman. But at a meeting of the Ministerial Committee in November 1957 the French delegate Edgar Faure declared baldly that unless the Treaty of Association for EFTA was roughly similar to the Treaty of Rome the French could not accept it.

The main stumbling block was food prices. In January 1958 the British circulated a paper which included provisions for commodity agreements in an effort to satisfy the French over food prices,* but it expressly excluded agricultural products from the vital obligation of the Seventeen to abolish import tariffs. The British paper was coldly received. On 14 January 1958 Maudling reported that the French were becoming more obstructive and were unready to make concessions on farming and Commonwealth preference.

Russell Bretherton of the Board of Trade minuted to Maudling on 31 January 1958 that the French reaction was 'a warning that the going would get tougher', and A. J. Edden of the Foreign Office noted: 'the negotiations are already becoming so difficult that we ought to consider

---

*No agreement had yet been formulated by the Six on agricultural policy.

doing a deal with the Six alone.' Bretherton concurred provided only that Britain did not incur 'blame' for letting down the other ten countries. Sir Roderick Barclay of the Foreign Office noted that 'the Danes think EFTA negotiations will break down and then the United Kingdom will quickly do a bilateral deal with the Six,' while R. W. (later Sir Richard) Clarke of the Treasury asked if it was really necessary to have Greece, Turkey, Iceland, Ireland and Portugal in at all. Greece and Turkey would be more trouble than they were worth and were asking for large sums of investment money on admission totalling not less than 100 million dollars. However if they were not admitted 'it might seriously undermine' their reliability as members of NATO and in the case of Turkey of the Baghdad Pact, and expose Britain to the risk of their flirting with the Soviets. Maudling in his role as European co-ordinator had a difficult task in the face of conflicting advice from the officials in Whitehall.[3]

From the start the protectionist-minded French were hostile to the idea of EFTA of the Seventeen, believing that it was a British attempt to sabotage the Common Market of the Six. On 3 January 1958 the British Ambassador in Paris, Gladwyn Jebb, wrote:

> French opinion is suspicious of FTA at the moment. The Government do not like it because, as now conceived, it involves economic concessions without (in their view) adequate compensating political advantages, and French business circles and officials fear these economic concessions would expose the French economy to competition which the French as a whole dislike in principle and which in their view would aggravate in practice the difficulties which the Common Market must create anyway ... recently the anti-FTA campaign in the French press has increased noticeably in volume and in shrillness of tone.

A further letter from Jebb on 9 January 1958 stated: 'Pineau [the French Foreign Minister] remains in favour of FTA in principle but says there is increasing opposition to the concept in France and that it will therefore be impossible for France to go fast in the direction desired as we now seem to be going.' Jebb also reported that a French counter-plan was in preparation.[4]

Maudling saw Faure, the French Prime Minister, at Chequers on 17 January 1958 and was left with the impression that 'Faure is genuinely working for FTA although strictly on terms which he considers will be acceptable in France and which will secure our co-operation. He will not lightly countenance a breakdown in the negotiations, and is sincerely desirous of being constructive.' A. J. Edden minuted: 'It may not necessarily be a bad thing if the French come forward with some ideas of their own instead of continually criticizing ours ... it is quite essential from our point of view that the FTA should come into effective operation at the same time as the Common Market.'

By 3 March the French had put proposals to the permanent representatives of the Six in Brussels; these included general harmonization of tariffs among the Seventeen with a sector by sector approach, and a common agricultural policy, and elimination of tariffs within three years. The Germans and the other four expressed 'almost unanimous opposition' and the French agreed to rewrite the plan. Revised French proposals sniped at Commonwealth preference while at the same time trying to claim some of the advantages of Commonwealth preference for themselves.

The immediate Foreign Office reaction was 'We must stop this by taking no official initiative but by seeking indirectly to kill the idea,' while Maudling stated: 'but for the attitude of the French there would be no difficulty in getting agreement. The Five were trying to work out proposals that would be acceptable to the French on the one hand, and to the rest of the Seventeen on the other.'[5]

On 17 March 1958 Maudling had a long discussion with Macmillan, on which Macmillan wrote the following note, showing that both he and Maudling thought a breakdown likely well before de Gaulle came to power.*

> Mr Maudling came to see me about the present position. As we know the main difficulty is with the French. First they are protectionist. Secondly they are as jealous of Britain as the British people seem now to be of America. Thirdly there is the question of Commonwealth preference which keeps coming up. The position of the Six as a whole is that they do not want to quarrel with the French but at the same time would like to get an agreement.
>
> The French have put forward a new plan which is unacceptable because it wants to deal with the question industry by industry. All the other Six seem to realize this ...
>
> Although Pineau and, outside the Government, Mollet [Prime Minister at the time of Suez] want to get this matter settled there is a very strong opposition from the Independents and in the present French Assembly nothing can pass which they oppose ... The key to the whole question is Germany. The German position is as follows: Erhard [German Foreign Minister] is as keen as ever to reach a full European agreement. Hallstein [recently elected President of the Commission] since his new appointment is rather antagonistic. Everything therefore depends on Adenauer. Adenauer takes no interest in economics but if he can be assured that the British really would react if necessary by isolating themselves from Europe together with

---

*No reference is made to this note in Macmillan's memoirs.

any friends they can collect, e.g. Scandinavia, Adenauer may shrink from dividing Europe. He only thinks about the political issue.

We ought to try a special treatment for France in order to get the thing through. But it would be wiser for special treatment for France to be put forward by one of the Six or possibly by Spaak, not by us ... The next meeting – 22 April – might lead to a final breakdown of the whole negotiations for if the French Plan is supported by the Six there is very little more to be done. On the other hand the French are very unwilling to be regarded as guilty of destroying Europe. They are particularly unwilling to incur German criticism. There is therefore a hope that something may well be done to avoid a break. Maudling feels that unless real progress is made this summer the impetus will go out of it. We should then have to turn to quite different solutions, political and economic.

An article in a French magazine, *Combat*, gave a good indication of French feeling. Maudling, according to the headline, was threatening France with all-out economic war, and there was a fundamental difference between the EEC and the Maudling plan because Britain wanted to keep Commonwealth preference and a low tariff on imports of raw materials while at the same time taking advantage of customs-free entry into Europe.[6]

The course of negotiations changed when at the end of March 1958 Guido Carli, the Italian Finance Minister, put forward new proposals over tariffs. Outside the Six external tariffs varied enormously and there was no suggestion of harmonizing them. Under the Carli plan goods would move freely throughout the EFTA area provided the external tariffs applied by the producing country were within a specified margin of an agreed norm. If countries retained external import tariffs above these margins 'compensatory tariffs' would be levied on goods partly produced within the free trade area.

Maudling has described Carli as 'one of the most able men I have had the good fortune to encounter', and admits that his plan held the floor in the discussions of the Ministerial Committee. In the Carli plan there was the germ of a solution because it allayed French fears of unfair competition in their markets since no goods could come in customs-free if they had been produced with the help of cheap imported materials. The flaw was that the issuing of certificates of origin was too complicated and Carli's Italian Customs were least capable of operating such a system.[7]

Carli told Sir Frank Figgures, Director of Trade and Finance at OEEC in Geneva, that there was no possibility of an agreement on a free trade area during 1958, and he had put forward his plan 'to ensure there was no discrimination after the Six made their internal tariff reductions on 1 January 1959', and that he saw it almost as a trick to get the free trade area of the Seventeen adopted by the French and Italian Parliaments. The Foreign Office advised that it would not be in our interest to kill the Carli plan at birth because it might go some way towards removing French hostility and it was useful to have some positive proposals which did not emanate from Britain.

As it became clear that the Carli plan was too complicated to be practical the Foreign Office reported: 'the negotiations are in a very difficult stage, and in many ways the best outcome would be some sort of special status for France in an agreement which otherwise broadly meets our needs.'

The group of trade experts of the Seventeen discussed the Carli plan for four days from 29 April to 3 May, as did the steering board of officials on 8 May. General agreement on low duties for raw materials, the UK representatives stated, would go a long way to solving the problem of origins. The Foreign Office reported that 'this idea may provide a basis for future negotiations and they would seek the views of the Commonwealth.'[8]

Controversy arose over the involved question of 'origin controls' in the Carli plan – that is, the definition of goods which if only part-produced within the free trade area would have to be discriminated against. The technical difficulties of operating 'origin controls' were immense but this problem was bound to arise in a free trade area which had abolished internal import tariffs but did not have a common external tariff. 'Origin problems' were exhaustively examined by OEEC working parties for the Maudling Committee, but as might be expected with unsatisfactory results. In principle the French, Belgians and Italians wanted heavy restrictions on goods not originating entirely within the free trade area, while the British and Scandinavians wanted more liberal treatment. How anyone ever thought workable arrangements could emerge defeats the imagination but with the Carli plan there was more optimism over the successful outcome of the negotiations for the Seventeen than at any other point.

In early 1958 both the French and the Germans indulged in the misplaced hope that they might themselves obtain advantages out of imperial preference like the UK. In April 1958 Christopher Steel, Ambassador to Bonn, wrote to the Foreign Office that 'the Germans have an idea of using the free trade area as a means of getting a cut out of imperial preference,' but he had told them 'we paid dearly for our privileges,' and as the Germans would never admit Commonwealth food free of duty this 'worked well on them'. (German farmers, hopelessly inefficient and out of date at the time, were receiving large state subsidies to stimulate production.) In a confidential talk with the Federation of British Industries Maudling said the most objectionable part of the

French plan was their attempt to secure for themselves a preferential position in Commonwealth markets.[9]

While the Carli plan was under debate the French produced their own memorandum (the Faure plan). In March 1958 Prime Minister Faure travelled to the other capitals of the Six explaining his proposals. They were unpalatable to the British; they stipulated that the Commonwealth countries must accept at preferential rates a quota of Continental goods which would pay only the old imperial preference duty. Faure complained bitterly that the British would not open their markets to Continental farm produce and because of this there must be substantial compensation in other fields.[10]

As details of the Faure plan became available in Britain speculation increased that EFTA would never come into being and that Britain would have to take harsh counter-measures against the Six. The French were blamed for dividing Europe. This was not fair: it was Britain who had divided Europe by cold-shouldering the Schuman Coal and Steel Plan and the Messina congress. However the rest of the Six would not approve the Faure plan either, and the Common Market partners gave Roger Ockrent, the Belgian permanent delegate to the OEEC, the near impossible task of trying to find a common position acceptable to the Six which also stood a chance of being acceptable to Britain and the other ten European OEEC countries. However in April 1958 the French Government fell, and all negotiations with France were suspended.

With France without a government the visit of Adenauer to London in mid-April 1958 seemed opportune. Maudling understood only too well that many among the Six were deeply suspicious of British motives in promoting the Seventeen. This becomes clear from his briefing of 11 April 1958 to Macmillan for the Adenauer meeting:

> The French have been working hard on him recently ... He will probably have been told:
>
> (1) That the British never liked the Common Market and the Free Trade Area is merely a plan to sabotage it.
>
> (2) That the British are trying to put pressure on France (unjustifiable) to fall in with a scheme designed to meet British interests.
>
> (3) That the British are trying hard to have it both ways particularly in maintaining Commonwealth preference while claiming access to the Common Market.

Maudling added that Adenauer disliked economic policy and would think of EFTA purely in political terms. A hopeful sign was that Walter Hallstein, head of the EEC Commission, had said he could not come to London with Adenauer because he was working day and night to try to effect a reconciliation between the proposed free trade area and the views of the Six.

The Macmillan–Adenauer talks – in which Maudling and Dr Ludwig Erhard, the pro-British German Finance Minister, also took part – resulted in the Germans promising to try to pressurize the French into a satisfactory settlement. With France without a government and on the verge of civil war in Algeria the outcome initially seemed promising.

However in a gloomy report on 5 May 1958 Bretherton wrote that, in the absence of an effective French government, prospects of an agreement before the inauguration of special tariffs on 1 January 1959 were bleak, and Britain should consider negotiating a free trade area with Scandinavia, Switzerland, Austria and Portugal. This was the first serious mention of such an alternative to the Seventeen.[11]

When the French Government under Félix Gaillard, Faure's replacement as Prime Minister, had fallen in mid-April 1958, the committee of officials of the Six under Ockrent's chairmanship had drawn up a paper recommending agreement by a sector to sector approach to tariffs. It was considered on 22 April by the Ministers of the Five together with French officials but in the absence of a French government they could not reach agreed conclusions. A meeting of Ministers of the Six eventually took place in Brussels on 20 and 21 May, but in view of the French elections Faure persuaded the rest of the Six to postpone any decision on the free trade area for a month, and obtain Maudling's consent for an adjournment of negotiations until early July.

Meanwhile a crucial meeting between Maudling and his advisers had been held on 6 May. There it was stated that the negotiations were taking a 'new turn', with the Six not only making claims for Commonwealth preference but also putting forward proposals on origin under the Carli plan which, if accepted, would make the free trade area a quasi-customs union so that there was danger that the Commonwealth would begin to suspect the new developments. Maudling foresaw the possibility of a break and said that 'if it came to a break [with the Six] it was important not to find ourselves in isolation. We should firmly resist the suggestion that we owe the Six some form of compensation for Commonwealth entry.' However if this was denied to the Six there was no chance of an agreement, and Maudling was overplaying his hand.

On 1 June 1958 de Gaulle became Prime Minister of France and it was immediately clear that Britain faced an even tougher struggle. Faure when Prime Minister had genuinely tried to get an agreement for the Seventeen, but he was out of the Government and this was a serious blow. Maurice Couve de Murville became de Gaulle's Foreign Minister and was to prove a nasty thorn in the British flesh.* Still Selwyn Lloyd reported optimistically that on 16 June he had spoken to Dr Luns, the Dutch Foreign Minister, and had been told that the Dutch promised full support for the original British policy and would tell de Gaulle so when they met in fourteen days' time.

When Maudling held a meeting with his officials on 19 June he stated arrogantly that he would make it clear that 'we were not prepared to bring Commonwealth preferences into the negotiations but that if the Europeans chose to negotiate with Australia and New Zealand they were free to do so.'

False hopes were raised by Gladwyn Jebb, British Ambassador in Paris, who wrote that 'there was no reason to suppose that he [de Gaulle] would have any *a priori* dislike of a free trade association', while Edden minuted misleadingly: 'the more we hear of Couve de Murville, the more hopeful his appointment sounds.'[12]

At the end of June Macmillan and his Foreign Secretary, Selwyn Lloyd, went to Paris to meet the new French leader. Although EFTA was a major priority for Macmillan it was of less significance to de Gaulle whose mind was dominated by the Algerian crisis. Nothing of importance was said about EFTA by the two leaders, but Maudling was authorized to talk to Couve. They held abortive talks in Paris where there was no meeting of minds and no evidence that the French would accept any compromise over EFTA. Although de Gaulle had always been a 'scornful critic' of the Messina plans it soon became clear that he had even less time for the free trade area.

Meanwhile the Commission of the EEC had made strenuous efforts to get agreement on the basis of the Ockrent Report. They had submitted the report to the Maudling Committee in June 1958 with the proposal that when the first tariff cuts were made by the Messina powers on 1 January 1959 all the other OEEC powers should cut their tariffs with one another by 10 per cent for a provisional period of eighteen months; during this period definitive arrangements between the EEC and other OEEC countries could be worked out and finalized.

Finding negotiations neither with France nor with the Commission easy going, the British tried to make progress in bilateral discussions with the other Five. This produced suspicion in France that the British were trying to isolate them. During the multilateral discussions in the Maudling Committee which followed on the Ockrent Report the French

---

*Macmillan in his diary described Couve as 'a functionary not a politician and a cold Protestant fish . . . de Gaulle sees him but rarely' (29.11.61). Macmillan considered that all decent French statesmen should be Catholics.

took a harder line and pressed the British to accept arrangements which amounted to a customs union. Olivier Wormser, the chief French negotiator, head of Economic Affairs in the French Foreign Office, stated that if EFTA came into being the Seventeen must always negotiate within GATT* 'with a single point of view discussed between them beforehand'. Although Wormser was a civil servant, not a Minister, he now became the chief French negotiator.

Not surprisingly the Maudling Committee made no progress in the early autumn of 1958. Only clear-cut and far-reaching political decisions by France and Britain could save the negotiations, and neither government showed any inclination to change their stances or define their minimum terms. On 10 October de Gaulle stated that France would not be interested in any arrangement which excluded agriculture and given France's many concessions, it was now up to the United Kingdom to make some. The Foreign Office minuted: 'I fear this must be regarded as evidence that since his meeting with the Prime Minister de Gaulle has learned nothing and forgotten much about the free trade area.'[13]

Bernard Clappier, a French member of the steering board, told Bretherton on 13 October that it would be impossible to get any important decisions out of France before February 1959. On 22 October Maudling gave the Six an intentional shock in a speech at Baden-Baden, saying that Britain would be forced to take defensive measures if negotiations were not in sight of a conclusion by the end of the year.[14]

By July 1958 the Carli plan and the Faure plan were dead ducks. Apart from the political divide between the French and the UK, the complications of devising workable formulas for 'origin controls' and the degree of autonomy which individual countries were to have over their own import tariffs were insuperable. Over all the negotiations loomed the unpalatable fact for the Six that Britain insisted that Commonwealth food and raw materials should enter Britain on a most favoured nation basis free of duty or at low preferential rates. This would give Britain unacceptable advantages in cost over the Six who would impose their common external tariff on all Commonwealth imports. As well as this the British had gravely misjudged the strength of the movement towards unity within the Six and the suspicion and hostility aroused by their clumsy efforts to wreck the Messina powers' purpose. The British archives reveal an air of unreality over all the negotiations. Britain was skirting the main issues; the Maudling Committee had become bogged down in detail over trivialities without seeking a clear-cut understanding with the French and the other Five on fundamentals.

---

* General Agreement on Tariffs and Trade: a 'code of international fair trading practice' accepted by thirty-eight non-Communist countries.

Even if de Gaulle with his iron hand had not finally vetoed further negotiations, EFTA of the Seventeen was always doomed to failure.

During the autumn, negotiations over the Carli plan and the Ockrent Report continued, with Maudling still firmly vetoing any suggestion of curtailing Commonwealth preferences in the British market or any agreement over agriculture. With this attitude the negotiations could make no headway, and Jebb wrote on 6 November that when he mentioned the free trade area the 'General' visibly 'winced'.[15]

Maudling's hopes of a successful conclusion to his labours were finally dashed when Couve de Murville came to London on 6 November 1958. At the Foreign Office Couve emphasized to Maudling and Lloyd that the free trade area as originally proposed would expose the French economy, which was highly protected, to unacceptable foreign competition, and the original proposals would have meant the disappearance of the Common Market. However he was open to finding a solution. Unfortunately he felt that discussion between the Seventeen had been too cumbersome and amounted in effect to discussion between France and the United Kingdom 'by proxy [*par personnes interposées*]' and so far there had been 'no real discussion aimed at finding a compromise'. Couve continued that he could not agree to complete free trade among the Seventeen (which of course was Britain's objective).

Despite Couve's uncompromising attitude Maudling thought negotiations should continue but Lloyd disagreed, saying, 'It would be much better to break today rather than go on under an illusion [that agreement with France was possible].' They then adjourned to 10 Downing Street to see the Prime Minister. Lloyd stated that he and Couve had just 'finished a bad meeting' at which the French had finally 'torpedoed the free trade area'; Maudling, he said, was very depressed. According to Lloyd, the French could not contemplate any arrangement which did not allow the Six a special position between themselves. Couve agreed that there was an impasse.

Macmillan said that, with the French position continually changing, no serious progress had been made during the last year and it depressed him that the French Government had decided that 'Sparta and Athens must quarrel.' The Russians were getting stronger and stronger all the time and here was the free world voluntarily weakening and dividing itself. 'History would regard this as a tragic decision and the crowning folly of the twentieth century in Europe.'

Macmillan gives no details in his memoirs of this conversation with Couve on 6 November 1958. The next day he wrote a letter to de Gaulle stating that 'we have been negotiating at cross-purposes' and begging the French leader to do something to prevent 'the erection of barriers between two halves of Europe' which would start on 1 January 1959. This letter was unproductive.[16]

A week later, 13 November, on de Gaulle's orders Jacques Soustelle, the French Minister of Information, announced to the press that 'It was not possible to form a free trade area as had been wished by the British to result in free trade between the Six and the Eleven other OEEC countries unless there was a common external tariff and harmonization in the economic and social spheres.' Maudling showed surprise as well as dismay at the announcement, and postponed the meetings of his committee. It never met again. The Free Trade Area of the Seventeen was dead.

At the end of November de Gaulle and Adenauer met at Bad Kreuznach and both sides agreed to veto the free trade area. Adenauer promised the closest co-operation with France in the development of the Common Market, and they agreed that negotiations for EFTA should not be reopened through OEEC. However as a sop to Britain and the rest of Europe they agreed that Walter Hallstein, the German President of the Commission, should be asked to produce a plan for 'a multilateral association' or *modus vivendi* between the Six and the other OEEC countries. The tariff reductions and lowering of quotas within the Six scheduled for 1 January 1959 were endorsed by de Gaulle and Adenauer and the prospects for a rapid increase in EEC trade were confirmed.

After the Soustelle announcement there was much recrimination against France in the British press. On 18 November 1958 a percipient *Times* leader stated: 'Many parts of the Treaty of Rome were tailor-made for France. She has done extremely well out of it . . . France wrecked the negotiations single-handed.' This was correct; France was highly protectionist and protectionist-minded. They were alarmed even at free trade with the other Five and thoroughly frightened at taking on tariff-free competition from a further Eleven.

The previous day in the Commons Maudling had been more statesmanlike, but no one believed him when he disingenuously implied that this was the first time the French had called into question the basis on which the negotiations had been proceeding. Barred by tariffs from the expanding market of the Six Britain desperately needed a new policy, and on 12 December Macmillan authorized a further study of the Uniscan plan for a free trade area of seven comprising Britain, Norway, Sweden, Denmark, Austria, Switzerland and Portugal.

With considerable difficulty Britain persuaded the Six to hold a meeting of the OEEC Ministerial Council on 15 December 1958. The meeting was stormy with 'heated discussion' between Maudling and Couve. European trade was at that time bedevilled not only by import tariffs but by quotas. David Eccles, President of the Board of Trade, for

Britain, argued that the Treaty of Rome quota remissions due on 1 January should also apply to all OEEC countries who wished to apply them on a reciprocal basis. The French refused, whereupon Eccles declared that in that event 'defensive measures' might be taken by the British. This infuriated Couve, the French delegate, who refused to negotiate further 'under threat'. Lloyd, however, promised not to 'modify our commercial policy to defend our interests' before the next meeting on 15 January, although he reported to Macmillan that the meeting had been 'difficult' with 'trouble over the *modus vivendi* with the French wanting as a matter of principle to discriminate in favour of the Six against the non-Six'.

At this OEEC meeting differences and tensions between France and her partners in the Six came out into the open for the first time; the civil servants' briefing for the British Cabinet stressed that the objective must be to 'maintain and if possible increase French isolation'. With the other Five deeply suspicious of British motives this came to nothing. Immediately after the OEEC Ministerial meeting the French devalued the franc by 17½ per cent which gave them a big advantage in all export markets at the expense of Britain and other OEEC countries.

Foster Dulles had also been in Paris for the stormy Ministerial meeting of OEEC on 15 December. The following day further gloom was shed by the account which he gave Lloyd and Jebb of his talks with de Gaulle. De Gaulle had insisted to Dulles that there must be trade discrimination between the Six and the Eleven; he also wanted a 'tripartite organization' for global policy, the participants being France, the UK and the USA. De Gaulle told Dulles he was sure there was a secret Anglo-American planning body, and he was determined France should be admitted to this mythical body. The conference 'had not gone well', Dulles said, given a foretaste of the French President's prima donna ways.

Meanwhile Macmillan sent a telegram to Selwyn Lloyd that he had been 'shocked' by a story from an 'unimpeachable source that a very highly placed United States official who had recently visited Europe was actually if incredibly saying that the United Kingdom was out to sabotage the Common Market'. Although the Macmillan Government was at least trying to dilute the EEC if not to sabotage it, the Prime Minister wanted Lloyd 'to put a stop to this sort of thing'.

Selwyn Lloyd saw de Gaulle two days after the OEEC meeting and continued to issue strong pleas for France to accept Britain's now defunct plan for an EFTA of Seventeen. De Gaulle was unmoved although he said he did not want to rub salt into old wounds and would not aggravate the situation. Macmillan's private secretary, Philip de Zulueta – who enjoyed a great influence with the Prime Minister – minuted on the report of the Foreign Secretary's meeting with de Gaulle:[17]

not very encouraging . . . de Gaulle had quite dismissed the idea of the Free
Trade Area . . . I cannot help feeling that the Free Trade Area is now
finished. In the economic field we do not seem to have any effective cards
to play, and the only pressures we could bring would therefore be political . . . our main card is NATO, and our contributions to the defence of
Europe particularly Germany. If we try to use threats of withdrawal from
Germany and perhaps an independent policy about such questions as Berlin
we should certainly alarm the Germans, but probably not the French. My
own conclusion is therefore that our only course is either to try and break
up the Common Market or watering it down and securing the best possible
terms. The first course would probably involve stimulating anti-German
feeling in France, and the second course may involve forming a grouping
of the non-Six. Both are disagreeable and would have bad political
consequences and short of a change of heart by the French there seems little
else to do.

Macmillan minuted that he favoured 'watering down', but Britain was
out to wreck the EEC, as de Zulueta had hinted.[18]

With these quarrels at the OEEC, not surprisingly little effort was
made to reopen negotiations with the Six, who now gave overriding
priority to hastening on the development of the Common Market. Led
by Britain the Eleven turned their attention to efforts to secure a *modus
vivendi* with the Six to minimize discrimination when the Six's tariff cuts
came into operation on 1 January 1959. At a meeting of the Ministers
of the Eleven on 17 December, Maudling stressed the gravity of the
forthcoming tariff discrimination by the Six and dispelled any idea that
the Eleven would take it lying down. He summed up: 'there should be
constant contact and the Eleven should do all they could to impress on
the Americans the real nature of the issue.' It was agreed to consider
action if the Six refused to offer reciprocity – the equalizing of tariffs
between the two organizations.[19]

The Foreign Office sent out instructions to British Ambassadors that
the breakdown in the talks was to be represented as a postponement and
not a rupture of negotiations but admitted 'there is nothing but a blank
prospect,' although the Eleven had pressed for some solution before 1
January to prevent 'discrimination'.

So the British attempt to secure some arrangement before discrimination on tariffs and quotas was introduced on 1 January 1959 came
to nothing. Britain alleged that it was the responsibility of the Six to
suggest a resolution of the situation. The Six did not see it that way,
and expected the Eleven to put a proposal before OEEC. But Maudling
did not want any get-together of the Seventeen, thinking that the present
split should mark 'the dividing of Europe by France'. The British hoped
that the rupture would draw down criticism on France from the other

Five, but the Five were determined to maintain the solidarity of the EEC and would not allow a wedge to be driven between them.

Paul Gore-Booth of the Foreign Office wrote to Sir Harold Caccia, British Ambassador in Washington:

> when the French attitude became clear Ministers were upset to the point of fury. This was not at all surprising because Maudling had been working for one and a half years on a basis accepted by OEEC including France only to find out that France had *not* accepted the basis. There was therefore at any rate for a few days a certain amount of fierce talk which worried us considerably in the wider context of the world situation.

For a moment Britain considered bribing France into an agreement, and a telegram was sent to Jebb in Paris: 'We should like to see negotiations of FTA go forward on a basis of France being given a "special position".' Macmillan too had written to de Gaulle, suggesting that 'the growing tension in Europe and the world makes me feel it is imperative that a solution be found,' but the manoeuvre was dropped when de Gaulle's reply poured cold water on further negotiations.[20]

Smarting under the French snub Macmillan attempted to fall back on the special relationship between America and Britain in which he had always proclaimed great confidence. This was fruitless. The US administration were so elated by the way in which German membership of the EEC had firmly removed West Germany from the Soviet orbit that they were determined to do everything in their power to encourage Franco-German friendship. The State Department therefore took de Gaulle's side against Macmillan. When on 23 December 1958 the Cabinet decided to try again to enlist American support and to write to her putting 'our actions in the most favourable light', this was already a lost cause.

The biggest shock to Macmillan and Maudling was delivered by one of the US delegates to OEEC in Brussels, John McCarthy. He could put no pressure on the Six, he declared to Gore-Booth, because his instructions from Washington consisted of 'fulsome praise' for the Six, and he was fighting 'an uphill battle with his own people who moan about British threats ... the United Kingdom had not got through to either Dulles or Dillon.' Dulles wrote a polite letter to Lloyd refusing any help in preventing the introduction of the new discriminatory tariff measures by the EEC on 1 January 1959.[21]

When the crunch came over the EEC the special relationship with America, so valued by Macmillan, proved a broken reed. The Macmillan Government's European policy lay in ruins. They had managed to alarm the Commonwealth, antagonize the Six and displease America. Fortunately for the Conservatives all this was successfully covered up during the 1959 General Election.

CHAPTER 8

EFTA of the Seven

AFTER THE SOUSTELLE statement Macmillan, more than any other member of the Cabinet, was determined to strive for an agreement with the Six over the level of import tariffs; he was convinced that British economic interests would otherwise suffer gravely as a result of her exports' exclusion from the rapidly expanding industrial market of the Six. For the next three years the problem was seldom out of his mind, and coloured his approach to both foreign and home economic policy. Unfortunately he continually overplayed his hand and like Eden failed to realize that although Europe was grateful to Britain for saving them from Nazi dominion during the war years, Britain's influence was on the wane, and unless she toed the line and genuinely accepted the principles and ideals of the Treaty of Rome the Six would go their own way regardless.

Maudling remained in charge of policy towards Europe. After his unrewarding experience in negotiations with the Six he had a clearer understanding of the difficulties than the Prime Minister (or his successor, Edward Heath) and the archives show how realistic and sceptical was his assessment of the outcome.

Following the Soustelle statement, Maudling sent a memorandum to Macmillan on 27 November 1958 stating that the French supported the Hallstein thesis that the OEEC was an 'anachronism', and felt there was no longer any need for a specifically European organization: from this position the Six would treat Britain and Sweden on the same commercial basis as the United States and Canada or for that matter Costa Rica and San Salvador. He continued:

> this enables the French and the Commission to pose as leaders of liberal thought, outward-looking, progressive, anti-restrictionist. They say we want trade with the whole world through GATT not merely with Europe, but in examination their actual proposals for tariff reductions are nothing like as liberal as they pretend, but the matter is complicated enough for them to get away with it and, of course, it has immense attractions for the Americans . . . it would be folly to commence another negotiation unless we

126

can be reasonably confident of success although we are pressed by the Swiss, Austrians and Danes to ask for urgent negotiations with the Six, and in the absence of negotiations we shall have increasing difficulty in keeping our flock together.[1]

This assessment, outlining the path the Six would follow, was far from the advice Macmillan wanted; he and his Foreign Secretary, Selwyn Lloyd, ignored it and instructed the officials to explore every avenue that could lead to an understanding between the Six and the Eleven. They were chasing a will-o'-the-wisp; only by accepting the ideals and principles of the Treaty of Rome could Britain have access to Europe. Frenzied efforts to find a *modus vivendi* between the Six and the Eleven came to nothing.

The air was thick with talk of retaliation and Europe was deeply divided. As a result of an initiative by de Gaulle a sop was given to the non-Six countries, when the Common Market countries reduced their tariffs by 10 per cent towards the remainder of the OEEC with effect from 1 January 1959. As Miriam Camps points out, these arrangements would not eliminate discrimination within the OEEC, and were accordingly considered inadequate by Britain and the other members of the OEEC. Severe discrimination clearly lay ahead under the Treaty of Rome. Apart from this gesture de Gaulle was intransigent, and the likelihood of a permanent *modus vivendi* between the Six and the Eleven remained dim.[2]

However in a personal letter to the Prime Minister on 20 January 1959, Gladwyn Jebb gave a sanguine account of talks he had held with Antoine Pinay, French Minister of Finance, on the free trade area. He pointed out that with the devaluation of the franc Britain was not likely to sell very much more than at present to the French but, over-optimistically, he felt that a 'quick bargain' could be made provided we abandoned our position on the principle of complete non-discrimination. He felt the other Eleven would like to see Britain come to 'some practical arrangement which would hold the fort for the time being', and allow the negotiations for the free trade area to proceed 'in a reasonable atmosphere'. Macmillan was attracted by Jebb's idea.

Paul Gore-Booth of the Foreign Office advised Macmillan that Jebb 'had missed the point' because 'our friends among the Eleven have very considerable interests in exporting goods to France', and the problem could not simply be solved by the French and British coming to a mutually agreeable bargain. Gore-Booth thought an Anglo-French bargain could be struck but this would let the Eleven down and prejudice a sensible multilateral association such as the Uniscan idea now being put forward, which Britain might want to seek in default of any better prospect.[3]

Hopes of this type of *modus vivendi* were finally dashed on 16 February

1959 when Walter Hallstein, President of the Commission, accompanied by his deputy Robert Margolin, met Maudling and his advisers in London. For the Commission they stated that this problem was part of the relations of the EEC with the outside world, and there was no easy solution; it would be useless to bring the Seventeen together again at this stage since they would quickly come up against all the difficulties which had caused the breakdown. Maudling agreed, and both sides decided that a *modus vivendi* was a long-term, not an immediate hope.

In an effort to retaliate against the EEC the British now took the lead in trying to form a free trade area with six other countries out of the Eleven (Portugal, Norway, Sweden, Denmark, Austria, Switzerland); this would be an EFTA of Seven, otherwise known as Uniscan. This move limited Britain's freedom of action in direct talks with the EEC, who regarded the plan of an EFTA of Seven as a hostile riposte to their dismantlement of internal quotas and tariffs. The British Government now abandoned all hope of successfully negotiating an association with the Six that would not involve accepting a customs union: a condition they refused to consider. The British also wanted to prevent other European countries being drawn into the orbit of the Six; there was a real danger that Denmark at least might take this course. The British aim was to form a strong group of seven to bargain with the Six.[4] As early as 18 December 1958 *The Times* was reporting that a joint meeting of the British FBI and the Swedish counterpart had recommended the formation of 'a body to be known as Uniscan'. However time was too short for EEC tariff discrimination on 1 January 1959 to be avoided.

By 4 December 1958 British Ministers were discussing setting up the Uniscan Free Trade Area. The first important Foreign Office minute upon it noted: 'a Uniscan FTA has many drawbacks. It will serve to divide Europe even more deeply and our initiative in promoting it would provoke US displeasure.' The British tried to obtain support for the new formation from the US, but when Caccia talked to Under-Secretary of State Douglas Dillon in Washington Dillon said he could do 'nothing': America was too keen on Germany and France drawing together within the Six to sponsor a rival European grouping.[5]

In February 1959 Maudling and Heathcoat Amory began to suspect that Macmillan was toying with the idea of applying for full membership of the EEC and was lukewarm about an EFTA of the Seven. On 17 February Amory sent the Prime Minister a long paper prepared in the Treasury setting out the reasons why Britain should not join the Six. Maudling had read it and agreed, and Amory wanted it circulated to all the Cabinet; Macmillan agreed to do so.

The Treasury pointed out that three quarters of our trade was with the world outside Europe whereas three quarters of the trade of the Six was with Europe; the things 'that are fundamental to us appear marginal to them'. They added that the open market in Britain for Commonwealth food producers would be bound to disappear if Britain was part of the EEC, and it could not be assumed that the Six would be prepared to have Britain in on terms 'which would begin to safeguard the Commonwealth producers'.

Maudling followed up the Treasury statement with a strong letter to the Prime Minister on 3 March 1959:

> The fact is the French do not want us in Europe at all. The Community of the Six has become a Paris/Bonn axis, with Paris at the moment the dominating partner on the basis of Adenauer's personal policy. The other four countries are no more than satellites ...
>
> In these circumstances the need for some positive action to hold together our friends outside the Six seems to be growing. The recent discussions among officials have shown an encouraging degree of interest in an alternative free trade area, not only in Scandinavia but also among the Swiss, Austrians and Portuguese. The Norwegian and Swedish governments are now taking the initiative in trying to produce a possible plan of association. This, of course, is what we hoped would happen as we did not want to take any initiative ourselves ... I remain convinced that if we were to reject the idea of forming some alternative association with our friends outside the Six we should be left without a friend in Europe and we should thoroughly deserve such a fate.

These letters from colleagues in whom Macmillan had confidence appeared to persuade the Prime Minister after all to push ahead with plans for an EFTA of the Seven. His confidence was misplaced, as events were to show.

Prompted by Maudling and Heathcoat Amory, Rab Butler expressed support for the Uniscan project, writing to the Prime Minister on 24 March 1959 in his own particular style: 'I think myself that in certain circumstances the plan [Uniscan] might do the trick ... much depends on the timing of the Uniscan project in relation to our own election ... it is all very difficult, but if we do nothing we are a sitting rabbit.'[6]

At a Cabinet meeting on 7 May 1959 the Chancellor of the Exchequer made it clear that with the failure of the EFTA negotiations there was a serious danger that unless other European countries could work out some commercial policy each would become constrained to make the best terms they could with the Common Market. Since Britain could not join the Common Market on satisfactory terms there was a possibility of her becoming isolated and her trade and economic strength suffering. It was therefore in her interest to co-operate in the Swedish initiative for a free trade area. Although the 'immediate' Swedish proposal was limited to a free trade area for industrial goods some concession might be given on Danish bacon. With the Cabinet's backing, negotiations with the Swedes were speeded up.[7]

On 22 May 1959 the definitive new British policy towards Europe was set out in a despatch to Ambassadors abroad. It stated:

> the Swedish Government intends to announce probably on 27 May that invitations to the United Kingdom, Denmark, Norway, Austria, Switzerland and Portugal to attend a working party to establish a possible basis for a Free Trade Area between the 'Outer Seven' have been accepted. The working party is expected to start work in Stockholm on 1 June . . . chance of an early revival of multilateral negotiations on the lines of those which took place in Paris in 1957 and 1958 seems remote. Adopting a merely passive attitude would be dangerous. Discrimination against us in the Common Market will be growing to the disadvantage of export trade and it would be very likely to extend if other European countries found themselves obliged to come to terms with the Six . . . the only positive policy open to us is to try and reach our objective of free trade and close economic co-operation with Western Europe by another route . . . the overriding objective and hope would be . . . a bridge of a wider arrangement providing for free trade between that Group, the Rome Group and the rest of OEEC. It would provide an incentive to the Six to put pressure on their more reluctant members to move faster to enter into negotiation for a wider association. Criticism must be expected on the score that the Stockholm Group would further split Europe politically and wreck OEEC. Europe has already been divided by the Six . . . Any suggestion that our action is retaliatory should be firmly rebutted.[8]

Ministers of the Seven met near Stockholm on 21 July 1959 and quickly approved the convention for EFTA of the Seven. A schedule of tariff reductions was designed to put the Seven on an equal footing with the Six by 1 July 1960. At the same time the Stockholm Convention tried to take advantage of the thousands of man hours that had been wasted on 'origin controls' in the Carli plan to prevent any country taking unfair advantage of their complexity. Following the example of the Six it also provided for the total elimination by the end of the transition period of all quotas and tariffs between the signatory nations. The convention declared that the Seven would 'do all in their power to avoid a new division in Europe', and that their new association was 'a step towards an agreement between all member countries of OEEC'. They also recorded their readiness to negotiate with the Six.

With the creation of EFTA Britain hoped to link the Common Market and the Seven by a harmonization of internal tariffs (although external tariffs against the rest of the world would remain at the discretion of the Seven). There was initial enthusiasm for the plan in Britain as a reaction to the humiliation suffered at the hands of France by the outright rejection of the proposed association between the EEC and EFTA of the Seventeen. But by the time the convention was ratified on 20 November 1959 this enthusiasm had largely vanished. Businessmen realized that the Six offered far greater opportunities for trade, and the Government was beset by complaints from industry. Little effort was made to exploit the opportunities within the Seven. During the three years 1960, 1961 and 1962 when Britain had a large tariff advantage in the markets of the Seven, and a tariff disadvantage in the markets of the Six, exports to the EEC rose by 55 per cent while exports to EFTA went up by only 33 per cent.[9]

At the end of November 1959 the Six decided to accelerate their tariff reductions* in excess of the requirements of the Treaty of Rome. Meanwhile the monthly trade statistics offered dramatic proof that Britain was backing the wrong horse. Gravely concerned, the Government appointed Sir Frank Lee (who moved from the Board of Trade to be head of the Treasury on 1 January 1960) to chair a Treasury committee to examine the whole field of possible solutions to the European problem: to report on how the Six could join the new EFTA of the Seven as a unit, and how Britain could join a customs union while retaining the advantages of imperial preference on trade with the Commonwealth. The two propositions were incompatible; the Six had no intention of joining EFTA 'as a unit' and would not consider Britain entering their customs union while she enjoyed even a limited form of free or preferential entry for Commonwealth food and manufactures. Macmillan also asked Lee to work on the principle that Britain would accept a customs union provided all agricultural products were excluded: again this was unrealistic as the Messina powers were now embarked on formulating a common agricultural policy. Nevertheless it showed that Macmillan had at last accepted the feasibility of Britain being in a customs union rather than a free trade area, and was prepared to put this proposition to his Cabinet.

During his visit to London in December 1959 the US Under-Secretary of State, Douglas Dillon, admitted to Macmillan that the United States had 'accepted the Six' but had not pressed for a 'wider association' – although they had no intention of opposing the Seven. The idea of a

---

*Eventually all quotas between the six EEC countries on industrial goods were abolished on 31 December 1961; tariff reduction during the first stage was increased from 30 to 50 per cent. This was highly damaging to British trade in Europe. Attempts were also made by the Six to speed up the common agricultural policy.

'bridge' between the Six and Seven had never been enthusiastically received in the United States, he said, but he agreed to work 'closely with the United Kingdom and the rest of the OEEC to see if a framework could be found ... and if some wider association could be achieved they would accept it but without unbounded enthusiasm.'[10] It was crystal clear that the USA wanted the United Kingdom to join the Six and abandon its reliance on the special relationship with the United States. Dillon firmly turned down the idea of a North Atlantic free trade grouping – a plan which had support in Canada and from influential quarters in the City of London – and in talks with the Chancellor of the Exchequer and the President of the Board of Trade continued to emphasize the USA's desire for Britain to join the Six.

On 10 December 1959 Macmillan minuted to Heathcoat Amory that the result of the talks with Dillon

> represents a considerable setback to our policy ... the responsible American newspapers had made it clear the USA would back the Six rather than the Seven, and did not favour negotiations between the Six and Seven as groups. Although we knew what the American attitude was likely to be this is the first time (I believe) that their position has been made public in such explicit and unfavourable terms. I had hoped that we could have got them to be more impartial ... Unless some way can be found of avoiding the economic damage which we should otherwise suffer from the Six the whole of our political relationship in Europe will have to be revised. Although we have failed with Mr Dillon that is what we have got to get the United States and the Six to understand.[11]

On 15 December, after a further talk with Dillon, Macmillan sent the Chancellor another minute recording that the meeting had been 'useful'; he and the Foreign Secretary had impressed on Dillon Britain's need to consolidate and stand by the Seven, and tried to make him understand 'that the purpose of the Seven is to prevent the political as well as the economic division of Europe and that it can and will be used to make the Six more liberal'. Macmillan also expressed his grave concern to Dulles about the serious consequences to Britain's exports of the policies of the Six.[12]

With his discussion with Dillon having raised doubts in his mind about the validity of the special relationship – a relationship on which he set much store, more especially because of his personal friendship with Eisenhower – Macmillan now wrote to Lloyd on 11 December 1959:

> One of our basic reasons why we could not integrate with Europe was our desire to maintain a special relationship with the United States. *Just what does that now mean?* [Author's italics] Is the pattern changing – will the Six

replace us as the major ally of the United States? Why is it difficult to make the United States realize that the Six which they support for the sake of European political unity is in fact (because of the economic threat to the United Kingdom and others) a threat to European unity?

Lloyd hastily collected a briefing from his Foreign Office team and replied on 13 December:

Our Special Relationship with the USA
It does exist. It means preferential treatment for us in discussion and in certain types of knowledge (nuclear, intelligence, etc.). It gives us considerable influence on United States policy.

We ceased to be on an equal basis with the United States and USSR when we gave up the Indian Empire. We have been in retreat since . . . I do not believe size or physical military power will decide the future.

But even if it is so we must prevent the Six supplanting us as the principal influence on United States policy. (I admit our special relationship might *end* when Eisenhower and Herter* go, but I rather doubt it.) To achieve this, we need to play in the game both as pro-Europeans and pro-Atlantic community.

We must go flat out with the President, Herter, Merchant and Co to convince them that they make a profound mistake in taking the continued political unity of Western Europe for granted.

Macmillan had a knack of asking the right probing questions but even when he agreed with the answers he constantly failed to put the lessons learnt into practice. The Foreign Office were correct, and the special relationship only existed insofar as Britain was an ally of the USA in nuclear affairs and defence. Otherwise Britain enjoyed no special position in American eyes and the Americans, obsessed with the need to promote the EEC so as to keep France and Germany permanently immune to Soviet influence, refused to take the British side and help to bridge the gap between EFTA and the EEC. Unfortunately Macmillan, despite the frank Foreign Office answer, refused to admit that there was no special relationship on which he could call to persuade the USA to coerce de Gaulle into cushioning Britain against the economic disadvantages of tariff discrimination which it incurred under the Treaty of Rome. He realized that when Eisenhower retired his own influence with the USA was bound to diminish.

A Western summit of the heads of state of America, France, Germany and the UK was held in Paris between 19 and 21 December 1959. In a minute to the Chancellor of the Exchequer the following day, regarding the Paris discussions, Macmillan wrote:

---

*Christian Herter became Eisenhower's Secretary of State in April 1959 following the resignation through illness of John Foster Dulles.

> Far the most important from our point of view (I mean the economic side)
> was the tripartite Rambouillet [Eisenhower, Macmillan and de Gaulle] on
> Sunday and my talk with de Gaulle ... I believe that de Gaulle will play
> the game, and at any rate I am now in a position to bring a lot of pressure
> on him ... I want as you can see to play the political support that I am
> now – owing to President Eisenhower's rather unexpected attitude – in a
> position to give to de Gaulle without disloyalty to the Americans. I must
> play this to the full in order to get an economic quid pro quo.

At this meeting the British and Americans had discussed with de Gaulle
the formation of a tripartite defence committee which would give him
equal access with them to atomic warfare secrets, and Macmillan had
formed a wildly over-optimistic opinion of the effect of this on de
Gaulle's attitude towards a *modus vivendi*. But de Gaulle at no time made
any move to support British efforts for an agreement between the Six
and the Seven. Macmillan was indulging in wishful thinking when he
wrote the above minute.[13]

After talks between Eisenhower and Adenauer on 20 March 1960
the two leaders issued a joint communiqué giving 'explicit approval'
to EEC acceleration of internal cuts in import tariffs – a move, as
The Times indicated, that was being taken on American initiative.
Maudling reacted angrily and wrote in a letter to Heathcoat Amory that
'this amounted to a public smack in the face for us, and confirmed what
we thought, that Dillon in these matters is working against us and the
rest of the administration neither understand nor care.' The time had
come, Maudling said, for the Prime Minister to lodge a protest with
Eisenhower since the communiqué had been issued on presidential
authority:

> we really must tell the Americans that it is not in accordance with our
> relations with them that they should continue to ride rough-shod over
> fundamental British interests ... we are now facing a serious payments
> problem which arises from continuing military expenditure overseas and
> from sharply increased government aid.
>   At the moment it is American policy to urge us to maintain the military
> expenditure and to increase the aid. The acceleration of the Treaty of Rome
> will mean a serious damage to our trade, and therefore a further threat to
> our current surplus. In these circumstances the Americans must understand
> that we shall have to revise our attitude both to military expenditure and
> to overseas aid ... The American move will have a serious effect on some
> of our colleagues of the Seven. The people in Denmark and Austria, for
> example, who dislike EFTA will be greatly strengthened in their opposition.
> As for the stout-hearted, as you know they already are very angry with the
> Americans and suspect us of being dragged at the American chariot wheels
> ... there is a further need for urgent study of what our publicly stated
> position should be.

Macmillan minuted to de Zulueta that Maudling was 'of course right to be annoyed' with the Americans and said he would raise it in Cabinet on 23 March 1960. However he did not, and refused to have a show-down with Dillon. Instead Heathcoat Amory, not Macmillan, wrote to Dillon and told him that 'we cannot expect a permanent solution of the European trade problem in the near future,' and must therefore concentrate on a solution to the 1 July problem of the acceleration of the reduction in internal tariffs amongst the Six. He went on that 'our overriding preoccupation is to mend the breach in Europe' since the present division would lead sooner or later to damaging political divisions in Europe; he emphasized that the Seven were ready after a meeting in Vienna to reduce their tariffs with the Six if the Six reciprocated. Dillon replied unhelpfully: 'We are faced with a situation for which there are no perfect solutions.' The Americans wanted the Common Market to succeed and made no bones about the fact that they thought Britain should accede to the Treaty of Rome.[14]

On 7 April Macmillan asked de Gaulle to halt the acceleration, emphasizing that if the Six accelerated their tariff reduction on 1 July there would be 'serious discrimination against other countries with an important stake in European trade'.

> The trade of the United Kingdom will suffer severely in the Benelux and German markets; the trade of some other countries – for instance Switzerland and Austria – will suffer even more. If the arrangements for the Common Market on 1 July were spread over a longer period this would enable all concerned to work out an accommodation and to discuss the situation calmly. But if the so-called 'acceleration' is introduced by the Common Market on 1 July there will be an immediate accentuation of the economic division which has been created in Western Europe. This could have serious effects on the economy of the other Western European countries, and I fear that it would not be long before there were serious effects in the political field as well. I therefore believe it to be of the greatest importance that the operation of the Common Market should not be accelerated on 1 July 1960. I do not think our difficulties can be solved unless Heads of Government, and especially yourself, give the lead and interest themselves personally in these problems. Experts do not solve problems except under the direction of the leaders of nations.

Macmillan attached to his letter statistics showing the harmful con-sequences for British trade 'if the acceleration plans of the Six are carried out'. On 13 April de Gaulle replied tersely that the statistics sent by Macmillan depicted 'in somewhat too pessimistic colours the situation which would face British trade in Europe if the Common Market Treaty were accelerated'. He sent a technical paper playing down *inter alia* the 'handicap to Anglo-French trade'.

Macmillan was still hoping on 22 April that a 'minimum discrimination arrangement' could be agreed, but his private secretary Fred Bishop pointed out that this was open 'to gravest objection in our own interests in the view of all the experts'. Convinced that 'the more the problem is examined the clearer it becomes we are in a most serious position', Bishop feared that if Britain made a favourable unilateral arrangement with France it would wreck EFTA as Britain would then be in a more favourable position than her EFTA partners.

On 10 May Macmillan replied to de Gaulle's letter of 13 April enclosing some technical comments on the French analysis and claiming that 'your advisers were underestimating the difficulties we are facing'. The annexe to his letter stated that the French analysis did not deal with the real matter of concern to the United Kingdom 'which is not accelerated reduction of tariffs among the Six, but the accelerated increase of the national tariffs against British goods in Benelux and Germany'.[15] Macmillan does not give details of this unrewarding correspondence in his memoirs, but the letters make clear the strained relations between him and de Gaulle.

On 22 April 1960 Sir Frank Lee presented the report which he had been commissioned to write as soon as news came about the 1 July acceleration of tariff reductions by the Six.* It was sent immediately to the Prime Minister. In it Lee stated:

> It is almost certain that after 1 July next the two economic groups – the Six and the Seven – will go their separate ways at least for the time being. Each will discriminate against the other and against the rest of the world. The extent of the immediate discrimination will depend on whether one or both groups decide to accelerate the tariff reductions between themselves . . . the economic divisions of Europe will confront the United Kingdom with a most serious situation . . . From the economic standpoint the immediate and overt effects will not be disastrous (only 14 per cent of our exports go to the Six, and it is reasonable to hope that a substantial part of this trade will continue despite tariff discrimination against us). But even in the short term the fact that our exports will be increasingly at a disadvantage in the markets of the Six (where the rate of economic growth has been high and is likely to continue so) will be a serious matter at a time when our balance of payments position once more gives cause for concern.

Lee thought the creation of a 'bridge' between the Six and the Seven was 'improbable', and in the longer term the situation would be 'still more serious' with the Six discriminating against us and the rest of the world while themselves constituting a block with a high rate of

---

* Lee's Inter-departmental Committee consisted of representatives of the Foreign Office, the Board of Trade, Colonial, Commonwealth and Agriculture Offices.

economic growth. With the strength which their internal market gave them, the Six would develop into 'most formidable competition' in UK markets. As a result, Lee went on, there was 'dismay' amongst leading industrialists at Britain being 'yoked indefinitely with the Seven' and 'cut off' by tariff barriers from the Six.

> The prospect is seen of three powerful economic groupings – the USA, the USSR and the Six – able to develop internal markets of scale and therefore strong and competitive industries based on such markets, whereas the UK will have a preferential position only in the Seven and in Commonwealth markets (where we face tariff barriers in any event and where our position is likely to weaken rather than grow stronger).*
>
> The conclusion is inescapable – that even if one can leave the political factors on one side, from an economic standpoint we *must* maintain our broad objective of having the UK form part of a single European market unless a still wider grouping – say, an Atlantic Free Trade Area – became a possibility.

Any proposal by the Seven to resume negotiations for a single market would, he believed, be regarded as further evidence that they were trying to 'delay or prevent' the formation of the Six as a separate unity. Lee also emphasized that the fact there was no prospect of successful negotiations must not preclude us from 'taking action', and he reiterated the point that the US Government wanted nothing to impede the Six.

> We shall not get the solution which we want on the cheap. There is nothing to show that we are desperately needed in Europe – e.g. to oppose German hegemony in support of the French. That has become the way of illusion. Therefore we shall have to be prepared to pay for the sort of settlement we want – in political terms or in terms of inconvenience for or damage to some of our cherished interests – the Commonwealth, domestic agriculture, our tariff policy, perhaps indeed our political pride and sense of self-reliance.

He expected that in the months ahead important sections of UK industry would press for Britain to join the Common Market; there had been in recent weeks 'a marked drift among serious commentators in favour (with Lord Plowden and Lord Robbins being two notable converts)'.† He foresaw great difficulties over joining the EEC: first, it would weaken Britain's links with the Commonwealth and imperial preference could scarcely survive; second, the Six would not welcome

---

* Commonwealth countries were imposing duties on imports of British goods to protect their own growing manufacturing industry.
† Lord Robbins was the prominent Professor of Economics at the London School of Economics, and wartime Director of the Economic Section of the War Cabinet. Lord Plowden was a former Economic Adviser to the Government.

her because it would mean rewriting the Treaty of Rome; third, Britain's accession would break up the Seven.

According to Lee if Britain could not join the Common Market (which was the course he strongly preferred) she should try for 'near identification with the Common Market' by which he meant 'an arrangement between the Six and the Seven which would go as far as possible towards acceptance by the Seven of most of the essential features of the Common Market without formal absorption in it'.[16] Lee's views carried great weight with the Prime Minister, who, swayed by the report, changed course and determined that, regardless of prestige, the Commonwealth or the Seven, Britain must eventually become a member of the EEC.

After the Lee Report had been digested by the Cabinet, government departments were asked to examine the Treaty of Rome article by article and to report on the implications of accepting the main provisions of the treaty. At the same time Douglas Dillon spent a week in Europe discussing the Six and Seven, and again emphasized that the USA favoured Britain joining the Six, and thought it was impossible to breathe new life into OEEC. Most top civil servants were in favour of Britain joining, but the predominant feeling in the Cabinet was that this should be avoided and instead some arrangement short of full membership excluding agriculture and retaining a strong measure of imperial preference should be negotiated.

An important Cabinet meeting was held on 13 July 1960. They had before them the report by officials based on Lee's recommendations about 'the political and economic considerations which should determine whether or not the UK should seek to join the Community'. Heathcoat Amory, Chancellor of the Exchequer, said 'his personal conclusion was that we should be ready to join the Community' provided it did not substantially impair our relations with the Commonwealth. Maudling said it would be 'disastrous' to begin negotiations until there was a political will within the Community to reach an accommodation with Britain; he pointed out that France feared British membership of the Community would threaten her leadership, whilst the present US Government favoured the development of the Community regardless 'of what difficulties this would cause for the United Kingdom'. Maudling did not want the Government to be pushed into hasty decisions by the press campaign, and wanted an authoritative statement in which the Government would make it clear that this was not 'a suitable moment' to begin negotiations, and would emphasize the fundamental objections to UK membership. This constituted major disagreement from the most knowledgeable member of the Cabinet.

Duncan Sandys, Minister of Defence, a convinced European, disagreed

strongly with Maudling and wanted Britain to join the Community where she 'might hope eventually to achieve leadership'. He thought an 'association short of membership could not secure us enough influence in the Community to make the price worth paying'. However he emphasized that even if Britain secured full membership special terms were necessary to guarantee the interests of the Commonwealth.

The Cabinet agreed that they could not become members on the terms of the Treaty of Rome, and some members argued that although the time 'was not ripe for negotiations we should prepare the ground for later negotiations by holding discussions with other Commonwealth countries and by strengthening the Community links with EFTA'. It was also argued that both the advantages of joining the Community and the dangers of staying outside had been exaggerated. For the time being it was decided that in the Commons debate on Europe, due on 25 July, the Government should state that there were 'insuperable difficulties' in the way of accepting Community membership under the provisions of the Treaty of Rome.[17]

Macmillan however had broken the ice. Although a majority of the Cabinet were strongly against making an application to join the Six, a customs union was not opposed, and belatedly the Government discovered that by forming EFTA of the Seven they had created a serious handicap in negotiations with the Six. Their hurriedly conceived plan had recoiled.

On 27 July 1960, upon Heathcoat Amory's retirement from politics, Selwyn Lloyd was taken away from the Foreign Office to become Chancellor of the Exchequer. Lord Home was promoted from Commonwealth Relations Secretary to be Foreign Secretary, and Edward Heath, Minister of Labour, was made number two at the Foreign Office to speak on Foreign Affairs in the Commons and to take over responsibility for negotiations with Europe from Reginald Maudling; Heath became Lord Privy Seal. Unlike Maudling, Heath was an enthusiast for the Common Market, and in his maiden speech in 1950 in the Commons had criticized the Attlee Government for spurning the Schuman Plan for a European iron and steel community to include Britain.

False hopes for an early improvement in the situation were raised by Adenauer when he and Macmillan talked in Bonn on 10 and 11 August 1960. Adenauer indicated to the British Prime Minister that his Government were anxious to bring the United Kingdom into closer association with the Six, and were ready to consider what arrangements Britain would have to make for such an association to be possible. Similar hopes were raised when Heath visited Rome at the same time. Accordingly the Commonwealth Relations Office instructed their representatives abroad to warn their respective governments that at the meeting of Commonwealth Prime Ministers in September 1960 there might be discussion over the continuance of Commonwealth preference as some abrogation might be a *sine qua non* of any settlement with the Six. This was not seriously pursued, Macmillan describing the 'exploratory' talks as 'very guarded'.[18]

From Paris Jebb poured cold water on hopes of the French agreeing either to a readaptation of the Treaty of Rome to suit Britain or to a scheme by which the Six would join EFTA as a unit. He wrote on 10 September 1960:

> the idea of founding some major new negotiations on the assumption that the Six could join the Seven as a block is a non-starter. But worse than that if we ever put it forward seriously the French at any rate would simply think that it represented a new effort to torpedo the Common Market. In other words we would be back to Square One.

The astute Jebb was one hundred per cent correct. But Heath did not agree and in the autumn of 1960 began cautiously and secretly to test the ice by instructing Ambassadors to make informal contacts within the Six. Rumours of these moves circulated and Jebb, now retired with the title of Lord Gladwyn since October, said in a widely reported speech on 7 December 1960: 'Negotiations cannot get started unless the UK goes further than she has so far been prepared to go, and specifically to negotiate on the basis of a common external tariff.' According to the Foreign Office this speech 'gave much satisfaction in Community circles'.

British enthusiasts for Europe had high hopes when Macmillan went to Rambouillet in January 1961 for talks with de Gaulle. According to the official account de Gaulle offered him no encouragement, but Macmillan recorded: 'Broadly speaking I think we made good progress.'[19] Particularly discouraging was de Gaulle's remark to Macmillan that he did not see how it was possible for the Commonwealth and the Six to make an economic community without destroying one or the other; one day, de Gaulle added, possibly in three years' time, there would be a great advantage in having 'one economic system for Europe' but the way had not yet been found. When Macmillan suggested that experts ought to be asked to work with a 'directive', de Gaulle replied that French experts were having such difficulties with the Common Market that the prospect of yet another negotiation would be too daunting, although he agreed that they might take another look at the difficulties of an accommodation between the Six and the Seven. When Macmillan first asked whether experts from France and Britain might meet to discuss 'with an open mind' an accommodation between the Six and the Seven de Gaulle did not reply. However later, having questioned how long Britain could pursue both a European and an American policy, de Gaulle expressed the hope that tripartism over nuclear defence might work, and agreed that British experts might meet the French for economic discussions. The President advised Macmillan to take his time and move little by little, and said France had to move faster because she was frightened of Germany.

The newly appointed British Ambassador in Paris, Sir Pierson Dixon, who was present at the talks, was doubtful of a successful outcome to any negotiations. He wrote to the Foreign Office after the meeting: 'We are committed to talks with the French ... If the prospects of their advancing matters are as bleak as I fear we shall have to be careful not to appear to be attaching too much importance to them or give the impression that should the experts separate without having reached any useful conclusions we shall necessarily despair.' Olivier Wormser, he added, who was in charge of economic affairs in the French Foreign Office, was being very awkward.

On 23 January 1961 the French Ambassador in London, Jean Chauvel, talked to Heath and gave only cold comfort. Heath reported to Macmillan that Wormser, the principal figure in all French negotiations, 'gave the impression he was not very interested in reaching a solution and it seemed extraordinary that one man and that an official should apparently be in a position to be the arbiter of the fate of Western Europe.' Heath told the French Ambassador that in view of the common tariff British firms did not feel confident of being able to sell their goods in Europe, and agencies within the Six were already refusing to act for British firms on account of the common tariff.

Christopher Steel, British Ambassador in Bonn, when told early in January that in the opinion of the Foreign Office de Gaulle was the 'key', replied that rather he was the 'lock', and that the German Finance Minister Dr Ludwig Erhard had told him the French had no intention of letting us into their private Europe. However Anthony Rumbold, Minister at the British Embassy in Paris, was more optimistic, writing to the Foreign Office: 'General de Gaulle would welcome our involvement on a basis of equality with France provided France was not expected to pay a price for it, and provided we were not trying to get the best of two worlds.'[20]

Talks started between British and French experts. Sir Roderick Barclay, Foreign Office Adviser on European Trade Relations, and Sir Frank Lee of the Treasury saw Wormser at the Foreign Office on 27 and 28 February 1961. It was an inauspicious meeting. According to the Foreign Office account, 'Not much common ground was found.' Wormser made it clear the French would not consider any arrangement under which the Commonwealth and British farmers received special treatment, and he complained bitterly about a speech by Heath to the WEU Council on 27 February, which had received great publicity, and expressed Britain's hope of joining the Common Market whilst retaining their farm subsidies and Commonwealth preferences.* The Foreign Office discovered that the Quai d'Orsay briefing after this speech of Heath's was that 'British proposals were so complicated and subtle that several years of effort would be required to produce a real association between Great Britain and the Continent.' Barclay's instructions were far removed from any terms which the Six were likely to grant to Britain.[21]

When Frank Lee met Wormser again on 3 May Wormser informed him coldly that Britain would have to depart from their traditional cheap food policy, but he assured Lee that if Britain decided to apply to accede to the Treaty of Rome the response would be one of 'unreserved welcome', although he recognized her difficulties in relation to the Commonwealth and agriculture. Lee minuted: 'He gave no indication that the French would meet us halfway in an effort to help, and was definitely unresponsive when I referred to the importance of ensuring satisfactory arrangements for our EFTA partners.' Wormser's 'unreserved welcome' could safely be offered since he knew from Macmillan's and Heath's speeches that Britain had no intention of accepting the Rome Treaty as it stood, and he knew also that if Britain insisted on continuing her own system of farm subsidies and Commonwealth preference de Gaulle would veto her entry.[22]

A later Foreign Office note clarifying the questions raised at the Barclay–Wormser discussions should have been a grave warning to Heath of the almost insoluble problems ahead. According to this, Wormser had insisted that the 'external tariff' must apply to all imports whether industrial or agricultural, and must apply to all countries not members of the Common Market. Wormser had also emphasized that farm prices must be identical for all main agricultural commodities, and he wanted these to be fixed in a way which would be remunerative for farmers; all the same he could not disguise the fact that European farm production was already in surplus, and the member countries together as a whole would be responsible for dealing with the problem of surpluses. Worst of all he made it crystal clear that the United Kingdom would have to impose the common duties at the frontier on all imports from non-member countries including the Commonwealth.

Neither Heath nor Macmillan accepted the full gravity of this grim Foreign Office note which should have dashed any hopes that Britain could continue to have the benefit of cheap food from Commonwealth

---

* French farmers under the EEC common agricultural policy would sell their produce at the farm gate at an artificially high price because levies on imported food kept up the market price. British farmers sold their produce cheaply at the farm gate, and were then reimbursed up to the guaranteed price by taxpayers' subsidies.

sources once they joined the EEC. Wormser had emphasized that there
could be no *modus vivendi* between what he called 'the two regional
economic systems – the Commonwealth and the EEC'.[23] His gut impression of the British attitude must have been reinforced by Macmillan's
remark in the Commons on 9 May, in reply to a Parliamentary question,
that any US intervention with the Six on behalf of Britain would be based
on 'Britain's entering the Common Market in agreement with our EFTA
partners and having regard to Commonwealth commitments and to the
interests of British agriculture'. Macmillan was living in a dream world
blissfully ignoring the fact that the French would not consider allowing
Britain to join the EEC unless she abandoned Commonwealth preference
and her cheap food policy. Already in March, when British officials had
been instructed to emphasize to civil servants of the Six that agriculture
must be excluded from any prospective negotiations, the Foreign Office
had warned that this was giving 'the worst impression' to the French.
Macmillan and Heath ignored this.[24]

Nonetheless, despite these gloomy predictions, Roderick Barclay
minuted on 11 May 1961: 'I think we can say that the outlines of a
reasonable solution are visible,' and the Foreign Secretary, Lord Home,
commented: 'Yes. I think a solution is coming into sight . . . Agriculture
will be the big snag.' Evidence of the French attitude, however, as
disclosed in the archives, shows that this was over-optimistic, although
there were signs that Holland and Italy were keen on British entry,
whilst Germany was ambivalent, with Erhard enthusiastic for it.[25]

A long minute from Heath to the Prime Minister revealed that he was
thinking in terms of accepting

> only a limited common external tariff, and that [is] sufficient evidence of
> our good intentions.
>
> Unless we are prepared to change our agricultural support policy or accept
> the institutions of the Treaty of Rome this is the only means of negotiation
> we have. The more we extend it the more we shall please the Six, but the
> more we shall come into conflict with the Commonwealth and the EFTA.

Heath confirmed that in talks with the Six, British officials had been
authorized to say that if the Six would meet the British over
Commonwealth trade and agriculture 'the UK will be ready, subject to
consultation with their EFTA partners, to consider a system based on
the acceptance of a common or harmonized external tariff on raw
manufactures and manufactured goods from countries other than the
Commonwealth and the Thirteen'. The French, he went on, would 'find
it very difficult to reject' an offer to accede to the Rome Treaty with
derogations to cover our agricultural and Commonwealth difficulties and
EFTA problems. He was wrong, and badly briefed: the British Embassy
in Paris was sending contradictory advice.

Macmillan instructed Heath to continue on this basis. But both the Prime Minister and the Lord Privy Seal were far removed from reality, and were overplaying their hand *vis-à-vis* the Community. The Six were unanimous in rejecting the possibility of cheap Commonwealth food coming into Britain after accession.[26]

Ominous confidential accounts of the French determination to block British entry had already reached the Foreign Office. Edward Tomkins, Minister at the British Embassy in Paris, reported on 23 March 1961 that he had been informed by a French diplomat closely connected with Wormser that the Quai d'Orsay were seriously worried that the UK might wish to adhere to the Treaty of Rome and 'had set up an ad hoc committee of some of their most intelligent members to think up ways of keeping us out'. Tomkins followed this up in April with a report that the French diplomat Jean-Pierre Brunet had told him the French had made up their minds not to let Britain in, and would regard it as a calamity if we said we wanted to join. On 29 April Sir Frank Figgures reported from Geneva that he had been informed by a French diplomat 'who can be taken as reliable' that Wormser had told him that he (Wormser) intended in the next round of discussions with the British to be absolutely firm and inflexible about agriculture, and expected this would put a stop to any question of a British offer to join the Community; if however, contrary to his expectation, there was a British offer, it would receive no consideration until the autumn, and no negotiations would start until 1962 when the objective would be to bring the British to give way on every point. The Washington Embassy reported that another French diplomat had told them in strict secrecy much the same, but the informant was considered notably unreliable. These rumours do not appear to have been reported to the Prime Minister although Heath initialled the papers. They were only too true, as events in June showed.

Christopher Soames, Minister of Agriculture, went to Paris with Eric Roll of his Ministry and met Wormser and other French officials on 14 April 1961. Wormser found it convenient to leave the meeting early and was playing a double game. When Soames asked for French intentions over the common agricultural policy and expounded the British method of subsidies, Wormser did not argue but gave the impression that the main problem would be the effect on Britain's balance of payments as a result of her having to pay more for food imports. In further conversations with French officials after Wormser's departure Soames said he could take the conversation no further without referring to the Prime Minister.

Wormser also told Soames that the French Government were 'very divided' over Britain joining and that Michel Debré, the French Prime Minister, hated the Common Market and would like to see Britain join, believing that would wreck it, while de Gaulle was schizophrenic – sometimes wanting Britain in, sometimes fearing that her Anglo-Saxon habits would prevent him from getting the best he could out of it.

Barclay reported the Soames–Wormser conversation to Heath, saying that the French attitude 'was in general much better and there was nothing in Wormser's general approach to confirm Figgures' report of his intention to block British entry'. It might have been better if Wormser had been frank rather than courteous. With hindsight it is obvious de Gaulle had told him to do nothing to facilitate British entry.[27]

On 25 April 1961 the Cabinet held a marathon meeting to discuss whether or not to apply to join the Six. The Prime Minister opened by stating categorically 'the time had not yet come' to apply to join the Common Market because the Commonwealth and EFTA would have to be consulted. In discussion it was pointed out that up till now they had been thinking of an 'economic settlement' between the Sixes and Sevens but this was 'no longer practicable nor sufficient' while the United States wanted to prevent the Seven developing as a separate political force in Europe.

Some Ministers argued that with a population of 160 million the Six would constitute a market the size of the United States which would be very damaging to the British economy, and as the economic strength of the Common Market grew it would be difficult to hold EFTA together. The pessimistic view was voiced that 'a great weight of sentiment could easily be aroused against any policy that could be represented as a threat to the Commonwealth and British farmers, especially within the Conservative Party', while the National Farmers' Union had published a pamphlet very hostile to the Six. However, at the previous Cabinet on 20 April Christopher Soames, the Minister of Agriculture, had said that British farmers would not suffer from joining the Six as the present subsidy system could not last (while the EEC agricultural subsidies would); he had not been able to tell the French how far we were prepared to go over farming policy. He wanted 'further progress with the detailed negotiations' before any final decision.

Summing up, Macmillan said that for some time after the war Europe had been dependent on American aid and content to accept Anglo-Saxon leadership, but she had now regained her strength and there was a new situation in which the economic state of Britain might be undermined. Therefore it was in our interest to join the Six if we could gain admission on terms which would be tolerable. De Gaulle did not want us in since he wanted to hold the reins in Europe but his attitude might change if he saw that the West 'could not prevail against the Communists unless its leading countries worked together'. But Macmillan hoped that the new US President, John F. Kennedy, would bring his influence to bear on de Gaulle during his forthcoming visit to Paris so as to persuade the French leader to accept a wider basis for European political and economic association.[28] Little by little the Cabinet were groping their way towards the Six blissfully believing that substantial concessions for the Commonwealth would be given.

Rab Butler was usually careful to hide his true feelings about the EEC; however at this Cabinet meeting more than at any other time he openly expressed his hostility to Europe, stating that the Cabinet had already agreed the previous year that there were 'insuperable difficulties' in accepting membership of the Treaty of Rome; apart from the Commonwealth difficulties there was the question of the surrender of national sovereignty, the significance of which had been highlighted in recent official reports. He was also concerned about British farmers and said that the Government would be 'in very grave political difficulties' if they could be represented as having broken their pledges to farmers. At the General Election British farmers had been promised no substantial change in the subsidy system in the life of the next Parliament, while the NFU at this period was strongly opposed to the Common Market and its President, Harold Woolley, continually made speeches to the effect that joining would mean letting down 'our kith and kin' in the Commonwealth and colonies.[29]

Heath told the Cabinet that his discussions had shown the French would prefer our full membership to association, but we would have to give 'concessions' on Commonwealth trade and agriculture. This was an understatement. Heath, like Soames, had been misled about French intentions. After Anglo-French talks had been held in Paris on 2 and 3 May he circulated an optimistic memorandum to his Cabinet colleagues emphasizing Wormser's insincere remark to Lee on 3 May that the French response would be one of 'unreserved welcome' if the UK acceded to the Treaty of Rome, and declaring: 'In general our talks with the French, the Germans and the Italians revealed an inclination on their part to be more accommodating and flexible than we had expected.' If this were true British original expectations must have been rock bottom.

The memorandum was drafted forty-eight hours before a realistic letter from Pierson Dixon sent on 12 May sounded a note of caution:

> It is generally agreed General de Gaulle would not be able to turn down point-blank a genuine offer from us to join the Six. On the other hand I still do not believe that either he or many other people in the administration are positively enthusiastic for us to join. In any case we can be sure that they will drive a hard bargain . . .[30]

On 29 May Lord Perth, Minister of State for the Colonies, sent Heath an encouraging note about a weekend he had spent with Jean Monnet, the French architect of the European Community who was now out of office. Monnet told Perth that de Gaulle

> would not and could not object because de Gaulle's views were coloured and guided by thinking of how history would judge his actions. If he opposed our joining he would go down in history with only a small name whereas constructive support of European unity would assure his fame.

Monnet spoke highly of Wormser who he believed was a convert 'to the UK coming in'. He also said he hoped a New Zealand association could be achieved.

Unfortunately Monnet was not in touch with French Government thinking. However here was a crumb of comfort for Heath after much gloom from the Foreign Office and Treasury: so pleased was he with Perth's letter that he invited him to dine to discuss Monnet's ideas although Lord Perth, who had never served in the Commons, cut little ice with either his Ministerial colleagues or in the Conservative Party.*

Monnet reiterated his hopes for a successful conclusion to negotiations to Lord Gladwyn and to James Marjoribanks (an Assistant Under-Secretary of State in the Foreign Office), even telling Gladwyn that it would be possible for the UK to be a full member by 1 January 1964. This was reported to Heath and again encouraged false hopes.[31] However Monnet, although he still had great influence both with the Five and French civil servants, was completely ignored by de Gaulle and his subservient Ministers.

At the beginning of June 1961 Macmillan wanted to make another direct request to de Gaulle to push on the negotiations; he was dissuaded by Dixon and Heath. Instead he decided to call a weekend discussion meeting of Ministers at Chequers and then, if he could get their agreement, to take the plunge.

Accordingly he instructed the Foreign Office to send a questionnaire to all the British Ambassadors in the EEC capitals asking whether the operation of the Community had impinged on the 'attributions [sic] of the national parliament', and how the parliaments reacted to Community regulations which ran counter to national legislation or national practices; also whether the EEC was gaining or losing popularity. He looked for reassuring replies in order to gain the support of the anti-Market members of his Cabinet for an approach to the EEC.

The answers were satisfactory for the Prime Minister, with Dixon stating that in France 'no conflict had arisen between the operation of

---

* Perth's father, as Sir Eric Drummond, had been Secretary of the League of Nations in Geneva in the twenties, and a close friend of Monnet's.

the Community and the French Parliament', and he did not foresee any arising in the immediate future. Dixon, a keen European, added:

> apart from the long-term economic advantages for ourselves the addition of the United Kingdom would strengthen Europe and broaden its outlook and give it windows on to a wider world ... The Six with United Kingdom, Danish and perhaps Norwegian membership, and with almost all the other countries of Western Europe associated economically with this broadened Common Market would be a still more important economic entity and more beneficial political influence in world affairs.

Ashley Clarke from Rome wrote that the Common Market had caused 'no serious stresses' in Italy, who viewed the Community as a bulwark behind which to expand, and 'her progress has been remarkable since the Common Market came into force', while her general political attitude towards the EEC 'has always been enthusiastic', and she had no difficulty in absorbing regulations made by the Community. He added that Italy would like to see the United Kingdom accede although 'we can expect she would take no steps to weaken the bonds which at present tie her partners to her'. The 'Community idea', according to Clarke, was gaining popularity in Italy, and the country as a whole was better off since the formation of the Community.

Christopher Steel from Bonn reported that there was 'no effective opposition to the Community in West Germany ... and all in all there is satisfaction ... with the Community'. Sir John Nicholls from Brussels affirmed the growing popularity of the Community in Belgium. From The Hague Andrew Noble wrote that the operations of the Community impinged hardly at all on the Dutch Parliament, and the Community idea was popular; while Freese-Pennefather from Luxemburg thought that Luxemburgers in every walk of life 'consider themselves committed to their country's membership'. These were exactly the replies Macmillan wanted, and he ordered them to be printed and circulated to the Cabinet and junior Ministers in preparation for his next move.[32]

On 22 and 23 June a nasty hiccup occurred when Roderick Barclay and Eric Roll held talks at the Quai d'Orsay with Wormser and other French officials. Wormser refused any concessions and expressed disappointment at the British inability to say 'anything new on agriculture and the Commonwealth'. Although he admitted that special arrangements could be made for the Commonwealth he stressed that these must not 'be too far reaching and must not conflict with the principles of the Treaty of Rome'. He emphasized his particular disappointment with the British refusal to accept the principle of variable levies – that is, taxes on imports of Commonwealth grain and dairy products paid to the Community budget, to be paid out as subsidies to farmers in the Six so as to bring their farm gate prices up to the levels which would be agreed in the EEC common agricultural policy.

The paper submitted by Wormser to this meeting made no mention of special arrangements to overcome Britain's Commonwealth and agricultural problems, while it emphasized that the French insisted on common food prices within the Community with variable levies on imports from all other countries and common responsibility for the disposal of surpluses. He made it plain that the Community intended to give price advantages to their own farmers: to allow low tariff food imports from the Commonwealth 'would cause a breach in the system'. He accused the British of having retreated from their position at the last meeting. De Gaulle had obviously told him to pour cold water on the talks.

On the second day Wormser was even 'more pessimistic', saying that there had been no progress because the UK's position was rigid and he saw no point in further discussions. He insisted that as there had been no progress in these talks the press statement should not include any reference to their 'usefulness', although in the end an anodyne press statement was agreed. Wormser had not given ground on any important points, Barclay afterwards reported to Heath.[33]

These Paris discussions should have been the red light and made it clear to Heath and Macmillan that only minor concessions would ever be wrung from the French, so that Britain would either have to accept the Rome Treaty hook, line and sinker or stay out. Maudling, who had far more experience of European negotiations than Heath, saw it that way, and sent a minute to the Prime Minister arguing that Britain should not apply for membership since Wormser had categorically rejected arguments about the special position of the UK. Maudling wanted the Chequers discussion to focus on the 'wholly negative French attitude and the need for a complete change in our tactics'.

In my earlier minute today I expressed my doubt as to whether the French had in any way changed their attitude to British participation in a European economic system.

I have now seen the translation of M. Wormser's memorandum which is attached to the Lord Privy Seal's minute to you of 14 June. If I understand this correctly this amounts to a categorical rejection of the arguments we have been putting forward about the special position of the UK. On all the points concerned, Commonwealth, agriculture, and EFTA, M. Wormser takes a completely negative attitude. He even dismisses the Lord Privy Seal's speech on 27 February as being inadequate even as a basis for discussion. In view of the fact that this speech involved considerable concessions from our side, I think this is particularly disappointing.

If this really is the view of the French Government, and in my view what

evidence we have suggests that it is, then it seems to me to be pointless
to be talking about any negotiations with them. They have in fact rejected
in advance any proposals on the points of vital interest to us.

I am glad we are going to discuss this at the weekend. As you know
I have always been doubtful of the wisdom of trying to entice an unwilling
France to the conference table by successive concessions on our side. So far
the concessions we have made have only been of United Kingdom interests
but if we were to go further and try to make concessions involving the
Commonwealth and EFTA, even if this be with their consent, we might
find ourselves earning the hostility of our friends without getting any
advantage with the French. As I recall it one of the essential features in the
programme we were envisaging for European negotiations was that there
should be a real change in the French attitude which we hoped would take
place as a result of President Kennedy's visit to President de Gaulle. I should
like to suggest that one of the things we might discuss this weekend is
whether in the light of this wholly negative French attitude a complete
change in our tactics may not be necessary.

I am sending a copy of this minute to the members of the European
Committee [a Cabinet Committee on European negotiations, chaired by
Butler].[34]

Maudling, who had spent much time in abortive negotiations with
European countries, could read the Foreign Office accounts with an
expert eye; the Prime Minister, who had a high opinion of Maudling,
was nonetheless not persuaded by him that the French would torpedo
any negotiations unless Britain jettisoned her EFTA partners and the
Commonwealth.

Heath's optimism too, though flimsily based, was undeterred, and at
the Chequers weekend of 17–18 June 1961 there was a majority in favour
of making a formal application to join the EEC, provided that special
terms were allowed for the Commonwealth and British farmers.

Already on 18 May 1961 Christopher Soames, Minister of Agriculture,
had sounded a warning note on this subject to the Prime Minister:

Some of us, including myself, would not be ready to go in unless we could
satisfy ourselves that it was politically possible for us to do so. I should be
anxious about deciding in principle . . . and then finding ourselves precluded
by pledges from going in. We must obtain certain pre-conditions in the
sphere of agriculture and the Commonwealth before we go in. We must
be able to top up farmers' incomes unilaterally through consumer subsidies
for ten years after joining. We can then honestly meet the strong criticism
of our Conservative back-benchers that we are handing over control of
British agriculture to Brussels. If we do not fulfil our election promises to
maintain the support prices under the 1957 Act we would be disingenuous.
If we did, the only honest course is as in 1923 to have an election. I am
not in favour of an election if it can be avoided. Ted Heath at the last
meeting referred to pledges to our farmers and this was well received, and

reinforces what I say. I do not believe the French or other members as yet know that we have any similar conditions in our mind.

However, Soames had then dined at Birch Grove with Macmillan and made a U-turn, writing to Macmillan on 22 May 1961:

I now incline to the opposite view to that which has hitherto been current in Whitehall about future agriculture. I am now firmly of the opinion that not only could we with benefit alter the system of our support for agriculture in the interests of associating ourselves with the Six, but regardless of the Six we should in any event be giving thought for the future health of our agricultural industry.

Our present system of support was devised in 1947 when food and currency were both scarce . . . It has achieved a momentum which is hard to check. If we stay out of Europe in the late sixties I envisage . . . the net result would involve a net bill to the Exchequer of something like £400 million . . . This would not be healthy . . . I think we should give serious thought to shifting the emphasis of protection from agriculture to the consumer. This leads me to question whether we are not making it unnecessarily difficult for ourselves in our European discussions in refusing even to consider changing our system of agricultural support as one of the prices to pay for joining the Six.[35]

Despite the advice of the Minister of Agriculture, however, Heath contended in negotiations over the next eighteen months that the deficiency payment system of support for British farming must be retained for a lengthy period after the date of accession, and only at the last moment did he give way on the point. Negotiations would have been easier if the Soames view had prevailed, and he was correct in forecasting that rigidity over the British farm subsidy system would alienate the Six.

Evidence that Macmillan at the Chequers weekend was considering bribing the French into acquiescence by firm promises of more US nuclear know-how and a possible tripartite nuclear policy in partnership with Britain and the US appears in a revealing minute from de Zulueta two days before the Chequers conference: 'If we cannot bully the French we shall have either to try to persuade them or bribe them. The tripartite and military bribe is not really in our hands . . . Kennedy seems ready to help up to a point. Help over Anglo-French strategic deterrent might help.' However de Gaulle knew that Britain could deliver nothing on these lines.

As regards Commonwealth quotas it was decided at Chequers that 'some permanent provision for at least the main Commonwealth imports into the United Kingdom at something like the present level of trade' must be permitted, while on home agriculture it was agreed that Britain might have to terminate Exchequer support to her farmers, and change over partly to the EEC plan.

At the Chequers weekend only Maudling opposed making the application for entry; 'we should apply to accede', he said, 'only on the basis that we want some amendment of the basic principles and objectives to meet our special requirements.' The Government would have been spared much humiliation if they had taken Maudling's advice.[36] Macmillan himself noted of the weekend, 'We got *somewhere* – but not very far . . .' and also commented prophetically: 'even with satisfactory transitional arrangements it would be very difficult to preserve the Commonwealth's traditional rights in the United Kingdom.'

A Cabinet meeting was held following the Chequers discussions. The conclusion had been reached at Chequers, so Macmillan stated, that it was 'undesirable' to leave the Commonwealth in suspense much longer on whether the United Kingdom proposed to apply to the Six. As it was not possible to obtain 'any clear indication' of the conditions of entry in discussions,* Ministers should be sent to the Commonwealth countries to say we were 'inclined' to think that the right course was to apply to accede to the Treaty of Rome in order to find out 'whether we could secure acceptable terms and conditions that would safeguard the essential interests of other Commonwealth countries and also meet our own requirements and those of the other members of EFTA'.

Objections were expressed by some members of the Cabinet but it was agreed that Ministers should be given a directive to this effect by the Prime Minister. The main purpose of the exercise was to allay fears within the Conservative Party that the Government had decided to spurn the Commonwealth for the sake of Europe. However the Cabinet advised the itinerant Ministers to emphasize that 'our talks with the Six had made only limited progress', and to warn that, if Britain did join, the policy of unlimited Commonwealth access to British markets would have to be modified.

Maudling opposed these visits and his Permanent Under-Secretary, Sir Richard Powell, had written a strong letter to the Prime Minister's office on Maudling's behalf on 29 May 1961: 'to make a further approach so soon after the meeting of Commonwealth economic officials who had spent a whole day on European problems would cause all Commonwealth countries to feel we were concealing something which in good faith we should have revealed.' Powell's letter added that the Board of Trade were concerned because Wormser had spoken of only 'small adjustments to meet UK problems over the Commonwealth. It seems to me it is an attempt to pick them off one by one and that this may

---

* As has been seen, Wormser had been brutally frank about the essential conditions. Macmillan was distorting the facts by this remark.

make them more resistant than they would be likely to be at a collective meeting at which certain countries would come out on our side.' He also emphasized that the provision of officials to accompany the three Ministers was putting a great strain on Whitehall, and insisted that the Commonwealth be offered a Prime Ministerial or Foreign Ministerial conference instead.

The reports in the archives reveal that the trips were almost counter-productive. The Ministers could add little to Macmillan's letter to the Commonwealth Prime Ministers introducing them:

> We had previously thought it would be possible to find out by informal discussions whether there was reasonable hope of agreement before entering formal negotiations. It now appears that unless we are prepared to enter formal negotiations with the Six collectively we shall not be able to ascertain what special conditions they would be prepared to accept.[37]

As soon as he heard of Sandys's visit Keith Holyoake, Prime Minister of New Zealand, wrote on 22 June 1961 to Harold Macmillan:

> the continuation of unrestricted and duty-free access for our primary products to the United Kingdom market seems to be the only method by which New Zealand can avoid economic disaster ... We find it difficult to believe that the disastrous nature of these consequences is thoroughly understood and appreciated in the United Kingdom. Fears are expressed about the future isolation of the United Kingdom should it stay outside Europe; but how much more serious is isolation for a small country like New Zealand.

This was a warning of the emotional reaction that was likely to result from tampering with Commonwealth preference. Heath himself went to Cyprus in July 1961; Perth went to the West Indies. Sandys had a difficult time in Australia and had to work hard to get them to soften their hostile press statement. In New Zealand he met protests that entry must have grave consequences for the New Zealand economy, and Holyoake wrote to Macmillan a second time deploring the proposed approach, which letter Sandys advised the Prime Minister only to acknowledge formally. Peter Thorneycroft, now Minister of Defence, went to India, Pakistan, Ceylon and Malaya, while John Hare, Minister of Labour, went to Sierra Leone, Nigeria and the Central African Federation. Reading their voluminous reports confirms the impression that Powell was correct when he said that this exercise was largely a waste of valuable civil servants' time.[38]

At a Cabinet meeting on 26 July 1961 memoranda by the 'missionaries' were produced. Sandys said that in Canada, Australia and New Zealand he had found 'serious anxieties' about Britain joining the EEC. There was no disguising the fact, he said, that 'if we did join the Community this would be an initial shock to the whole Commonwealth system . . . if on the other hand we did not join the Community the decline in our economic strength would eventually lead to a permanent weakening of the whole Commonwealth.'

Soames, Minister of Agriculture, said that considerable opposition must be expected from British farmers who 'were taking the extreme position' and claiming their interests could only be safeguarded by continuing the existing subsidies, although it was increasingly being recognized in Parliament and elsewhere that the Government could not maintain the subsidies indefinitely whether or not the United Kingdom joined the EEC.*

After a long discussion the Prime Minister summed up by saying it was 'evidently' the view of the Cabinet that we should enter into negotiations with the EEC to find out on what terms we could join; he emphasized that the decision to negotiate was 'a very different matter' from the later and much more critical decision to join the Community. Macmillan said he would draft a public statement in which it would be necessary to achieve a 'delicate balance' between creating the impression that we had already decided to join on whatever terms we could obtain and on the other hand 'suggesting to members of the Community that we had no real will to join'.

Macmillan circulated a draft of his statement to another Cabinet meeting on 27 July (when he was absent). With Butler in the chair it was approved with minor amendments. The final draft made clear that no commitment would be made without consulting the Commonwealth and EFTA.[39]

On 31 July 1961, after fortifying himself with a good lunch, a highly nervous Macmillan announced in the House of Commons that Britain was applying to join the EEC. Jo Grimond, the Liberal leader, brought a smile to the Prime Minister's face when he congratulated him on the statement, but the smile froze when Grimond added, 'and for doing what the Liberal Party has been urging for years'.

Macmillan was worried that there had been no mention of the Common Market in the Conservative 1959 General Election manifesto, and much of his nervousness was due to fear of an adverse reaction in the Commons from entrenched pro-Empire Conservative MPs. He sent a minute to Heath:

> I think our chief difficulty at the moment is to carry the House with us. Of course we have to show reasonable enthusiasm towards the Europeans. When it comes to negotiations it will hang on two points:

---

* The cost of the deficiency payments to British farmers to maintain their guaranteed prices was soaring and putting an excessive burden on taxpayers.

(a) Whether de Gaulle (becoming more and more Napoleonic and self-centred) really wants us in or not. This he will settle on political grounds and instruct Wormser accordingly.

(b) Whether even if de Gaulle wants to settle we can work out terms which are fair to the Commonwealth and our EFTA partners.[40]

Given this awareness, it is surprising that Macmillan should have ignored both Foreign Office warnings of implacable French hostility and Heath's unsatisfactory talks with Wormser at the end of June.

Why had Macmillan changed his mind about the Common Market? Only sixteen months before, a reputable Continental newspaper had reported him as saying: 'The EEC would mean a revival of Nazism in Europe and force Britain into an alliance with Russia as in the days of Napoleon.' Although he always denied using these exact words this had been roughly his attitude.* The watershed for Macmillan had undoubtedly been the Lee Report and his meeting with Kennedy earlier in 1961 when it became clear that the present US Government no longer considered they had a special relationship with Britain and that future economic co-operation would be dependent on Britain taking part in European integration. Macmillan's original hope that an arrangement between EFTA and the EEC would be possible without Britain becoming a signatory to the Treaty of Rome had vanished with the acceleration in the reduction of the internal tariff duties of the EEC and the abolition of all internal quotas together with the maturing of their farming policy. Macmillan disliked those sections of the treaty which would edge Britain into political integration, but had come to the firm conclusion that much of British industry protected by high tariffs was flabby, and needed the cold wind of price competition from Europe.

The debates which opened on 2 August 1961 went well for the Government. Macmillan told the Commons that our future prosperity depended on our bringing down industrial costs, and that, whether or not we joined the EEC, we could not continue to exist with our industries sheltered against price competition by an 'isolated protective system'. Both Macmillan and Lord Plowden† (in the corresponding Lords debate) advanced the cogent argument that the United Kingdom no longer offered a large enough market behind her customs barrier to support industrial units of the most economic size. This was particularly

---

* As late as July 1961 the Conservative Newsletter, the monthly briefing from the Conservative Central Office, said: 'The Liberals call on the Government to apply forthwith to join the Common Market. It is foolish advice.'

† Edwin Plowden, a former Treasury Chief Planning Officer, and now Chairman of Tube Investments, had been recalled to the Treasury part time in 1961.

true of the latest technological industries such as petrochemicals and plastics, where only the largest modern automatic production lines could give the great savings in costs required to compete with other industrial countries. Faced with the prospect of recurring economic crises, Macmillan had reluctantly accepted Treasury advice that rather than play about with unilateral action to cut industrial costs it was simpler to take the plunge into the EEC customs union.

In the Lords Plowden advanced another powerful economic argument (obviously concerted with Macmillan) by pointing out that the Commonwealth required large amounts of capital both on public and private account in the immediate future for essential industrial development. He emphasized that we could not possibly provide this unless we achieved a permanent surplus on our balance of payments, and there was no possibility of achieving this necessary surplus without access to the large new mass market on the Continent. The Dominions too were protecting their own infant industries by high tariffs, and they could not be expected to open their markets to the full blast of competition from Britain. Therefore, Lord Plowden argued, we were deluding the Commonwealth if we pretended that Britain could ever provide them with the capital they required unless she had tariff-free access for her industrial goods into the expanding markets of Europe to compensate for the loss of free entry to her former colonies.

Macmillan obviously had high hopes that once we had a customs union with the EEC it would be possible to pass on Commonwealth claims for development capital to EEC institutions, and that this would afford welcome relief to Britain's fragile balance of payments which was put under fresh strain with every request for loans by the Commonwealth.

About the political consequences of joining the EEC Macmillan was lukewarm. He and the other government spokesmen in the August debate played down the inherent necessity for the transference of some sovereignty to supranational institutions under the Treaty of Rome to an extent which caused considerable concern amongst the Six. The Government rallied their supporters by minimizing the sovereignty issue, Home in the Lords saying, 'The surrender of sovereignty is restricted to economic matters,' for all the EEC's clearly expressed desire to move towards supranationalism. Despite these assurances both Derek Walker-Smith in the Commons, a former Junior Minister, and Lord Salisbury in the Lords though it a 'pretence' that the Common Market was purely an economic alliance, while Lord Attlee felt so strongly that the transference of sovereignty might make it impossible for future Labour governments to pass Socialist legislation that he stampeded the Labour Peers into abstaining on the Common Market resolution.

The Conservative Whips had expected thirty abstentions amongst their back-benchers; there were only twenty-two. The Government had jumped their first hurdle. The Conservative Party Conference also gave overwhelming support.

Neither in Parliament nor at the Party Conference did Macmillan or his Ministers make plain the political implications of joining the Six. They feared that if they did so public opinion would turn against entry and the Conservative Party would not give them a mandate. Their plan was to educate the public while the negotiations progressed. Some observers felt that the Government were deterred from giving too strong a lead because expressions of enthusiasm would cause the Six to harden their terms. This is not the author's view.[41]

The Government also ignored Maudling's warning that attempts to secure concessions for the Commonwealth would fail, and discredit the Conservative Party. EFTA commitments were an embarrassment, and the possible alienation of the Commonwealth was a nightmare: throughout the negotiations the Cabinet looked back over their shoulders at the effect on Conservative opinion of sacrificing Commonwealth and farming interests. Yet only by jettisoning Commonwealth preference and snubbing both the NFU and the Tory land-owning lobby could quick agreement be achieved, while on top of this Heath and Macmillan had to convince the Six that they were sincere in their support of the ideals and principles of the Treaty of Rome.

Thus Heath in the autumn of 1961 embarked on a supremely difficult task. The negotiations soon became slow and ponderous, and eventually de Gaulle, rigidly opposed to British entry, seized his opportunity and barred the way.

CHAPTER 9

EEC Negotiations

THE DECISION TO apply for entry into the EEC was one of the most important political turning points of the twentieth century. It had a more lasting effect on British history than any other act of the Macmillan Government. It meant that Britain would no longer base her trade policy on the Commonwealth preferences of the Ottawa Agreement, but instead eventually be part of the rapidly expanding European industrial market. It also meant that with American approval the special relationship with the United States would become of declining importance. The basic reason for this decision was economic: being excluded from the customs union of the Common Market in 1961 placed British industry at a disadvantage in this fast-expanding market. Although there was strong opposition from pro-Commonwealth Conservative MPs, the majority of Conservatives understood Britain's economic weakness and her crying need to be part of the EEC's rising prosperity.

Macmillan's problems were twofold: how to reconcile Commonwealth interests without upsetting the Six, and to persuade the Labour Opposition and the British electorate of the need to join. He realized that most of his Party and the nation did not share European enthusiasm for a move to federalism and supranational institutions. Yet he had to convince the Six that Britain would co-operate in the ideals and principles expressed in the Treaty of Rome. He had a further difficulty to overcome in that the 1959 Conservative manifesto had promised British farmers no change in the system of farm subsidies during the life of the next Parliament.

The Conservative Cabinet were divided on Europe. Christopher Soames, Minister of Agriculture, and Duncan Sandys, at first Minister of Defence and then for Commonwealth Relations, were enthusiastic Europeans like Heath. Butler was lukewarm; Lord Hailsham, President of the Council, and Reginald Maudling, soon to be Chancellor of the Exchequer, were opposed. British industrialists were keen to join, but the National Farmers Union, still a powerful political force, was strongly hostile. The trade unions were ambivalent and many prominent Labour politicians rejected the EEC as a capitalist club, while a few influential Labour figures like Douglas Jay were virulent in appealing to insular opinion by opposing the abandonment of the cheap food policy and any encroachments on British sovereignty. Macmillan and his Ministers were reluctant therefore to espouse supranationalism or federalism, and preferred to argue for entry on economic grounds. As a result some politicians in the Six intent on the ideal of a European state were sceptical of the British approach.

In much of the Commonwealth there was concern and alarm; New Zealand, Australia and to a lesser extent Canada, relied heavily on tariff preferences in the British market especially for their exports of temperate foodstuffs,* and the approach to the EEC was disruptive of Commonwealth unity. The British Government hoped against hope that the Six would make slashing concessions over Commonwealth temperate food imports but to do so ran counter to the EEC common agricultural policy which was in the process of formulation and outlined in the Mansholt Plan, a 300-page document completed in June 1960.

A perpetual thorn in the flesh of the Conservatives during their attempt to join the EEC was Lord Beaverbrook. Passionately devoted to the British Empire he put his immense wealth and powerful newspapers at the disposal of the opponents of EEC entry. At first he tried to persuade the former Prime Minister Anthony Eden to spearhead the opposition. Though believing that Britain should not join Europe, Eden, who still possessed great influence and popularity within the Conservative Party, wisely refused to play. However Beaverbrook's national news papers, the *Daily Express*, *Sunday Express* and *Evening Standard*, were full of anti-Common Market propaganda. In the 1960s the *Daily* and *Sunday Express* were more up-market than today with higher circulations; they exercised great influence over their Conservative readers. Given the importance the Conservatives attached to success throughout the long-drawn-out negotiations, their failure when it came left a policy vacuum that was exceedingly damaging to their popularity.

The Six agreed that Heath should make an 'introductory statement' regarding Britain's application at a Ministerial conference in Paris on 10 October 1961. Immense trouble was taken by the civil servants over Heath's speech. Heath was on the horns of a dilemma. He had to satisfy the Six that Britain would not try to slow down the pace of unification and at the same time show opinion at home that if the negotiations were unsatisfactory Britain would withdraw. 'In saying that we wish to join

---

*Meat, butter, cheese, barley and wheat.

the EEC,' Heath told the Ministers of the Six on the day, 'we mean
that we desire to become full, whole-hearted and active members of the
European Community in its widest sense and to go forward with you
in the building of a new Europe.'

Here he was on treacherous ground. The Government had decided to
accept the common external tariff of the customs union, but he had been
told to bargain hard for preferential treatment for the Commonwealth
and to try to keep Britain from being drawn into the common agricultural policy for a considerable number of years although it was
evident that the CAP was evolving fast; Britain also wanted to resist
any strengthening of supranational institutions.

Over the three major problems, Commonwealth trade, British farming and EFTA, Heath declared that these solutions

> must be compatible with and not disruptive of the Common Market . . .
> I am sure you will understand that Britain could not join the EEC under
> conditions in which this trade connection [between Britain and the Common-
> wealth] was cut with grave loss and even ruin for some of the Common-
> wealth countries.

This last sentence produced adverse comment from the French.

Heath then pointed out that the Treaty of Rome had given generous
treatment to France and others with overseas dependencies, notably in
the special protocol which gave former French African colonies and
Tunisia access to the French market. This was a fair point well made
but, although the negotiations were to result in similar treatment for
the African, Caribbean and Pacific parts of the Commonwealth, together
with India, Pakistan and Ceylon, Britain was too late for the rest of the
Commonwealth countries. The Six were not now going to water down
their arrangements and allow a major breach in the plan for a common
agricultural policy by agreeing to the continued entry to the UK of cheap
Commonwealth temperate foodstuffs, nor accept the competition of
low-priced manufactures from the Commonwealth.

On the common agricultural policy Heath said he would want the
transitional arrangement for British farmers to continue for a period
of 'between twelve and fifteen years'. This was asking too much from
the Six, who were intent on plans to support their own farmers,
and this point was also received badly. Heath was making an opening
gambit by stating Britain's extreme position; it was obviously open to
compromise.

Within the Six Heath's speech was taken as meaning that Britain
would insist on sweeping exceptions for the Commonwealth and try to
boycott the CAP. However Heath made it clear that there was a fundamental change in British policy: the UK was now prepared to accept

the common external tariff and take some part in European supranational institutions. He hoped Britain could have a strong influence on the formulation of the Six's agricultural policy. This expectation came to nothing.

There was no discussion of Heath's speech at the October 1961 meeting, and although Heath attended another Ministerial meeting in November, by the end of the year no progress had been made in the negotiations. It was hard to gauge the chances of success, and Treasury, Board of Trade and Ministry of Agriculture officials in Whitehall poured cold water on Heath's optimism.

Meanwhile the Six pressed ahead with their agricultural policy without consulting Britain. In December 1961 they decided that levies must be paid on all imports of food and these levies used to subsidize their farmers so that farm gate prices could be kept artificially high and surpluses dumped abroad cheaply. Such a policy made Heath's negotiating position difficult.

On 26 November 1961 de Gaulle visited Macmillan's country house, Birch Grove, in Sussex. The main issue under discussion was Berlin, but the possibility of Britain entering the EEC was also discussed. The British Ambassador in Paris, Pierson Dixon, briefed the Prime Minister before the talks: 'It is fairly certain that he [de Gaulle] considers our presence among the Six to be a risk which is worth taking only if he can get us in on his conditions that make it difficult for us to resist the general direction in which he would like to steer the formation of Europe.' Macmillan minuted of the talks that they were 'very friendly but not very fruitful . . . it would be premature to despair [over the EEC] since General de Gaulle like all great men never yields to argument but only to facts.'[1]

As 1962 opened, the British tried to speed up the negotiations in the hope that the United Kingdom could become a full member by January 1963. There was a reluctance on both sides to negotiate over the Commonwealth for fear of causing a breakdown. However the French insisted that the British must accept the 'letter' of the Treaty and should expect only minor concessions. More understanding was shown by the Dutch and Italians, especially by Dr Joseph Luns, the Dutch Foreign Minister, and Emilio Colombo, his Italian counterpart.

On 22 January 1962 Eric Roll, who had been posted to Brussels as deputy head of the British delegation, talked to Robert Margolin, deputy head of the EEC Commission, and told him he was 'unhappy' at the way negotiations were going. Margolin replied that five out of the Six were 'most anxious' that we should succeed. 'However the French were not at all keen to have us in; on the other hand they were most anxious not to be seen as the ones to have stopped us.'

On 23 February 1962 Heath and Roderick Barclay, of the London negotiating team, talked to Attilio Cattani, the Italian permanent representative with the EEC; Heath told him he was

> not happy with what had emerged so far from the discussions about manufactured goods from the old Commonwealth or from the Asian countries.
>   It was no good talking about a short transitional period. The Commonwealth system would continue and must be protected from anything which would seriously damage the interests of its members. It would not be possible from the internal political point of view in the United Kingdom to accept arrangements which caused such damage.[2]

It would be difficult to accept that Commonwealth countries should retain permanent advantages in the United Kingdom market, Cattani replied, although it should not be 'too difficult' to work out satisfactory arrangements for the African members which would not place them at a disadvantage *vis-à-vis* the ex-French countries. Here was the writing on the wall. Heath was franker with the more co-operative Italians than he was with the French, but the Commonwealth problem was left hanging in the air.

On 5 March, Ashley Clarke, Ambassador in Rome, wrote that Cattani did not think the British had yet taken into account the full implications of the arrangements recently concluded between the Six for agriculture. Britain appeared to think that she could come to some arrangement with the Six while retaining her preference in favour of Commonwealth food as before, and Cattani thought 'this was a serious misapprehension.' Cattani also told him that the whole conception of Commonwealth preference was at variance with the principle of the Common Market, and warned that during the recent internal negotiations over agriculture the French Foreign Minister Couve de Murville had been the toughest contender, although on several occasions he proved willing to make concessions without having been previously authorized to do so by de Gaulle.[3]

Two inter-departmental teams of British civil servants had been formed for the EEC negotiations. One operated in London; the other in Brussels under Pierson Dixon who was also Ambassador in Paris. Some critics have suggested that this put too heavy a burden on Dixon. However Sir Edward Heath told the author that he had insisted on Dixon's appointment to this post; knowing that French agreement was the key to success, he wanted to put the man who was closest to them in charge in Brussels. In spite of the strain on Dixon from the two jobs, Heath believes he was the correct choice. In the successful negotiations in the seventies Sir John Hunt (later Lord Hunt, head of the Civil Service and Secretary to the Cabinet) was in charge of the negotiations, and this according to the Foreign Office was a better arrangement. However with his experience of the 1961–3 negotiations Heath as Prime Minister in 1970 then had 'everything at his finger tips'. Both teams were composed of the brightest officials selected for their competence, and no blame for the failure can be attached to them.

The London officials team was chaired by Sir Frank Lee of the Treasury, and on 26 February 1962 they stressed to the Ministers involved that the UK concept of an extended transitional period for domestic agriculture and assurances to the Commonwealth of 'comparability of outlet'* were 'unnegotiable'. The Ministry of Agriculture and the NFU rejected this out of hand. Roger Jackling, an Under-Secretary in the Foreign Office team under Sir Patrick Reilly, noted that the Community would be unwilling to give any long-term undertakings about Commonwealth access which were not given to third countries generally.

These two factors were the crunch for Heath. He wanted the Commonwealth to be promised precise 'comparable outlets' for exports of food to the EEC after they had lost their preference on trade with the UK. British officials by February 1962 had given clear warnings that this was not on, but Heath refused to admit this disagreeable fact.

From his post in Geneva as Secretary-General of EFTA, Sir Frank Figgures of the Treasury had a ringside view of the controversies within the Six. On 28 February, he was pessimistic, saying:

> he doubted whether our present tactics would resolve the Six/Seven problem and were causing real distress not only to our friends among the Six but also to some countries within the Seven ... the only hope was the acceptance of the Treaty of Rome subject only to special arrangements for the Commonwealth, and adoption of their agricultural policy would be necessary. We should not underestimate the *feeling of hatred* against the UK which was being put out at all levels by both the European Commission and the French administration. This is very real and a factor to be reckoned with. It is reflected in the mass of information which comes to EFTA headquarters from all sorts of sources (including American businessmen and bankers visiting here) and indicating a highly organized and well put over operation.[4]

There was truth in Figgures's diagnosis of 'hatred against the UK' shown by the French. This was due not to the claims by Britain for adjustment of the Treaty of Rome to accommodate British farmers and the Commonwealth but to a more fundamental issue – the refusal of

---

* 'Comparable outlets' were tariff-free quotas equivalent or in ratio to the volume of previous year's sales.

Britain to help France to become a nuclear power, and the British insistence that the American policy of 'non-dissemination of nuclear weapons' must be strictly applied to France.

Heath alone in the Cabinet appreciated the depth of the problem with the French. He expressed this clearly in a minute to the Foreign Secretary on 10 March 1962 after Pierson Dixon had confirmed in a talk with him in Brussels that the reaction of the French to the British application for entry 'would depend to a great extent on whether France is now considered to be a nuclear power'. (Technically France lagged far behind Britain.) In the minute Heath emphasized that French diplomats had made clear their Government's strong opposition to the US policy of non-dissemination of nuclear weapons, and 'one could hazard a good guess what de Gaulle's attitude would be':

> What alarms me more than anything is that, at the same time as we are trying to negotiate our entry into the EEC – in which we have all too few cards to play – we are giving every indication of wishing to carry out political policies which are anathema to the two most important members of the Community. This can only increase the mistrust and suspicion already felt towards us in the political sphere. Dr Adenauer's statement in *Le Monde* yesterday may only be an indication that he is fast losing his grip; on the other hand, it may be the manifestation of a growing belief that whatever we may say in the negotiations, we are not interested in becoming a genuine partner with the members of the Community in the future development of Europe.
>
> We must never forget that the countries of the Community are interested in two things; first, in jointly increasing their own prosperity – in which they regard us as a possible liability and the Commonwealth as an undesirable complication; secondly, in strengthening their defence against what they regard as the persistent and menacing threat from the Soviet Union and her satellites along beside her – as to our attitude towards this, they can only judge by the proposals we put forward for dealing with it. What they see here is our apparent determination, with the United States, to prevent the French from developing their atomic and nuclear defence; an apparent tendency to negotiate away German interests in order to appease the Russians in Berlin; a desire to introduce a variety of aspects of disarmament along the Eastern areas of the EEC in order to place a no-man's land between the Communists and the Anglo-Saxons – in which they realize only too well that it is the Community countries who will pay the price . . . an apparently irresistible urge to settle these matters in favour of the Anglo-Saxons at the expense of the Europeans by rushing – regardless of the possibilities of success or failure – Gaderine swine-like down the slope towards the summit! Of course, for good measure, at the same time as we demand that the cost of keeping our forces in BAOR should be paid by the Germans, we give a variety of indications that we intend to run down and withdraw a considerable body of these forces.

In fact, our colleagues have instructed us to carry out a negotiation for our entry into the EEC at the same time as they – showing a complete lack of understanding of European attitudes and problems – are carrying out contrary policies in the political and defence fields. It is no wonder that these negotiations, already sufficiently difficult and complicated, threaten to become almost unmanageable . . .

I cannot see how we can continue much longer to pursue such divergent policies at the same time.[5]

Although this important minute shows Heath, at this early stage in the negotiations, correctly diagnosing the acquisition of nuclear technology as the key factor in securing French agreement to British entry into the EEC, the Foreign Secretary and Prime Minister failed to appreciate the importance of the issue. Nor was it further questioned in Cabinet whether Britain should refuse to follow the American line on the non-dissemination of nuclear weapons to placate de Gaulle.[*]

By April Frank Lee was also pessimistic; he told Paul-Henri Spaak, the Belgian Foreign Minister, who was keen on Britain's joining, that our entry could never be carried 'here in Parliament and in the country' unless satisfactory arrangements had been made and could be seen to have been made 'not only for Commonwealth temperate agriculture but also on Associated Overseas Territories arrangements [Colonies and Commonwealth] and certain nil tariffs, domestic agriculture and EFTA'. On 14 April Roll too recorded that he was very worried about the slow progress of negotiations, saying: 'We should now perhaps be speaking to the Five in plainer and tougher terms because the Five are used to following the French.'

On 10 May further gloom was caused by a despatch from Dixon reporting a talk with Couve, who had stressed the dire difficulties 'inherent in many of the problems, particularly "comparable outlets" which he said was the core of the whole affair. We should not be justified in assuming from Couve that the French will be any more helpful than they have been in finding solutions.'[6]

On 16 May 1962 Dixon sent to the Foreign Office a long memorandum about the French attitude to the British application.[†] This was so gloomy that it should have served as the red light to Macmillan and Heath that the General did not want negotiations to succeed, and hoped that we would abandon our attempt to join. However Dixon thought it was unlikely that de Gaulle would ever say 'explicitly' that he was opposed to British entry because it would get him into 'serious trouble'

---

[*] See Chapters 14 and 15.
[†] The report was written for the Ambassador by Sir Michael Butler, then First Secretary at the Paris Embassy.

with the other Five, and precipitate a major row which he did not want. Dixon thought that Wormser and Kojeve of the French Foreign Office had been deliberately inciting the Commonwealth to stand out against our entry while the American experts at the US Embassy in Paris had believed for more than three months that de Gaulle was opposed to it. In addition the British Embassy had learnt that Gaullist party headquarters were briefing their speakers to explain why it would be against the interests of France if the British application were allowed to succeed.

In his diary for 10 May Macmillan wrote: 'Pierson Dixon who has the most subtle mind in Whitehall thinks that de Gaulle has now definitely excluded us. But he [Dixon] believes if we play our cards well we can put him into an untenable position.' This was a correct appreciation of Dixon's analysis but unjustifiable optimism soon sprang up with both the Prime Minister and the Lord Privy Seal; not, however, within the Paris Embassy where a cold sense of realism prevailed. Dixon from his position as Ambassador in Paris and also as head of the Brussels delegation was better placed than anyone else to gauge the chances of success.

Confirmation of the gloomy prospects came when on 23 May 1962 Dixon talked again to de Gaulle, who made it clear he could not envisage Britain joining the EEC, because the Community would not make sufficient exceptions in favour of the Commonwealth to satisfy them, and it would be 'too difficult to bridge the gap' so that Dixon very much feared 'it was too early for us to enter the Common Market'. The full implications of these authoritative reports were lost on the Cabinet Common Market Negotiating Committee chaired by Rab Butler.[7]

When Britain had informed the Six of her desire to open negotiations on 21 July 1961, de Gaulle's response had been, according to his memoirs: 'the English attack again . . . having failed to prevent the birth of the Community they now plan to paralyse it from within.' In his view there were so many conditions attached to the application about the Commonwealth, EFTA and home agriculture that there was no hope of a successful outcome, and since his partners did not have the courage to say 'No' the day would come when 'I would have to accept the challenge and either put a stop to the time wasting or pull France out of a venture which had lost its way as soon as it began.'

Heath was displeased when it was suggested by some of the Five that further negotiations should await Macmillan's proposed meeting with de Gaulle at the Château de Champs on 2 and 3 June 1962, and he sent a personal message to Colombo: 'I can assure you this is not our view . . . it would be damaging to public expectation in all countries if the idea should get around that we were stuck in our Brussels talks and that personal intervention at high level was necessary.'

The Champs meeting of the two leaders was unrewarding; although Macmillan claimed that the discussions were 'fairly satisfactory', the archives do not support him.* Macmillan hoped to dangle before de Gaulle the carrot of access to American nuclear know-how in a tripartite association with the USA and UK, if Britain joined the EEC. But Macmillan was in no position to deliver the goods and the Frenchman knew this. De Gaulle made it clear he preferred the Six without Britain, mainly because Britain was too close to America. After Champs Macmillan wrote to the Queen: 'I did not expect any dramatic change as a result of our talks but I would think the danger of the French imposing a resolute veto to our application has been avoided for the time being.'

The impression was confirmed by Margolin who told Roll on 30 June that he did not think 'the negotiations could fail. The French could not say "No" and we [UK] could not retreat.' Roll replied cynically, 'You should not assume the latter but I am glad you think the French would not say "No"!' The hope was misplaced.[8]

Heath told the Cabinet on 25 June 1962 that on temperate foodstuffs from the Commonwealth, the most critical problem, little real progress had yet been made, and that on present indications negotiations were likely to continue into August. He added later in the discussions that the Six were taking the line that after 1970 the Commonwealth would be treated on the same basis as any other third country: surprisingly, the Cabinet were not unduly alarmed. Regarding British agriculture Soames stated that 'reasonable arrangements' could, he believed, be negotiated, although it was unlikely the farming community would see them in that light.[9]†

---

* His official biographer Alistair Horne agrees.
† In their 1959 election manifesto the Conservatives rather unwisely pledged themselves not to alter the guaranteed price to farmers contained in the 1957 Agricultural Act. This meant that the guaranteed farm gate prices were increased on a cost plus basis (less an allowance for increased efficiency) automatically. Changing to the EEC system would mean a technical breach of this election pledge which worried Ministers because of both the influence of the NFU in rural Conservative constituency associations and the importance of the farm vote in certain constituencies where a menacing challenge came from the Liberals after the Orpington by-election of 1962.

Harold Woolley, President of the NFU, had, according to the Ministry of Agriculture in 1962, lost confidence in the Government's determination to stand by this undertaking and feared farmers would lose heavily if the UK joined the EEC. Accordingly the Prime Minister and Soames gave Woolley a private interview on 9 July 1962 after Woolley had written an article strongly hostile to the EEC in the NFU journal *British Farmer*.

Woolley told them that statements by Heath and Macmillan gave him the impression that Britain was already in the Common Market and farmers were worried. Macmillan said he could not understand Woolley's remark. Woolley later said 'he did not believe the Government would succeed in getting satisfactory guarantees for Commonwealth and British agriculture.' (He was very pro-Commonwealth and acted as self-appointed spokesman for Commonwealth farmers.)

At the Cabinet meeting on 5 July 1962 Heath complained bitterly about the French, saying they refused to enter into substantive discussion of their objections when the United Kingdom was present but were active in pressing them at meetings of the Six. However he gave an optimistic statement about Commonwealth temperate foodstuffs, saying that 'encouraging progress' had been made: it was agreed that the transitional period should continue at least until 1970, and it was accepted that if by 1970 no world-wide agreements had been negotiated for a particular commodity it would be necessary to negotiate with the Commonwealth countries 'continuing arrangements', while existing members of the EEC had said they would be prepared to operate their price and production schedules so as to 'give reasonable access to Commonwealth foodstuffs'. This was far from a correct version of the attitude of the Six and Heath was still over-optimistic compared with the officials.[11]

By July it was increasingly likely France would say 'No'. To safeguard Commonwealth prosperity the British had suggested that after the transitional period was over specially favourable trade terms should be offered to them under the categories of 'access arrangements' and 'comparable outlets', and asked for a 'review' to be carried out by the Six in conjunction with Britain and the Commonwealth countries. This would have been a cumbersome process. Regardless of France, the other Five would have nothing to do with it; they were formulating their agricultural policy based on high levies on all food imports, and were anxious to push ahead with it. The Six were also unanimous in rejecting the British suggestion of a twelve-year transitional period for British agriculture. (This, unlike Commonwealth preference, was negotiable

---

He would not support any agreement which did not secure adequate safeguards. The Six had no common plan; France hoped to be the granary of Europe. He feared high target prices would preclude imports and even import levies would not be sufficient to support European agriculture. He feared there was too much guess and hope in the Government's policy, and frankly he did not think the assurances to British farmers were 'firm enough'. They amounted to a hope of a policy and therefore would be very difficult to discuss seriously; he was worried that the agricultural theories of the Six would not make sense. It would be more difficult to upset them if the UK were committed to the Commonwealth.

Woolley was garbled and prejudiced. Before the meeting Soames briefed the Prime Minister: 'Woolley is by temperament an anti-Common marketeer; his article left the impression he has already made up his mind against the Common Market without knowing the terms.'

On 21 September Hailsham wrote to Butler as Chairman of the Common Market Committee: 'Last two meetings of Cabinet have convinced me agriculture is crucial; I do not believe EEC can be got through Parliament if the farming constituencies are fundamentally unconvinced and took exception to artificially high price of wheat and corn in EEC.' Butler replied that the NFU was not fully representative of agricultural industry and farming should do well in the Common Market.[10]

and the British eventually agreed to all special arrangements for British farmers ceasing by 1970.)

In early July Heath informed Macmillan that the most difficult problem to solve would be temperate foodstuffs from Canada, Australia and New Zealand; he wrote:

> Here it will be necessary for them to have opportunities to sell on the sort of scale on which they have sold in the past on fair competitive terms, and whatever arrangements are made in the years immediately ahead they must not end suddenly. There must be provision for discussion and consultation to safeguard the Commonwealth in the longer term.[12]

This was what the French were determined to avoid. On 19 July Heath told the Cabinet: 'If we could not at this stage secure reasonable compromises on the main issues in dispute there would be no question of negotiating further concessions later since all prospect of the United Kingdom being able to enter EEC would have gone.' In the ensuing discussion it was decided that such a measure of agreement on Commonwealth matters should not be reached with the Six as would then place the UK under pressure to make unjustified concessions on British agriculture. However the problem of Commonwealth food imports was far from solved, as will be seen.[13]

There was a further bad omen on 16 July. After a moderate speech by Gaitskell taking more or less the Government's line, Paul-Henri Spaak, the pro-British Belgian Foreign Minister, said the next day that Britain expected the Governments of the Six 'to beg on their knees for her to join because of the conditions they were demanding for the Commonwealth'.

Another bleak note from the Paris Embassy arrived in the Foreign Office on 23 July stating that Wormser had 'made it clear at the end of last week to Barclay that he would only be willing to continue beyond 28 July if by that day some really substantial progress had been made. In the event of the negotiations becoming deadlocked he would see no advantage in stopping the clock.' Harold Caccia, now returned from Washington to be Permanent Under-Secretary at the Foreign Office, minuted that he hoped the message from Wormser 'would not be the end of negotiations, let alone the end of the world'. Home, now Foreign Secretary, minuted: 'Yes, it looks fairly sinister but Couve never reflects these alarming messages. However perhaps they play it that way.' Despite Wormser's threat Heath went back to Brussels on 24 July hoping for success. He was soon disillusioned. The Cabinet at this stage thought the state of negotiations so unsatisfactory that no White Paper could be published, as they had originally intended.

On 25 July 1962 formal negotiations were resumed by Ministers in

Brussels. That same day the Six turned down the proposal for 'comparable outlets', and Heath fell back on the arguments that instead there should be 'world-wide agreements' for temperate foodstuffs specifying the maximum amount of each foodstuff which the EEC would allow to be brought in on favourable tariff terms from the Commonwealth. These agreements, Heath argued, must be tied to 'a reasonable price policy' for internal food supplies within the EEC because otherwise EEC food production would expand so rapidly that there would be no room for overseas suppliers in their market.[14]

Eugène Schaus, the Luxemburg chairman of the Ministerial meeting, stated that the Six would accept 'world-wide agreements' and a reasonable farm price policy but they would not accept consultation with the Commonwealth as Heath had suggested. 'World-wide agreements' were not endorsed by the French and as a sop to Heath, Schaus suggested: 'if it appeared world-wide agreements could not be considered the enlarged Community would be *disposed* [Author's italics] to have consultations with third countries and especially the Commonwealth.'

The next day, 26 July, when Heath argued for a low level of farm prices within the EEC, Couve attacked him, saying he would not agree to low prices and 'I am opposed to consultations with the Commonwealth.' The French Foreign Minister was backed by Sicco Mansholt, the EEC Agricultural Commissioner, who said, 'It is impossible to make specific exceptions for the Commonwealth.' There was an impasse.

A marathon series of meetings began the next day, 27 July. Schaus began by saying that the Six 'believe they have made concessions over the Commonwealth' which offered a fair solution. His view was echoed by Walter Hallstein, President of the Commission: 'The British have not appreciated what the Six have done to meet their point of view because they had rephrased their recommendations to suit the Commonwealth. What we cannot do is to commit ourselves for an unlimited period to continue the present [Commonwealth] trading pattern.' The Six, Hallstein pointed out, had agreed to the Commonwealth being given a special position during the transitional period [up to 1970] but 'we cannot concede complete equal footing with the Community. This would amount to admitting the Commonwealth to the Community without political obligations.'

The German delegate Dr Rolf Lahr supported Hallstein. So did the Belgian Foreign Minister Spaak who said the British and the Commonwealth deserve to be told clearly that 'We cannot give outsiders more specific guarantees than are given to Community producers' and there was 'a fundamental difference' between the Six and the British. With negotiations in disarray the delegates dispersed, agreeing to meet on the following Wednesday for what was still hoped to be a final four-day session preparatory to agreement.[15]

The Times for 28 July reported a crisis in Brussels, with the negotiations reaching 'complete deadlock' and 'no way out'. Negotiations, the British national newspapers made clear, were foundering over Commonwealth food. Dixon flew back to London, and briefed the Prime Minister at Chequers on the unsatisfactory state of play. On Monday, 30 July, Dixon reported to the Cabinet Common Market Negotiating Committee chaired by Butler, and saw Macmillan a second time.[16]

Tense Cabinet meetings on 31 July and 1 August were not told of the full extent of Dixon's gloom. However Heath admitted that the Six would not accept either his proposals for comparable outlets for Commonwealth food, or precise undertakings about continued access for our traditional suppliers, and 'very little progress had been made in the discussion of the complex arrangements for the transitional period before any world-wide agreements could come into effect.' The Six, Heath said, had affirmed their intention to pursue a reasonable farm price policy but there was no likelihood they would commit themselves 'to more precise definitions which would carry conviction in this country or in the Commonwealth'; and he explained how price policy could be used to deny access by the Commonwealth to Community markets. It seemed 'highly improbable', he added, 'that agreement could be reached in a few days'.

The Prime Minister summed up by saying the general view of the Cabinet was that 'if at all possible' a breakdown at Brussels should be avoided; a price policy must be obtained which had due regard for the Commonwealth, and if the Six would not in Brussels 'make any further move towards us' discussion on the question of Commonwealth food should be adjourned. Whatever the result, given the great importance of this issue, it was essential that there should be the 'fullest opportunity' for the Government to discuss it with the Commonwealth; the idea of a separate protocol for New Zealand should also be pressed. This was a clear decision to stand by the Commonwealth.[17]

It should have been clear to the Cabinet however that the French would block our entry unless we abandoned the Commonwealth. On Monday Heath had trouble with the Opposition in the Commons on this very point. Although the written minutes do not convey how bad the situation was, Dixon had scared Ministers at the Cabinet Common Market Negotiating Committee who recorded: 'The terms of any agreement which the Six might be prepared to accept at this stage would be open to effective challenge in Parliament and at the London meeting of the Commonwealth Prime Ministers in September.'

On 1 August the Ministers met again in Brussels. Heath complained that he had been given no reaction to his proposals about Commonwealth food. Couve replied that the Six had commented 'by counter-amendments or silence'. The day's proceedings ended in a chilly atmosphere.

Late on 29 July Dr Hoogwater, a senior Dutch diplomat, had called on the Commercial Counsellor at the British Embassy at The Hague and told him, 'the French are determined to block us, and will succeed unless they can be faced with firm opposition inside the Six, and the Italians will not fight the French, so that the only chance would be for the Dutch and Germans acting together to try to move the French from their present insistence on absolute preference for Community agriculture.' He suggested that Heath should invite Dutch and German Ministers with two officials in each case to lunch, and that the Germans might then be in the mood 'to accept our final assessment of what we could get through Parliament and would join the Dutch in standing out for this inside the Six'. The Germans, he added, were disgusted 'by French intransigence'. However before Heath could host this lunch party there was deadlock.[18]

On 30 July Sir Arthur Tandy, the British representative in Brussels of the Foreign Office accredited to the EEC (who had a separate office to the delegation), talked to Eugène Schaus of Luxemburg who was to chair the 4 August Ministerial meetings. Schaus told him that the intransigence on guaranteed access of Commonwealth temperate foodstuffs was not only French but 'a genuine common position', and he thought there was no possibility of the Six making a concession; if we were not prepared to accept their position, Tandy said, 'there was a real danger of a breakdown' and 'he [Schaus] did not dissent when I suggested this would be to fall into a long premeditated French trap in which the UK would incur the responsibility and odium of the failure of negotiations.'

An ominous message to Macmillan arrived from Adenauer on 3 August 1962 in answer to a letter from Macmillan indicating that only after the discussions with the Commonwealth Prime Ministers early in September would 'we be in a position to decide whether it is possible to proceed or not'. 'I fully understand the importance of maintaining good relations within the Commonwealth,' Adenauer wrote. 'At the same time however we are obliged to respect the interests of European agriculture and of the consumers in accordance with the spirit of the Treaty of Rome.' It seems likely that Hoogwater had exaggerated German opposition to the French line on agriculture. Adenauer, originally amenable to British entry, was becoming in his old age dazzled by de Gaulle's warmth towards him.[19]

A breakdown in the Conference of Ministers on 4/5 August at Brussels took place not over Commonwealth trade with the EEC, but over the financial regulation which was being designed by the Six to raise a considerable income by means of levies on imported food, to be used for general purposes by the Commission of the EEC. Britain, by far the largest importer of food, would be much the biggest contributor to this fund. The break came when this item arose at the final session starting on the evening of 4 August.

As early as 22 March 1962 the British delegation in Brussels had reported receiving from secret sources a provisional draft of EEC Regulations 199–209 regarding the financing of farm support, and they were perturbed that there was nothing about refunding levies on food imported into the Community to the countries collecting them. In May Dixon told the Officials Committee of the Six in Brussels that 'the financial regulation' was unacceptable to Britain as it stood. It is hard to understand why this key question was left unresolved. The archives show that Heath and the British negotiating delegation in Brussels ignored it, not realizing its supreme importance; they assumed that the Community would agree to part of the monies received from import levies, over and above the British assessed contributions to the EEC Budget, being returned to the British Exchequer.

The French had prepared a trap for the British over the financial regulation. It was deceitful of them not to inform Dixon, the head of the British official delegation in Brussels, of a detailed memorandum they were preparing which, despite Dixon's statement in May that the retention by the Commission of all British levies on food imports was unacceptable to Britain, declared that no monies received from levies would be returned to the countries where they had been collected. Dixon was under the mistaken impression that his objections were being considered by the Six, and a compromise was being drafted for discussion.

The head of the Dutch delegation in Brussels, Dr Grooters, had raised British hopes in a talk with Raymond Bell, one of the Treasury members of the delegation in Brussels, on 5 July 1962. Grooters was asked by Bell what would be the position under the agricultural finance regulation if the levy contribution amounted to more than the country's assessed contribution in the Community budget.* Grooters replied that once a country had paid in from levies, tariffs, etc. more than their assessed contribution 'any balance remaining above the assessed contribution of any country reverted immediately to that country'. But ominously Grooters warned that this was an issue which should be handled 'with

---

* The Community Budget set agreed total contributions by all the members which would vary annually.

great caution', and Grooters himself thought 'we have been unwise to raise the issue so precisely as we had.'

It is difficult to follow his reasoning because if the key problem was not solved how could there be any real agreement? Grooters went on:

> we [the UK] should not press for greater precision. Our position was very clear from our statement and we knew that we had the support of Germany and Benelux. If we asked for any more definite commitment we should reopen the question among the Six; it would have to go to Ministers and eventually take many months to solve . . . because such decisions had to be taken with unanimity. He could not see what we risked by letting the matter lie as it was.[20]

Grooters obviously thought that any excessive payment of levies by the British could be reduced in renegotiations after accession.

Fierce opposition to the draft financial regulation proposed by the French had been expressed to Heath by the Australian Deputy Prime Minister, John McEwen, on 12 July when he was in London:

> A price basis as you suggested would mean that Britain would be paying for Australian wheat substantially less than would be paid from a supplier in the Community. She would be collecting on Australian wheat levies at least part of which could very well be used to subsidize exports of Community wheat to our disadvantage in other markets. This is a situation to which we would have strong objection.

The comment was devastating because it showed how difficult it would be for the Government to secure Commonwealth or Parliamentary approval if they entered the EEC with such a commitment. It put Heath in a dilemma. In his memoirs Macmillan wrote: 'We were encouraged by Mr McEwen's general attitude to the Common Market.' This cannot be true.[21]

Saturday, 4 August, had been scheduled as the final day before the recess for discussions by Ministers. The French were alarmed that the British by giving in might after all win the day and secure a *vue d'ensemble* (heads of agreement) for a treaty of accession, and were determined to postpone discussions until after the long summer holidays. At 6 p.m. there was an adjournment; Bernard Clappier, a French diplomat, called on Dixon and told him in confidence that Couve had informed the other Five that the French were going to 'wreck' the negotiations by refusing any concessions over the financial regulation.

Reporting to the Foreign Office on Clappier's call, Dixon wrote that the French stand, so he had told Clappier, amounted to saying that unless we were prepared to accept terms which fitted in with present French policies the French would try to block our entry into Europe. Clappier did not demur, even though as a former Directeur de Cabinet to Robert

Schuman in 1951, Clappier wanted Britain to join the EEC and disapproved of the French tactic of using the financial regulation to balk her entry.[22]

The talks resumed after dinner and went on past midnight; then to the surprise of the British, at 3 a.m. on the morning of 5 August Couve produced a French paper which gave a new interpretation of what had been agreed by the Six about the financial regulation; not even the gist of this important document had been given to the British delegation in advance. If the French proposal was agreed the worst fears of the Australian McEwen would be realized, and the levies on Commonwealth food would be used to subsidize both French and other cheap exports of food from the EEC while the British contribution to the Budget would be sky-high with no refunds allowed.

Heath protested at being given this paper at 3 a.m.; the paper, he said, ignored the fact that Dixon, at a meeting of officials on 22 May, had declared this version of the financial regulation 'unacceptable'. The French paper, in Heath's view, went further than anything which the Six had already agreed, and no firm decision had yet been taken by them that levies would go into the Community budget without some return to the country paying them if they exceeded their budget contribution. He had already been irritated because, despite repeatedly raising the point, he had been unable to get any indication from the Farm Commissioner Sicco Mansholt (former Dutch Minister of Agriculture) or the Ministers of the Six what they meant by a 'reasonable price policy' for food; he said that when faced with the direct question Mansholt and Couve went off at tangents. Couve had also repeated to Heath that assurances to Commonwealth countries of comparable outlets 'were not acceptable'.

Heath refused to discuss the new French paper, and reserved his position on 'comparable Commonwealth outlets' until he had studied the matter carefully with his financial and legal advisers. It was left that the financial regulation would be re-examined when negotiations were reopened.

In his diary Pierson Dixon wrote that the night of 4/5 August was 'the end of the Brussels negotiations'. He did not mean that prospects of successful negotiations from then on were non-existent, but that the French had succeeded in preventing an agreement on the outstanding points which would have made it impossible for de Gaulle to prevent Britain signing a treaty of accession. Dixon was sure de Gaulle would use the same tactics again to prevent Britain succeeding.[23]

Couve's action, Sir Patrick Reilly has written to the author, was 'outrageous', but he goes on to say: 'What happened in August was not a "breakdown". It was certainly a pity that we failed to get a *vue d'ensemble* by the recess although it is certainly true that the financial regulation at the end was unfinished business which might have caused

us considerable trouble.' Eric Roll adds: 'On the question of the financial
regulation in connection with the CAP our original attitude as expressed
by Pierson Dixon on Treasury instructions on 22 April was undoubtedly
a major error. It gave the French a handle for considerable obstruction
even after Heath's withdrawal in August of [his] 15 May statement
[about the financial regulation].'

De Zulueta telephoned Downing Street and told Harold Evans,
Macmillan's press secretary, 'The French have succeeded in sabotaging
the EEC negotiations'; Evans recorded that he had had confirmation of
this from other sources. On 6 August *The Times* commented: 'disappointment was great.' Heath told journalists that the issue of 'comparable
outlets' for the Commonwealth was on the way to being solved, and
mentioned difficulties over the financial regulation; he made no mention
however of the French demand for the whole of the levies to be paid
into the Community budget and then used to subsidize Common Market
enterprises – a stand which the British public would have found
unpalatable.[24]

John Marshall, Deputy Prime Minister of New Zealand, said hope-
fully, 'The death sentence has been pronounced.' Arnold France of the
Treasury, a member of the British delegation to Brussels, minuted that
the French

> had tried to bounce Heath by highly discreditable means into a formal
> agreement that the levies on food imports could be used for the Commission
> budget. France with a high proportion of own food would pay only small
> levies while Britain would be paying large levies.
>
> The Commission have to decide in good time how under Article 201 the
> budget of the Community is to be financed from the various receipts but
> it should be the intention of the majority of the Six that the appropriation
> of the receipts under each head shall be so arranged that each member of
> the Community shall make an equitable contribution to the budget.[25]

By this he meant that any surplus from the levies should be repayable
to the country paying them.

Heath was now faced with the problem of insistence from the Six that
the Community should keep all the levies regardless of how much Britain
contributed to the Budget and there was no prospect of compromise
since the other Five supported France. Anthony Rumbold, Minister at
the British Embassy in Paris, wrote that after talks with French officials
he had concluded that de Gaulle had instructed the French delegation
'to see to it that as hard a bargain as possible' was driven with the British
consistent with such action not resulting in a breakdown for which the
other Five, and especially the Germans, would hold the French primarily
responsible. De Gaulle

does not think that the accession of Great Britain is a desirable end in
itself . . . he had no incentive to make it easy for us by sacrificing French
agricultural interests.

[The French] felt it would be in their interests for the negotiations to
drag on into the winter as our position would become weaker and [they]
thought we were in a 'hurry' because a British General Election had to be
held shortly, and the Government wanted to negotiate entry beforehand so
as to be able to point to it as a great achievement accomplished.[26]

Rumbold had correctly interpreted de Gaulle's attitude.*

Neither Macmillan nor Heath accepted Dixon's view that all was over.
At a meeting of the Common Market Negotiating Committee on 6
August, with Dixon present, Heath said that the disposal of the levies
on imported foodstuffs had not yet been agreed but the French wanted
'the whole of the levies to be at the disposal of the Community' for
exporting agricultural surpluses; other countries however considered that
some of the levy should be repaid to the countries making larger contributions, and it seemed unlikely that the Five would agree with the
French. There was no need to take a pessimistic view of matters in public
discussion: there had not been in any sense a 'breakdown' in the negotiations. It was agreed that officials should start at once on a detailed
study of the paper by the Six on the 'financial provision'. It would
have been better if such a study had been carried out several months
earlier.[28]

On 6 September 1962 Heath spoke to Secretary of State Dean Rusk,
about possible US help if negotiations broke down. Rusk promised
generous political support but said he would have to look at specific
issues on their merits. Heath told the American:

There is no reason to suppose at this stage that we shall be unable to negotiate
terms of entry which can be presented to the Commonwealth and British
public opinion as demonstrably fair and reasonable . . . This may however take
time unless we can impart a new political stimulus to the negotiations and
thus recover the ground which has been lost through our inability to reach
a *vue d'ensemble* [with the Six] at the beginning of August and the summer
adjournment. The success of the negotiations now depends in a large measure
on the ability of and readiness of the Germans to stand up to the French and
to help us to obtain tolerable terms of membership . . . Adenauer is becoming
increasingly preoccupied with the need to set a seal on the Franco-German
entente. He is strongly influenced by the views of de Gaulle . . . all the signs
are that Adenauer is completely isolated.[29]

---

* That astute observer Miriam Camps believes there was a 'lack of generosity' amongst all the
Six, and that it was not at this stage confined to France.[27]

De Gaulle now hoped that the imminent Commonwealth Conference and Tory Party Conference would express such strong opposition to Britain's joining the EEC that Macmillan would be forced to abandon the project. He was disappointed.

The Commonwealth Prime Ministers Conference began in London on 10 September while the Brussels negotiations were adjourned. Disregarding assurances to the contrary from Macmillan and Heath, John Diefenbaker, Prime Minister of Canada, made it clear that if the UK joined the Community, Commonwealth links would inevitably be weakened and Canada would be increasingly drawn into the orbit of the United States. Diefenbaker, like the other Prime Ministers, felt the terms were too imprecise for any 'final judgement' but as far as they were known they were 'unsatisfactory'.

Keith Holyoake, the New Zealand Prime Minister, was reasonable and willing to accept the British terms of entry but spread anxiety by claiming that the terms agreed were far too vague to give New Zealand the assurances needed to save his country from 'economic disaster'. Robert Menzies, Prime Minister of Australia, was also highly critical of the terms so far agreed both for their vagueness and because too much of the final price seemed to be payable by the Commonwealth – thus echoing the devastating criticism made by his Deputy Prime Minister McEwen in July regarding the financial regulation and its effect on Australian wheat.

However by dint of persuasion by British Ministers and civil servants the Commonwealth Prime Ministers were induced to agree an anodyne press statement, in which they declared: 'The Prime Ministers took note that the negotiations in Brussels were still incomplete and that a number of important questions had still to be negotiated. Only when the full terms were known would it be possible to form a final judgement.' Given the quicksand over the unsolved issue of 'comparable outlets', and the proposed annexation of import levies by the Community, the conference had gone well from the British point of view.

With great finesse Macmillan manoeuvred so that the communiqué involved no British Government promises to the Commonwealth beyond that of 'bear[ing] in mind Commonwealth fears'. The communiqué was so ambiguous that the press were divided about its implications. Some commentators argued that it meant Macmillan was so 'hell bent' on joining the EEC that the Six in Brussels need not bother about terms. *The Times*, however, said it flashed a 'dim' not 'bright' green light; while the Common Market correspondent of the *Spectator* wrote on 21 September:

The communiqué reduced British officials to acute rage ... There are demands which cannot or will not be met by the Six and therefore constitute an effective barrier to our entry. The Australians demanded an impossible amount of provision in the guarantees they were being offered in Brussels.

Paradoxically the same day, 21 September, according to Macmillan's memoirs, Butler told the Prime Minister over lunch at Buck's that he had belatedly made up his mind and that in spite of '(a) the farmers; (b) the Commonwealth; (c) the probable break-up of the Conservative Party, he had decided to support our joining the Common Market.' Butler repeated this at the Cabinet meeting the next day.* It seems that, though chairman of the Cabinet Common Market Negotiating Committee, he had not fully appreciated how deep was the crisis, and the risk of a break.

Preparations were now in hand for the Conservative Party Conference at Blackpool in October. At their Assembly shortly before, the Liberals had shown great enthusiasm for entry to the EEC, but at the Labour Conference Gaitskell had taken a firm stand against the EEC, defying one third of his MPs who were pro-Europe and obtaining a substantial majority for an anti-Common Market motion.

On 11 October the Conservative Party Conference rejected an anti-Common Market amendment moved by MPs Robin Turton and Sir Derek Walker-Smith, former Conservative Ministers, with only 50 out of 4,000 voting for it.† Both Heath and Butler made impressive speeches in favour of Europe with Butler making a much-appreciated rejoinder to Gaitskell: 'For them a thousand years of history. For us the future.' So enthusiastic were Conservative Party delegates for the EEC, especially after Macmillan's winding-up speech, that Heath feared it would give the Six the impression that we would join at any price and thus weaken his bargaining position in Brussels.

Heath's optimism remained undimmed. On 27 September he had told Macmillan at a meeting of Ministers that the attitude of the French was likely to be difficult. But he felt that, 'if we could agree with the

---

* Contradicting the accepted view that Butler was hostile to the EEC, Sir Edward Heath has told the author that, as Chairman of the Cabinet Sub-Committee on Common Market Negotiations, Butler was never obstructive but instead pragmatic, frequently stressing the importance of educating British public opinion to accept membership of the EEC and pointing out other difficulties that had to be overcome. Butler's widow, Mollie Butler, has told the author that Rab was never opposed to the EEC; she herself addressed many Conservative Ladies Associations during this period, and she was invariably briefed by her husband, who wanted her always to give the impression that Britain ought to join. The myth that Butler was anti-EEC was given credence by Macmillan who spitefully quotes the above letter from Butler out of context, to give the erroneous impression that Butler had been a consistent opponent and only a late convert.[30]
† Macmillan, who was not at Blackpool on the day of the debate, had written a Conservative Party pamphlet setting out the advantages of entry; this had a considerable effect on the delegates.

other Five, proposals which were manifestly reasonable and sensible on
merit the French would not in the last resort be prepared to reject them
publicly.' He appeared not to appreciate the extent to which the atmosphere had deteriorated in London and Brussels, despite warnings from
his advisers that 'negotiations must run into the sand.' The Lord Privy
Seal now embarked on a tour of the capitals of the Five for the purpose
of analysing the chances of agreement.[31]

An important meeting took place at the Palazzo Chigi in Rome with
the Italian Prime Minister Emilio Fanfani and Foreign Minister Colombo
who had chaired the fatal meeting when the breakdown occurred on 5
August. Heath stressed to him that the Commonwealth Conference 'had
gone well'; the Commonwealth had been told that there would be
opportunities in the EEC for them, and 'we had reaffirmed our determination to protect the vital interests of the Commonwealth [in the
Brussels negotiations].' However Britain had not come away from the
conference with a shopping list and was free to proceed with the
negotiations in Brussels and determined to push ahead as quickly as
possible.

Colombo recognized the serious differences of viewpoint over the
financial regulation and Commonwealth temperate foodstuffs; his view
was that the differences must be reconciled by the officials and in private
talks with the Six, and that controversy about them at the forthcoming
Brussels Ministerial meetings must be avoided.

Heath then explained that he had agreed that the levies on food
imports should be paid into the Community budget, and that the disagreement with the French was only over the use to which they should
be put. In August the French had presumed that the Council of Ministers
had already taken a decision that they should not be repaid to member
countries even if their agreed contribution to the budget had been
exceeded. If the French had their way, importing countries like Britain
and Italy would be paying into the budget huge levies which would then
be used to subsidize exports. 'This would be an intolerable situation and
one which the British Parliament would certainly not accept.' The
French, Heath told the Italians, were using the negotiations with Britain
to obtain a concession which they had tried but had failed to get from
the other Five, and Britain must insist that the extent to which member
states should contribute to the total expenses of the Community must
remain 'open'. Colombo offered little comfort, but he admitted the Six
would have to devise a formula for the apportionment of the revenue
from import levies.

The Rome meeting had been preceded by a long discussion at
Chequers on 21 September between Heath and the Dutch Foreign
Minister, Dr Luns. Strangely they did not discuss the key question of

import levies but confined themselves to discussing procedure. Heath admitted that British public opinion was moving against entry, and that opposition from the farmers was increasing. However he thought 'we were now in a position to surge ahead and would be prepared to meet at any time in order to press the negotiations forward to a successful conclusion.' Dr Luns said British entry into the EEC depended on a political decision the key to which was in Paris. 'The French were resigned to UK entry although they would still welcome a situation in which the negotiations broke down provided the blame did not fall on them.' He added that Wormser was 'very negative' although Pompidou was 'well disposed'. Heath and Luns agreed that the problem of the levy on temperate foodstuffs should not be raised at the next two Ministerial meetings. Yet without its resolution there was no chance of a quick end to negotiations.[32]

A memorandum on the British support system for farm prices was submitted to the Commission in preparation for the October Ministerial meeting; in discussions British officials were unable to reach agreement with the Commission and battle over farm policy and the length of the transitional period was resumed at the Ministerial meeting on 25 October. The Six stressed that they wanted the British system of deficiency payments to farmers abolished as soon as Britain entered the Community, and that the transitional period must end on 31 December 1969, which was the date fixed by the Six for entering on the single market. However the Six were 'willing to envisage special transitional measures designed to cushion the possible repercussions of the agricultural regulations upon the [British] price level both to consumers and producers', and they were prepared to envisage the British giving consumer subsidies.

Heath emphasized that if Britain acceded on 1 January 1964 they would only have six years to change over to the Common Market system and the change would be greater for British farmers than for farmers in the existing member states. He asked for a transitional period at least as long as the one which the Six themselves had, otherwise it would be difficult to carry Parliament's opinion; it was, he said, 'a political question'. To announce to British farmers that their present system must disappear without knowing what system was to replace it 'would undermine the confidence of the farming community'. However, Heath declared, Britain would eventually apply 'the Common Market agricultural system without restriction' – a statement that was well received by the Six apart from France.

For France Couve stated that Heath was proposing that Britain would be 'isolated from the Common Market for the whole of the transitional period', and the levies from third countries on food imports would be

introduced only gradually; he pointed out that although the British
Government would face political difficulties regarding the changeover,
there would be 'reactions' in the member countries of the Community
if British farmers received 'more favourable treatment' than them in the
transitional period. Couve asked Heath to accept the new system from
the start rather than 'keep matters hovering on uncertainly for several
years'.

Replying, Heath reminded Couve that there would be no common
agricultural market until the end of the transitional period, and there
were bound to be differences in the levy during the time they were
moving towards the Common Market proper. Finally he warned that
if there were 'very sudden' increases in UK prices British farm production
would leap, and this would not be in the interests of those countries
who wished to export to Britain.

Mansholt disagreed with Heath's view that there would be no common agricultural market during the transitional period: the Six would
have 'one single system during that period and none of them could
deviate from it'. The time had come, Mansholt added, to examine what
the Community system had to offer, product by product; such detailed
consideration of the Common Market plan would show Heath that the
system was one which could afford confidence to British farmers. After
an adjournment it was agreed to appoint a committee of investigation,
to meet and report on the problems raised in time for the Ministerial
meeting in December.[33]

Heath reported to the Cabinet Committee on Common Market Negotiations on 1 November that the October Ministerial meeting in Brussels
had been 'difficult', mainly because of unpleasant interventions by the
French Minister of Agriculture, and the Six felt after the Commonwealth
and Conservative conferences that Britain would accede to the Community on almost any terms so that the Six need only bide their time to
succeed in the negotiations. 'We should have to make it clear that this
was not the case.' However he said he had no reason to doubt that we
should substantially attain our objectives 'but if we did so it would be
mainly upon political grounds.'[34]

In his speech to the Party Conference Macmillan had said that the
Government had 'insisted from the start that arrangements must be made
to safeguard the Commonwealth, home agriculture and fellow members
of the EFTA' – a repetition of his message to the Commons in the July
1961 debate on Britain's application to join. The theme was taken up
again by Macleod in a speech on 3 November, in which he stated that
Britain must not pay too high a price for membership, and must secure
a long transitional period for agricultural prices; while three weeks later

Fred Erroll, President of the Board of Trade, declared that it would be 'no disaster' if Britain stayed outside the Community. These last two clearly co-ordinated statements may have been a ploy to impress the Six that Britain would not join unless the terms were satisfactory; more probably it was to prepare the British public for a failure which would discredit an unpopular Government.[*]

It is impossible to be specific about the effect of such speeches on the Five in Brussels. The Five wanted Britain to join but these reservations must have caused them to doubt whether Britain really shared their enthusiasm and commitment to a united Europe.

The Conservatives' difficulty was that although the Cabinet believed that Europe provided the right future for Britain the Party itself was split. There were many more landowning and farming Conservative MPs then than now, while the strong Empire lobby who followed Lord Salisbury and Lord Beaverbrook were awkward bedfellows. Macmillan was thus forced continually to express reservations which he personally thought unnecessary and which were poorly received by Britain's friends among the Six.

This looking back over his shoulder by the Prime Minister gave the Six grounds for criticism of British motives in trying to join the EEC. The Conservative Party between 1959 and 1963 were the wrong party for him to lead in his European adventure and only the Liberals, then minuscule in numbers, went the whole way with him. Gaitskell, with his out-and-out opposition to Europe in defiance of one third of his MPs, was gaining anti-Common Market votes at by-elections at the expense of the Conservatives. Thus, at the moment when entry into the EEC was of supreme importance to Britain, Macmillan with his cautious temperament feared that public opinion was not sufficiently educated, and that by evincing too much enthusiasm for the Common Market he might provoke an internal crisis in Conservative ranks which could bring down his Government or make it impossible to win the next General Election. Alistair Horne, Macmillan's official biographer, confirms that Macmillan told him many times that he was acutely conscious 'his Common Market policy was still opposed by substantial sections of public opinion while he had to carry along both a divided party and a hesitant Cabinet.' Sir Edward Heath does not entirely agree; he believes that only Butler, Maudling and Hailsham were lukewarm, whilst the entire Cabinet were conscious throughout of the problem of carrying Parliament with them.

*   *   *

---

[*] On 13 December forty-seven Conservative MPs signed a motion urging the Government to remain firm in the negotiations even if it meant breaking off.

By October, it had become increasingly clear to the British teams in London and Brussels that the difficulties which the French were raising over domestic agriculture and Commonwealth food imports were not due to any intrinsic problem of principle but solely to de Gaulle who was seeking to raise the stakes so high that Britain would be forced to withdraw. Then suddenly a dramatic political crisis blew up in France. On 5 October the Pompidou Government was unexpectedly defeated, and on 10 October the French Parliament was dissolved with 25 November scheduled for a General Election. Simultaneously de Gaulle called for a referendum on his presidency.

Although a similar period of political uncertainty in Britain would incline British civil servants to compromise, in Brussels Couve stuck rigidly to de Gaulle's instructions as if in no doubt about the result of the referendum and election. The timetable and agenda for the official and Ministerial meetings in Brussels had been fixed well in advance, and the French opposed any move towards an early agreement on agriculture and the Commonwealth.

The referendum had nothing to do with Britain's application to join the EEC and de Gaulle made no mention of it in his campaign. Nominally it was about the method of electing the French President, but de Gaulle turned it into a vote of confidence in his leadership. In his television appearances de Gaulle made it clear he would not be satisfied with a 'scratch' majority and unless he got a proper mandate he would quit. He won his vote of confidence with 61 per cent in favour and 29 per cent against.

The Gaullist political parties also won convincingly in the General Election. Had de Gaulle lost there can be no doubt that in the current state of negotiations, and given the attitude of the other Five, a treaty of accession could quickly have been agreed; this would have made a great difference to the subsequent history of both Britain and the Community. But as a result of the referendum and the General Election de Gaulle was in an impregnable political position from which he could flout the wishes of both the Five and pro-British opinion in France, and block British entry without having to search any longer for an excuse to put the blame on the British.

The Ministerial meetings at the end of July and August, and especially Bernard Clappier's secret intimation that de Gaulle had instructed Couve to find any excuse to wreck the British application, should have made it clear to the British that the interval between the defeat of Pompidou's Government and the elections was the moment to press for final agreement on all unfinished business. With the future of Gaullist rule in France in the balance, de Gaulle was for a short period in no position to bar Britain from the Community against the wishes of the other Five. This opportunity was lost.

Unfortunately the Permanent Under-Secretary at the Ministry of Agriculture, Sir John Winnifrith, a former Treasury official, was fiercely anti-Common Market. (After he retired he was prominent in anti-Common Market organizations.)* Instead of oiling the wheels his Ministry made difficulties and were abetted by the National Farmers Union. Sir Patrick Reilly told the author that the attitude of the Ministry of Agriculture was often obstructive during the autumn of 1962 – despite the Minister, Christopher Soames, being a keen European – especially over the length of the transitional period about which the NFU were particularly sensitive. There is a mystery why Christopher Soames allowed this.

After the 'difficult' meeting of Ministers in Brussels at the end of October, the Ministry of Agriculture accentuated rather than resolved the dispute between the Six and the UK over the length of the trans-itional period which – once Heath had agreed the financial resolution – became the main stumbling-block. A memorandum from the Ministry of Agriculture to Heath is indicative of their opposition to entry; the line which the Six took about transitional arrangements for UK agri-culture at the Ministerial meeting on 25 and 26 October, it said, was 'disappointing': 'To require the United Kingdom to change its whole system of support overnight could hardly be said to conform with the principle of gradualism which is clearly laid down in the Treaty of Rome.' It suggested that in his talk with Colombo Heath should make the points:

> It is unreasonable, as the Six are doing, to ask the United Kingdom to make what amount to fundamental changes in its support arrangements in the space of a few years ... There was no indication that during the Ministerial meeting [in October] the Six had seriously considered the proposals put forward in the United Kingdom memorandum. The UK is prepared, as the memorandum explained, to give undertakings which would ensure that the elimination of consumer subsidies would take place gradually and progress-ively and would be completed within a reasonable period ... If the UK is to maintain the confidence of its producers the arrangements for the transitional period would have to be seen to be reasonable ... The UK is simply asking for transitional arrangements which fit its special circum-stances. The sort of sweeping and rapid changes which the Six have proposed that we should make on accession could not be defended in Parliament or to the country generally.[36]

---

* Sir Michael Franklin who at this time was private secretary to the Minister of Agriculture, Christopher Soames, wrote in his diary for 13 May 1961 that Winnifrith is 'the great negative force and believes rightly that we are going to have lots of trouble from the farmers'. On 16 February 1962 Franklin wrote: 'The Treasury regard Winnifrith, a former Treasury man, as a traitor.'[35]

Sir Patrick Reilly commented to the author:

> It was always understood that we would adopt the CAP fully at the end
> of the transitional period as the Six had. The Six were insisting that the
> transitional period should end at the end of 1969. In October/November
> Heath was still standing out for a much longer period although Soames in
> August 1962 was prepared to accept 7½ years.

Lord Roll also confirms that

> At the Ministry of Agriculture there were European-minded officials who
> shared Christopher Soames' views including myself. But the basic protection-
> ist attitude of the Ministry and its anxiety not to accept changes in our
> agricultural support system that might be difficult for the NFU to swallow
> or the strong anti-Europeanism of John Winnifrith explain the differences
> between the official and the Ministerial attitudes. The criticism of our tactics
> which you quote is undoubtedly correct.[37]

Although the NFU had great influence within the Conservative Party
in the early 1960s the stress laid on a long transitional period was unjustified. The changeover had to be made at some stage, and the difficulties would not have been greater if a short transitional period had been
fixed. In any case the current British subsidies to farmers were doomed
on account of their soaring cost. As the Commission President Walter
Hallstein was to comment to the press on 25 November: 'negotiations
might well fail; on agriculture the UK asked for 7½ years to do what
the Community had done in 4½ months.'[38]

A circular letter to all British Ambassadors and to overseas Governments from the Foreign Office on 26 November gives an interesting and
revealing picture of the Government's attitude. It was more pessimistic
than the statements being made by Cabinet Ministers:

> Press reports have presented a picture of alternating success and deadlock ...
> we now have to deal with a wide variety of problems some of which raise
> substantial political difficulties both for the Six and ourselves but which must
> be settled on reasonable terms if the final settlement is to be acceptable in
> the United Kingdom.
>
>   There have been suggestions that as a result of the successful outcome
> of the Commonwealth Conference and the support given to the Govern-
> ment's policy at the Conservative Party Conference we are now prepared
> to enter the Community on whatever terms we can get. This is an assump-
> tion which is both false and dangerous. During the debate on 7 November
> the Lord Privy Seal made it very plain that there are bound to be formidable
> negotiations ahead and that the outstanding problems are some of the most
> difficult with which we have to deal ... there can be no question of
> sacrificing negotiating objectives for the sake of speed ... The response we
> have had from the Community has been frankly disappointing. We have
> naturally expected that, joining an established community, we should have

to move some way to meet the Six . . . It is quite out of the question for us as the Six have suggested to abandon our whole [farm] deficiency payments immediately upon entry.

It is essential that we should secure reasonable arrangements to safeguard Commonwealth interests . . . The successful outcome of the Commonwealth Conference should not be allowed to obscure the very serious misgivings which exist and which we must strive to meet.

While we are wholehearted in our desire to join the Community we can only do so on the basis that satisfactory arrangements are made to report the essential interests . . . There is no question whatever of any date having been arranged even tentatively between the Six and ourselves or of our negotiating to a deadline.[39]

This circular letter shows the caution of the Macmillan Government and confirms Macmillan's statement that he had a 'divided Party and hesitant Cabinet'. It is also evidence of the serious doubts among top civil servants.

An important draft paper, summarizing the pros and cons and based on the Brussels delegation's assessment of what was negotiable, was now being prepared by William Armstrong of the Treasury for presentation to the Cabinet. It would be an important paper, Armstrong wrote to Caccia, 'on which Ministers may well have to take decisions as to whether the likely outcome of the negotiations is one which we could accept or not'; he asked for an appointment to discuss it with the permanent secretaries of all the Ministries involved and Eric Roll before submitting it to Heath.

Armstrong's draft memorandum pointed out the slow progress of the negotiations, and that the task was not made any easier by the impression current for some time among the Six 'that we were now ready to join the Community on almost any terms which they were prepared to offer us'. However, 'there was almost complete provisional agreement on matters such as association for the Caribbean and the colonies and the position of India, Pakistan and Ceylon.' Any settlements reached for agriculture, comparable outlets or import levies, Armstrong felt, 'will clearly be open to attack and fall short of what we had originally hoped to attain' so that the question arose 'whether the settlement will be so inadequate in some vital respects as to justify our refusing to try and reach agreement on the terms likely to be available'.

It had always been thought that a break, if it came, would be over the Commonwealth and not over any UK interest. To break over UK agriculture would put us in an impossible situation. There would be little understanding, much less sympathy. It was essential to break therefore – and to be seen to break – on a Commonwealth issue – for example the price policy for cereals for New Zealand.

Reilly commented on 19 December that the paper still gave him 'the impression of being a little too optimistic in general but it is clearly difficult to hit just the right note'. Caccia, head of the Foreign Office, minuted that he agreed with Reilly and would submit it to Heath after Christmas.[40]

A meeting called by Armstrong, which Winnifrith and the other Permanent Under-Secretaries involved would have attended, was fixed for 4 December but cancelled, and the Armstrong draft never became an official memorandum from the Lord Privy Seal because, so Heath told the author, he rejected it on the grounds that the way in which it was being prepared meant that it would be bound to incorporate the 'maximum' demands of each of the six Ministries and would provide a base from which it would be impossible to negotiate satisfactorily. Heath wanted it replaced by two memoranda – one on agriculture, the other on 'unfinished business'.[41]

At the 11 December Ministerial meeting on agriculture the Six adopted a tough line, with the chairman stating firmly that the Six had come to the conclusion that the British system of farm support should be 'adapted to that of the Community as soon as the United Kingdom acceded', and that the price guarantees granted to British farmers through deficiency payments must cease, although the Community was prepared to study technical difficulties which might arise; any transitional measures which the British Government found necessary must come to an end on 31 December 1969.

Heath pointed out that under the EEC farm policy the price of beef would have to increase by 50 per cent, of butter by 100 per cent, while the British price of cereals was considerably lower. 'These increases in the United Kingdom would be achieved during the transitional period steadily and gradually.' Heath also declared that he could not accept the short transitional period for farm support ending on 1 January 1970.

Sicco Mansholt, the Farm Commissioner, said that what Heath proposed would be unfair 'because it allowed British farmers advantages which the present members of the Community would not have'. Heath countered that he could not see why 'this changeover should be at the point when Great Britain entered the Community rather than at the end of the transitional period'. Here the discussion reached such an impasse that a break was called, Heath pointing out that the British had accepted the Common Market agricultural policy in the making of which they had had no part, and this was 'a very considerable commitment'.

When the meeting restarted the chairman issued a written statement saying 'Any subsidy system either to producers or consumers must be digressive and disappear by 31 December 1969.' Heath said he could scarcely see what new features were contained in these latest proposals which seemed to him to be going 'backwards as compared with other discussions', and he asked to be told what were the difficulties and 'what harm it would do if the British system was phased out gradually during the transitional period'. A confused discussion followed, which Heath ended by saying he could not accept being faced with the immediate abolition of the British deficiency payment system. It was then decided to postpone the problems of British agriculture to a future meeting.[42]

In some ways it was shadow boxing. The Six did not so much object to British farmers having a more beneficial price system but to the fact that under the British system food prices in the shops were lower than in the EEC which in turn gave British manufacturers advantages in wage negotiations over their Continental competitors.

In the December debate in the Commons on the EEC Harold Wilson, now leader of the Opposition, said that an enormous revenue would go to the European Fund partly to subsidize European agriculture and partly to subsidize exports of high-costing European produce to third countries and 'have the effect of penalizing further Commonwealth producers who have already been pushed off our market'; we cannot, he declared, accept the agricultural programme if it is based on the penal import levy. This was damaging to the Government and Heath was clearly uncomfortable. A Gallup poll published in the *Daily Telegraph* three days before the debate on 12 December showed that the numbers in favour of joining 'on the facts as you know them at present' had declined from 40 per cent in October to 29 per cent, and the figure for those opposed had risen from 28 to 37. This was coupled with a poll showing a decline in Conservative popularity.

Meanwhile, on 15 and 16 December, Macmillan and de Gaulle were meeting at Rambouillet. According to Macmillan's memoirs, the talks became a 'wrangle'. With his position consolidated by the October referendum and the November General Election, de Gaulle was even more autocratic than at Champs in June.

De Zulueta's record of the talks shows that de Gaulle soon made it clear that he disliked the dependence of both Germany and Britain on the United States, and said that if a serious European organization was to come into existence all European countries must be 'independent'. It became clear that by independence he meant that all Europe should follow the leadership of France – a leadership which he hoped would render Europe as important a power bloc as the Soviet Union and the United States. Regarding federation de Gaulle asserted that those who wanted a federal Europe really wanted a Europe without a policy which would be run by Jean Monnet in accordance with US policy. (De Gaulle was known to think that Monnet's federal plans were an abomination.)

This line of conversation was getting nowhere so Macmillan brought it back to the Brussels negotiations, saying that they should be 'brought to a quick conclusion' and it was not good for Europe that they should go on much longer. The Prime Minister added that Britain had 'fully accepted the Treaty of Rome, and nothing which Britain had asked for was outside the Treaty of Rome'. When they had met at Champs, de Gaulle had expressed doubts whether he, Macmillan, would be strong enough with the Commonwealth and with his own Party to bring the negotiations to a successful conclusion. Macmillan now had secured their agreement but he could not hold the position in Britain much longer, and he hoped that the negotiations could be brought to a successful conclusion in one or two months.

De Gaulle replied that it would be wrong to think the difficulties of the negotiations came from the 'obstinacy or short-sightedness of [French] Ministers or experts'. The negotiations were difficult, especially over agriculture, and if they went too fast everyone faced even greater problems. Macmillan then dismissed the difficulties over agriculture, but said it would be wrong to produce too much food in Europe, thus dealing a fatal blow to other countries from whom Europe now imported food. The first day's meeting ended with the Prime Minister reiterating his wish that negotiations be brought to a conclusion 'in the fairly near future'; whilst de Gaulle said that he was not surprised the negotiations had been 'difficult and long'. It was an unpromising start, but worse was to follow.

When the two leaders met again at 10 a.m. on Sunday, 16 December, de Gaulle stated that there was a lack of will in the EEC for a common policy and his effort to promote the political unity of Europe had failed; he thought it would make little difference if Britain joined – comments aimed at the Five's refusal to show their independence of the USA under French leadership. De Gaulle followed this up by stating bluntly that 'it was not possible for Britain to enter tomorrow and he felt the arrangements inside the Six might be too rigid for the United Kingdom.'

Macmillan expressed himself 'astonished and deeply wounded' at these remarks. He had overcome all obstacles, including de Gaulle's fear at Champs that the Commonwealth would make it too difficult for Britain to enter Europe; now de Gaulle was saying that because the French-conceived Fouchet Plan had not been accepted the whole European idea had failed.

De Gaulle said that he was against any supranational plan (clearly he wanted to abolish the Commission which he disliked) but he had favoured the Fouchet Plan which was his own idea and which envisaged regular meetings of Ambassadors plus a secretariat, and he had hoped this would operate, particularly in the military field. Macmillan confirmed that the Fouchet Plan had coincided with British ideas in its insistence that governments should govern and that everything would not be run by civil servants.*

The admission of British mistrust of the Commission was not enough to placate de Gaulle. The discussion became heated, Macmillan saying that 'Britain had better abandon her European ideas and make a life of her own.' Anyway, de Gaulle interjected, Britain did not accept the Treaty of Rome as it was. Macmillan replied tersely that this was untrue; all Britain wanted was certain arrangements to take care of particular interests: 'this was no more than France had obtained at the beginning of the Common Market, and the main problem was agriculture.'

Tempers cooled and de Gaulle said there appeared to be a pause in Brussels; French agriculture must be prosperous and France must be able to ensure that her surplus was consumed within the Common Market. Macmillan said he agreed, but production must not be over-stimulated and if Britain joined they would create a good market for French food. De Gaulle said that France would never be able to consume all her production of food; this was the result, Macmillan interjected, of internal prices for agricultural produce being too high.

At this stage Macmillan should have realized that de Gaulle's references to French agriculture were just a pretext for refusing admittance to Britain; Pierson Dixon, as head of the British delegation in Brussels, had already made this plain to him. The conversation then turned to affairs outside Europe, and they adjourned for half an hour until noon.

When talks were resumed de Gaulle said that if Britain joined she would be followed by Norway, Denmark, Ireland and Portugal and perhaps even Spain. Something could be 'worked out gradually' and although Macmillan had said the reasons for the delays in the Brussels negotiations were not 'very important' the difficulties for France over agriculture were 'real'. The existing arrangement on agriculture had been 'worked out' with the utmost difficulty and the real point for France was that her agricultural products 'must be eaten. In Brussels the delegates were disagreeing about hard realities.'

Macmillan then said it would be 'immoral' for Europe to adopt such a selfish attitude as to refuse admission to the £2,500 million worth of foodstuffs which came to Europe at the moment, and there must be 'a reasonable price level'. The negotiations, he repeated, could not be allowed to drag on much longer; Britain could either abandon her traditional role and become a mere client of the United States or she

---

*In fact the Fouchet Plan was a try-on by de Gaulle to substitute inter-governmental co-operation for institutional integration, and was a forerunner to Maastricht.

could help to build up a strong Europe in close alliance with the United States. If she took the latter course Europe would have the 'capacity, the population and resources to equal the United States and Russia'.

De Gaulle's last point however was profoundly depressing. Because of her strong position within the Six, he said, France at the moment could say 'No' to any policies with which she disagreed. Once the United Kingdom and Scandinavia joined, things would be different. The implication again was that France's leadership of the EEC was paramount and that he was averse to Britain joining. Nettled, Macmillan said this was 'a most serious statement', and de Gaulle was putting forward a fundamental objection to the whole idea of Britain's entry. 'If this was really the French view it should have been put forward at the very start.'[43]

The Common Market negotiations had run up against a brick wall: de Gaulle clearly intended to veto British entry. In his diary Macmillan recorded that the discussions were 'about as bad from the European point of view as they could be'. Sir Michael Butler has told the author that following that meeting Macmillan was deeply distressed and almost in tears when relating to staff in the Embassy library that de Gaulle intended to block Britain's entry and all the preparatory work had been in vain.

However false hopes quickly sprang up in Macmillan's breast. On the first day of the talks the nuclear deterrent had been mentioned. From the way in which de Zulueta has written the record it appears that de Gaulle indicated that he had no real interest in nuclear weapons, which France could not manufacture; but for the prestige of France he wanted a token *force de frappe*. Macmillan misunderstood this and believed that if he, as an intermediary, could prevail on President Kennedy to allow France nuclear weapons this might soften de Gaulle's attitude to British entry. At Nassau therefore, on 19 December, he persuaded Kennedy with difficulty to supply both Britain and France with Polaris launchers. This, he hoped, would be the necessary quid pro quo to induce de Gaulle to change his mind about British entry to the EEC. He could not have been more wrong. On receipt of the news, Couve immediately told the US Ambassador in Paris that the 'Polaris deal' would make British Common Market entry 'more difficult'. This should have made it clear that de Gaulle had already decided to veto British entry and that the offer of Polaris only strengthened this resolve.[44]

When Peter Ramsbotham,* Minister at the British Embassy in Paris, saw Jacques de Beaumarchais, de Gaulle's Directeur d'Europe and later French Ambassador in London, on 9 January the Frenchman told him that de Gaulle had hinted to Macmillan at Rambouillet that if there was

*The Hon. Sir Peter Ramsbotham was later Ambassador in Paris and Washington.

Anglo-French co-operation over nuclear missiles he would soften his attitude towards British entry into the EEC. However the General had deleted this from the French transcript because he did not want to appear as a *demandeur* (beggar). De Beaumarchais told Ramsbotham it was unfortunate that an agreement about Polaris had been concluded so soon after Rambouillet: de Gaulle looked on our decision to buy Polaris as 'confirmation that we prefer to do business with the Americans and not with the French'. According to Ramsbotham the French Government were now trying to make out that the Prime Minister had rejected a proposal from General de Gaulle that Britain and France should co-operate in the manufacture of missiles.[45]

De Gaulle, who was very conscious that France could not manufacture or launch atomic warheads, in fact looked on the offer of Polaris as irrelevant. He knew France would never use an atomic weapon in anger, and only wanted atomic know-how for the sake of prestige. Some historians believe the offer of Polaris decided de Gaulle to veto Britain's entry. De Gaulle himself gave the idea currency.

Sir Edward Heath told the author that his firm view was that de Gaulle was intensely annoyed at the Nassau agreement, and the patronizing way in which Kennedy and Macmillan offered France a share in a NATO nuclear deterrent subject to strong American strings, and that if it had not been for Nassau a marathon session in January 1963 would have been successful and a treaty of accession agreed. This view is not altogether shared by survivors of his two negotiating teams, and the staff of the British Embassy in Paris at the time. The truth surely is that de Gaulle had little interest in the Nassau discussions, and it would have been far more tactful if Macmillan and Kennedy had not made their offer to him in a remarkably back-handed manner.[46]

There is disagreement about what was actually said by de Gaulle to Macmillan at Rambouillet about a French nuclear deterrent because Macmillan did not insist on an interpreter, and de Gaulle doctored the French version.[*] Rumbold informed the Foreign Office that according to French diplomats de Gaulle had told his Ministers that he had felt very sorry for Macmillan and had almost said, 'Ne pleurez pas, milord.'

British diplomats at the Paris Embassy later learnt from their French counterparts that at a party on 5 February 1963 de Gaulle claimed to have told Macmillan that 'we ought to unite our two nuclear forces and pool everything', and then try to associate within the European framework independent of America, and it was the Prime Minister's actions at Nassau that changed the tone of de Gaulle's press conference on

---

[*] This is not available to British researchers in the Quai d'Orsay Archives.

14 January. Pierson Dixon commented that de Gaulle 'was given a good idea of what was in Macmillan's mind about Nassau; he also considers that sovereignty of France cannot be assured unless she has at her disposal atomic arms . . . This nuclear power, the guarantee of independence, will become still more necessary when Europe, having made progress towards its unity, will appear as the third great power.'[47]

Despite the gloom shed by de Gaulle at Rambouillet the Cabinet still hoped agreement could be reached at the marathon session of Ministers due to begin on 14 January 1963. On 20 December Heath accordingly submitted to the Cabinet a paper drafted for him by the UK Brussels delegation asking the Cabinet to give him general authority to negotiate a settlement on all the outstanding issues. The Armstrong draft was dead and buried. Over the financial regulation Heath stated that Britain had made it clear she accepted the text without qualification:

> Our interpretation of the regulation is that whilst it amounts to a decision by the Council establishing with binding effect the principle that agricultural levies will be the property of the Community, it would be open whether the levies should replace to a certain extent the contributions which member States made to the Community Budget, and if Britain's share were equal to that of France and Germany it would be about 22 per cent which we should regard as reasonable.

He pointed out that the French, who originally thought the financial regulation protected their interests, were no longer satisfied this was so, and wanted to reopen the subject and to force further concessions from the Germans, in particular making this part of their price for agreeing to our entry; the French attitude had brought them into conflict with the other five governments and in consequence the Six were unable to reach an agreed position which could be discussed with us. Heath pointed out that Britain and Germany had a common interest in keeping their contribution to the financial regulation levy low, and in the last resort some concession might have to be made to the French; 'any proposal that Germany would accept should also be tolerable to us.'

The settlement reached for the developing Commonwealth countries in Asia, Africa, the Caribbean and for most of the colonies, Heath thought good; 'I do not expect any great difficulty in justifying and defending it in Parliament.' On domestic agriculture, EFTA, and the details but not the principle of the financial regulation, there was, he emphasized, unresolved business.

> These questions must be settled to our satisfaction, and if this should prove to be impossible the question would arise whether there was any purpose in pursuing the negotiations.
> If we are able to secure satisfactory arrangements on the key questions

which I have mentioned together with solutions on all the other matters such as those outlined above, I believe that we can in fact bring the negotiations to a successful conclusion. At that stage when we have the whole picture before us we shall have to decide whether we should be justified in presenting it to Parliament.

My expectation – and certainly my hope – is that we shall be able to achieve satisfactory arrangements. Beginning on 14 January there will be a series of Ministerial meetings in Brussels as a result of which I hope to bring the negotiations to a successful conclusion.

Heath asked for 'a general authority from the Cabinet to negotiate a settlement with the Six on all the issues now outstanding within the terms of his Paper and its Annexe'. The Cabinet gave him the mandate he asked for. Even after Rambouillet Heath appeared hopeful, although he did not rule out failure.[48]

The marathon session never took place. Instead on 14 January de Gaulle vetoed Britain's entry. Would the marathon session have been successful? With hindsight, and taking into account the successful negotiations for entry into the EEC ten years later when Heath was Prime Minister, it is likely that all outstanding matters could have been agreed. However it was exactly because de Gaulle realized that agreement was dangerously close that he decided on a veto.

Sir Edward Heath told the author that he could have agreed all the 'unsettled business' at a marathon conference with the Six in January. He was ready to make concessions; so were the Six, and the other members of the Ministerial Committee apart from the French were also confident that agreement would be reached. Heath's firm opinion is that de Gaulle imposed his veto on account of the decision at Nassau not to allow France, without the strings of US control, the technical knowledge to become an important nuclear power.

The late Sir Pierson Dixon did not agree with Heath. His view was that by the summer of 1962 de Gaulle had decided to keep Britain out, and was using the negotiations to find an excuse. Sir Patrick Reilly also disagrees, and told the author that in his view, as the official in charge of the Foreign Office end of negotiations, there was so much unfinished business including the difficulty of Britain's EFTA partnership that no agreement would have been possible before Easter even if the French had been co-operative. He notes too how in 1967, when the Labour Government under Wilson reapplied, de Gaulle would not even allow negotiations to begin.[49]

In his important minute to Home on 10 March 1962 Heath had set out clearly his view that if the Government supported the Americans in their policy of barring France from nuclear expertise through the US non-dissemination policy the negotiations 'would be very difficult'. He was right. Macmillan and the Cabinet never realized that they must break with America on non-dissemination if Britain was to gain entry into the EEC. For Home and Macmillan it was more important that Britain should be an independent nuclear power than that they should enter Europe. For this, future generations of historians are likely to criticize them. The cost of nuclear weapons crippled the British economy; in return Britain may have had greater influence at international conferences. But was the game worth the candle?

According to Dixon, Heath was unjustifiably confident and ignored the evidence of the chilly meeting at Rambouillet when he cheerfully discussed voting procedure at the 19 December Ministerial meeting. Dixon saw de Gaulle three times fruitlessly in the early days of January 1963 with messages from Macmillan that France ought to accept Polaris. In his own words 'he was unable to dent the monolith.' Couve met Heath at lunch at the Embassy on 11 January, and concealed the fact that de Gaulle was about to veto Britain's entry. Couve gave Heath the impression that he was not as hostile as de Gaulle to Britain's entry; but he was only the servant and had no intention of resigning over treatment of the British no matter how strongly he disagreed with his master.[50]

On 14 January 1963 de Gaulle, at a now famous press conference, declared Britain 'unfit for membership'. It was an absolute veto. The negotiations had foundered and the Macmillan Government was sorely humiliated. Heath was in Brussels preparing for Ministerial meetings when news of de Gaulle's bombshell arrived from Paris. He sent several frantic telegrams to London that day; these show that he could hardly believe it was the end of the road. On 16 January he reported to the Foreign Office:

> The scene is constantly changing. During the morning I saw first Monnet and then Spaak and Fayat [of the Belgian delegation]. Monnet thought the only possible tactic for us and the Five was to continue on the line that the negotiations must go on, and said the Five had been deeply offended by the dictatorial manner of de Gaulle's statement; the General was wrong in saying little progress had been made in the negotiations; it was clear solutions could be found to the outstanding problems.

Later that day Heath reported that Spaak, Fayat, Luns and Colombo wanted a Commission set up to take stock of the provisional agreements reached and make proposals for solutions of the outstanding problems, but Heath told them this would be a waste of time if at the end the French imposed a political veto. Heath also emphasized to them that if the negotiations were postponed *sine die* it must 'emerge' that the French were solely responsible.

At a Ministerial meeting of Britain and the Six on 16 January all except

France favoured forming such a Committee under Colombo to try to find a solution. During this meeting Couve left and talked by telephone to de Gaulle; returning, he said 'there was no point in negotiations' but mentioned the possibility of Britain being 'associated'. Heath then expressed scepticism over the utility of continuing negotiations, making it clear he could not agree to the establishment of any group which did not 'constitute a continuance of negotiations.'

France openly took the blame for the breakdown. A press statement was issued after the meeting of the Seven: 'The French delegation has requested that the negotiations with Great Britain should be terminated. The five other delegations of the EEC and the British delegation have opposed this. Discussion of this question will be continued in the course of the next session of the Conference.' Heath had an unpromising discussion with Hallstein, and until 28 January talked with all the other Ministers except the French. The French flatly refused to give the Commission a mandate to review the state of the negotiations.

The suggestion was made orally by Ministers of the Five that they should negotiate with Britain without France; the Cabinet approved this suggestion on 23 January. There was a flurry of diplomatic activity with all the British Ambassadors to the Five talking to as many politicians and important officials as possible but no formal written suggestion was made of negotiations with the Five.

De Gaulle had by now got Adenauer firmly on his side and convinced him that the decisive factor in his (de Gaulle's) rejection of British membership of the EEC was Harold Macmillan's 'deceitful deal' with Kennedy at Nassau. Steel's repeated assurances in Bonn that this was false were unavailing. The German Finance Minister Erhard however disagreed totally with Adenauer and flew to Brussels to assure Heath that negotiations 'must continue'.[51]

By January 1963 Adenauer was almost senile; he had become bewitched by de Gaulle who flattered the geriatric Prime Minister with the romance of concluding a lasting Franco-German friendship based on the power of their own personalities. Originally Macmillan had got on reasonably well with Adenauer, and the German had shown mild enthusiasm for Britain's European participation. Whilst Erhard and the rest of his Cabinet were keen to admit Britain to the EEC, Adenauer obstinately went off on the opposite track. Thus only a week after de Gaulle's veto Adenauer signed a high-falutin Franco-German treaty of friendship in spite of a 'chorus of dissent' in Bonn; in so doing Adenauer condoned de Gaulle's veto. Perhaps Macmillan made a mistake in visiting de Gaulle four times and Adenauer only twice, but the British Prime Minister found Adenauer trying, and placed mistaken reliance on his wartime friendship with de Gaulle.

How important was disagreement over the financial regulation? Pierre Forthomme, of the Belgian delegation, told Arnold France of the British Treasury on 17 January that 'you had done great damage by not allowing the financial regulation to be settled in August in Brussels . . . the French thesis that the levies must belong to the Community was primarily based on their view that if national economies benefited from the levies there would be a built-in inducement to import.' This is a specious argument. Indeed ten years later Heath negotiated entry to the EEC by accepting a financial regulation similar to that proposed by the French in July/August 1962, which Harold Wilson's third Government was later able to amend in our favour, while the Thatcher Government in the 1980s got very considerably better terms.[52]

The archives show that the Macmillan Government was apprehensive about the reaction of Parliament to the financial regulation: it was expensive and detrimental to the Commonwealth, and the Labour Opposition under Gaitskell would have opposed it tooth and nail. When the Heath Government was in power and accepted the financial regulation as a condition of joining, the Opposition under Wilson were less hostile to Europe and the links with the Commonwealth had loosened considerably in the intervening ten years.

It is significant that Raymond Bell, one of the Treasury delegates in Brussels, advised Heath in January 1963 that the financial regulation 'could be the sticking point for us', and 'it was a formula which was visibly grossly unfair to us, and the sort of thing at which the Commons might rebel, while the German interest in it was the same as ours.' (Germany was also a big importer of temperate foodstuffs.) Gerhard Schroeder, German Minister of Foreign Affairs, emphasized in one meeting with Roll that he thought there would be a compromise solution establishing the principle of equitable sharing of burdens. Rolf Lahr of the German delegation told Heath the financial regulation was a sticking point for France and a settlement of this point was a precondition of a final settlement of all other points – 'Germany and the UK ought to press for an assurance that there would be an equitable sharing of the financial burden. There was certainly a risk that the French might not be prepared to accept this but it offered some advantage to both parties.' Lahr had sent his proposal for a compromise solution to Colombo, Fayat and Schaus, all of whom he expected to respond favourably; he then proposed to tackle Wormser.[53]

Dixon was firmly of the opinion that the dispute over the financial regulation was contrived by the French to block British entry: the archives support him. Ignoring his warnings and similar ones from the Treasury and the Foreign Office Heath went to the July/August 1962 meetings confident that marathon sessions would bring success and all the issues would be amicably solved. His plan was to accept the financial regulation in principle, and then in later negotiations to amend it in Britain's favour.

Is the criticism sometimes made of Heath that he was slow and ponderous in the negotiations and thus jeopardized success justified? Sir Patrick Reilly has written to the author:

> his performance was surely extraordinary. He put into his task an immense amount of devoted work and showed remarkable energy, drive and stamina. His mastery of the very complex subject matter of the negotiations was complete. He won the complete loyalty of a delegation representing six different Ministries where there might easily have been friction. He took immense pains with all the Ministers of the Six with whom he had to deal, seeing them frequently in their capitals or at Chequers – including Couve, whom he saw for the last time on 11 January 1963, when the latter gave him his notorious assurance that there would be no political veto.[54]

An inter-departmental enquiry or post-mortem into the negotiations was prepared for use if they were ever resumed. This reveals clearly Heath's problems.

> A point on which our opening position was certainly misguided was our attitude to the regulation on the financing of CAP. The Treasury had of course good cause to be worried about the possible effect of this regulation. We doubt however whether it was wise to take a position our instructions obliged us to do that went beyond the position taken by the German Government. It was unquestionably a mistake to suggest that the expenditure out of the Agricultural Guidance and Guarantee Fund should be reasonably balanced between member states. It may have been a mistake to raise openly this question of equity even in regard to contribution to the fund instead of simply stating as we began to do from early July that we accepted the regulation and leaving it until after entry into the Community to join with the Germans and possibly other delegations in efforts to ensure that we were not obliged to make any excessive overall contribution to the expenditure of the Community.
>
> If we had dealt with agriculture commodity by commodity a damaging confrontation in an issue of principle might have been avoided and the French might have been denied an opportunity of which they took ready advantage to make it appear that we were seeking to avoid having to change over to the Community system of agricultural support.
>
> A damaging factor was the acceptance by the Six of the thesis that although the conference was between all seven Governments the Six would not negotiate with us on any subject until they had discussed it amongst themselves and reached a unanimous decision. This process had to be repeated if on any point the unanimous decision was not acceptable to us . . . It gave the French very great leverage on the Five. The French attitude was

hostile and at times they resorted to open warfare. We never succeeded in establishing that the conference was a place where seven Governments were together seeking solutions which would permit British entry.[55]

Professor Henry Kissinger, then of the US State Department, told Heath in June 1963 that on a visit to Brussels he had found the EEC Commission in a state of 'severe malaise' over Britain's exclusion, and that Heath was the 'hero of the hour', while no one seemed prepared to accept de Gaulle's ideas about the way Europe should go. Heath replied that 'the General was confident he could steer Europe the way he wanted, France was riding high; the economy was growing fast so that by 1970 they would be the richest and most populous country in Western Europe.' The EEC negotiations had failed, Heath felt, simply because de Gaulle saw British membership as frustrating French domination of Europe.[56]

There was blunt speaking from the Five who offered both sympathy and moral support for Britain. Spaak and Erhard were particularly outraged. However when it came to the crunch none of the Five would defy France. Much as they wanted Britain in, they were more frightened of breaking up a Community on which their economic prosperity now depended. They also felt that negotiations had gone on too long and, though up in arms about French arrogance, were paying only lip-service to Britain's fury. The Five stuck by the Treaty of Rome, and refused any negotiations with Britain without France. Even so they succeeded in maintaining the Europe dreamed up by Monnet, holding out against de Gaulle's attempts to dominate the movement until finally he disappeared. John Robinson, Secretary of the British delegation in Brussels, summed up the position well in a note to the Foreign Office: 'Anger at French action continues. But for many this anger is based more on the damage done to Community co-operation than on the resulting exclusion of Britain from the Community.'[57]

Heath's last meeting with the Foreign Ministers of the Six took place on Tuesday afternoon, 29 January. The speeches were intended for the record, and not to persuade. The Ministers of the Six, apart from Couve, stated that they would have liked the negotiations to continue and that they wanted Britain within the Community. Couve denied that the French had unilaterally terminated the negotiations; they had 'merely noted the negotiations had been making no progress since October, and it was better to face the facts. Britain at present is not in a state to accept the discipline of the Rome Treaty, notably of carrying out the Community's common agricultural policy.' There was an element of truth in the French statement.

Heath aroused great sympathy from the Five by declaring that agreement had been near on all the remaining items of dispute. He continued:

> We in Britain are not going to turn our backs on the mainland of Europe or on the countries of the Community. We are a part of Europe by geography, tradition, history, culture and civilization. We shall continue to work with all our friends in Europe for the true unity and strength of this continent.

'It was obvious,' states Sir Patrick Reilly, who was present, 'that he had won the respect, admiration and sympathy of everyone there apart, no doubt, from the French. His closing speech was perfect. There were few dry eyes among the British present.' Nora Beloff, the *Observer* correspondent, wrote: 'For the first time in history an international economic negotiation was ending in tears.'[58]

In a broadcast about the breakdown of the negotiations on 30 January 1963, Macmillan said: 'When in the last few weeks it became clear that the remaining points could be settled then the French brought the negotiations to an end.' This is what Macmillan and Heath wanted to be believed so that the whole blame for failure could be thrown on the French.

Thus in January 1963 Macmillan's European policy lay in ruins. The negotiations with the Six had alienated the Commonwealth, and done irretrievable harm to the old links. In return there was nothing to show except that Britain might never have joined after the fall of de Gaulle without this first try.

When announcing Britain's intention to apply for membership, Macmillan had sounded lacklustre and unenthusiastic, and the string of guarantees which the British then demanded persuaded the Europeans that Britain wanted the best of both worlds. To be realistic the Macmillan Government had to choose between Europe and the Commonwealth – a decision that was never made because the Government believed that Britain's accession would be so valuable to the EEC that they would gain the wanted concessions for the Commonwealth. Macmillan gave the Six the impression he had no commitment to the EEC; Heath tried but failed to dispel this.

De Gaulle, always hostile to British entry, had from the start decided that he would not allow Britain into the Community unless she toed the line over agricultural policy, and kept out Commonwealth temperate foodstuffs and agreed to make massive contributions to the budget from levies on food imports. Finally, frightened that the Five might give way and allow substantial concessions to the British, he used his strong position after his victories in the autumn elections to exercise a veto, putting forward the excuse that Britain would not accept the principles of the full common agricultural policy. Dixon termed this Britain's 'Achilles heel', and the French mercilessly exploited it. However Heath and his advisers had gone to the conference table at the end of July 1962 unprepared for the pitfalls laid for them by the French.

The Macmillan Government had missed the boat in their first few weeks of office. In 1957 they could have joined with the Messina powers on the ground floor, and got satisfactory conditions for the Commonwealth and agriculture. The Treaty of Rome was tailor-made for the French, giving them generous terms for their former overseas possessions; similar terms could have been negotiated by Britain if she had taken the plunge in 1957.

In 1961 the Macmillan Government again missed the boat. If instead of sitting on the fence and demanding unacceptably favourable terms for the Commonwealth Britain had settled for entry immediately following her application, de Gaulle would not have been strong enough politically to block Britain. By allowing the negotiations to drag on until de Gaulle was in an impregnable political position the opportunity was lost.

It is strange that Macmillan, after being told in August 1962 by Dixon, of whom he had the highest opinion, that the Brussels negotiations were likely to founder, should have had the élan to bring the Commonwealth Conference to a successful conclusion over the EEC and have persuaded the Conservative Party Conference that he was about to lead Britain triumphantly into Europe. In his memoirs Macmillan says that by convincing the Conservative Party that it was right to join the EEC he had put Britain 'in the straight'. Alistair Horne writes in the official biography that Macmillan was ignoring 'all the British reservations, the cautious Brussels overtures and the prolonged delays in the discussions'. These had not only given the French the excuse to veto Britain's entry but also made the other Five doubt our sincerity.

In his diary Macmillan wrote despairingly, 'All our policies at home and abroad are in ruins,' and in his memoirs that he felt it would be a mistake in retaliation to 'organize even more strongly a combination with EFTA and the Commonwealth countries'.[59] At the Commonwealth and Conservative conferences he had been playing a charade, pretending he had won a victory which in his heart he must have known was in doubt. He acted so well that the blow to his personal rating as Prime Minister and the damage to the Conservative Party was vastly greater when the French veto came in January 1963 than it would have been if he had admitted the problems faced in Brussels after 5 August.

On 6 February 1963 when the curtain had finally come down, Heath outlined his new policy to the Cabinet as confined to thwarting de Gaulle in his attempt to dominate NATO; the reluctance of the Five to split with France ruled out any 'new institution'. On 7 February Dixon consulted with Macmillan in London and they decided in retaliation to cancel Princess Margaret's forthcoming visit to Paris as 'it might be interpreted by other European governments as having political significance'. On 1 March the Cabinet Common Market Negotiating Committee under Butler's chairmanship rejected as unacceptable to the rest of EFTA a plan by Spaak for a customs union on industrial production between the Six and Great Britain – a plan which was 'liable to involve us in another round of unsatisfactory negotiations with the Six. Instead we should work towards curtailing our commitment to NATO in order to maintain and reinforce our position east of Suez.'[60]

On 18 May 1963 de Zulueta drew the Prime Minister's attention to the charge that Heath was being 'a bad loser' and was continuing to make speeches in public raking over the ashes of the EEC controversy:

> What do such speeches achieve? The French say they merely make Anglo-French relations more difficult without doing any good and it is probable that some of the rest of the Five regard them as embarrassing. On the other hand it may be said that such speeches had to be made for the record, and to show the French we are not beaten yet. The French say we are showing ourselves to be bad Europeans. I am sure you ought to raise this with the Lord Privy Seal.

There is no trace of what Macmillan actually said to Heath,* but after reading de Zulueta's note he minuted to the Foreign Secretary, Home, that our policy should be:

> (a) No further signs of our displeasure. Margaret and Queen Mother will not go to Paris. That is right. There must be no intimacy
>
> (b) Correct attitude on points of principle agreed e.g. continuation of supersonic aircraft and discussion of military deals with Messmer i.e. weapon deals.
>
> (c) An attitude of reserve on all matters of high policy. The French can be smoked out by the Americans and the Five.
>
> (d) Generally an attitude of waiting to see on our part.

Home replied without comment that he agreed. Macmillan was taking defeat in a statesmanlike manner but he had run out of constructive ideas.[61]

---

*On 17 July 1963 Macmillan wrote in his diary: 'Heath is so bitterly anti-French as to be almost unbalanced in his hatred of de Gaulle, Couve etc.' However Macmillan had himself been bitter about the French in speeches which Heath considers to have been more hostile to the French than his own. In the summer of 1963 Heath went for a holiday in the South of France and, feeling enmity must not be allowed to continue, lunched at Couve's house where they resumed their friendship.

CHAPTER 10

After the Veto

As MACMILLAN HIMSELF admitted, de Gaulle's veto on 14 January 1963 on British access to the EEC left the Government without a positive economic policy. The Prime Minister was always conscious that British industry was soft and uncompetitive because of high import tariffs; he expected one great boon from joining the Six to be price reductions as a result of competition from EEC manufactures paying lower import duties, and he hoped that this would halt both price inflation and excessive wage settlements. His immediate reaction to the cessation of the EEC negotiations was to insist that the Cabinet Economic Policy Committee considered urgently all the means of increasing price competition which had been strongly recommended in the Report of the Prices, Productivity and Incomes Commission (COPPI) in July 1961; then their advice had been ignored because the Government had just decided to apply for EEC entry, and expected that the desired extra price competition would be achieved more readily by reductions in import duties on EEC goods as soon as the Treaty of Accession had been signed.

In 1957, during the first few months of Macmillan's premiership, as has been seen in Chapter 2, there had been serious concern in the Cabinet at the strains on the economy – concern which eventually in September 1957 caused the Chancellor of the Exchequer, Peter Thorneycroft, to raise bank rate from from 5 to 7 per cent and to put a ceiling on both capital spending and bank advances. Disturbed at the Government's lack of success in controlling wage push inflation, Thorneycroft then decided to create COPPI as an authoritative body intended to pronounce on wage levels and educate the public in an effort to restrain rising wages by offering a 'guiding light' for wage levels. COPPI was officially set up on 12 August 1957; Lord Justice Cohen was appointed as chairman and the distinguished but controversial economist Dennis Robertson was with difficulty persuaded to join. (Robertson was an old-school Liberal, a free-marketeer and a believer in deflation and unemployment as a means of controlling inflation.) Sir Harold Howitt, a leading City accountant, was the third member. As Robert Hall, Economic Adviser to the

Government, commented, 'they were a distinguished body and I should think highly competent as these things go.'

Thorneycroft hoped the council would act as a substitute for an official incomes policy, but as Samuel Brittan has commented, 'there was never any chance that the council would take upon itself the odium of producing a "guiding light" for wage increases.' Instead, after taking a great deal of evidence in camera, the first three reports restricted themselves to arguing the case for monetary deflation.

Lord Cohen resigned, and for their fourth report Lord Heyworth, former chairman of Unilever, a company with a strong free-trading bias, and the able economist Professor Henry Phelps Brown had been recruited. Issued by the council in mid-July 1961, the fourth report contained strong advice. Paragraph 17 spotlighted the fact that home industries were sheltered against price competition by high import tariffs and thus could raise their prices at will whenever they were faced by rising wages or other increased costs:

> One is the case of selling in the home market – a case sheltered by high tariffs. How high these tariffs are is not generally appreciated within the UK itself. Perhaps because the tradition that this is a free trade country has persisted through the thirty years in which it has ceased to be so; or because the extent of tariff reductions in other countries has not been realized . . . the UK now ranks as a high tariff country. [This was illustrated by a chart.] So firms relieved of effective foreign competition in the home market have not had to look overseas to find enough buyers but have given priority to satisfying customers in the home market who were ready buyers at prices that yielded a comfortable profit.
>
> But those who have been trying to sell abroad have been impeded by a second factor, namely the progressive rise in their costs. Firms themselves limited by the prices at which they can sell in export markets have had their labour drawn away by others who could cover the higher earnings they offered by higher prices in the home market. In other countries costs have been rising less or not at all. The rise in relative costs helps also to explain why in recent years a steadily increasing proportion of the import bill has been made up by goods which compete with the output of British manufacturing industry – why for instance exports of footwear and motor cycles, clothing and cameras, were smaller last year than imports. What a general policy can do is rather to provide that profits can only be made in fields that are open to buyers and sellers generally and not sheltered or restricted; that costs have to stand the test of competition and that profitability is the mark only of efficiency in meeting demand.

There were two ways in which the Government could remedy the situation, the report continued:

> One is to take action against agreements for price maintenance . . . The other way is to reduce import duties. We have pointed out that the UK now

ranks amongst high tariff countries and that many firms are able to maintain their profit margins simply by raising prices in the home market.

There is a growing body of opinion in favour of a reduction of duties on imports. This may seem untimely when the balance of payments is giving trouble. But it is agreed that the best remedy is not to keep imports down but to get exports up. A sheltered home market works against this. On the one hand exporters have lost much of the preferences, formal or informal, that they used to enjoy in markets overseas. On the other hand the home market has been easy to sell in and has offered little resistance to rises in costs. To remove the bias means making profits less easy to come by and prices less easy to raise in the home market ... we would emphasize that the effect of greater competition from overseas in the long run will not be to weaken the balance of payments but to strengthen it.

The council turned down statutory price controls although they pointed out that the damage done by administered prices and 'cost plus' made them attractive, but failed to point out how trade unions always went for the maximum increases in wage negotiations because they knew it did not matter much to most employers how steep were wage increases because they could be passed on to the consumer by higher prices with consequent grave damage to the economy.[1]

Shortly before the fourth report was published the Cabinet had decided to disband COPPI and replace it with the National Economic Development Council and the National Incomes Commission.* These would meet and hear evidence in public, not in private like COPPI. The Cabinet were told such bodies would be more acceptable to the trade unions who had declined to co-operate with COPPI. This was a false estimate.[2]

The fourth COPPI Report was an excellent diagnosis of the malaise of the British economy. It must have strengthened the Cabinet's resolve to apply for membership of the EEC in order to take advantage of their lower tariffs, but the recommendations were ignored while the EEC negotiations lasted. The Cabinet believed that entry into the EEC with competitively priced imports would keep down inflation, and that lower tariffs would make British exports more competitive within the Six without further legislation.

Under the Attlee Government the Monopolies Act 1948 had established the Monopolies Commission to report on certain industries selected by the President of the Board of Trade, and declare whether or not they made price rings or indulged in other practices contrary to the public interest. The Attlee Government promised Parliament that when

* See Chapter 5, pages 77 ff.

the Commission disclosed practices against the public interest the Board of Trade would make orders under Section 10 of the Act declaring them illegal. By the beginning of 1963 there had been twenty-four reports by the Monopolies Commission; eighteen had disclosed price-fixing practices contrary to the public interest but only two orders had been made under Section 10: following an adverse report in 1951 the Attlee Government had declared certain practices in the supply of dental goods illegal, and in 1953 the Churchill Government had prohibited certain restrictive practices by timber importers. However in the remaining fourteen cases reported under the Conservative administration where the Monopolies Commission had found price fixing against the public interest, no orders had been made.[3]

This failure to take action on Monopolies Commission reports caused widespread indignation but in 1956 the Eden Government found an excuse for inaction by passing the Restrictive Practices Act 1956, claiming that the new Act would be a more expeditious way of dealing with price agreements against the public interest. Under the new Act all price-fixing agreements had to be registered with the Registrar of Restrictive Trading Agreements. The industry concerned had then to justify to the Restrictive Practices Court that their agreement was in the public interest. If they failed, the court would declare the agreement void.

A number of industries reported on adversely by the Monopolies Commission gave up their written price-fixing agreements in the Restrictive Practices Court, but the Liberal Party pointed out that in most cases no extra price competition resulted because the industries concerned were protected by high tariffs, and quite legitimately continued to eliminate price competition by unwritten price leadership even after an adverse verdict in the Restrictive Practices Court. In the United States price leadership is defined as 'conscious parallelism' and is banned, but the practice flourished unchecked in Britain after 1956.

In the second report of the Registrar of Restrictive Trading Agreements published in January 1961 Rupert Sich, the Registrar, admitted that the Restrictive Practices Act was frequently ineffective against price rings because in many cases the abandonment of a written price-fixing agreement in his court made 'no effective difference' to price competition since, instead of operating the price ring through a formal written agreement, the industry was able to obtain the same result by informal unwritten agreements. As the Liberal pamphlet *Expansion Without Inflation* commented:

Mr Sich said that all the parties to the abandoned written price agreement could agree to circulate amongst themselves their price lists and details of all trading terms. Mr Sich considered that this regular exchange of information about prices could be used by unscrupulous concerns to promote effective price rings, and therefore should have come under the Restrictive Practices Act, but under the present law he is impotent to do anything about them.

What Mr Sich's report did was to reveal that there were loopholes in the anti-price-fixing legislation through which industries could drive a coach and four.

By spotlighting this part of Sich's report and publishing a list of the industries criticized by the Monopolies Commission the Liberal Party succeeded in embarrassing the Government, exposing the fact that these industries were all protected by out-of-date import duties and that in ignoring Monopolies Commission reports the Government was allowing price rings to flourish, inflating the cost of living and pricing British exports out of the market.

The Cabinet Economic Policy Committee were concerned at these charges, and at their meeting on 5 November 1962 Fred Erroll, President of the Board of Trade, admitted that his references to the Commission were decided on political grounds, not grounds of national interest:

> In view of the political agitation [by the Liberals] earlier this year for a more active and positive policy towards monopolies I think it would be expedient that we should make two further references to the Monopolies Commission. If these are particularly of a kind which will attract public interest and support we should be better able to stave off further complaints of inactivity.

Among manufactures suggested for reference were household detergents, soap powders and colour films. The Commission was already at work on petrol solus sites* and wallpaper. No export references, Erroll said, had been made since 1952, but there was no reason why they should not be made provided cases were avoided in which British firms had agreements with European firms. Additional candidates suggested for investigation were razor blades, plate glass, sporting cartridges, financial newspapers and periodicals. No decision was taken about further references to the Commission.[4]

After de Gaulle's veto in January 1963 on Britain entering the EEC, the Cabinet Economic Policy Committee, at their meeting on 13 February, had to think out an alternative economic policy to fill the void left by the failure of the EEC negotiations. Fred Erroll ruled out any new anti-monopoly legislation before the General Election because of the crowded Parliamentary timetable. Other members disagreed and urged the need to 'rehabilitate the economy'.

---

*Petrol stations owned by oil companies selling only one brand of petrol.

These divergences produced a far-reaching discussion on economic policy in the light of the failure of the Brussels negotiations. The committee wanted a fundamental re-examination of present agricultural policy and noted that the present heavy unemployment resulted largely from the long-term decline in shipbuilding, mining and heavy engineering which was likely to persist for some time. One possibility was to continue to pin faith in free enterprise and competition; if the Government wanted to be taken seriously in their drive for economic growth they must be prepared to face unpopular decisions in order to introduce a higher degree of competition. The case for the abolition of resale price maintenance should be reconsidered; amendments to the legislation upon monopolies and restrictive practices should be examined, while consideration should be given to unilateral suspension of tariffs. The committee invited Erroll to submit proposals for the abolition of resale price maintenance, and for amending legislation on monopolies and RPM, and to circulate a memorandum on the advantages and disadvantages of unilateral suspension of import tariffs. In addition Heath, Lord Privy Seal at the Foreign Office, was invited to report on the possibility of securing accelerated tariff reductions by some if not all of the member countries of EFTA. On reading these minutes Macmillan ordered a sub-committee of the Economic Policy Committee – the Monopolies Sub-Committee – to be set up to consider the recommendations in the fourth report of COPPI.

Board of Trade officials were asked to produce a brief on unilateral tariff suspensions with the object of 'exposing British manufacturing industry to greater foreign competition'. Erroll suggested they worked on a 25 per cent suspension of the present level of industrial tariffs with farming and market gardening unaffected, and Commonwealth preferences preserved.

A civil servants' memorandum of 4 March 1963 proposed that any suspension should be made across the board and not be selective between industries so as to preserve the principle of equality of treatment. They felt the figure of 25 per cent was the minimum likely to produce any significant effect on competition:

> anything else would look timid, and anything more might be thought too severe and likely to have too great an effect on imports. It would need to be made clear that the suspension would be for an indefinite period but it would no doubt have to be reviewed when the results of the Kennedy Round of tariff negotiations were known.

A unilateral suspension would be an innovation in British practice. Hitherto tariffs have been changed only as a result of international negotiations or of applications from domestic interests, either producers or users. There could be no prior consultation with industry, and no discrimination between industries some of whom would be hit harder than others . . .

Arguments in favour
It is generally accepted that the right policy for the country would be to increase the efficiency and improve the competitiveness of British industry. The reduction of protection from foreign competition is one obvious means of putting this policy into effect. The stimulus which entry into the European Economic Community would have provided has vanished; it will be a long time before whatever reduction of trade barriers may emerge from the Kennedy Round will come about, and this reduction may in the event amount to very little, as the difficulties of securing international agreement will be formidable. Unless we are to wait indefinitely and acquiesce in what may be a disappointing result, we can only act on our own in order to apply the necessary stimulus.

Arguments against
Industry would certainly dislike a unilateral cut, which they would regard as giving their foreign competitors an uncovenanted benefit in the domestic market while leaving them to face not only the present obstacles to trade presented by the protective tariffs of foreign countries but also the new disadvantages arising from the progressive dismantling of the internal tariff within the Common Market. At a time when business confidence is still low and trade has not yet begun to revive noticeably either at home or overseas, they would view with concern action which would be expected to cut further into their profit margins, and so reduce the funds available to them for new investment.

An indefinite suspension would reduce our bargaining power, for what this is worth, in the Kennedy Round, but we would bind reductions only in return for adequate concessions in the negotiations.

To the extent that reductions in the m.f.n. [most favoured nation] tariff reduced non-contractual preference margins enjoyed by Commonwealth countries, these countries might be encouraged to bargain away our non-contractual preferences in their markets more quickly than they otherwise would. However, since we should only be anticipating what we should be willing to do anyhow in the Kennedy Round, this is hardly an important consideration.

In the short term at least, there would probably be some increase in imports and, to the extent that more competition curtailed the production of weaker firms or drove them out of business, more unemployment (though the effect of a 25 per cent cut would probably only be marginal). There might also be some short-term effect on the balance of payments, and some loss (perhaps about £25 million) of revenue, though this would be reduced to the extent that imports increased. The beneficial effects flowing from increased efficiency would take longer to show themselves.[5]

The Dillon Round of GATT negotiations for reductions in import duties had been completed in the spring of 1962. They had originated from American efforts to secure substantial reductions in the EEC common external tariff and were warmly welcomed by Britain. Tariff duties on some industrial goods were reduced by one fifth but the average was only in the range of 7–11 per cent.

The Kennedy Round of GATT negotiations opened in May 1963 and were essentially a blatant bargain between the USA and the EEC although Britain was an enthusiastic participant anxious for the maximum cuts so as to reduce the tariff discrimination against British goods exported to the EEC. Unfortunately the Kennedy Round was not completed until June 1967 when it resulted in substantial cuts of about 40 per cent in most import duties.

On 13 March 1963, with Maudling as Chancellor of the Exchequer in the chair, the Economic Policy Committee considered unilateral tariff cuts as a means of revitalizing the economy in light of the failure to join the EEC. Erroll had written a memorandum maintaining that the target of a 25 per cent reduction in industrial tariffs would stimulate British industry by removing protection from inefficient or insufficiently competitive business. However a measure of this kind would only be appropriate and effective as part of a larger programme of 'deliberate stringency' such as he had described in February, and preferably at a time of industrial prosperity. Ministers considered that it would not be expedient to proceed to any general suspension of tariffs which would almost certainly have 'immediate and unacceptable effects on the balance of payments'. However there might be a good case for considering the reduction of protective tariffs in particular instances where, for example, some identifiable section of industry appeared to be deriving undue benefit from a position of monopoly. Erroll was examining 'possible application of such a remedy to the various parts of the economy which might appear to warrant it; in most cases, however, there were serious practical difficulties in the way and piecemeal measures of this sort would lack most of the advantages to be derived from a general suspension.' The committee agreed that it was 'inopportune' to make any general cut in the level of industrial tariffs, and took note that Erroll was examining 'selective cases of quasi-monopolies'. They agreed to resume discussions.

The Cabinet Sub-Committee on Monopolies first met on 7 May 1963. Before them was the question whether monopolies legislation should be amended and strengthened by allowing the Commission and not the Board of Trade to select cases for investigation, and by giving the Board effective powers to deal with the Commission's findings, including the power to break up monopolies and ban price rings. The Government were still under strong attack by Liberal propagandists for ignoring Monopolies Commission reports and allowing price rings to inflate the cost of living. As Jo Grimond had commented in a speech which received

considerable publicity, it was useless to keep watch dogs and then ignore
them when they barked.

At the 7 May meeting it was agreed that the Government were
exposed to unnecessary criticism as long as the Board of Trade lacked
specific powers to deal with the Monopolies Commission's findings; they
could only 'plead' or pass legislation. (This overlooked the Government's
power to make orders.) The Monopolies Commission, it was stated,
gave the appearance of being both prosecutor and judge although this
was not in fact the case. They debated whether it would be practicable
to arrange for the appointment of counsel to the Commission who
would be distinct from the Commission and whose task would be to
argue the case against the industry. The sub-committee also considered
extending the Monopolies Commission to services. Summing up, Erroll
said the sub-committee had shown anxiety about powers to deal with
mergers; favoured administrative tribunals to initiate enquiries; were
against including services, but were generally agreed that the Monopolies
Commission should be strengthened and given specific powers to deal
with the findings of the Commission.

On 27 May the sub-committee met again and agreed that since there
was no Parliamentary time to prepare a bill for the next session it would
be useless to make any announcement in the Queen's Speech, but that
the situation would be different if there was an autumn election, when
plans would be made for legislation in the next Parliament.

The sub-committee met for the third time on 14 June 1963. Erroll said
he wanted no radical changes in the Restrictive Practices Act 1956, but
loopholes in the Act needed 'to be blocked'. The worst loophole, he said,
was information agreements; another was the bilateral agreement in which
only one party accepted restriction. Edward Du Cann, Minister of State
at the Board of Trade, favoured 'emphasizing the economic importance
of strengthening the law against practices which impaired competition'.
Erroll thought the report should 'relate to strengthening the Monopolies Commission to discharge its existing function'. He thought wilful
failure to register a restrictive agreement should be a criminal offence.[6]

Following these meetings the Cabinet Sub-Committee on Monopolies
submitted a report to the Cabinet Economic Policy Committee in July
stating that the existing legislation was

> widely known to have very serious defects. For example, the Monopolies
> Commission works extremely slowly and the powers to implement their
> recommendations are inadequate; the findings of the Restrictive Practices
> Court are easily circumvented by 'information agreements' and other devices.
> To let this situation continue would be deeply damaging because:
> (a) it would rob of its potential effectiveness one of our weapons in the
> struggle to attain the 4 per cent growth target;

(b) since the defects of the existing legislation are widely known, inaction might be taken as indicating that the Government were not serious in advocating a more competitive economy.

Considering the state of the present law and its possible extension, the sub-committee submitted the following conclusions and recommendations:

We think that the Government's present 'neutral' and uncommitted approach to monopoly is right. But we also think that the Monopolies Commission needs to be made more effective, to be given greater authority, and to be enabled to act far more quickly than at present.

The Commission should have the responsibility for instituting enquiries into monopolies (the essential condition of which should continue to be that control of at least one third of the market rests in the hands of a single undertaking). In our view it is better that the Government should take no specific action about any individual case of monopoly until an independent body has made its investigation and reported on the public interest. But the Government must have effective powers for dealing with monopolies which abuse their dominant position in the market. The present powers are inadequate and should be made fully effective to deal with any abuse. They should include, for the extreme but very rare case, powers to divest interests or even to require the break-up of monopoly, subject to Parliamentary safeguards.

To enable the Commission to act more quickly it would have to be enlarged so that the work could be done by small groups. An enlarged and strengthened secretariat would be indispensable.

We have noted that industry complains that the Commission act as both judge and prosecutor, and that they go into unnecessary detail. We think that a reconstituted Monopolies Commission should aim to streamline procedures and that further consideration should be given to the possibility of doing something to meet these particular criticisms.

Another section of the sub-committee's report dealt with the operation of the Restrictive Practices Act 1956. It concluded that the Act must not be weakened and 'we must resist industry's desire to have some easier grounds of defence' for unwritten price agreements which inhibit price competition.[7]

But there are loopholes which are bringing the Act into disrepute. The most serious of these is the 'information agreement', which must be brought within the scope of the Act. There is a practical problem here. Many information agreements are harmless, indeed useful, but it would not be feasible to make a statutory exemption for such agreements without opening the door again to abuse. We can deal with this by including a wide definition of information agreements in the Act, but without making registration automatic. Instead, the Board of Trade would have power to call up information agreements for registration class by class. We would make a start on those types of information agreement which are obviously being used to get round the Act, e.g. the price information agreement. Other classes would not be called up unless and until there was evidence of abuse.

Another loophole is the series of apparently unconnected bilateral agreements, in each of which only one party accepts a restriction. We can deal with this by amending the Act to make restrictions which are accepted by only one UK party registrable. In order to avoid catching as well some ordinary commercial transactions, it would be necessary to extend the present provisions by means of which such transactions are specifically excluded.

The grounds of defence in the Act would not be appropriate for information agreements. We propose that there should be a new ground; the parties to an agreement – an information agreement or any other agreement – should be allowed to argue that it was not against the public interest because it did not restrict or deter competition.

The absence of any effective sanction against wilful failure to register a restrictive agreement is also a serious weakness in the Act. The remedy lies in making this a criminal offence. We recommend that this be done.

The sub-committee finally concluded that if their colleagues approved the proposals they were advocating it would be 'undesirable' to expect a bill to reach the statute-book before the end of the next session so that it might be 'unwise' to make any policy announcement before the Queen's Speech at the beginning of the next session since the absence of reference to legislation might be taken as suggesting 'that the Government were not in earnest'. They therefore thought it preferable to delay an announcement until the late autumn on the assumption that there would not be an election by then; if there were, the announcement would have to be brought forward.[8]

If Macmillan had survived as Prime Minister after the recess of 1963 there is little doubt that when Parliament reassembled in the 'late autumn' he would have insisted on legislation to implement these findings of the Cabinet sub-committee. In his memoranda about economic affairs he frequently referred to British industry being 'non-competitive' and 'soft'. However, following Macmillan's departure from the scene, the incoming Prime Minister Alec Home took no further interest in the subject while the Chancellor of the Exchequer Reginald Maudling also failed to pursue it. The sub-committee never met again after the issue of their memorandum to the Economic Policy Committee and nothing materialized from this part of their report.

However the sub-committee also dealt in this memorandum with resale price maintenance, and concluded that the case for getting rid of it was 'overwhelming'. Here they achieved action in the shape of the Resale Price Maintenance Act 1964. They proposed:

We should use the Monopolies Commission. We would take one by one the classes of goods in which resale price maintenance is at present operated, and in each case ask the Commission to look into the practice and report on whether it was against the public interest. Where the Commission condemned the practice, the Government should be ready to prohibit it for the goods concerned. (The Commission have twice considered resale price maintenance in the course of their investigations – they condemned it in the case of electrical equipment for motor vehicles, but they exonerated it in the tobacco trade.)

The advantages of using the Monopolies Commission to deal thus with resale price maintenance seem to us to be:

(i) the Government could take the line that they were opposed to it when it was against the public interest;

(ii) people would have an opportunity to argue the case for it in the circumstances of their own particular trade;

(iii) the Commission would be looking at each case on its merits and there would be the presentational advantage that there would not even be a presumption that the practice was against the public interest;

(iv) we should avoid making resale price maintenance a statutory offence.

New legislation would be required to give the Government the necessary powers to –

(a) refer the practice of resale price maintenance to the Commission;

(b) prohibit it for any class of goods where the Commission found that it operated against the public interest.

In each instance, the practice would be prohibited by an order, and, if this were disobeyed, procedure would be by way of a court injunction (with an action for contempt in the last resort).

There would be presentational advantages if the enquiries into resale price maintenance were held in public, and this would be the normal way of proceeding, but the views of the Chairman of the Commission should be sought before finally deciding on it.

In the Cabinet reshuffle following Alec Home's succeeding Macmillan as premier Edward Heath became President of the Board of Trade. He confirmed Erroll's view that the timetable was too short before the General Election was due to allow wide-sweeping legislation to curb monopolies and price fixing, but he was attracted to the Cabinet sub-committee's view about making resale price maintenance illegal. Any preliminary doubts he may have had about taking action were removed when John Stonehouse, a Labour MP, introduced a private member's bill for its abolition, while another MP who had come second in the private members' ballot threatened a bill to abolish Green Shield stamps* which were already making nonsense of resale price maintenance.

---

* Vouchers given as a discount which could be accumulated and used to buy many classes of goods.

Heath plumped for abolition, side-stepping the Monopolies Commission and instead allowing the right of judicial appeal in respect of any type of product found in retail shops. Only with great difficulty was Heath able to persuade his own Parliamentary Party to accept the bill,* and in the following year the Resale Price Maintenance Act 1964 made it unlawful for a supplier of goods which had not been exempted in the Restrictive Practices Court to fix a price at or below which the goods might not be resold. Heath told the author that he was sure abolishing resale price maintenance was necessary as a step towards holding down the cost of living. However the bitter opposition it aroused from Conservatives in Cabinet and in Parliament is evidence of how much greater difficulty Heath would have encountered if he had tried to implement the proposals of the Cabinet sub-committee on monopolies or price rings.[9]

In January 1964 the Home Government produced a White Paper, *Monopolies, Mergers and Restrictive Practices*; this proposed a Registrar of Monopolies to be responsible for investigating the issues of public interest involved in particular cases and made the Commission nearer to a solely judicial body. The Registrar could investigate proposed mergers where a monopoly of one third of the market might be created or added to. Such mergers would be prohibited or only be allowed subject to conditions if the Monopolies Commission ruled them to be likely to be against the public interest. 'Information agreements' were to be registrable, and the supply of services included in the field of the Monopolies Commission.

The defeat of the Conservative Government in the October 1964 General Election put an end to their overhaul of competition policy; it did not altogether appeal to the following Labour Government who in their Monopolies and Mergers Act 1965 produced major alterations to the plan contained in the Conservative White Paper.

Each Government after Macmillan's claims it kept competition policy under review, and the issues discussed by the Economic Policy Committee and the Sub-Committee on Monopolies in early 1963 reappeared in subsequent years. The relative toughness of the law against written price agreements meant that mergers between the former parties became a popular alternative once the written price-fixing agreements were proscribed or discontinued. This led the Wilson Government by the Monopolies and Mergers Act 1965 to extend the Monopolies Com-

---

*Heath's biographer claims that with the introduction of the Resale Price Maintenance Act Heath presented himself as the man who was modernizing the Conservative Party, and this was a potent factor in his becoming the Party leader and Prime Minister.

mission's powers to examine monopolies in services where one third of the market was held by a single company. It also filled the gap identified by Erroll in the powers possessed by the President of the Board of Trade in relation to the break-up of enterprises. As before, reference to the Commission continued to be a political decision exercised either for economic reasons or political expediency.

In 1963 the House of Commons Estimates Committee and the Public Accounts Committee received incontrovertible evidence that cables and transformers for nationalized industries were only being supplied at fixed prices in spite of manufacturers' assurances to the Board of Trade that their common price agreements had been abandoned following a Monopolies Commission ruling that they were against the public interest. By the time this issue was raised in Parliament the Labour Government had superseded the Conservative, and the President of the Board of Trade, Douglas Jay, gave a disarming reply although there was clear evidence that the Monopolies Commission had been ignored. In fact the Labour Government showed more faith in a new creation of their own aimed at keeping prices down – the National Board on Prices and Incomes chaired by a former Conservative Minister, Aubrey Jones.

The NBPI employed leading firms of accountants to carry out quick surveys of the profits of certain firms to verify assurances given by these companies of only 'reasonable profits'. These accountants only established the percentage of profits on assets employed, and the grave weakness of this procedure was that it was impossible for the accountants to challenge the nominal value of the assets as claimed by the firms. The accountants were not allowed to investigate the book value of these assets and could not cast doubt on items inflating them such as goodwill, out-of-date factories or abortive research which should have been written off, nor could they query excessive salaries to directors and senior management and unwarranted high pay settlements with trade unions in wage negotiations. All these factors could obscure unduly high profits; the right yardstick, as pointed out by commentators at the time, should have been not the percentage profit on paper assets but comparisons with prices charged in other industrial countries and particularly in the EEC.

Glaring contradictions between the findings of the Monopolies Commission and the NBPI occurred. In October 1965 after a quick investigation the Board reported that although one firm had earned well above average profits, their price increases of $12\frac{1}{2}$ per cent to 20 per cent on their product were justified on account of higher costs. In 1966 the Monopolies Commission made a laughing stock of the Board when after three years' investigation it recommended price reductions of 20 per cent on that product because the firm had made excessive profits of 53.2 per cent and 23.4 per cent on capital.

A further glaring contradiction came in a Prices and Incomes Board Report in August 1965. In 1959 the Restrictive Practices Court declared the bakers' price-fixing agreements illegal, and stated there should be more price competition in baking. The Board brushed aside the court's ruling, declaring that price reductions to promote competition in the sale of bread would have to be at least a penny a loaf and 'such a cut would have a disproportionate effect on profit'.

In 1970 the Labour Government announced their intention to merge the Monopolies Commission with the NBPI, and the Department of Trade issued a consultative document setting out how the Government proposed to start a new Commission for Industry and Manpower to develop both competition and incomes policy in close consultation with the Government over planning. After Labour's defeat by the Conservatives in the 1970 General Election nothing more was heard of this plan, and the Conservatives abolished the NBPI in 1971. When Labour returned to power in 1974 the idea of a Commission for Industry and Manpower had been forgotten.

Meanwhile unwritten information agreements had continually replaced the formal written price agreements which were declared unlawful by the Restrictive Practices Court under the 1956 Act. As a result in 1968 the Wilson Government had passed a new Restrictive Trade Practices Act (only in relation to goods) which caught unwritten information agreements. The same Act provided for a civil remedy for those whose economic interests were affected by companies operating a registrable agreement which they had failed to notify to the Registrar of Restrictive Trading Agreements. This provision fell well short of the suggestion floated by Macmillan's Cabinet Economic Policy Committee in 1963 that such behaviour should be a criminal offence, and indeed it proved abortive – since 1968 there has been no award of damages in court under this provision although there is some evidence of the occasional out-of-court settlement.

The major change since the Macmillan days lies in the Fair Trading Act 1973 which repealed the Monopolies Act 1948 and the Monopolies and Mergers Act 1965. The most important innovation was the creation of a new officer, the Director-General of Fair Trading, who was given the task of referring monopoly cases to the renamed Monopolies and Mergers Commission. Whether or not to refer a merger remained a political decision, and the Director-General's role was simply to advise whether a reference should be made, and the Government of the day has on occasions rejected the director's advice. Again under this Act the Commission has no jurisdiction of their own to instigate an investigation; they only pick up the ball after it has been passed to them. The Director-General also took over the functions of the Registrar of Restrictive Practices which now included information agreements relating to services.

Few cases have come before the Restrictive Practices Court since 1973 because of the ease with which the Act could be avoided, so that its work has largely been confined to a few registrable agreements which companies had failed to register and which had been discovered. They were compulsorily placed on the register and the Director-General usually obtained an order prohibiting the agreement. Defiance of an order of the Restrictive Practices Court can result in the invoking of contempt powers involving imprisonment and fines. However no one has been imprisoned and the level of fines in practice has proved surprisingly modest.

In 1977–8 Hans Liesner, a former Cambridge economics don turned civil servant, undertook an investigation for the Department of Trade. He recommended no major changes. Ten years later the DTI published a White Paper, *A Review of Restrictive Trade Practices Policy*. This gave the impression that the Thatcher Government intended to merge UK and EEC competition law, and legislation was expected to this effect in 1991. Nothing happened.

Over monopoly policy the 'streamlining' desired by the Cabinet Economic Policy Committee in 1963 was partially implemented by the Competition Act 1980 which gave the Director-General power to investigate 'anti-competitive' practices. The stated intention was to avoid lengthy enquiries. However the streamlining was poorly designed. It took the Director-General a year to investigate and publish a report, and if his report was critical of a firm's behaviour everything went to the Commission for them to confirm the existence of an anti-competitive practice and to adjudge whether it was against the public interest. The process was far from speedy.

With Macmillan taking the initiative in 1963 his Government was beginning to get to grips with a realistic national policy to promote competition. In the intervening years this has gone astray, although the Competition Court of the EEC can be effective.

In the early 1960s a prominent economist, A. D. Neale, and an eminent Professor of Law, Robert Stephens, warned of the dangers of bringing courts of justice into the 'realm' of economic assessment because judges were not equipped to make economic decisions, and all the courts could do was to evaluate facts concerned with price rings and restrictive intent. They were correct; the Government alone should decide which industries should in the national interest be allowed to fix prices higher than price competition would allow. This lesson has never been accepted by British Governments.[10]

Because Britain was a free trade country after the repeal of the Corn

Laws in 1846 until the Import Duties Act of 1932 it is much overlooked that the 1932 Act gave British manufacturing industry high tariff protection against imports from other modern industrialized countries, which often eliminated price competition from abroad. In addition during the Second World War contracts for government supplies on a cost plus basis were common, and this created the cost plus mentality which was rife by the sixties. Trade unions, conscious that employers could raise their selling prices and maintain profit margins regardless of how high wage settlements were, exacted the last ounce of flesh and the employers remained complacent. As a result the unit cost of manufactures in Britain soared while it was falling in the EEC.

When in 1963 the shock of the de Gaulle veto exposed the glaring lack of an alternative economic policy the Macmillan Government nearly grasped the nettle and were, in the last months of his premiership, about to produce policies which would have forced the cold wind of price competition to blow through British industry. If this had happened, as Macmillan intended, the efficiency, which was eventually created by the onslaught of the Thatcher Government on trade unions together with price competition from Common Market imports, could have been produced much earlier without the wholesale closure of British factories and enterprises.

CHAPTER 11

Kenya

IN 1957 THE British Government accepted demands for independence from the Gold Coast Colony. In 1951 under a new constitution this colony had been given almost complete self-government, and in 1957 Dr Kwame Nkrumah became the first Prime Minister of a newly independent Ghana, the rechristened Gold Coast. A single chamber known as the National Assembly was elected by direct popular vote and four separate regions had their own assemblies.

Accepting Ghana's demand for independence was a historic step which set British Africa on the same path as India. The former Gold Coast not only possessed a competent administration but was one of the strongest economies in Africa. Though politically Ghana became a sad story, at first it was looked on as a model of decolonization – a textbook example of wise evolution – until Nkrumah was ousted from power in 1966 during his absence on a visit to China. However Ghana, unlike the other British African colonies, had been adequately prepared for independence by the presence of reasonable schools and a university and this gave her advantages over the other African colonies.

Nigeria became independent in 1960, and under its admirable president Sir Abubakar Balewa overcame internal divisions until his tragic death in January 1966. Sierra Leone, also on the African West Coast, became in nearly every respect independent in 1958, and fully independent following a constitutional conference in April 1961.

Ghana, Nigeria and Sierra Leone thus created a pattern of evolution from colonial status to full independence. The umbilical cords attaching the colonies to Whitehall, however, only became fully severed with full independence. The pace of change in these three colonies was faster than in India although in comparison with India there were far fewer people with sufficient education and experience of civil administration to take over the reins. Fortunately in these West African countries enough education had been provided to furnish a modicum of ministers and officials who were able to undertake successfully the difficulties of running the state. Unfortunately in the Central African

221

colonies and Kenya education of black people lagged far behind West Africa.

By 1959 although the educational system in Nyasaland, Northern and Southern Rhodesia and Kenya was inadequate for early independence, the march of events in Africa, which culminated in the swift departure of the Belgians from the Belgian Congo, was such that their independence could only be long delayed by the use of military force. Alan Lennox-Boyd, who was Macmillan's first Colonial Secretary from 1957 to 1959, wanted to curb the pace of change towards self-rule in Central and East Africa and to maintain the *status quo* for as long as possible.

Kenya was a white man's country with economic power firmly in European hands. Kenya's farmers, many of them British ex-servicemen, who had gone to the country with the financial support and encouragement of successive British governments, including the post-war Attlee Labour Government, were prospering. With its varied altitudes and rainfall, Kenya provided profitable farming for white settlers, and in the White Highlands, the most fertile area, blacks were not allowed to own farms.

Neither the Colonial Office in Whitehall nor the colonial administrators in Kenya in the late fifties faced up to the coming inevitability of black rule and independence, and they ignored the events in West Africa. With Ghana independent in 1957 and the Nigerian approach to that status gathering momentum, the Central and East African colonies, although more backward, could not remain an oasis bypassed by the move to black rule.

The Governors of Kenya, Sir Evelyn Baring until 1959, and Sir Patrick Renison later, and their European officials were less enthusiastic for a quick change to African rule than their counterparts in other colonies, and ruled it out because of the number of European settlers and the fact that new arrivals had been sponsored since the war by both the Labour and Conservative governments; government-aided farm settlement schemes for white people were still in operation in 1959, enabling European settlers to farm in the fertile areas reserved for them in Kenya with the aid of cash grants. As late as 1958 Lennox-Boyd had announced in a well-publicized speech at the Conservative Party Conference that the British Government would maintain their responsibility for Kenya into the future. The settlers, and especially the assisted post-war ones, had every reason to believe that Kenya would continue almost indefinitely as a self-governing British colony under white rule. Suddenly at the end of 1959 Macmillan decided to move quickly towards African majority rule.

Since 1952 there had been a state of emergency in Kenya because of the atrocities and widespread terrorist activities of the Mau Mau, a secret society of the Kikuyu (20 per cent of the population) who had revolted against white rule under the leadership of Jomo Kenyatta; he and around a thousand of his leading activists were now in prison, but the terror and violence were so extensive that a large British military force had to be sent to Kenya to put down the rebellion.

By the time the British army had restored law and order and put a stop to the barbarity, there had been appalling loss of life amongst both Africans and Europeans. 80,000 Africans, mainly members of the Kikuyu tribe, were detained in custody at the end of hostilities, though by the end of 1959 all but 4,000 who were serving prison sentences and 1,000 'hard-core incorrigibles' in special camps had been released.

Because of the great number of white settlers earning a livelihood in this beautiful country and enjoying paternal relations with their African employees, the situation in Kenya was quite different from Ghana and Nigeria. The white population could not believe that after being encouraged to settle there by both Conservative and Labour governments they would be asked to hand over their farms to the black people. The atrocities of the Mau Mau rebellion had also created a revulsion amongst those who lived through it; they deemed the African leaders unfit for government. As late as January 1959 the Macmillan Government were giving the Kenyan white settlers the misleading impression that African majority rule was a long way off. Lennox-Boyd presided over a conference in London attended by the Governors of the three East African colonies, Tanganyika, Kenya and Uganda, at which it was tentatively decided and published that Tanganyika might achieve independence by 1970; Kenya by 1975 and Uganda somewhere between the two. In the event Tanganyika became independent in 1961, Uganda in 1962, and Kenya in 1963.

In 1959 there was a tragedy at the Hola detention camp in Kenya. Eleven Mau Mau detainees died in circumstances which aroused serious dismay and indignation and produced a censure motion in the Commons. The deaths were initially attributed to lack of water, but when the truth emerged it was crystal clear they had died from beatings by warders: these were attempting to use forced labour to break the hard core of fanaticism among detainees who were resisting the work of pacification already successfully accomplished amongst many thousands of members of the savage Mau Mau cult. In a Commons debate on 17 July 1959 the Opposition charged the Government with lack of Ministerial responsibility, and claimed that the camp superintendent had been made a scapegoat when the authorities in Kenya and the Colonial Office knew, or ought to have known, of the danger of these deaths. Lennox-Boyd denied that there had been any attempt at 'white-

'washing' but announced that a special commissioner would be appointed to oversee the detention camps and the policy of rehabilitation of the Mau Mau.*

In an article in the *Weekend Telegraph* on 12 March 1965 Iain Macleod suggested that the Hola Camp incident had achieved more than the Nyasaland emergency† in making Macmillan change his mind about the pace of transfer of power from whites to blacks in Africa. Macmillan never denied this.

Following the October 1959 General Election Macmillan decided that Iain Macleod should replace Alan Lennox-Boyd as Colonial Secretary, with the general brief to speed up the rate of advance towards African rule which had been curbed by Lennox-Boyd. Macleod had been outstandingly successful as Minister of Health and Minister of Labour and National Service; Macmillan had faith in him. Unfortunately, by the end of Macleod's term at the Colonial Office they were on bad terms. Macleod felt passionately about issues and his views on the need for a rapid move towards self-rule in Africa were too radical for the Prime Minister.

In the Commons Macleod had command of the House. His election speeches had been highly successful and he was probably the Minister most popular with the electorate. However his manner was often abrupt, impatient or cold, and many considered him rude. He disliked wasting his time and became restive in the face of muddled thinking and discussion of irrelevant matters. This was a grave drawback in solving sensitive problems such as those at the Colonial Office. Fortunately he was warm and pleasant with the African leaders – less so with the white settler lobby. The civil servants were all on his side and much appreciated his mastery of detail and capacity to make quick and firm decisions.

The first problem confronting him was Kenya. White settlers occupied all the best farm land which was alienated from the Africans. At the end of the Second World War the population consisted of 5¼ million Africans, 30,000 Europeans and 124,000 other non-Africans, mostly Indians and Arabs. Kenya had become a Crown Colony in 1920, and the Government was in the hands of white settlers though nominally subject to Whitehall.

With the aim of considering a new constitution and a move to majority rule, Macleod inaugurated the Kenya Conference at Lancaster House in London in January 1960; it lasted six weeks. Prior to its opening

---

* A full enquiry into Hola by W. H. Gouldie, a senior resident magistrate, was published in June 1959 (Cmd 778).
† See Chapter 12, pages 232 ff.

Macleod had taken the important decision to suspend the state of emergency and to release all the terrorist detainees apart from Kenyatta and a few hundred ringleaders: he was determined to set up a new constitution for Kenya with power in the hands of the Africans.

In his opening speech Macleod, to the horror of Lord Salisbury and the right-wing Conservatives, announced that the time had come to recognize that majority rule must come in Kenya; the Africans were the majority race. The African delegates immediately demanded the release of Kenyatta. Macleod took a strong line and refused even to discuss it.

The conference was stormy and marked by walkouts; for a moment indeed it looked as if the conference would not take place at all because of African insistence that Kenyatta, who was still under restriction, should take part. Macleod throughout took the line that the future of Kenya lay with the Africans, and he refused to be deflected by the strenuous opposition of Lord Salisbury and other influential Conservatives, although Macmillan had qualms that the Parliamentary Conservative Party would become dangerously split.

In the absence of Kenyatta Tom Mboya led the African delegation. Fortunately he was a moderate, while the radical Michael Blundell who had farmed in the White Highlands since the twenties acted as a bridge between the settlers and the Africans. Blundell at first formed the impression from Macleod that the British Government were planning a delay of between eight to twelve years before independence was granted, and Lord Salisbury was told by a senior Minister that British control would continue for at least ten years. However, as discussions went on, Blundell and his colleagues accepted that Macleod favoured a reasonable timetable for government by Africans.

Macmillan was travelling in Africa during the Kenya Conference but was kept abreast of things by numerous telegrams from Macleod. At this stage the Prime Minister and his Colonial Secretary were agreed on the rough timetable for the handing over of power in Kenya to Africans; later they were to be in bitter disagreement over it.

The conference produced an agreed new constitution for Kenya with only Captain Briggs of the extreme right-wing European Party dissenting. The plan envisaged a council of Ministers composed of four officials and eight 'unofficials' of whom four were to be Africans, three Europeans and one Asian. In addition there was to be a legislative council of sixty-five members elected by 1¼ million Africans and the Europeans. This meant eventual government by Africans.

The decision by the British Government at the 1960 Kenya Conference to opt for African majority rule caused much heart-burning within the Conservative Party; Macleod was savagely criticized and became mistrusted and disliked by a section of his own Party. However, to delay a decision in favour of the Africans would have plunged Kenya back into civil war, and as Michael Blundell writes, 'The only alternative was to shoot Africans with bullets for the next ten years.'

Macmillan agreed with reluctance. Symptomatic of his state of mind was his alarm at press reports on 21 April 1960 of the imminent release of Kenyatta. Macleod soothed him with a minute: 'There is not, and never has been, any intention of releasing Kenyatta. There is no comparison between Nyasaland and the seven-year tragedy of Mau Mau . . . The end of the emergency is very near . . . It is conceivable that the day may come when it might be advisable to release him out of Kenya perhaps to Ghana.' Macleod then instructed the Governor of Kenya, Sir Patrick Renison, to make a firm statement that Kenyatta would not be released, and himself made a similar statement in the Commons.[1]

In fact at the Kenya Conference, in a moment of pique, Macleod had spoken off the record of his intention to release Kenyatta. The Governor, Renison, was strongly opposed and soon afterwards made a speech describing Kenyatta as 'the leader to darkness and death'. Macleod for once held his fire and did not comment on Renison's provocative remarks; nor did he sack him although he seriously considered it. At that time few Europeans foresaw the golden opinions they would form of Kenyatta after he came to power. Duncan Sandys, who in 1960 was opposed to Kenyatta's release, said of him in 1964: 'If every Commonwealth statesman was as wise, as co-operative and as helpful as Jomo Kenyatta there would be no problems in the Commonwealth.'

In March 1961 a General Election, fought largely on the emotive issue of Kenyatta's release, was held in Kenya. Inevitably the two African parties KANU and KADU obtained a large overall majority but Tom Mboya, leader of KANU, the more popular party, refused to take office unless Kenyatta was released, thus throwing away a glittering opportunity of being Kenya's eventual leader in place of Kenyatta. Renison refused Mboya's condition so that KADU formed an interim administration with the help of the European New Kenyan Party under Ronald Ngala, leader of KADU. The African electorate and politicians were extremely sensitive to suggestions that Britain would not really allow them to be free, and that African majority rule was a hoax. Fortunately many of the candidates chosen by the European voters in the primary contest were not elected to the legislature because the Africans voting on the common roll rejected them in favour of more progressive Europeans who were less ready to hold out for white privilege.

With the problems of forming a government in Kenya after the March 1961 election Macleod again seriously considered Kenyatta's release. On 18 April 1961 Lord Home, Foreign Secretary, minuted to Macmillan that Lord Swinton, an influential former Cabinet Minister, had said release would cause a revolt in the Conservative Party and he (Swinton) 'would be among the rebels'. Home gave it as his own opinion that 'The idea of release was repugnant to decent-minded people.'[2] Kenyatta's release was demanded not only by the Africans, but also by a number of progressive younger Conservative MPs, together with the Labour and Liberal parties. However Macmillan became increasingly concerned at the opposition of a large and important section of Conservative MPs and influential peers and temporarily stalled.

Finally early in July 1961, after consulting with their Whitehall advisers, Macleod and Renison made the decision to release Kenyatta, moving him as a first stage into Kikuyu country twenty miles from Nairobi. Here Kenyatta consulted with other African political leaders. He proved mild and moderate in talks, and obviously a good influence on the disputing KANU and KADU parties. In mid-July 1961 Macleod told Macmillan orally that he had decided to set Kenyatta free. Macmillan demurred, and hoped to postpone the announcement: he had just taken the decision to announce Britain's application to the EEC and, worried about the knock-on effect on the Conservative Party, did not want another controversy simultaneously.

Macleod was furious and sent an agonized memorandum to the Prime Minister on 26 July 1961, implying that he was considering resignation if he did not get his way. 'We shall never be in a better position to take this decision than now,' he stated, and he was concerned at the effect of a refusal on his personal position within the Party:

> There is almost universal agreement in Kenya that Kenyatta should be released, and overwhelming support here. No doubt Lord Beaverbrook[*] will be angry, but the rest of the press I am certain will not be, particularly as we can say that the senior members of the administration in Kenya and the police and the Kikuyu loyalists believe this is the right thing to do. Overwhelmingly again, the two Houses of Parliament are reconciled to this action, and expect some sort of statement before the recess. The position is becoming almost impossible to hold in Kenya where yesterday the Governor [Renison] had to telephone from Nairobi that the resignation of his Government was imminent unless we could make a statement on Kenyatta fairly soon. That would be a disastrous outcome of all our work in Kenya particularly now that Kenya with luck has turned the corner.
>
> In the House of Commons yesterday I thought it likely seeing that debate took place on my salary that we would have a number of abstentions and even possibly a number of votes against. In the end nobody abstained and even Turton [a notorious pro-settler Tory MP] came into the Division Lobby. But all this is going to be jeopardized if I shuffle off with a statement

---

[*] Still a great supporter of imperialism and white supremacy.

on Friday of next week [the last day of the session].* Moreover this will be disastrous in the Lords where our strongest critics are not even sitting on the day and will be justifiably incensed at what they would regard as a back door approach to a difficult decision. If I have to make the statement on the Friday I know that all the careful relationships which I have re-established even with my critics in the House of Commons are going to go by the board, and although I recognize to the full the arguments for postponing the statement to Friday I do hope you will consider letting me make it on Tuesday ... I must say frankly that I will feel deeply and personally unhappy if I have to put this statement off until Friday, and I am convinced that it will do a great deal of harm in Kenya where I may not be able to hold the Government together (see for example this morning's *Guardian*), and also to my own personal position in the House. Everybody expects a statement from me and indeed I have virtually promised it and no one will, I am sure, expect me to make it on the Friday ... the issues at stake are very important.[3]

With the Common Market issue weighing so heavily on his mind Macmillan was not prepared for a showdown with the volatile Macleod and could ill afford a dramatic resignation of the kind which his letter seemed to contemplate. Instead of arguing, the Prime Minister caved in and asked the Chief Whip to make arrangements for Macleod's statement to be made both in the Commons and the Lords the next day.

The following morning, Tuesday, 27 July, the matter was put to the Cabinet. There was opposition, and misgivings were expressed, but the 'balance of opinion' was that there was no alternative because the Government would be strongly criticized if they made the announcement during the recess; on the other hand the announcement would not be well received by a section of government supporters, and if it were made in the following week it would add to the Government's difficulties over the Common Market announcement. According to the minutes no Minister argued against Kenyatta's release.[4]

In November 1961 Kenyatta came to London nominally as a private citizen but in fact as the national leader of the majority KANU party which was solidly behind him. Kenyatta made an excellent impression on politicians and civil servants although a member of the League of Empire Loyalists threw the entrails of a sheep wrapped in a *Times* newspaper at him during a press conference at the Eccleston Hotel, shouting 'Take that, you bloody butcher Kenyatta.'

It now became clear that, despite his disreputable connection with the Mau Mau, Britain would have to recognize Kenyatta as the ruler

---

* This is obviously what Macmillan had suggested to him in an effort to get the EEC announcement out of the way first.

designate of Kenya. A constitutional conference was held in London in February and March 1962. Several times it came near to breakdown but finally, by astute chairmanship, Maudling, who had replaced Macleod as Colonial Secretary, persuaded KANU and KADU to agree to the formation of a coalition national government with equal status for Kenyatta and Ngala, the leader of KADU. Maudling manoeuvred both parties into accepting a constitution which provided for a strong central government with regional governments enjoying wide autonomous powers of which the most important were control of most land (except the controversial White Highlands) and the police.

Kenyatta and his KANU colleagues were convinced that Kenya instead ought to have a strong unitary government, and it was a sterile negotiating triumph for Maudling when he persuaded KANU to agree to a regional policy; British colonial officials in Kenya were also opposed to regionalism. On 2 March 1962 Kenyatta wrote a letter to *The Times*, pointing out that KANU had won 67 per cent of the votes against 16 per cent by KADU, and stating, 'You cannot suppress and frustrate a majority without serious risks.' As KANU were categorically opposed to regional government this should have been the red light for the Macmillan Government: it made clear that the regional government constitution disliked by KANU was little more than pie-in-the-sky. For eleven months KANU and KADU wrangled in committee over the boundaries of the regions.

The Maudling constitutional framework could not easily be put into legal form and Duncan Sandys, who had become both Colonial Secretary and Commonwealth Relations Secretary when Maudling was made Chancellor in the summer of 1962, spent three weeks in Kenya in February 1963 trying to sort out the quarrels. On 18 April 1963 the most complicated constitution ever devised for a former British colony was produced two days before nomination day for the May elections. It contained 233 clauses covering 223 pages. For a government which maintained that proportional representation was too complicated for British voters to understand it was a monstrosity for an emergent African country.[5]

In the General Election in May KANU, as was inevitable, won a large majority, and immediately the Kenyatta Government declared their intention of changing the constitution. Successive British governments had been culpably dilatory in training Africans for civil service posts and the process of creating a regional administration was proving beyond the capabilities of the experienced British colonial officials.

In September and October 1963 a fundamental dispute over the type of future government for an independent Kenya arose, with considerable display of ill will, at the final pre-independence conference in London,

KANU demanding the end of the regional system and KADU fighting to preserve it. The British Government's problem was that they had to launch Kenya into independence with a constitution acceptable to the ruling party; otherwise an independent government would immediately tear it up.

On 19 October 1963 Sandys announced that he would back-pedal on the Maudling agreement of the previous year 'in the true interest of Kenya in the years ahead', and in a revised constitution he strengthened the central government and weakened that of the regions. Ngala of KADU accused Sandys of dishonesty, but this was no more than point-scoring. The Macmillan Government had no other option than to revise the Maudling 1962 constitution; to have insisted on it would have been irresponsible when KANU rejected it. Had Macleod's 1960 policy been followed, and Maudling been prevented from imposing the regional provisions of the 1962 constitution, the independence of Kenya would have begun on a far happier note.

A large sum of British taxpayers' money was provided to buy out the farms of the white settlers who refused to accept African rule, and on 12 December 1963 Kenya became independent. Kenyatta proved a wise leader and statesman, and against all Macmillan's fears and predictions it was Britain's most successful effort at decolonization, thus completely contradicting misgivings expressed by Macmillan in his diary at the end of 1961: 'If we have to give independence to Kenya, it may well prove another Congo. If we hold on, it will mean a long and cruel campaign – Mau Mau and all that.'[6] Instead most white settlers continued to live on in their farms more or less in harmony with their African rulers.

CHAPTER 12

Wind of Change

MACMILLAN WROTE IN his memoirs that the concluding years of his premiership were haunted, not to say 'poisoned', by the growing tension in the Central African Federation. He made himself chairman of the Cabinet Africa Committee in October 1959, and followed every move in detail until in desperation he suddenly handed control over to Butler in March 1962.[1]

Eden as Prime Minister fussed his Ministers with phone calls and notes, and was much criticized for this. This was nothing to the state into which Macmillan worked himself over Welensky and African majorities in the preparation of a new constitution for Northern Rhodesia. The Government's behaviour is best described by W. P. Kirkman, *The Times* African expert, who followed events closely, 'as negotiations went on continually and often acrimoniously. Decisions were made and unmade. Pressures were brought to bear; threats were uttered, tempers flared. The British Government staggered through it all, battered on all sides, conducting matters of high policy in a hole in a corner fashion, speaking through different Ministries with different voices.' The archives support Kirkman.[2]

The Central African Federation was created by the Conservative Government of Winston Churchill in 1953 out of the three British colonies, Southern and Northern Rhodesia and Nyasaland. The fusion had the blessing of the Labour Party but was against the wishes of the black majority. The Federal Government under their Prime Minister Roy Welensky were responsible to the Federal Parliament which was elected by the voters (mainly white) of the three territories. Its status in some ways resembled that of an independent member of the Commonwealth but each former colony retained a colonial governor and had an elected governing council. The Federal Government over its own affairs dealt with the Commonwealth Relations Office; in respect of its responsibilities towards Northern Rhodesia and Nyasaland it dealt mainly with the Colonial Office. In a final resort the British Government had a right of veto over the Federation and over the other three elected bodies.

Economically the union made sense because it combined the rich copper belt of Northern Rhodesia (Zambia) with the agricultural countries of Southern Rhodesia (Zimbabwe) and Nyasaland (Malawi). However Southern Rhodesia had a European population out of proportion to the mix in the other two colonies and this wealthy white minority were determined to continue indefinitely with European rule – a situation which was clearly impossible, except in the short term, in Nyasaland and Northern Rhodesia where there were few Europeans.

The creation of the Federation was violently opposed by the Africans in all three territories; apart from everything else, they felt strongly that the protection of the Westminster Parliament was being withdrawn, leaving them at the mercy of the European settlers.

Little provision had been made for African political advancement, and the strength of African feeling against the creation of the Federation was largely ignored. Government of the Central African Federation was placed in the hands of the whites as Sir Roy Welensky became Prime Minister. The British Government in 1957 effectively gave up control of the internal affairs of the Federation which resulted in nothing being done to satisfy African aspirations for more political power and eventual majority rule. The Federal leaders under Welensky were dedicated to preserving white supremacy, and there was no question of black and white partnership. There was one coloured Minister, Jasper Savanhu, and he resigned in 1962 on the grounds that the Federal Government had never made any effort to implement a policy of partnership.

The Colonial Secretary in early 1959, Alan Lennox-Boyd, was an enthusiast for the Central African Federation and had strong support from Lord Salisbury and the settler lobby of the Conservative Party in the Lords and Commons. However the Labour and Liberal opposition were conducting an effective propaganda campaign against the existence of the Federation, drawing much attention to the right-wing views of Roy Welensky and his Dominion Party colleagues who had a majority in the Federal Parliament.

The Macmillan Cabinet were already worried about the Federation when serious riots broke out in Nyasaland as a result of which a state of emergency was declared by the Governor, Sir Robert Armitage, on 3 March 1959. It was no longer impossible to disguise the weight of opposition to the existence of the Federation by Africans in all three territories. The immediate appointment of the Devlin Commission* to enquire into the causes of the Nyasaland riots soothed public opinion temporarily but grave disquiet about the whole future of the Federation

---

*See below, pages 238–42.

and the overall problems of the three territories were expressed at a Cabinet meeting on 12 March. A constitutional conference on the future of the Federation had already been scheduled for the following year. Concluding the 12 March discussion, Macmillan said: 'The wider problem – can the Federation continue in its present form? – must be studied before the Constitutional Conference agreed for 1960.'

On 17 March 1959 the Cabinet decided to set up a Royal Commission to 'advise upon the future of the Federation' and to provide evidence for the discussions at the forthcoming constitutional review. Macmillan said in a speech that the aim of the Royal Commission was 'to dispel widespread ignorance of the purpose and working of the Federation'. Sir Walter Monckton, who had been a member of the Eden Government at the time of Suez, was invited to head this Royal Commission. He had a good reputation as an appeaser of the trade unions from his time as Minister of Labour during the Churchill Government of 1951–5 and Macmillan hoped he would be acceptable to the Opposition.[3]

Immediately Welensky and his Federal Ministers expressed violent opposition to the creation of the Royal Commission. Earlier that month Lord Perth, Minister of State for the Colonies, had been sent out to try to conciliate him – unsuccessfully. Perth was followed by Home on 1 April. Home warned Welensky that if Labour came to power in the forthcoming election they would almost certainly allow both Nyasaland and Northern Rhodesia to have the option of secession and that would destroy the Federation. Welensky replied that all the Africans had to do was to have a riot and then a Commission would immediately be sent out from England 'to decide whether or not they were right', and if there were Labour Party members of the Commission they would be sure to issue a minority report advocating secession.

The Prime Minister wrote to Gaitskell pleading with him to nominate Labour representatives to the Monckton Commission, writing: 'Unless we can succeed in creating a common mind on the next stage of evolution for the Federation there is a prospect of real trouble.' Gaitskell refused to co-operate unless the terms of reference of the Commission were extended to include the possible liquidation of the Federation. However, soon after the General Election of 1959 he proposed that James Callaghan, the Shadow spokesman on Africa, should join.[4]

At the suggestion of Callaghan's joining, Welensky frantically urged Macmillan to abandon the Commission altogether. Macmillan soothed Welensky to a certain extent by assuring him that he would on no account extend the terms of reference to include examination of secession and the UK Government would not allow the Commission to be made an instrument of attack on the Federal or territorial colonial governments. (The three territories had their own white-dominated elected governments under the Federal Government of Welensky.) Macmillan explained to Welensky that Labour opposition to joining the Commission was due to the Government's insistence that 'secession' was outside its terms of reference.[5] Callaghan was not appointed.

Dr Hastings Banda, an intelligent and charming medical practitioner in London, and a man of great charisma, became president of the Congress Party of Nyasaland, the main African party. In June 1958 Banda had told a crowd in Nyasaland, 'I am not anti-European, still less am I anti-British. My task here is to bridge the gap of disunity.' However six months later in December he had been so antagonized by the rigid policies of Lennox-Boyd and the Governor of Nyasaland, Sir Robert Armitage, who refused to support the Nyasaland Africans against the reactionary policies of Welensky and the white majority in the Federal Parliament, that he had completely changed his tone. He proclaimed that civil disobedience, passive resistance and non-violence would be the policy of his Nyasaland Congress Party, and stated: 'In Nyasaland we mean to be masters and if that is treasonable make the most of it.'[6]

On 3 March 1959, in a debate in the Commons following the serious disturbances in Nyasaland in February, Lennox-Boyd quoted information which had reached the Governor of Nyasaland to the effect that plans had been made by Dr Banda and his political party for widespread violence and murder of Europeans, Asians and moderate African leaders – in fact that a massacre was being planned. This was cited as justification for the Governor's declaration of the state of emergency that day. Fifty-two Africans were killed by security forces in the period following the declaration of the state of emergency.

In the early hours of that morning, 3 March, in an operation known as 'Sunrise', every influential African leader – in practice almost all the office-bearers of the African Congress Party – had been arrested, including Dr Banda. In the Commons the Opposition refused to accept Lennox-Boyd's explanation of the need for a state of emergency, and the Government's Commission of Enquiry was duly appointed under the High Court judge Lord Devlin, with Sir J. Ure Primrose, Sir P. Wyn Harris and Sir Edgar Williams as members.*

The Devlin Report was finalized in early July; the last part described the retaliation of the Nyasaland Government against those who supported Dr Banda's Congress Party and how houses were burnt, implements confiscated and unnecessary force and punitive toughness used in arrests. The last lines queried 'whether sound administrative reasons can

---

* Sir Edgar Williams was Warden of Rhodes House, and during the Second World War Field Marshal Montgomery's Chief of Intelligence at 8th Army; Sir John Primrose was a Scottish farmer; Sir P. Wyn Harris was a Chief Native Commissioner in Kenya.

justify breaches of law'. Its most damaging conclusions were that 'no evidence' had been produced to support the Government's assertion that the Nyasaland Congress Party had been plotting 'massacre and assassination' which the Government alleged as the reason for imposing the state of emergency; 'Nyasaland is – no doubt temporarily – a police state where it is not safe for anyone to express approval of the policies of the Congress Party.'

The Devlin Report was highly critical both of the Governor and the Colonial Office, and as soon as Lennox-Boyd read it he cabled to the Governor, Sir Robert Armitage, 'As we both expected it is a very hostile report'; he was having urgent discussions about the next step and would possibly hold up publication until 'we have a full counter-blast ready'. The date of the General Election had already been tentatively fixed and Macmillan was concerned at the harm the Devlin Report might do to Conservative popularity.

On 16 July the Prime Minister held a meeting at 10 Downing Street with Lennox-Boyd, the Minister of State Lord Perth, Commonwealth Relations Secretary Lord Home, and Sir Norman Brook, Secretary to the Cabinet. The evening before, Lord Perth had discussed the report with Devlin in the House of Lords when the judge had said Britain must choose between benevolent despotic rule or else releasing responsibility to the natives; 'colonial administration', he had added, 'did not seem to concern itself with the law as such.' Devlin told Perth he would be prepared to consider some changes in his report. After discussing the report Macmillan and his advisers thought that 'the best step would be to omit Appendix One' and Lord Perth was asked to take this up with Devlin again.[7]

Appendix One was a summary which the Commission had included so that 'people who do not think it necessary to read the whole narrative may wish to know what conclusions of fact we have reached'. In his talks with Perth Devlin agreed that 'any summary' would be the only part read by the press who would pick out sentences to the exclusion of everything else in the report. He finally agreed to omit Appendix One.

Normally the Cabinet would not be able to discuss the contents of such a report and ask for changes but by some extraordinary oversight the Stationery Office had sent the proofs to the Colonial Office and Welensky, whereas their duty was to send them in strict confidentiality only to the Secretary to the Commission. The Government seized upon this breach of protocol to press Devlin for amendments. They got only small change out of him.

Meeting to consider Perth's approach to Devlin regarding alterations to the report, the four members of the Commission – Devlin, Williams, Ure Primrose and Wyn Harris – decided reluctantly that it would be better to stick to recording facts without saying anything which could be considered to be comment, 'however outrageous some of the facts may be'. As a result, Sections 289–95 which formed Appendix One were deleted and a new section headed 'Governmental Responsibility' was inserted in its place.*

Wyn Harris was unhappy about this and in his own words 'argued passionately' with Devlin, because he did not agree that the first draft was 'in any respects unfair' and he was 'very disturbed' at this doctoring of the report. He was particularly anxious that it should be made clear that the police had 'gagged suspects' and that one of the senior policemen, he considered, did not regard the people he was arresting as 'human beings'; he was 'disgusted' at the treatment of detainees in the camps, and by the refusal of the British police giving evidence to express remorse for their actions. However when Devlin assured him that the report had lost none of its significance by the changes he fell into line.

On 21 July Perth wrote to Devlin: 'My dear Pat ... Whatever the reactions to the Report may be, it is very clear that the Commission have done their best to evaluate the facts and to present them fairly. You have performed a great service in the face of many difficulties.' Perth's letter was not for publication but it was a great contrast to the abuse which his Conservative colleagues showered on Devlin in the Commons and the Lords.

Macmillan told Lennox-Boyd and Home the Government must make a reply 'of a robust nature' and that Armitage, who was arriving from Africa the next day, should be taken down to Chequers by Lennox-Boyd for a working weekend to prepare the 'counter-blast'. Lennox-Boyd was particularly perturbed by the words in the Devlin Report, 'these illegalities were expressly or implicitly authorized from the top', in relation to the charge of burning houses.

After a hearing of six weeks in Africa and taking evidence from 465 individuals and 1,300 in groups, the Devlin Report disclosed that 44 men and 4 women had been killed by gunfire, 3 by batons or bayonets, while 79 had suffered bullet wounds. The report vindicated the Government's declaration of a state of emergency, but was highly critical of the action taken by the police and military once the state of emergency had been declared. According to a memorandum by Norman Brook, the Government would find it particularly difficult to rebut charges that 'unnecessary violence was used in the initial round-up of Congress leaders' and 'the policy that every crowd must be dispersed if necessary by shooting

---

* Welensky has compared the draft and final Devlin reports in his book *4,000 Days*, pages 131–4. The draft is in the Rhodes House archives, but not in the Public Record Office.

was precipitate and unacceptable.' However Brook commented: 'The need to enforce respect [for law and order] is infinitely greater in places like Nyasaland where a handful of white people are controlling hordes of primitive people. If crowds are once allowed to get out of control anything may happen ... The report does at least uphold the sincerity of the motives of the actions taken by individual officers in the riots.'

Brook thought Devlin showed that the suppression of the Congress movement and the assertion of government authority were undertaken in a tough and punitive spirit; the report had some pretty stiff comments about the use of force in villages, the burning of houses and confiscation of implements, and it found that a general policy of toughness was authorized expressly or implicitly by the Government of Nyasaland. The Cabinet immediately decided to reject the Devlin Report. William Kirkman, *The Times*' Africa correspondent at that period, has written that the decision to reject it was 'by any standards a depressing example of the triumph of expediency over principle' and 'a shameful exercise in electoral expediency'. It is impossible to dissent from his judgement after reading the archives.[8]

When Macmillan read the Devlin Report he was angry both at the content and with Devlin. In his diary he wrote:

> The poor Lord Chancellor [Lord Kilmuir], the sweetest and most naïve of men, chose him. He was able; a Conservative runner-up, or nearly so, for Lord Chief Justice. I have since discovered that he is (a) Irish – no doubt with Fenian blood that makes Irishmen anti-Government on principle. (b) A lapsed Roman Catholic. His brother is a Jesuit priest.[9]*

Macmillan also felt that Devlin had been bitterly disappointed at 'my not having made him Lord Chief Justice'. Macmillan was astray in attributing the Devlin Report to anti-Government bias on the part of Devlin and his colleagues. All were Conservative sympathizers and Devlin himself was right wing; that Devlin even discussed alterations in the report with Lord Perth is evidence of his sympathy for the Government. The Devlin Report was an unprejudiced and accurate account of reprehensible government action in Nyasaland.

At the same time as the Devlin Commission reported, the Government, and Lennox-Boyd in particular as Colonial Secretary, were under heavy fire over the Hola detention camp incident in Kenya in March 1959. There, as explained above, eleven Mau Mau detainees had died in circumstances which gave rise to grave dismay and indignation and extensive adverse press comment: initially the deaths were attributed to

---

*This was correct; his brother Christopher Devlin was a Jesuit.

lack of water but the evidence showed plainly that they had died from beatings by warders who were using them for forced labour.*

The full enquiry into the Hola incident by W. H. Gouldie, a senior Kenyan resident magistrate, published in June 1959, showed that the deaths were due to 'multiple beatings'. There was no doubt, Gouldie stated in the White Paper, that there had been a failure to provide efficient control because responsibility was shared between two Ministers in the Governor's Council. Unfortunately the Colonial Office had just given an MBE to one of the officials criticized by Gouldie.

On 16 June Hola was debated in the Commons. For the Opposition Sir Frank Soskice, the former Attorney-General, made a strong case against both Lennox-Boyd and the Governor based mainly on the coroner's report. Lennox-Boyd in a long speech frankly admitted mistakes and muddles over Hola but gained sympathy by emphasizing how the original 80,000 Mau Mau detainees had been whittled down to 1,000 by effective rehabilitation.

After the debate, with Labour crying out both for his resignation and a public enquiry, Lennox-Boyd thought he must accept responsibility for the Hola tragedy and resign. With difficulty Macmillan persuaded him to withdraw his resignation, arguing that it would force the Governor of Kenya, Sir Evelyn Baring,† to resign as well, 'which would be a tragic end to a fine career of voluntary service in Africa'.

Macmillan suggested to Lennox-Boyd that he should write a despatch to the Governor giving his view of the affair, laying down certain principles for the future and asking what the Governor now proposed to do; the Governor in his reply should set out the organizational changes he envisaged, while the most notorious figures concerned with Hola would be transferred to other jobs or colonies. This correspondence should then be published. Lennox-Boyd agreed with the Prime Minister; he sent instructions to the Governor and these with the Governor's reply were published as a White Paper. This put the blame on the camp superintendent who was sacked, while another official took early retirement. No blame was cast on anyone higher up.[10]

This second Hola White Paper came at a bad time for the Government, coinciding in late July 1959 with completion of the Devlin Report in the last fortnight of the final Parliamentary session before the 1959 General Election.

Lennox-Boyd, who had decided to leave the Commons at the coming General Election, again wanted to resign. He now faced on consecutive days in the Commons debates on the report on the Hola

---

* See Chapter 11, pages 223–4.
† Later Lord Howick of Glendale.

Camp deaths, and the Devlin Report. He felt a sense of guilt and knew it would be difficult for him to justify the actions of the Colonial Office under him over both Hola and Nyasaland. *The Times* wrote: 'Tactically Lennox-Boyd could not be more vulnerable because he cannot attack Devlin'; he was 'in a tight corner', while the Government were facing the most dangerous and electorally damaging ordeal of the session. It was a mistake, the newspaper pointed out, to have appointed a 'judicial' not a 'Parliamentary' Commission for Nyasaland: a Parliamentary Commission would almost certainly have produced a majority report exculpating the Government over Nyasaland, and a minority one by the Opposition members condemning them.

Macmillan and his colleagues were horrified at Lennox-Boyd's renewed suggestions of resignation with the General Election only weeks ahead. They decided to bluff it out over both Hola and Nyasaland and to go over to the counter-attack.

On 20 July a tense Cabinet meeting was held in which the issue of Lennox-Boyd's resignation over the Hola Camp and Devlin reports was put to each Cabinet member in turn. All insisted there was no need for him to go, and he withdrew his resignation. Macmillan claims he told the Cabinet, after the 'decision' had been reached, that had it gone otherwise he himself would have resigned as Prime Minister. This is unlikely to be true although he may have uttered the words.

Over the weekend following this critical Cabinet, Armitage was summoned to Chequers. There with his help Lennox-Boyd, Julian Amery (Colonial Under-Secretary) and the law officers Lord Kilmuir (Lord Chancellor) and Reginald Manningham-Buller (Attorney-General) wrote at speed a counter-blast to Devlin, to be published as Armitage's 'despatch' on the same day as the Devlin Report, 23 July; it served to undermine Devlin's credibility and justify the Government's handling of the Nyasaland crisis.

Lennox-Boyd's Commons ordeals were scheduled for 27 and 28 July, with Hola on the first day and Devlin on the second. At the 1922 Committee he was criticized over Hola by the Tory MPs Enoch Powell, Lord Lambton and John Astor. In the Hola debate to everyone's surprise Powell, the former Treasury Minister who was being tipped for another Ministerial post, was very critical, saying 'it was a great administrative disaster' and 'we could not, we dare not, in Africa of all places fall behind the highest standards in the acceptance of responsibility – responsibility must be carried where it properly belonged, with the Kenyan Minister of Defence and Minister of African Affairs. Instead only the camp superintendent had been punished.' The effect of his speech was weakened when he added, 'Lennox-Boyd was without a jot or tittle of blame.' Still he sat down to prolonged Labour cheers.

The Opposition led by Michael Foot called for Lennox-Boyd's resignation, alleging that the facts were still covered up and complaining that Lennox-Boyd had allowed a junior officer to take the rap. George Thomas called also for Evelyn Baring as Governor to carry responsibility and resign. In order to get the debate on Hola into the Parliamentary programme before the end of the session Labour arranged the debate on the Appropriation Bill which meant it was impossible for them to force a vote. The debate also took place so late at night that it got little press coverage. Macmillan recorded in his diary that if there had been a vote 'there might well have been quite a number of Conservatives voting against the Government or abstaining.'

The Devlin Report and the rival despatch from Armitage contradicting its main findings had been published simultaneously on 23 July 1959. Although it was unusual for a Government to reject an independent judicial enquiry the Conservatives had a satisfactory press on 24 July both in the news columns and the leader comment. *The Times* drew attention to the number of interviews carried out by the Commission and to the numbers killed, and noted the fact that Devlin had shown it was right to call a state of emergency on 3 March, although British policemen in Nyasaland had consistently misreported Banda's speech by exaggerating his calls for violence. On the whole the press thought the Governor's replies were 'convincing'. Despite a damaging headline the *Manchester Guardian* had a 'fair' leader, while as would be expected the *Telegraph*, *Mail* and *Express* were favourable to the Government. Only the *News Chronicle* and the *Mirror* were hostile.

The Government motion in the Commons for the 28 July was that only part of the Devlin Report should be accepted. Reginald Manningham-Buller, the Attorney-General, denied unconvincingly that the Government in March had used the phrase 'murder plot' which Devlin had emphasized was a misnomer. However he had to admit that Lennox-Boyd had said 'massacre' and Julian Amery 'conspiracy to murder' in relation to the political activities of the Nyasaland Congress Party. Manningham-Buller also made play of the Governor's view that Devlin went 'against the weight of evidence' in saying that Banda would never have approved a policy of murder.

In an effective speech James Callaghan, Shadow Colonial Secretary, suggested that the Cabinet had refused to accept Lennox-Boyd's offer to resign purely 'on electoral grounds' and the Government had winnowed through the report 'sieving out, dredging out everything that would support their case and averting their eyes from anything which might in the slightest degree be embarrassing to them'. His criticism was convincing.

Despite previous murmurings from dissatisfied Conservative back-benchers whom Macmillan described as 'frondeurs', there were no Conservative abstentions and the Government had a majority of 63 against 'full acceptance' which was around the usual mark. However word got out in Conservative circles of Perth lobbying Devlin to alter the wording of his report, and in an article in the *Spectator*, owned and edited by Ian Gilmour, soon to be a prominent Tory MP, Bernard Levin wrote: 'The Government refused to accept the the Devlin Report because it told the truth, and relied instead on a despatch from the Governor who had shown himself to be unfit for the job because his White Paper on 4 March had tampered with the evidence and was, Devlin showed, a simple falsehood.'

Christopher Hollis, the recently retired Conservative MP, also defended Devlin stoutly in the *Spectator*, writing that Devlin was a Conservative who had helped him in his constituency, and that the Conservatives would have been glad to give him (Devlin) a safe seat, but he preferred the law. Devlin, he added, would be an ideal Lord Chief Justice. In the Lords Lord Coleraine, a former Conservative Minister, has described Devlin as 'intellectually dishonest' and 'naïve': to apply these words to Devlin, Hollis wrote, was 'inept'; Devlin was a man of the highest integrity. 'Why', Levin wrote in another article in the *Spectator*, 'is Lennox-Boyd clinging to office after the total collapse of his Suez policy and when the Hola outrage like the Nyasaland tragedy has turned out to be a falsehood?'

In his autobiography published in 1964, Welensky disclosed that Devlin had altered his draft report. He wrote of the report that 'it was moulded by British prejudices rooted in ignorance or misunderstanding of African thought, feeling and customs and profoundly antipathetic to the Federa-tion', and drew attention to extensive excisions and omissions from the 'final page proof copy'. On 12 August 1964 Devlin wrote to Sir Edgar Williams, criticizing the Colonial Office for having sent the draft report to Welensky; he thought it 'improper' for Welensky to publish extracts from the draft five years after the event, for the purpose of criticizing his report, and wondered whether they should not now 'take a brief side-swipe' at Welensky. Though it would 'not be wise' to do anything during the General Election which was currently taking place, if they waited, Devlin wrote to Williams, too much time would have elapsed after the publication of Welensky's book and the affair would be 'stone cold'; something would have to be done to 'put the record right sooner or later in some way'. The papers relating to this episode were deposited at Rhodes House where they have recently been released. They disclose how the report was changed as a result of Perth's intervention, and raise important general questions about whether a Government should ever be furnished in advance with a draft report from a Commission.

The Devlin Report had produced a nasty hiccup for the Macmillan

Government, and they got off the hook only by the ruthlessness and speed with which they produced Armitage's rival report. Behind the scenes Lennox-Boyd had given the Cabinet a great fright. He had only with difficulty been persuaded by Macmillan not to resign over Hola in June: with Devlin coming so soon after Hola in July he felt strongly the need to satisfy his conscience. If he had gone, Lord Perth, Julian Amery (Macmillan's son-in-law and Under-Secretary to Lennox-Boyd) and Sir Robert Armitage would have been forced to resign or be dismissed, as would Sir Evelyn Baring, Governor of Kenya. In the run-up to the General Election such an upheaval would have been a serious threat to Conservative electoral fortunes. By adroit manoeuvres the Conservatives had managed to defuse both Hola and Devlin so that neither became important issues in the General Election three months later.

However it was in Sir Edgar Williams's words 'a disgraceful episode', and the above details never before revealed are immensely detrimental to the Macmillan Government and out of keeping with their normal behaviour when faced with a political crisis.[11]

With the General Election safely out of the way Macmillan decided to begin his tour of Africa in January 1960. He had never visited Africa and asked Burke Trend, the senior Treasury official upon whom he placed great reliance, to make a preliminary visit so as to provide him with a comprehensive briefing. Trend was chairman of an inter-departmental Cabinet committee of officials on Kenya, Northern and Southern Rhodesia and Nyasaland.

In a long private report to Macmillan in October 1959 Trend analysed the possible alternative lines of constitutional advance; the Federation, he reported, suffered from the handicap of the opposition of the Africans, and the reluctance of the European-dominated governments of Southern Rhodesia, Northern Rhodesia and Nyasaland to make Federation effective; apart from Roy Welensky, Prime Minister of the Federation, there was 'no outstanding Minister capable of taking the machinery of government by the scruff of the neck and making it work'. Welensky was divorced to a startling extent from the departmental machine, whilst he and the Prime Ministers of the three countries in the Federation had met only three times since the Federation was inaugurated in 1953.

One of the troubles with the officials of Southern Rhodesia, Trend considered, was that they were too well aware that they could cut adrift and join South Africa,* and there was no concept of partnership between

---

* This is surprising because H.F. Verwoerd, the South African Prime Minister, had already made it clear he did not want Southern Rhodesia in. Although there was a white government, the whites were mainly English; and worse, from Verwoerd's point of view, was that each white Rhodesian would bring thirty blacks with him. (Information from Sir David Hunt)

Africans and Europeans, while severe discrimination against Africans in the new multiracial university at Salisbury was practised. His verdict was that the atmosphere in Southern Rhodesia was 'unhappy', and 'the colony's selfish preoccupation with the maintenance of the white man's complete social dominance is one of the greatest obstacles in the way of Roy Welensky's enlightened policy.'

In Northern Rhodesia Trend found the officials considered Federation just 'one more complication in their daily life'; the Governor had told him that whenever some sign of co-operation began to appear a maladroit public statement by Welensky would set everybody at odds again. The Governor also expressed his fear that the visit of the Monckton Commission might force him to declare a new state of emergency.[*] Trend found there was resentment also that they, as the largest and richest member of the Federation (because of the copper belt), should be controlled (however ineffectively) from Salisbury.

Trend thought the atmosphere in the lovely country of Nyasaland with its green trees, mountains and water was far better. He found people there 'Epicureans as opposed to Stoics in Northern Rhodesia', and wrote:

> no reasonable person in Nyasaland doubted that she must become a black
> state in the not too distant future because of the great disparity between
> the numbers of whites and blacks, while the three territories were largely
> unaware of federation as an effective principle in their daily lives, and there
> was no feeling of 'belonging' to Salisbury or for sharing a common burden
> of responsibility.

According to Trend, 'The African opposition to federation was absolute and universal.' One African chief had said in 1953: 'What have we done wrong that the great Queen has withdrawn her protection as a punishment?' Trend continued:

> The root cause of all this trouble is that federation as it exists in Central
> Africa is not federation as it exists elsewhere. The settlement was not a
> voluntary or agreed one. It was imposed against the wishes of the Africans
> as they expressed them at the time and still express them . . . The result
> was an attempt to combine without subordinating one to the other two
> forms of government which in the last resort are as incompatible as oil and
> water, i.e. a system of parliamentary government at the Federal centre (and
> to some extent in Southern Rhodesia) and a system of direct government
> by the two Northern territories. In the end one of these two systems must
> prevail or the Federation must break up . . . The Colonial Office are bound
> to oppose any closer assimilation of the two Northern territories to the
> Federal authority on the grounds that the existing arrangements are the only

---

[*] Mainly because of African resentment that Dr Banda, their national leader, then in prison, would not be permitted to give evidence. For the Monckton Commission, see page 233.

ones which enable us to discharge our responsibilities to the Africans or British protected persons.

Macmillan thought it 'a most interesting paper and should be sent to the Colonial Secretary and Commonwealth Secretary'. Trend had painted a gloomy but accurate picture of the deficiencies of federation, and pointed out the difficult and almost insoluble problems. However Macmillan at that moment refused to admit that the Federation was a failure or that it should perhaps be brought to an end. Trend omitted any reference to the key problem, the limited educational opportunities afforded to Africans in the three territories involved: with the dearth of secondary schools and university places a totally inadequate number of Africans were being given the education needed for successful self-government. For this successive British governments were to blame.[12]

Welensky may have wanted a partnership with the Africans but only one with a paternal basis. Trend was probably over-generous about Welensky's good intentions, and this coloured Macmillan's attitude, causing him as will be seen to retain false hopes that Welensky would act in a moderate and statesmanlike way.

By December, with Macmillan vetoing Callaghan's appointment to the Monckton Commission because of the animosity it aroused in Welensky after the Shadow spokesman's strong remarks in the Commons on the Hola Camp and Devlin reports,* the Opposition had decided against nominating members to the Commission. But at the last moment Macmillan succeeded in persuading Sir Hartley Shawcross, the former Labour Attorney-General, to join. Soon the fat was in the fire. Shawcross said in early January 1960 in a television interview that he felt quite free to recommend to the Monckton Commission the break-up of the Federation if he felt it desirable, and 'the future of Africa must be settled in accordance with the will of the majority of the inhabitants. That means a counting of heads.'[13]

In January 1960 Macmillan set off on his tour of Africa. The Southern Rhodesian leaders were already up in arms because of a gaffe of Macmillan's at Accra on 13 January, soon after his arrival in Ghana. When asked by journalists about his plans for Nyasaland and Northern Rhodesia Macmillan said: 'The people of the two territories will be given an opportunity to decide on whether the Federation is beneficial to them.' This contradicted his previous assurance to Welensky, who on hearing of the Shawcross television statement had issued a press statement that this would be the 'first thing' he wanted to discuss with Macmillan on his

---

* In a pen-portrait of Macmillan, Harold Wilson remarked in his only adverse criticism: 'This was one of his few churlish actions.'

1. HM campaigning with Dorothy in the 1959 General Election

2. With Eisenhower at Chequers, 1959. HM extracted maximum electoral value from the American President's visit

3. Khrushchev welcomes the international statesman. This visit too had an electoral
purpose but, despite hiccups, was also a breakthrough in the Cold War

4. Peter Thorneycroft: his resignation in 1958, together with Enoch Powell and Nigel Birch, HM dismissed as a 'little local difficulty'

5. Derick Heathcoat Amory, Thorneycroft's successor, resigned in 1960, afraid that expansion was going too fast

6. Selwyn Lloyd, brutally sacked in 'the night of long knives', 12 July 1962

7. Reginald Maudling, the most able and to HM the most sympathetic of his Chancellors. He narrowly missed becoming Prime Minister at the height of the Profumo Crisis in 1963

8. Edward Heath confidently negotiates British entry into the EEC, which de Gaulle plotted to block. Pierson Dixon, Ambassador in Paris, is on the left

9. HM with de Gaulle during the frosty talks at Rambouillet in December 1962. They resulted in the French veto

10. Duncan Sandys, pragmatic Commonwealth Relations Secretary. Like HM he realized Empire was over

11. Iain Macleod and Reginald Maudling, Colonial Secretaries in succession one to the other, but both in HM's view over-zealous in pursuit of his Africanization policy

12. Roy Welensky, Prime Minister of the Central African Federation, likeable but a tough defender of the *status quo*

13. Lord Devlin, whose devastating report on the Nyasaland disturbances cast a long shadow over the Government

14. Dr Hastings Banda, Nyasaland nationalist leader, lost no time in pursuing independence after his belated release from gaol

15. Jomo Kenyatta, hailed a national hero in Kenya. On the verge of full release he was still, in this photograph, obliged to stay in a wire compound

16. Rab Butler. A flummoxed HM finally placed the problems of decolonization in Central Africa in his capable hands

17. Nikita Khrushchev, the Soviet leader whose aggressive stance over Berlin and Cuba so
disconcerted the West

18. HM with Jack Kennedy: there was some friendship but
little meeting of minds

19. Jack Profumo,
Secretary of State for War,
at the time of his resignation

20. Christine Keeler on her way to give evidence

21. Lord Denning, who reported on the security angle of the Profumo case

22. Alec Home arrives in Downing Street with a mandate from the Queen
but not from all his colleagues

23. Reginald Maudling, Quintin Hailsham and Rab Butler: each was
strongly tipped but all were unsuccessful

arrival in Salisbury. However in London the civil servants had already advised that the Shawcross interview was 'unimportant'.

Of course once Shawcross became a member of the Monckton Commission he was free to recommend dissolution of the Federation if he considered this desirable, and there was no power to prevent him doing so. Macmillan's promise to Welensky that secession would not be on the agenda was worthless. Macmillan must have regretted this rash promise.

In a memorandum to the Prime Minister on 3 December 1959 Macleod had summed up his policy for Nyasaland saying,

> there has been a fairly swift release of detainees [only 380 remained in detention in Nyasaland] . . . I do not believe we can possibly justify for long the continuance of the emergency. We would have no chance of defending our action before the Human Rights Commission [of the United Nations] . . . there is no question, as there was in Kenya, of these people being of the Mau Mau type . . . Not only are they acceptable now, but they are also their accepted leaders . . . I have no doubt at all that some time we will have to deal with Banda . . . I am convinced, although this may sound paradoxical, that Banda is the most likely African Nyasa leader to keep Nyasaland within the Federation.

Macmillan discussed and approved this brief with Macleod; it was anathema to Welensky and Sir Edgar Whitehead, Prime Minister of Southern Rhodesia. The British Prime Minister faced a tricky situation when he arrived in Salisbury on 18 January 1960 to meet them.

Welensky had a genuine enthusiasm for the Federation which he sincerely believed to be the right vehicle to bring prosperity to both Africans and Europeans. Whitehead was less enthusiastic; his view was that Southern Rhodesia should secede if power in the Federal Government passed to the Africans, and even if necessary seek a union with South Africa (then still a member of the Commonwealth).

The atmosphere was tense when Macmillan met Welensky and Whitehead on the morning of 19 January. Welensky started by saying that Shawcross's unfortunate remarks 'had created a widespread impression within the Federation that the Commission would go outside their terms of reference', that is by recommending the secession of Nyasaland; he was concerned too at rumours of the impending release of Banda which he felt 'would substantially increase the security risks in Nyasaland'.

Macmillan ignored the Shawcross controversy, and affirmed his faith in the Federation. He also said there had been a misunderstanding about his statement at his press conference in Lagos but this did not convince Welensky whom he promised to consult about the release of Banda after his visit to Nyasaland, saying the timing of it must be 'largely a matter of tactics'.

On 21 January Macmillan went on to Northern Rhodesia where

he met leading members of all the political parties except Banda. Much to the Prime Minister's relief he had been advised beforehand that it was not necessary to see Banda in prison because arrangements had been made for him to talk to a delegation from Banda's own political party.[14]

Macmillan continued his journey to Cape Town and there addressed the all-white South African Parliament on 3 February 1960; the green benches were calm and full of senators and MPs but South Africa was in turmoil. Nelson Mandela with 155 others was on trial for treason. The militant Pan-African Congress had just split from the more moderate African National Congress, while the National Government under the Prime Minister, Hendrik Verwoerd, was pressing ahead with apartheid laws including banning Africans from 'white' universities and restricting nearly every aspect of their lives. Speaking to the Assembly Macmillan said:

> The wind of change is blowing through this continent . . . The great issue in this second part of the twentieth century is whether the uncommitted people of Asia and Africa will swing to the East or to the West . . . What is now on trial is much more than our military strength or diplomatic and administrative skill. It is our way of life.

He had a duty to talk frankly to South Africans, he added, and he urged them to create a society 'in which individual merit, and individual merit alone, is the criteria for a man's advancement'.

Dr Verwoerd was furious and replied: 'Mr Prime Minister, we have problems enough in South Africa without your coming to add to them . . . In South Africa justice must be done to the black man, but also to the white man'; while the Foreign Minister, E. H. Louw, asked whether Mr Macmillan would dare to criticize de Gaulle over Algerian policy or talk about race in the United States. But Macmillan had made it clear that no part of Africa could for long remain an exclusive white preserve.

The South African Government ignored the 'wind of change' speech. Apartheid went ahead, and the following month sixty-seven black demonstrators were shot dead at Sharpeville and the ANC and PAC parties were banned. But the speech was significant in proving dramatically to the South African Government that Macmillan and his Government believed there must be moves, however slow, to African majority rule everywhere, irrespective of the opposition of white South Africa to any form of African rule in its own country.

Sir David Hunt, then Assistant Under-Secretary in the Commonwealth Relations Office, accompanied the Prime Minister; he it was who coined the phrase 'wind of change' and wrote both the Accra and Cape Town speeches. The Accra speech aroused such little attention that Hunt thought it worth while to use the phrase a second time at Cape Town. But despite the world-wide publicity the speech received, Macmillan's ideas of a timetable, Hunt confirms, were vastly slower than those of his Colonial Secretary, Iain Macleod.

In between his visits to Nyasaland and South Africa, Macmillan had returned to Salisbury but had refused point blank to discuss the question of Banda's release with Welensky. On 2 February the Commonwealth Relations Secretary Lord Home sent a message to Welensky that since leaving Salisbury Macmillan had been in consultation with Macleod and the decision had been taken to authorize Banda's release, although the date was as yet undecided. Welensky protested vigorously and asked if either he could come to London or Home to Salisbury urgently.

Macmillan by now was on the *Capetown Castle* and travelling home by sea as far as Las Palmas. He described it as 'a most comfortable and agreeable journey' during which he had to deal with 'a considerable volume of business from home'.

In the Prime Minister's absence Macleod and the Commonwealth Secretary, Home, had clashed over Banda's release. Home was strongly opposed to release, at least while the Monckton Commission was in Nyasaland. Cabling to the *Capetown Castle*, he told Macmillan that there was a crisis in the Federation over the release, and that Welensky had asked for the visit to Africa of the Monckton Commission to be postponed. Home suggested that the release of Banda and constitutional advance in Nyasaland should be balanced by conceding to Whitehead that all the remaining restraints which under the constitution Britain could impose on Southern Rhodesia should be lifted* – though he admitted that, since the restraints had been put there for the protection of Africans, their removal was bound to be criticized. Home wanted Macmillan to settle the differences in direct conversation with Welensky and thought this would be preferable to Home himself going to Salisbury.

Macmillan did not fancy another face to face meeting with Welensky in London, and replied from the ship that he did not feel at all happy about bargaining our protective duties towards Africans in Southern Rhodesia against Whitehead's agreement to constitutional advance in Nyasaland:

> I am sorry you are having all this trouble through my failure to deal effectively with the Banda problem when I was with Welensky. My difficulty, of course, was not only the time factor but the ambivalent advice I received from the Governor of Nyasaland [Armitage] and to a lesser extent from the

---

* These restraints had been imposed when Southern Rhodesia had been given almost complete self-government in 1953. The British Government felt they must retain some residual powers in case the ruling white minority behaved badly towards the Africans.

Governor of Northern Rhodesia. I was therefore not in the position to say that this was simply a security problem which we could handle on our own.

Macmillan was correct. The crisis was his own fault for not being frank with Welensky and Whitehead and telling them of his Colonial Secretary's decision to release Banda, and that he as Prime Minister approved of this course. Macmillan added:

> Constitutionally, of course, responsibility for the release of Banda rests with the Governor and the Colonial Secretary, but the events of last year when we had to fall back on help from the two Rhodesias certainly gives them a status. That is what we have always meant when we promised to consult Welensky . . . It is clear there must be a meeting; we all seem to be agreed on that . . . Welensky is like Henry III of France surrounded by the Guises. Whitehead is the Duc de Guise.[15]*

The fact that the Duke was later assassinated at the King's instigation must have been overlooked by Macmillan as there was no question of Welensky trying to assassinate Whitehead. Macmillan continued: 'The question is how to hold Welensky and company during the next few days.' This was an acute problem because Welensky was very angry and was threatening to arouse the pro-settler lobby of the Conservative Party against Macmillan.

Evidence of how jumpy Macmillan was over the release of Banda came on 19 February 1960 when Macmillan read in the press that the Governor of Nyasaland, Armitage, would resign if Banda was released. He asked his press secretary, Harold Evans, about this; Evans replied that only the *News Chronicle* and *Express* 'had speculated and the Colonial Office feel certain there had been no public utterance from Armitage'. Macmillan then minuted: 'I am not so sure.'

Macmillan was deeply suspicious of Armitage. There had been a row during their talks in the Nyasaland capital Zomba when Armitage resisted all Macmillan's arguments to persuade him to release Banda, and spoke so insultingly to the Prime Minister that David Hunt stopped taking notes. After that Macmillan was determined to dismiss him, and was now apprehensive that Armitage would not wait for the sack but resign first and stir up a fuss. In the event Armitage decided to leave quietly.[16]

Macleod was determined to release Banda as soon as possible. Home, who had flown to Salisbury, refused to agree because of the strong opposition of the Federal Cabinet. Whitehead continued to argue

---

*Macmillan had taken Garrett Mattingly's book *The Defeat of the Spanish Armada* to read on the tour and was referring to Henry III's flight from Paris in 1588 when the third Duke of Guise, who had been responsible for the massacre of Protestants in 1572 and did not conceal his ambition to be king, entered the city.

that, if they gave their consent, all British restraints on the Southern Rhodesian Government must be lifted as a quid pro quo. This would have been anathema to the Africans, and Home feared that without agreement Southern Rhodesia might make a unilateral declaration of independence and even seek to join South Africa, so as to remain in the Commonwealth. In a panic Home cabled to Macmillan on 22 February: 'Unless we are careful the Europeans [in Southern Rhodesia] will do something rather desperate,' adding, 'Please do not say anything to Iain until I arrive home as I must talk to you alone.' Events overtook Home.

Disgruntled at Home's attitude, Macleod, at the Cabinet meeting on 23 February, announced his intention to resign since he refused to be associated with the proposal not to release Banda until after the Monckton Commission left Nyasaland. Macleod had given embarrassing assurances to Banda which had probably not been communicated to Home or Macmillan; he felt he was in an impossible position if the Cabinet would not support him. There is no mention of his resignation in the Cabinet minutes. Following the Cabinet meeting Macmillan cabled to Home in Salisbury: 'We are having serious difficulties here, and Macleod may resign.' He recorded in his memoirs that there was a real clash of opinion between Home and Macleod over Banda's release, and 'for a few days it looked as if I should be faced with the resignation of one or other of two colleagues.'

Macleod's resignation would have produced a serious political crisis for Macmillan. Fortunately for the Government hardly a whisper reached the press, and Macleod was persuaded to withdraw his resignation when Macmillan suggested that Banda should be released on 1 April 1960, which was three days before Monckton left Nyasaland instead of three days after. According to Macmillan, Macleod then became excited and said 'it would solve this problem.' As so little made such a difference to Macleod it must have been a clash of personalities rather than of substance. With great tact Home in Salisbury persuaded the Federal Cabinet to agree without strings to the suggestion of 1 April, although Whitehead still insisted he would only agree if Britain made concessions over the Southern Rhodesian constitution.[17]

Lord Dalhousie, Governor-General of the Central African Federation, wrote to Home on 24 February 1960:

> The right wing is hardening because of the impression given by Macleod that 'you can do anything provided your face is black' plus bias against the Colonial Office and mischievous press reports ... as to the idea of Iain synchronizing Banda's release with a visit, I can only say that the additional antagonism it would create out here towards Iain, which is already considerable, would seriously jeopardize any future dealing with this country ... he must at least appear to be open-minded.

The return of Banda, he added, would produce a dangerous situation for security. Dalhousie, who as Simon Ramsay had been a Conservative MP and Whip in the 1945 Parliament, was a political appointee. No member of the Colonial Service could have written such a letter about a Cabinet Minister, but it reflected accurately the views of the settlers and a part of the British Conservative Party.*

Macmillan was sent this letter by Home on his return to England, and despite the derogatory remarks about his Colonial Secretary the Prime Minister minuted: 'This is a very interesting and significant letter,' and he ordered it to be circulated to the various Departments. Macmillan must still have had cold feet about the release of Banda and wanted to hint to Macleod that he was going too fast. However it was a strange method of conducting a Government and a humiliation for Macmillan.[18]

This episode with Home and Macleod at daggers drawn shows how big a mistake Macmillan was making in allowing Central Africa to be handled by two different Departments of State even though he had made himself Chairman of the Cabinet's Africa Committee. The Commonwealth Relations Office was responsible for relations with the Federation and Southern Rhodesia; the Colonial Office for internal affairs in Northern Rhodesia and Nyasaland. It is surprising that Macmillan allowed this dual responsibility to continue for so long when the different approach of the two Departments and the policy clash between Home and Macleod had become known to the press. Probably he felt that Home at the Commonwealth Relations Office was a useful brake on Macleod who was taking the pace of Africanization dangerously fast.

On 1 April 1960 Banda was released from gaol and taken immediately to Government House in Zomba to meet Macleod. They got on well; Banda agreed he would do his best to keep Nyasaland calm, and succeeded. As Macleod's biographer writes: 'It was like the lancing of a boil.' Banda's beneficial effect on peace in Nyasaland exceeded Macleod's expectations, and his decision was soon vindicated. At the airport a few days later on his way to London Banda remarked to the press, 'Macleod is a great man,' and in Washington: 'He is a man with whom I can deal.'

Armitage minuted after the meeting that Banda was 'well and in a friendly mood' but 'immensely vain and will show up badly on television, etc.' He could not have been more wrong. Macleod wrote to the Prime Minister from Nyasaland on 3 April: 'Typically enough the United Federal Party [white settlers] objected to Banda making a speech ...

---

*Lord Home confirmed to the author that Simon Dalhousie was a very close personal friend of his.

there is really no measuring the bottomless stupidity of their members here and in all the three territories. They think of their party and Federation as one and the same thing, and will be too stubborn in the end for all our efforts.'

Macmillan agreed with Macleod but continued to seek a means of reconciling the settler lobby within the Conservative Party, and clung to the vain hope that somehow he could persuade Welensky to support the Africanization with which Macleod wanted to press on. On 3 April 1960 Macmillan wrote to the Queen that the arrival of Banda might mean the

> fears of violence and disorder in Nyasaland will prove exaggerated . . . The trouble will come when the extremists [Africans] fail to obtain their demands. Although the public [Europeans] in the Federation are certainly alarmed both by the constitutional advance in Kenya and by the disorders in the Union [South Africa] it is just possible that the European population in Rhodesia will learn the lesson in time.

Unfortunately they did not.

Banda flew to London where he was well received, and the Government announced there would be constitutional talks in June on Nyasaland. Welensky and his supporters were highly hostile to the idea of a new constitution for Nyasaland which they knew would mean an African majority and secession from the Federation. In an effort to propitiate Welensky Macleod sent a personal letter to him on 30 May, with general reflections on the constitutional position in Northern Rhodesia and Nyasaland. In his memoirs Welensky describes this letter as 'controversial'.

Macleod expressed disquiet about what would happen when Belgium gave independence to the Congo after 30 June 1960, and hoped that

> after a period of chaos some order will prevail. I believe firmly in the Federation, and I believe it is the best future for the three countries of Central Africa but I am realist enough to know that the odds at the moment are against its full success. I do not take as despondent a view as Whitehead does and I believe in particular that Walter Monckton's Committee will give us a clear guiding light . . .

The Nyasaland Conference, Macleod continued, looked as if it would have little chance of success, and Dingle Foot, the Labour MP who was advising Banda, was neither trustworthy nor efficient; while it would be far easier to hold Nyasaland in the Federation if it were given 'fairly swiftly a generous measure of constitutional advance'. Macleod must have had his tongue in his cheek, because he knew that once Banda took power under a new constitution he would demand secession from the Federation, and the Monckton Report would have no influence on him.

Banda himself was making no secret about his determination that Nyasaland should leave the Federation.[19]

The Constitutional Conference on Nyasaland took place in London in July 1960, and agreed the framework of a new constitution. It provided for a completely new system of direct election of Africans to the legislature with a 'qualitative franchise* on upper and lower rolls'. The system of election was complicated but Banda took it as meaning there would be an African majority; this was also the view of Macleod and his Colonial Office advisers. Macmillan tried to give the contrary impression in private letters to Welensky.

A running battle ensued between Macleod and Welensky over the details of the upper and lower rolls voting procedure and the nominated members of the council, and Macmillan kept intervening with some loss of dignity. Much against Welensky's wishes Macleod issued an Order in Council on 3 January 1961 to establish the new election procedure. It was now obviously only a question of time before Nyasaland seceded from the Federation.

Differences between Macleod and Home had continued after Macleod's threat of resignation on 23 February 1960. They had a mutual dislike for each other.[†] On 10 June 1960 Home wrote to Macmillan:

> I think a programme of advance culminating in independence for Nyasaland and Northern Rhodesia by 1970 would be accepted as reasonable and swallowed, although with great difficulty, by Southern Rhodesia. Anything shorter would, I fear, surely provide a campaigning period for the extremists on either side and give no chance of stability.

On 1 July he wrote again that Macleod was moving too fast 'by wanting low property qualification for the franchise [in Nyasaland] while 1962 is early enough for the next step in Northern Rhodesia'.

On 27 July 1960 however Home left the Commonwealth Relations Office to become Foreign Secretary. He was replaced by Duncan Sandys. With his sympathy for Welensky and the Europeans in Central Africa, Home had always favoured a slow pace of change and Welensky looked on him as an ally. Though favouring caution, Sandys was a realist who took the view that the days of British rule in Africa were over; once India had gone, the British Empire, he felt, had little to sustain it. Although Macleod did not have the same dislike for Sandys as for Home, the two were temperamentally incompatible. Sandys was an experienced

---

* A 'qualitative franchise' meant that only Africans with a certain amount of money or education could vote.
† It was evidence of Macleod's distaste for Home that he and Powell alone of Macmillan's Ministers refused to serve in the Home Government in 1963.

pragmatic politician and immensely hard-working; not one to be caught out on a question of detail. But he was ponderous and slow to make up his mind, and thus clashed with Macleod who was quick-witted, impulsive and emotionally involved, and believed that he had a divine mission to Africanize the former colonies. Both were well liked and admired by their civil servants, but there was continuous friction and jealousy over African policy while they were both Secretaries of State.

On 18 October 1960 the Monckton Commission published their report; it made it clear that the Federation was doomed. Their main recommendation was that the Africans who hitherto had occupied 12 out of the 50 seats in the Federal Parliament should have parity with the Europeans with 30 seats each in an assembly of 60. It recommended also an African majority in the Northern Rhodesian Legislative Council (the government subordinate to the Federal Government), and an 'unofficial' majority on its Executive Council (i.e. a majority of Africans over and above the combined number of officials and European members). This was the pattern the Cabinet had expected and Macmillan even commented: 'The general purport of the report is exactly what I minuted and said in Salisbury.'[20]

The report also declared that secession should be discussed at the Federal Review Conference due to start in December in London, and that the British Government should state its intention of allowing secession, while a new constitution for Northern Rhodesia should be drafted without waiting on a full revision of the Federal structure. The two African members signed a dissenting report saying the continuance of the Federation was unacceptable as it was not based on the consent of the inhabitants, and the British Government should provide for the immediate secession of any territory whose people demand it. The Commission also stated that the 'Federation' was hated by the Africans because it was associated with a policy of white domination, and they urged that it be altered. However they hoped the Federation would be replaced by a close form of association.

Sandys arrived in Salisbury with an embargoed copy of the report and found Welensky up in arms not only about the Monckton Report but because Macleod had promised to hold a Northern Rhodesia Conference early in 1961. Unfortunately Macleod had stated at Lusaka on 29 March 1960 that he had no plans to amend the Northern Rhodesia Constitution before the Federal Review Conference. Obviously a Northern Rhodesia Conference would produce a new franchise similar to that for Nyasaland which would result in an African majority government.

Welensky wrote to Macleod that the Monckton Report's recommendations 'play into the hands of African extremists ... and rule out any possibility of reasonable changes being made on merit'. Backed by

Lord Salisbury in London, he also attacked Macmillan on the grounds that the British Prime Minister had assured him beforehand that secession was not within the Monckton terms of reference. He got nowhere and when Macmillan offered to publish all his letters in a White Paper Welensky piped down. Macmillan came out well from this exchange.

Welensky and his associates acquiesced in the new constitution for Nyasaland, albeit unwillingly, because they did not care greatly whether she was within or outside the Federation and the number of Europeans there was small. They cared desperately however about retaining Northern Rhodesia within the Federation, not only because of its bigger white population but also because her rich copper belt was the jewel in the Federation's economic crown. Welensky's opposition to a new constitution for Northern Rhodesia thus became almost hysterical. This did not unduly bother Macleod, so sure was he that he was doing the right thing. However Macmillan became alarmed and did his best to satisfy the settlers – an impossible task – and his attempt to have the best of both worlds did nothing to calm the grave internal quarrel within the Conservative Party over Central Africa.

On the one side the Europeans in Northern and Southern Rhodesia and the Federal Parliament were determined that the white settlers should retain power. On the other, the Africans, especially after the Congo had gained independence, were equally determined to acquire power quickly. Power could be held by a black majority by consent of the mass of the population, or it could be wielded by a white minority only as long as it was backed by force. It could not be shared, and any system of parity was bound in the end to lead to disorder. Macleod realized this. Welensky had a blind spot which was shared to a degree by Macmillan, and completely by Lord Salisbury and the powerful Conservative settler lobby in the Commons and Lords. Consequently Macleod found the going much tougher during the Northern Rhodesia Conference, and with internal opposition to his plan within the Conservative Party whipped up to fever point, once again came to the brink of throwing in his hand and resigning.

The conference on the future of the Federation opened in December 1960; it achieved nothing and was adjourned *sine die*. It is best forgotten, and consigned to the dustbin of history.

The Northern Rhodesia Constitutional Conference got down to business on 8 February 1961. The white United Federal Party in Northern Rhodesia, probably on the instructions of Welensky, boycotted the conference. Welensky mistakenly thought this would put an end to the conference; it was a bad negotiating error. Macleod's aim for the conference was to give Africans in Northern Rhodesia parity for one Parliament, to be followed by an African majority. He knew well this would mean Northern Rhodesia seceding from the Federation and becoming independent. Welensky put pressure on Macmillan in one personal letter after another to try to prevent this; he was supported by the right-wing Conservative MPs and peers whose influence succeeded in weakening the resolve of the Cabinet to implement in full the details of Macleod's White Paper. This produced distrust amongst the Africans.

Welensky claimed that under the Federal Constitution the Federal Government had the right to veto changes in the Northern Rhodesia Constitution. This was at variance with the legal position according to the Commonwealth Relations Office but as a compromise the Cabinet, again because of Macmillan's desire to placate Welensky, allowed Welensky's representative Julius Greenfield to come to London to conduct parallel talks with the Commonwealth Relations Office. This made Macleod's task difficult and produced more friction between him and Sandys.*

Dalhousie, at Home's suggestion, tried to put pressure on Macmillan and alarmed him by a personal note on 31 January 1961:

> I cannot over-emphasize the seriousness of the situation *re* the Federation's continued existence which at present depends on Northern Rhodesia talks. Pressing Welensky or Whitehead beyond the point they will go will result in premature and immediate and certain break-up ... Welensky has informed us that the failure to agree a basis ... for Northern Rhodesia talks will result in his being forced to sever relations with HMG and go his own way independently whatever this means. Having questioned him I am convinced that he is not bluffing and might even consider holding some areas by force if necessary.[22]

Dalhousie was overstating the Welensky position, but Macmillan was by now powerless to curb his Colonial Secretary's drive to satisfy the Africans although he would have liked to do so.

Foreign Secretary Home showed his hostility to Macleod's plans by writing to Macmillan on 3 February that 'we cannot impose political conditions on Northern Rhodesia which would make it impossible for the Europeans to control the country if we were to go,' and he wanted the conference adjourned. On 27 January he had asked Macmillan for ten or twelve years' interval before African rule, otherwise the Northern Rhodesia franchise would break the Federation and 'the trouble was we had started the conference without previously working out a compromise franchise which the Federal Government would accept.'

Sandys on 31 January 1961 had cabled from Salisbury that Whitehead had formally told Welensky that 'if parity were conceded in Northern

---

* Macmillan had firmly turned down Welensky's request to have a 'Federal observer' at the conference, but later weakened by allowing Greenfield to come to London.[21]

Rhodesia he would come out for secession for Southern Rhodesia and
the break-up of the Federation.' Sandys urged Macmillan to keep in mind
during the Northern Rhodesia discussions 'how much was at stake – the
whole future of the Federation and the whole outcome of this great
experiment in racial partnership, not to mention the almost impossible
difficulties which would confront us if Welensky were to put himself
at the head of a campaign for independence'.

With Sandys and Home in head-on opposition to Macleod, Macmillan
was in a dilemma. He had rashly written to Welensky in January regarding Northern Rhodesia: 'Whatever balance we decide upon the Africans
will in fact remain in a minority in the Legislative Council'; he also gave
his opinion that there was material in Northern Rhodesia 'on which a
moderate non-racial centre party could very usefully play'. This was
wishful thinking and the hard-headed Welensky knew it for what it
was.[23]

Kenneth Kaunda, head of the African National Congress, was the
African leader at the Northern Rhodesia Conference and was on good
terms with Macleod. However he was agitated when he heard that
Welensky had called on Southern Rhodesian troops to stand by to
prevent disturbances, and looked on this as interference in the constitutional talks in London. From his headquarters in Gower Street he
wrote to Macmillan on 13 February asking the British Government to
order the Federal Government to withdraw their troops at once. It was
an explosive situation because the British Government had also concentrated forces at Nairobi, contemplating disorder and a rash act by
Whitehead with his troops.

Kaunda, at that time a mild and well-balanced man before absolute
power went to his head, was subject to great pressure from more militant
supporters at home, and had already committed a major tactical error
on 9 February by issuing a press statement saying that if the British
Government did not grant a clear majority to the Africans there would
be an uprising in Northern Rhodesia which 'by contrast would make
Mau Mau a child's picnic'.[24]* He regretted this statement and together
with Sir John Moffat, the leader of the Northern Rhodesia European
Liberals, went on a deputation to Macleod and Macmillan demanding
in much milder terms an African elected majority. The air was full of
rumours that Macmillan would overrule Macleod's Africanization plan
and give way to Home and Sandys because of the security dangers.

Macleod gave a preview of his intention to announce his decision
for an African majority in a speech to the conference on 14 February.

---

*Macleod tactfully persuaded Kaunda shortly afterwards to withdraw this statement. However
it enabled right-wing Conservatives to label Kaunda an extremist.

Welensky, who had been in almost continuous touch with Sandys by telephone, reacted violently, sending a message to Macmillan that this was a breach of the undertaking given to him by Sandys and a 'complete sell-out to African nationalism which would drive Southern Rhodesia out of the Federation'. Macmillan reminded Welensky that the conference did not end until Friday, 17 February, and there was time to straighten out the results of misunderstanding or bad drafting.[25]

The vital question of franchise qualifications for Northern Rhodesian Africans was still undecided as the conference met for its final session on 17 February 1961. Then Macleod, regardless of the divisions in the Cabinet, circulated a draft White Paper which if implemented would result in African control. It meant not parity, but an African majority.

When Macmillan read this White Paper on 16 February he was horrified: it confirmed Welensky's worst misgivings. He sent a hasty minute to Macleod asking him to revise it. The next day, 17 February, while the conference was still in session, Macleod and the Prime Minister met privately at Admiralty House. Macleod told Macmillan that in view of the latter's minute 'he had no option but to resign at once'. Macmillan asked him why. Macleod replied that 'We were continually giving way to Sir Roy Welensky and that he [Macleod] was not being allowed sufficient freedom in his own sphere of responsibility'; he would not, he said, amend his draft White Paper which had been circulated to everyone attending the conference that morning. Macmillan begged Macleod to finish off the conference that afternoon and then report to him again at around 6 p.m. when it was over. Macleod returned to the conference.

At 10 the next morning Macmillan held a crisis meeting with Kilmuir the Lord Chancellor, Home, Sandys, and the Chief Whip Martin Redmayne to discuss how to deal with Macleod. Sandys proposed a very different solution from Macleod's, with restrictions on the voting qualification for Africans and the Government emphasizing their desire for a multiracial community and no African majority at present. Macmillan said the Government ought to make a statement that objections to Macleod's proposals had been made 'from all sides' and there was no agreement, so that it would be a serious matter for the Government to impose a new constitution without the agreement of the responsible authorities while there were a number of proposals still open to discussion.

Macleod came to see Macmillan later in the morning determined to resign if he did not get his way. The meeting was stormy, and Macmillan ordered that there should be 'no circulation' for the record.[26]* The

---

*The previous day, 16 February, Macmillan had ordered his private secretary Tim Bligh that nothing was to be printed without his agreement, and what had already gone to the printer should be carefully scrutinized and brought to his attention, while Trend should always be consulted as well as Sandys. Macleod was angry with this clipping of his wings.

Prime Minister had with him the Foreign Secretary Home, the Lord Chancellor Kilmuir, in addition to Sandys the Commonwealth Secretary. Despite the opposition of this formidable combination Macleod stuck to his guns and against all odds won the day.

Macleod began by saying that telegrams had been received from Welensky and Whitehead which indicated that they would refuse to work with the Government if the White Paper was published as drafted. The others tried in vain to persuade Macleod to amend his proposals and agree to a statement which might be acceptable to Whitehead and Welensky. Macleod insisted that any agreement reached with them could not be consistent with his White Paper.

Kilmuir argued that the White Paper should not be published before there had been a period of consultation with Welensky and Whitehead. Sandys supported him, and said it was 'important to try to avoid an open break with Southern Rhodesia and the Federal Government'. Home agreed, and thought it would be dangerous to rush the matter through, and it was 'not out of the question that we should be able eventually to reach agreement within the terms of the White Paper'. This suggestion was divorced from reality.

Undeterred, Macleod insisted the White Paper must be published as the Government's plan and a statement made that there would be consultation before the proposals were implemented; he agreed there was a considerable risk that Southern Rhodesia might 'secede', but if we gave way 'there were other and possibly graver risks to the British position throughout the whole of East Africa'.

There were two possible courses of action, Macleod maintained: either to publish the White Paper; or for the Government to say that, as agreement was impossible, they did not think it right to propose a constitution and would carry out further consultations. The latter would be 'an honourable course of action', Macleod went on, but he could not support it as he was personally committed to the White Paper and had given 'too many personal pledges at the conference', so that if the White Paper was abandoned he would resign.

Kilmuir argued ineffectively that this was not a 'resigning matter'. Macleod hit back, saying that Whitehead's seceding from the Federation was of less moment than a black uprising in East Africa. Sandys intervened, saying that the balance of risks lay the other way because if Southern Rhodesia seceded they might try to annex the Copper Belt, and this could lead to 'war between black and white'.

Macleod successfully flouted the Prime Minister and his senior Cabinet colleagues, and two days later the Cabinet authorized him to proceed on the lines of his White Paper. Blatant insubordination by Macleod had seriously damaged the authority both of the Prime Minister and the

Foreign Secretary. However, having ceded complete victory to Macleod, Macmillan, Home and Sandys in the next few weeks continually sniped away at Macleod's formula for a new constitution in an effort to pacify Welensky and Whitehead.

Lord Perth, Minister of State for the Colonies, tried to pour oil on the troubled waters by writing to the Prime Minister 'to say how much I rejoice at the outcome of the Northern Rhodesia Conference. It must have been an exceedingly difficult decision for you, necessarily demanding great weighing up and courage ... It led us to a position we intensely disliked.' Evidently Perth like Macleod was on the brink of resignation. However his observation in this letter, 'Both Europeans and Africans will publicly oppose the scheme which I think shows it is right and fair', was apposite.[27]

In the Lords Salisbury bitterly attacked the February White Paper on Northern Rhodesia; he berated Macleod for 'being too clever by half' and said he 'could not be trusted by the white people of East and Central Africa'. In a television interview Macleod gave a dignified response: 'Salisbury may state "The pace in Africa is dangerously fast" but it might be more dangerous still if we went slowly.' However the Cabinet were deeply divided, as were the rank and file of the Conservative Party. It was Kilmuir's view that the Salisbury episode 'demonstrated how deeply Macleod had estranged opinion not only in Africa but on the extreme right wing of the Tory Party'.[28]

Welensky denounced the White Paper, and at his request all five European United Federal Party Ministers in the Northern Rhodesian Council resigned in protest against it. This proved helpful to Macleod because African aspirations were far from satisfied, and a wild condemnation by the settlers made the decision more acceptable to them. With great tact Sir Evelyn Hone, the Governor, succeeded in obtaining Kaunda's approval.

Drafted in a hurry, the White Paper had unfortunately left many points wide open, and this gave Welensky his chance to reopen the battle; he claimed there must be a European majority in the first Northern Rhodesia Parliament. Macmillan tried to do everything possible to keep Welensky happy, and with Macleod's reluctant approval Sandys went to Salisbury for talks with Welensky in June 1961.

Macmillan took an intense personal interest on the details of the new complicated voting system. There was a continuous flow of letters between him and Welensky on ingenious variations of the voting procedure, the Prime Minister even suggesting alterations which would entail ten different coloured ballot papers. A typical letter from Macmillan to Welensky read: 'We are bound by the spirit of the White Paper. You are concerned to see that Northern Rhodesia does not fall into the hands of irresponsible and extreme nationalists. I still think these can be reconciled. We have not yet found the answer, but I am determined to find it.'[29] Here the Prime Minister was demonstrating a mental blockage. The two positions were irreconcilable and it was the duty of his Government to make a decision between them.

It was unsuitable work for a Prime Minister, and his frequent messages to Welensky over the voting details encouraged the Federal Prime Minister to demand more. Over all the negotiations hung the shadowy awareness that it was only a mockery of democracy in a country with a population of 50,000 Europeans and over five million Africans. The final agreed electoral roll was to consist of 25,000 Europeans on an upper roll and 70,000 Africans on a lower roll; to qualify for the vote an African needed £480 per annum, or secondary education and £350 per annum.

The Cabinet insisted on back-pedalling on the February White Paper and departing from Macleod's original detailed voting proposals. Naturally this concerned Macleod deeply. As the proposed franchise became more and more complicated in an attempt to satisfy Welensky, the process of Africanization took a definite step backwards. As Kirkman writes: 'The new proposals were both ill conceived and imperfectly shaped.' Predictably they produced an adverse reaction from Kaunda, the Liberal white leader Moffat and the African politicians who with reason saw them as a breach of faith. Kaunda had only with difficulty been persuaded to agree to the February proposals and, as some of the proposals originally inserted to satisfy the Africans became altered or deleted, violence and sabotage broke out in Northern Rhodesia, while the Labour and Liberal opposition in the Commons clamoured for the Government to stick to the original scheme.[30]

In London Macmillan, with Home and Sandys on his side, disputed with Macleod. The sticking point for Macleod was that Africans should have parity in the first parliament, whereas Welensky was adamant there must be a 60–40 European majority. By 13 May Home was reporting from Nyasaland that any 'middle roll' even minimally attractive to Welensky would be impossible to sell to the other parties. He was correct.

At their negotiations in Salisbury Sandys and Welensky came to a provisional agreement. Macleod dissented. Immediately Kaunda sent a personal message to Macmillan that 'we can never accept the Sandys–Welensky plan, and imposition of this plan will mean ruling us at gun point.' Much alarmed, Macmillan dictated a four-page memorandum, and summoned Sandys who had returned to London, and Macleod, to two meetings on 17 June 1961. In an effort to find a formula acceptable to Welensky, Macmillan wanted a 60–40 European majority in the first parliament, insisting, 'We must try to meet him on this point.' Macleod told Macmillan he would not accept 60–40 as it was not within the February White Paper and 'would certainly lead to complete loss of faith by the Africans in the British'. Sandys now supported Macleod, so Macmillan had to give way. He was on the horns of a dilemma and told his two Ministers that 'whatever they did was wrong'. Eventually he agreed it was 'better to be honourable' and go for 50–50 as the best possible alternative to put to Welensky.[31]

Although the 50–50 formula meant that the Governor and colonial civil servants plus the European members would have a majority for the first parliament, Welensky was up in arms again when he heard of the proposal, which he claimed was less than Sandys had promised him. He said he would fly to London to protest personally and arouse the right wing of the Conservative Party. He had packed his bags and was waiting at Salisbury airport to board the plane when Sandys reached him by telephone. A long conversation ensued, and with great tact Sandys persuaded Welensky to accept the 50–50 formula, stressing that the balance would be held by the European officials. So instead of creating a row in London Welensky went on holiday.

Much relieved, Macmillan telephoned Buckingham Palace with a message to the Queen that 'he had solved Rhodesia.' He thought his worst African nightmare was over. Unfortunately it was not, and his satisfaction did not last long. His first disappointment came from Sandys at the Commonwealth Relations Office who wrote that he considered the proposals unsatisfactory, and feared that if they were carried out 'it would be impossible to avoid a major political crisis'. This was followed by disquieting rumours of his resignation.

However on 26 June a new White Paper incorporating what were erroneously called the 'Governor's recommendations' was published. This was an overture to the Federal Government and a dilution of Macleod's original principle. Macmillan recorded: 'By a miracle we have achieved a solution. Both Macleod and Sandys have agreed, so has Welensky.' Welensky wrote to Macmillan on the day the White Paper was published: 'I am glad the main points of the Rhodesia Constitution [North] have been settled. As you know I do not like the Constitution that they foreshadow but my one hope is that it will prove workable.' Welensky's view was that the new constitution 'had been inspired by doubtful principles overshadowed by political expediency ... and bedevilled by haste. Nevertheless I am now satisfied it is a reasonably workable instrument.'[32]

Welensky was placated but African reaction was disastrous. Kaunda announced his complete rejection of the proposals which he described as far worse and far more complicated than any previously presented. He flew to London and saw Macleod. After friendly talks he announced

that the end of the Federation was in sight, and once back in Northern
Rhodesia he stated he would wage 'a passive resistance campaign which
would crack every part of the Federation and shake the foundations of
British government in Northern Rhodesia', which he accused of giving
way to 'a political idiot and evil genius – Welensky'.

The campaign was not 'non-violent'. There were acts of hooliganism
and arson with destruction of schools and bridges. The situation in
Northern Rhodesia deteriorated rapidly, and the British Government's
departure from the original February White Paper (which had been
grudgingly received by the Africans) meant that there was now no hope
of the Africans compromising on a future association with the Federation. It soon became apparent that the June proposals were unacceptable
in Northern Rhodesia, and influential opinion urged the Government
to move back towards the February proposals.

Macmillan again became agitated about the situation, and both
Ministers and civil servants were alarmed by the amount of attention
the Prime Minister was giving to the intimate details of the Rhodesian
problem. In the archives there is a note from Macleod to Burke Trend,
the senior civil servant responsible to the Prime Minister for co-
ordination of Central African affairs, informing him that 'we are keeping
as many papers as possible from the Prime Minister.' Macmillan appears
to have twigged, since there is a note from him asking the Colonial
Office 'to keep him in touch on all points'. In his memoirs Kilmuir
recalled: 'The Cabinet found itself spending long hours and unnecessary
hours [on Central Africa] trying to handle small matters which should
never have come to its attention.' And of Macleod he wrote: 'one of
the most charming and kind of men his manner too frequently leads men
to view him with distrust and dislike.'[33]

On 6 September Macmillan held a meeting with Macleod and Sandys
to deal with the threatening situation. Macleod warned that unless
'we took action Moffat and the Liberals and African independents
[Kaunda's party had already withdrawn] would resign, and a period of
official government rule would have to follow with Kaunda and the
other Africans and Liberals boycotting the elections. This would
amount to a complete failure of our policy in a vital area of Africa.' He
had sent a draft to Moffat of a new constitution more favourable to the
Africans.

Macleod received only partial support from Sandys who said he was
'in two minds' and was much concerned about starting a new row with
Welensky 'who unless we were very careful might, with some reason,
charge us with bad faith'. He wanted to consult with Welensky very
tactfully. Macmillan had previously said he would never give way to
violence, and in discussion it was first suggested that nothing could be

done until 'violence came to an end', but they admitted the crux of the matter was the number of Africans qualified to vote.

At a second meeting on the same day it was decided that Macleod should send out drafts of more favourable treatment for Africans in the franchise, and they should aim to persuade Welensky 'to take a statesmanlike attitude, and make him recognize that if the elections were boycotted by the Africans the resulting situation would be thoroughly bad, and must do damage to the prospects of the Federation as a whole'. This was in fact giving way to violence, but there was no acceptable alternative.

Unfortunately Sandys's 'tactful approach' to Welensky did not produce a 'statesmanlike' reaction. Instead Welensky exploded at the idea of back-pedalling from the June White Paper. On 11 September Sandys minuted Macmillan that any statement on Northern Rhodesia should be postponed because of Welensky. This brought Macleod again close to resignation. After reading Sandys's minute to the Prime Minister he sent an ultimatum to Macmillan the following day calling for a statement to be issued either that day or the next:

> We cannot once more be put off from a decision because of the threats that Welensky will make a speech denouncing it. The whole facts of the matter in Northern Rhodesia are:
> (1) That over 2,000 arrests have been made.
> (2) That about 25 people have been killed.
> (3) That we have had to take emergency powers including the right to detain without trial in two of the provinces of Northern Rhodesia.
> We have certainly failed to achieve the minimum degree of acquiescence which we looked for hopefully in June. The Federal Government's assessment of the security risks at that time have proved disastrously wrong. You will remember that they urged on us even if we accepted their proposals African reaction would be slight and easily contained . . . Finally I attach great importance to speed . . . if Kaunda returns and no statement has been made his Executive will urge on him to implement Stage 3 as it is called of their plan which involves disturbances on the Copper Belt.* Once this happens the situation in Northern Rhodesia and indeed the cause of the Federation could be set back for years.

Once again Macmillan ignored Sandys and capitulated to Macleod. On 13 September the Government issued a statement about Northern Rhodesia, noting that there had been criticism of the June proposals and the Government were therefore ready to consider representations 'about the divergences of view which persist'.

On the same day Macmillan wrote to Welensky, pointing out that a

---

*Kaunda and his associates were known to have prepared a plan to seize the copper mines.

boycott of the new constitution by the Africans would lead to more
violence and setting up of concentration camps on the Kenya model*
which would

> embitter race relations throughout the Federation and the destruction of all
> hopes of securing African support for the Federal system.
>
> We intend to keep a complete open mind about whether or not to amend
> our proposals ... It would not therefore serve any useful purpose for any
> of your Ministers to come to London tonight. If we should later come to
> the conclusion that changes are desirable we shall naturally consult you
> before reaching any decision ... We have had no negotiations of any kind
> with Moffat or Kaunda, and have certainly not promised them that we
> would make any changes in the constitution.

In his memoirs Welensky relates that he did not reply to this letter
because the only answer he could have given would have been very rude.
He knew his aims had been thwarted by Macleod.[34]

By now Macmillan had had enough of Macleod and his threats of resignation. Macleod had won as before, but at the expense of his relationship
with the Prime Minister. In his memoirs Macmillan described Macleod
as 'not an easy colleague ... he is a Highlander which means that he
is easily worked up into an emotional mood; it also means he is proud
and ambitious.' As Nigel Fisher, Macleod's closest Commons friend,
writes in his biography of Macleod:

> a rift developed in the hitherto close relationship between Macmillan and
> Macleod. Previously when there was a division at ten o'clock the two would
> often come swinging into the lobby together, the Prime Minister's arm
> around Iain's shoulder and the two clearly in the closest harmony. But one
> evening in 1961 as Macmillan entered the lobby he caught Iain's gaze and
> his eyes flickered away. This made it clear that Macleod no longer had the
> Prime Minister's full confidence, and that he considered his Secretary of State
> expendable.[35]

In the late summer of 1961 with the Conservative Party divided over
both Europe and Africa, and with criticism of Macmillan's leadership
mounting, the Prime Minister could not afford Macleod's resignation.
Macleod was popular with the younger MPs and was being talked of
as a successor to Macmillan. He could not be sent to the back benches.
Instead Macmillan decided to remove him from the Colonies, and as soon
as Parliament reassembled on 9 October 1961, asked Macleod to accept
'promotion' and become Leader of the House and Chairman of the
Conservative Party. Macmillan recorded in his memoirs that Macleod

---

*In 1953 thousands of Mau Mau arrested by the British Army had been put into hastily
constructed camps.

accepted 'reluctantly', but later commented ruefully that his successor at the Colonial Office, Reginald Maudling, caused him disappointment because he was quite as 'progressive' as Macleod, and 'in some respects *plus royaliste que le Roi*'.

In promoting Macleod Macmillan was extremely harsh on Butler to whom both of these positions belonged, and who had been his loyal supporter through thick and thin. Though still Home Secretary, Butler felt the blow, and his widow told the author that the loss of the Chairmanship of the Party in particular made Rab for once depressed. As Butler wrote to Home:

> I was finally informed by Harold that I was to give up being both Chairman of the Party and Leader of the House in favour of Iain Macleod. I was told I was too old and had anyway done the House for six years ... I could have dug my heels in and refused to give up the Commons where I have much support.[36]

But Macmillan's problem was that Macleod would not accept the Chairmanship of the Party alone, and demanded the Leadership of the House as 'the price of moving from the Colonial Office'.

CHAPTER 13

The End of Federation

TO HIS SURPRISE Macmillan found it even more difficult to deal with the problems of the Central African Federation with Maudling as Colonial Secretary. Macmillan himself had devoted a disproportionate amount of his time to the Federation issue and wanted to dictate government policy. He found he now could not do so because the three Ministers involved were at cross purposes, while as Chairman of the Conservative Party Macleod, though no longer with direct responsibility, was very influential and still in the Cabinet, and ready to fight to the point of resignation to see that his African policies were implemented.

As Foreign Secretary, Selwyn Lloyd had taken no interest whatsoever in Africa. Coming to the Foreign Office straight from Commonwealth Relations in June 1960, Alec Home felt much involved, had strong views, and was much influenced by his close friend Lord Dalhousie, the right-wing Governor of Southern Rhodesia, who continually urged the Foreign Secretary to take a strong line against rapid Africanization and to make every effort to placate Welensky. Duncan Sandys, who had been moved from Defence to replace Home at Commonwealth Relations, had quickly got to grips with the problems and though frequently ambivalent was more favourable to Welensky than was Maudling. Lord Perth, who remained as Minister of State under Maudling, was insistent that Macleod's aim of giving the Africans a majority in government was right: he like Macleod was ready to resign if Africanization was negated. Maudling had stepped into a hornet's nest and quickly decided that Macleod's, not Home's, policy was the correct one.

Maudling has recorded that he accepted Macmillan's invitation to take on the Colonial Office 'readily' and that his predecessor, Iain Macleod, had come under 'a great deal of unjustified criticism from the right wing of the Party'. He thought resentment at the speed of change among the Conservative right wing and European residents of the colonial territories involved had focused upon Macleod because they thought he was deliberately and unnecessarily accelerating the pace of independence.

Macmillan's optimism that Maudling would reduce this pace of change was misplaced. Having studied the problem Maudling favoured early Africanization as keenly as Macleod, but was a less prickly colleague, being affable and pragmatic, while Macleod was abrasive and emotional. When Maudling visited Central Africa in the late autumn of 1961, he records in his memoirs that he had soon made up his mind to produce proposals for the new constitution of Northern Rhodesia designed to improve the position of the Africans in the forthcoming elections. Both sides, he discovered, expressed disapproval, the most vehement being the Europeans and Welensky; whilst the Cabinet was divided with Sandys taking the opposite view to his own. Thus Maudling found himself repeating Macleod's role.[1] Indeed his proposals for Northern Rhodesia went even further than Macleod's but Maudling claims that this was because events 'had marched on since the summer of 1961' with the outbreak of violence; his concern now was to avoid a degree of violence which would make a solution satisfactory to both sides impossible.

As Maudling took over from Macleod, Sandys as Secretary for Commonwealth Relations wrote to the Prime Minister that it was essential that a single Minister should be responsible for the protracted and complicated negotiations over the Federation which would be inevitable. Macmillan replied that 'dependent territories traditionally looked on the Colonial Office as their protector, and if it was all transferred to the Commonwealth Office powerful emotional reactions might be aroused sufficiently to outweigh the advantages of administrative convenience.'

However Macmillan was at first attracted by the idea and said he would mention it to Maudling and Trend before discussing it again with Sandys himself. A meeting was arranged for 25 October 1961. Meanwhile Sandys urged on Macmillan that all responsibility for the Federation be transferred to himself, although he admitted that Maudling would be bound to argue against this. The meeting was cancelled; at the time Macmillan hoped that Maudling, who seemed so easy-going, would pay more attention to his wishes even than Sandys. Macmillan's last word on the subject was to tell Sandys he had not found time to discuss the matter but 'I hope you will not pursue your suggestion'; it had already been agreed that Maudling should go out to Northern Rhodesia and Nyasaland to make contact with African leaders, and an announcement to that effect was about to be made. At the same time Macmillan asked Norman Brook, head of the Civil Service, to make it clear to Sandys that his suggestion was impractical. Five months later, in the middle of March 1962, Macmillan decided that one Minister must be responsible, but that Minister was not to be Sandys. Sandys was grievously disappointed, feeling with justification that such an assignment would have been ideally suited to his talents and political experience.[2]

Reviewing the situation Maudling has recorded that his initial reaction was that Federation was 'a dead duck', and that it would be better to have an African majority governing in Northern Rhodesia in a good frame of mind rather than an African minority in opposition in a bad frame of mind and never likely to agree to any form of federation. Sandys agreed with him that 'We can no longer be guided by logic and equity.'[3]

Macmillan discussed the next steps to be taken at a meeting with Maudling and Sandys on 14 November 1961. The civil servants' effort to prevent the Prime Minister getting too involved in details had failed, and Macmillan came up with detailed suggestions on altering the voting procedure marginally to the benefit of the Africans. The others thought it was pointless to go into such details before they had received written replies from the political parties in Northern Rhodesia as requested in September. However they agreed to the Machiavellian suggestion that they should ask Welensky to put forward his own proposals and try to get him to ask for more 'than we were prepared to give' so that if this was rejected the Government would seem to be taking the side of the Africans. This plan obviously originated with Macmillan.

Welensky was in London. After talking to him the next day Sandys wrote to Macmillan that he had suggested that Welensky 'should try his hand at an agreed solution', and that his thinking had advanced a long way. Welensky did not fall into the trap, and wrote to Sandys: 'Kaunda is asking for a built-in majority in middle roll seats, and this spells the end of Federation. If the [British] Government has already made up its mind all discussions would be a hollow sham.'

The British Cabinet juggled continually with variations on electoral rolls in an abortive effort to reconcile the irreconcilable: the slowing down of the attainment of African majority rule to placate the Welensky lobby and its acceleration to pacify African expectations. Voters on A rolls needed property, income and educational qualifications; the lower or B rolls called for lower qualifications of literacy or wealth. Few Africans could qualify for the A roll, and in general candidates for the A roll were European, and candidates for the B roll African. In proposals for Northern Rhodesia the Colonial Office had suggested a middle roll for which candidates had to have support from voters on both the other rolls, but despite the interest of Macmillan in such experiments the middle roll proposal foundered.

Before leaving for Africa Maudling told Macmillan that Banda was committed to secession for Nyasaland; the scenario was such that the new Colonial Secretary must have found it hard to believe that the Federation could still be saved as the Prime Minister wanted.[4]

Maudling, one of the most intelligent and clear-minded of Britain's post-war politicians with acute antennae for learning quickly, soon dis-

covered the true state of affairs abroad. In Salisbury he was unimpressed
with Welensky's and Whitehead's arguments; he was more in tune with
the Northern Rhodesian Liberal Moffat, and quickly got on good terms
with Banda and Kaunda. He returned home convinced there must be
a built-in African majority in the new Northern Rhodesia constitution,
and that both Nyasaland and Northern Rhodesia must be allowed to
secede from the Federation, although he still hoped fruitlessly that the
Federation might be replaced by a form of economic association. His
views were even less acceptable than Macleod's to the Prime Minister,
the Foreign Secretary and to right-wing Conservatives.

Trouble for Macmillan over East Africa loomed up in January 1962,
and he was again faced with threats of resignations. Meetings of
the Cabinet Colonial Policy Committee early that month produced
acrimonious disagreement. Macleod was asked by Macmillan to attend
one meeting, but refused. On 7 January Macmillan asked Macleod for
help in persuading Maudling to water down his proposals for Northern
Rhodesia. Macleod replied that he had found out from Lord Kilmuir
and Lord Perth exactly what changes in the June White Paper Maudling
advocated and that he, Macleod, wanted only moderate changes whereas
Maudling wanted sweeping changes which would be regarded as breaches
of faith after the June White Paper and the September statement. Of
Maudling's four points Macleod accepted only one and a half as essential.

Lord Salisbury fanned the flames of this bitter Tory dispute by writing
to Macmillan on 3 January 1962 that reopening the question of Northern
Rhodesia so soon

> would certainly be regarded as running counter to undertakings which
> Welensky had every reason to believe were binding ... You will know
> better than I what the effect will be on many Conservatives just as they
> are extremely sensitive about events in Katanga and Goa ... I am certain
> that I can speak for a considerable body of opinion in the Party that either
> you or Maudling should scotch the rumour – the sooner, the better.

In conversation and speeches Salisbury took every opportunity to vent
his disagreement.

After the Colonial Policy Committee meeting on 16 January both
Maudling and Perth were ready to resign unless the new voting system
for Northern Rhodesia guaranteed a black majority. The Chief Whip,
Martin Redmayne, sent Macmillan an alarming note that his soundings
amongst Conservative MPs showed that Maudling and Perth and their
under-secretaries had decided to resign, and that Macleod would almost
certainly resign in sympathy.[5]

Faced with a disruptive crisis which threatened the existence of the
Government Macmillan called on the long-suffering Butler for help. As

usual, Butler obliged. Butler talked to Sandys on 16 January 1962 and reported to Macmillan that at first Sandys said he had been 'through all the permutations' and did not know the best way simultaneously to stop his colleagues resigning, maintain law and order in Northern Rhodesia and avoid Welensky going off the handle. He thought the possible amendment of the June proposals about which 'we had agreed that I should speak to him would not satisfy Iain'. (This was a reference to a compromise solution discussed privately by Rab and Harold.) They then discussed how this compromise, which was slightly in the Africans' favour, would affect Welensky. According to Butler Sandys 'wanted to play this along and suggested he himself should go out to Rhodesia and sell whatever proposal we decided upon'. For this, he said, Sandys wanted more time, and in order to 'carry him along with us' he should renew contact in a few days.

Two days later, on 18 January, Butler talked to Macleod, remarking that he had heard the Northern Rhodesian situation was unsettled. Reporting Macleod's reply, Butler wrote:

> He [Macleod] failed to understand how Reggie Maudling had taken such an extreme view. It may have been because he, Reggie, was concerned about the law and order situation or because he had a great deal fed into him by his own Colonial people when he was out there. He thought that Reggie was not now in such an extreme mood as he had been. He asked how things were going and I said I thought you had in mind some small concession to suit the spirit of the September statement. He said he thought this was what was desired.

Macleod went on to tell Butler that 'his attitude to resignation would be very much governed by that of the two under-secretaries at the Colonial Office, Lord Perth* and Hugh Fraser', and although he was friendly with Maudling he cared less about him than he did about the two under-secretaries with whom he had worked.

Obviously Macleod was considering resignation in sympathy with Maudling over the Cabinet's refusal to allow a black majority in the Northern Rhodesia Government because he reiterated to Butler that he would be 'extremely uncomfortable unless he could carry at least Lord Perth with him'. Perth was taking a stronger line than Macleod, who now had other responsibilities. Butler then embarked on cloying political platitudes, remarking to Macleod how important it was for 'every man at his post to win back the situation by the next election because as was normal the Government was unpopular in mid term'. Macleod said he was willing to co-operate to try to find a way through.

---

*Lord Perth was in fact Minister of State.

Butler confronted Macmillan with the bleakness of the situation, and the Prime Minister decided to go further down the road to meet Maudling regardless of Welensky. On 31 January at a meeting at Admiralty House Maudling accepted a compromise over the electoral franchise for Northern Rhodesia, although the next day he had a blazing row with Sandys as to exactly what the agreement was, refusing to lunch with Butler and Sandys at Buck's to make up the quarrel.

Macmillan still feared Maudling might resign at the subsequent Cabinet meetings held on 26 and 27 February and recorded in his memoirs that he felt uncertain about the attitude of the Colonial Secretary to the proposed amendments in the Europeans' favour to the June White Paper on Northern Rhodesia; but after some three quarters of an hour's discussion in Cabinet on 28 February Maudling said that 'the Government were faced with such great problems in every field that – whatever it might be – he would accept the decision of his colleagues.' Maudling gives a different version in his memoirs, writing that 'while I disagreed with my colleagues, [I said] I would accept their decision because an open act of resignation would have grave effects in Africa and stir up just the kind of bloodshed which I was most anxious to avoid.'[6] Maudling also recorded that Harold immediately asked him to a most agreeable lunch at Buck's. There is no mention of Maudling's statement in the Cabinet Minutes. However Perth, who had decided in conversation with Maudling to resign with him, sent the Prime Minister his resignation in writing. In his diary for 26 February Macmillan wrote: 'This is pretty silly in view of his chief's [Maudling's] decision not to. I will see him tomorrow and ask JFS to see him this evening.' On 28 February Macmillan was able to write that Perth 'has unresigned'.

On 28 February 1962 Maudling announced the new franchise for Northern Rhodesia in the Commons. It paved the way inexorably for African majority rule, with consequences little different from those which Macleod's White Paper of February 1961 would have produced, and which had been so hotly disputed both in Cabinet and by Welensky. The alterations in favour of the Europeans were largely psychological.

In his memoirs Macmillan wrote: 'The alterations which had caused so much argument were of minor importance. What remains in my memory is the immense amount of trouble taken over the future of the African territories amidst so many other baffling problems, internal and external, with which we, like every other Government, had to contend.' In December 1960 Macleod had written to Macmillan after a weekend with Welensky at Chequers that he was thinking of somewhere around 'the point of parity for the new Northern Rhodesian Constitution, and there was reason to believe Welensky and his colleagues were thinking along the same lines, and Kaunda would be satisfied if there was the appearance of an African majority through the votes of the Governor and the officials on the elected Council.'

If Macmillan had kept to this solution, which he accepted at the time, and been firm with Welensky, the settler lobby within the Conservative Party would probably have acquiesced. By dilly-dallying and pandering to Welensky and Lord Salisbury over an absurdly complicated voting procedure Macmillan made them more obdurate. The Prime Minister recorded realistically in his memoirs: 'The delay between December 1960 and February 1962 achieved nothing.'[7] The only verdict can be that it antagonized the Africans without pacifying the Europeans, and the ambivalent attitude of the British Government gave Lord Salisbury every reason to make accusations of bad faith.

The tale unfolded above is one of a Government led by a man who constantly changed his mind, and worked himself into a nervous state by immersing himself in the details of African franchises until he could not see the wood for the trees. No wonder he puts a gloss over it in his memoirs. But the threat that Maudling's resignation would trigger off others was the last straw; it convinced Macmillan that he must shuffle off responsibility on to someone else. In March 1962 he asked the ubiquitous Butler to take charge of Central African affairs. Once again Butler obliged and firm government and clear policies replaced the dithering which had characterized the two and a half years since Lennox-Boyd left the Colonial Office.

Butler set up his new Central African Office in Gwydyr House, Whitehall, on 19 March 1962. In his memoirs he makes it plain that he had never been in favour of the appointment of the Monckton Commission; he felt that Macmillan and the rest of the Cabinet agreed to it solely from the point of view of home politics, hoping the Federation could be preserved if 'Church and middle of the road opinion could be reassured by a dispassionate and widely based enquiry' which would also persuade the Labour Party not to break up the Federation.

Butler felt that Monckton would be bound to highlight and not solve the political dilemma over the Federation which Butler attributed to its 'plural nature' – an overwhelming African majority, small Asian and coloured communities, plus a very sizeable body of Europeans upon whose capital, skill and enterprise the economic development of the Federation depended. He also mistrusted the disparity of the ratio of Europeans to Africans in the three territories – 1 to 13 in Southern Rhodesia; 1 to 30 in Northern Rhodesia; 1 to 300 in Nyasaland – although he had felt hopeful in 1953 that African suspicion of federation might 'evaporate' with rising prosperity. By 1960 he claims to have realized that the Federation had no future, given the swiftly rising tide of African nationalism, and when the Monckton Report concluded that Britain should allow the principle of the right to secede, he was sure the Federation was doomed. Although both Alec Home and Harold Macmillan tried to impress on him that there was hope for the Federation when he assumed his new post, Butler was unimpressed by their arguments and declares that he took up the job only out of a sense of duty.[8]

Nine months previously Dr Banda had won an overwhelming electoral victory under the new Nyasaland Constitution with a campaign advocating secession. Butler arrived in Salisbury with his wife on 11 May 1962 for a stay of fourteen days, having three days previously told a stormy Commons that Nyasaland would be allowed to secede if she insisted and other forms of association would be studied. According to Welensky, this meant he came as a 'liquidator' not a 'negotiator'.

On the day Butler arrived in Salisbury the seventeen-nation United Nations Committee on Colonialism endorsed a report (with the representatives of Britain, USA, Australia and Italy dissenting) that the position in Southern Rhodesia was grave and there was a danger of serious conflict if the existing constitution was maintained in the face of 'total African opposition'. This strengthened Butler's hand in arguing with Welensky that Southern Rhodesia could not secede from the Federation unless her constitution was modified to give better African representation.[9]

After brief and friendly talks in Salisbury with both Welensky's Federal and Whitehead's Southern Rhodesian Ministers in which Butler perceived that neither thought all was lost, he flew on to Zomba to stay with the new Governor of Nyasaland, Glyn Jones. Together with Glyn Jones, Butler then held three crucial talks with Dr Banda. Fortunately Butler and Banda got on together like a house on fire, and Banda became even more enthusiastic about Butler than he had been for Macleod.

The talks started at Government House on 16 May and continued with intervals throughout the day, being followed by a further meeting on 17 May. Butler quickly made it clear to Banda that, although the principle of secession from the Federation by Nyasaland had been conceded, he could not carry his Cabinet colleagues or the Conservative Party with him unless his advisers 'recommended' this course.

Banda insisted that whatever Butler's advisers 'recommended' he and his people were determined to secede, and that he was disappointed in the delay because Sandys had promised him a firm decision by the British Government in March, and he wanted to know how long Butler's 'expert advisers' would take. Butler said he could not get them 'on the ground' before June and then their work might take several months. Banda stated categorically he would not negotiate alternative forms of association with the other two territories until Nyasaland's secession had been implemented. Fortunately Banda was friendly and polite throughout, and he thanked Butler cordially for showing so much understanding of his territory's problems.

At the second session Banda stated that he wanted Nyasaland to move to self-government in July and the complicated business of detaching Nyasaland from the Federation completed by April 1963, when Nyasaland should be accorded independence within the Commonwealth. This timetable was too fast for Butler, who wanted a conference in London as a preliminary to self-government – a move which Banda thought unnecessary, though later in a conciliatory gesture he agreed to it.

Butler then embarked on the tricky matter of association between Nyasaland and the two Rhodesias after secession, and asked Banda whether there could be some arrangement about the army 'which would still be necessary for Nyasaland'. Banda said he would like the help of British officers for training but 'could not agree to any co-operation with Southern Rhodesia on military matters'. He also rejected any currency union with Southern Rhodesia; he wanted a direct link with London. Butler got the impression that any consultation with Banda about association with the Federation after independence would be only 'token'; he was correct. The atmosphere was still cordial but Banda was in a more excitable mood and, according to Glyn Jones, might easily have been provoked into a display of emotion.

The third meeting was more stormy. Banda declared with considerable heat that he must have independence in April 1963. Butler temporized, saying he could 'not go further' until he had consulted with his colleagues in London; he persuaded Banda to come to London for talks in June.

Violent disagreement erupted over Butler's determination that there should be a conference prior to the Nyasaland constitution being altered in favour of independent self-government. Eventually Banda was persuaded to agree to this provided that the conference fixed a date for Nyasaland's independence within the Commonwealth. Butler stalled again and said he could not commit himself in advance of the further discussions which would take place in London. Banda then 'strongly represented' that the work of Butler's advisers need not take more than two months, and he demanded a decision not later than September; he stressed that Butler's advisers must consult with his Ministers because 'the people must understand that Malawi Ministers were not being hoodwinked'. Finally Banda reiterated that it would be quite impossible for him to agree to any association whatsoever with Southern Rhodesia.

The meeting was 'again cordial', Glyn Jones noted, although at one time Banda grew 'very heated' – Jones suspected the heat was to some extent assumed. However the end-note was 'friendly in the extreme'.

Butler had done splendidly. He had delayed the precipitate departure of Nyasaland from the Federation; he could thus explain to Welensky and the settler lobby in London that negotiations were still proceeding. Undoubtedly Butler had by now made up his mind that the Federation was doomed, but he cunningly hid his conviction from both Macmillan and Home and the white politicians in Rhodesia while he set to work to prepare a *fait accompli*, with independence for both Nyasaland and Northern Rhodesia and the demise of the Federation. At the worst moment of the meetings, Banda had said petulantly that if the enquiry by the experts did not finish quickly and enable HMG to grant secession he would have to go to his people and say, 'I must now resign because my methods have failed to achieve the aims for which you chose me. You must choose somebody else who may have to adopt different methods.' This threat was not lost on Butler.

There were 'internal fireworks', Butler records, when he talked again to Welensky in Salisbury on his way home. He gave a guarded account of his discussions with Banda and left the misleading impression that it was his 'intention or hope' to create a constructive solution for the Federation. He persuaded Welensky to issue a press statement that no decision had been made 'other than to undertake an appraisal of the situation by a committee of advisers'. This hid Butler's true state of mind. Fortunately Butler's charm worked as well on Welensky as it had on Banda, and Welensky welcomed one Minister being in charge, saying that if anybody could find a reasonable solution it 'would be Mr Butler' while he, Welensky, would consider 'any reasonable suggestions for an adjustment of the Federation . . . Butler's visit had achieved a great deal of good.' As Butler's purpose was now to sell the Federation down the river this is a fine tribute to his tact.[10]

Butler wanted to lure Burke Trend away from the Treasury to head his official team of advisers. Ungenerously Macmillan would not allow this, so Butler had to be content with a team from the Colonial and Commonwealth offices headed by Mark Tennant and Duncan Watson, both of whom were able and experienced. By July they were in Salisbury and Home allowed Sir Roger Stevens from the Foreign Office to join them while Butler added the economist Professor Arthur Brown of All Souls and General Ralph Hone, a distinguished lawyer and soldier, to the team. Brown produced a lucid and ingenious plan for an African economic common market but, as Butler records, such constructive ideas stood no chance against the 'torrent of racial nationalism'; however Butler cleverly kept the ball in the air, giving the white settlers the illusion that there was some hope for the creation of another type of association to replace the 1953 Federation.

Despite these successes, in the 'night of long knives' in July 1962, Macmillan dealt a new blow to Butler: he decided to remove from him the Home Office and to appoint Henry Brooke in his place. Though accorded the unofficial position of Deputy Prime Minister with the official title First Secretary of State, Butler was greatly dismayed by the decision, as he wrote to Macmillan:

> I understand from Norman Brook and others that there will be no pre-cedence in the title Secretary of State. I will, therefore, lose my position as senior Secretary of State, as Home Secretary, and also all my connection with the Court and my duties with the Queen ...
>
> The last time that arrangements were made with the press to show that I was helping you very little came of it. I lost the Leadership of the House and Chairmanship of the Party – and the general impression was 'Butler Down'.
>
> Since then the African appointment has tended to improve the situation but you said, most emphatically, when I took on Africa that I must *not* do it alone.
>
> The latest proposal is that I become Secretary of State (*tout court*). I will to the public mind have no duties except Africa. Furthermore, without a classical office such as Lord President, I shall be out on a raft, as I was after Anthony Eden's decision in 1955. I know what this means: one has a per-sonal assistant and inadequate staff to transact business.
>
> I, therefore, think I shall be out on an African limb, as there has never yet been any clearly defined position for an undefined deputy.[11]

Butler must have been close to resignation, and coming so soon after the other sackings this would have put Macmillan into a difficult position. However, all Butler's working life had been devoted to politics, and the alternative of the back benches, or a peerage (which Macmillan had suggested), did not appeal to him. Much to Macmillan's relief Butler decided to soldier on, and the feeling of self-pity evident in his letter to Macmillan soon passed, so his widow told the author, as he re-immersed himself in Africa.

By October the report by Butler's advisers was complete; the docu-ment bears strong traces of Butler's own drafting. It concluded that Nyasaland's secession was inevitable and must lead to the dissolution of the Federation, and that Northern Rhodesia would insist upon secession as vehemently as Nyasaland. Thus it would be unwise to try to hold the two Rhodesias together in a federation even for a short period. It also stated that Southern Rhodesia would not want to remain, even temporarily, within a federation with a 'turbulent' Northern Rhodesia. Two questions arose, the advisers reported:

> (a) Would it be advisable to equivocate about the future of the Rhodesias even to the extent of telling Sir Roy Welensky that the Government for their part undertake to work for the closest practicable association between

Northern Rhodesia and Southern Rhodesia which would leave open the question of a continuing federal relationship between the two territories?

(b) When it is announced that the Government accept the secession of Nyasaland will Sir Roy Welensky at once conclude that this means the dissolution of the whole Federation and how is he likely to react?

By stating the problem in these terms Butler was placing on his Cabinet colleagues the onus of taking the decision that the Federation was dead, and making it impossible for them to argue for its continuation.

The advisers also pointed out that with Nyasaland seceding Northern Rhodesia would apply ever more powerful pressure not only for secession but also for rapid constitutional advance towards independence under a black African government. They added significantly that independence and the secession of Northern Rhodesia would precipitate equal pressure for independence in Southern Rhodesia under a predominantly white government which would place Britain *vis-à-vis* the United Nations and in other 'contexts' in difficulties because Southern Rhodesia would continue to be governed by the white minority, and at the United Nations it would be argued that 'human rights' were being denied to the Africans. In conclusion they warned that dissolution would prove costly to the United Kingdom but the cost would be less than that either of maintaining the present Federation by force or of failing to secure acceptance of another form of association in good time.[12]

By presenting this issue in the words of his advisers instead of as his personal view Butler torpedoed efforts by Macmillan and Home to work for a revised federation. Reluctantly they caved in, although the pretence that something could be saved out of the Federation continued for many months, mainly in an effort to pacify Welensky.

The Nyasaland Conference met in London and paved the way for independence with a Bill of Rights to safeguard the interests of the Europeans. The secession of Nyasaland from the Federation had been decided by the time the conference ended on 23 November 1962. Simultaneously the General Election in Northern Rhodesia produced a black coalition government under Kenneth Kaunda and Harry Nkumbula, while the Southern Rhodesian election resulted in the defeat of Edgar Whitehead and his substitution by Winston Field as head of a more extreme white supremacy party opposed to the continuation of Federation and in favour of independence.

On 19 December 1962 Butler announced to the Commons the secession of Nyasaland from the Federation: 'We were not', he said firmly, 'to be put off our duty.' Macmillan was in Nassau and Butler cabled: 'Nyasaland statement received quietly in Commons, but rude remarks were made in the Lords with Salisbury being very rude and difficult.' The British Parliament had every right to legislate to end Federation but influential right-wing Conservatives raised constitutional difficulties, alleging that the Government had breached pledges given in 1953 when the Federation was created. Lord Malvern, the first Prime Minister of the Federation and before that Prime Minister of Southern Rhodesia, flew back from Africa for the Lords debate and accused the Government of betrayal and paying more attention to 'a Messiah' (Banda) than to the white population. Similar charges and allegations of broken pledges were also made in the Lords by ex-Colonial Secretaries Oliver Lyttelton and Lennox-Boyd (now Lords Chandos and Boyd). However a White Paper disposed of their protests, establishing that no promises made in 1953 had been broken.

On 18 January 1963 Butler returned to Africa on a fourteen-day tour. His brief from Trend was to talk to the territorial governments and not to the Federal Government, and to tell them that 'our aim' was to develop an effective association between Southern and Northern Rhodesia, preferably with some political teeth, but 'it may be necessary to limit ourselves at the outset to purely economic ties and try to develop these later into political links'. Trend's brief must have been written to keep Macmillan quiet because at this stage the realistic Butler had no faith in any type of alternative association. The formation of any new association, Trend added, 'would be very complicated'. Perhaps he had his tongue in his cheek.[13]

Butler's Central Africa visit passed off quietly. He was the conquering hero in Nyasaland but was pressed hard in Northern Rhodesia to make a categorical statement announcing their secession. To avoid a confrontation with Welensky Butler refused to make this statement although what he expected to gain from delay is far from clear. Possibly he feared telegrams from Macmillan.

In March 1963 a deputation from the Federal Government led by Welensky arrived in London at the same time as a mission from Northern Rhodesia led by Kaunda. Butler had tendentiously told the Commons that the object of these missions was to discuss a future association between the two territories. This was patently untrue, and Butler has recounted that the ensuing days were 'the most laborious and painful of his career'. Macmillan told Butler: 'We must try to manage things in such a way that the Federation dissolves of its own accord – preferably as the result of the expressed wish of the two Rhodesias.' This must have been intended to satisfy right-wing Conservative MPs since it is hard to understand why Macmillan was still sensitive about Welensky.

On 25 March Kaunda told Butler he would not continue the talks unless the British Government announced his right to secede, and on 28 March, after a long meeting with Cabinet colleagues assisted by the

Governor and Deputy Governor of Northern Rhodesia, it was decided that Kaunda's request for secession must be granted immediately, although his mission had finally extinguished any hope that they would agree to an association with their neighbours in Southern Rhodesia. Butler told Roy Welensky and his delegation of this decision on 29 March, adding implausibly that he looked forward to a conference, preferably in Africa, to work out the new relationship, thus ignoring Kaunda's categorical rejection of any such idea. This produced an explosion from Welensky who refused to lunch with the Prime Minister at 10 Downing Street because 'the food would choke him'. Butler recorded that his interview with the Federation representatives was 'brief and painful'. Butler continued to explore the possibility of a conference to discuss new links between Southern and Northern Rhodesia but he must have known the exercise was futile: Macmillan and Home, however, still held vain hopes that something might materialize despite Kaunda's intransigence.

Butler's task now became more complicated by Whitehead's successor as Prime Minister, Winston Field, calling for independence for Southern Rhodesia. Such a request was unreasonable because under the existing constitution the rights of the Africans were not safeguarded, and Field's Government were resolutely opposed to any amendment of the constitution. Butler told Field he would consider independence but only if the constitution was amended in the Africans' favour on terms which Butler admitted he knew Field would never accept.[14]

Field's insistence that his country must have the right to become independent of Britain brought an agitated memorandum from Macleod to the Prime Minister, stressing that 'it would be indefensible to give independence to the present Government of Southern Rhodesia' and that 'everybody had now accepted the end of the Federation and the fact that Northern Rhodesia will go down the constitutional road under African Ministers. These are tremendous advances.' Macleod emphasized that these matters concerned him very much, and Macmillan realized that if he interfered with Butler at this late stage he would soon have another threat of resignation from Macleod on his hands.

Nyerere from Tanganyika and Obote from Uganda told Macmillan that they would leave the Commonwealth if the UK allowed independence to Southern Rhodesia. The Canadian and Australian governments also expressed alarm. Macmillan wrote to Robert Menzies, Prime Minister of Australia, on 28 April about Field's bid for independence – a bid now supported by Welensky:

> Unfortunately the policies followed by Edgar Whitehead's Government have not been followed by Winston Field's. It would be a difficult proposition to put to the House of Commons that with its present constitution and

legislation Southern Rhodesia should be granted independence by the UK Government ... on the other hand there is an even larger number of Conservative back-benchers, perhaps over 200, who feel that we should recognize Southern Rhodesia's right to become independent either before or at the same time as the other territories of the Federation.

If Southern Rhodesia was granted independence, Macmillan continued, she would probably be refused admittance to the Commonwealth. Despite the realistic tone of his letter to Menzies Macmillan was still being devious, writing to Welensky a week later that Southern Rhodesia might become independent after the Federation had been brought to an end.

The archives reveal that in the spring of 1963 the Cabinet were alarmed by rumours that Welensky might use the armed forces of the Federation to stage a *coup* that would effectively prevent the independence of Northern Rhodesia. These fears proved unfounded. However European politicians in Southern Rhodesia were extremely conscious of the importance of the mineral wealth of Northern Rhodesia to the prosperity of the Federation, and, disconsolate at the Copper Belt passing entirely to the Africans, certainly considered the use of force to prevent this.[15]

Having given up all hopes of a new association to replace the Federation, Butler now concentrated on organizing a conference which would bring the Federation to an orderly end with the co-operation of the three governments concerned. He had considerable difficulty in persuading Welensky and Field to attend the conference, and it is a great tribute to his political skill that they finally agreed to come. At that conference, at Victoria Falls at the end of June 1963, the final rites for the Federation were performed with dignity and without any assurance from Butler to Field that Southern Rhodesia could become independent under its existing constitution; Field only agreed to attend on the express condition that discussion of Southern Rhodesia's internal affairs would be altogether precluded. Welensky declared that he was attending the conference 'in a very co-operative frame of mind' as he had concluded that the only wise course was to proceed with orderly dissolution as soon as possible.

The Victoria Falls Conference ended amicably on 4 July 1963 and Macmillan cabled his congratulations to Butler, paying an effusive tribute to his 'leadership'. (Nevertheless a few weeks later Macmillan did everything he could to prevent Butler succeeding him as Prime Minister.) Having got himself completely bogged down in the complexities of the Central African Federation, Macmillan realized that while he had Maudling as Colonial Secretary there would always be acrimony and disputes. Butler not only relieved the Prime Minister of responsibilities which must have been driving him towards a nervous breakdown, but his efforts also culminated in the successful solution of two thirds of the problems. In addition he managed to present the dissolution of the Federation and the independence of Nyasaland and Northern Rhodesia in terms which the settler lobby of the Conservative Party had to accept.

Butler had achieved the orderly dissolution of the Federation and the establishment of the new states of Malawi and Zambia in place of Northern Rhodesia and Nyasaland. Unfortunately Southern Rhodesia was left with a strong army and its ruling clique were determined not to alter the constitution to allow for African aspirations.

It is apparent from the archives that when Field was in London in May 1963 Butler wanted to have a showdown with him and insist that independence was out of the question without important amendments to the constitution in favour of the Africans. Macmillan was opposed to the problem being put to Field in those terms. Conscious that over 200 Conservative MPS were adamantly opposed to any constitutional revision in Southern Rhodesia, and with the Government's standing in the opinion polls reduced to disaster level by the Profumo scandal and other events, Macmillan was in no mood to provoke a head-on clash with his Parliamentary Party by authorizing Butler to dictate terms to Field, as Butler would have liked to do. Butler with his limited mandate was therefore not to blame. Had he been authorized by the Prime Minister and the Cabinet, he would certainly have refused to allow the white settler Government to continue indefinitely in Southern Rhodesia. In 1970 he wrote that UDI and the Ian Smith Government offended him deeply 'as a negation of human liberty and dignity'.[16]

Ignoring the Southern Rhodesia constitutional issue at the time of the Victoria Falls Conference was a blot on the East African policy of the Macmillan Government. Obviously the correct time for dealing with this was when the dissolution of the Federation was on the agenda. The state of affairs left existing in the country after the dissolution of the Federation at Victoria Falls in June 1963 led inevitably to the unilateral declaration of independence by the Ian Smith Government of Southern Rhodesia in the following year. It was left to a future Government to deal with this running sore.

CHAPTER 14

Defence

THE LABOUR GOVERNMENT of 1945–51 stressed the importance of conventional forces for the defence of the nation and but reluctantly yielded to Ernest Bevin as Foreign Secretary in developing the nuclear deterrent. When President Truman hinted to Clement Attlee that the Americans might use nuclear bombs in the Korean War the British Prime Minister hurried over to Washington to warn him not to do so as British public opinion would be 'horrified'. However, under the Churchill Government of 1951–5 the bias of British defence policy moved positively towards nuclear weapons, and British nuclear capacity began to be integrated into NATO. By 1956 Britain had her own nuclear bombs ready for use.

In March 1956 there had been a clash between Harold Macmillan, then Chancellor of the Exchequer, and the Prime Minister, Anthony Eden. In his forthcoming April Budget Macmillan wanted to make savage cuts in spending on RAF fighters, arguing that fighter aircraft made little contribution to the defence of Britain: he wanted an immediate reappraisal of the long-term defence programme. Eden would not agree to any immediate cuts in RAF expenditure. However in his 1956 Budget speech Macmillan stated that there would be a comprehensive study of the 'whole programme' which would produce 'worthwhile savings'.[1]*

As soon as he succeeded Eden as Prime Minister Macmillan instructed Duncan Sandys, Minister of Defence, to undertake this long-term revision, and on 4 April 1957, in the annual Defence White Paper, Sandys announced massive cuts in spending. The White Paper expressed 'the commitment to nuclear weapons as the most effective deterrent to war ... on this basis large conventional forces are not required. A reduction of these forces allowed for the termination of national service

---

*As Minister of Defence in 1955 Macmillan had reported to the Cabinet: 'In regard to Europe if war comes in the next few years the Allies would have to make immediate use of the full array of nuclear weapons with the object of containing Russia's immediate overwhelming superiority of manpower. We must therefore plan on the assumption that global nuclear bombardment will become general.'[2]

and a cut in the Defence Budget.' In 1957 unemployment was minimal and the reduction in the number of servicemen and the abolition of conscription was welcomed by Norman Brook, Secretary to the Cabinet, as an opportunity of getting between 400,000 and 500,000 men into 'productive work'.

The 1957 White Paper announced the decision to restrict the role of Fighter Command to that of protecting the nuclear deterrent – that is, defence of the strategic bomber airfields. Duncan Sandys followed it up with a long memorandum to the Cabinet on 14 November 1957 which restated the reliance on nuclear weapons and sealed the fate of the RAF fighter force. The case for the retention of Fighter Command, as Sandys put it, turned on the question whether the absence of fighters would 'materially increase' the risk of the UK bomber force being knocked out before it could take off, and it was hardly conceivable that the Russians would make an unprovoked surprise attack on the British except in conjunction with a simultaneous attack upon the American air bases in the United States. According to Sandys:

> Our Intelligence services would have twenty-four hours' notice to bring our bomber forces into operation readiness, and once it had been so alerted the warning period provided by the radar system would be enough for the whole of medium bomber force to take off loaded with their bombs before Russian aircraft could reach our airfields.

Under these circumstances, the report claimed, 'the absence of fighter defence would have no effect'. In conclusion, the report stated: 'A decision to disband Fighter Command might be badly received by the United States who look to us to defend their bomber bases in Britain. Nevertheless if the arguments for dispensing with our fighter defence convince us, it should not be beyond our ability to convince our Allies.' Fighters were to be retained in Britain only for training and to provide a 'backing for the squadrons abroad'. Instead ground to air guided missiles were the most 'feasible method of destroying the long distance powered bomb launched from a stand off aircraft'.

In place of Fighter Command Sandys wanted a limited number of fighter aircraft to intercept hostile reconnaissance planes at great altitudes and to identify enemy raids; this task, he considered, could be more efficiently undertaken by a NATO single force. As might be expected George Ward, Secretary of State for Air, who had joined the RAF in 1927 at the age of 21 and had a distinguished war record as a flier, was opposed; he sent a minute to the Prime Minister on 20 December 1957:

> I have read the MOD's paper recommending that fighter aircraft should no longer be provided for the defence of B airfields. I must leave you in no doubt that my advisers and I disagree entirely with this recommendation.

It is important that the Ministers attending your meeting on Monday should
have before them a short account of the realities of the air defence situation.
I enclose copies for them.

He enclosed sheets of statistics.[3]

The Air Ministry's objections were overruled by the Cabinet who
accepted Sandys's arguments. The aircraft programme was reviewed in
the light of Sandys's policy, and the 1958 White Paper defined even more
clearly the switch-over to reliance on nuclear weapons with the numbers
of fighter aircraft severely reduced.

> If Russia were to launch a major attack [on the Western powers] even with
> conventional forces only, they would have to hit back with strategic nuclear
> weapons. In fact the strategy of NATO is based on the frank recognition
> that a full-scale Soviet attack could not be repelled without resort to a
> massive nuclear bombardment of the sources of power in Russia.

The Macmillan Government were aiming for an 'independent nuclear
deterrent' over which they could exercise national control, and in return
for American assistance had, as will be seen, always to keep in mind that
they must have something to offer.[4]

By the time Macmillan became Prime Minister the British delivery
system for nuclear bombs was out of date. It consisted of purpose-built
V bombers which had now been superseded by American modern ground
missiles with atomic warheads. In 1957 Britain therefore embarked upon
the development of a liquid-fuelled rocket called Blue Streak – the copy
of an American Atlas ballistic missile – which was to be carried on aircraft. Its manufacture was suggested by the Americans when Sandys had
been sent out to Washington by Macmillan a few weeks after he became
Prime Minister. Here Sandys had a frank exchange with Dulles, saying:
'We all felt badly let down [over Suez] and it would require a big effort
by the Americans to restore British confidence in them.' Dulles did not
take these aggressive remarks in bad part.

As has been seen in Chapter 1, when Eisenhower offered Macmillan
Thor at Bermuda in May 1957 the Prime Minister accepted with open
arms. Thor was a ballistic missile with a range of only 1,500 miles which
rendered it useless from American bases. To reach Russia it needed
European bases which America wanted to site in Britain. The agreement over US bases in Britain and Thor reached at Bermuda was
important not only for post-Suez Anglo-American relations, but also as
a landmark in Anglo-American nuclear relations until the sale of Polaris
in 1962.[5]

The Americans did not consider Britain's small nuclear force carried
in warheads on V bombers of serious military importance, and they had
a rooted dislike of it as an independent nuclear deterrent mainly because

they thought this might lead to proliferation. On the other hand the Macmillan Government, conscious of Britain's world-wide commitments, believed strongly that it was important to remain a nuclear power so as to have the maximum influence on world policy. This was a source of constant friction in relations between the two countries, especially between officials. Contrary to the American view the Macmillan Government was insistent not only that they must have independent control of Thor and any future acquisitions from the United States, but also that these should not be assigned to NATO, despite American pressure to do so. Instead Macmillan interpreted his Bermuda talk with Eisenhower about Thor as a formal agreement that it was to be solely under UK control – a misunderstanding that did not improve relations at the official level.[6] British defence chiefs considered Thor unsatisfactory, and they accepted it more on political grounds as a symbol of partial 'post-Suez rapprochement' in Anglo-American relations than on technical grounds, some British defence chiefs arguing that US Thor bases would make Britain a much more attractive target for Soviet missiles.

At first the British thought the American concession over Thor would be followed by sales of other American missiles to which UK-manufactured warheads could be attached. However British resources were inadequate to make such warheads. The United States Atomic Energy Act of 1946 had inhibited nuclear co-operation between the US and the UK and allowed only strictly limited information to be passed; by 1957 therefore Britain had become very much a junior partner, although originally – like the French – British scientists had been far ahead of their US counterparts in research into nuclear fission. With the entry of America into the Second World War in December 1941 US scientists were given access to all British nuclear secrets, and in a few months they had not only caught up, but moved well ahead. The British Prime Minister, Winston Churchill, was told firmly in July 1942 by his civil servants that the necessary production plant would be so 'huge' that 'its erection in this country is out of the question during the war'. From then on nuclear research became almost wholly American-based.[7]

A more permissive United States Atomic Energy Act in 1954 allowed for more exchange of nuclear information, and in May 1957 Britain exploded her first thermonuclear (hydrogen) bomb and became a mature nuclear power. President Eisenhower therefore felt able to propose amendments to the 1954 Act to permit greater exchange with countries which had made substantial progress in the development of nuclear weapons; this meant only Britain.

The British Chiefs of Staff and Harold Caccia, Ambassador in Washington, felt that American concern over the successful launch into space of the Russian Sputnik in the summer of 1957 would lead to their being more anxious to make concessions to Britain. They were correct, and when Macmillan went to Washington in October 1957 to meet Eisenhower for a second time the two agreed that there should be joint studies into defence co-operation with particular reference to missiles. This agreement quickly led to the 1958 Atomic Energy Act which put no limit on nuclear technology being imparted to the British.

The British air chiefs were enthusiastic for an independent nuclear deterrent which would be airborne, but the Admiralty and War Office were sceptical. Mountbatten, formerly First Sea Lord, and now Chief of the Defence Staff, frequently reminded his colleagues of 'the possibility of war fought with conventional forces'.[8]

Sandys however insisted that Britain must have her own ground-based ballistic missile, Blue Streak, in addition to Thor. Heathcoat Amory, Chancellor of the Exchequer, opposed Blue Streak on grounds of cost, while the Admiralty disliked it because they wanted a submarine-carried nuclear deterrent which the Americans were developing. Ewen Broadbent, private secretary to the Secretary of State for Air, minuted on 1 January 1958: 'If a decision was taken to do away with Blue Streak and if we are then left with Thor with American nuclear heads then the Navy, with a British seaborne ballistic missile, would in fact take over the deterrent from the mid 1960s onwards.'[9]

Thor was despised by all the British defence chiefs as an inferior 'first generation system' which would soon have to be replaced. Armed with their support Sandys tried to rally his Cabinet colleagues in favour of continuing the Blue Streak programme although this weapon could not be operational until six years after Thor. On 5 November 1958 a final Cabinet decision was deferred after Amory had opposed Sandys's recommendation. Sandys told the Commons on 25 February 1959 that Blue Streak was going ahead, 'but we shall naturally continue to watch progress of other developments in America'.

However by February 1960, in addition to the argument about excessive costs, it had become clear to the Ministry of Defence experts that Blue Streak was out of date as a result of advances in propellant fuels and the vulnerability of its fixed sites. It then became known that the United States had plans to create a NATO force of submarines fitted with Polaris missiles with a range of up to 1,500 miles – a much more attractive proposition for the defence of the UK than Blue Streak. At first the Polaris project was not viewed favourably by all the Cabinet, but the matter was clinched when on 17 January 1960 Sir Richard Powell, Permanent Secretary to the Ministry of Defence, reported that Blue Streak was 'vulnerable to pre-emptive attack', and was effective only if fired first in reply to a Soviet attack with conventional weapons. The view of Harold Watkinson who had replaced Sandys as Minister of

Defence in October 1959, was that 'A large and ever-increasing number of [Russian missiles] were targeted on Britain and could wipe out Blue Streak without any possibility of reply'.

On 20 February 1960 at the Cabinet Defence Committee Sandys, now Minister of Aviation, and Harold Watkinson discussed whether or not to cancel Blue Streak. Following this meeting Macmillan recommended in a memorandum 'doing away' with Blue Streak, and the Cabinet decided provisionally to abandon it and to try to purchase the superior 1,000-mile range US missile Skybolt from America.[10] Skybolt's great attraction for the British Government was that it could be fired from an aeroplane and so gave the nearly obsolete V bombers another generation of life, while avoiding the problems implicit in a fixed site missile; in this crowded island these could never be located far from a centre of population which would inevitably be targeted by Russian missiles.

At first American officials were reluctant to allow Britain an independent Skybolt, wanting to reserve this for NATO. However at a meeting with Eisenhower at Camp David at the end of March 1960 Macmillan succeeded in obtaining agreement from the President for the purchase by Britain of Skybolt without warheads. In April the Commons were told that Blue Streak had been abandoned and that Skybolt would be bought from America.

Cancellation of Blue Streak made Britain even more dependent on the United States at a moment when an alternative policy of European collaboration in missile development might still have been followed. In the Commons debate on scrapping Blue Streak the Government escaped damaging criticism largely because the Opposition were divided on the need for any nuclear deterrent.

As part of the Skybolt deal at Camp David Macmillan had promised Eisenhower that the Americans could use Gareloch on the Clyde for a new US Polaris base – the British quid pro quo for American agreement over Skybolt. Gareloch was looked on by the British both as a stick and carrot to the Americans, and firm arrangements for an American base there were deferred until a signed agreement for Skybolt was forthcoming. Macmillan himself told the Defence Committee on 25 May 1960 that 'It would be preferable to refrain from taking any initiative in reply to the American proposal for a submarine base in Scotland until Watkinson in Washington has made satisfactory arrangements with the Americans for the provision of Skybolt.' The idea of an American base for submarines with nuclear warheads caused a fiercely hostile reaction in Britain, more especially since it was to be located on the Clyde close to a densely populated area. The resulting demonstrations caused grave misgivings within the Cabinet.

Meanwhile friction and misunderstandings arose with the Americans over the precise nature of the agreement between Eisenhower and Macmillan at Camp David. The Americans wanted to take advantage of Macmillan's consent at Camp David to send a dry dock to the Clyde in the summer of 1960 to service Polaris submarines. A meeting between Harold Watkinson and Thomas Gates, United States Secretary of Defence, was held in Washington on 1 June 1960. Watkinson emphasized to the American the political difficulties facing the British Government, and said that these could only be overcome if the project could be presented to the British public as a joint US-UK effort. He also expressed misgivings about the site on the Clyde being close to a populous industrial area, saying the British Government must be satisfied that there were no undue risks involved in the storage and maintenance of the nuclear warheads.

Gates replied that, although he could see 'no military difficulty' in having a joint US-UK base for Polaris submarines, 'there might be serious political difficulties'; Congress wanted America to provide NATO with submarines equipped with ballistic missiles, and he said it would be embarrassing to come to a bilateral agreement with the United Kingdom alone over Polaris. He was prepared to examine establishing the base in a more remote area although this would add greatly to the expense.[11]*

Writing a hurried report for the Prime Minister on the flight back to London Watkinson pointed out the differences between his position and the Americans'. He emphasized that the Americans considered the provision of Skybolt closely linked to Gareloch and that they were likely to press Britain to accept a NATO joint project for a European nuclear deterrent. He found it impossible to get the Americans to accept 'a swop of Gareloch facilities for a Polaris submarine' because of Congressional opposition, whilst the Americans were at the same time insisting that Britain had already made a commitment to support European submarines. If the Americans were not given the base at Gareloch, Watkinson warned, they would ask and succeed in getting the Germans to give them Bremerhaven as an alternative.

Watkinson advocated British support for 'a very limited' NATO submarine MRBM† force of about fifty missiles; with American help Britain should build one Polaris submarine to American design and make warheads for it, and then assign it to NATO; Gareloch should also be a joint project, the Americans training crews for the first British nuclear

---

*As an alternative base to Gareloch, Gates mentioned the possibility of Loch Linnhe (on the west coast of Scotland), but nothing came of this.

† Medium Range Ballistic Missile.

submarine which would be based with theirs at Gareloch and share US facilities. Britain must be in 'both the air-launched and undersea-launched missile business', Watkinson stressed, 'if we are going to be able to exert a continuing influence on the Americans'.

As private secretary dealing with these exchanges, Philip de Zulueta was disturbed at this report and minuted to Macmillan that the Americans had already offered the Chief of Defence Staff, Lord Mountbatten, 'to lend lease two or three submarines to the UK until we were able to build our own';* whereas now the Americans were proposing to exchange Gareloch for the right to buy Polaris missiles minus warheads provided these were assigned to NATO:

> This arrangement does not seem a very good bargain from our point of view; it also has the presentational disadvantage that the Americans would like to put equipment in the Clyde in 1960 whereas our submarines would not be available until 1966. Consequently the Gareloch base could not at all easily be presented [to the British public] as a joint base from the beginning unless we bought a nuclear submarine from the US.[12]

Although the Americans claimed that at Camp David in March the Prime Minister had agreed to the US use of Gareloch, no details of the bargain had been discussed, de Zulueta emphasized, although Watkinson had given the impression that Britain had promised to support some kind of NATO MRBM scheme with or without the French. According to de Zulueta Britain had made no such commitment. Failing agreement with Britain, there was a danger that America would quickly make an agreement with the Germans to use Bremerhaven which might be a breach of the Brussels Treaty obligations,† but if Britain objected she would be put in the position of being 'the only people ostensibly opposing German military ambitions'. De Zulueta felt sure Macmillan should take the matter up with the President personally.

Macmillan was disturbed. On 15 June he held meetings with Lloyd, Heathcoat Amory and Watkinson and told them that there were no agreed details of his understanding with Eisenhower at Camp David. As regards America's proposal to send a dry dock to the Clyde in early July and place a Polaris submarine tender there in the late autumn,

---

* The proposal of the loan of Polaris submarines by the Americans may have been wishful thinking on Mountbatten's part, and only a suggestion by a junior US official, not an offer by Gates. Always a breezy optimist Mountbatten was anxious to secure Polaris so that nuclear defence would be in the hands of the Royal Navy not the RAF.
† The Brussels Treaty was signed by the victorious European powers – Britain, France, the Netherlands, Belgium and Luxemburg – in March 1948. It was a guarantee against revived German aggression, and placed restrictions on the siting of atomic or chemical weapons on German soil. It was still policed in 1960.

The proposal to use the Clyde was particularly difficult in view of the proximity of the population and industry of Glasgow. It would not be easy to resolve legitimate anxieties on safety grounds. It would be much easier to present this project if the base were in some more remote area in north-west Scotland. Fort William might be an alternative.

To satisfy public opinion, Macmillan continued, the arrangements must be presented as a partnership, and as part of the project we ought to obtain an option to purchase one or more Polaris submarines of our own or obtain their design rights in case we wished to manufacture them ourselves. It was also essential to be able to say that the Polaris submarines we obtained 'would be under the sole ultimate control of the UK Government'.

On 15 June Macmillan sent a message to Eisenhower referring to the Gates–Watkinson talks about Skybolt:

As regards Polaris, as I told you at Camp David, I shall do my best about a suitable arrangement for the use of Scottish ports. You will realize that this is a pretty big decision for us to take. It will raise political difficulties for us in view of all the pressures and cross-currents of public opinion here. I must therefore put it to my Cabinet colleagues . . . I hope it will be possible for us to make a mutually satisfactory arrangement.

On 20 June Eisenhower replied: 'I hope you will find it possible to proceed this year with the arrangement [about Gareloch] on which we reached agreement in principle at Camp David.' On this letter Macmillan noted, 'I did not, repeat not, agree to this at Camp David,' and set about preparing drafts of a letter to Eisenhower. He contemplated denying the existence of an agreement but Caccia cabled from Washington on 22 June advising that we should spare Eisenhower another humiliation.[13]

In a carefully redrafted letter, Macmillan warned Eisenhower on 24 June that facilities for Polaris submarines in Scotland would cause

serious political controversy in our country at this time . . . Our people are inevitably conscious that this duty of providing the advance base exposes them to special risks. This means that we must be able to present this project in a way which will command public support.

It would be a serious mistake from your point of view as well as ours [to use the Clyde].

It would surely be a mistake to put down what will become a major nuclear target so near to the third largest and most overcrowded city in this country. As soon as the announcement was made Malinowsky [the Russian Defence Chief] would threaten to aim his rockets at Glasgow and there would be not only the usual agitation of the defeatists and pacifists but also genuine apprehension among ordinary folk. But a more immediate difficulty is that a city of this size inevitably contains large numbers of people who would be quick to take the opportunity of making physical demonstrations against us both. Security problems would certainly be much greater here than in less populated areas.

Macmillan suggested for these reasons that Loch Linnhe would be a far better location to meet operational requirements. It was near Fort William and 'a robust population of three or four thousand highlanders' at Fort William, Macmillan thought, would be 'much more to my taste' than the rather mixed population of the city of Glasgow.

Moving on to his second point Macmillan stressed to Eisenhower that Gareloch

> should be run as a partnership, it must be made publicly clear from the outset that we shall have an option to come in ourselves on the operation of Polaris submarines. In other words we give you the facilities for the floating dock and the tender and we get in return the option of buying from you and/or building submarines so that we can make in the years to come a contribution to the Western deterrent as effective as our bomber force now is.

Macmillan's third and most important point was the question of control. In order to obtain political approval for a Polaris base on the Clyde it was essential, he felt, to give the public impression that the British finger would also be on the trigger.

> We have a firm understanding that your bombers would not undertake operational missions from British bases without our prior agreement. With the submarines all that has been suggested so far is that they should not without our consent fire their missiles from within our territorial waters. I am wondering whether this could for presentational purposes be extended to something like a hundred miles.

Several drafts of this letter had been made before it was actually sent, and Macmillan hoped that Eisenhower would sign a memorandum agreeing to its points. On 30 June, however, Eisenhower replied with a complete rebuff – a point-blank refusal to accept any of Macmillan's three points. It was a real snub and further proof of Britain's junior role in defence matters and the withering of the special relationship. Eisenhower's letter stated tersely that he was compelled 'reluctantly' to decline the offer of Loch Linnhe, whilst 'the other points raised in your letter would present difficulties for us'. This scotched any prospect of a Polaris deal outside a NATO MRBM scheme – the very contingency Macmillan was determined to avoid.[14]

In a minute to Macmillan de Zulueta expressed his dismay at this letter and pointed out that Eisenhower's reply might indicate that he thought (albeit wrongly) that Macmillan had gone back on an agreement reached at Camp David; however there was nothing that could be done to restore the situation: the present administration was dying and the President's influence was steadily decreasing (Eisenhower had suffered a stroke). As it would be difficult to keep 'the cordial and intimate relations going for the next six months', he recommended Macmillan to do nothing for the present and instead try to establish a special relationship with the next President. It would be a mistake, de Zulueta emphasized,

> to take any precipitate action but it might be necessary to recognize that our 'special relationship' with the United States is not worth much in real terms even with President Eisenhower so that we had better start reinforcing ourselves *vis-à-vis* the Americans by an independent policy in concert with someone else, e.g. the French.

De Zulueta was certainly correct in remarking that relations between Macmillan and the Americans had fallen to a low ebb, and much of the ground regained since Suez had been lost.

On 2 July Macmillan sent a further message to Eisenhower:

> I am sorry you feel that Loch Linnhe will not do in spite of its obvious advantages, from many points of view, over the crowded area of the Clyde. However, I do see the technical advantages of the Gareloch and if this is the really vital point for you, I will have the question reopened. It would be very sad if such a valuable strategic plan had to be abandoned.

By 12 July Macmillan had received no reply and asked the Washington Embassy for advice as he 'did not quite see how to deal with the President's silence'. He was reassured by the British Embassy at Washington that this should not cause concern, and on 15 July 1960 Eisenhower replied:

> Our Navy still insists that Loch Linnhe won't do from a technical standpoint and I therefore am happy to accept your offer to reconsider this question. Indeed this has become a matter of some urgency as we need a firm basis now for locating the submarine tender this fall either in the Gareloch or elsewhere. Although our Navy is keeping the dry dock in the US this year, we would expect to locate it in the Gareloch next spring if you find the Gareloch can be used for the tender. We agree that our Polaris missiles would not be launched within your territorial waters without your consent. To extend any form of dual control beyond territorial waters would however present us with a number of problems . . . A bilateral arrangement with the UK on Polaris missiles outside the NATO framework could jeopardize favourable consideration of the NATO MRBM programme.[15]

As to Macmillan's proposal that there should be no firing within 100 miles of Britain's waters without British consent, this, the President added, would form a 'most difficult precedent' with respect to the utilization of weapons in other waters such as the Mediterranean and the

Caribbean. In an effort to be conciliatory he offered to work out 'such co-ordinating measures as may be necessary'.

Macmillan minuted de Zulueta on Eisenhower's letter: 'I do not know how we can deal with this before the end of the session. But we must do so – at least in some temporary way. Also I must report to the Cabinet. What do you think?' Replying, de Zulueta described Eisenhower's letter as much better than the last one, but it 'does not meet us at all on any of our conditions':

The Deterrent Control
I do not think that it will be enough for this country if the submarines are only controlled within our territorial waters. On the other hand the Prime Minister's suggestion of 100 miles was fairly arbitrary. I think the important thing is to establish the Polaris as a joint enterprise and ... that some studies on control possibilities might be undertaken ...

NATO MRBMs
This is the worst part. The Americans are in great confusion. I think we should say firmly that if NATO agrees on a MRBM programme we would agree to work our Polaris into the scheme ... If this question is resolved we would certainly be prepared to put submarines we have into NATO but meanwhile let us make arrangements privately between ourselves.

At this stage Macmillan appeared to be relying more on advice from his private secretaries de Zulueta and Bligh than the Foreign Office, or the Ministry of Defence or the Chiefs of Staff, and in a further note to the Prime Minister de Zulueta wrote: 'Unless we have an option to buy or build Polaris we ourselves get nothing out of giving the Americans facilities in Scotland.'

In scotching the possibility of a Polaris deal outside NATO, Eisenhower had made it clear that any acquisition of Polaris by Britain would have to be part of a British contribution to NATO – exactly the situation Macmillan wanted to avoid. Frustrated he admitted defeat, and realizing the need to retain US goodwill at all cost he advised the Cabinet to accept Eisenhower's Polaris plan. The Cabinet at their meeting on 28 July agreed; the Prime Minister informed Eisenhower of Britain's agreement, and he and the President decided that negotiations should thereafter be carried on at official level.[16]

From August 1960 the Government concentrated on trying to obtain an agreement over control which might satisfy the British public. Caccia was instructed on 3 August that arrangements for the control of the Polaris submarines using British territory 'inevitably have to be both of a general nature and secret; the public position to be adopted will require careful thought.' Caccia was asked to suggest the following formula to the Americans for Macmillan to use in public, explaining that 'joint decision in emergency' referred only to UK territorial waters although it would be desirable outside them ('we should prefer not to spell this out publicly'):

> In accordance with the spirit of the arrangements in force concerning joint consultation over the use in emergency of United States Air Force and missile bases in the United Kingdom, I have obtained the agreement of President Eisenhower to arrangements that ensure wherever necessary full and timely consultation and joint decision in an emergency concerning the employment of United States submarines using United Kingdom facilities.

The only formal agreement with the Americans related to the Thor missiles which by 1960 were operational in Britain. The agreement of 1957 read: 'The decision to launch these missiles will be a matter for joint decision by the two Governments. Any such joint decision will be made in the light of the circumstances of the time.' In his 3 August 1960 instruction Caccia was told: 'We cannot hope for a formal agreement on lines similar to the Thor agreement but we should like to be able to say that the arrangements will be broadly as effective and of the same nature as the arrangements for the Thors and the United States aircraft operating from United Kingdom bases.'

The Americans proved difficult, and no full written agreement was arrived at. All they would allow was that the Prime Minister might state: 'Some decision of this kind would not be taken rashly or foolishly or except upon general consultation with those concerned.' In a discussion with the Prime Minister in New York in October 1960 Eisenhower and Secretary of State Herter had at first agreed the formula: 'The US Government would use their best endeavours to consult with their British and other allies as regards the use of Polaris missiles as well as about the use of nuclear weapons generally.' Afterwards Herter told the British that the Pentagon found it impossible to be committed to a formula under which the US Government might be committed to consult with their other allies before using nuclear weapons, and the Americans reneged on this suggestion.

On 17 October Caccia reported that the Pentagon were 'adamant' against making any American public statement on 'control' and would rather forgo their facilities on the Clyde than make one. Their reasoning, he explained, was that any statement would whet the appetite of their allies, 'especially as regards the Far East, and would oblige them to give a series of assurances and undertakings which they would find embarrassing and hampering to operations'.[17] Eisenhower, recovering from his stroke, was not fully in charge of his administration and anti-British feeling among officials in the Pentagon was allowed to carry the day.

As Parliament reassembled in the autumn Macmillan was forced to make a statement about control of firing from the Scottish-based Polaris submarines, and at Question Time on 8 November he was pressed to say whether there was an oral or written agreement. 'Wherever these submarines may be,' Macmillan replied, 'I am perfectly satisfied that no decision to use these missiles will ever be taken without the fullest possible previous consultation . . .'

Since there was no such agreement this was a gaffe and American officials in Washington immediately pointed out to the press that the US had given no such commitment to Britain. The *Daily Mail* gave the story a banner headline and it was made much of by other national newspapers and the Opposition. Concurrently Chapman Pincher wrote an article in the *Daily Mail* stating that Britain had no veto over the US starting a nuclear war which might bring about Britain's destruction, while Emmanuel Shinwell was prominent in the Commons in expressing doubts whether Macmillan had told the truth.

Ten days earlier, Macmillan had informed Eisenhower that he would be saying something about control in Parliament and gave him this text: 'As regards control we shall continue to rely on the close co-operation and the understanding which exists between us and the United States on all these defence matters and which the President has recently reaffirmed.' This seemed completely 'satisfactory', Eisenhower had replied. Unfortunately in the Commons on 8 November 1960, Macmillan, who had intended to say 'no decision would be taken without the fullest possible previous consultation with those concerned', omitted the words 'with those concerned', and added inadvertently 'wherever these submarines may be'. The matter was soon smoothed over with the Americans but is evidence of the tension between the USA and Britain during the dying days of the Eisenhower administration.

As over Thor Macmillan wanted a formal published agreement for the Polaris missiles. Alec Home and Watkinson were asked to report. They concluded that the talks had 'ruled out as impractical any formal joint consultation prior to the firing of the missiles by US submarines within a given radius of the UK or within a limited sea area', and there could be no public formal agreement as over Thor. However they maintained that the UK should have the right to emergency consultation wherever possible before nuclear weapons were launched, and an agreement to this effect was eventually signed on 31 October. By early 1961 important details over this agreement still remained unresolved, with Macmillan still asking for the inclusion of a firm declaration about control arrangements. Caccia advised him that the new President John Kennedy would take this amiss as US ships were about to arrive at the Clyde base on the Holy Loch, not far from Loch Gare.[18]

Eventually Macmillan was persuaded by Home that a personal message from Kennedy on 6 February 1961 about an Anglo-US secret under-standing over the use of UK bases and nuclear weapons could be inter-preted as an admission by the new US administration of the need for a 'joint decision' so far as UK territory and territorial waters were con-cerned. Home advised that in these circumstances it would be unneces-sary 'as well as psychologically unwise' to ask for anything further. Macmillan then concurred.

There was also a protracted but unresolved dispute about the amount of financial liability which would fall on the US if there was an accident with the nuclear warheads stored at the Holy Loch base.

Meanwhile the Americans shilly-shallied over signing a firm agreement for the supply of Skybolt. Summing up the position for Macmillan at the end of August 1960, de Zulueta wrote: 'It is very tiresome that the Americans are holding up the Skybolt agreement until they get the Polaris one [for a base on the Clyde]. I do not think this is really at all in the spirit of the Camp David agreement exchanges where no bargain was really struck.' Although records of the Camp David con-versations had been made, difficulty lay in the different interpretations put on these by Macmillan and Eisenhower and their officials. Eventually a formal Skybolt agreement was signed on 23 September 1960 and Watkinson sent the Prime Minister a minute which showed the British determination to link Skybolt with the Holy Loch base. He also forecast accurately the disappointment over Skybolt:

Skybolt and the Holy Loch
The final signature of the Skybolt Agreement is taking place today. An Anglo-American planning conference on the project has just been concluded at which the American authorities gave an assurance that the programme was being given, and would continue to be given, top development priority. The conference showed that all the major milestones in the programme are being prepared on time, or substantially on time, with delivery of the first four missiles to the Royal Air Force planned for March 1964.

We have accepted the American proposals to establish a base for their Polaris submarines in the Holy Loch.

It would be most helpful if in welcoming these mutually advantageous arrangements you could emphasize to the President that we have accepted their proposals for the Holy Loch, which will certainly cause us some difficulties, in view of the arrangement which they have agreed for the supply of Skybolt, and that we regard the whole transaction on a reciprocal arrangement, in accordance with what was agreed at Camp David. It is important that the Americans should recognize that if Skybolt should meet with serious trouble and have to be abandoned they would have a moral obligation to help us to overcome, in one way or another, the difficulties which this would cause for us. After all they have got the Holy Loch and we certainly have not got Skybolt for some years yet. This would give us the necessary standing to reopen the Polaris submarine question or take any other action that seemed necessary if Skybolt fails.

Now with Skybolt firmly in the bag Britain tried, in the words of the Cambridge military historian Ian Clarke, 'to spend the cheque a second time', and obtain Polaris as a second quid pro quo for the base on the Clyde. It was an uphill struggle, with the US administration determined to equip NATO and not Britain alone with Polaris missiles, whilst Macmillan and his Cabinet were rigidly opposed to merging Britain's nuclear deterrent into NATO.[19]

When John Kennedy defeated Richard Nixon in the presidential election in the autumn of 1960 the United States changed from a Republican to a Democratic Government. Eisenhower's principal policy advisers departed as President Kennedy brought in his own team of talented advisers, many from the academic world. The military top brass did not change but the British found it easier to work with the new administration. Robert McNamara replaced Tom Gates as US Secretary of Defence.

Kennedy's design was for an integrated European system of defence. In this he was frustrated by de Gaulle's intransigence, whilst at the same time the Democrats disliked the idea of an independent British nuclear deterrent as much as the Republicans.

Harold Watkinson went to Washington for talks with McNamara accompanied by Solly Zuckerman, Chief Scientific Adviser to the Ministry of Defence, and a strong team of advisers on nuclear matters. Although they signed a formal undertaking for a policy of greater interdependence, little came of it. Watkinson attributed this to the pressure of the American arms lobby and a desire on the part of the Kennedy administration to recover a share of the cost of policing the world by selling arms and equipment. This materialistic view may be unfair on the Americans, and Watkinson, a businessman, probably overstated the pressure of the US arms industry. In a memorandum of April 1961 for the Prime Minister on his agreement with McNamara Watkinson pointed out that, as weapons became more and more complex, Britain would have to buy more equipment abroad or do without.[20]

However feuding between the Pentagon and the Ministry of Defence continued and there were persistent allegations of American claims that the British nuclear deterrent was 'unnecessary'. In the end McNamara issued a formal statement saying there was no truth in these allegations. This is controverted by recently released American archives which disclose that Kennedy and McNamara made strong efforts to dissuade Britain from continuing with her nuclear deterrent – a move which must have been deeply disconcerting to Macmillan, although he reveals no hint of this in his memoirs.

A US National Security Council paper on 21 April 1961 is significant:

> We must try to eliminate the privileged British status ... Our minimum objective should be to persuade the Prime Minister to commit his atomic warhead to the NATO atomic stockpile and his delivery weapons to NATO commanders. Beyond this we should try to move him to cease the production of fissable material for weapon purposes.

The President approved, minuting: 'It would be desirable for the British in the long run to phase out of the nuclear deterrent business since their activity in this field is a standing goad to the French.'

A year later McGeorge Bundy, the President's Special Assistant for National Security, wrote to the French political commentator Raymond Aron: 'If we had to do it over again today we should not encourage the British in this nuclear effort, and it is our guess that over a period of time all merely national deterrents will become uneconomic and ineffective.' The attitude is corroborated by an unsigned and undated paper in the National Security Council archives, which states: 'It is doubtful that the benefits the Alliance receives from the special US/UK relationship at least in the military sphere outweigh the costs in resentment and loss of prestige others suffer.' Confirmation is also given by Peter Thorneycroft, who succeeded Watkinson as Minister of Defence in July 1962, and has recorded in an oral interview that there were 'a great deal [sic] of Americans working jolly hard to do away with the British deterrent'. According to McGeorge Bundy, Kennedy's view was that 'the British deterrent was a political necessity but a piece of military foolishness, although he did not put much pressure on the British personally to drop it.'[21]

Under the influence of the Russians' successful launch of Sputnik in 1957 President Eisenhower had looked on British nuclear forces as an asset against Russia, but by 1961 the Kennedy administration thought such a contribution by Britain unnecessary and out of date in view of US technological advances. Instead McNamara advocated an increase in British conventional forces to fight the Russians if they attempted a *coup* in Berlin or attacked the Western Allies in Europe – a proposal unwelcome to the British Government.

On 18 March 1961 Caccia had sent a warning to Macmillan that the Americans were favouring a build-up of conventional forces. General Lauris Norstad, head of Allied forces in Europe (1956–63), was strongly of this view, as the US archives confirm, and had impressed on the President the opinion that the UK's contribution on the Continent since

1956 had been inadequate, and that she must be forced to increase the size of her conventional forces.[22]

Sir Solly Zuckerman knew Kennedy's advisers well and at the end of February Kennedy talked to him frankly for three quarters of an hour. Zuckerman told de Zulueta on 2 March 1961 that he had a 'fairly clear' idea of what the Americans wanted. De Zulueta recorded Zuckerman as saying:

(a) President Kennedy hates and despises President Eisenhower.

(b) Your visit will be our last chance to influence the policy of the new administration before it crystallizes.

(c) The new administration will not respect you if you pull your punches with them.

(d) President Kennedy is really determined if he can to get away from the immobile strategy of the last few years. He is serious in his disarmament plans and hopes that he may achieve a position in which the peace of the world is maintained by quite small nuclear forces.

(e) He is preoccupied with the dangers of purely nuclear strategy, and feels that conventional forces are too small. But since they want to reduce nuclear armaments the American administration will not be receptive to the introduction of complications (e.g. the position of France) into their plan for an Americo-Russian détente based on nuclear disarmament.

(f) President Kennedy is very anxious to get a position in which the free world can start building up its economic strength. He realizes that America cannot do this alone. He wants ideas.*

Macmillan arranged to see Zuckerman at Chequers on 9 March and their long talk had considerable influence on Macmillan's tactics with Kennedy whom he was due to meet in Washington in early April 1961.[23]

When on 6 April 1961 Macmillan and Home met Kennedy and his advisers, with Dean Rusk and McGeorge Bundy replacing Eisenhower's foreign affairs team, on board the President's yacht Macmillan suggested that the reason why Khrushchev could not pursue a policy of détente was because of domestic difficulties in the Soviet Union. While Kennedy said that it would be a mistake to remove the impression that the Western powers would take a 'stiff' line on Berlin, the British expressed the view that 'it might be possible to tolerate a Soviet peace treaty with East Germany and a joint guarantee of a Free City for all Berlin.' This met with a cold response from the Americans, although Kennedy said this could be looked at 'afresh' together with a revised military plan for Berlin. However these first talks between Kennedy and Macmillan were remarkably unfruitful.

---

*In a letter to the author McGeorge Bundy has pointed out that in his experience Zuckerman used to listen, and then believed the views expressed were those he wanted to hear.

When Macmillan and Kennedy met again at the White House the President, with the help of the former US Secretary of State Dean Acheson, left the Prime Minister in no doubt about American determination to build up conventional forces in Europe with the purpose of being able to enforce a 'pause' of two or three weeks after any Soviet attack and before any need to resort to nuclear means. The British Chiefs of Staff disagreed; they thought 'the longer the conventional battle we allow, the more we are in danger of being unable to avoid escalation to all-out [nuclear] war.' In a memorandum of 1 May 1961 Home and Watkinson stated: 'It is not so much the lack of conventional capacity on the part of NATO that might lead to Soviet aggression as doubts about NATO's will to resort to nuclear weapons in its own defence.'

In the event of attack on Berlin by Russia Macmillan and his Cabinet were prepared to accept defeat rather than invoke an all-out nuclear war. It is impossible from the archives to form an opinion of what the Americans, the senior partner, would have done. However the continued American pressure for larger British conventional forces was anathema to the Prime Minister.

The dispute with the Americans about the size of the British contribution to NATO conventional forces in Europe erupted into a first-class row with the publication of the Defence White Paper of February 1962. In deference to the clearly expressed views of the Americans the White Paper had moved marginally from exclusive reliance on the nuclear deterrent which had featured in the earlier Macmillan Government Defence White Papers to saying, '. . . if we had nothing but nuclear forces this would not be credible. A balance must be maintained, therefore, between conventional and nuclear forces.'[24] Even so the White Paper remained ambivalent, carrying no plans for a quick build-up of British NATO forces to meet the increasingly dangerous Berlin situation[*] and proposing to end conscription in 1962. It again emphasized, to the Americans' annoyance, the importance attached to the British nuclear deterrent. Overall the White Paper claimed the new defence policy would lighten the burden on the British economy.

As soon as he had read it President Kennedy took the unprecedented step of writing a personal letter to Macmillan expressing his 'deep concern' and making strong criticisms. He tried to soften the pill by ending his letter with the words: 'I could not raise a matter of this sort in this way with any other man – at the head of any other country – and I am sure you know that I only do so because we can both be so confident of our continuing partnership.'

---

[*] See Chapter 15, pages 355 ff.

Kennedy's main complaint was at the White Paper's failure to mention any increased build-up to meet the emergency in Berlin. He pointed out that America had considerably increased its combat forces 'deployed in Europe' at great expense, and it had done so with one central goal: to impress on Khrushchev 'the seriousness of our purpose'. The President alleged that the other NATO allies had only given an unsatisfactory response, and he attributed this to British 'weakness'. The British Army in Europe was under strength, and he felt this could not be remedied without continuing conscription.

He also deprecated the policy expressed in the White Paper of the United Kingdom maintaining 'its independent nuclear strategy' which would not only discourage those in France who were opposed to de Gaulle's policy of spending vast sums in developing a French nuclear weapon, but encourage unwelcome Franco-German co-operation in nuclear research which America opposed vigorously as part of their effort to prevent the spread of independent national nuclear arms.

This unusually governessy interference in British affairs was ill received in Whitehall. Watkinson called it an 'odd communication' resulting from American domestic difficulties caused by an 'over-expansion of their conventional forces in Europe, calling up drafts, and generally giving the American public grounds for alarm or even hysteria'. He cautioned against taking umbrage at this lecture from the President and suggested it was written by Paul Nitze, Assistant Secretary of Defence, who probably had 'misinterpreted' the advance copy sent to him. There were now undoubted 'divergences' between British and American thinking on defence, Watkinson pointed out, because the Americans had moved from over-emphasis on a strategic deterrent under Eisenhower to over-emphasizing the role of conventional forces under Kennedy.

Macmillan tried to take the sting out of the quarrel by writing to Kennedy on 23 February 1962:

> I am glad that you feel able to write to me in this way. It may be unusual but it is really helpful. After all, I am not a General . . . I frankly do not myself see at the moment how it will be possible to devise a NATO deterrent. All this argument comes back to the question of command and veto over the use of nuclear weapons.
>
> The major decision must rest with you as our contribution is necessarily small . . . the existence of a British deterrent did not encourage the French and Germans to develop their own nuclear capacity, and one can argue quite plausibly that the existence of the British nuclear force gives some comfort to those Europeans who fear that the United States might, in the last resort, shrink from using the nuclear deterrent for the defence of Europe and to those who contrariwise are worried lest America might use it too precipitately.

He also pointed out that British nuclear forces with Blue Steel and V bombers would be effective throughout the sixties.*

In an emergency, Macmillan asserted, Britain could rapidly send 60,000 trained reservists to reinforce British troops in Germany, while Britain alone amongst NATO countries maintained considerable conventional forces in the Middle East and Asia – forces which operated in areas difficult for the United States to reach and which were of great value to the world. He also emphasized the strain on the British economy of stationing troops in Europe and took a quiet dig at America by writing that 'Britain had hoped to obtain a much larger share of German armament orders but your own people were quicker than we were, and have pretty well scooped the pool.'

The author has been unable to find evidence of how this letter was received in the White House. However the remarks about the merits of a British nuclear force were in direct contradiction to the President's stated views and must have exasperated him. These letters are evidence of the wide split between British and American views on defence. There is no mention of them in Macmillan's memoirs.

Just as it seemed that Anglo-American defence relations might be on a more even keel, McNamara started another rumpus by declaring at Ann Arbor on 18 June 1962 that 'independent national nuclear forces within NATO' were 'dangerous, expensive, prone to obsolescence and lacking in credibility as a deterrent'; he emphasized that American nuclear weapons were trained on military and not civilian targets which gave 'a possible opponent the strongest imaginable incentive to refrain from striking our own cities'. Relatively weak nuclear forces directed at cities, McNamara continued, would not only be insufficient as a deterrent but might actually encourage an enemy to conduct a pre-emptive first strike if he thought they might be used independently: 'In the event of war the use of such a force against the cities of a major nuclear power would be tantamount to suicide whereas its employment against significant military targets would have a negligible effect on the outcome of a conflict.'

This argument was obviously aimed at both Britain and France but McNamara took a further swipe at France by stating that 'the creation of a single new independent nuclear force would encourage the proliferation of nuclear power with all the attendant dangers.' Ormsby-Gore, who had succeeded Caccia as Ambassador in Washington in March 1961, commented correctly to Macmillan: 'The more McNamara or any other American attacks the French deterrent the more it makes the General

---

*Blue Steel was a missile launched from a V bomber expected to go into service by 1962 as a stopgap before Skybolt became available; its range was 600 miles.

and those around him determined to carry on with their present nuclear policy.'

This statement created a furore in the world press and put the British in a delicate position over their Common Market negotiations with the French at a time when they had no wish to see the differences between British and French about nuclear weapons emphasized. Controversy over whether the British nuclear deterrent was truly independent flourished. Macmillan minuted:

> I see some extraordinary statements ... Legally the President can use the American deterrent without my agreement. I can use the British deterrent without his approval. We have a gentleman's agreement to consult with each other if there is time to do so. All that is being said to the contrary is just anti-British propaganda.

Replying to the Prime Minister de Zulueta commented that it was 'doubtful whether we could in fact use our deterrent independently. I understand there are no serious operational plans for us to do so.' Macmillan was disconcerted.

In an effort to play down the quarrel McNamara commented:

> British bomber command aircraft with their nuclear weapons have long been organized as part of a thoroughly co-ordinated Anglo-American striking force and are targeted as such although of course their *political* control remains with the British ... We in the US appreciate the important role which the British bomber command plays in our co-ordinated strike plans.

The phrase 'political control' was ambiguous, and this statement intensified the controversy whether the British deterrent was truly independent. In the debate in the Commons on 26 June Macmillan did badly, saying: 'I am not responsible for what Mr McNamara may have said.'

This row over McNamara's Ann Arbor speech brought Anglo-American relations to a temporary low point and the Macmillan Government grew deeply suspicious of the Americans. Thus when the Skybolt crisis erupted at the end of 1962 the climate was bad.[25]

Fortunately, despite the dispute over control, relations over defence between the Kennedy administration and the Macmillan Government never sank to the same low level as they had done in the last months of the Eisenhower administration, and this was due to co-operation over the use of the British possession Christmas Island for nuclear tests by America, and the vast underground Nevada caverns for similar testing by the British.

American atmospheric nuclear tests had originally been carried out from the Eniwetok Pacific atoll which was a United Nations trust territory under American control. Although legally the Americans could use Eniwetok,* so Kennedy told Macmillan, the UN position of the islands could expose them to criticism. Christmas Island had been discovered by Captain Cook in 1777 and annexed by Britain as a colony in 1888. It was used as a coconut plantation employing Haitian labourers, and was the site of the 1957 British atmospheric atom bomb experiment. Around 500 British army officers and men were stationed there.

The use of Christmas Island by the Americans was first raised on 30 October 1960 when Glenn T. Seaborg, Chairman of the United States Atomic Energy Committee, wrote to Sir Roger Makins, his British counterpart, stating that British underground testing in Nevada was 'feasible' and suggesting in return that Britain might allow the Americans to stage operations from Christmas Island.

When a formal request for the use of Christmas Island for nuclear bomb testing came from America in October 1961, Macmillan was delighted, seeing this as a means of remedying the breach between Britain and America over defence policy. The Americans asked for a reply within a few days; Macmillan minuted: 'This is unreasonable and the full Cabinet must decide.' From Washington Ormsby-Gore advised on 15 November: 'if we agree to the American request we shall be in a much stronger position to influence the way they carry out the programme.'

Macmillan was unable to agree a public announcement of the proposal with Kennedy. For internal political reasons neither wanted to give the impression that they would be too dependent on the other. Macmillan told the Commons on 31 October: 'If I were convinced that a particular atmospheric test was necessary in order to maintain the balance of the deterrents and to preserve freedom in the world, Britain would be bound either to co-operate in or support its conduct.' On 1 November the President said:

> No nuclear test in the atmosphere will be undertaken, as the Soviet Union has done, for so-called psychological or political reasons. But should such tests be deemed necessary to maintain our responsibilities for Free World security, in the light of our evaluation of Soviet tests, they will be undertaken only to the degree that the orderly and essential scientific development of new weapons has reached the point where effective progress is not possible

---

* Eniwetok and Bikini in the Pacific Marshall Islands had been the sites of atmospheric nuclear bomb tests by the Americans after the Second World War. In 1919 under the Treaty of Versailles Japan was appointed 'mandatory' to these former German possessions in the Pacific north of the Equator consisting of 100 islands and atolls. In 1946 the US agreed to administer these former Japanese mandated islands as a trusteeship for the United Nations. Bikini and Eniwetok were placed outside the jurisdiction of the trust administration, and the inhabitants were transferred to other atolls and in 1957 paid half a million dollars in compensation by the USA.

without such tests – and only within limits that restrict the fall-out from such tests to an absolute minimum. In the meantime, as a matter of prudence, we shall make necessary preparations for such tests so as to be ready in case it becomes necessary to conduct them.

Worried by the disparity between the two statements Macmillan consulted Norman Brook, Secretary to the Cabinet, who pointed out: 'There is in fact no disparity in the criteria. You said: "necessary in order to maintain the balance of the deterrent and to preserve freedom in the world". The President said "necessary to maintain our responsibilities for Free World security".' However, according to Brook there was a notable 'difference' in that Macmillan had spoken of 'a particular atmospheric test'; Brook believed that at some stage the Prime Minister would have to 'gloss over' this, to make clear he had used 'test' as covering a series of explosions in a single test. If the British were to allow the Americans to use the facilities at Christmas Island, Brook continued, it would be important that Macmillan make it plain in public that Britain should also put herself in a position to carry out such tests, if it were thought necessary. A statement should be made by Macmillan along the lines of the President's, in case we and the Americans co-operated in further atmospheric tests.

Accordingly Macmillan wrote to Kennedy on 3 November 1961 that he was sorry they had not been able to agree 'a joint declaration', and that in the Commons the official Opposition did not dissent from what he had said, although there was hostility from the left wing of the Labour Party.

> What I felt, and still feel, is that the present series of Soviet tests, particularly the large explosions set off in direct defiance of a United Nations resolution, has put the Russians in a very bad posture throughout the world. I know that the Neutrals are always much readier to criticize us. All the same I have no doubt that they do resent the callous Soviet behaviour. I believe that this is a situation which we can use and that it is very important to set out our position clearly and firmly. Otherwise if it does seem essential later on for you to hold further atmospheric tests, the full weight of Neutral opinion will turn against us or will at least succumb to the argument that there is nothing to choose between the Russians and the West. That was why I believed and still believe that some solemn joint declaration by the two Western nuclear powers would have real value. I think that our public statements this week mean that the time for such a declaration has passed for the moment. But if you do decide to resume atmospheric tests, my own feeling is that a solemn declaration broadly of the kind which I have suggested may still be desirable when that decision is announced.

Britain had strong technical reasons to test a device for Skybolt called Super-Octopus, which needed to be tested underground. As there were no suitable underground sites in the British Isles Macmillan asked Kennedy to allow this device and others to be tested in the Nevada caverns.

Anxious as he was to give his consent to American use of Christmas Island, Macmillan was worried about the political reaction at home; at this time the Campaign for Nuclear Disarmament was active and gaining support even amongst Conservative voters. Following his usual presidential method of government, rather than consulting the Foreign Secretary* and obtaining the advice of the Foreign Office officials Macmillan asked Norman Brook to give his considered opinion in a memorandum designed solely for the Prime Minister's eyes. This was reminiscent of the way Neville Chamberlain at the time of Munich bypassed the Foreign Office and relied on his personal adviser Sir Horace Wilson. Brook's reply was cautious. In a memorandum dated 13 November 1961 he stated:

Christmas Island
The special difficulties about this are: –

(i) it is not enough that the President should be satisfied that further atmospheric tests are necessary. You must also be satisfied, if the tests are to be made at Christmas Island. And you must be in a position to justify these to public opinion here. This means that you must have access, at the appropriate moment, to the military and scientific assessment on which the President's judgement is based: indeed, it must be something very like a joint judgement by the President and yourself.

(ii) Ideally it would be logical to take this decision first – before making the preparations which are necessary to enable further tests to be carried out at Christmas Island. For, once those preparations begin, they cannot be kept secret. And, once they are known to have started, those opposed to further testing will assume that we have made up our minds to conduct tests and we shall be exposed to public pressures to stop. We shall thus become involved in controversy before we have taken the main decision. And, if we should eventually decide not to conduct any further tests, it will be said that we have been forced to this decision by public pressure.

(iii) The public pressures in the United States will be, mainly, in favour of testing. Those here will all be against it. This will tend to divide us from the Americans, on a matter on which we should stand firmly together.

(iv) Unfortunately, it is impracticable to postpone all preparations at Christmas Island until the decision of principle has been taken. For it may take as long as six months to put the facilities there in a condition in which tests can be made. The Americans are bound to press us to get ahead with this as quickly as possible.

---

*During all these Anglo-American negotiations Macmillan took the matter into his own hands, thereby bypassing his Foreign Secretary Lord Home who had a much keener interest in defence than in the Common Market; Home, unable to speak in the Commons, was pushed to the sidelines.

Brook advised sending out a small party – two or three from either side – to reconnoitre and produce an up-to-date report on the situation at Christmas Island.[26]

Brook also advised the Prime Minister to send a message to the President that if the tests were to be made, both the President and the Prime Minister must be satisfied on military and scientific grounds that they were necessary within the meaning of the public statements 'so that they can be justified to world opinion on that basis', and therefore Britain must have full information about the military and scientific justification for whatever programme of tests was proposed. He insisted that British technicians must be fully consulted, and that Macmillan should not guarantee in advance that he would concur in the President's decision:

> This will be a matter for his judgement, and your judgement may in the event differ from his. It is also conceivable that you may feel unable to go along with him for political reasons; and on that account he may wish to prepare alternative facilities at Eniwetok in case he feels obliged in the end to 'go it alone'.

In a final recommendation Brook suggested that the Prime Minister's message to the President should include a statement to the effect that

> In the event you are satisfied that the tests are 'necessary' to preserve the balance of the deterrent you will be ready to agree to the use of Christmas Island and ready to reactivate the facilities there . . . But you would like to reserve for the moment your decision about the date on which overt preparations could begin.

Macmillan based his policy on Brook's advice. Kennedy had replied to Macmillan's letter of 3 November agreeing to British underground tests in Nevada, and offering the assurance that the Americans would not conduct any atmospheric tests on Christmas Island unless these offered the likelihood of improvements 'of substantial military significance' which could not be obtained in any other way, and that 'rigorous steps' would be taken to avoid or reduce fall-out.

Christmas Island lies in an area which is the concern of Australia and New Zealand. Accordingly Macmillan on 1 November 1961 wrote to their Prime Ministers, Robert Menzies and Keith Holyoake, saying he favoured giving consent to American use of Christmas Island because

> if we help the Americans over this we shall strengthen our claim to continue to enjoy the widespread collaboration which we now receive from them in the defence and nuclear fields, and consequently if we decline we may prejudice our chances of this. Dependence on our facilities might lead to closer understanding in regard to test progress generally.

Menzies sent his agreement, but Holyoake replied that his Government looked on the resumption of testing 'as a matter for deprecation rather than for any show of welcome', and only reluctantly acquiesced.

In a telephone conversation with Kennedy on 9 November 1961 Macmillan indicated that the British Cabinet would approve and that he was only waiting for acquiescence from Australia and New Zealand. However the Prime Minister was put out when informed by Watkinson on 15 November that American government scientists were already talking as if the US would shortly cease testing underground and carry out all tests in the atmosphere. 'This was very bad,' Macmillan noted, and three days later he wrote to Kennedy that opinion in Britain

> is running in the opposite direction to your own. But I am much more deeply concerned about our joint position in the face of world opinion. On both these grounds I feel that before we take our final decision we ought to have the fuller information which I have suggested . . . It will then of course be necessary for a more formal agreement to be drawn up dealing with the many related issues which would flow from such a joint enterprise.

Brook again cautioned that Britain must decide in conjunction with the Americans whether an explosion in the atmosphere was really necessary. Without having seen Brook's paper, Home wrote a paper for the Cabinet advising that Britain should allow the Americans to start construction work on Christmas Island 'in 23 weeks'. Watkinson disagreed, and wrote to Macmillan that this would put the Government in a difficult position in the Commons, because it would mean that Britain had committed herself to allowing a series of American tests and the Opposition would immediately ask what 'assurances about safety, etc.' had been received from the Americans and what was the military necessity. Watkinson reminded the Prime Minister of his Commons statement on 31 October and argued that to prevent 'a quite indefensible position in the House' a substantive reply to the President should be delayed for ten days; he asked Macmillan to consider a memorandum by Zuckerman who had advised Watkinson that the Americans had 'not thought this out'. But Zuckerman's paper was no help to Macmillan who, faced with Zuckerman's involved arguments, minuted: 'This is a very confused paper. Any classical scholar could have done better.'

Sir William Penney, Deputy Chairman of the UK Atomic Energy Authority, was more favourable to the resumption of tests than Zuckerman, believing that any decision by Britain and America not to pursue further tests would 'put us in a condition of decisive inferiority if the Russians produced a new series of tests'. He thought Britain could wait a few months, perhaps up to a year or more, without 'really serious ill-effects. However Zuckerman had emphasized that the recent Russian tests had not altered the strategic balance of nuclear power between east and west.' Noting in December 1961 how the two experts disagreed, Macmillan delayed going ahead with an agreement over the use of Christmas Island.[27]

On 20 December 1961 Kennedy and Macmillan met in Bermuda for face-to-face talks about resuming atmospheric nuclear testing while their retinue of scientific advisers discussed technical details. The news from Russia was bad; they had built a new town of 20,000 people for nuclear workers and had developed a 100-megaton bomb. Macmillan made a strong appeal to the President for another effort 'despite Russian trickery and bad faith' to put a stop to this folly. They agreed to make preparations for renewed atmospheric tests at Christmas Island and to hold their hand to see whether progress could be made on Berlin and disarmament.[28]*

Writing to Kennedy on 3 January 1962, on his return to London, Macmillan confirmed his agreement to the series of tests the Americans proposed to make from Christmas Island within the definitions they had set out together in October and November 1961. However Macmillan insisted that the announcement of the decision to hold the tests should be accompanied by an appeal to Khrushchev to abandon tests and co-operate in the disarmament conference being held in Geneva – an announcement which might take the form:

> We are therefore determined to make every effort to pull the world out of this rut, and are making proposals to the Russians to this end (of which we can give a short outline); we hope that the result of our proposals will be to enable the nuclear powers to stop testing altogether as the first move towards general disarmament.

Replying, Kennedy said that he saw no prospect of success in direct appeal to Khrushchev for test bans, and pointed out that American opinion would be hostile to it.

Tests on Christmas Island began on 25 April.† However Macmillan succeeded in persuading Kennedy in August to agree to offer the Russians the option of either an atmospheric ban or a total and comprehensive ban to include underground tests with a reasonable number of inspections. Khrushchev gave an ambiguous reply on 5 September 1962, but efforts to reach an agreement with Russia were overtaken by the Cuba crisis, which effectively overshadowed everything.[29] ‡

* * *

---

* See Chapter 15.
† The residents of Christmas Island were transferred elsewhere. Tests were fixed for early May in the danger area around Christmas Island.
‡ See pages 351 ff.

Meanwhile there were disquieting rumours about technical problems in the Skybolt development programme but the British 1962 Defence White Paper reported Skybolt as 'making good progress'. Yet in January 1962 President Kennedy had told the Secretary of State for Air, Julian Amery (Macmillan's son-in-law), that Skybolt had 'problems'. By the autumn of 1962 there was good reason in Whitehall for believing that all was not well with the project and the news of its cancellation in December did not come quite as a bolt from the blue.

On 8 November Ormsby-Gore had talked to US Secretary of Defence McNamara who had stated that the development costs of Skybolt had doubled and the US Government were considering alternative systems. The British Ambassador warned that any threat to Skybolt would be 'political dynamite' and could put Anglo-American relations 'under the sorest strain'; he went so far as to suggest that cancellation might be seen 'as a means of bringing pressure upon the British Government to abandon their [independent] nuclear deterrent'. McNamara sought to soothe him by suggesting that America would supply Britain with alternatives, including possibly Polaris.

The next day, 9 November, Watkinson's successor as Minister of Defence, Peter Thorneycroft, talked to McNamara on the telephone, emphasizing the political embarrassment which cancellation of Skybolt must cause, and 'the need for any alternative British deterrent – whether Polaris or any other – to have the same degree of independence as Skybolt would have'.[30]

On 7 December Thorneycroft sent an important memorandum to Macmillan, confirming that if Skybolt was lost he would broach the issue with the Americans of their making available an alternative on the same basis 'with no political or other strings'. Assuring the Prime Minister that he would reject 'inadequate substitutes', Thorneycroft declared that 'the only efficient alternative was Polaris'. He proposed buying enough US Polaris missiles for seven British-designed submarines which could be ready by 1974, and during the intervening period Britain would borrow two or three US submarines equipped with Polaris missiles.

The archives reveal a measure of disagreement between Thorneycroft and Macmillan. Initially, so Bligh records, the Prime Minister felt that 'Our best plan would be to try and play Skybolt along for another year in order to avoid political difficulties at home. It was clearly in our interest to get on to a Polaris deterrent at some stage but we had made a number of statements, and it would be a little easier if that continued for the time being.' Doubtless Macmillan did not want to reopen discussion within the Cabinet, some members of which queried the enormous cost of the British deterrent, and at the same time feared the unpredictable reaction of the French and the effect this might have on Common Market negotiations which were then at a crucial stage.

McNamara agreed to come to London for talks, carrying instructions from Kennedy and Rusk to offer Polaris provided Britain agreed to 'assign' it as the British contribution to a NATO multilateral force. When McNamara talked to Thorneycroft on 11 December 1962 the British Minister of Defence was horrified at the American's proviso that Polaris would only be supplied with strong political strings, the most important being that the United Kingdom should 'participate in a seaborne MRBM force under multilateral manning and ownership [i.e. NATO]'.

Kennedy and Macmillan had now agreed to meet in the Bahamas, and Macmillan suddenly became a wholehearted convert to Thorneycroft's proposals to dump Skybolt and plead for Polaris. The Prime Minister instructed de Zulueta to write to Ormsby-Gore explaining that at his Bahamas meeting with the President, Macmillan would press for the purchase of Polaris and the loan of US submarines. Realizing that Kennedy was likely to find Congress difficult over such an agreement, Macmillan told de Zulueta to write:

> The Prime Minister feels that the President could take the line with Congress that the agreement about Skybolt and the agreement about Holy Loch were really part of the same arrangement, and that by lending us the three submarines he would simply be carrying out legally the spirit of his predecessor's undertakings to an ally.

Ormsby-Gore used this argument to good effect with the President.

There is evidence in Macmillan's diary that he at first suspected the Americans of plotting to use technical difficulties over Skybolt as an excuse to force Britain 'out of the nuclear club', although he later wrote that they killed Skybolt 'on good general grounds – but they handled things in such a way as to make many of us very suspicious'.[31]

By the time Macmillan and Kennedy met at Nassau in the Bahamas between 19 and 21 December the Americans had already been pressing for several months with little success for a NATO multilateral force (MLF). The US idea was to head Germany off from her own nuclear programme in which they perceived grave dangers. The British did not oppose MLF openly for fear of antagonizing the Americans and prejudicing Polaris. The Foreign Office brief to the Prime Minister for Nassau included a report from the Washington Embassy that hints had been received from the State Department that Pentagon officials were saying our prospects of getting an adequate alternative to Skybolt would be good 'if we made some open move to multilateralization, and pretty poor otherwise'. In private Whitehall officials treated MLF with 'utter disdain' and Macmillan dismissed the idea as 'politically dangerous and unwarrantably expensive'.[32]

At Nassau on 18 December Kennedy first proposed to Macmillan that their two countries share the development costs of Skybolt equally, although production would be solely for Britain's use. Tentatively Kennedy stated that the US might be prepared to provide Britain with Polaris 'under certain circumstances', but it could not be decided straight away and would need considerable discussion, while the disadvantages of Skybolt were 'relative'; he wanted a small committee set up to discuss Skybolt and report during the winter of 1963. This was unsatisfactory to the British and Thorneycroft twice told the President bluntly that Skybolt would be 'late, expensive and unreliable', and it would be difficult for him to recommend it to Parliament. Thorneycroft also said America had a responsibility to provide an 'alternative'.[33]

As an alternative to Skybolt Kennedy offered the US missile Hound Dog which he claimed would be operative until 1970. Macmillan rejected this abruptly on the grounds that it would be too difficult to fit Hound Dog to British V bombers. He then deployed the skilful argument that by allowing the USA to station their Polaris depot ship on the Clyde and to place an early warning radar station at Fylingdales Britain was 'running all the dangers' and exercising 'none of the power'. He declared that he himself was satisfied that Skybolt was now 'unacceptable', and it would suit Britain better to go in for a missile fired from a submarine, and as they already had a nuclear submarine programme planned, this could easily be converted to take missiles. Britain would, if necessary, be prepared to divert funds by making savings 'elsewhere in the defence programme'.

Warming to his theme, the Prime Minister told the President not to be under any illusion about such a decision:

> If they had to go ahead and develop a submarine-fired missile themselves this would lead inevitably to a deep rift in United States–United Kingdom relations. That was not to say that the Government would in any way lessen their efforts to co-operate with the United States. But public opinion could not be controlled.

By accepting his offer of Skybolt, Kennedy pointed out, the United Kingdom could prolong the effectiveness of their nuclear deterrent from 1966 to 1970 for as little as 250 million dollars, while to give Polaris to Britain was certain to cause dissension in Europe. Macmillan rejected this renewed proposal of Skybolt, using the picturesque argument that 'the proposed marriage with Skybolt was not exactly a shotgun wedding; the virginity of the lady must now be regarded as doubtful': no one believed in the effectiveness of Skybolt.

When the meeting was resumed in the afternoon of 19 December Kennedy offered to supply Polaris without warheads on the understanding that Britain 'assigned' her force to NATO and would only use it independently *in extremis*. There was bitter argument between the Americans and the British about the terms on which it would be 'assigned' and in what circumstances Britain could use Polaris independently: the rooted objection of Kennedy and his advisers to Britain or any NATO country having a small independent nuclear deterrent proved difficult to counter.

A draft statement, to be used in answer to questions whether the agreement reached meant that the United Kingdom was giving up its independent nuclear deterrent, was produced by the Americans and read:

> Only in the event of a dire national emergency – an emergency in which it might be necessary to act alone – an emergency which we cannot envisage and which we all trust will never occur – would HMG be faced with a decision of utilizing such forces on its own.[34]

The British delegation made it clear that this wording was unacceptable. Immediately after the afternoon meeting on Wednesday, 19 December, Thorneycroft minuted to the Prime Minister his strong objections to the American draft statement, saying that under their proposals we would not have an independent nuclear deterrent, and their proposals for NATO would mean a return to conscription 'plus a very big bill for conventional equipment or withdrawal from east of Suez'; his advisers thought even the most liberal interpretation of the word 'assigned' would make it impossible for Britain to be able to pose continually the deterrent threat in accordance with the Government's policy. He advised giving up the attempt to find a formula

> which glosses over the very wide chasm between us because if such a formula was found it would lead to a series of public disagreements.
>
> Public reactions in Britain are easy to forecast. We shall be accused of spending vast sums of the taxpayers' money to create a force not under our control in order to subscribe it to NATO.
>
> In the circumstances and with great regret my advice is that these talks should be wound up with a communiqué saying that the Americans have decided to withdraw their support from Skybolt, that whilst they have (in accordance with the 1960 agreement) given us the option of continuing it at our own expense, we have decided not to do so, not only because of the uncertainties as to cost and date of completion but because of the doubts the Americans have themselves expressed as to its success and reliability; possible alternatives have been discussed but it has not been possible to reach agreement.

Macmillan replied to Thorneycroft that the President's formula, with the words 'dire emergency', was 'too restrictive' but he was hopeful that he could work on a form of words and devise a formula which would seem reasonable to ordinary people. 'If we break, our formula and theirs will be published so we shall have to defend our own and all the consequences . . . The Americans may some time on Friday [21 December] give in to us. I have not given up hope.'

The next day, 20 December, Macmillan cabled to Butler in London:

So far the Americans have felt unwilling to offer us the Polaris missile on terms that are acceptable to us. They wish to *assign* the whole of the British Polaris force to NATO or a multilateral nuclear force. Such an arrangement would not give us an independent British contribution to the nuclear deterrent in any real sense of the word independent, since, under the American proposal we would only be able to withdraw the force from NATO in a dire national emergency. It would therefore not be available outside the NATO area or play a role in strengthening our NATO foreign policy.

Our feeling is that it would not be tolerable to British public opinion that we should pay about £300 million for a force which would then become, as it were, the property of NATO. Alec Home and Peter Thorneycroft are giving me splendid support in their different ways. We are going to try again tomorrow [21 December] but I do not know how far we will be successful . . .

The real trouble is that the Americans:

(a) feel they have enough nuclear power for the West and cannot see why anyone else should question their willingness to defend us, and

(b) are most anxious not to stimulate the French and especially the Germans to ask for favours similar to what we should get if we were supplied with Polaris without strings.

Our difficulty is that if we accept the American proposal as it stands we should be spending some £300 million or more without preserving freedom of manoeuvre in the future for foreign policy in general and action in any part of the world. Of course we do in fact intend that should we be supplied with missiles our Polaris fleet should normally be deployed in support of NATO as some of the V bombers are. But as you will see the Americans wish us to go further than this in the assignment of the fleet to NATO or a multilateral force. They think that possible reaction from Germany and even France makes it essential for them not to give us favours in the field. They claim that Polaris is different in kind from Skybolt.

I should be grateful if you would consult as many Cabinet Ministers as are available in London tomorrow, Friday, and give us your advice.[35]

The next day, 21 December, Macmillan met with some success. He and Kennedy discussed this formula:

These forces would be made available for inclusion in a NATO multilateral nuclear force. The Prime Minister made it clear that except where Her Majesty's Government may decide that supreme national interests are at stake these British forces will be used for the purposes of international defence of the Western Alliance in all circumstances.

Macmillan referred this statement to the Cabinet. In London there were reservations about the deal, especially about the conditions and the cost, and after chairing a Cabinet discussion Butler asked Macmillan to try to ensure that the clause emphasized 'more clearly and unambiguously the British right to use the force independently'. The Cabinet suggested the following draft:

> The Prime Minister made it clear that except where Her Majesty's Government may decide that the supreme national interests are at stake these British forces would be used only for the purposes of international defence of the Western Alliance.

This rephrasing would have made little difference, and sensibly the Cabinet assured Macmillan of their confidence in his 'final decision'. Macmillan ignored this telegram; he knew he had wrung the last drop of blood out of the Americans.

After Sandys and Thorneycroft had discussed Kennedy's proposed clause again with Macmillan and Home in Nassau, Macmillan cabled to Butler that they felt they could defend it 'in the House and the country as maintenance of independent British contribution to the nuclear deterrent'. Macmillan emphasized that he would make public that the agreement he had with President Eisenhower, now repeated with President Kennedy, was that neither side would use nuclear weapons without first consulting the other, and this would apply to Polaris submarines and missiles.

However Martin Redmayne, the Chief Whip, was intransigent and felt that Macmillan would have difficulty in convincing the Conservative Party that Britain still had her own nuclear deterrent. He sent a rather silly cable to the Prime Minister in Nassau late on 21 December:

> I am not sure that Cabinet have sufficiently considered the political repercussions of the Polaris decision. Although I realize that you have had a great battle to win any ground it may well be thought that what you have won is not worth the cost in that it has little but prestige value until 1968 at earliest. Moreover it will be denigrated because it will have been so hardly wrung from a nation which will be clearly seen to regard it only as a sop to our pride.
>
> I am afraid that you personally will be thought to have been driven with the need to come back with something at whatever cost.
>
> Would it not be better to pause and study at leisure here whether there

are not practical alternatives which even if more costly might well be more acceptable politically.

Macmillan paid little attention to Redmayne's objections and only three trivial alterations were made in the press statement. Macmillan does not describe the dispute in his diary, writing:

> Nassau was an exhausting experience: three days' hard negotiations – nearly four days. The Americans pushed us very hard . . . the discussions were protracted and fiercely contested. They turned almost entirely on 'independence' in national need. Whether Parliament will think we have done well or badly I cannot tell yet.

On 21 December Kennedy and Macmillan issued a joint press statement, confirming that the US would make Polaris missiles without warheads available for British submarines which Britain would construct, and containing the important words that the British Polaris missiles could be used independently 'when supreme national interests were at stake'.

> The President and the Prime Minister agreed that the United States will make available on a continuing basis Polaris Missiles (less warheads) for British submarines . . . The United Kingdom Government will construct the submarines in which these weapons will be placed . . . The Prime Minister made it clear that except where Her Majesty's Government may decide that supreme national interests are at stake these British forces will be used for the purposes of international defence of the Western Alliance in all circumstances.

The wording was deliberately ambiguous so as to allow Macmillan to claim that he had preserved Britain's independent nuclear deterrent while paying lip-service to Kennedy's multilateralist policy.

As part of the bargain Britain was forced to agree to increase her 'conventional' contribution to NATO – the shortfall that had worried Kennedy when he read the 1962 British Defence White Paper. The Cabinet was concerned about this reference to conventional forces, some members fearing that it could be used as an excuse for not delivering Polaris if Britain defaulted on this part of the bargain.[36] However the promising proposal for the loan of three US submarines equipped with Polaris missiles fell by the wayside. There is nothing in the archives to explain the lapse of this arrangement, and it remains a minor mystery.

Kennedy flouted the views of his advisers in giving Polaris to Britain. At a pre-Nassau meeting on 16 December McNamara, Ball, Rusk and Bundy had all expressed serious doubts about the offer. But one factor which weighed with the President was the need to lend support to a British Conservative Government; the alternative Labour Government, he thought, would be opposed to British entry into the EEC, and would 'want to spend more on social welfare and less on defence'.[37]

As the Cabinet and the Chief Whip feared, the Nassau communiqué received a bad press in Britain. Nassau was the lead story in all the Saturday morning newspapers on 22 December. The *Express* and *Herald* had hostile headlines. However the *Guardian*, while questioning the decision to continue with a British deterrent at all, said that given that decision the Polaris solution was 'sensible'. The *Express* headline was 'The Sell Out' and René McColl, its diplomatic correspondent, stated that Britain would obtain Polaris at the cost of being shoved politically and militarily deep into Europe; the paper's lobby correspondent expected Macmillan to return to the most serious political crisis of his career, while its editorial said that 'the public will accept nothing less than our own nuclear deterrent.' Of course the *Express* was giving Lord Beaverbrook's view but the paper had an enormous influence with the public at that time.

Macmillan's reaction to this attack by the Beaverbrook press was to send a minute to Lord Hailsham, President of the Council:

> Lord Beaverbrook talks as if Skybolt were an English weapon rather than the long bow at Agincourt. I am sure it would do an immense amount of good if you felt able to expound in a speech what we have done, bringing out the two concepts of interdependence and independence which you understand so well.

'Macmillan's Nuclear Folly' was the *Herald*'s headline and their lobby correspondent dismissed the independence of the deterrent as 'meaningless'; he expected a political row but thought the Tories would accept the agreement as the best Britain could get. More serious for the Government were the *Telegraph*'s criticisms. These questioned Macmillan's ability to retain the confidence of the Conservative Party, and stated that the Opposition had seldom been presented with more favourable ground for attack. The *Telegraph* editorial stated that Britain had 'very much the worst' of the bargain, and argued that instead of rattling our chains we should make ourselves truly independent by going ahead on our own or with those in Europe with similar interests.

Television news bulletins and press reaction in America on the same day were also critical and concentrated on the disagreements and ill-feeling between the two sides. Kennedy was incensed at this, and was even more angry when the next morning McNamara authorized the issue by the Defence Department of the news of the first successful firing of Skybolt. Kennedy realized the trouble this would cause in London, and insisted that further statements were published correcting the impression. According to Ormsby-Gore Kennedy was particularly 'vexed' at accusations that the United States were using the troubles over Skybolt 'to

drive Britain out of the nuclear business', and Kennedy insisted that the
story of Skybolt's success must be killed since it would add to the
administration's problems with Congress over their decision to abandon
Skybolt, which the President thought likely to be formidable. Kennedy
wrote to Macmillan: 'I was more annoyed than you with the Skybolt
test and especially with the way in which it was announced. The degree
of its success was greatly exaggerated, and as you know we have now
gone forward with our own cancellation of production plans.'[38]

At the Cabinet on 3 January 1963 Macmillan countered criticism by
saying first that he was forced to agree to 'commit Polaris in some way
to NATO as a condition of the US supplying the weapon'. He emphasized that it would remain subject 'to the ultimate authority of HMG,
and could be withdrawn if the supreme interests of the country required.
It was a realistic compromise between independence and interdependence
and we had acquired a far more effective weapon than Skybolt.' Some
members of the Cabinet expressed reservations about any written agreement to commit Polaris to NATO; also about the cost which would
'involve even more drastic contraction of defence expenditure than
had previously been contemplated'. However the Nassau agreement
was unanimously endorsed and the Commons debate was fixed for 31
January.[39]

By then Nassau was overshadowed by the de Gaulle veto on Britain's
entry into the Common Market. Macmillan opened and wound up the
31 January debate with impressive, well-argued speeches, and in spite
of fears by the Government Whips there were no Tory abstentions and
a majority of over 100 in favour of the Nassau agreement. Redmayne's
misgivings, which had been echoed by many Conservative MPs and
lobby correspondents, had proved unfounded, owing primarily to
Macmillan's powers of persuasion; the acceptance of the Nassau
agreement was a political triumph for him.*

---

*There was a strange sequel to the Nassau communiqué. In December 1963 when Home was
Prime Minister Ormsby-Gore reported that the White House were perturbed at the bad press
the Nassau agreement was receiving in Britain. With Home's permission de Zulueta allowed
the *Sunday Times* Washington correspondent, Henry Brandon, to see the official transcript of
the Nassau conversations which were only revealed to historians thirty years later. On 8
December 1963 Brandon wrote in the *Sunday Times* that the Nassau communiqué was 'a
compromise formula' which did not contradict Kennedy's own policy of multilateralism and the
prevention of the spread of nuclear weapons, yet made it possible for Macmillan to claim he
had saved Britain's independent nuclear deterrent: 'Thus Kennedy paved the way for a graceful
transition in British history.' This article was well received in the White House. Professor
McGeorge Bundy in a letter to the author described Brandon as the most highly regarded
European journalist in Washington, whom Kennedy particularly liked because he always respected
the difference between 'on the record' and 'off the record' comments while his own comments

At Nassau Kennedy agreed to make a similar offer of Polaris missiles to France. As soon as this was agreed on 21 December Macmillan instructed Pierson Dixon in Paris to inform de Gaulle, hoping that the General would receive the news favourably. His judgement was wrong. De Gaulle treated the offer with bad grace. When he saw him, Dixon reported, de Gaulle had already heard from Kennedy but had retorted that the offer was not of practical interest to France:

> The French were constructing missiles. They would have Mirage 4 bombers next year ... He expressed no criticism of the idea of 'a NATO nuclear force' to be composed of national units working together. On the other hand he expressed no interest in it. From everything he said it must be assumed that he is unlikely to accept this conception for France.[41]

Despite Kennedy's and Macmillan's hopes, de Gaulle entirely discounted the Polaris agreement concluded at Nassau. He was only interested in a completely independent French *force de frappe*, and when announcing his veto on British entry into the EEC on 14 January 1963 he also announced that he could not accept the kind of nuclear arrangement the Americans had proposed at Nassau. The Americans' 'entangling terms', de Gaulle asserted, showed the unbridgeable differences between Europe and Anglo-Saxons:

> In case of a general atomic war there would inevitably be terrible and perhaps mortal destruction for both countries. In such conditions no one in the world and in particular no one in America can say whether or where or how or when or to what extent American nuclear weapons would be used to defend Europe.[42]

Some air chiefs were unhappy about the substitution of Polaris for Skybolt, with its implication that V bombers would soon be obsolete. Dermot Boyle, Chief of Air Staff until 1959, criticized Thorneycroft for purchasing Polaris 'without any reference to the Chiefs of Staff', while Sir John Slessor, Chief of the Air Staff 1950–2, wrote: 'It is a really appalling thought that a couple of Ministers and a zoologist can skip off to the Bahamas and, without a single member of the Chiefs of Staff Committee present, commit us to a military monstrosity [Polaris] on the purely political issue of nuclear independence – which anyway is a myth.'[43]

'were often illuminating'. Kennedy nearly always acceded to Brandon's requests for an interview. Brandon had promised Ormsby-Gore in Washington that his article would have a favourable slant, and he told de Zulueta that he would show it to Downing Street before it was published, and allow them to make corrections. The article included the comment that 'It was one of Macmillan's finest hours.'[40]

At Nassau Macmillan achieved his goal, returning with a modern independent nuclear deterrent in place of Skybolt. At home he played down the conditions attaching to the deal that Polaris should be part of a NATO MLF, and emphasized that in a national emergency Britain's finger alone was on the trigger. After initial difficulties this proved to be a convincing political formula, and with this platform he convinced the electorate that he had served them well by using his special relationship with the President to make a good bargain.

During the last three weeks of Macmillan's premiership the military historian Professor Michael Howard told an important Government-convened Anglo-American conference at Ditchley in Oxfordshire:

> An independent force under ultimate British control provides in the eyes of a substantial section of public opinion – a section particularly well represented in Whitehall – a certain sense of assurance even if the defence analyst can prove rationally that this assurance has no valid foundation. This assurance is not for the eventuality of our being abandoned by our allies in face of the existing threat. It is for the possibility of the whole pattern of world politics changing in the future as radically as it has changed in the past . . . What the future holds in store no one can tell.

Sir Bernard Burrows, then a Deputy Under-Secretary at the Foreign Office, reported to Edward Heath about this conference:

> The whole American team and practically the whole of the non-official British team expressed strong disapproval of the retention of an independent deterrent by the UK. They argued that its military value was slight and that in spite of its assignment to NATO its existence played an important part in encouraging the French to continue with their plans to have an independent deterrent, and even more dangerously was certain to lead the Germans in the same direction. Instead the Americans argued that it was largely the existence of the British and French deterrents which made the MLF necessary. The Americans emphatically stated their view that it would be far better for the alliance if the UK nuclear deterrent were scrapped and resources devoted instead to increasing conventional forces both in Europe and in Asia.

Macmillan was always conscious of the 'sense of assurance' described by Howard, and seeing an independent British deterrent as a vote-winner also, he attached great political importance to retaining it. In this he was not alone. There had been a long continuity of policy between Labour and Conservative governments over the British independent nuclear deterrent. As early as December 1945 a highly secret Cabinet Committee had authorized the construction of an atomic plant at Windscale to produce plutonium. In October 1946 there was a 'hiccup' in the Cabinet when the escalating costs of the factory came under scrutiny. In the absence of Ernest Bevin, the Foreign Secretary, Hugh

Dalton, Chancellor of the Exchequer, and Stafford Cripps, President of the Board of Trade, argued strongly against continuing the Windscale project. On Bevin's late arrival the Prime Minister, Clement Attlee, summed up on the lines taken by Dalton and Cripps. Bevin intervened:

> No, Prime Minister, this will not do. I do not mind for myself but I do not want any other Foreign Secretary of this country to be talked at or to by the Secretary of State of the United States as I have just been by Mr Byrnes. We have got to have this thing over here whatever it costs and we have got to have a bloody Union Jack on top of it.[44]

Seventeen years later the Prime Minister, Alec Home, was challenged in the Commons in November 1963 by Jo Grimond, the Liberal leader, about the need for an independent British nuclear deterrent. Home said: 'The way we shall get to the peace talks is to be taken of right because of nuclear power.' This doctrine, Grimond replied, made it impossible to argue against proliferation to Germany, China or anywhere else.

Both Bevin and Home ignored the fact that, although it may be convenient to be asked to the conference table by virtue of possessing an independent nuclear deterrent, it made proliferation far more probable. However the doctrine of the need for a British deterrent went unchallenged in the Cabinet during Macmillan's premiership. Future generations of historians must decide whether this judgement has turned out to be in the best interests of the nation.[45]

CHAPTER 15

Khrushchev and the West

WHEN BERLIN WAS occupied by the Allied armies in June 1945 the central government of Nazi Germany ceased to exist. The French, British, American and Russian commanders-in-chief exercised their authority in four separate zones under the Allied Control Council. Greater Berlin was excluded from the zones and each power was allocated a sector of the city, the commandant of which was to sit on the Kommandatura answerable to the Control Commission. The authority formerly exercised by Hitler had thus passed legally to the Allied Control Commission. In June 1948, without Russian consent, the Allies agreed on a federal government for the three western zones of Germany, causing antagonism between the two blocs.

In the summer of 1948 the three Western powers decided that a reform of the currency was imperative. The Russians objected. The Soviet representative withdrew from both the Allied Control Commission and the Kommandatura and the Russians cut off all road and rail traffic with West Berlin. By blocking all communication and supplies to the city, the Russians planned to force the Western Allies to withdraw from the government of West Berlin and remove their occupying troops. But in an airlift lasting ten and a half months the British and Americans succeeded in supplying the west part of the city and the Anglo-American troops with their essential needs, and finally in May 1949, frustrated in their plan, the Russians lifted the blockade and road and rail traffic from the west reached Berlin normally again. The Russians undertook to provide the Allies with 'free and unhindered access from West Germany to Berlin'.

In September 1948 the City Assembly, which was supposed to represent both parts of the city, moved from East Berlin to West Berlin. Elections were held in West Berlin and a leading Socialist, Ernst Reuter, was elected Mayor. Although nominally part of the Federal Republic of West Germany, West Berlin was in political and geographical isolation and its representatives had no vote in the Federal Parliament of West Germany at Bonn.

After 1949 – when the Russians created in the eastern zone the German Democratic Republic (Deutsche Demokratische Republik, or DDR for short) – Berlin led an extraordinary life. The Deutschmark was worth six times as much in the west as in the east, and from time to time communications between east and west were interrupted by the Russians. An uneasy *modus vivendi* existed until 1958, when in November there was a sudden crisis, which was to last until the end of Macmillan's premiership. On 10 November Khrushchev demanded the withdrawal of all Allied troops from Berlin and ten days later told Adenauer that Russia intended 'to liquidate the occupation statutes concerning Berlin'. The uneasy peace which had lasted since 1949 was at risk. As usual in a crisis Macmillan immediately gathered the reins into his own hands.

Badly shaken, Adenauer sent an urgent personal message to Macmillan begging him to dissuade Khrushchev. However the next week, 27 November, the Soviet sent an official note to the three occupying Western powers declaring that Russia looked on the existing arrangements within Berlin as 'null and void' and that Russia would sign a peace treaty with the East German Government, after which the Russian and East German governments together would negotiate with the Western Allies on the basis of West Berlin being a 'demilitarized free city'. The declaration was accompanied by an ultimatum that unless a new agreement was reached within six months all military traffic from the west to Berlin would be blocked as in 1948.

The West Germans and French were horrified at the Communist threat. Such a treaty, the French and Germans argued, involving recognition of the East German Government, would make a non-Communist united Germany impossible, and the two governments adamantly refused to contemplate recognizing the DDR, accounting it no more than a Soviet puppet. The Americans began a staff study of military plans to force entry. Macmillan took it all calmly, minuting that he was 'confused as to what the argument was about', and he could not visualize what the Russians proposed should happen when the six months were up. He summarized his views in a memorandum:

Land traffic from the west to Berlin consists partly of military and partly of civil traffic. Since there are only about ten thousand Allied troops in Berlin the military traffic must be small – a few tons of supplies a day. The civil traffic I imagine runs into very large figures.

What is all the row about? Is it about the civil traffic whether from the west to Berlin or to other parts of the DDR territory? Is there to be any change in the procedure about this? Do not the Western Germans (who are so anxious that we should not deal with the East) in fact deal with the

DDR every day? What is the form in which these German dealings take place? In any case is there any reason to suppose that when the six months are up there will be any change in the situation on civil traffic?

As I understand the Russian move it is just to go away and leave us to make our own arrangements with the DDR. We say, and rightly, that this is a breach of an understanding which the Russians cannot do unilaterally. This is what the European countries said to Castlereagh when we abandoned the Holy Alliance.* Is it that they are, as it were, passing their rights to the DDR? If that is so, I do not see how we can have a world war or take action which endangers peace on a point of this kind.

If, of course, the DDR refuse to allow our lorries to go through, that is another thing, but you cannot have a war or military action about that. You can have a war about facts – about whether you are prevented from going to the play, but not about whether you buy a ticket from the theatre or from Keith Prowse.

Macmillan's diagnosis was correct. Khrushchev's main aim was to force West Germany and the Western Allies to recognize the DDR as the legitimate government of East Germany. As the Foreign Office advised, Khrushchev wanted to force the three Western powers to give 'some sort of *de facto* recognition' to the DDR Government so that he would be in a stronger position to force Adenauer to negotiate reunification direct between the two German governments; even if the Russians handed over their sector of Berlin to the DDR it would be extremely unlikely that 'Soviet forces will be withdrawn from East Germany'.

Khrushchev also hoped to divide the Western Allies over Berlin, and up to a point he succeeded. The prospect of Federal Germany obtaining nuclear arms, so the Foreign Office pointed out to the Prime Minister, gave a sense of urgency to Khrushchev's attempt to loosen the Western hold. This appears to have been the correct explanation; with hindsight it is clear that Khrushchev was bluffing, but this, though suspected by the British, was not obvious at the time.[1]

On 13 December Khrushchev sent an ominous letter to Macmillan:

The Soviet Government's main aim in proposing the abolition of the last vestiges of the occupation regime in Berlin is to eliminate a dangerous, indeed extremely dangerous source of friction and tension which complicates the relations between our countries and creates an abnormal atmosphere in Europe as a whole.

---

* The Holy Alliance was a treaty signed in September 1815, following the final defeat of Napoleon, whereby Russia, Austria and Prussia pledged themselves to rule as fathers of families and to observe the principles of Christian charity in international affairs. It had no political significance.

Khrushchev ended his letter with the bald statement that if agreement on Berlin was not reached within six months Russia would sign a treaty with the DDR. A week later Khrushchev called for a Summit conference to resolve the dispute.[2]

Macmillan showed more statesmanship than the Americans, French or West Germans. He decided that while the West must maintain her right of access to Berlin it was imperative to avoid giving Russia no choice other than humiliation or war, and that the Western Allies had no legal right even to protest if Russia gave the same recognition to East Germany as the West had to the Federal Republic. In his diary he wrote: 'I doubt whether therefore we can make the question of whether Russians or East Germans approve the bills of lading or punch the railway tickets into a *casus belli*.' To his dismay, however, the Americans pushed ahead with plans to keep the routes to Berlin open by force.

In the week before Christmas Adenauer wrote to Macmillan emphasizing that in 1948 both the Russian and the Allied sectors of Berlin were 'equally poor'; today the western sector had a great deal to lose. Adenauer objected to beginning negotiations with Russia while the deadline of the ultimatum existed. The American State Department told the British that they would attempt to reopen access 'by force before considering an airlift as in 1948'. The British Chiefs of Staff disagreed, reporting on 1 January 1959 that

> it would be impracticable to open the autobahn for the use of convoys by means of limited action, and no attempt should be made to force access unless the risk of global warfare is accepted, and all preparations including mobilization have been made to demonstrate the determination of the West.
>
> As a test of Soviet/DDR intentions air probing action involves much less immediate risk of global war than a land action. It would give them an opportunity to make concessions without loss of face.
>
> An airlift would not provide a final solution to the maintenance of the whole of West Berlin ... Undertaking an unsuccessful land action will compromise a subsequent resort to air action.

The British and American Chiefs of Staff were at cross purposes. However the German, French, British and American Foreign Ministers agreed at a meeting on 2 January 1959 that 'in no circumstances would they deal with the DDR as the agent of the Soviets', but adding the important proviso: 'We consider that to deal with the DDR in substitution for the Soviets and even to recognize them would be vastly preferable to a general war.'

According to the Foreign Office the US position was 'that if we make a show of force on land to show our determination the Russians will not oppose it except to the extent of supporting harassing tactics by the

DDR which would stop short of actual military force'. The Foreign Office thought this 'a very questionable and dangerous assumption'.

Sir Patrick Reilly, Ambassador in Moscow, wrote on 2 January 1959:

> I believe Khrushchev's calculation is based on the belief that Western public opinion will not support a Western military initiative which would appear to be a provocation to a general war, and that matters can be so managed by an initially accommodating attitude by East Germans to allow communications, by new offers of negotiations and by peace propaganda that the West will have great difficulty in finding a specific issue on which to take a stand.

If war appeared imminent, he continued, the Soviet Union would snatch advantages for herself, probably as the outcome of a hastily convened conference for which there would be strong popular pressure given the threats of a nuclear bombardment of Western Europe which would have been touted. In face of a direct military challenge, Reilly thought that Russia would be unlikely to back down for reasons of 'face', but the Allies could not be so sure that they would do so in face of an airlift which would 'have the great advantage that it would put on them the onus of the first forcible action'.

Macmillan used the Foreign Office briefings as the basis for messages to de Gaulle, Adenauer and Eisenhower. France, only fourteen years after the end of the Second World War, was strongly opposed to the reunification of Germany, for fear that she might become a military menace again; Macmillan, a veteran of the Somme, was not unfamiliar with such feelings. The British Foreign Office was correct in advising Macmillan that Khrushchev was not envisaging total war, and they were less alarmist than their American counterparts who were concentrating on 'contingency' military planning for the moment when the six-month ultimatum expired. Then, on 10 January, as Anglo-American dissension was building up, the Berlin crisis was to a certain extent defused when Khrushchev himself made a new move: he invited the three Western powers to a Summit peace conference 'to include a discussion of Berlin'. This was better received in London than Washington.[3]

On 22 January 1959 the *Washington Post* carried an article by the well-known European correspondent Don Cook spotlighting British differences with the Americans over the use of troops to break the Berlin blockade and the reasons for British opposition to land operations, in strong contrast to the position taken by the White House. Then on 6 February Sir Harold Caccia, British Ambassador to Washington, cabled London, enclosing a copy of another article, this time by Joseph Alsop, an even more influential Washington columnist, which stated: '. . . in the talks about the Berlin problem that have been held here between

Deputy Secretary of State Robert Murphy and the British and French Ambassadors . . . British objections to a firm and clear contingency plan brought the talks to a virtual impasse.'

Caccia was indignant, reporting that he had repeatedly pressed the Department of Defence and the State Department for clarification of their policy on contingency planning, and he had himself spoken to Dulles on 21 January and 1 February expressing the hope that as a result of Dulles's forthcoming visit to London, Paris and Bonn 'this essential work [military contingency planning] should be done without further delay'; Murphy had agreed, saying 'We must hope contingency planning would get started as a result of the Dulles tour.'

After reading the Alsop article Macmillan minuted: 'Foreign Secretary – This is interesting because I have no doubt that Murphy and Co have inspired this. This is Algiers form.* They are angry with Dulles and the President. It also makes me realize how fatal it would be if Dulles had to retire from health or other reason.'[4]

Khrushchev had made it plain that he would like a visit from Macmillan. Macmillan himself felt that he was the only Western political leader who could break the deadlock and solve the immediate crisis. As a statesman he foresaw that he could play a useful role as a peace broker between America and Russia; and as a politician he could see the electoral advantages of doing so.

After a long discussion at the Foreign Office Macmillan had sent a telegram to Dulles on 20 January 1959 asking the American Government to agree to his accepting an invitation from the Russians to visit Russia. In his memoirs Macmillan writes that Eisenhower and Dulles offered him 'great encouragement'; this is incorrect. As the Eisenhower archives disclose, Dulles told the President that Macmillan wanted to go to Moscow solely because there would shortly be a British General Election and he wanted to be 'the hero who finds a way out of the Cold War dilemma'. Eisenhower's and Dulles's immediate reaction was to say 'No', but coming to the opinion that Macmillan would be 'speaking only for himself', and that 'the trip would react adversely', they decided it would cause offence if they objected.[5]

Like Eisenhower, Adenauer looked on Macmillan's proposal as an election manoeuvre, and stressed that under no circumstances should recognition be given to East Germany – this was always his priority; de Gaulle gave a more statesmanlike response. News of the trip was well

---

* In 1944–5 Murphy and Macmillan had been their countries' representatives in Algiers. Among several complimentary references to Murphy in his memoirs, Macmillan reports that the two of them got on well, but there have always been doubts about this, and this minute confirms the existence of friction.

received in all sections of the British press and Commons, and the British party duly arrived in Moscow on 21 February 1959.

In initial discussions Khrushchev stuck to his guns, and argued forcibly that West Berlin must be set up as a 'free city'. Macmillan countered with three alternative suggestions: that Germany should be reunited; that East Berlin should go to East Germany, West Berlin to West Germany; or finally, that all Berlin might be established as a free city. Khrushchev then asked why the West wanted to prolong 'the state of war'. The discussion on this subject was calm and promising, and the talks turned to the possibility of a Summit, a meeting of Foreign Ministers of the Four, and the Soviet draft of a peace treaty with East Germany.

Macmillan then left on a tour of Russia, and while he was away Khrushchev delivered an aggressive speech in which he castigated the Western powers for proposing a Foreign Ministers' conference on Berlin and Germany without the presence of the Foreign Ministers of Czechoslovakia and Hungary – overlooking the fact that these two governments were Soviet puppets. Khrushchev went on to criticize Eisenhower, Dulles and Adenauer, but unexpectedly offered Britain an immediate non-aggression pact in an ill-contrived attempt to divide Britain and America: he was well aware of their current divisions of opinion on how hard a line to take over Berlin.

When Macmillan and Khrushchev met again on Macmillan's return to Moscow the British Prime Minister stressed the need for a Summit or Foreign Ministers' conference within the next few weeks or months, saying that Berlin was otherwise a 'dangerous prospect'. He viewed Khrushchev's belligerent speech as a clumsy attempt to separate the Western Allies, which he made plain to the Russians was impossible. He then left on a trip to Kiev. Khrushchev, who had planned to accompany him, cried off because of toothache.

When the British party returned once more to Moscow the Russians were again affable and Macmillan cabled to London and Washington: 'The Russians seem anxious to make amends for the discourtesy of Khrushchev's speech. They are like children. They like to have the last word in argument and they have fits of sulking. The Russians have been showing us a fair face since the scowl last Wednesday.' Khrushchev and Macmillan now agreed on the need for an early Summit; the chief difference being that Khrushchev and Gromyko considered that all the problems could be solved by a few days of talk between Khrushchev, Eisenhower, Macmillan and de Gaulle, whereas Macmillan and Lloyd insisted that the Foreign Ministers must carry out a great deal of negotiation beforehand if a Summit was to have any chance of success.[6]

Macmillan and Lloyd had done well in Russia, remaining courteous under grave provocation. Their visit did much to improve relations and, if the same spirit had been shown by Eisenhower and de Gaulle, early agreement over Berlin and East Germany and even over withdrawing Soviet troops from Eastern Europe might have been reached.

In a despatch on 2 March, the day before Macmillan's return to London, Caccia wrote scathingly from Washington about the Anglo-American rift over Berlin:

> There is no such thing yet as an American position over Berlin, and there is no apparent effort by the administration to do anything but drift; the ordinary American has still no idea that he may have to compromise or fight before the year is out ... The President's usual routine is golf and quail shooting ... the impression is that Berlin is just another affair like Lebanon or the offshore islands* and that provided the US Government stands firm all will be well with no bones broken and the *status quo* preserved.
>
> This general happy-go-lucky attitude is promoted by the Pentagon. The Chairman of the COS affects to be spoiling for a showdown and talks in terms of clobbering the Russians. Of course if a showdown of this kind suits us and we are ready to run the risks there is something to be said for letting things drift as they are. Admittedly there would always be a danger that the Americans would run out when they have woken up and see the crunch coming. But meanwhile it would have been made far more difficult for the US Government to retreat ... we should seize the earliest opportunity of getting down to a discussion of ends with the US Government. There is grave danger in this that we shall be accused of being yellow and shall lose some of our standing in America. This may be the lesser evil.
>
> If we choose this course it means getting as soon as possible at the only American who in the last resort will have to make the decision, namely the President. As over the offshore islands last year it would be surprising if he were not a great deal less belligerent and less ready to let things reach the brink than many of his advisers.
>
> I recommend the Prime Minister and Foreign Secretary visit USA as soon as they can after their return from Moscow. Mr Herter† said he would welcome them at any time. Herter said he shared much of the concern expressed in this letter.

On 8 March Macmillan cabled to Caccia:

There are only four alternatives:
(a) The Russians will climb down.
(b) We shall reach an acceptable compromise.
(c) The West will suffer a resounding diplomatic defeat and the loss of West Berlin.
(d) We shall have a war.

---

* The offshore islands of Quemoy and Matsos: see Chapter 16.
† Foster Dulles's Deputy, soon after to be Secretary of State.

Because of the necessity of momentous decisions, Macmillan added, a meeting of heads of government was essential. Caccia was unable to persuade the US State Department to accept this realistic assessment.

But one favourable result of the Prime Minister's visit was soon noticeable. Khrushchev softened his line over the six-month ultimatum on Berlin, and in a speech at Leipzig on 4 March 1959 said 'the deadline of 27 May had no particular significance. If the West did not like it they could name another one'; the three Western powers, he added, might keep forces 'for police purposes' when it became a free city, but Russia would also have token forces there.

On 5 March Caccia sent a further note from Washington: 'There is a tendency to drift here in the direction of a showdown with the Russians or of finding objections to any proposals for avoiding it,' and at a press conference Eisenhower unkindly refused to agree that Macmillan's Russian visit had been a 'success'.[7]

Eisenhower's national television broadcast on foreign affairs on 16 March was unhelpful. In it he listed seventeen different types of nuclear missiles now with the US armed forces and stated: 'The US had a great retaliatory force capable of reaching any target on earth', whilst 'for every soldier we have under arms our allies in NATO have five.' He left the question of a Summit open. However, as another promising result of Macmillan's Russian visit, a long private letter from Khrushchev reached him on 14 April 1959 agreeing to a Foreign Ministers' meeting in Geneva as a preliminary to a Summit.

Meanwhile American military contingency planning continued for keeping open the routes to Berlin. Macmillan disliked this initiative which he looked on as 'brinkmanship', writing on one report of current US plans: 'I suppose we must agree. One can only say this is much less silly than it was four months ago.' (The US had scaled down the initial reaction.) In a memorandum to the Foreign Secretary he wrote:

> British, French and US military authorities should plan precautionary measures in Europe which will not create public alarm but will be detectable by Soviet Intelligence, plus more elaborate military measures to be put into effect only after the Soviets have turned over their check-points to the DDR or our traffic is obstructed forcibly.

The Foreign Office view was that every effort should be made to continue normal traffic by autobahn and rail, even if the DDR took over the check-points, and that an attempt at an airlift would be 'inadvisable'. The Americans however wanted far stronger measures.[8]

On 15 April Dulles resigned for reasons of health and died six weeks later; he was succeeded by his deputy, Christian Herter. Though far-sighted and intelligent, Herter lacked charisma and was to have only a short term as US Secretary of State.* On 11 May Gromyko, Lloyd, Herter and Couve de Murville assembled in Geneva for the Foreign Ministers' Conference. Simultaneously officials began disarmament talks, concentrating on suspension of nuclear testing. The outlook was promising with Khrushchev ready to extend his six-month ultimatum to one year.

The Americans continued to accuse Britain of softness over Berlin. Writing in the *New York Herald Tribune*, Joseph Alsop not only accused Britain of being 'soft' but alleged that she was widely separated from the other Allies by reason of having given massive financial credits to Russia following Macmillan's visit; he castigated David Eccles, President of the Board of Trade, for going to Moscow to seek better commercial relations, and the Federation of British Industries for opening offices in Moscow. He even maintained that Russia had ordered Arab Communist parties not to disturb British oil interests in the Middle East in return for British undertakings to be more sympathetic to the Russians there. From Geneva too the British diplomat Anthony Rumbold reported that there was 'disquiet' amongst the French and US delegations about 'our softness'.

The Foreign Ministers made a good start in Geneva. Russia had produced a Soviet draft treaty and the West a 'plan'. Talking with Lloyd on 18 May, Gromyko said there were three possible solutions over Berlin: complete demilitarization of West Berlin – his preferred solution; the stationing in West Berlin of symbolic forces of the four powers; or, finally, the replacement of these forces by symbolic forces of neutrals. He stressed in addition that the Soviet Union attached great importance to the question of guarantees for the Free City and for access to it.

Three days later Lloyd sent this witty report to the Prime Minister:

> The French and Germans are deliberately putting it about that we are soft. The French motives are varied. There is a little bit of natural dislike ... their primary motive is to turn the situation to their advantage in two respects: first to break the closeness of Anglo-American relations, and secondly to prevent a rapprochement between the United Kingdom and Germany over economic matters ... Some of the Germans are genuinely frightened of a détente between East and West. They want a divided Germany but dare not say so ... If the *status quo* is to persist it is reasonable to give more recognition to East Germany.† If they give more recognition to East Germany it will start the rot in West Germany. Standing pat is easier than thinking out the future.

---

* Kennedy appointed Dean Rusk in his place as soon as he became President.
† Adenauer's Government was terrified that Communism would spread through West Germany if normal relations were begun with the DDR.

The United States are confused and perplexed and one school of thought feels it is too dangerous to talk at all to the Soviets. The Soviets are completely untrustworthy. The whole process is a trap in which good simple men like Eisenhower and Herter are bound to be outwitted by the Russians and let down by the Allies. There is another school of thought that it is necessary to have the talks but that the best way to negotiate with the Russians is to hit them as hard as we can on the nose as frequently as possible ... The Soviet delegation, I suspect, are enjoying themselves. The result is a curious atmosphere; a feeling of detachment – almost of isolation.

On the first day the attitude we took was that the West was absolutely right to insist on a different status, i.e. separate tables for the German advisers. The danger is the French want the conference to end in deadlock and no Summit [because of de Gaulle]. Mr Khrushchev is unpredictable; although he is anxious to come to a Summit I do not think we should forget his mixture of sensitiveness and cockiness. He must know that in fact the West will not go to war over who stamps a pass. There is little or no prospect of reaching agreement at this conference. The most that we can expect is agreement on how to define our disagreements with a possible tacit or perhaps explicit understanding that the Soviet Government will for the time being refrain from unilateral action about Berlin or a separate peace treaty.

There was now reason to hope that a conference along the lines of Macmillan's plan would pave the way for a successful early Summit, despite Lloyd's perception of the de Gaulle-inspired French 'death wish' and US ambivalence towards it. In the negotiations Lloyd did his best to facilitate a Summit; Herter too was anxious to tie up Berlin with a Summit but Eisenhower was still reluctant to attend one.[9]

On 16 June Macmillan suggested that Eisenhower should come to Chequers for an informal meeting to discuss the Berlin problem; Eisenhower turned down the suggestion, writing that the public would see no difference between an 'informal' meeting and a 'Summit'. This was no more than a snub.

After a truculent speech by Khrushchev and an ambivalent paper by Gromyko, both of which left the impression that the Berlin deadline had been extended to eighteen months although the threat to access was still operative, Macmillan proposed an 'interim' agreement on Berlin to produce a prolonged pause in the negotiations. To Macmillan's chagrin Eisenhower reiterated that there was 'insufficient' progress in Geneva to justify a Summit. Instead Eisenhower suggested a recess of a few weeks for the Geneva Conference, and after six weeks in session the conference adjourned on 20 June. As it adjourned Gromyko told Lloyd 'he very much liked Macmillan's attitude towards holding a Summit but doubted whether Eisenhower wanted one.'[10]

On 25 June Macmillan sent a message to Caccia that he felt it was 'one of the most critical moments of his life' and he was determined to press the Summit one way or the other; the President, he said, 'must be brought right up against this issue within ten days or so. We must not lose the initiative over the Summit meeting.' The next day the Prime Minister sent a note to Lloyd: 'We must be very careful not to drift into a situation like 1914 when our 1912 obligations forced us to go to war because of our commitment to contingency plans.' As a result of Macmillan's pressure the Foreign Office instructed Rumbold to go slow in talks with the Americans on 'contingency planning' and to call it 'ground access'.

When the conference in Geneva resumed on 13 July 1959 the atmosphere was friendly; all four governments expressed their belief in German unity, free elections and a peace treaty covering both Germanies. For the first time the DDR was represented and Gromyko even admitted the validity of Western rights in Berlin. Macmillan told Lloyd he thought a negotiated settlement could be reached which preserved the Western position in Berlin, but that this could only be achieved by a Summit meeting. The Prime Minister asked for a Summit meeting on 25 August; Eisenhower at first agreed, but later demurred.

By now Macmillan had decided to hold a General Election early in October, and electoral considerations were strongly on his mind. If he could show that he had achieved a *modus vivendi* over Berlin it would be a trump card for the Tories. However, quite apart from party politics, Macmillan felt at this moment that he was on the brink of a diplomatic triumph from which he was separated only by American intransigence.

Eventually Lloyd reported Herter as saying that Eisenhower might come to a Summit in September or October. This put Macmillan into a near panic as it would clash with the date he had decided on for the General Election. He cabled to Lloyd in Geneva: 'I would be completely sunk, and all my plans disarranged. I really cannot take this risk.' The latest date for the Summit, he insisted, must be 1–10 September. From the electioneering point of view, so Macmillan wrote in his memoirs, a Summit, he felt, would be better as a future prospect 'than a modified success or even failure in the past'. Nevertheless the US President would not have it.

Meanwhile the good news was that with the Geneva Conference atom bomb testing had been suspended by both the Americans and Russians, although the Conference of Experts on the final cessation of tests was making, in Macmillan's words, 'snail's progress'.

At the end of July Eisenhower took the sudden decision to invite Khrushchev to America – an invitation not linked with a Summit. Moreover he wrote to Macmillan on 30 July that he was much disappointed in the Geneva Conference's lack of progress; he made it clear that no arrangements for a Summit could be made until after Khrushchev had visited America although he hoped this visit might pave the way for an eventual Summit. The President also proposed a meeting of the Western heads of government in Paris towards the end of August.

On 13 August Khrushchev sent a long personal letter to Macmillan, stating that 'If the West persists in finding difficulties over Berlin the USSR will have to go ahead alone and make its peace treaty with Eastern Germany.' With the letter Khrushchev enclosed a transcript of a conversation he had held with Vice-President Nixon and Llewellyn Thompson, the American Ambassador in Moscow. Rash remarks from the Americans had led to a row, and in disclosing its details Khrushchev once again hoped to drive a wedge between the two Allies. Thompson had said imprudently: 'If you force a crisis on the Berlin question this is fraught with dangerous consequences for peace as it is difficult for us to see how it accords with your statements about your desire for peace.' Predictably Khrushchev flew into a rage and replied:

> You are threatening us in the event that we try to bring about a settlement of the question. Take care, Mr Ambassador, do not use such words . . . we are very sensitive to such threats. If we did not want negotiations we would ourselves have signed a treaty with the DDR without warning you in advance. It is our right; it is the right of any country sharing a frontier with East Germany. Tell us if we sign a peace treaty will you declare war?*

Nixon protested in vain that Khrushchev had misunderstood the Ambassador. Not unnaturally, the Americans had failed to inform the British of this unfortunate gaffe.

In his important letter of 13 August, about which Macmillan is reticent in his memoirs, Khrushchev wrote that 'conditions were ripe for more fruitful discussions to include the American President about disarmament, nuclear test bans, and limitation of armaments up to complete disarmament'; he wanted to maintain the independence of West Berlin, he stressed, and would guarantee access and the social system desired by the inhabitants and make peace treaties with both Germanies which would lead 'to the liquidation of the Cold War', and the removal of international tension. However he was adamant that

---

* Khrushchev's anger over this gaffe may possibly have been feigned. He got on well personally with both Thompson and Nixon. When Thompson left Moscow in July 1962 Khrushchev, to everybody's surprise, after a long tour of the north gave up five hours of the next day for his leave-taking; whilst Nixon, as President, in 1972 signed agreements with the Russians for co-operation in space and on trade, covering not only the supply of American wheat to the Russians but also a halt to the deployment of ballistic missiles, and a general fostering of détente.

Russia would sign a separate peace treaty with East Germany failing agreement on Berlin with the West.[11]

Adenauer above all, he claimed, had adopted an entirely unrealistic position: he was fearful of a peace treaty, and the Russians wanted the other Western powers to put pressure on him as he was 'the only person interested in maintaining international tension'. Reasonably enough Khrushchev wrote:

> We are prepared to agree that West Germany should remain in NATO and East Germany in the Warsaw Defence Treaty until conditions are ripe for the liquidation of military blocs. Finally we are prepared to agree to withdraw our troops from the GDR, Poland and Hungary if on the other side troops are withdrawn from corresponding territories . . . We naturally feel justified in expecting an equally flexible approach on the part of our Western opposite numbers.

In a note which was kept secret within his private office Macmillan immediately minuted his private secretary de Zulueta on his reaction to Khrushchev's letter:*

> The more I read Mr K's letter the more I admire it. It may be insincere but it is specious and to most people it would seem pretty reasonable.
>
> He asks us to recognize that there are in fact two Germanies. Their unification he argues can only come about by agreement between them. Here of course he is comparing like with unlike. The Eastern German Government is a puppet of Russia. No one could call Adenauer a puppet.
>
> He says we must make peace after all these years and that means the end of military occupation of Berlin. In our hearts we too know that these rights of conquest are wearing pretty thin. Would anyone go to war for them? Khrushchev says he will not yield on this at least indefinitely.
>
> When he comes to the status of West Berlin he is more flexible. I cannot help thinking that the ultimate settlement (as Rumbold foresaw) will be something on the lines of the Free City with appropriate guarantees for its freedom and access. Khrushchev mentions access specifically.
>
> His remark about troop withdrawals is very significant. I assume he means withdrawal of non-German troops. His letter if published would be thought by British public opinion as pretty good. Mr Gaitskell would go to town on it.
>
> But I cannot hope to get the Allies to accept this sort of thing yet. After eighteen months or two years of moratorium perhaps.
>
> So we must get our election over first, in an atmosphere of hope but without too much detail. That is why I am so anxious about the letter. If Khrushchev agrees I will show it to President Eisenhower (as I have

---

* Macmillan does not quote this minute in his autobiography. It is possible that he did not keep it in his private archive which at the time of writing is not accessible to historians. He may have thought its disclosure would be badly received in America.

described in my minute to Mr Profumo).* I am not, repeat not, in a
hurry. For the President (who has learned his lesson about our rights very
thoroughly) will start by going off the deep end. What we want is:

(a) A pleasant visit by Mr Khrushchev to the USA.

(b) Perhaps a moratorium (Khrushchev only refers to indefinite occupation
as inadmissible).

(c) General Election.

(d) A pleasant return visit by President Eisenhower to Russia.

(e) During the moratorium a real negotiation. Of course if Adenauer is
still functioning there is not much hope, for de Gaulle will stick to him.

But much could happen in eighteen months – and if withdrawal of
Russian troops from East Germany and Hungary is really a possibility this
is something which must be treated seriously.

Meanwhile my chief anxiety is about the timing and programme outlined
[above]. My reply to Mr Khrushchev must be very carefully written in order
to achieve this. A 'sharp reply' (just to please Adenauer and de Gaulle who
are not really treating this question seriously or in the long term) will not
do. It would be very difficult to defend to our public if Mr Khrushchev
chose to publish this letter.

Our reply must be of a kind that can be published. Indeed it might suit
me to encourage publication. But that requires much thought – especially
as to timing.[12]

The fact that this was minuted only to de Zulueta shows how Harold
Macmillan took it upon himself to act as his own Foreign Secretary.

Khrushchev's letter was confidential and could not be released to
the press where it would have created a sensation and led to anti-
American feeling. With Khrushchev's permission Macmillan allowed
Eisenhower to read it in strict confidence, but it was kept secret from
Adenauer and de Gaulle. When Eisenhower came to Britain in August
1959 Macmillan, taking his cue from Khrushchev's letter, unsuccessfully
tried to impress on him the necessity for a comprehensive agreement
banning all nuclear tests, but Eisenhower was not taking the bait.[13]

On 27 August Khrushchev wrote to Adenauer suggesting a
Confederation of both Germanies and emphasizing the power of Soviet
weapons; the West German Government, he said, was more intent on
plans for rearming itself with nuclear weapons than on the reunification
of the country:

> You are fighting to preserve the aftermath of the war and it would mean
> atom bombs in Germany. Try to find courage to overcome your prejudices
> against the DDR and other socialist countries. Should anyone commit an
> action of aggression against us because we sign a peace treaty he would be
> branded by history as the most vicious of criminals.

---

* Jack Profumo was then the popular and successful Minister of State at the Foreign Office.

It was a telling letter. Adenauer replied by calling for the limitation of nuclear arms, and obligingly passed the Russian letter and his reply to the British Ambassador.

On his way to America in September Khrushchev stopped off in London. Gaitskell and Bevan impressed upon him that they would never accept the incorporation of West Germany into East Germany, whilst Khrushchev made it clear that reunification of Germany was 'off' except under the DDR.

Khrushchev's visit to the USA can be rated a success. He made himself affable, and in talks with the President concentrated on disarmament and the Berlin problem. At a final press conference on 29 September Eisenhower said his objections to a Summit had been reluctantly overcome, and a Summit was fixed for May 1960 to be preceded by a meeting of Foreign Ministers.[14]

Prospects for a successful Summit meeting in May the following year were good, despite a declaration by Khrushchev that if the Summit produced no agreement on Berlin he would make a separate peace treaty with East Germany which would place the DDR in control of access to Berlin, and 'if the West then attacked, the USSR had the bombs ready.' On the other side of the balance sheet there had been some progress in Geneva over banning nuclear tests, with the Russians offering to allow Western inspection teams to visit the site of any earth tremor in the Soviet Union whether due to natural or artificial causes. Macmillan pressed Eisenhower to promise no further American nuclear testing; the President would not give a positive reply; instead he asked Macmillan to visit Washington to discuss the matter in March. Meanwhile on 19 March 1960 Macmillan was 'elated' at the friendliness of a letter from Khrushchev which boded well for the results of the May Summit.

In the Prime Minister's Washington meetings with the President during 27–31 March 1960, Eisenhower accepted the principle of a one to two years' moratorium on underground testing as a response to the Russian proposal of a four- to five-year moratorium. Macmillan now had high hopes of the May Summit; it represented the culmination of his long and strenuous efforts to secure an East–West rapprochement, and by his personal intervention he had been able to secure the apparent goodwill of Khrushchev and to overcome the opposition of de Gaulle and the Americans and the downright hostility of Adenauer. He felt he was 'on the eve of a great step forward' and hoped future generations 'would look back on this meeting as the beginning of a new era'.[15]

On 5 May there was disaster. An announcement came from Moscow that four days previously an American U-2 spy plane had been shot down over Russia; the pilot, Captain Gary Powers, who parachuted to safety in Russian hands, admitted that he had been on a spying mission over Russian territory, and the latest sophisticated US reconnaissance photographic equipment had been recovered from his aircraft. Unwisely Eisenhower immediately stated that there had been no authorization for Powers to overfly Russia: this was patently untrue.

On 8 May Khrushchev sent Macmillan a letter of complaint in which the Russian leader doubted the sincerity in which the American contingent were approaching the Summit; he also complained of their support for Adenauer and of Eisenhower's glib remark that he would not stay in Paris, where the Summit was to be held, for more than a week. Macmillan replied in a friendly letter assuring Khrushchev that de Gaulle and Eisenhower were coming to the Summit 'with a serious determination to do their best for the peace of the world and the future of mankind'. *The Times* wrote on Downing Street authority that Khrushchev was optimistic about the Summit.

On 9 May Herter contradicted the initial denial by the US, stating that Eisenhower had ordered the gathering by unarmed aircraft of 'every possible means of information required to protect the US against surprise attack',* and at his press conference on 11 May Eisenhower – in complete contradiction of his earlier statement – confirmed that the U-2 flight had been made 'with his knowledge and approval'. Macmillan was appalled at the clumsiness of the Americans in handling the incident. It would have been far better if they had expressed contrition and stated that it was a mistake to allow such spy flights on the eve of the Summit. *The Times* described the flight as 'reckless folly'. Clearly it was.

On 15 May Khrushchev and Macmillan had tea together at the British Embassy in Paris. It looked for a moment as if the Summit could be saved. However when Eisenhower arrived in Paris he categorically refused to apologize to Khrushchev. The Russian had a mercurial temperament, and with a fulsome apology from the American President Macmillan felt Khrushchev might have been brought round and the Summit held on course. But all Eisenhower would say in Paris, and this only under pressure, was that he had ordered the abandonment of U-2 flights. Khrushchev was not satisfied: it would be impossible to continue the Summit, he declared, unless Eisenhower (a) condemned the air spying; (b) apologized; (c) said it would not recur; (d) punished the criminals. Eisenhower would not comply so the Summit broke up without any discussion taking place between the heads of government.

---

* There is evidence that this misguided statement by Herter justifying intelligence flights and making it clear they were carried out in conformity with a directive from the President without any attempt at an apology helped to work Khrushchev up into an ugly mood, and was an important contributory factor to the failure of the Summit.[16]

Reilly's view was that Khrushchev may have failed to understand that his conditions were bound to be unacceptable: on 16 May, with every appearance of sincerity, the Russian was urging Macmillan to persuade Eisenhower to accept his conditions and expecting him at least to concede the first two points. By pitching their terms so high, Reilly has written, Soviet leaders were aiming to make Eisenhower 'eat humble pie'; but it may not have been as obvious to them as it was to others that in doing so they were automatically wrecking the conference before it could begin.

Prior to the conference the Soviets had proposed an interim agreement on Berlin, and had been told in reply that the West was convinced that only the presence of Allied troops in West Berlin could guarantee West Berlin being a free city. The two sides were not far apart, but, as a pointed insult to Eisenhower, Khrushchev announced that the Summit must be postponed for eight months, by which time Eisenhower's term of office would be over. The test ban conference in Geneva was allowed to continue.[17]

Khrushchev's behaviour over the Summit was difficult to explain. From his vantage point as British Ambassador in Moscow Patrick Reilly had observed the Soviet leader closely, and in an important despatch stated that Khrushchev's appreciation of diplomatic issues

> urged him to follow a carefully charted course which demanded prudence, patience and consistency. His own pragmatism, his belligerence, his vanity and the rest tend to interfere with these plans. It is almost fair to say that he would like to be a philosopher, but human nature keeps creeping in. In face of Mr Khrushchev's irresponsibility we on our side must be patient and vigilant.

If Reilly's assessment of Khrushchev is correct the reason for the failure of the Paris Summit must have been the Russian's sudden fury at the blow to his pride when Eisenhower refused to apologize for the U-2's invasion of Soviet air space. Undoubtedly in the spring of 1960 he was hoping and striving for a détente: he was being criticized at home for this and the spy plane incident gave ammunition to his critics. According to Reilly, the U-2 setback to rapprochement and to Khrushchev's personal relations with Eisenhower not only embarrassed him at home but left him 'vulnerable to criticism'.[18]

In his post-Paris speeches Khrushchev rebuked Macmillan and de Gaulle for not having the courage to condemn the U-2 flight, but his 'hottest fire' was reserved for Eisenhower, who he felt had deceived and insulted him. Determined to avenge this blow to his self-esteem the Russian leader made personal attacks of extraordinary brutality on the President but it remained his declared policy that further negotiations with the West should take place after Eisenhower had been replaced by a new President.

Leaving Paris Khrushchev took pains to make it clear that he still favoured détente and saw advantages in negotiation with the West. On 28 May and 3 June he indicated that he was still looking forward to the expansion of trade and cultural exchanges with the West, and Soviet officials were ordered to be co-operative. Further confirmation was received at Geneva where the Foreign Office had expected the disarmament talks to be halted after the Paris fiasco. Their continuation for a period impressed the Foreign Office as evidence that the Soviet Government genuinely wanted agreement on disarmament despite Khrushchev's personal vendetta against Eisenhower and his frequently renewed threats of immediate retaliation against US military bases in Europe and Turkey should further spy flights take place.[19]

Before they left Paris on 19 May Eisenhower, de Gaulle and Macmillan talked. As might be expected they discussed military tactics for keeping access to West Berlin open, and came to an agreement on 'contingency planning', but they laid down that 'on no account should it be revealed that contingency had been discussed in Paris.' At this gloomy meeting, which Eisenhower spoke of as 'his last', he appears from the archives to have been oblivious of his failure to do anything positive to try to save the Summit. Although admitting in his memoirs that he had made a big error by issuing 'a premature and erroneous cover story', Eisenhower remained convinced that the Summit, if held, would have been a 'failure'.

When Macmillan spoke in the Commons about the failure of the Summit he added: 'Curiously all was going "very smoothly" at Geneva; perhaps experts are better than politicians.' However this harmony was short-lived: the Russians stalked out of the disarmament conference on which Macmillan was so keen on 30 June.

Macmillan has recorded that the fiasco in Paris was 'the most tragic moment of my life'; de Zulueta too thought it was a real watershed for him, and he 'never saw him more depressed'.[20] But history must salute Macmillan for his brilliant statesmanship in steering the East and West close to agreement in 1960. It was heart-rending for him that his dreams should suddenly have been shattered by unreasonable American behaviour, and it was probably owing solely to their refusal to apologize for the U-2 incident that the Summit was aborted. In his memoirs Macmillan glosses over his anger against Eisenhower and the American State Department but he had every reason to be resentful. All that he had gained with Khrushchev during his visit to Moscow in March 1959 and his ceaseless diplomatic manoeuvring for a successful Summit thereafter had come to nothing. He had been on the brink of success. Instead there followed a period of 'ice'.

The weight of evidence continued to show that the Soviet Government had not reversed its policy of conducting negotiations with the

West, although Khrushchev's brutal personal vendetta against President Eisenhower was unremitting. Further negotiations between heads of government were scheduled to follow the expiry of Eisenhower's term of office. However Khrushchev's attitude to a Summit had hardened and he was arguing for China, India and Indonesia to be included, though he was probably not serious about this. There was evidence that many in Russian governing circles were uneasy about Khrushchev's handling of the Summit, and a war of nerves against countries harbouring American rocket bases continued. As long as Khrushchev remained the Soviet leader the West were justified in believing there would be no fundamental change for the worse in Soviet foreign policy.[21]

In January 1961, following the presidential election, John Kennedy succeeded Eisenhower as President. Kennedy belonged to a younger generation and the US administration immediately recovered an energy and decision which had been lacking in the last days of Eisenhower's Government when both the President and his Foreign Secretary Foster Dulles were in bad health. Kennedy has been well described as 'sensitive, ruthless and highly sexed'. He knew Britain well from his time in London when his father was US Ambassador to Britain.

Dean Rusk, who replaced Herter as Secretary of State, came from academic life; he was an intelligent but quiet Southerner lacking in charisma. He had been a Rhodes Scholar at Oxford which had given him a love of the University but not of the British, while his experiences serving in the Far East in the war had left him resentful of British arrogance. Professor McGeorge Bundy, another academic, was given the important post of Special Adviser to the President on Security. Bundy was no anglophile and together they attempted to diminish the special relationship and downgrade the British nuclear deterrent so as to put Britain on an equal footing with West Germany and France. Bundy frequently pointed out that Britain would be more important in American eyes if she joined the EEC and became its natural leader.

Macmillan replaced the professional diplomat Harold Caccia as Ambassador in Washington with a political appointment – David Ormsby-Gore, a Conservative MP and a Junior Minister at the Foreign Office, and an old personal friend of the new President. As a result of this friendship Ormsby-Gore, as British Ambassador, had privileged access to Kennedy which Macmillan considered a great advantage. However this irritated Kennedy's personal advisers.[22]

On 31 May 1961 Kennedy came to Paris with his wife on his first official visit as President. Here he had talks with de Gaulle and Macmillan. His visit was a great popular success; the French were enchanted by the American couple's good looks and charm, and his wife

Jackie's elegance made a great appeal to the Parisians. Kennedy's talks with de Gaulle however became chilly. De Gaulle was intent on an independent French nuclear deterrent, whilst Kennedy was strongly opposed to France 'acquiring a nuclear weapons capacity' and was determined not to raise de Gaulle's hope of US co-operation in this field. In addition Kennedy was not pleased at de Gaulle's reservations over Britain's chances of joining the EEC.[23]

The Kennedys went on from Paris to Vienna to meet Khrushchev. But despite a glittering reception at the Hapsburg palace of Schönbrunn, where the Vienna Ballet danced in front of the two heads of state, their official meeting was a ghastly failure. They found no common ground either over Berlin or a nuclear test ban. Khrushchev warned the American that he intended to sign a peace treaty with East Germany by 31 December 1961, and that would be 'the end of American occupation rights in West Berlin'. Kennedy insisted that US rights in West Berlin rested on the Potsdam Agreement. Khrushchev retorted vigorously that if the US wanted to go to war over Berlin, 'This is your problem.' Kennedy snapped back, 'It is you, and not I, who wants to force a change.' Shocked at Khrushchev's coarse and arrogant behaviour, Kennedy remarked to his aides that 'there was no area of compromise' between him and the Soviet Union.

On 4 June the Kennedys arrived in London to a warm reception. But the American President was in a prickly mood and suffering from shock at the brutal treatment dealt him by the Soviet leader, and he let his hair down in a private talk with Macmillan complaining about Khrushchev's behaviour. Apparently, so Macmillan remarked to Pierson Dixon afterwards, Kennedy had hardly been able to get a word in during the Khrushchev interview, and was surprised to find that 'Khrushchev does not react to charm.' McGeorge Bundy, Kennedy's special foreign affairs adviser and his closest confidant, has commented that 'this first meeting was the most difficult of their several encounters.'

T. C. Sorensen, Kennedy's biographer, considers Macmillan the Western leader 'he liked best and saw most often', and McGeorge Bundy, who was often critical of Macmillan, has described Macmillan's advice on nuclear matters as 'important and highly valuable to the President, even if occasionally long-winded'. In his memoirs Macmillan gives the impression that there was a warm friendship between himself and Kennedy, and a close harmony of views. The archives do not support this generally accepted picture and show that there was tension and acute disagreement, especially over the Far East, Berlin and the British independent nuclear deterrent.[24]

*   *   *

During the first half of 1961 an uneasy peace prevailed over Berlin. Khrushchev's threat, with its postponed deadline for a separate peace treaty with East Germany, hung over the city like a cloud; yet in spite of the débâcle of the Paris Summit in May 1960 Khrushchev showed some signs of moderation and a desire to appear reasonable towards the West in the eyes of the world. The international situation then worsened when on 1 September 1961 Russia began a series of large-scale atom bomb tests which were reported to be 'very dirty'. The conference in Geneva on banning nuclear tests had become in Macmillan's words 'a farce'.

West German industry in the late 1950s had started to boom, while East Germany stagnated. As a result refugees from East Germany were pouring into the West to take advantage of job opportunities and high wages; this exodus was removing a large proportion of key workers with technical skills and was potentially a mortal blow to East German industry.

By August 1961 the flood of refugees from East to West Berlin escaping the low standard of living in the Communist sector had risen to the fantastic total of 2,400 per day. This was too many for Khrushchev, and on 11 August he threw up a monstrous wall through the middle of Berlin to seal off East Berlin, some East Berliners even jumping at the last moment from their windows into the West before the bricklayers could seal them up. Although there was nothing illegal in the act, the Wall was an inhuman measure which brought the Berlin crisis to fever point and the flow of refugees to a sudden halt. The UK and USA were divided over tactics. A Gallup poll showed 71 per cent of Americans were ready to fight for Berlin whereas only 46 per cent of the British and 9 per cent of the French were.

Macmillan gathered the reins into his own hands. Sensing that Khrushchev was only bluffing and that he wanted to negotiate, he tried to play down the crisis, telling journalists that it had been got up by the press and no one was going to fight over West Berlin. The Americans took a tougher line, and de Gaulle categorically refused to be bound by any settlement that altered the *status quo* in Berlin.[25]

The Western Allies could not defend West Berlin by conventional means. Field Marshal Lord Montgomery and Basil Liddell Hart had obtained great publicity for asserting this obvious truth in the *Sunday Times* in the spring of 1961. Thus if Khrushchev was not bluffing and intended to hand West Berlin and its access over to the DDR, the Allies' only choice was to fight with nuclear weapons or capitulate.

Despite strenuous opposition from the British, Kennedy announced that the USA would resume underground atom bomb tests (but not atmospheric tests), and the Russians responded with a series of atmospheric nuclear tests including high calibre bombs and one of 50 megatons on 30 October. Khrushchev blew hot and cold. Nevertheless there were reports of Soviet aircraft buzzing Allied planes in the air corridor to Berlin, and in October both Soviet and American tanks moved into the centre of Berlin within gun range of each other. This was brinkmanship.[26]

The atmosphere improved when on 13 December 1961 the Russians suggested an eighteen-nation committee to discuss both nuclear and conventional disarmament in Geneva. On the same day Khrushchev sent Macmillan a long letter suggesting means of reducing tension in Europe. There was little fresh in it. Khrushchev wanted peace treaties with both Germanies and all occupying troops withdrawn from West Berlin. If the West left their troops in West Berlin then there must also be Russian contingents although he would agree to the garrisoning being taken over by United Nations troops.

Macmillan replied to Khrushchev that the ultimate solution of the German crisis was a peace treaty with East Germany and a freely elected East German Government as envisaged in the Potsdam Agreement of 1945. He knew this was asking too much; in the interim, he went on, they must find a practical plan. The British Prime Minister also told Khrushchev that the Russian idea of a free city in West Berlin could not be 'viable' because she would be surrounded by territory controlled by 'other authority' and prohibited from relying for defence on her natural friends. Macmillan suggested a *modus vivendi* provided that Russia would guarantee the right of access to West Berlin, and gave an outline of his proposed *modus vivendi* which lasted until the tearing down of the Wall and reunification of Germany in 1989.[27]

Meanwhile a conference between Macmillan and Kennedy had been arranged in Bermuda for mid-December 1961. Fortunately, after this conference Kennedy moved closer to the British position over Berlin, rejecting the calls of West Germany and France for toughness. As a result Berlin remained a stalemate, and Khrushchev never fulfilled his threat of signing a separate peace treaty with East Germany.

On 4 January 1962 the US Ambassador Llewellyn Thompson had a two-and-a-half hour meeting with the Russian Foreign Minister Andrei Gromyko in Moscow. Gromyko said the main US preoccupation was 'access'; Thompson disagreed, saying the main problem was to achieve a peace treaty with both German states including an agreement about access to Berlin. The West, Gromyko maintained, had recognized the DDR *de facto*, but in advance of a peace treaty Gromyko told Thompson that Russia would consider a quadripartite agreement on access. Here was some progress.

Two days later Dr Kroll, the West German Ambassador in Moscow, was handed a memorandum from Khrushchev stating that Russia wanted a peace treaty with West Germany

> but the Western Allies positively want the Cold War continued and are encouraging revanchism even at the risk of causing a war; the interests of the German people can only be assured on a basis of friendly relations with Russia, and the Wall cannot come down until legal bonds are established between West Berlin and the DDR.[28]

This was a crude effort to detach Adenauer from Britain, France and America.

Gromyko got as far as preparing a protocol for a free state and demilitarized city of Berlin which was handed to Thompson on 12 January 1962. The following day a hopeful statement came from Gromyko, stressing that 'the formalization of the existing borders of Germany, respect for the sovereignty of DDR, prohibition of nuclear weapons for both Germanies and a non-aggression pact between the Warsaw Pact countries and NATO should be considered simultaneously.' However Llewellyn Thompson reported from Moscow that in his view the Russians were 'getting ready for a break' in order to go ahead with their peace treaty with East Germany. Both the State Department and the British Foreign Office disagreed, the Foreign Office stressing that in their view Thompson was wrong and the Russian aim was to keep talks going. Dean Rusk, Kennedy's Secretary of State, told the British he was prepared to discuss everything if the Allies were assured of access to Berlin.

Macmillan too was in favour of talks in the course of which, he was sure, agreement would be found. However, on 27 January 1962 the State Department asserted that there was 'no base for negotiations' since the Russians would not start talks except on the basis of a change in the *status quo* of West Berlin and acknowledgement of the sovereignty of East Germany. However Alec Home thought the conversations between Gromyko and Thompson were 'running into the sand', and he suggested on 6 February that the West German Ambassador in Moscow, Dr Kroll, should have a further round with Gromyko.[29]

It is difficult to tell how close Khrushchev was to reaching an agreement over Berlin in early 1962. A British historical researcher is not helped in coming to a conclusion by the blanket closure of all the Foreign Office files on Berlin from 1961 to 1963, although some of their contents must be duplicated in the Prime Minister's files.

Early in February Kennedy told Ormsby-Gore that he was taking day-to-day responsibility for US policy on Berlin. This may have had some influence in aligning British and American policy and healing the differences in the British and American approach to Berlin. Kennedy also said he was prepared to attend a Summit provided the Geneva negotiations on disarmament made progress. Meanwhile, on a report which arrived from Washington showing that the US planning agreement on contingencies included a military 'reconnaissance' if the access roads were closed by the Russians, Macmillan minuted: 'I do not mind if this is being discussed as an academic exercise. But it must be clear, as I assume it is, that specific political approval is necessary even for reconnaissance.'

On 16 February 1962, in a long letter to Macmillan, Khrushchev proposed an immediate Summit meeting of eighteen heads of government in Geneva without any preparation or any experts present. This was a variation on his similar suggestion of 13 December and a move in the right direction. Macmillan wrote to Kennedy: 'We must remember that it is not altogether impossible that Khrushchev really wants to get in touch with us for some constructive purpose.' Kennedy replied on 28 February: 'It may be that Khrushchev really wants to talk to us but I must say his last letter is a strange way of showing it. You and I know that when heads of government really want to meet they make their arrangements in other ways, and so does Khrushchev.' Kennedy and his advisers were clearly less forthcoming than Macmillan who, having been convinced during his trip to Russia that a bargain could be struck with Khrushchev over both Berlin and disarmament, was determined still to play the role of peace broker.[30]

Eventually Khrushchev agreed to a British request that there should be a preliminary meeting of the Foreign Ministers of the eighteen, preceded by a meeting of the three Foreign Ministers of the UK, USA and USSR. This preliminary meeting of the three took place in Geneva on 11 March between Dean Rusk, Lord Home and Andrei Gromyko.

At this meeting Gromyko stated that Russia was prepared to sign an agreement halting atom bomb tests either before – and independently of – a solution to other disarmament questions or in conjunction with such a solution. Rusk declared the United States' readiness to engage in serious discussion of both problems. However friction developed when they got on to Berlin, after Rusk had referred to 'serious harassment by the USSR of Western air and ground access to Berlin'. Home, perhaps inadvisedly, recalled a previous warning he had made to Gromyko that harassment of the Berlin access might lead to war, and would jeopardize 'chances of agreement in Geneva on much bigger things'. Gromyko replied that he rejected Home's warning and Home 'should keep such language to himself because their task in Geneva was to ease the situation and solve the questions rather than give warnings'; he also categorically rejected accusations that there had been any Russian harassment. This meeting was an unpromising start to the eighteen-nation conference.

Rusk and Home co-operated well in Geneva, mooting various schemes of inspection to monitor any violation of a test ban treaty. The Russians were evasive, and on 21 March Home reported that there had been no progress at all in Geneva. America had delayed her atom bomb tests due to start on Christmas Island, and on 9 April Kennedy and Macmillan delivered a joint statement to the Russians:

> We hope . . . the Soviet Government may express their readiness to accept the principle of international verification . . . But if there is no change in the present Soviet position the Governments of the United States and the United Kingdom must conclude that their efforts to obtain a workable treaty to ban nuclear tests are not now successful and their test series scheduled for the latter part of this month must go ahead.

In reply Khrushchev categorically refused to allow any inspection on Russian soil. The die was cast and the US atom bomb tests took place on British soil on Christmas Island, the announcement that the tests would take place being made by Macmillan in the Commons on 28 April. Gaitskell had been informed in advance and accepted their necessity so that there was little opposition in Parliament, but the anti-nuclear lobby in Britain worked themselves up into a frenzy as the bombs began to explode in the Pacific.

Macmillan had become agitated at the belligerency of the contingency measures planned by America, and when de Zulueta tried to soothe him, suggesting that General Norstad, the US NATO Commander, was a restraining influence, Macmillan minuted: 'Yes. Norstad is the most sensible American.' To Macmillan's horror, the American newspaper *Saturday Evening Post* on 28 March 1962 carried a statement by Kennedy that 'under certain conditions the US would be prepared to be the first to use nuclear weapons.'[31]

The Russians became milder over Berlin after this statement, and on 13 April Khrushchev suggested to Thompson (as he had done the year before) that the West might change the status of their occupational forces to 'something akin to police'. The Foreign Office told Ormsby-Gore:

> The next round of talks with the Soviet should take place in Washington. There is a strange lull in the Berlin situation. The Russians show no sign of being in a hurry and Marshal Koniev [the Russian military commander] has suggested further efforts to improve local conditions . . . The Americans wish to get the next round of negotiations started before the resumption of nuclear testing.

Meanwhile planning continued on tough contingency measures in case the Russians closed the routes to Berlin, the British remaining reluctant to agree to anything likely to provoke a war. The Americans and West Germans proposed that NATO ships should close areas of the sea on the pretext of exercises, and use depth charges and gunfire with naval patrols to stop Russian ships in the Orkneys–Norway Gap and the western basin of the Mediterranean to the south of Sardinia. But as de Zulueta pointed out to Macmillan on 2 April 1962, the Russians could retaliate, and as the NATO merchant shipping fleet was so much larger, the Russian retaliation could cause more annoyance 'to us' than the NATO measures to the Russians. Macmillan agreed with him.

After minor difficulties with the Berlin check-points, General Watson, the US Garrison Commander in Berlin, retaliated by preventing the Soviet commander and his political adviser from driving into West Berlin. When Macmillan heard of this he minuted: 'All this is highly foolish and dangerous. Ought not some effort be made through Ambassador Bruce [US Ambassador in London] to stop it?'

On 7 April 1962 David Ormsby-Gore, the British Ambassador in Washington, cabled that the Americans were asking for a 'strong reaction' from the West to prevent Soviet harassment in the air corridors, and wanted 'maritime measures' prepared whereby Russian ships, as a counter-measure, would be stopped on the high seas. He wrote:

> The Americans do not deny that the maritime counter-measures involved some *risk* but on balance they thought these measures could be decisive in persuading the Russians that it was to their disadvantage to increase or continue air harassments . . . Since Soviet harassment may be resumed at any moment the Americans are pressing for an early discussion.

Backed by Macmillan's comment that we should make clear to the Americans that 'these maritime counter-measures are not only absurd in themselves but also untimely', Alec Home, the Foreign Secretary, told Ormsby-Gore that both the Foreign Office and the British Chiefs of Staff were much opposed to the measures:

> if we were to introduce these measures now when our aircraft are getting through to Berlin without hindrance and Soviet harassment in the corridors is hardly worthy of the name, public opinion here and in several other NATO countries would think we had taken leave of our senses especially as there is no reason to suppose that the measures contemplated would be likely to achieve their aim. The impression we should give is that we are much more worried about the Soviet actions than in fact we are and far from bolstering Berlin morale we run the risk of undermining it.

During the first week in May Macmillan and Home went to Washington. There Kennedy told Home that he wanted a bilateral Summit, not a quadripartite one. Macmillan was offended at the proposal to exclude Britain but later remarked that the atmosphere in Washington was far more cordial than in Ottawa. (The Canadian Prime Minister, John Diefenbaker, always was Macmillan's *bête noire* and when Macmillan visited Ottawa on his way home the two did not hit it off.)

On 16 June the newly appointed British Ambassador in Moscow, Frank Roberts, reported that there was a 'curious lull' over Berlin:

A simple explanation of the seeming anomaly represented by the absence of any energetic drive for the avowed Communist objective in Berlin coupled with no sign of any willingness to compromise could be that faced with Western firmness Khrushchev cannot go forward; equally because of the extent to which his own and Soviet prestige is involved he cannot retreat and he is therefore prepared for the time being to mark time.

Kennedy wrote to Macmillan:

If the real situation can be stabilized in a written *modus vivendi* we think the Russians might be able to have their peace treaty without serious consequences to our own position though we do not plan to say so directly ... if they want to make real and rapid progress all they have to do is to fire Ulbricht [Prime Minister of East Germany] and put a more civilized man in his place. And finally I am of a mind to say that if serious progress could be made on this sort of thing I would, of course, be glad to go to a meeting of heads of government to get it settled. Rusk is authorized to make quite private explorations in this direction in Geneva.

On 24 June Dean Rusk had a discussion with Macmillan and Home in London, and appeared less hopeful of a Berlin settlement than Kennedy had been in his letter. Home suggested that if Khrushchev wanted to save face and allow Western troops to stay in West Berlin after a peace treaty with East Germany, the West might help him by either converting their military occupation forces into police, or expressing their occupation as a trusteeship. If the Allies did not help him, Home feared, Khrushchev would sign a separate peace treaty within the next month or two. It was Rusk's view that there would be no Russian move for six months but he would be agreeable to call 'our troops' constabulary, or alternatively 'United Nations forces'.

In July a report came from Roberts that Khrushchev looked perilously close to making a peace treaty with East Germany. This was not believed by the Foreign Office, but lively contingency planning continued for immediate retaliation against Russian shipping. The main sanction now was to be in the field of trade; West Germany and the whole of NATO would break off trade with East Germany, although Western military plans were designed from the very start to persuade the Russians that the Allies were determined not to be denied access to Berlin.

On 23 July 1962 Home and Gromyko had an amicable but

unconstructive talk in Geneva, Gromyko complaining that as the Americans refused to start serious negotiations, Russia must sign a separate peace treaty with East Germany unless negotiations were conducted genuinely; 'troops of France, Britain and America must withdraw from Berlin and it should cease to be a NATO base'. There was hardly any difference, Gromyko went on, 'between what happened in Hitlerite Germany and what was happening in West Germany today, and no difference between the statements now being made by Strauss [German Finance Minister] and Göring' – only the other day Strauss had said that Germany would have to have atomic weapons. A peace treaty was necessary, Home would surely see, because Berlin was 'a powder keg which could explode at any moment'.

Home countered by arguing that West Germany could not be aggressive as long as she remained part of NATO, whilst the presence of troops in Berlin prevented Berlin being 'a powder keg'. As long as the Wall existed there must be incidents and escapes because relatives were not allowed to meet. If Russia insisted on the withdrawal of Western troops Home could not help, nor could he answer for what would happen if the Soviet Union handed over full powers in Berlin to Ulbricht. The West's attitude, Gromyko asserted, was exactly that of Lloyd George and Clemenceau after the signing of the Versailles Treaty – 'They too had said Germany could not constitute a danger to peace.' The remark was both untrue and irrelevant but the two parted on good terms.[32]

During the Geneva discussions in August 1962 Britain and America offered the Russians an option either of an atmospheric ban or a total and comprehensive ban with a reasonable number of inspections. Khrushchev sent a moderate, albeit ambiguous, reply on 5 September, and the Geneva talks went on in Macmillan's words 'tediously' and without coming to a head. Kennedy, who had by now recovered from his fury at the battering he had received from Khrushchev in Vienna, allowed the State Department to initiate proposals to the Russians over Berlin. These included a five- to ten-year *modus vivendi*, an all-Berlin free city, and the use of Berlin as a UN headquarters. These came to nothing but the fact that negotiations with the USA were known to be in progress appeared to make it easier for Khrushchev to accept inaction without loss of face.[33]

Berlin was stalemate. The Home–Gromyko conversation of 23 July showed that matters had progressed no further since the abortive Summit Conference of May 1960. Both sides were repeating what they had said since 1959 about Berlin, and progress towards bans on nuclear tests and general disarmament was minimal. Then came what looked like Nemesis.

* * *

The dangers to world peace inherent in the long-running Berlin crisis paled into insignificance in comparison with the alarming news on 21 October 1962 that the Soviets had planted medium-range missile sites in Cuba. According to an urgent message from Kennedy to Macmillan six sites had been identified, and two of them were possibly already operational. In his message Kennedy stated that he had demanded their immediate removal as 'a nuclear threat to our hemisphere'; although Khrushchev's main intention may have been to increase his chances in Berlin, Kennedy went on, it was essential that he should discover 'that if he is counting on weakness or irresolution, he has miscalculated'.[34]

There had been tension between Cuba and the US since April 1961. Cuba had become Communist under a militant dictator, Fidel Castro, who had ousted the right-wing dictator Fulgencio Batista early in 1959. Castro proceeded to confiscate factories and installations belonging to American businesses, and threatened to seize oil refineries including Shell. In July 1960, in a personal letter to Macmillan, Eisenhower stated that his Government intended to 'create conditions' in which anti-Communist and democratic Cuba would regain control of the island's Government. The Americans wanted the British Government to take economic sanctions against Cuba, including a slashing reduction in the Cuban quota for sugar imports to Britain.

Because of the bad balance of payments position the British Government was reluctant to comply, and refused to ban British tanker owners carrying oil to Cuba. In a personal reply to Eisenhower Macmillan stressed the importance of the US avoiding any action which might create the impression that the United States was actively intervening in Cuba 'because of the state of feeling in other Latin American countries'. Eisenhower had hinted in his letters that the US might be contemplating an invasion but gave no indication that an invasion plan had been prepared.

However in March 1960, even before Eisenhower wrote to Macmillan, an invasion plan for a US landing in the Bay of Pigs had been drawn up in strictest secrecy. This was pigeon-holed until Kennedy became President, but the new President decided on a landing on 17 April 1961 by a brigade of anti-Castro guerillas who had taken refuge in Florida. The force consisted of 1,500 men, trained and equipped by the Americans and supplied with US tanks. The original plan was for this force to have the help of US military planes manned by Cubans, but at the last moment Kennedy lost his nerve and withdrew the aircraft.

The operation was a military disaster. If Kennedy had allowed the guerillas to use US combat planes or ordered an intervention by the USAAF it might have succeeded, but no more than forty-eight hours after the landings, it was all over; the invaders had been mopped up.

The Bay of Pigs has rightly been described as the biggest blunder of Kennedy's career as President.

The British were not informed of the operation beforehand, and Macmillan, seeing the special relationship set aside, felt strongly that this would not have happened had Eisenhower still been President. Even so, pressed by the Americans along with her NATO partners to withhold sales of arms to Cuba after the Bay of Pigs incident, Britain complied; the other NATO countries were reluctant. The Foreign Secretary Alec Home wanted the Board of Trade to ban both trade and credit for Cuba in order to propitiate the Americans, writing to Fred Erroll, President of the Board of Trade: 'The existence of the Communist regime in Cuba is a matter of deep concern to us, but for the Americans a calamity. A further rebuff to the Americans would lead to a major row.' But Cuba was a valuable source of British trade and Erroll replied to the Foreign Office: 'While we are vigorously enforcing a ban on the shipment of arms and military supplies to Cuba, we are not prepared to extend this to other forms of trade or to commercial credit.' Macmillan supported Erroll against the Foreign Office to the annoyance of Kennedy and his advisers. A request to the NATO Council by the Americans for a total ban on credits for Cuba was rejected, and on 30 October America announced that she was going to block all her ships trading with Cuba.[35]

The Bay of Pigs attack together with the prolonged American trade sanctions transformed Castro into an implacable enemy of the United States. Accordingly in 1962 he succumbed to pressure from Khrushchev to allow Soviet missile bases to be installed so that Russia could threaten the mainland of the USA with nuclear attack; there is no evidence that Khrushchev would have allowed the Cubans to launch such weapons themselves.

On the morning of 21 October 1962 David Ormsby-Gore was asked to enter the White House 'unseen' for a talk with the President – a long confidential talk which bore evidence to Ormsby-Gore's own special relationship with Kennedy as a personal friend. The situation in Cuba, Kennedy told him, had completely changed during the course of the last week because two types of 'medium-range offensive missiles' had been installed with a range of between 1,500 and 2,000 miles. Kennedy had already made his position 'very clear', he said, having declared on 13 September that if Cuba became an offensive military base then 'the United States would do whatever must be done to protect its own security and that of its Allies'.

In Kennedy's view there were two alternatives: either the US could order an immediate air strike to 'take out all the known missile sites', and follow it up with a blockade of Cuba, or they could impose a blockade without carrying out an air strike. This would mean leaving the Cubans with their present offensive capacity but would demonstrate America's determination not to allow the build-up to continue.

Asked for his view, Ormsby-Gore replied that he saw 'very serious drawbacks' in an air strike because very few people outside the United States would consider the provocation offered by the Cubans 'serious enough', so that America would be damaged politically, and he could not believe that the missiles so far landed constituted any significant military threat to the United States; he also thought they should bear in mind possible repercussions on Berlin: the air strike 'might well provide a smoke screen behind which the Russians might move against Berlin'. He therefore favoured a blockade, not an air strike.

He and his colleagues had come to the same conclusion, Kennedy said, and would go ahead with the blockade and not an air strike. There were two other possible courses, the President added. They might carry out a full-scale invasion of Cuba and 'finish with Castro once and for all. They might never have a better opportunity.' Or again they might 'do nothing', but this was politically impossible and too dangerous: 'If he did nothing his friends and allies would come to the conclusion that he was afraid to move and Khrushchev would be bound to assume that the Americans for all their tough words would be prepared to sit supine and inactive whatever Khrushchev did.' An invasion would be 'most unwise', Ormsby-Gore reiterated, because there was no evidence that the conditions in Cuba were such that the Americans 'could expect any widespread support' and 'the idea of a puppet regime kept in power by American marines was not a happy prospect'.

On Kennedy's instructions this whole discussion was to be kept secret and communicated only to the Prime Minister and his closest advisers. However Ormsby-Gore's intimate account of his interview with the President did not reach Macmillan until after Ambassador Bruce had given Kennedy's brief message to Macmillan in London regarding the Cuban threat. Macmillan's reaction differed from both his Ambassador's and the President's. First he drafted a message to Kennedy advising him to invade Cuba 'and have done with it; at any rate avoid drifting into the situation which we had done at Suez'; but receiving Ormsby-Gore's memorandum, he decided not to send this message. Instead, seeming almost pleased that the US were now, as Britain had been for several years, within range of a nuclear attack, he remarked to Kennedy, 'If you live on Vesuvius you do not bother much about the eruptions,' which was ill received in the White House.[36] Macmillan believed correctly that Khrushchev was bluffing and was less panicky than the Americans; nevertheless he wrote in his diary on 22 October that it looked as though 'the world was closer to war than at any time since the Berlin blockade of 1948'.

If America had carried out an air strike they would have killed and wounded many Russians as well as Cubans, and both an air strike and an invasion carried grave risks of a Russian move for prestige purposes over Berlin which would have probably resulted in fighting between Soviet troops and the Western Allies. Any combat over Berlin would have been hazardous and carried the deadly danger of elevation into all-out war. To Kennedy's exasperation Britain rejected a call by General Norstad of NATO for British troops to be put into a higher state of readiness in Europe.[37]

On 23 October, two days after Kennedy's ominous message about Cuba, Macmillan asked the Labour leaders Hugh Gaitskell, Harold Wilson and George Brown to see him at Admiralty House and there gave them the latest news on the Russian threat to the United States. It was likely, Macmillan said, that Khrushchev wanted to force an international conference which he could then face 'with two cards on the table' – hoping to secure an advance over Berlin by appearing to make a concession on Cuba – and this might be a brilliant diplomatic *coup* by the Russians. The Opposition leaders accepted the news and the Prime Minister's diagnosis calmly, and according to the note of the meeting soon proceeded to discuss the Vassall case,* having agreed to say nothing at all about their meeting. The next day in the Commons Gaitskell gave his support to Macmillan.

At an emergency meeting on 23 October the Security Council called on Cuba to dismantle and withdraw the nuclear weapon sites under the supervision of the United Nations. When Ormsby-Gore reported from Washington that Kennedy did not mean to seize Cuba by force, Macmillan advised Kennedy to continue 'with your military build-up for any emergency'. As it was obvious this was exactly what America was doing this message was superfluous.[38]

The Cuba crisis was short and sharp, with a series of escalating manoeuvres on both sides which were finally defused by international mediation by the UN Secretary-General U Thant. In the final round of negotiations Cuba agreed to halt the construction of missile bases if the United States desisted from 'threats and aggressive actions against Cuba, including the naval blockade'. President Kennedy, in a letter to Khrushchev, described as 'generally acceptable' proposals by the Soviet leader that America should lift the quarantine and guarantee Cuba's territorial integrity, and that Soviet missile systems should be removed from Cuba under United Nations supervision. Work on missile sites

---

* See Chapter 18, pages 452 ff.

however must cease first and there must be 'measures to render such weapons inoperable, under effective international guarantees'.[39]

On 29 October Ormsby-Gore signalled from Washington that 'it now looks as though Khrushchev has decided on virtually a complete climb-down over the Cuban missile bases' and the newspapers carried the text of a letter from Khrushchev to Kennedy:

> I have learnt with great pleasure of your reply to U Thant that steps will be taken to exclude contact between our ships and thus avoid irredeemable fateful consequences . . .
>
> Your rockets are situated in Britain, situated in Italy, and are aimed against us. Your rockets are situated in Turkey.
>
> You are worried by Cuba. You say that it worries you because it is a distance of 90 miles from the coast of America, but Turkey is next to us. I therefore make the proposal: We agree to remove from Cuba those means which you regard as offensive means; we agree to carry this out, and make a pledge to the United Nations. Your representatives will make a declaration to the effect that the United States considering the uneasiness and anxiety of the Soviet state will remove its similar means from Turkey . . . Let us agree to some period of time, but not to delay; two or three weeks, not more than a month.

Khrushchev complained at the violation of Soviet air space and Cuban air space, and concluded by saying that he had sent Vasily Kuznetsov, Deputy Minister of Foreign Affairs, to New York, to assist U Thant in 'liquidating the present dangerous position'. He guaranteed that the Soviet Union would not attack Turkey if America gave a reciprocal guarantee over Cuba.

Apologizing in his reply for the accidental entry into Soviet air space of a US aircraft (in sharp contrast to Eisenhower in 1960), Kennedy welcomed Khrushchev's message, saying 'developments were approaching a point where events could have become unmanageable'. The President asked for priority to be given to 'a great effort' for a nuclear test ban. Macmillan also wrote to Khrushchev asking for a test ban agreement, but let it be known that Britain would support Kennedy's demand that the dismantling of Soviet rockets in Cuba must precede any negotiations.

In a further letter to Khrushchev Kennedy insisted that the missile bases in Cuba must be rendered inoperable under UN arrangements which would enable the US to give assurances 'against an invasion of Cuba'. Khrushchev's suggestion of a bargain between missile bases in Turkey and Cuba received short shrift – Macmillan records in his memoirs that he would 'never have consented'. The West were in a strong position and Khrushchev knew this. An American invasion of Cuba could not be halted by Russia, and if there was a nuclear war the US and NATO had considerably greater fire power than Russia, while

Russia had no nuclear warheads capable of reaching the US. Khrushchev had decided to cut his losses, and knew he could not insist on a quid pro quo in Turkey.[40]

With the Soviet climb-down over Cuba the British nation and the whole world breathed a sigh of relief. A nightmare was over. Christopher Booker has described the country as being hypnotized for a full week 'by what appeared to be the most dangerous crisis in its history with the world teetering on the brink of disaster and England forced to look on stupefied and powerless'. That Britain was powerless to influence events is certainly true, but there was no danger of nuclear war unless either Kennedy or Khrushchev lost his head and committed some rash act on impulse. British opinion was divided during the crisis and an enormous demonstration outside the American Embassy in Grosvenor Square chanted for hours 'Hands off Cuba'.

In the debate on Cuba in the Commons the Opposition speakers Wilson and Gaitskell, supported by some press opinion, argued that in failing to consult the British Government and treating it with contempt, the Americans had exposed the hollowness of the 'special relationship'; Britain gained nothing from being a nuclear power because America had risked total war without bothering about Britain or Europe. According to the press reports, honours were divided equally in the debate.

Macmillan and his official biographer Alistair Horne give the impression that Britain played an important role in the Cuba crisis. This cannot be substantiated. Alistair Horne writes that there were lengthy transatlantic calls between the Prime Minister and the President at the height of the crisis and although these fell short of 'consultation' in the strict sense of the word they were certainly more than just 'informative' since there had already emerged a deep, almost instinctive harmony of views between the two men. This ingenuous theory is contradicted by McGeorge Bundy, Kennedy's closest confidant during the Cuba affair, who stated baldly after Kennedy's death that Macmillan's advice on the Cuba missile crisis 'was not very important'.[41] The only real Anglo-American consultation over Cuba was Kennedy's talk with his personal friend Ormsby-Gore on 21 October, quoted above. The long telephone calls between Kennedy and Macmillan, transcripts of which are in the Public Record Office, reveal that Kennedy held the reins throughout the Cuban crisis himself and only consulted Macmillan to seek the approval of Britain and her European allies for what he was doing.

Cuba had no effect on the special relationship. Although Kennedy was aware that Khrushchev had faith in Macmillan's appeal for nuclear disarmament and a détente, and accordingly valued the British Prime Minister as a useful peace-broker, in no sense did he look on Britain as an equal partner in his confrontation with Russia.

On 28 October 1962, just as Khrushchev's humiliation over Cuba was complete, Ormsby-Gore suggested to the Foreign Office that the result of Cuba was 'a pawn in the hand':

> Ought we not to make an explicit link between the continued inviolability of Cuba and the continued inviolability of West Berlin? The three Western powers should offer an assurance that no offensive weapons would be introduced into Berlin and would agree that compliance should be verified by the United Nations. In return the Soviets would be asked to guarantee the inviolability of Western Berlin and it could be made abundantly clear that any external or internal threat to West Berlin by the Soviets would immediately relieve the US of their obligations to refrain from interfering in Cuba ...
>
> I see the following advantages in such a more or less direct link between Cuba and Berlin. It gives us full value of Cuba as a pawn at our mercy. It gives increased security to West Berlin and the Soviets would be put on notice that any undue pressure on us there would result in the disappearance of the Castro regime in a matter of hours.[42]

This was not a sensible suggestion and was probably inspired by the President himself or his immediate entourage. It was essential to allow Khrushchev to retreat from his Cuba impasse with dignity so that he would be inclined to begin negotiations over a test ban treaty. The Foreign Office were horrified by Ormsby-Gore's suggestion and, briefed by Caccia, Home turned it down out of hand; Macmillan reiterated Home's advice, writing:

> an explicit link between them might even encourage Khrushchev to feel that he might take Berlin at the risk not of nuclear war, but only of the loss of Cuba. It is surely possible that Señor Castro may one day be overthrown by a spontaneous revolution, and we should not get into a position in which such a development might seem to justify the Russians in seizing Berlin.

From Moscow Roberts wrote that the significant feature of Cuba was that Khrushchev had backed off when the chips were down; if during a moratorium the West insisted on raising the Berlin issue with a view to obtaining advantage without offering any fresh concessions it would appear to Khrushchev that we believed him to be on the run, and he would dig his toes in. 'He can no longer believe, as he seemed to recently, that the Americans would in no circumstances resort to nuclear war.'

On a Foreign Office memorandum stating that 'the only signs of panic during the [Cuba] Crisis occurred in the satellite countries (particularly in Prague) and that the Russians did not get the usual "spontaneous" expressions of support by means of demonstration in the satellite capitals,' Macmillan minuted: 'This is interesting; I wish Editors of

Observer, *Times* and *Sunday Times* to be informed.' The memorandum continued:

> it might be easier to discuss Berlin as part of a general discussion about a détente in East/West relations and possibly some form of non-aggression pact between the NATO and Warsaw pacts. Berlin remains in an exposed position and a hostage to the Russians. So on the whole it seems desirable to try and make progress about it and about other questions such as nuclear tests so that the West keeps the initiative they have gained over Cuba.

Macmillan minuted on this: 'This is the whole issue. As to method it must be the President as to modability [*sic*].'[43]

Khrushchev was not abashed by his total humiliation over Cuba. On 27 November he wrote to Macmillan a cocky but conciliatory letter linking Berlin with a nuclear test ban – just what Macmillan was planning.

> It is necessary to seek an improvement of British-Soviet relations and also that the existing international issues can and must be settled through negotiations ... Steps have been reciprocally taken which have diminished the acute danger of the situation in the Caribbean area and it has proved possible to avert the sliding of the world into a precipice ... The rocket weapons which the President termed 'offensive' have been removed from Cuba and the US Government has been given an opportunity to ascertain this ... It is to be hoped now that the negotiations on the final settlement of the Cuban conflict, including the formalization through the United Nations of the pledge that Cuba will not be invaded ... will be successfully completed.
>
> I fully share your view as well as that of President Kennedy that the Cuban crisis has led to a better understanding of the need for a prompt settlement of acute international problems. The Soviet Government has been and will go on doing its utmost in order to reach agreement on general and complete disarmament and thereby secure inviolable peace on earth ... Now that mankind has experienced what was probably the most imminent possibility of a thermonuclear war there are grounds to expect that the Western powers will also display a more constructive approach to the disarmament problems. It is necessary at the present time to agree on the conclusion of a treaty to stop all tests of nuclear weapons. The Soviet Government has no doubts that the national means of detecting nuclear explosions owned by states are quite sufficient to assure effective control over such agreement.

Whilst maintaining firmly that Russia would not agree to international inspection of its territory, Khrushchev conceded that, according to Soviet scientists, automatic seismic stations could be installed in Russia which might even include 'participation of foreign personnel'. About Berlin Khrushchev wrote:

At the same time the Soviet Government still believes that the most important question which requires urgent solution is the conclusion of a German peace treaty and the consequent normalization of the situation in West Berlin. Unless we settle this question we may jump from one crisis into another ... We are in favour of seeking economic solutions for the problems confronting us; we are in favour of removing the roadblocks ... if goodwill is displayed by all the parties concerned it should be possible to find a mutually acceptable solution for all outstanding problems.

Macmillan was enormously encouraged by the tone of the letter which he felt opened the road to a solution of both the West Berlin problem and a test ban treaty. The only drawback to the letter was a complaint from Khrushchev about the British Foreign Secretary who had remarked that after the 'sobering Cuba crisis the Russians might reconsider their role in international society'; if this erroneous conception of the situation was perpetuated, he said, 'there is hardly any hope that we shall be able to achieve success in the negotiations on the problems facing us'. Khrushchev obviously resented Home's assumption that Russia's international standing had been damaged by her being forced to withdraw her missiles from Cuba and that it was only she who had lessons to draw from the Cuban crisis.

But with this letter in his hands Macmillan went to meet President Kennedy in Nassau on 18 December 1962 full of optimism. With similar optimism the Foreign Secretary wrote to the Prime Minister on 14 December: 'I do not think it surprising that the atmosphere in West Berlin has improved since Cuba or that Ulbricht should be making conciliatory speeches.' However Home felt the Russians were only shelving the Berlin issue.[44]

Unfortunately at Nassau President Kennedy was uncompromising over Berlin, and the chance to arrive at an agreement with Russia on the subject was lost. After a dinner party given by the Prime Minister on 19 December Kennedy said that US tactics over Berlin had been 'foolish':

They had involved themselves in rows with the French and the Germans over possible initiatives which had then been rejected by the Russians. Thus no progress had been made but a lot of ill feeling inside the alliance had been engendered. At present there seemed no prospect of the Russians accepting reasonable terms.

As things stood Kennedy saw no point in taking the initiative: he and his advisers had been sent Khrushchev's letter of 27 November, but clearly read into it very different meanings from the British.

Answering Kennedy, Home said that it worried him that the West should be consigned to a position of complete immobility: 'If we made no attempt to settle the Berlin question now the Russians might build up their strength over the next months and years and would precipitate another Berlin crisis and the West would then be inhibited from negotiating "under threats".'

Thompson, understanding far more about Khrushchev than the others from his years as Ambassador in Moscow, supported Home against the President,* saying bilateral talks between the Americans and the Russians over the past year 'had brought out clearly the elements of a deal if the Russians wanted one. The basic elements were a Russian guarantee of access and a greater measure of Western recognition of East Germany.'

Was there any hope of an all-Berlin solution, Home then asked. But replying instead of Thompson, David Bruce, the US Ambassador in London, stated that Russia would never surrender control of East Germany: it was part of their plan to bring West Germany within the Communist orbit, and Berlin was the one issue which could precipitate a world war.

The talk ended with Thompson urging strongly that the channels of communication with the Russians over Berlin should be kept open, and that Britain and America should discuss the form which any settlement might take. However Kennedy and his advisers were adamant that no move should be made towards Khrushchev over Berlin, and once again there was an acute clash of opinion between Britain and the Americans.

Kennedy however had just received a promising letter from Khrushchev about a test ban treaty, on lines similar to the one sent to Macmillan. He was ready to take up this issue, and suddenly the focus of Anglo-American policy towards Russia shifted from Berlin to nuclear disarmament and a ban on nuclear tests. Happily this produced vastly better results than the long abortive unfinished dialogue over Berlin.[45]

In his letters to Kennedy and Macmillan of December 1962, Khrushchev had taken a big step forward in stating Russia's willingness to consider two or three on-site inspections each year. This was a distinct advance on anything the Russian delegation at the Geneva disarmament talks had suggested although the Americans did not consider two or three annual inspections enough.

In Washington progress towards a test ban treaty was not all plain sailing. Paul Mason of the British delegation to the disarmament conference in Geneva, after a visit to Washington on 26 February 1963, reported that 'pressures in Congress and elsewhere against signing a test ban treaty have built up to an exceeding high level ... although the

---

* Thompson had been appointed by the Eisenhower administration and his appointment had been terminated by Kennedy; this explains his forthrightness.

President was as anxious as ever for an agreement, he was under heavy fire so that it would be out of the question for him to make further concessions.' William C. Foster, Director of the US Arms Control Agency, had told him after an hour with Kennedy that the President felt it was impossible to make any further concessions to the Russians. Mason's view was that Britain's standing in Washington was 'worse than it had ever been', and that this was linked with Cuba on which a great deal of indignation had been worked up so that 'distrust of Russia was at a peak'. During this period a strong body of public opinion in America felt that Kennedy had been weak over Cuba, and should have invaded and toppled Castro from power. It was widely believed that Macmillan had persuaded Kennedy to be 'soft'. According to Mason Rusk was contemplating sending a message to the British Foreign Secretary urging 'that we stick together very closely because of all these difficulties'.

In Geneva the American delegation made a small step forward by suggesting they might agree to seven on-site inspections in Russia annually. William Foster told Ormsby-Gore that he was annoyed because the British delegation in Geneva had inadvertently leaked this offer to the press, and, in his talk to Mason, Foster emphasized that this leak had been 'highly embarrassing both to the President and his staff'.

Rusk had written to Home on 13 February 1963 urging that they should work 'closely together' in test ban treaty negotiations. He was pessimistic about Russia's genuine wish for a treaty, and indicated that the critics in America of 'our efforts to reach a test ban treaty had been very vocal of late'. Rusk emphasized that such criticsm would not prevent them engaging in serious negotiations. He doubted whether France or China would sign a treaty but nevertheless such a treaty would be 'worth while' because it would prevent a great number of countries from trying to develop a nuclear weapon capacity.

In Geneva no progress was being made and on 8 March 1963 the seventeen-nation disarmament conference broke up in total stalemate. Macmillan as usual wanted a Summit meeting to capitalize on Khrushchev's more flexible attitude to a test ban treaty, and told Ormsby-Gore he was 'certain' there was no hope of agreement with the Russians without a meeting of the three heads of government. Ormsby-Gore suggested this to Kennedy but it did not find favour. Kennedy was too conscious of the rebuff he had received from Khrushchev in Vienna in 1961 and would not consider requesting another Summit meeting.[46]

Macmillan then considered taking the initiative himself by way of a letter to Khrushchev. However Sir Humphrey Trevelyan, British Ambassador in Moscow in succession to Frank Roberts, warned the Prime Minister that any London initiative would entail the risk of a rebuff from

Khrushchev because he was so sensitive to suggestions that he had been soft on Cuba, and it would help him in his internal politics if he could be publicly rude without risk. Ormsby-Gore suggested that the best plan would be to send a special emissary from Britain and another from America to negotiate with Khrushchev in Moscow.

Macmillan told Kennedy he would be very ready to take part personally in the negotiations if a preliminary conference made good progress, and a meeting of heads of government seemed appropriate; he suggested that negotiations should be opened with the offer of five annual inspections through the Geneva negotiators, and a personal message from Kennedy to Khrushchev proposing either Averell Harriman, the elderly and much respected American diplomat, or the President's brother Bobby to go to Moscow to find out 'whether there was a chance of settling round about five [on-site inspections] or by some juggling with numbers'.[47]

This letter to Kennedy started the ball rolling. Kennedy replied on 18 March that the climate in America was adverse, and the State Department would not accept less than seven annual on-site inspections but he was prepared to write to Khrushchev. On 15 April Macmillan and Kennedy sent a joint letter to Khrushchev:

> Your acceptance of on the spot verification of unidentified events has been of great value . . . the actual difference between the three inspections which you have proposed and the seven for which we are pressing – important though this is, should not be impossible to resolve. We have a duty to humanity. President Kennedy and I therefore believe that we ought to make a serious attempt by the best available means to see if we cannot bring this matter to a conclusion with your help. President Kennedy and I would be ready to send in due course very senior representatives to speak for us in Moscow directly.

Khrushchev replied that he had only agreed to two or three inspections a year as 'a political necessity in order that the President could satisfy the United States Senate', but instead of accepting this offer in the spirit in which it was put forward 'the West had started to haggle'. More importantly Khrushchev agreed to continue to seek agreement and to receive 'your highly placed representatives'.

At the end of May a joint Macmillan–Kennedy reply to Khrushchev was sent, proposing that new talks on a test ban treaty should be held in Moscow by high-level British and American emissaries 'as a sign of the West's earnest intention to forget past misunderstandings and reach agreement'. On 8 June Khrushchev agreed to open negotiations. In an important speech that same day at the American University in Washington announcing the talks Kennedy said:

We do not want a Pax Americana enforced in the world by American nuclear weapons of war . . . not merely peace for Americans, but peace for all men; not merely peace in our time, but peace for all time. We must conduct our affairs in such a way that it becomes in the Communists' interest to agree on a genuine peace. The United States will never start a war. We do not want a war. We do not now expect a war. We shall also do our part to build a world of peace where the weak are safe and the strong are just . . . Confident and unafraid we labour on – not towards a strategy of annihilation but towards a strategy of peace.[48]

This important speech was a reward for the years Macmillan had spent in nudging America towards a test ban treaty with Russia, and from then on negotiations took place for the most part directly between the two main powers. Macmillan nominated Lord Hailsham, Lord President of the Council, as the British emissary, and Kennedy nominated Harriman for America. Kennedy immediately made it clear that he wanted Harriman, not Hailsham, to play the main part in conducting the negotiations and do 'most of the talking'.

British newspapers hailed Kennedy's 8 June speech as a great step forward, with the *Manchester Guardian* writing that it was 'one of the great state papers of American history'. The American press in general underplayed it with some hostile Congressmen calling it 'a soft line that can accomplish nothing . . . a shot from the hip . . . a dreadful mistake'. However Khrushchev was to tell Harriman when he got to Moscow that it was 'the best speech by any President since Roosevelt'.[49]

His success in negotiations with the Russians over a test ban treaty came at a time when Macmillan was depressed at a succession of political troubles at home culminating in the Profumo scandal.* He was buoyed up when Kennedy accepted an invitation to stay at Birch Grove for talks on outstanding world problems at the end of June.

Originally three full days of talks were envisaged, and Macmillan called for a series of briefs from Government Departments contemplating a wide agenda on eight topics: test bans; the Kennedy round of tariff reductions; the European political scene; Laos and the Far East; Malaysia; Sino-Soviet relations; Greece, and the East Africa Federation. Word came from the White House that Kennedy wanted to raise the Middle East (primarily Yemen and Pakistan) so further briefs were hastily produced.[50]

One day was chopped off the visit when Kennedy decided to search out his Kennedy ancestors in Ireland instead of flying direct to Britain, and further disappointment was caused when he decided to cut short the talks on the first day by spending the morning at the grave of his sister

---

* See Chapter 18, pages 454 ff.

Lady Hartington who was buried at Chatsworth in Derbyshire. This produced a petulant note from de Zulueta to David Bruce, the US Ambassador: 'We cannot have the President gallivanting around, and Chatsworth will presumably be filled with airmen trying to find somewhere for the helicopter to land without spoiling the geraniums.' Kennedy went to the Derby airport of Waddington and then motored to Chatsworth; this made him late and Macmillan had to wait at Gatwick for him on the afternoon of 29 June. Thus the President spent only twenty-four hours at Birch Grove.

However the biggest disappointment for Macmillan was a message from Washington that Kennedy had told Ormsby-Gore that in discussions at Birch Grove British Guiana would be as important a topic as any of the others and he supposed Duncan Sandys, Secretary for Commonwealth Relations, would be there for this. Hurriedly a brief on British Guiana was prepared for Macmillan. Kennedy also asked for Dean Rusk to have discussions with Lord Home, the Foreign Secretary, and Duncan Sandys in Whitehall about British Guiana before the Birch Grove meeting.[51]

There is no mention of British Guiana in Macmillan's memoirs, but it was of high importance after the Cuba missile crisis, being a British colony situated close to the south-east coast of the USA which would be as ideal a location for Russian nuclear missiles as Cuba.

In the summer of 1963 there was grave fear that, with the Communists under Cheddi Jagan now the governing party, British Guiana would fall under Russian influence. At a London conference in 1960 it had been promised the 'principle' of full internal self-government. In August 1961 in a General Election held under the British system of first past the post, the Communists under Jagan won 41 per cent of the votes, only a slender margin above the opposition party led by Forbes Burnham, but the Communists became the majority government in Parliament. In November 1961 they asked for full independence. The colony had become paralysed by strikes in protest at Jagan's method of government, and the London conference was reconvened in October 1962; but no agreement could be reached with Jagan's Government. In February 1962 Jagan's premiership had been discussed in talks at the White House, and in April the Foreign Office warned the State Department through the US Embassy in London that early independence under Jagan was impossible because of doubts about his ability to keep order, and he left the way open for Cuban domination.[52] Consequently in June 1963 British Guiana posed a serious strategic risk to the Americans.

Ormsby-Gore wrote to Macmillan: 'There is no doubt that the situation in British Guiana is causing the Americans the gravest concern in the whole context of the "cold war"; they see it as a most vulnerable point where Communism might easily take over and start a landslide in Latin America.' He added that Kennedy thought British Guiana could be damaging to him in the forthcoming presidential election as his political opponents were accusing him of having been soft on Cuba and expected him to take strong action to remove the potential menace of Communism in British Guiana.

The Birch Grove agenda was hurriedly rearranged, and in addition to talks at the Commonwealth Office in Whitehall between Dean Rusk and Sandys and Home on 28 June, two sessions on British Guiana were scheduled for Birch Grove. At the Whitehall discussion Rusk told Sandys that the United States objected strongly to British Guiana being given independence under Jagan's Communist Government and he wanted the British Government to delay the proposed independence 'until there was no risk of British Guiana going Communist'. Sandys replied that the only practical way of doing this was to suspend the constitution and reimpose direct rule, and it was undesirable for Britain to 'expose herself' in this way for the sake of a territory in which she had no profound interest because it would have 'very considerable long-term political, military and financial implications'.

Rusk contradicted Sandys, saying he was certain that Britain had a very large interest in British Guiana in the context of wider Anglo-American relations, and that he wanted Britain to seek agreement with the Labour Party of that country on resuming direct rule. Lord Home said it would be impossible to reach agreement with Labour, and reversion to direct rule would destroy 'Britain's image as a decolonizing power' and create the greatest possible difficulties in dealing with Africa, particularly Southern Rhodesia. However Sandys thought it might be possible to make direct rule work provided the United States gave generous financial and economic aid. Rusk insisted that direct rule offered the only really satisfactory solution and the whole question would have to be considered by the Prime Minister and President at Birch Grove.

Sir Hylton Poynton, Permanent Under-Secretary at the Colonial Office, said that in discussions between US and British officials it was agreed that Jagan would try to establish a Castro-type Communist Government; the US officials thought Jagan was bound to seek Communist assistance, but the British officials thought the local opposition would stop him.

Sandys then asked Rusk how far the United States would help Britain in the general colonial field if Britain reimposed direct rule in British Guiana, arguing that it was reasonable to ask for help in other directions if Britain helped America on this one. Rusk would not be drawn, saying that British Guiana was 'different', and he ended the meeting testily by saying that both sides would have to do some more thinking on the problem before the talks at Birch Grove.

Two long discussions about British Guiana were held between Kennedy and Macmillan at Birch Grove. At the first meeting Rusk demanded that Britain should resume direct rule. Sandys countered by proposing a change in the constitution so that instead of the first-past-the-post system of elections there should be proportional representation which was likely to deprive Jagan of his overall majority. Rusk then said that if Jagan was replaced by Burnham, the leader of the opposition, America would 'move rapidly' over economic and social aid, and might possibly reactivate the American wartime base there granted in 1940 by the Churchill Government. It was derelict but the Americans had the right to use it at any time. Kennedy was attracted by the idea of proportional representation and was pleased when Sandys agreed that it would be possible to resume direct rule. However Home pointed out that this would be embarrassing because it would be asked why Britain should not do the same in Southern Rhodesia.

Kennedy stated that he was worried that Jagan would take Guiana into the Communist camp, and move in technicians and many Cubans, and Latin America was the most dangerous part of the world because many countries might go Communist at any minute. There were elections next year in America, and if Guiana had gone Communist meanwhile 'there would be pressure for the United States to take action against Cuba which would be impossible for any administration to resist'. He asked the British Government not to give British Guiana independence; he was prepared to put up with a great deal, he added, to prevent British Guiana going Communist.

At the end of the meetings Kennedy emphasized that it would be very important to play down any stories of British and American discussions about British Guiana, and the press should be told that it had only been very briefly discussed by Rusk and Sandys with no mention of the President and Prime Minister taking part.

In the official Birch Grove communiqué there was no mention of the subject. However something was leaked to *The Times* which reported: 'Both US and UK representatives did their best to play down hard differences of view existing about British Guiana. The British view is that it is up to them to decide whether or not to suspend the constitution.'

Sandys was sent to British Guiana a fortnight after Birch Grove to allay US fears. A general strike had been in operation there for fourteen weeks, and there had been daily clashes between strikers and the Communist Government resulting in the suspension of mail services in and out of the country. The British trade union leader, Robert Willis, had already gone out unsuccessfully to try to settle the strike. Sandys used the excuse of the disorders to call another constitutional conference in October 1963. At this the voting procedure was changed to proportional representation and in the ensuing election Jagan held only twenty-two seats against twenty-nine by his opponents: with the Communists always in a minority, independence was eventually granted in April 1966. Thus this potential source of friction between America and Britain was laid to rest.

The meetings over British Guiana took up a disproportionate amount of time at Birch Grove. After the conference Macmillan issued a note to his Ministers:

> The twenty-four hours which the President was at Birchgrove House were of tremendous activity ... an international meeting of unique character because it could only have taken place between the British and American governments. It is inconceivable that a series of agreements could have been reached on such a wide number of difficult topics except by people who regarded themselves almost as brothers and partners in a joint undertaking.

The private discussions he had with Kennedy settled the main issues, he added. There were important discussions on the test ban treaty, as has been seen, and on the multilateral force (MLF).[*] But in truth there was little time for more than these in the crowded schedule and his highfalutin claims about their importance in his memoirs are belied by the archives.[53]

On 8 July, after talking to David Bruce, the American Ambassador, Harold Caccia reported to the Foreign Secretary that apart from 'tests'

> British Guiana was the issue of by far the greatest importance to the President. If British Guiana became independent under a leader commonly believed in the United States to be a Communist the President would be vulnerable to damaging attack from all those who were far from content with the present position in Cuba. The Ambassador hoped that after what had been said we were in no doubt about the weight which the President attached to this issue. It would be of little avail to us whether the President's views coincided with ours or not on a variety of foreign issues if he was unable to be re-elected next year. It was as simple as that.[54]

Macmillan in his memoirs described the Birch Grove meeting as an overwhelming success, writing that 'a fantastic, even romantic atmosphere prevailed during those thrilling hours'. The claim is unreal. Professor McGeorge Bundy, Kennedy's personal foreign affairs adviser,

---

[*] See Chapter 14.

points out in a letter to the author that at Birch Grove Macmillan was in a 'low' as a result of the political difficulties over Profumo which seemed likely to bring him down, while Kennedy was on a 'high' after his triumph in Berlin, though he is sure the two men 'liked each other a lot'. With hindsight it looks as if Kennedy fussed unnecessarily at Birch Grove over British Guiana, but McGeorge Bundy also points out that as a result of Kennedy pressing so hard, Sandys not only went out there, but two constitutional conferences were held to keep Jagan out of power. It was therefore good statesmanship on Kennedy's part and he achieved his aim. This point is undeniable.

Other Americans viewed the meeting in a different light. Even Alistair Horne, Macmillan's official biographer, writes: 'For Kennedy it was perhaps the least heartening of all the encounters he had with Macmillan' and he was disappointed that the British Prime Minister seemed 'so disconsolate, so fatigued and so lacking in new ideas'.[55]

From Birch Grove Kennedy travelled on to Paris. Here he was shocked at de Gaulle's adamant refusal to sign a test ban treaty and at the withdrawal of French naval forces from the NATO Fleet. From France Kennedy flew to Italy, and in Naples on the last leg of the European tour his entourage talked frankly to journalists about their experiences.

The Washington correspondent of the *Sunday Times* reported that the President and his party when they came to see Mr Macmillan at Birch Grove 'felt a distressing casualness in dealing with important principles'. *The Economist* thought this alarming and referred to their own correspondent's talk of 'British splutters'. However the *Daily Express* put the cat amongst the pigeons. Their reporter René McColl was a renowned British foreign correspondent, in an age when journalists on national newspapers could achieve a celebrity reserved today only for the television performer. He sent the *Daily Express* this authentic account of the American reaction to Birch Grove from Naples on 2 July 1963 and it was published the next day:

> It must now be put on the record that his meeting with Macmillan last week is sorrowfully referred to by the American party as one of the low spots of the tour.
>
> Members of the White House privately reported that President Kennedy is both 'disappointed and resentful'. He was disappointed at what he took to be Mr Macmillan's lack of grip on international affairs.
>
> The resentment arises from these factors: Mr Macmillan flatly refused to give British approval to MLF and would not put forward any alternative. The Americans contended that the British negotiators had not done their homework. There were, they complained, no concrete proposals put forward by Mr Macmillan and his advisers had no new ideas. The Americans

were also critical of Mr Macmillan personally. They say he seemed to be in a state of disarray following his recent domestic disasters. And whereas officials hoped to find a constructive and positive approach to the problems of the day they say they found the British team 'bumbling and old-fashioned'.

There was agreement on one question: the approach to the Russians concerning the East–West nuclear test ban.

President Kennedy is understood to have said after leaving Mr Macmillan that he hoped the US negotiator *not* Lord Hailsham will be allowed to do most of the talking to Khrushchev when the talks start in Moscow on 15 July.

Roy Wright, the former *Daily Express* editor, told the author that René McColl was completely reliable; he was proud of his reputation and would never manufacture a 'story' and, although he was inclined to sensationalism, he had the confidence of British and overseas diplomats and politicians.

De Zulueta discussed the *Daily Express* report with the Prime Minister, and sent a cable to Ormsby-Gore stating that the Prime Minister presumed this represents 'briefing by disgruntled mixed manners in the State Department Party'; he asked Gore whether he thought the White House 'could do anything to put the matter right'. Then followed a correspondence between McGeorge Bundy and de Zulueta; the letters indicate that McColl was correct. Bundy strongly denied that he himself was responsible for the leak but admitted, 'I cannot promise you that no American has said anything untoward to a reporter.'

On 5 July, in a personal letter to the Prime Minister praising Lady Dorothy Macmillan's cook, Kennedy wrote:

> I have also started immediate enquiries on British Guiana in the light of our conversations and I think I should warn you that our people do not think there is any realistic prospect of success in strengthening Burnham's numerical support. But I have told them to have another hard look and on the basis of what they tell me next week I will be in touch with you again.
>
> The big problem before us is the mission of our two colleagues to Moscow.[56]

The most important discussions on the test ban treaty took place not at Birch Grove but during the preliminary talks in Whitehall which Dean Rusk held with Home and Heath. The transcripts show an identity of view between the Americans and British but important decisions, such as Macmillan refers to in his memoirs, were not made either in Whitehall or at Birch Grove.

At the Foreign Office on 27 June Home and Rusk agreed that if no progress could be made on a 'comprehensive' ban they should consider 'a partial treaty, and allow underground tests to continue'. When Home raised the possibility that Russia would refuse to sign without French participation Rusk replied that an agreement must first be obtained between the three nuclear powers [Russia, UK and USA], and then if France and China did not adhere they would 'look at the situation again'. Rusk said:

> The Americans would probably not feel it necessary to withdraw from a treaty just because the Chinese carried out one or two tests, and the same should go for the Russians as regards French tests. He did not think the Russians really believed the French were testing devices for the United States and United Kingdom.

There was sufficient agreement at this level for a memorandum of the points agreed in discussion to be prepared for the Prime Minister and President Kennedy at Birch Grove.[57]

> The following conclusions were reached in discussions between Mr Dean Rusk and Lord Home on 27 June.
> Mr Harriman's and Lord Hailsham's visit to Moscow might well provide the last chance of agreement on a nuclear tests ban. Every effort should be made to take advantage of this.
> The first object should be to secure a *comprehensive treaty*, with adequate verification of uncertain events underground. This involves some on-site inspections, but Mr Harriman and Lord Hailsham should in the first stages avoid argument in justification of any particular number. Their opening line should be:
> (i) Our aim was to secure a treaty which would last. For this purpose each side must have confidence that the other was observing the rules.
> (ii) National detection systems were not adequate to identify all uncertain events underground. A proportion of on-site inspections would be necessary for this end.
> (iii) Such inspections could be carried out under strict safeguards against the possibility of espionage . . .
> As regards numbers, we should be ready to discuss the possibilities of aggregating the inspections over a number of years (with a maximum for say one year); or of dividing the quota of inspections between seismic and aseismic areas. Our own experts should again work these ideas out in detail at this stage.
> If the Russians refuse to budge on a comprehensive treaty, our next object should be a *partial treaty* covering tests in all environments except underground, with no restrictions on underground tests. This might be offered either as something separate, or as the first stage of a further continuous negotiation for a comprehensive treaty.
> If they refuse to accept a partial treaty in these forms, we should explore the possibility of some intermediate position between a comprehensive and a partial ban. Thus we could offer to conclude an atmospheric ban combined with some *annual limit* (by number and/or size) on *underground*

tests (our experts should develop some specific examples of such offers).

The Russians might press for a partial treaty with an indefinite moratorium on underground tests, and might hope to secure at least a *limited moratorium*. It would be politically impossible to sign an agreement with them binding ourselves explicitly to any kind of moratorium. It might, however, be possible, if the state of negotiations seemed to warrant this, to declare our intention not to test underground for a limited period.

If the Russians try to make a nuclear tests treaty conditional on *French signature*, our line should be that we would do our best to secure the adherence of all other Powers if a treaty were signed; and we would count on the Russians doing the same in respect of China.* In any case, the 'withdrawal clause' was designed to meet the contingency that tests by a non-signatory Power threatened the security of a signatory Power.

The Russians are likely to sound us on *non-dissemination*. We should be prepared to discuss this, bearing in mind that it was important not to go too far without bringing in the French. We should try to get the Russians to accept our existing formula as a basis for further talks including the French . . .

Another subject which the Russians might well raise is a *non-aggression pact* between the NATO and Warsaw Pact Powers. Our attitude should be that it would be time to start discussing this further after the conclusion of treaties on nuclear tests and non-dissemination.

An hour and a quarter's discussion between Macmillan and Kennedy at Birch Grove on 30 June added little. Kennedy emphasized that his difficulty was that he had 'no majority in the Senate in favour of a treaty, and indeed, a strong majority against. Both the Armed Services Committee and Atomic Energy Committee were opposed to a nuclear test ban and far from having the two thirds majority which he needed for a treaty in the Senate he probably had only fifteen Senators in favour'. Sir Solly Zuckerman, the British scientific nuclear expert, and Dr Long, his US counterpart, were called in but added nothing important.[58]

Khrushchev began talks with Harriman and Hailsham in Moscow on 15 July and three and a half weeks after the Birch Grove meeting the test ban treaty was agreed. On 2 July Khrushchev made an important speech suggesting he would agree to a 'partial' ban and not just 'all or nothing'; he also proposed a NATO–Warsaw Pact powers non-aggression pact. The Foreign Office pointed out that if a firm link were established between such a pact and the test ban de Gaulle could place a veto on the conclusion of the test ban treaty, and this would almost certainly mean no treaty. They advised Macmillan that the test ban and non-aggression must be treated as separate subjects. The Americans agreed.

---

* The Americans and British were far too optimistic about the influence the Russians would have over the Chinese. In the event the Chinese refused any co-operation.

In order to get de Gaulle to adhere to the treaty Kennedy proposed that the French should be given vital information about nuclear technology – information, Macmillan commented, 'which had been so long and so jealously withheld from us'.

Although the Foreign Office and Ministry of Defence were alarmed at this American proposal, Macmillan was in favour of accepting, and on 18 July the Cabinet agreed. Still harbouring thoughts of Britain joining the EEC, he persuaded the Cabinet to support the Americans. On that day Macmillan wrote to Kennedy: 'We could also consider arranging to provide them [the French] with nuclear information, and perhaps also supplying them with fissile or other material in such a way as to save them time and money, and of course above all *to obviate the need for further French tests*.' However de Gaulle knew that the 'Anglo-Saxons', as he called the British and Americans, would demand in return for this know-how that the French nuclear deterrent should only be used with American authority, and he had no interest in a French *force de frappe* with a double key. He insisted that France must have her own completely independent nuclear deterrent like Britain, no matter what carrot was dangled under his nose.

During the Moscow discussions it became clear to the Americans that there was no chance the Russians would agree to a system of on-site inspections which the Senate, outraged by the Cuba crisis, would accept. Kennedy therefore decided to settle for a treaty which did not 'preclude underground testing'. This was the political price he had to pay for Congressional support.

There were two further obstacles. The Russians tried to insist that the treaty should include the non-aggression pact referred to above which was unacceptable to Britain and America because of the possibility of a French veto; whilst the British asked for a non-proliferation or non-dissemination section. At one moment these inclusions threatened to torpedo the negotiations. However once they were excluded it was plain sailing and agreement was reached on 25 July.[59]

The partial test ban was a tremendous advance. Apart from its implication for future world peace the atmosphere was becoming dangerously and permanently polluted by thirteen years of American, Russian and British tests on top of the pollution caused by the Hiroshima and Nagasaki bombs dropped in anger in 1945. Without the treaty immeasurable further damage would have been done to mankind.

The Campaign for Nuclear Disarmament celebrated the test ban treaty with a victory rally in Trafalgar Square, but their joy was cut down to size by an article in the *Manchester Guardian* on 30 July by a leading campaigner, Peggy Duff. She wrote: 'We see the Moscow Treaty as a small but important step towards Peace ... It is only a partial treaty. The nuclear powers will be able to continue to test triggers and small weapons underground.' She did not mention the environmental advantages resulting from the banning of atmospheric tests.

The British press were ungenerous to Macmillan for his part in securing the treaty. It was true the negotiations were in effect conducted between America and Russia with Hailsham instructed to behave as a junior partner. Yet Macmillan had been the mediator and without his continual pushing there would have been no test ban treaty. Ignoring Britain's role, *The Times* referred to Russia and America as 'the two Titans of the post-war world' but argued that the world's political atmosphere hardly showed any signs of a general lowering of tension with China and France delaying any general rapprochement; the treaty could also lead to the switching of resources to other forms of defence expenditure rather than to peaceful purposes so that a swift reduction in defence spending seemed as far away as ever.

In the House of Commons Macmillan's announcement of the treaty was received more enthusiastically. From the Opposition benches Michael Foot hailed it as 'the most important achievement in that area ... possibly Macmillan's greatest'. Macmillan's star, which had seemed to be setting with Profumo and other damaging domestic issues, started to rise again.

In America the fears which Kennedy had expressed at Birch Grove of opposition in the Senate turned out to be unfounded. When the roll was called only 11 Democrats and 8 Republicans were against, with 55 Democrats and 25 Republicans in favour. Kennedy in the short period before his assassination always emphasized that it was only the beginning of détente and that there was still a long way to go. However historians agree that the 1963 treaty led without doubt to the later and much to be desired advances of the non-proliferation treaty of 1968, and the comprehensive test ban and the Strategic Arms Limitation treaties (SALT) of the late seventies and eighties. For the 1963 treaty and the subsequent developments mankind should be grateful to Macmillan who began it all in August 1959 by urging Eisenhower to agree to a comprehensive test ban.

Thirty-seven nations adhered to the test ban treaty, but not China or France. The French attacked the treaty for preserving the inequality between 'great and small powers' and the French, like China, argued that 'it would perpetuate the atomic monopoly of certain powers'. *Pravda* denounced de Gaulle for his alleged intention to begin French nuclear tests in the Pacific.

Both Macmillan and Kennedy wrote to de Gaulle calling him to sign the treaty and promising nuclear know-how, perforce with strings. De Gaulle's answer came at a press conference on 29 July:

The United States . . . sees tempting prospects opening up before it. Thus for example, all the separate negotiations between the Anglo-Saxons and the Soviets – which, starting with the limited agreement on nuclear testing, seem likely to be extended to other questions, notably European ones – until now in the absence of the Europeans, which clearly goes against the views of France.

When a journalist who must have had some idea of the Macmillan–Kennedy offer of nuclear help asked the General whether he would sign the treaty, 'thus establishing France as a fourth nuclear power', de Gaulle replied: 'You know that France's signature is not given to a series of hypotheses, none of which until now has even begun to be implemented.' This was a firm rejection.

Dixon wrote from Paris: 'If de Gaulle agreed [to the offer of nuclear help in return for signing] it would no longer be reasonable for him to keep us out of the EEC. Indeed he might even be prepared to facilitate our entry. But I must stress that I do not think it likely that he would accept any proposals such as those we are considering.'[60]

Kennedy himself was so anxious to obtain de Gaulle's signature to the treaty that, in return, he was ready to go a long way in giving the French help with nuclear research. However the State Department had turned very sour on de Gaulle and he was so unpopular with Congress that it was improbable they would sanction release of nuclear know-how to France under the McMahon Act. In a letter to de Zulueta of 21 August intended for Macmillan's eye Bundy wrote that he saw no chance of meaningful talks with de Gaulle and 'there could be no question of France obtaining important nuclear weapons without paying a proper political price'; that is, France in return would be expected to sign the treaty and co-operate fully in NATO. On this letter Macmillan minuted: 'We should give any British technical information of value to France.' Over this he would have found himself in difficulties with the Americans. But on 31 July Caccia had already noted that 'I cannot for a moment see US Congress authorizing the transfer of American nuclear information on such a basis.'

De Gaulle hoped against hope that in return for his signing the test ban treaty the United States Government would make an offer without any strings. Dean Rusk told Caccia this in a conversation on 5 August, adding that the Americans had a direct report that de Gaulle 'was going to make the Americans go to Canossa but the US Government was not interested in a Canossa of this sort'.[61]

On 5 August de Gaulle replied to Macmillan with a categorical refusal, making it clear that he would conduct high-level nuclear tests in the atmosphere in two years' time as he already planned whatever the political price. It was a clear decision, as Macmillan's advisers pointed out, not to co-operate with the Americans either in the organization of the Western Alliance or over détente with the Soviet Union.

In September Kennedy pondered making a further approach to de Gaulle to sign the treaty and seeing how much help over nuclear technology he could offer without upsetting Congress. Eventually, after discussions with Ormsby-Gore, he decided not to send a letter but to instruct Charles Bohlen, his Ambassador in Paris, to approach de Gaulle on the following lines:

> You should express our regret that French Government has not chosen to accede to the limited test ban treaty. You should refer back to the President's letter to General de Gaulle and make it clear that there are two quite different elements to the problem of any possible nuclear co-operation between our countries, as the President sees it. While we believe that co-operation in major nuclear weapons technology would clearly require a level of agreement on related political problems which does not currently appear to be possible, the particular question of the French need for atmospheric testing seems to us quite different. It is our belief that underground testing by the most modern techniques would in fact permit France to assure herself of the satisfactory development of her current plans in the nuclear field, and we would be prepared to co-operate with France in the technology of underground testing with no other political condition than a French accession to the test ban treaty. You should express the President's hope that General de Gaulle may wish to give renewed consideration to this possibility.

A copy of this instruction was sent to Macmillan; he held a discussion with Home and other Ministers at Chequers on 16 September, and recorded his view that 'the only possible bargain between us and France [was] French signature of the treaty in return for American know-how in conducting underground tests and [he] as Prime Minister would give any British technical know-how of value to France.' The Prime Minister followed this up with a minute to Home which reveals more clearly than his memoirs his attitude to France's having their own independent nuclear warheads:

> We discussed last night the general question of our approach to the French ... we agreed that it would be quite all right if the Americans offered the French full knowledge about underground tests in exchange for French signature of the nuclear test ban treaty. We would hope that they would not give them anything more, not for instance full design knowledge of nuclear weapons or, of course, actual warheads. For these we ought to ask a much higher price. We also agreed that perhaps the best course, once the policy was agreed with America, would be for the President to send the message setting out his offer in detail and for us to have a shorter message

delivered at the same time saying that we associated ourselves with the Americans' proposal.[62]

It is surprising that Macmillan, after having put so much effort into the test ban treaty, should have balked at the Americans giving France 'full design knowledge' or 'actual warheads'. His 'much higher price' must have been an offer to allow Britain to join the EEC; there is no evidence he was much worried by France's reluctance to co-operate in NATO. Kennedy of course could not offer France the 'actual warheads' which were given to Britain since the offer would not receive the assent of Congress.

On 3 October after Habid Deloncle, Second Minister at the Quai d'Orsay and French Secretary of State for Foreign Affairs, had suggested in a speech that Britain should co-operate with France and not the United States over nuclear defence, Lord Home circulated a printed memorandum to the Cabinet pointing out:

> Anglo-American know-how is so closely enmeshed that the provisions would in practice prevent us passing any information about sophisticated weapon designs of a kind in which the French would be interested without United States consent. In present circumstances there is no prospect that either the United States Administration or Congress would be willing to give such consent particularly if the information would assist the development of the French national deterrent.

The Cabinet decided to take no action on the Habid Deloncle initiative during Macmillan's last week as Prime Minister, and it turned out to be a damp squib.

Both Macmillan and Kennedy were soon to depart from the corridors of power, and no new concessions towards de Gaulle were given by their immediate successors so that France's nuclear bomb research went ahead with test explosions causing grievous damage to the atmosphere. There is reason to believe that if Macmillan and Kennedy had remained in power they might somehow have reached agreement with de Gaulle to give him full control over a French nuclear deterrent and prevented this regrettable development.

CHAPTER 16

The Far East

DISAGREEMENT OVER FAR Eastern policy bedevilled Anglo-US relations throughout the period of the Macmillan Government as it had the Churchill Government of 1951–5. In 1954 and 1955 the Far East had been in turmoil. The French colonial war in North Vietnam against the Nationalist Vietminh under Ho Chi Minh had begun in December 1946, and by 1953 after seven years of fighting was internationalized, with the Communist Chinese supplying ever increasing help to the Vietminh across their common border while the USA continuously stepped up their help to the French. The Vietnamese and Chinese were traditional enemies but in North Vietnam they sank their differences in the cause of their common socialist principles.

Originally the United States had disapproved of the French action in Vietnam, viewing it as a colonial war, but once Moscow and Peking had recognized the Nationalist Vietminh revolutionaries in North Vietnam as the legitimate Government and started supplying them with arms, the United States took the side of the French against the Communists, furnishing them with arms and money as the war escalated. Despite their dislike of colonial wars, the USA recognized that the French had established a form of independence in Vietnam in 1948 while the other parts of the former French empire in Indo-China, Laos and Cambodia, had been given independence within a French union in July 1949.

By 1953 the Americans had become thoroughly alarmed at the French lack of military success; it was feared that Chinese Communists would occupy not only all Vietnam but also Cambodia and Laos, thus posing a threat to Thailand and British Malaya where the Americans had important economic interests in the tin and rubber-manufacturing industries. Eisenhower and Dulles did everything they could to prevent a French military collapse, and by the end of 1953 America was paying half France's military costs in the Vietnam war. When the Communist Vietnamese General Vo Giap occupied half Laos and considerable areas in Cambodia on the western frontier of Vietnam there was serious alarm in Washington.

In December 1953 Eisenhower, Churchill, the Foreign Secretary Anthony Eden and the French Foreign Minister Georges Bidault held a meeting in Bermuda; all three agreed that the French war effort in Indo-China was of the utmost importance. But Churchill was shocked when the Americans said categorically that they were prepared to use atom bombs if the Korean truce broke down. Eisenhower told Churchill's secretary John Colville, 'Whereas Winston looked on the atomic weapons as something entirely new and terrible, he [Eisenhower] looked upon it as just the latest improvement in military weapons.' According to Colville Eisenhower implied there was no distinction between 'conventional weapons' and 'atomic weapons' as all weapons became in due course conventional weapons. Only with difficulty did Churchill persuade the Americans to leave out of the official communiqué the words 'free to use the atomic weapon' and substitute the phrase 'reserving the right to use the atomic bomb'. As Eisenhower explained to the British, 'the United States public would not understand failure to use weapons on which so much had been spent, and which are now regarded in the United States as established weapons of war'. In his report on Bermuda to the Cabinet, however, Eden wrote:

> In communicating with the old Commonwealth governments . . . we should affirm in particular that the consequence of the use of atomic weapons against an enemy in the Far East might be so serious for the United Kingdom that we cannot agree to such action in advance and must insist on being consulted at the time before it is taken.[1]

Meanwhile the tragedy of Dien Bien Phu began to unfold. The French General Henri Navarre reported that the considerable French forces at Dien Bien Phu in mid-Vietnam, concentrated there as a result of a grave strategic error, would have to surrender unless there was early American intervention. Field Marshal Sir John Harding, Chief of the Imperial General Staff, confirmed to the Cabinet that the French were in a very dangerous position. Believing that disaster was imminent for them in Vietnam Dulles stated that the possibility of 'the imposition on South-East Asia of the political system of Communist Russia and its Chinese ally . . . should be met by united action which might involve serious risks'. The great risk for humanity was the Americans wanting to use atom bombs.

Fortunately Stalin had died a few months previously and when Vyacheslav Molotov, the Soviet Foreign Minister, suggested a five-power conference in Geneva involving China, Britain, France, America and Russia, Dulles agreed on the understanding that the USA would not recognize the People's Republic of China. The conference was scheduled to begin in Geneva on 26 April 1954.

In the stand they planned to take at this conference Eden and Dulles were poles apart. With the concurrence of President Eisenhower Dulles and his military advisers were planning American air strikes to relieve Dien Bien Phu, while Eden was bent on a cease-fire and partition leaving the French in control in South Vietnam and the Communists in control in the North. Eden was adamantly opposed to British armed intervention and would not contemplate either American intervention or a long-term anti-Communist regional military alliance while there was a chance of success at Geneva.

Forty-eight hours before the Geneva Conference was due to begin Dulles became less bellicose and told Eden that although the Americans would not intervene at Dien Bien Phu 'because no intervention could now save the fortress' (he soon changed his mind), they thought that 'if the French were confident that we would join in the defence of Indo-China they might not capitulate altogether on the fall of Dien Bien Phu' and assurances to this effect would keep the French in the fight. The Americans were apprehensive that without Anglo-American backing France might abandon the whole of Vietnam, and leave the country to the Communists.

Churchill was alarmed at this rift between Eden and Dulles and tried in vain to pour oil on the troubled waters. But when Churchill suggested he attended the Geneva Conference because 'I would like to have met Molotov again and Chou En-lai for the first time', Eden was horrified; the last thing he wanted at Geneva was his master interfering in his negotiations with the Russians and the Chinese.[2] And since Churchill was due at any moment to retire, Eden, the undisputed crown prince, was able to put his foot down and refuse to allow Churchill to interfere in his Far Eastern policy. This was as well because at Geneva Eden secured the greatest triumph of his diplomatic career.

In Geneva Chou En-lai, China's Premier and Foreign Minister, was at first aloof, and refused to consider any compromise. Fortunately Molotov was helpful but Dulles refused to speak to Chou or any member of the Chinese delegation.

On 27 April Dulles complained that Eden was pressing the French towards a cease-fire which would in the American's view be fatal to the French military position in Vietnam. Eden denied this, maintaining that a cease-fire was only possible within a political settlement; Dulles countered by postulating that there was no chance of the French staying in the fight without a common defence system in alliance with Britain and the USA.

In London on the same day the British Chiefs of Staff were told that the American plan was for Super-Fortresses from Manila, 1,200 miles away, to bomb the Vietminh supply-lines leading to Dien Bien

Phu – the object being to free the French Air Force so that it could concentrate on close support of the fortress of Dien Bien Phu. The British Chiefs of Staff advised that such attacks would 'not be effective'.

At a dinner on 1 May in Geneva relations between Eden and Dulles reached a new low point when Dulles informed Eden that Britain and America were in 'complete disarray'. Eden replied that he had no idea what Britain was being asked to do; she had refused to intervene with armed forces, and if America entered the Vietnam war it would not be long before the Americans and Chinese were fighting each other 'and that was in all probability the beginning of the third world war'. Nettled, Dulles replied that he was only asking Britain for 'moral support'. According to Eden it was 'a highly disturbing conversation': the Americans were deeply aggrieved at 'our refusal to support them in military measures', whilst Eden foresaw himself having to get up in the Commons, once American forces had landed in Indo-China, to answer the question: 'Did you know of and approve this move?'[3]

On 3 May Dulles left Geneva in a huff; Walter Bedell Smith, Under-Secretary of State, was put in charge of the American delegation, and immediately the atmosphere improved. Dulles left a letter to Eden proposing secret talks between the USA and Britain about Thailand and the South-East Asia position generally, which he wanted kept secret from the French. His last message to Eden was: 'Could not the British Government reconsider its position at least to the extent of enabling us to help and provide Bidault with some hope which might enable him to gather the political strength to hold off from the surrender which otherwise seems inevitable?'

Bedell Smith and Eden got on well. Eden reported that on 3 May, when they had dinner together, the American was most receptive and eager to find some way of ending the misunderstanding, and told Eden that there could be no question of sending American ground forces. 'They will go in over my dead body,' he said. On 7 May Dien Bien Phu fell and Eden's plan for partition and a cease-fire became more acceptable to both French and American opinion. Eden's attitude to Dulles is revealed by his telegram to the Prime Minister on 12 May:

> The situation here gets steadily more confused and difficult. The French have their thoughts in Paris, but we are doing everything we can to try to get them to make up their minds upon their minimum terms, so that we can go into action in support of them.
>
> Washington, until very recently, has been trying to get wholly unreasonable terms. Meanwhile Dulles' daily commentary multiplies confusion and exasperates everybody.

Churchill gave orders that this message was not to be shown to other members of the Cabinet; he was determined that his special relationship with Eisenhower should not be wrecked by the Eden–Dulles row. The Americans too were clear that Churchill had more sympathy with their viewpoint over Indo-China than Eden, and Eisenhower had written personally to Churchill on 27 April, 'I am deeply concerned about the seemingly wide differences in the conclusions developed by our respective governments.' Winston wanted Bedell Smith to fly to London to talk to him direct; Eden curtly refused this suggestion.[4]

In June Joseph Laniel was replaced as Prime Minister of France by Pierre Mendès-France, who almost immediately declared that the French would not continue to fight in Vietnam. Since this made American intervention impossible, Eden's task in bringing the conference to a successful conclusion was considerably simplified.

Right up until the last minute the result was in doubt. On 17 July 1954 Eden reported that Chou En-lai had told him he was concerned that the Big Three meant to split South-East Asia, and he insisted that 'the three associated states must be independent, sovereign and neutral', and that there was still doubt whether Dulles would insist on Laos and Cambodia being incorporated in a regional security organization. This would mean US military bases in those countries, which Chou En-lai would find unacceptable. On the same day Churchill wrote to Eden: 'I am sorry to read in the newspapers that things are looking adverse on your front.' The press had reported fears that Molotov might break off negotiations and denounce the non-Communist delegations or make unacceptable demands.

Frenzied last-minute negotiations by Eden were effectual and agreement was reached between all parties on 21 July 1954. Dulles instructed Bedell Smith not to sign; instead America took note.* There was to be a cease-fire; Vietnam was to be partitioned at the 17th parallel; Cambodia and Laos were to be independent; and elections were to be held in Vietnam within two years. In addition, an international supervisory commission, presided over by India and composed of representatives of Canada, Poland and India, was to prevent 'revocations' of the treaty.

The Geneva result was rightly hailed as a triumph for Eden. He had proved that China and Russia were willing to talk and to attempt to co-exist. But, perhaps more important, it had put a stop to American designs to settle the Far East crisis by a war in which they would crush the Communists with atomic weapons.

---

*Although America refused to sign the Geneva agreement they declared that 'they would respect the settlement'. The sullen and unhelpful position taken by Dulles, so Macmillan recorded, was a grave, even disastrous error and made a deep impression on the other governments.[5]

An American-sponsored South-East Asia Collective Defence Treaty followed the Geneva Conference, and a pact was signed by eight nations (the UK, France, New Zealand, Australia, the USA, the Philippines, Thailand and Pakistan) in Manila on 8 September. Dulles went to Manila, but not Eden. Surprisingly Dulles did not try to spell out America's exact military commitment, and a Council, the South-East Asia Treaty Organization (SEATO), was established to keep the military situation under review.

The treaty was primarily a declaration of intent, and only authorized military action under closely defined circumstances. However the Manila powers were satisfied that it gave adequate protection to the non-Communist states in Indo-China, and the guarantees given by America and Britain made it clear to Chou En-lai that there was a strong joint Anglo-American policy over former French Indo-China. With Manila, the Anglo-American quarrel was temporarily buried. The French had been enabled to withdraw their troops from North into South Vietnam in good order although after the Dien Bien Phu surrender the remnants of their army had been in a disastrous situation.

Unfortunately the promised democratic elections in North Vietnam never took place and nearly a million people voted with their feet by crossing the frontier from North to South Vietnam. The International Control Commission barely functioned; the Canadians always took the non-Communist side, and the Poles the Communist. Thus the Geneva agreement produced only a breathing space, and after a long truce war flared up again in December 1960.[6]

It had been hoped that Laos and Cambodia on Vietnam's western frontier would act as buffer states. Unfortunately this did not happen and, abetted by the Chinese, the North Vietnamese constantly violated Laotian territory in order to transfer armed men and military supplies into South Vietnam. The people of Laos were on the side of neither Communist North Vietnam nor American-supported South Vietnam; they only wanted to be left in peace. The same was true of Cambodia. However Laos with its common frontier with Communist China and North Vietnam became the centre of a cold war as the Americans tried hard to prevent the Chinese and North Vietnamese from using Laos and Cambodia for the passage of supplies to guerillas in South Vietnam.

In November 1954, after the closure of the Geneva Conference Don Katay, a strong and active politician, formed a non-Communist government in Laos. Wanting to replace the French colonial links with Vietnam by closer relations with Thailand and Cambodia, he strengthened his economic links with Thailand, at the same time improving railway communications. Unfortunately when French and Vietminh forces withdrew from Laos following the Geneva agreement, the Pathet Lao, a Communist organization, took over the two northern Laotian provinces. Talks between the Pathet Lao and Katay went on until the end of April 1955 with the Pathet Lao refusing to implement the Geneva accord.

Suddenly a ray of light appeared. At the end of April delegations from twenty-nine nations assembled at Bandung in Java. Representing 1.4 billion people from the countries of Asia and Africa, it was the first authentic meeting of the emergent regimes. Present at the conference was Chou En-lai, who had gone to Bandung expecting to hear little but abuse of the former colonial powers and America; instead he was surprised at the amount of pro-Western sentiment and had a change of heart during the proceedings which culminated in his making an offer to sit down with the United States to seek a solution to their differences.

After the Bandung Conference general elections took place in the fourteen provinces of Laos not held by the Communist Pathet Lao. There was a prolonged political crisis with Katay unable to command a parliamentary majority but finally, on 18 November 1957, the Pathet Lao entered a coalition government headed by Prince Souvannaphouma. The Pathet Lao delegation settled down in the capital, Vientiane, and functioned as a normal political party. American aid to Laos was stepped up. Then in fresh elections held in May 1958 the Pathet Lao obtained more parliamentary seats largely because American aid had been shown to have been misappropriated by the Government in the capital and had failed to reach the necessitous rural areas.

A Congressional enquiry revealed massive corruption in the administration of US aid and at the end of June 1959 America suspended aid to Laos in an effort to drive Prince Souvannaphouma out of office. Simultaneously the International Control Commission was withdrawn in spite of vigorous protests from the Polish members who saw it as providing support for Pathet Lao interests. The West was glad to see it go. In August Prince Souphanouvong, the moderate left-wing leader of Pathet Lao, resigned, and went to Paris as Ambassador, and Phoui Sananikone formed a new government. He aimed to prevent further electoral gains by the Pathet Lao and secured a renewal of American aid.

At Geneva the Pathet Lao were not at first recognized but Souphanouvong was able to claim that the Pathet Lao needed to hold two of the northern provinces pending an internal Laotian settlement. This was conceded at Geneva because the North Vietnamese were clearly in control of these provinces.

When Phoui Sananikone asked for American military aid the Communist bloc denounced it as a breach of the Geneva agreement, and on 18 May 1959 civil war started in Laos with the Pathet Lao portion of the army slipping out of the Plain of Jars and going to an isolated valley on the North Vietnam border. The Laotian Government declared that the Pathet Lao had committed an act of open rebellion, and that there must be a military solution. The North Vietnamese reinforced the Pathet Lao battalions and in August and September heavy attacks were made by the rebels on government positions. As there were torrential rains the fighting was not as heavy as the press reports made out but there was wild talk in Congress of sending US troops to Laos and on bombing the 'invaders' with US Navy and Air Force planes. Units of the US 7th Fleet were sent to the danger zone in the South China Sea.

On 29 December 1959 Katay died of an embolism, and the King dismissed Sananikone the next day. A new government was formed, dominated by General Phoumi. A military regime, it was much disliked by the West. Then in August 1960 Captain Kong Lae carried out a political *coup*; his aim was the ending of the civil war and the removal of all foreign troops from his country. With difficulty Souvannaphouma and Phoumi restored the situation in the capital but fierce fighting broke out, with the Pathet Lao being heavily reinforced by the North Vietnamese who launched attacks on government troops from the Vietnam frontier. Three groups were now fighting in Laos: Kong Lae's, Phoumi's government army and the Pathet Lao.

On 27 September 1960, the United States, Britain and France issued a statement confirming their support for the Government of Souvanna-phouma. By now Phoumi and he had quarrelled, and Souvannaphouma went into open rebellion. On 13 December Phoumi attacked the capital Vientiane with overwhelming forces and on entering the city claimed they had defeated the Communists. This was a fiction to which the US subscribed. Kong Lae now allied himself with the Pathet Lao, and together they captured and held the Plain of Jars. Here they received Russian and Chinese military aid with airlifts by Soviet planes.

The Eisenhower policy towards Laos has been well summarized by Ted Sorensen, the trusted adviser to President Kennedy on the Far East:

> The Eisenhower administration spent some 300 million dollars and five years in the hopeless effort to convert Laos into a clearly pro-Western, formally anti-Communist military outpost on the borders of Red China and North Vietnam ... As the Kennedy administration prepared to assume office the situation was deteriorating rapidly. The Soviet Union was airlifting an estimated 45 tons of arms and ammunition out of Hanoi every day to the Pathet Lao and Viet Cong forces were steadily expanding their positions in north-east Laos and on the strategic Plain of Jars. The United States was airlifting supplies to General Phoumi's forces further south ... The British and French still favoured Souvanna but he had fled to Cambodia. General Phoumi had committed himself to a new offensive into Pathet Lao territory. His troops though superior in numbers and American-trained and American-

equipped gave way to panic upon hearing that the more toughened North Vietnamese might be fighting on the other side.

In short a Communist conquest of almost every key city in the entire kingdom was an imminent danger.

In a conference with the incoming President Kennedy on 19 January 1961, Eisenhower told him that Laos was the most difficult and dangerous 'mess' he was passing on. 'You might have to go in there and fight it out,' he said.[7]

Charge and counter-charge began between the Soviets and Americans about intervention in the Laotian civil war, while a strong counter-attack by Phoumi's forces in the Plain of Jars was defeated in March 1961. This caused alarm bells to ring in Washington.

On 22 March 1961 Macmillan received a message from the Americans that the Royal Laotian Army had been decisively beaten by the Communists, and that urgent intervention was necessary to save at least part of the country. The British Cabinet decided to call for an immediate cease-fire, the return of the International Commission and reconvening of the Geneva Conference. They were adamantly opposed to military intervention either by SEATO or by America on its own – a course now being advocated by the US State Department and the Pentagon. Macmillan went to Trinidad, and on 25 March received a message asking him to meet the newly elected Kennedy at the giant US military base of Key West. Macmillan consulted Rab Butler who was in charge of the Government in his absence, and got Cabinet backing for a refusal to undertake any commitment for British military support.

To his great relief Macmillan found Kennedy ready to overturn Eisenhower's aggressive policy of US military action in Laos, the new President telling Macmillan that 'he did not want to go it alone' but wanted action by SEATO. Sorensen gives a picture of Kennedy's thinking about Laos.

If we used nuclear bombs, the President asked, where would it stop, how many other Communist movements would we have to attack, what kind of world would it be? No one knew. If we didn't use nuclear weapons, he asked, would we have to retreat or surrender in the face of an all-out Chinese intervention? That answer was affirmative. If we put more forces in Laos, he asked the Chiefs, would that weaken our reserves for action in Berlin or elsewhere? The answer was again in the affirmative. If neither the royal nor the administrative capital cities fell, and the cease-fire squabble was merely over where the truce was to be signed, would these risks be worthwhile? No one was sure.

Once in, how and when do we get out? he asked. Why cannot air and naval power suffice? Do we want an indefinite occupation of an unenthusiastic, dark-skinned population, tying up our forces and not those of the

Communists? Is this our best bet for a confrontation with Red China – in the mountains and jungles of its landlocked neighbor? Would forces landing in Vietnam and Siam [Thailand] end up defending those regimes also? Above all, he asked, why were the Laotian forces unwilling to fight for their own freedom?

Kennedy was given contradictory advice by his military and diplomatic advisers, and was undecided whether to provide military backing for the pro-Western forces in Laos or not. After the Korean War the army commanders had vowed never again to fight without atomic weapons in a country with no seaports, no railways and almost no usable aerodromes. General Douglas MacArthur, who had commanded in Korea, solemnly warned Kennedy against 'committing American foot soldiers on the Asian mainland', and Kennedy never forgot this advice.[8]

During his first conference with Kennedy at Key West on 26 March 1961 Macmillan made it clear to the new President that the United States would be 'largely alone' if they launched a major military operation in Laos. Kennedy replied that the US had changed policy over Laos, and in his view it had been a mistake of the Eisenhower administration to encourage the Royal Laos Government to believe that America would always support them militarily; his administration proposed instead to encourage a 'genuinely neutral country'. Macmillan said that if there was a SEATO operation in Laos the United Kingdom could not at this stage enter into 'an unlimited commitment'; the British Chiefs of Staff were not in favour of the current SEATO plan for intervention, which involved the despatch by air to Vientiane of 31,000 troops.[9]

Kennedy then asked bluntly twice: if the only way to save Laos was to send a force in, 'would the British join in?' Macmillan hedged, saying he would have to seek the views of his Cabinet; Laos was a bad place to fight in and an alternative would be to make a stand in Thailand. However he was prepared to put it to his Cabinet that the United Kingdom might make 'a small military contribution to a limited objective'.

Macmillan then asked Kennedy the really important question – ' "Was the thing worth doing at all?" Everybody agreed that a military operation intervention was futile. Was it not futile politically? Those Laotians who were supported by the Americans did not seem disposed to do any fighting at all whereas the other side [Pathet Lao] did.' Kennedy dodged the issue and asked if Britain would participate in planning 'definitely limited intervention for limited goals?' Macmillan stressed that the UK could not agree to an open commitment but he would put it to his Cabinet.[10]

At Key West Macmillan did his best to thwart US plans for military intervention against the Communists in Laos, and Kennedy shilly-shallied. The President wanted to bluff Khrushchev into believing that if it came to the crunch America would fight and might use atomic weapons. His attitude undoubtedly was instrumental in stopping Khrushchev overplaying his hand, whilst the British were chary of refusing all military support to SEATO, as Macmillan was disposed to do, for fear of doing lasting harm to Anglo-American relations.

Informed by a telegram from Macmillan of the purport of the talks, the Cabinet were 'sceptical about the effectiveness of military intervention' although they fully appreciated the importance of not allowing the situation to deteriorate further or of letting the Russians think they could get away with things. They agreed that planning should take place on that basis, and that Britain should be prepared to play her part in such action, but decided that the Cabinet must be consulted again before any military action was taken, and at the SEATO meeting anything implying that Britain was automatically committed to intervention should be avoided.[11]

The Minister of Defence, Harold Watkinson, minuted to the Prime Minister: 'Military intervention in Laos has always been a nonsense, but if the Americans are determined on a limited intervention we can play our part ... We must not risk being dragged into a major war ... There are no military advantages in holding small bridgeheads in Laos. But it is militarily feasible'. Even so the marked difference in policy between the Americans and the British continued, with the British unwilling to commit British forces in the area while the American Chiefs of Staff believed that unless they intervened militarily in Laos they would lose the country to the Communists, who would also take over Thailand 'which would jeopardize SEATO so that in five or six years all South-East Asia would be lost in a trail of disaster'.[12]

By now (March 1961) the much-heralded success of the 1954 Geneva Conference had turned sour. Three fifths of Laos was in the hands of insurgent forces operating alongside the Communists, and the North Vietnamese were able to infiltrate guerillas and arms into South Vietnam at will through this area of Laotian territory.

In April, with the military situation deteriorating fast, Phoumi approached the US for urgent military help, alleging that 60,000 North Vietnamese were in the field against him. On 19 April the 400-strong US military mission in Laos put on their uniforms. On 24 April 1961 Britain and Russia called for a cease-fire, to be followed by a Geneva Conference. An armistice was proclaimed on 3 May, by which time the Pathet Lao had acquired all the territory they planned to occupy.

The second Geneva Conference opened on 16 May 1961 with the same

participants as in 1954.* Meanwhile provisional plans for armed intervention were drawn up by the Americans, the British giving only lukewarm support. In June the conference had to be adjourned because fighting
had broken out again and it was impossible to maintain an effective cease-
fire. However the conference restarted on 12 June 1961 with Alec Home,
the British Foreign Secretary, as joint Chairman. The British Government
asked the Australian and New Zealand governments to co-operate in
contingency military plans. They agreed but without enthusiasm.

The Americans had placed heavy military equipment in Thailand, and
Watkinson, the Minister of Defence, pressed Macmillan for Britain to
do the same. On 22 June Tim Bligh, Macmillan's principal private
secretary, minuted to Macmillan that if Britain did not follow the
Americans' lead 'the Commonwealth Brigade might in the event of
serious operations developing find themselves fighting for a period of
perhaps four weeks without artillery, armoured cars and other heavy
equipment alongside American forces who were properly equipped'.
Cabinet approval was thereupon given to the movement of British and
Commonwealth heavy equipment to Thailand.[13]

Meanwhile all was not going well in Geneva, although the addition
to the US team of Averell Harriman, who was head and shoulders above
his fellow American diplomats, helped to oil the wheels.† Macmillan
cabled to Home in Geneva on 5 July 1961:

> I have been thinking over our conversation. It occurs to me to wonder if
> the situation of the Laos Conference is not very similar to that of the Tests
> Conference. Here again if Berlin is settled we may hope for some progress;
> and if it is not the war in Laos will seem very small beer. So ought not
> our tactics to be to keep the conference going as long as we can, adjourning
> it from time to time if necessary? Of course we would hope that the three
> Princes might manage to settle it between them. But our purpose would
> be to keep on talking for we know that the end of the conference would
> mean the beginning of vast new expenditures for whatever version of Plan
> Five [the US plan for large-scale military intervention] was by then in favour.
>
> In putting this suggestion to Rusk [US Secretary of State] could you not
> also point out that, whether by Soviet design or unlucky accident, we and
> the Americans are in danger of getting entangled in all sorts of troubles
> around the world just as Berlin is coming to a head. These entanglements
> must please the Russians very much; they want to lead us further into the
> net and so we should try to keep clear of it.

---

*Britain, France, North and South Vietnam, Cambodia, Laos, USA, Russia and Communist
China, together with the members of the International Control Commission: India, Canada and
Poland, plus the remaining two neighbours of Laos: Burma and Thailand.
†Averell Harriman, former US Ambassador to Moscow during the Second World War, had
been appointed Assistant Secretary of State for Far Eastern Affairs.

Home replied the next morning:

> We are in an immediate difficulty because the Canadians are cutting up rough about the treatment by the Russians, Chinese and Pathet Lao of the ICC. They are trying to hamstring its activities, and if this goes on much longer the Canadians may withdraw their man. In response to Mr Khrushchev's general attitude the American attitude is tougher, and I fear they may have left the impression with Phoumi that they will support him if he takes a tough line. He is not interested in a peaceful settlement. It won't be easy to keep the conference going if these issues come to a head, but I think we can succeed.

Later that day Home sent Macmillan a second message from Geneva:

> *Military Planning for Laos*
> Admiral Felt [Harry Felt: US] and Admiral Luce [John Luce: UK] have now held their talks in Okinawa and have made some progress in sketching out the sort of operation which SEATO could conduct in Laos if the Geneva Conference breaks down. We have been invited to send an officer to Honolulu to maintain contact with Admiral Felt's staff. Nevertheless there are still important points of difference between ourselves and the Americans. The Chiefs of Staff and I therefore consider that we should hold further political talks with the Americans to get final agreement on the terms of reference under which Admiral Felt should finish his planning. While I am doubtful if he will consider himself bound by such a document once fighting begins, I am sure we should insist upon it as a proper basis for planning and because we must have a firm agreement with the Americans about why we are going into Laos and what we hope to do there.
>
> Before we go back to the State Department, there is one matter for which I would like your approval. There is a risk that when SEATO troops enter Laos they may find Pathet Lao forces already in some of the bridgeheads which we are to occupy. Both United Kingdom and United States military planners would like, on military grounds, to be free to attack these Pathet Lao and expel them without having to wait for specific political authority. I am sure that is right and essential from the military point of view. I therefore suggest that the initial political decision to intervene in Laos should carry with it authority for our forces to attack and expel Pathet Lao forces from the areas within our bridgeheads.
>
> I am sending copies of this minute to the Minister of Defence and the Commonwealth Secretary.

At that time Macmillan, as has been seen, was highly nervous about the British economy, and he sent the following gloomy message in reply to Home's two cables: 'I am really beginning to get very unhappy at all this. If we were to be involved in Laos following Kuwait and in the middle of our other difficulties, I think it might mean the final collapse of the economy. Do you think we ought to review our whole position regarding SEATO?"[14] Earlier that year Selwyn Lloyd, Chancellor of the Exchequer, had cabled the Prime Minister on 31 March:

> Our view is that the effect of military action in Laos, whether it took the form of a joint US/UK holding operation or of a joint SEATO operation, could only be to increase the present nervousness in the foreign exchange markets ... these fears would affect the dollar as well as sterling and the most likely outcome would be the resumption of buying of gold on a substantial scale ... the present movement of sterling into Continental currencies would be still further accentuated ... there would be considerable risks for both sterling and the dollar. All this is apart from the actual cost of the operation. I am afraid that sterling is having a poorish time.

This message, which grossly exaggerated the danger to sterling, obviously affected Macmillan who was always conscious of the difficulty of maintaining the value of the pound.[15]

Watkinson sent a minute to the Foreign Secretary on 12 July pointing out that, although the Cabinet had approved sending heavy equipment to Thailand, Australia and New Zealand were expressing hesitations in case the 'pre-position' of this heavy equipment in Thailand might provoke the Pathet Lao to break the cease-fire and take offensive action. Macmillan minuted on the Defence Secretary's memorandum: 'I hope we will do *nothing* at all'.

Home was more in tune with the Americans and he replied to Macmillan's minute of 7 July on 14 July.

> I do not think we can decide now to quit the Far East; there would be too many adverse repercussions. The Chancellor's proposed economies do not so far touch the Commonwealth Brigade, so that we could provide at least a small force for a SEATO exercise with a limited role. We would have to make it clear to the Americans if it came to a show-down on Laos that we could not provide more than this token.
>
> I realize that even this might involve considerable additional expense and man-power worries in bringing our units up to fighting establishment and keeping them supplied with ammunition, etc. There would also be works and communications costs in Laos. I would propose to warn Rusk when I see him that if it did come to hostilities we would probably have to ask that we should be helped to meet the additional cost. I hope you will agree that I should do this.
>
> I am sending a copy of this minute to the Chancellor of the Exchequer.

A revealing minute from the Foreign Secretary to the Minister of Defence on 18 July is further confirmation that Home was not as alarmed about the consequences of a build-up of Anglo-American, Australian and New Zealand forces in Thailand as the Prime Minister.

In your minute of 12 July you asked my views on certain political considerations affecting this matter. You will no doubt since have learnt that the Prime Minister minuted on his copy of your minute that he hoped that we would take no action at all. It is in any case very difficult for me to say at this stage whether we are likely to have to intervene in Laos or not. This depends entirely on how much we can get out of the Russians and Chinese during the negotiations in Geneva and whether, in the last resort, the Americans are going to want to fight if the conference is a failure. They have not yet made up their minds, but if they do feel that they must intervene, I do not think that we can very well ourselves back out and I have made this clear in my minute to the Prime Minister of 14 July. I think, however, that we shall have ample warning of any likelihood of the conference breaking down and that we can so plan ahead as to give ourselves plenty of time to get into a good military position once we see that this is likely to be required.

I therefore suggest that we should leave this matter over for the moment but that the Foreign Office should review it every week in the light of events in Geneva and in Laos and that I should let you and other Ministers know immediately if I believe that we are heading for a breakdown and may have to resort to force. We can then take an immediate decision on whether to pre-position or not.

If we had to do so I do not think that at that stage we would need worry very much about the risk of prejudicing a peaceful settlement. In any case, the Americans have had heavy equipment and aircraft pre-positioned in Thailand for some time. There has been no leakage (at least to the press, though presumably the Communists know what is going on) and no adverse effect at Geneva. If there should be any leakage, either with regard to our equipment or that of the Americans, it could possibly have a salutary effect by convincing the Communists of our determination to resist by force if necessary.

On reading this Macmillan minuted: 'This operation is really getting more and more unreal.' He felt that Home was exceeding his instructions in his co-operation with the Americans, and minuted to de Zulueta on 23 July:

I do not want to harry the Foreign Secretary but I am afraid there may be some misunderstanding in the Foreign Office as to the position.

I do not, repeat not, regard the Cabinet as having given agreement to Plan 6 [the current SEATO plan for military operations in Laos] being put into operation without a specific and new policy decision by the Cabinet.

In other words the approval to what we did before, at and after Key West has lapsed.

In the present circumstances and with the increasing pressure on sterling etc I feel it unlikely that the Cabinet would agree. The question arises should the Foreign Secretary warn Rusk privately, or should I warn the President (also privately) or should we say so officially for the record? I feel there is a danger of misunderstanding. I would be grateful for your thoughts about this.[16]

In spite of Home's more co-operative attitude to American military plans, Macmillan and Kennedy were several times close to a rift. On 11 September the Prime Minister, the Minister of Defence and the Foreign Secretary held a meeting to discuss the new American proposal for military intervention in Laos. According to the map supplied by the Americans, it was in Watkinson's words 'really a plan for partition' which involved putting a screen of US troops between Thailand, South Vietnam and Cambodia and the Communists. The Americans thought this the only feasible method of preventing military infiltration by the North Vietnamese into South Vietnam through Laos; they wanted to seal off the Communists from Laos, Cambodia and South Vietnam. The operation required a great number of troops who would be mainly American.

Home emphasized that it was being put by the Americans as a serious military proposition, and Watkinson said he was unwilling to ask the British military chiefs to 'take an obstructive attitude' since he feared that if they did it would only harm their relations with the Pentagon 'to no good effect'. Home offered to discuss the matter 'frankly with Rusk'.

Macmillan agreed that the Ministry of Defence could authorize planning and examination of the new American proposal 'on a purely military basis', but in doing so the military must point out the size of the conflict involved. The Prime Minister instructed Home to talk to Rusk in Washington and to point out that one branch of the US administration seemed to be pursuing its own policy contrary to that of the President, and Home must try to bring Rusk face to face with this 'reality of which he seemed, however, to be personally quite unaware'. Indeed, in October Harriman told the British delegation in Geneva that 'some very unwise advisers in Washington were urging contrary policies on Kennedy and there was a danger of the President being unduly influenced by them'. Fortunately, despite wavering, Kennedy stuck to the line that the US must try to scotch plans for full-scale military intervention.

Negotiations at Geneva became bogged down as Phoumi and Souvannaphouma failed to agree either over the composition of a new government or, more especially, on how much representation the Pathet Lao should be given. Sporadic fighting continued and the Pathet Lao nibbled away, successfully acquiring more territory. In Geneva British diplomats found the Chinese and North Vietnamese delegates impervious to reason, although progress could be made with the Russians in spite of their lack of civility.[17]

On 15 May 1962 the Pathet Lao made a major attack across the Mekong valley and took the town of Nam Than. Mainly for internal political reasons, Kennedy now determined to show that he would not allow the Communists to take Laos by force. Under the formality of a request by Thailand for help under the SEATO Treaty, US naval forces and two air squadrons were moved to the area. More than 5,000 US marines and army combat troops were landed in Thailand together with a few British, Australian and New Zealand units. The Pathet Lao then stopped, convinced that the Americans meant business, and the negotiating atmosphere in Geneva suddenly improved.

On 6 June 1962 Watkinson produced a paper stating that 'probably the best military solution would be to hold the line to the 17th parallel itself', but 'even this would be a major military operation in which large forces would be required initially with an almost unlimited commitment for reinforcements after general hostilities broke out.' He did not want to get involved in any planning with the Americans even on the most uncommitted basis until the Cabinet had come to a decision. Macmillan continued to express reservations, minuting: 'I think we should be extremely cautious over all this.'

Fortunately the new sense of urgency at Geneva had resulted in agreement to form a Laotian government of national unity under Souvannaphouma on 11 May 1962, and the Geneva Conference ended on 23 July 1962 with a treaty signed by fourteen countries which gave Laos the freedom to work out its own destiny as a politically unaligned buffer state. This solution was fortunate for Anglo-American relations because it is doubtful whether the Macmillan Government would have agreed to support the massive military action in Laos which the Americans were planning.[18]

Unfortunately although the Russians and Chinese were ready to honour the accord the Vietminh and the Pathet Lao were not. Khrushchev even showed his sincerity by writing a letter to Macmillan purring with satisfaction at the Soviet role in achieving the Geneva agreement; alarmed at Chinese aggressive intentions the Russian wanted to preserve the *status quo* in this part of the Far East. The treaty signed at Geneva on 23 July 1962 proved more brittle than the one of July 1954 although it contained formal statements of intent and solemn undertakings by all the nations to respect the neutrality of Laos. If these undertakings had been honoured by the Vietminh, the dangers to world peace implicit in the Laotian situation would have disappeared.

That autumn, to the dismay of the Thais, SEATO troops left; prisoners on both sides were released, and over 1,000 American and Philippine troops were withdrawn, being counted out by the Control Commission. However during the winter of 1962–3 the Laotian situation deteriorated. The Vietminh refused to keep their part of the bargain and withdraw from all Laotian territory. The Americans, alarmed by the weakness of the Laotian Government, increased their military aid, supplying *inter alia* helicopters and amphibious vehicles, and training in counter-insurgent methods. They also stationed more troops in Thailand.

As a riposte the Vietminh flagrantly breached the Geneva agreement by placing eleven battalions in the main passes between Vietnam and Laos.

Although the Laotian Government expressed themselves satisfied that the Vietminh cadres had left the country, the Americans knew this was far from being the case. Because of the coolness between the Russians and the Chinese the Russians gave up their airlift to the Pathet Lao troops in the Plain of Jars, but the Chinese more than made up for that. Artillery and mortar duels began in the Plain of Jars between the Pathet Lao and government troops, and these skirmishes developed into a battle front. On 1 April 1963 after assassinations of some of their ministers, the remaining Pathet Lao ministers withdrew from the capital to the North, where Prince Souvanouvong had already gone. Thus within ten months of the Geneva agreement the Laotian coalition Government upon whose existence the whole arrangement depended had in effect broken up.

Nevertheless no one, including China, wanted to bring the Laos issue to a crisis point again for fear that this would bring in the other side on a scale which threatened a major war. The archives reveal that the British Ministers, particularly Macmillan, exercised considerable influence on America in steering her away from a massive military operation in Laos which might have triggered off a major war including the use of atomic weapons, and this should be rated as one of Macmillan's finest diplomatic achievements.

Once the Geneva agreement was signed, the Americans wanted to give financial aid to Laos and pressed Britain to make a large contribution. Macmillan was dubious and minuted on 8 October 1962: 'If you give money it would go straight into the Paris bank accounts [of Souvannaphouma and his associates].'[19] In a memorandum for the Cabinet Home wrote that President Kennedy was 'much disturbed' at the small British contribution:

> His view is that the settlement in Laos is the outcome of a triple policy which America accepted at the instigation of the British and the French. He wishes to continue this common policy but believes that America's allies should share economic as well as political responsibility . . . The Geneva agreements were designed to terminate the American dominance over Laos, and the Americans are justified in thinking it can only lead to trouble if they alone carry the main weight of the economy . . .
>
> I think that our policy of close co-operation with the Americans in South-East Asia has been the right one. It is more likely we should have been faced with a local war in the area in 1960 or 1961 if we had not been able to persuade the Americans to take the right line. The risk of a disaster in Vietnam, Laos or even Cambodia is still considerable.
>
> Because of the decisions taken by President Kennedy and the personal efforts of Harriman we have got back to the closest possible relationship

with the Americans in that part of the world but they expect that we will not leave them in financial isolation if this high degree of co-operation is to be maintained. I think it would be right to provide £1 million a year for three years to finance more imports into Laos over and above the £1.35 million worth of development aid already offered over the next five years.[20]

Sir William Armstrong, Joint Permanent Secretary at the Treasury, replied to Home on 2 November 1962:

Your new proposal is . . . far more than I would regard as justified by the normal standards for a country such as Laos. I am not altogether convinced moreover that by pressing us to go to an even higher figure the Americans are activated solely by the political needs of the situation in Laos. This is one of a number of interchanges that we are having with them over a wide field about how the burden of overseas aid should be shared and I cannot help feel that they are using the specific circumstances of Laos to drive a hard financial bargain.

The euphoria within the Foreign Office at the restoration of Anglo-American relations, following the success at Geneva, was evidently not shared by the Treasury. However the Treasury 'reluctantly' agreed to the Foreign Secretary's proposals 'in view of the importance and priority he attached to the matter'. In the event the British made a contribution still considered inadequate by the French and Americans of £1.35 million for capital and technical assistance over five years together with £3 million for financing essential exports or technical assistance.[21]

In the last months of the Macmillan administration the situation in Laos deteriorated. Fighting escalated between the Pathet Lao and government troops, while Pathet Lao leaders refused to co-operate with the Control Commission on which the Poles were again at daggers drawn with the other two powers – the Indians and Canadians. Khrushchev tried to avert further trouble, and was instrumental in arranging for another cease-fire in April 1963.

After talking to Khrushchev Harriman had an interview with Macmillan on 29 April 1963, and told him that Khrushchev's attitude was 'satisfactory' on Laos:

He had appeared rather bored with the subject and had been inclined to take the view that there were only two million people in Laos and that its importance had been overrated. He had however reaffirmed his agreement to work with the West to maintain the neutrality of Laos.

Macmillan wrote to Kennedy after talking to Harriman:

On South-East Asia it does seem as if the Russians were not anxious to see troubles develop on a large scale. They have their commitments the same as we have but I would guess from what Averell said that if they could do so without letting down their friends they were quite willing to see the general arrangements carried out at any rate for the present.

Summarizing matters in his memoirs at the end of summer 1963, Macmillan described the situation in Thailand as 'relatively quiet'; in Cambodia, 'anxiety' and 'suspicion at violations of the frontier by the North Vietnam'; in Laos, inconclusive fighting with the Pathet Lao backed by the North Vietnamese on the offensive; in South Vietnam, gloomy prospects for 'any successful defence against the Communists from the North'.[22]

He was right. Having refused to help the French to regain control of Indo-China in 1945 on the grounds that the French were fighting a colonial war, the Americans were obliged from 1963 onwards to build up their forces in South Vietnam and thus to involve themselves in a ten-year war against the Communists. It would have been better if they had realized after the Japanese surrender in 1945 that the French were fighting an anti-Communist and not a colonial war: then they would not have fallen into the fatal trap of attempting to stop the inexorable advance of Communism in the Far East. The Macmillan Government tried in vain to persuade the Eisenhower and Kennedy administrations that large-scale military intervention in former French Indo-China would be in vain. Had President Kennedy lived, this advice might have been heeded, but after his assassination America plunged herself into the long and disastrous Vietnam War.

At the end of the 1954 Geneva Conference there had been a bitter clash between the British Foreign Secretary Anthony Eden and his US counterpart Foster Dulles, the repercussions of which were to last through both Eden's and Macmillan's days as Prime Minister. The subject was the Chinese offshore islands of Quemoy and Matsos.

When the Chinese Nationalists under Chiang Kai-shek had been forced to evacuate all mainland China by the Communists in 1948 they retreated to Formosa (now Taiwan), the Pescadores and the offshore islands of Quemoy, Matsos and Tachen. From these bases Chiang Kai-shek threatened to invade the mainland, while the Communists threatened to liquidate Formosa.

On 11 August 1954 Chou En-lai made a vicious anti-American speech, declaring: 'It is imperative to liberate Taiwan and the traitorous Chiang Kai-shek group. Taiwan has been converted into a US colony and they have the wild ambition of restoring criminal fascist rule and converting the whole of China into a US colony.' Eisenhower retaliated by stating that any invasion of Formosa 'would have to run over the American Seventh Fleet'.

In September General John Hull, commanding Far East American forces, reported to Dulles that 'atomic bombs' would have to be used against the Chinese mainland to break up Chinese dispositions if the offshore islands of Quemoy and Matsos were attacked by the Communists. Dulles then wrote a memorandum for Eisenhower stating: 'almost certainly a committal under present circumstances to defend Quemoy etc. would alienate world opinion and gravely strain our alliance both in Europe and with ANZUS [Australia and New Zealand]. This is the more true because it would probably lead to our initiating the use of atomic weapons.' Dulles was on edge when he came to London for talks with Eden on 17 September: on 5 September the Chinese Communists had begun to shell Quemoy and Matsos, which lay only five miles from the mainland. The Nationalists replied with their own artillery and announced that they 'would fight to the finish'.

Dulles told Eden that the US National Security Council was in favour of US forces defending Quemoy because 'any further Communist success coming so soon after the Indo-China settlement would suggest that the United States was not willing to stand and fight at any point in Asia and damaging inferences would be drawn both by the Communists and by America's allies . . .' Withdrawal from Quemoy 'would have a disastrous effect on morale in Formosa', which was essential to US Pacific defences and needed the aid of the Chinese Nationalists for its defence. Eden replied that he wanted the neutralization of Quemoy, leaving Formosa and the Pescadores under Chiang Kai-shek, and direct negotiations with the Communists for a guarantee that, if Quemoy was abandoned to them, they would leave Formosa 'in peace and quiet'.

Dulles suggested that the offshore islands would have to be defended by atomic weapons even at the risk of a third world war; this alarmed Eden, who had just been given a secret report by the British Chiefs of Staff that Quemoy and the offshore islands were indefensible 'except at the cost of great exertions by the US Fleet', and they were not essential to the defence of Formosa.

In January 1955 the Cabinet approved Eden's proposal that the British should refuse to support Dulles in any American guarantee to Chiang Kai-shek to defend Quemoy and Matsos. The Americans, with New Zealand backing, wanted the offshore islands dispute to be considered by the United Nations. According to Humphrey Trevelyan, the British representative in Peking, Chou En-lai would not hear of this and refused to separate the question of the offshore islands from Formosa. On 20 January 1955 Eden instructed Roger Makins, British Ambassador in Washington, to put it to Dulles 'very strongly' that the Chinese would never acquiesce in the coastal islands remaining in Nationalist hands; that the United Nations could take no effective action; and that as long as the Nationalists occupied the islands 'there will be a continuing danger of friction and fighting'.

This drew a personal letter from Eisenhower to Prime Minister Churchill, obviously drafted by Dulles, dated 25 January 1955: 'We are convinced that the psychological effect in the Far East of deserting our friends on Formosa would risk a collapse of Asiatic resistance to Communists'; he also decried Churchill's opposition, in a previous letter to the President, to the use of atomic bombs in the Far East:

> We believe that the consequences would not be as far-reaching as you describe. I refer to the extraordinary increase in the value of tactical or strategic surprise brought about by the enormous destructive power of the new weapons and the probability that they could be delivered over targets with little or no warning ...

According to the President, the Kremlin and Peking were driving forward with plans of political and military nibbling in relative safety, 'knowing we in our democracies abhor the thought of mass destruction'; he added ominously: 'there can be "local" deterrents as well as "global" deterrents.'

Eisenhower wrote again on 10 February to Churchill in an effort to persuade him to soften Eden:

> certain groups in the USA wanted us to take a much stronger even truculent position. The number that would like to see us clear out of Formosa is negligible. I know that on your side of the water you have the exact opposite ... the Nationalist troops and Chiang himself are not content now to accept irrevocably and permanently the status of 'prisoners' on the islands. They are held together by a conviction that some day they will go back to the mainland.

He argued that Quemoy and Matsos must be defended. Both Churchill and Eden felt the idea that Chiang Kai-shek's forces might attack the mainland was 'arrant nonsense', and it must be doubtful if Eisenhower really believed this himself.

Churchill replied to Eisenhower that a war to keep the coastal islands for Chiang 'would not be defensible here' and he could see 'no decisive relationship' between the offshore islands and an invasion of Formosa.

> It would surely be easy for the US to drown any would-be Chinese invaders of Formosa whether they started from Quemoy or elsewhere ... I do not think it would be right or wise for America to encourage him to keep alive the reconquest of the mainland to inspire his faithful followers.

He also urged Eisenhower to use the present lull to remove the 50,000 Nationalist troops from Quemoy and Matsos. On 16 February Dulles made a speech containing the phrase that 'further one-sided concessions are not the way to proceed'.

On 19 February Eisenhower replied to Churchill: 'What we have done has apparently been interpreted by the Chinese Communists merely as a sign of weakness ... further retreats become worse than a Munich.' He continued that he suspected the Chinese of being really interested in Formosa, and later on Japan; that the coastal islands were marginal, and that the Americans had not the 'capacity' to drown anybody who tried to cross the Formosa straits and therefore had to rely on 'a loyal and dependable force of Nationalists on Formosa to deal with the attackers'. The letter ended with what Eisenhower obviously thought would be a cogent argument:

> It would surely not be popular in this country if we become involved in possible hostilities on account of Hong Kong or Malaya which our people look on as 'colonies' which to us is a naughty word. Nevertheless I do not doubt that if the issue were ever framed in this way, we would be at your side.

Churchill wrote to Eden: 'It is a much better letter ... it is a real and sincere attempt to make us understand the American point of view. They do not mean to let Japan go red.'

With Dulles angry at Britain's refusal to join in a guarantee of Quemoy and Matsos, and Eden alarmed at the Americans' intention to use atomic weapons to defend the islands, their meeting on 23 February 1955 produced another clash. Dulles refused point-blank to have anything to do with the British plan for the Nationalists to withdraw from the islands in return for a pledge by China not to attack Formosa. Dulles told Eden aggressively that surrendering Quemoy and Matsos would increase the potential for a successful Chinese attack on Formosa and 'greatly weaken the morale of the Nationalists'.[23]

After Eden became Prime Minister on 6 April 1955, with Macmillan as Foreign Secretary, he remained convinced that the American refusal to allow the evacuation of Quemoy and Matsos was likely to start a third world war, and was ready to antagonize the Americans rather than alter his policy. On 19 April 1955 he told the Cabinet that they must be prepared for a Chinese Communist attack on Quemoy and Matsos during the election campaign, and on 4 May the Foreign Office produced two drafts of alternative press statements to be issued in the event of such an attack. One was to cover the eventuality of the Americans coming to the help of the Nationalists; the other in case the Americans decided not to oppose the attack. Both stressed that Britain had no commitment. Eden minuted to Macmillan: 'I would think that it would be better not to show them to Dulles at least while S-E Asia climate lasts.'[24] That Eden was prepared to put Anglo-American friendship at risk out of a conviction that a deal must be done with Chou En-lai is

evident from his minute to Macmillan of 23 April: 'It is only too clear
that so long as the Americans are unable to get Chiang out of the coastal
islands a Chinese attack on them would place our alliance in jeopardy.'

Macmillan had a better personal relationship with Dulles, but he toed
the Eden line, knowing that any attempt to depart from it would be
ill received by his temperamental master. In his memoirs he is unenlight-
ening over his attitude to the offshore islands controversy, although a
hint that as Foreign Secretary his views were at variance with Eden's
is given in an extract from his diary which states that he had thought
Eisenhower's reply to the British suggestion that Quemoy and Matsos
should be evacuated and a stand made only in Formosa and the Pescadores
was 'certainly a powerful, well-argued and persuasive document'.[25]

Fortunately the 1955 crisis over the offshore islands disappeared as
quickly as it had come, when the Chinese stopped bombarding the
islands. There followed a lull of three years; then, on 23 August 1958,
the Chinese Communists restarted the massive artillery bombardment of
Quemoy and Matsos. A daily event, it threatened to be a preliminary
to invasion. Although the islands were not an essential part of Formosa's
defence, being close to the mainland while Formosa lies comfortably 85
miles to the east, Chiang Kai-shek had positioned 80,000 of his best
troops (out of half a million) on Quemoy. Eisenhower's 1955 declaration
that the islands, like Formosa, would be defended by the USA still held
good in 1958, as it does today.

In early September 1958 Dulles escalated the crisis by giving a public
warning that the USA might use atomic weapons against China if it
invaded Quemoy. The British Government's view was that Dulles was
bluffing, and that the Americans would not take steps which might lead
to atomic war with Russia on account of these valueless islands. Selwyn
Lloyd, the Foreign Secretary, was on holiday when Macmillan received
a letter from Dulles on 4 September, following his statement that
America might use atomic weapons.

> It is no doubt regrettable that so much should now seem to hang upon two
> small islands such as Quemoy and Matsu [sic] which are so close to the China
> mainland that they are not readily defensible. We have in the past made
> serious efforts to bring about disengagement of the Chinese Nationalists
> from these islands. We have, however, never pushed these efforts to the
> point of attempted coercion because we have come up against realization
> of the hard fact that the ability to keep Formosa in friendly hands has not
> been separable from the National Government holding on to these islands.
> If we force their surrender, or if we allowed the Chinese Communists to
> force their surrender, there would, we estimate, be a rapid deterioration of
> the situation on Formosa.
>
> We have had a very careful study of the situation made by our intelligence

community, by the State Department officials, by the Joint Chiefs of Staff, and they are unanimous to the effect that if Quemoy were lost either through assault or surrender, this would have a serious impact upon the authority and military capacity of the present government on Formosa; that it would be exposed to subversive and military action which would probably bring about a government which would eventually advocate union with Communist China; that if this occurred it would seriously jeopardize the anti-Communist barrier, including Japan, the Republic of Korea, the Republic of China, the Republic of the Philippines, Thailand, and Vietnam; that other governments in South-East Asia such as those of Indonesia, Malaya, Cambodia, Laos and Burma would probably come fully under Communist influence; that Japan with its great industrial potential would probably fall within the Sino-Soviet orbit, and Australia and New Zealand would become strategically isolated.

There is also a question as to whether if we did intervene we could do so effectively without at least some use of atomic weapons; I hope no more than small air bursts without fallout. That is of course an unpleasant prospect but one I think we must face up to because our entire military establishment assumes more and more that the use of nuclear weapons will become normal in the event of hostilities. If this is not to be the case, then we face a very grave situation indeed in the face of the massive manpower of the Sino-Soviet bloc.[26]

Macmillan was horrified; Dulles's reference to atomic weapons made it clear than he was in deadly earnest about using them despite the risk of a major atomic war with Russia. Conscious of how Eden's robust opposition to Dulles in 1954 and 1955 had led to a serious deterioration in Anglo-American relations, he pursued a gentler and more statesman-like line: he was also worried because the Chinese were again making threats over Hong Kong. He wrote to Dulles on 5 September 1958:

From your analysis, it is obvious that you do not feel that as things now are, the position in Quemoy and Matsu can be abandoned without endangering the strategic balance in the Far East which is vital for the defence of the whole Free World. At the same time, you do not hide from yourself or from me that we may be on the edge of operations which could be the prelude to a third world war.

The new Commonwealth countries – India, Malaya, Ceylon, Ghana and etc. – will of course be against any action. I do not attach overwhelming importance to that, because they are always neutralist, but they have a considerable influence on Asiatic opinion at least. So far as Pakistan is concerned, I should think they would hope that the Chinese would not risk war, but would like to see some kind of settlement. In any case, they are not, I am afraid, very strong, either politically, economically, or in general influence.

Now for the old Commonwealth countries. You know the Canadian position well yourself, but I feel sure that they will be cautious at the best.

Australia, which is normally robust, will have anxieties about this area. On the one hand, they will be fearful of trouble which might involve them. On the other, they will no doubt be impressed by your analysis of what may happen if the Communists get away with it. Unfortunately, they are just approaching an election. New Zealand, also a robust little country, under Nash's leadership will tend to favour words rather than actions. South Africa will keep aloof.

As for this country, as I warned you in my first message, public opinion will not be easy to steer. We are on record in 1955 as having said that Formosa and the off-shore islands were in different juridical categories, and Churchill took the line that 'a war to keep the coastal islands for Chiang would not be defensible here'. This of course was in a private letter to the President but represented fairly the instinctive reaction of the man in the street.

I feel I should let you have this analysis of opinion because these are important factors in the problem. For if we have to face war, we also know from experience that even in the more tolerable contests of the past, something like unanimity of peoples is the only basis on which they can be induced to hold fast under its hardships.

Having said all this, which is not an attempt to do anything but set out the facts as objectively as I can, I agree with you that a Communist triumph by force, or even by the threat of force, might perhaps prove a Munich for the East.

What then are we to do? There is of course the possibility that after the President's statement, the Chinese Communists will avoid direct assault and try, at any rate in the first place, to make the position of the islands intolerable by ground bombardment and by blockade. I imagine their 12-mile Declaration is intended to give some legal cover to the latter, and it might well be that you could enable the defenders to withstand blockade by action that did not in itself lead to anything like the operations envisaged in your message. This would only follow, presumably, if you had to attack the air bases. But a sort of half-war could not continue indefinitely; there would be the risk at any moment of its enlarging itself in the way that you envisage, perhaps even, as you suggest, the use of atomic weapons.

Demilitarization can be, as I say, put forward publicly. If so, there are different ways in which it could be done: either in the Security Council or in a public statement by the British Government, or by some friendly but uncommitted government. Alternatively, we could approach the Russians privately.

It is possible that the Russians have privately agreed with the Chinese only to press the issue to a certain point and not to the point of war. In that case, they will have no serious anxieties; but it may be that they are themselves uncertain what will happen, and such a proposal then might be one by which, in one form or another, they would be attracted and press upon their allies. I can hardly believe that they and the Chinese have agreed to want a war. That would be contrary to the general Russian attitude.

But, of course, they may think that they can frighten you out of it by the weakness of your allies. It is that that I am determined to avoid if I can. It is in that spirit that I am sending you my personal appreciation of certain factors and the only positive proposal that seems at all practicable.[27]

On reading Macmillan's letter to Dulles, Eisenhower replied to the Prime Minister on 6 September:

> One major factor which may not be readily understood by those not in direct touch with the situation is Chiang's temperament and purposes. Any proposal that seems to him to imply retreat from his position as head of the only legitimate Chinese Government, any thought of abandoning a single foot of his defense perimeter, is automatically rejected. Indeed such rejection is so emphatic as to imply that if coercive efforts should be made to override his objection that would end his capacity to retain Formosa in friendly hands.

On 11 September Lloyd, having returned from a Spanish holiday, wrote a letter to Dulles trying to deter him from committing America to a war against the Chinese using atomic weapons:

> First, I share your views as to the Communist menace in the Far East. I believe in the importance of your containing line, i.e., Japan, South Korea, Okinawa, Formosa, South Vietnam, with such support as our position in Malaya and Hong Kong may afford. I believe that there is now beginning to be a wider recognition of the importance of this line than before although I must admit that for the past ten years Syngman Rhee and Chiang Kai shek have been exceedingly unpopular figures in the United Kingdom. Therefore, it should be an object of Western policy to seek to maintain and not to weaken this line until there is a change in the attitude of the Chinese Communists (if ever).
> Secondly, I must say that I feel that this line is weakened not strengthened by Chinese Nationalist retention of Quemoy and Matsu. The supply of their forces on the islands is hazardous, the islands themselves are very vulnerable to harassing fire by the Communists and their defence against attack is difficult. If that defence were to involve the use of even tactical nuclear weapons, then the risks involved for all of us by a process of chain-reaction are obvious. My view is that if a Nationalist withdrawal could be effected in a reasonable manner, it would strengthen not weaken Chiang Kai-shek and the anti-Communist line.
> But what is a 'reasonable manner'? I fully realize that if there is to be a withdrawal the Nationalists must have something to show for it. If the matter were to be referred to the Security Council, the Communist Chinese might refuse to take part in any discussion on Article 2(7) grounds and that refusal might help us. There are obvious dangers of the matter going to the General Assembly as an item although it is bound to be a subject of discussion in the General Debate. We await your views on a demilitarization solution although in their present frame of mind I doubt very much whether

the Communists would accept this even if the Nationalists did ...

Having regard to our 1955 statements, we are perhaps in a good position to float any idea which you do not want initially to sponsor yourself.[28]

Meanwhile, in response to a query about the military importance of Formosa and the Pescadores from the Prime Minister, Watkinson produced the Ministry of Defence appreciation, and on 11 September Lloyd wrote to Dulles:

What Churchill, Eden and Harold himself, when Foreign Secretary, stated in 1955 as our position over the off-shore islands is well-known to you. I have myself, whenever questioned, referred back to those statements as representing our views. Had Parliament been sitting now, no doubt I would have had a flood of questions designed to elicit the same answer.

Nevertheless, we want, as Harold put it in his message, to steer our public opinion towards an understanding of what is involved and to help and support you in any way that is possible. Your troubles are our troubles. In these days this is a matter of hard fact, not just sentiment. Therefore I want, so far as is possible having regard to our previous statements, to prevent any open difference of opinion as to how to handle the present situation being revealed between us and to try to work together towards a common position.

Formosa is of little direct military value, and the West would probably have been better off if Chiang Kai-shek had never managed to hold on to it. On the other hand if he were pushed out of it by Communist Chinese the resulting loss of face for the West might well set off a chain reaction throughout South-East Asia which would totally undermine the morale of the SEATO alliance and sooner or later make Malaya and Singapore untenable.

In Washington Harold Caccia, the newly appointed British Ambassador, talked to Dulles, and the American gave the ambassador the impression of being 'extremely worried' and 'aware' that he had not got the full support of his public, let alone of the outside world, for a tough policy over the offshore islands. Caccia commented: 'it would be only human for him to look round for a scapegoat. I trust that by following our present line we shall avoid the role.'

On 15 September the leader of the Opposition Hugh Gaitskell took a hand, writing to Macmillan expressing concern:

Like your predecessor [Anthony Eden] we regard Quemoy and the other offshore islands as part of mainland China. We therefore consider the claim of the Peking Government to them legitimate and that they should long since have been evacuated by the Chinese Nationalists instead of being reinforced. We do not accept that from the military angle they are of any importance to the defence of Formosa.

Britain should not support, still less participate in, a war to defend these islands, Gaitskell insisted, and it was the Government's duty to do everything possible to dissuade the US from engaging in such a war. He was also disturbed by reports that the US were prepared to use nuclear weapons to defend Quemoy; public opinion in Britain and Europe was completely opposed to war over Quemoy.

The immediate problem, Macmillan replied, was not the present or future status of the offshore islands; it was whether a dispute of this nature should be settled by force. On that point Macmillan said the Government strongly supported its American friends, and 'we should be playing into Communist hands to allow ourselves to take a public attitude on difficulties with the Americans which we hope jointly to overcome'. Macmillan intentionally sent his reply to Gaitskell late in the evening so that the leader of the Opposition was plagued by journalists in the early hours of the morning. John Wyndham, Macmillan's political secretary, minuted to Macmillan the next day: 'the press including the members of the opposition press, e.g. the *Daily Mirror*, think that your reply to Gaitskell last night and the manner in which it was effected was a *tour de force*. Your technique is the talk of Fleet Street tonight.'[29]

On 19 September Lloyd went to Washington for talks with Dulles; there Dulles told him that 'if the United States were seen to give in to Chinese Communist force which was backed by the Soviet Union the US would be finished everywhere in the Far East. The whole area was so brittle and so dependent on the US as a prop.' Dulles also outlined the difficulties the Americans were having with Chiang Kai-shek. The situation was not expected to become critical for a week or two, Lloyd reported, but if no negotiated settlement had been reached by then and the supply situation had become impossible it was the intention of the Americans to permit the Nationalist forces to attack the Communist shore batteries; and if this proved ineffective the Americans would then take action themselves.

> I still think that they will try first with conventional explosives but if that is not speedily effective they will very soon use nuclear bombs. Whether and if so we should attempt to dissuade them from this course in the circumstances of the imminent collapse of the off-shore islands is a matter which requires very careful consideration.

US public opinion, Lloyd concluded, was still unaware of the genuine efforts Dulles was making for a negotiated settlement. Eisenhower himself told Lloyd he was more worried about Quemoy than anything else in a long time; it had lost him sleep and put him off his golf.[30]

After seeing the President Lloyd reported his conclusions to the Prime Minister:

(a) The President realizes very well in what a bad posture the United States' Government is over the islands. He said again and again that it did not stand to reason to fight for these two islands. If there had to be a fight, the four imprisoned United States airmen were a much better issue. The American people understood about them but not about Quemoy and Matsu.

(b) A retreat enforced by Chinese military action is impossible for the President to tolerate.

(c) His personal views on the use of nuclear weapons against the Communist batteries are reassuring.

(d) He did not reject the idea of a Foreign Ministers' meeting if the Warsaw talks [between China and the US, regarding the Formosa/Matsu question] failed. With regard to it being between Dulles and Chou, he seemed to consider it a practical proposition. With regard to a wider meeting, I cannot put it higher than that he was politely interested.

(e) He, like Dulles, is ready to go a long way in pressure on the Chinese Nationalists. He is even considering the possibility of an alternative regime to Chiang. He is anxious to have a full discussion with us about the implications for the Western Powers of changes in American policy over Formosa. For example, how to handle the overseas Chinese.[31]

Fortunately the British Cabinet never had to face up to a decision whether or not to support the Americans in the use of atomic weapons against the Chinese in defence of the offshore islands. In October China suddenly and unexpectedly announced that the heavy bombardment would only take place on the odd days of the month, and in March 1962 it ceased altogether. The crisis was defused. Why the shelling ended remains a mystery even today. Almost certainly Khrushchev influenced the Chinese to desist; and the fear of a nuclear war, with the Americans much stronger technically than the Russians or Chinese, was a potent factor. The author has produced much hitherto unknown detail from the official archives because it has been insufficiently realized by historians how near the world was to a major nuclear war, and how the Macmillan Government came closer than either the Eden or Churchill governments to supporting the Americans in the use of nuclear weapons.

---

*At the end of 1957 there were 450 US subjects imprisoned in China (including some USAF personnel) as a result of the Korean War. Mothers had been allowed to visit prisoners but Chou En-lai refused leniency. The case aroused much publicity and indignation in America.

CHAPTER 17

Home Affairs

AFTER FIVE YEARS of deliberation the Royal Commission on Capital Punishment reported in 1953, but not until 1954 was Parliament given time to debate its conclusions; even then the Government only wanted to take note of the report. The Royal Commission was barred by its terms of reference from concluding whether or not the death penalty should be abolished. However the report was clear enough in its conclusion: 'In this country a stage has been reached where little more can be done effectively to limit the liability to suffer the death penalty and . . . the issue is now whether capital punishment should be retained or abolished.'

This was encouraging for the abolitionists, and the Howard League for Penal Reform, the pressure group monitoring the administration of criminal justice, pointed out that the question of abolition or retention 'had always been the basic issue and that Parliament should not shirk it now'. The Churchill Government wanted to shirk it, but the Labour MP Sydney Silverman had made up his mind that they should not be allowed to do so. After the defeat of his amendment refusing agreement to a government motion that the Royal Commission Report 'be noted' and urging action instead, he presented in November 1955 a private member's bill which the Prime Minister, Anthony Eden, generously allowed a second reading on 12 March 1956. This bill proposed total abolition of the death penalty, and during the committee stage all the amendments for retaining it in certain cases were defeated except for the one concerning those already serving life sentences. This was a sop to the prison service who were worried that abolition might result in murders of warders by convicted murderers. However it was pointed out that there had been no such murder for 150 years, since a prisoner in Newgate had used a beer tankard to brain a warder who had been playing cards with him.

On its second reading in the House the Silverman Bill obtained a majority of twenty-four. Just enough Conservative MPs voted for it, defying their Conservative constituency associations who were all vehemently opposed to abolition. On the third reading in the Lords the Lord

Chancellor, Lord Kilmuir, urged the bill's rejection. A former Home Secretary, he denounced the bill as 'an unwise and dangerous measure, the presence of which on the statute book would be a disaster for the country and a menace to the people'. The Lords rejected the Silverman Bill by 238 to 95. In the *New Statesman* Silverman wrote that the peers who voted against the bill 'came from the hills and forests of darkest Britain; the lame, the deaf, the obscure, the senile and the forgotten, the hereditary peers of Britain united in their determination to use their medieval powers to retain a medieval institution.'[1]

Silverman, however, had made it clear to the Government that there was a majority in the Commons in favour of reform of the death penalty. Accordingly a Cabinet committee under Lord Kilmuir was set up to examine the issue, and produced a Cabinet memorandum recommending limited abolition. The Cabinet could not make up their collective mind to accept this, and on 26 July were told that it was open to doubt whether a sufficient number of Conservative MPs would find such a bill acceptable. On 31 July 1956 it was pointed out to the Cabinet that the Government would be embarrassed if it 'failed to assume responsibility for a matter which so closely affected law and order', and when Parliament reassembled at the end of October the Cabinet authorized Kilmuir to introduce a bill based on the memorandum he had produced for the exemptions of certain categories of murder.

At the Conservative Party Conference at Llandudno in October 1956 there were thirty-three motions favouring the retention of capital punishment – more than on any other subject. A resolution in favour of retaining capital punishment was passed with tremendous enthusiasm, one delegate exclaiming: 'Thank God for the House of Lords.' The only delegate who spoke in opposition was howled down and asked by the chairman to leave the rostrum without finishing his speech.

No Tory abolitionist MP was in evidence. Richard Hornby, who had recently won the Tonbridge by-election, had voted for the Silverman Bill. When asked by the author why the abolitionist MPs kept quiet at Llandudno, he replied that by securing a majority for the Silverman Bill they had forced the Government to take action; in doing so he, like the others, had incurred the wrath of his constituency chairman. 'There was no need for us to put our heads on the block again when we had done the job,' he said.

Eden, however, ignored the conference, telling the Commons on 23 October that the Government would introduce a bill to curtail but not to abolish capital punishment. Although this did not satisfy the abolitionists, the will of Parliament had in part been accepted by the Cabinet.[2]

The Homicide Act 1957 abolished the death penalty for certain degrees of murder. The crime was divided into two categories: 'murder' and 'capital murder'. Clause 5 preserved the death penalty for murders in the course or furtherance of theft; murders by shooting or by creating an explosion; murder of police officers and murder of prison officers. Clause 6(1) preserved the death penalty where a person convicted of murder had previously been convicted of another murder.

Abolitionists like Sydney Silverman bitterly criticized the bill; Silverman emphasized that it was ridiculous to single out murder by firearms as a special kind of murder liable to the death penalty, pointing out of Ruth Ellis, the last woman to be hanged after shooting her lover, that 'If only she had used a hatchet she would have been all right.' On the government side there was little complaint against the bill, but scarcely any enthusiasm for it.

After Eden's resignation as Prime Minister the Homicide Bill had its third reading in the Commons on 21 March 1957, after passing its third reading in the Lords on 19 March 1957; it received the Royal Assent on 21 March 1957. From then on judges and juries had to decide what was capital murder and what was simple murder. This was a difficult enough matter for the courts and the question of reprieve was made even more difficult for the Home Secretary, as Rab Butler soon found out.*

Butler has recorded that as Home Secretary he inherited the 'rather curious Homicide Act of 1957' which restricted the death penalty not to the types of murder which were regarded as the most wicked, but to those in which the deterrent effect of capital punishment was believed to be most likely to operate to the maintenance of law and order. To reach a decision on a reprieve he had to shut himself up in the Home Office 'for two days or more'. His widow, Mollie Butler, told the author that when Rab first became Home Secretary he was not an abolitionist, but his experiences there made him change his mind; before he left the Home Office he was a convinced abolitionist. (Lady Butler was always an abolitionist after her first husband had been concerned with capital punishment as High Sheriff of Essex.) Butler himself recorded that at the end of his time at the Home Office he was convinced that 'the system could not go on.'[3] His most difficult decision, he writes, was whether to reopen the case of Timothy Evans who had been hanged for the murder of his wife and child; but despite his initial doubts he refused to reopen the case. He was also disturbed by the execution of Derek Bentley, who had been hanged although his younger accomplice, Christopher Craig, who was under age, had actually committed the murder.

On 8 February 1961 Butler submitted a memorandum to the Cabinet

---

*Under the 1957 Act 48 people were sentenced to death for capital murder; 19 were reprieved.

pointing out that he was under 'considerable pressure to do something about capital punishment'. The Howard League and the National Campaign for the Abolition of Capital Punishment had been obtaining a good deal of publicity, arguing for abolition and spotlighting the miscarriage of justice in the cases of Ruth Ellis, Derek Bentley and Timothy Evans. Many Conservatives, so Butler pointed out in his memorandum, wanted him to restore the death penalty for all murders, arguing that the murder rate had risen; the abolitionists as usual maintained that there was no evidence that the death penalty 'has a uniquely deterrent effect and that the only thing to do is to abolish it altogether'.

Butler's view was that if the present law were to be changed there were only two alternatives – either to restore the death penalty for all murders or to abolish it altogether; it would be neither practical nor desirable to modify the present categories of murder. He therefore proposed to leave the law unchanged. He was also anxious to prevent it becoming an election issue: an abolition bill at this moment, he told his colleagues, would be opposed by a majority of their own supporters, whilst a bill restoring the death penalty for all murders would be opposed by a vocal minority of Conservatives as well as the Opposition.

On 12 February 1961 the Cabinet endorsed the Home Secretary's recommendations, and capital punishment was not debated again by the Cabinet during Macmillan's premiership.* With the swing to Labour in the 1964 General Election many of the Conservative MPs adamantly opposed to abolition left the Commons and were replaced by Labour MPs who were abolitionists. Consequently when in December 1964 the Wilson Government allowed time for the Silverman private bill for the abolition of the death penalty, it had an easy passage through Parliament.[4]

The problem of immigration from the Empire began to attract attention in 1954 and 1955 under the Churchill Government. Churchill was ready to legislate to control entry, and secret plans were drawn up by the Cabinet. The Cabinet archives show that the problem was stated with admirable clarity but no firm decision was ever taken. The dilemma

---

* The release in the PRO of the 1964 archives shows that in September 1964, a month before the General Election forced the Conservatives out of power, Alec Home, the Prime Minister, and Henry Brooke, the Home Secretary, had agreed that the 1957 Homicide Act was unworkable following a civil service minute that the distinction between capital and non-capital murder was 'inherently unsound'. But with public opinion on the issue divided, they decided to do nothing. However a note of their conversation ends with the conclusion: 'The next Home Secretary of whatever party will have to abolish the death penalty.'

for the Churchill Government was that, although there was an acute shortage of labour, grave problems were being caused in south London and elsewhere by the influx of West Indian workers from Jamaica.

Well-publicized complaints were made by white residents in Brixton and Tiger Bay, Cardiff, while Mr Macpherson, Jamaica's Minister of Labour, stated with considerable publicity that he would take no steps to stop emigration 'because there were jobs for all in Britain'. Churchill was concerned and the Colonial Office reported to Downing Street that an estimated 40,000 to 50,000 'colonial people' were resident in Britain with the greatest concentration in London, Liverpool and Cardiff. The main source was Jamaica with an average of 3,000 immigrants a year from 1945 to 1952.[5]

Reviewing the situation in a Cabinet memorandum in January 1954, the Home Secretary David Maxwell-Fyfe (before his elevation to the Lords as Lord Kilmuir) reported that colonial governments were trying to stem the flow by tightening up dock control to prevent stowaways. Over and above this, Maxwell-Fyfe advised that immigration officers should be given powers to deport British subjects to their places of origin, but 'there could be no question of seeking such power to deal only with coloured people' because it would be a 'complete break with the traditional principle that any British subject had a right to enter freely and remain in the UK'. When in October race riots in London were reported in the national press Churchill asked for details from the Home Office and was told that the reports of widespread violence against blacks were exaggerated.[6]

In October 1954 Gwilym Lloyd George, replacing Maxwell-Fyfe as Home Secretary, quickly decided that there was a need for laws to curb coloured immigration and he found the Prime Minister ready to act. In November Lloyd George told the Cabinet that 'the rate of immigration had greatly increased in recent months, and it was now expected that about 10,000 would come to this country from the West Indies in 1954, as compared with a little over 2,000 in 1953.' In three or four years, his memorandum continued, this would 'raise the coloured population to a total of something like 100,000', and as the law stood, there was 'no means of putting any limit on the number of Commonwealth citizens from overseas who may choose to settle here'; the only way to restrict immigration was to impose control similar to that imposed on aliens, but it should not be extended to Ireland. Lloyd George asked for a Departmental Committee to report, and for permission to make a Commons statement; and he suggested that the Prime Minister should mention it first to the leader of the Opposition.

The Cabinet agreed to a Departmental Committee, but not to an approach to Attlee nor a statement in the Commons. In the course of discussion Lord Swinton, the Commonwealth Relations Secretary, suggested that if Ireland were excluded from immigration controls the Government would be criticized in Commonwealth countries for giving more favourable treatment to a country which had left the Commonwealth than to countries which had remained within it. But in this Swinton was a lone voice; though influential and able, he was a relic of the Baldwin and Chamberlain Cabinets with their commitment to the Empire.

Alan Lennox-Boyd, the Colonial Secretary, was the rock on which immigration control foundered. In a paper dated 4 December he told the Cabinet he would have 'the gravest misgivings' if legislation applied predominantly to coloured persons. On 6 December the Cabinet revoked its previous decision to appoint a Departmental Committee on the grounds that it might produce a minority report which would make government action difficult; instead they asked for a draft bill.[7]

On 12 January 1955 Norman Brook, Secretary to the Cabinet, minuted to the Prime Minister that the draft bill would empower immigration officers to prohibit the entry of immigrants unable to support themselves. However, the next day the Cabinet postponed the issue by asking for a White Paper to set out the existing restrictions imposed on the entry of British subjects into other Commonwealth countries. The civil servants found it impossible to draft such a White Paper satisfactorily because of the complexity and number of these regulations. Harold Macmillan (then Minister of Defence) was not satisfied, and sent a note to Eden (then Foreign Secretary) proposing a private bill in the House of Lords, legislation being 'hopeless' unless it was agreed beforehand by all parties.

Meanwhile sections of the Conservative Party had become agitated, and Cyril Osborne, a right-wing MP, introduced under the ten-minute rule a bill restricting coloured immigration. On 27 January the Conservative Parliamentary Party's Commonwealth Affairs Committee discussed the Osborne Bill. According to the Government Whip present, Osborne explained his draft but 'had not carried the committee', and the Whip stated that in his opinion debate on the bill would degenerate into a colour bar wrangle, and 'an administrative solution giving the Home Secretary power to deport undesirables after conviction' would be much more effective than controversial legislation. The Whip continued that an awkward situation would arise if leave to bring in Osborne's ten-minute rule bill was refused by the House, as was likely, because then the Government's hands would be tied. Osborne had replied to the discussion and lost his temper. There was 'grave disquiet' in the committee and the feeling that, if Osborne persisted, 'he will, because he is so easily baited by the Opposition, put his foot right in it'.

The Cabinet discussed the Whip's report on 31 January, but decided not to act. A fortnight later they revoked their decision to publish a White Paper on the restrictions on immigration operated by other Commonwealth countries, because it would be too difficult to get all the countries to agree its contents.[8]

On 16 March the Cabinet was informed that at the meeting of the Central Council of Conservative Associations, to be held next day, attention would be drawn to the increasing immigration of black and Asian workers, and laws requested to enable undesirables to be deported. This was the last time the Churchill Government discussed immigration, and they had reached no conclusion.

On 20 April 1955, after Eden had succeeded Churchill, Lloyd George minuted the Prime Minister that although he had a draft bill ready he preferred a Departmental Committee of Inquiry prior to legislation. During the General Election of that year Lloyd George wanted to make a speech saying that, if the Government were returned, it would legislate against uncontrolled immigration; but the Cabinet would not agree to this.[9]

On 10 June 1955, following the election, Lloyd George in a Cabinet paper estimated that in 1955 about 20,000 coloured persons would come from the West Indies to Britain; they tended to congregate in overcrowded streets, especially in the Midlands and certain parts of London, 'which is beyond the resources of the housing authorities concerned to prevent or alleviate'. There were no means of controlling the influx, he felt, without legislation. His draft bill, he continued, would be 'highly controversial', but controversy would be reduced if the bill were based on the recommendations of an 'impartial committee'. He suggested the formation of a Departmental Committee to report in time for legislation in 1956, under the chairmanship of Lord Radcliffe, with as its other members the Earl of Crawford and Balcarres; John Sparrow, the Warden of All Souls, or Sir David Lindsay Keir, Master of Balliol. He said that the Commonwealth Secretary, Lord Home, agreed with his recommendation, but that the Colonial Secretary, Lennox-Boyd, had reservations.

The Cabinet jibbed at setting up so imposing a committee and decided instead to ask the Home Secretary for an Inter-Departmental Committee of officials to prepare a report suitable for publication on the growing influx of coloured workers. On 18 August this committee, chaired by William Cornish, Under-Secretary at the Home Office, produced a long report, together with an appendix suitable for publication. It pointed out that reaction in India and elsewhere would be much greater to a statement about 'coloured people' than to one about West Indians alone, and that immigration from the 'old Dominions' had 'never given rise to difficulties'.

The Irish were included within the terms of reference of the committee; an estimated 750,000 had entered the UK since the end of the war, and were prepared to live in condemned premises and put up with conditions which English people would not normally tolerate, but there were not the same difficulties over the Irish as over black and Asian people because 'the Irish are not . . . a different race from the ordinary inhabitants of Great Britain'. Controls on the Irish were not proposed, and the committee thought the Government should argue boldly that the whole British Isles were for historical and geographical reasons 'one'. The report went on that the absence of laws to restrict immigration, in a world in which other countries with similar or better standards of living universally exercised such powers, is 'hard to defend'.[10]

The appendix for publication stated that the recent influx of West Indians, probably amounting to 20,000 a year, was a new development, and that taking into account 8,000 Indians and Pakistanis some 30,000 black and Asian immigrants a year were coming to the United Kingdom. However, there was no evidence that these immigrants were finding it difficult to obtain work, and they had made 'a useful contribution' to manpower resources. Nor was there evidence that they were making undue demands on National Assistance, although there was evidence that West Indian men in London played a large part in illicit drug trafficking in cannabis and accounted for 'a disproportionate number of the convictions in London for living on the immoral earnings of women'. They found no evidence of racial tension, apart from one or two isolated incidents, and black and Asian workers made a favourable impression on buses and trains.[11]

However, the bulk of the immigrants had congregated in relatively few areas, mainly in London and the Midlands, where there was already an acute housing shortage, and there had been 'scandalous overcrowding' with several single people or even families sharing one room. This had created a grave problem for the housing authorities, whose resources were quite inadequate to cope with the problem. It was known that many of these immigrants hoped to bring their families here, and should any large-scale influx of families take place 'the situation might quickly become critical'. A further significant influx into areas of unsatisfactory housing 'might well lead to developments in which it would be difficult to avoid racial problems arising'. There was no power to prevent any British subject, whatever his origin, from entering Britain, and no control was possible without an amendment of the law, which could be drafted to exclude Commonwealth citizens and the Irish, and to apply only to certain categories, such as West Indians.

The report concluded that there would be little difficulty in administering a scheme to restrict entry to those who had employment permits and suitable living accommodation, and that such controls ought to be supported by making approved employment or continued residence in suitable accommodation 'a condition of continuing stay'; enforcement of any system of entry control could be carried out by the Immigration Service, if it was enlarged, although this would involve delays at the airports. The statement emphasized that controls must not prejudice the widespread practice among people of all parts of the Commonwealth from visiting this country for study, business and recreation.[12]

As he was going to be abroad when the matter was discussed in Cabinet on 30 August, Lord Home wrote a memorandum for the Cabinet, in which he emphasized that the Government did not want to keep out immigrants of good type from the old Dominions, and that it was politically impossible to legislate for a colour bar. He was prepared to agree to discrimination against West Indians, but took up the cudgels for citizens from India, Pakistan and Ceylon, though agreeing that the number of working-class Indians coming to Britain had increased in the last year and 'unless checked this could become a menace'. However, he thought the governments of India and Pakistan were 'genuinely ready to do what they can to stop immigration'. He felt there was a danger that India and Pakistan might introduce retaliatory restrictions on the entry or residence of the British business community, and he wanted the reference to the 8,000 Indians and Pakistanis arriving each year deleted from the published document.

When the Eden Cabinet met to discuss immigration on 15 September they had before them the Committee report and Lord Home's memorandum. The civil servants were sure that curbs on West Indian immigrants would be put in hand. After all, here was an authoritative report written in sombre, matter-of-fact language which made it crystal-clear that Britain had a problem which was on the brink of becoming critical and could only be solved by legislation. It seemed inconceivable that the Eden Cabinet would flout the civil servants' advice. But that is what happened.

On 15 September the Cabinet accepted the principles of the report and asked Lloyd George to circulate a draft bill with permissive powers to prohibit the entry of overseas subjects who had neither a home nor a job. On 3 November the draft bill was discussed by the Cabinet. They had before them a memorandum by Lennox-Boyd, dated 31 October, stating that 'I must go on record that I could not agree to legislation confined to colonial immigrants.' This indicated a clear intention to resign if the bill was proceeded with, and this threat stopped Eden from acting. Lennox-Boyd was witty and flamboyant, popular in the Conservative Party, and a close friend of Eden's.

In Cabinet on 3 November Lloyd George spoke in favour of his draft bill. Lennox-Boyd argued against it, saying that it was 'inexpedient' and would be criticized as 'social discrimination'. He suggested rather implausibly that 'the preferable course was ... to disperse the colonial immigrants more evenly over the UK.' It was stated, almost certainly by Lord Salisbury, Lord President of the Council, that 'if immigration from the colonies and, for that matter, from India and Pakistan, were allowed to continue unchecked, there was a real danger that over the years there would be a significant change in the racial character of the English people.'

The Cabinet discussed admitting immigrants to work for a period 'not exceeding five years', after which they might be sent home – a proposal that might meet the present need for labour with less prejudice to social conditions. Such a scheme would have resembled the *Gastarbeiter* scheme under which West Germany was recruiting Turkish workers for employment but not for settlement. The view was also expressed on economic grounds that 'immigration was a welcome means of augmenting our labour resources.'

Eden summed up and effectively killed the draft bill by saying that further thought needed to be given to the problem before the Cabinet could decide whether legislation should be introduced.[13] Churchill had been ready for strong action, but Eden was not, and refused to follow up Churchill's move to close the door on unrestricted immigration. Eden loved the rhetoric of a new multiracial Commonwealth, and disliked the prospect of controversial legislation which might spoil his image as a moderate in home politics.

A supplementary report was presented to the Cabinet in November 1956 when Eden was away ill. Opening the discussion, Kilmuir, the Lord Chancellor, gave it as the view of the committee set up under his chairmanship to review the problem that, even if regulation of Commonwealth immigration was decided upon, there were 'solid reasons for excluding the Irish Republic'; moreover the demand for black and Asian immigrants in employment had not yet reached 'saturation point', while 'the acceleration in the rate of immigration which had been the cause of concern in recent years seemed to have been checked.' Lennox-Boyd noted that the reports of conditions in Britain which immigrants were sending to their families and friends were less optimistic now, and that this was likely to check the flow.

Lord Salisbury said that he remained disquieted, and if regulation was instituted he doubted whether it would be right to continue preferential treatment for the Irish. There was support for Lord Salisbury's anti-Irish view, but the committee concluded also that the trend of coloured immigration and of unemployment amongst coloured people had disclosed nothing to make the problem more urgent than when it was last reviewed in July, and it was agreed that there should be a further report in the following spring. That was the end of the immigration controversy under the Eden Government: the nation might have been spared many tears if the draft bill had been put to Parliament in 1955.[14]

Becoming Prime Minister in January 1957, Macmillan was sensitive about immigration, and on 21 June he minuted to Butler, the Home Secretary, and Lennox-Boyd, the Colonial Secretary: 'What is the position now about the West Indian immigrants into the United Kingdom? You remember at one time we were considering dealing with this problem by legislation. Is the flow increasing or decreasing? Do you think this is something we ought to face or not?'

On 3 July Butler replied that the problem had been kept under constant review by the Lord Chancellor's committee set up by the Eden Government:

> The total number of West Indians in this country continues to increase but the flow of immigrants has displayed a continuous and striking fall since last summer. The total net immigration in 1957 is unlikely to be anything approaching the figure of 29,000 for 1956. Immigration from India and Pakistan, however, although on a smaller scale, shows no sign of abating. The presence of some 120,000 coloured people in this country has not so far given rise to such difficulties as to make legislation imperative, and the Lord Chancellor's Committee will be reporting accordingly, although it will recommend that the trend of immigration should be closely watched.

The ensuing report to the Cabinet by Kilmuir's Committee made the point that since the peak rate of immigration was reached in June 1956 arrivals had dropped steeply, and although numbers had tended to rise slightly for the first five months of the year they were running at rather less than half the level of the previous year. However even this reduced rate of immigration was capable of giving rise to problems, particularly 'where it produces black pockets of population who monopolize housing'.

Although public opinion, Kilmuir continued, would not at present accept introduction of legislation to restrict the flow of immigrants, the Government should be ready to take action if the situation deteriorated; in that event these powers should take the form not of a quota system which would raise considerable difficulties but of the prohibition of entry into the United Kingdom of any British subject from the Commonwealth who could not demonstrate that he had both authorized employment and suitable housing.

Burke Trend, Deputy Secretary to the Cabinet, advised the Prime Minister that the committee's proposals were 'eminently reasonable', and suggested that the Lord Chancellor's Committee ought to make a further report on the situation in six months' time.[15] Macmillan accordingly advised the Cabinet that no action on curbing immigration was necessary.

In September 1958 however there were disturbing race riots in London and elsewhere, and Macmillan minuted to Home on 2 September 1958 that the time had come to consider legislation again. The police reported to Butler, the Home Secretary, on 4 September that in certain areas of London there was widespread resentment over the influx of black and Asian people, and much resentment that black landlords were trying to get rid of white tenants, 'and much hostility caused by coloured men known to be living off the immoral earnings of white prostitutes'. This had produced serious disorders on 30 August after local incidents in June and July; these latest disorders were caused by white hooligans but there was no reason to believe the disturbances were in any way organized from outside. 'The most disturbing feature was that the people concerned were carrying the most damaging offensive weapons such as razors and leather-studded straps and this had led to an increase in the number of coloured people carrying offensive weapons.'

When Butler, Home and Lennox-Boyd met visiting Ministers from the West Indies on 8 September Butler referred to the recent disturbances and assured the West Indians that the Government had no intention of making any changes in the traditional policy of free entry to immigrants from the Commonwealth, but he warned that if there was unemployment black immigrants should be discouraged from coming in substantial numbers. Norman Manley, Chief Minister of Jamaica, said that none of the West Indian governments would want to legislate to restrict the flow. Two days later Lennox-Boyd held a discussion with the West Indian Ministers and reported to them the Ministry of Labour view that Britain had reached 'saturation point'. The West Indians agreed to publicize the serious unemployment situation in the United Kingdom, and to take action to slow down the issue of passports, perhaps extending the period between application and grant of passport from five days to six months. 'They all argued strongly that they should not be asked to stop the issue of all passports even for a limited period, as this would be politically impossible and lead to a serious loss of faith in the United Kingdom.'

By February 1959 the situation had deteriorated and Kilmuir's Committee recommended to the Cabinet that a comprehensive Immigration Bill should be studied, but they were satisfied it need not be introduced in the present Parliament on the grounds that the flow of immigrants was showing a marked reduction which reflected the success of discussions with Commonwealth governments, and also the less favourable prospects of employment in the United Kingdom. However the majority of the committee favoured a bill during the present Parliament legalizing the deportation of undesirable Commonwealth immigrants.

The committee set out for the Cabinet the arguments for and against legislation; these turned on whether the Government would lose more face by failing to take action than by introducing a bill 'which involves a departure from our traditional policy of avoiding discrimination between British subjects as regards entry to this country'. The committee pointed out that there had been no recurrence of race riots and immigration seemed to be declining so that 'it may be thought unwise to stir up what may probably become a controversial matter at this stage in the life of the present Parliament: it might be preferable to defer action until the next Parliament.'[16] At the 1958 Tory Conference the previous October, in reply to a motion calling for curbs on immigration, Butler had said in an unguarded moment: 'We should maintain the long and respected tradition of allowing Commonwealth citizens to come here . . . It is very unlikely that the Government in the new session [1959] will seek a power of deportation.'

The Lord Chancellor's Committee raised the question of whether there should be any statement on control and deportation of immigrants in the Conservative 1959 election manifesto. However in view of Butler's downright statement at the 1958 Tory Conference it was decided to avoid this. Surprisingly immigration was not an issue in the 1959 General Election except in North Kensington where Sir Oswald Mosley, the former Fascist leader, argued that as many immigrants as possible should be sent home at government expense.

After the 1959 General Election the immigration problem became more acute. Fred Bishop, Macmillan's private secretary, wrote an important brief for the Prime Minister on 25 July 1960, pointing out that in the first six months of 1960, 19,500 immigrants had arrived –

> a good deal more than for some years past – and this has given rise to representations to the Home Secretary from both sides of the House. The Home Secretary [Butler] does not suggest any action at present other than trying to persuade the governments of the West Indies to discourage their immigrants from setting out. But he says if this is not successful it might be necessary to control immigration and to consider some form of statutory control.[17]

The Cabinet agreed that no legislation should be introduced for the time being. However immigration continued to increase, and at a meeting of Kilmuir's Commonwealth Immigrants Committee on 16 February 1961 there was agreement that 'the present level of immigration raised problems which could not be ignored' as the various problems of housing, health and unemployment became more acute, and a serious situation would eventually arise.

Butler reported to the Kilmuir Committee on 17 May 1961 that the figures for black and Asian immigration for the first four months of 1961 were substantially larger than for the corresponding period of 1960 which was itself a peak year.

> These latest figures suggest that the total net intake for 1961 would be in the order of 150,000, or possibly over 200,000 compared to 58,000 in 1960, and by the end of the year the coloured population would amount to half a million. As in previous years the majority of immigrants came from the West Indies although the highest rate of increase was for Pakistanis. The passport control introduced by the Indian and Pakistani governments seemed to have broken down completely. Immigrants readily obtained passports for the Middle East, and then came on to this country . . . it was now accepted by government supporters that some form of control was unavoidable if we were not to have a colour problem in this country on a similar scale to the USA.

Both Butler and Iain Macleod, who had replaced Lennox-Boyd as Colonial Secretary after the 1959 General Election, were in principle opposed to controls but in the face of these statistics they could not maintain their objections. However in the ensuing discussion Macleod said that an immediate announcement might have 'grave repercussions' on the current moves to establish a federation in the West Indies (in the event this federation was a failure).

The Minister of Labour Edward Heath reported to the committee that his department had produced a scheme by which immigrants would be divided into three categories – skilled workers; immigrants coming to a job with a named employer, and others. The first two categories would be allowed in without restriction but those in the third category would have to apply by post to the Ministry of Labour who would grant 'permits on a first come first served basis' but with absolute control over the total number admitted. The committee agreed this was the most promising method so far considered.[18]

The committee decided to recommend to the Cabinet that 'the balance of advantage lay in favour of legislative control in the face of the sharp rise in figures and despite the objections of principle.' The committee's view was accepted by the Cabinet, and the Commonwealth Immigrants Bill was drafted. Butler as Home Secretary, and Macleod, now moved from Colonial Secretary to Leader of the House, had to see it through Parliament.

Irish citizens were excluded from controls. In his report to the Cabinet on 26 May 1961 Kilmuir wrote:

> I see no alternative but to be frank about the Irish if the question is raised, taking our stand upon the same consideration which led us in the context

of nationality to treat Irish citizens as if they were British subjects – a useful precedent in the present circumstances. It would also be impracticable to have a comprehensive control of Commonwealth citizens entering this country via the Irish Republic; for the rest we would hope to obtain – as we do over aliens – the co-operation of the immigration authorities of the Irish Republic in operating a control similar to ours.

Kilmuir advised that there should be proposals for deportations on the lines agreed in the draft bill of 1958–9 which would enable the courts to recommend the deportation of Commonwealth citizens with less than five years' residence in the UK and not belonging to the United Kingdom by birth, descent or naturalization, who were convicted of any offence carrying liability to imprisonment.[19] The Cabinet agreed and a bill was prepared on the lines of Kilmuir's memorandum and was given a place in the Queen's Speech, while Butler informed the Tory Conference in October 1961 of this intention – doing so in Macmillan's opinion with 'no great distinction' although he recorded that Butler handled the debate in the Commons 'skilfully'.

The bill was published in November and came under heavy attack, Macmillan claiming that he had never seen the Commons in 'so hysterical a mood'. Macmillan was particularly indignant at the attacks in *The Times* by its editor, Sir William Haley, who stated: 'it would be best if the bill could be thrown out altogether.'[20]

In the debate on the Queen's Speech Macleod revealed his deep distaste for the bill, saying 'I detest the necessity for it in this country,' but when charged with acting in unseemly haste Macleod replied with truth that 'We have taken years to consider it.' To the 1922 Committee Macleod stated: 'If steps had not now been taken there might have been 250,000 immigrants next year.'[21]

Gaitskell for the Opposition denounced Butler and Macleod as 'hypocrites', and the bill was opposed so fiercely that the guillotine became necessary. However according to Enoch Powell, who six years later was to make his famous 'rivers of blood' speech on the same subject, it was a pretty watered down affair. Indeed the Wilson Government in 1965 had to increase their powers to curb immigration – which was a far cry from Labour's bitter hostility to the bill before it became law on 1 July 1962.

Plans for a tunnel under the Channel date back to 1802 when the Prime Minister, Henry Addington, made the Peace of Amiens with Napoleon, and the Whig statesman Charles James Fox visited the Emperor in Paris. Fox was desperate to prevent the resumption of war and admired the principles of the French Republic. He and Napoleon got on splendidly and during their friendly talks agreed that a Channel tunnel would be advantageous for both countries. They discussed plans with French engineers and said 'It was one of the grand things they would do together.'

Unfortunately the Peace of Amiens lasted only a year, but meanwhile a French engineer Albert Matthieu had produced a design for two tunnels one above the other. The upper would be paved and carry horses and carriages; the lower would carry drainage water into reservoirs at each end; in mid-Channel there would be a large artificial island where horses could be changed, and a series of ventilation pipes would be built to above sea level at regular intervals. The continuation of the Napoleonic wars put paid to the project, but a similar plan was revived in 1834 as railways began. In 1834 the first scheme for a railway tunnel was produced using iron tubes lined with bricks after the sea gap had been narrowed by massive jetties 8 kilometres long jutting out from both the French and British shores.

When the Rotherhithe to Wapping tunnel was completed by the Brunels in 1843, the French engineer de Gran pioneered a scheme for a train tunnel with an island in mid-Channel. Unhappily the attempt to assassinate Napoleon III in January 1858 by Felice Orsini, who had come from England with an English bomb, dampened the interest of the French, whilst the Franco-Prussian war of 1870 further obscured the issue. Soon after this war British public opinion, which at first had been in favour of the Germans, swung back to the French, and in the mid-1870s both the French and British governments renewed their enthusiasm for the project. The French Channel Tunnel Company and the British Channel Tunnel Company were formed; shafts and headings were sunk both at Dover and Sangatte near Cap Gris and water pumps and ventilators installed. Geological conditions were better than expected. In 1880 a start was made on digging the tunnel. By 1882 pilot tunnels were a mile out under the sea from the French and British sides and were advancing by more than 100 yards each week. However in 1883 Joseph Chamberlain, President of the Board of Trade, appointed a Parliamentary Select Committee to investigate, and their majority report decided against the project as a result of military objections raised by the Duke of Cambridge and General Garnet Wolseley. Their objections were ridiculous, but work stopped.

In August 1913 Prime Minister Herbert Asquith received a deputation of fifteen MPs who presented a memorandum in favour of a Channel tunnel. Asquith was non-committal, and the project was examined by the War Office, the Board of Trade and the Admiralty. The Committee of Imperial Defence had the last word and on 13 July 1914, three weeks before the First World War broke out, they reported adversely. The scheme was off again.

Sir Maurice (later Lord) Hankey, Secretary of the Imperial Defence Committee from 1912 to 1938, was always hostile to the tunnel project on grounds of security; he was also instrumental in preventing Prime Ministers Lloyd George and Bonar Law giving a tunnel scheme the go-ahead shortly after the end of the First World War, although both men were in favour.[22]

In 1924 the Labour Prime Minister Ramsay MacDonald showed an interest in the scheme. Hankey once again torpedoed it. When in 1929 the Labour Government's Economic Advisory Council produced a majority report recommending the construction of a Channel tunnel, Hankey poisoned the mind of Ramsay MacDonald against it; following debate on a pro-tunnel motion in the Commons on 30 June 1930 after the publication of a negative White Paper, 172 members voted 'for' and 179 'against'. It was a close call.

Although in March 1949 200 MPs of all parties tabled a motion in favour of planning a Channel tunnel neither the Attlee Government nor Winston Churchill's 1951 Government was interested. On 2 February 1955 the Conservative Minister of Transport, John Boyd-Carpenter, said his Ministry did not favour the project 'and saw no possibility of private firms undertaking the work'. However on 16 February 1956 Harold Macmillan, then Minister of Defence, in reply to a Parliamentary question: 'To what extent do strategic objections still prevent the construction of a tunnel under the Channel?', announced to general surprise: 'Scarcely at all.' At last the British Government had given the green light.

At that date the Suez Canal Company, whose 99-year concession to operate the Suez Canal would expire in 1968 and was unlikely ever to be renewed by Egypt, wanted to be associated with the Channel Tunnel Company, but not until 1958 when the Egyptian Government offered compensation for the nationalization of the Suez Canal were they in a position to participate. Then with the help of the British and French governments and US capital the old London and Paris Channel Tunnel companies financed a Channel Study Group to survey the sites and make a feasibility study. They still owned the sites, and when the 1882 tunnel workings were inspected they were found to be intact and in good condition. Channel Tunnel shares were still quoted on the London Stock Exchange (being first quoted in 1881) and within a few days they soared from 4d to 57s. A syndicate of international bankers was formed with René Massigli, the former French Ambassador to London, as President, and Sir Ivone Kirkpatrick, the recently retired head of the Foreign Office as a director.

Jules Moch, a former French Minister of the Interior, in combination with Lord Gladwyn, who had recently retired as British Ambassador to Paris, headed a rival group who enthusiastically promoted a bridge in place of a tunnel. The supporters of a bridge called themselves the Channel Bridge Study Group (Société d'études du pont sur la Manche) and were backed by the Union Routière, a French company with massive road transport interests. The giant British steel firm Dorman Long designed a bridge for them. Unfortunately the financial projections were shaky, and eventually it was admitted that the profit would be so infinitesimal that they would be unlikely to be able to raise the necessary private capital. However the great attraction of a bridge was that it would provide almost unlimited capacity for both road and rail traffic without ventilation problems.[23]

Encouraged by the Macmillan Government the Channel Study Group commissioned independent surveys of schemes including bridges, a bridge–tunnel combination, and a road-cum-rail tunnel. They considered a cross-Channel dam along the top of which would run a motorway, with swing bridges to allow ships to pass. Road tunnels were soon ruled out since the concentration of carbon monoxide was found to be unacceptable. A bridge was technically feasible but twice as expensive, and with the concentration of shipping in the Channel and the necessity of obtaining permission from around eighty maritime powers who regularly used the Channel, there was little hope of solving the legal problems. A bridge–tunnel scheme would permit cars and trains to leave shore on a bridge, drop into a tunnel, and then land from another bridge: alas, the cost was excessive. Finally, the Study Group concluded that the most acceptable scheme on engineering and financial grounds would be two parallel 21-foot diameter one-way railway tunnels. The distance between the terminals would be 32 miles with 23 miles sunk some 125 feet below the seabed, and the train engines would be powered by electricity.

The Channel Study Group submitted their report to the French and British governments in March 1960 and produced financial projections showing the total cost of constructing the tunnel at £130 million (a fraction of its eventual cost). However the two state railways were expected to pay for the railway terminals and rolling stock which would cost £30 million. Thus a net £100 million was required. The Study Group proposed that a large proportion of the necessary private capital should be raised in the international money market with a big contribution from the United States, and to make it possible to find this capital the Study Group proposed that when the project was completed the British and French governments would lease the tunnel on a long-term basis, and sub-lease it to their respective nationalized railways. This would provide the government backing which would enable the promoters to raise the requisite private capital. These financial proposals did not find favour with the British Government, and they were turned down by the Economic Policy Committee on 2 November 1960, and by the Cabinet on 25 November, although the Cabinet authorized the opening of talks at official level with the French.[24]

Meanwhile on 14 July 1960 Leo D'Erlanger, the chairman of the Channel Tunnel Company, had held a press conference in the City of London where he faced two hours of heckling and questions. He acquitted himself admirably, and press coverage was favourable to the project.

In July 1961 the British Government applied for full membership of the Common Market, and it was announced that Anglo-French talks would be opened to compare the feasibility of the two schemes – the tunnel and Jules Moch's bridge – and in November the two Ministers of Transport, Ernest Marples and his French counterpart Marc Jacquet, agreed to set up an Anglo-French working group of officials under the joint chairmanship of Sir David Serpell, Deputy Secretary at the Ministry of Transport, and Jacques Ravanel, the French Commissaire de Tourisme, to report on the respective merits of the two schemes both operated with private finance.

Jules Moch and Lord Gladwyn continued their endeavour to whip up support for a bridge but with little success: senior members of the Royal Navy were contemptuous of an attempt to 'clutter up the gut', as they affectionately called the Channel.

De Gaulle and Macmillan discussed the options during their talks at Champs in June 1962, Macmillan telling de Gaulle that the bridge versus tunnel controversy represented no more than the rivalry between the French and British steel and cement industries. However at their meeting at Birch Grove in October, after discussions with experts from the Channel Study Group, both leaders came out firmly in favour of a tunnel. This was not universally accepted, and on 2 November 1962 in a Foreign Office minute the Lord Privy Seal, Edward Heath, commented: 'Even if the bridge cost two or three times as much as the tunnel it might be a better long-term investment; we might find that after all a bridge is a necessity after a comparatively few years.'[25]

The shock of de Gaulle's veto in January 1963 on British entry into the EEC caused some British Cabinet Ministers to blow cold on the Channel link. On a Foreign Office report that the French Minister of Transport, Jacquet, was putting a sense of urgency into the French side of the scheme and 'all is geared to producing an agreed report by 31 March 1963 with the established contacts giving the impression that at the technical and economic level Anglo-French relations were unimpaired [by the veto]', Heath minuted: 'But is a tunnel justified now that we are not going into the EEC? We must play hard to get [sic] and show no enthusiasm at all. It will in any case be difficult enough to get past the Chancellor of the Exchequer and the Cabinet. A pause will not matter.'

Heath asked for comments from the Foreign Office on this minute; one was:

> The existing facilities are worn out, old-fashioned and inadequate whatever assumptions we may make about our future economic and political relations with Europe. Dover for instance must decide whether to embark on expensive new constructional work. The cross-Channel ferries are reaching the end of their life.

Another on 21 February 1963 read:

> The reasons for pursuing this project seem to me even stronger than going along with the supersonic airliner project [Concorde] which has so far been unaffected by the breakdown at Brussels. Our interest in the Channel tunnel is if anything greater now than it was before the breakdown and . . . a delay now would damage us more than the French.

Heath's minute contributed to delay by British officials, although the British Embassy in Paris reported that de Gaulle's objections to the UK's application to join the Common Market had no bearing on the French attitude to the tunnel project, and that the General 'took a favourable view of the project'.

In Paris the French Minister of Information, Roger Peyrefitte, sounded far more enthusiastic for the fixed link than Marples in the Commons who talked about 'evaluating opinion first'. This brought the acid comment from *The Economist* on 21 September that the British were being 'sticky not from hostility but from sheer unwillingness to govern'. From Paris the British Ambassador, Pierson Dixon, reported:

> Now that the General for his own reasons has chosen the tunnel, and that this fact is becoming known, we must expect the French propaganda machine to blame us for any delay in following suit and to represent this as lack of decision and a lack of a European vocation on our part.[26]

There was by no means universal acceptance of the Channel link in Whitehall. Sir William Armstrong, Permanent Under-Secretary at the Treasury, wrote a memorandum cautioning against acceptance of the scheme without consideration of the economic return compared with other forms of investment, the benefit to British trade, the effect on roads, railways and airlines, and the effect on the Government's policy of stimulating development in the north and seeking to restrain the drive to the south-east, as well as its implications for Britain's relations with Europe. This was seized on by other civil servants as a cogent argument for delay, and Sir Patrick Reilly, Under-Secretary at the Foreign Office, alarmed at these proceedings, minuted to the other Departments involved on 21 September: 'I would be very grateful if you would do all you can to keep the sub-committee [Economic Steering (General) Committee] to the target date. Considering the report has been available for months it seems extraordinary that examination of its implications in various fields was not put in hand much earlier.'[27]

The report of the Anglo-French working group of government officials and the report of the Anglo-French Study Group were ready by March 1963, but not published until 18 September 1963 when they appeared jointly and simultaneously in Paris and London. The British version – a White Paper, *The Fixed Channel Link* – was given a mixed reception by the press. *The Times* leader the next day stated: 'A Channel tunnel had much to commend it but it should not be started with the dismal prospect of "continuously leaning on public funds", and relying on tax reliefs was a confession the project is unlikely to be a paying prospect.'

A comprehensive report by the Economic Steering (General) Committee, a standing committee of civil servants, on the feasibility of a fixed Channel link concluded that the only link worth Ministers' consideration was a rail tunnel. The French Government, they stated, had made it abundantly clear in private that in its view 'the rail tunnel is the only practical choice, so that the real choice before the Government lies between providing a rail tunnel or relying on the existing services by sea and air'.

> It is the policy of Her Majesty's Government in the circumstances following the breakdown of the Brussels negotiations to maintain and foster the European-mindedness of the United Kingdom and to demonstrate to the rest of Europe that Her Majesty's Government have not 'turned their backs on Europe'. This policy was set out in the European Economic Relations Committee paper (63)5, which was approved by Ministers, in the following terms –

>> Our success in securing and maintaining effective influence over Community policies will depend in large degree on the impression created by our own actions of our desire to work towards unity in Europe, outside as well as inside the sphere of economic relations. Moreover a continuing objective of eventual membership of the Community will need to be supported during an extended period of exclusion by measures to cultivate a European outlook on the part of the United Kingdom itself.

>> It is also our policy to develop practical links with European countries, in the interests of United Kingdom trade and Western solidarity.
>> In our relations with the French specifically, it is our policy to pursue co-operative enterprises which are of positive advantage to the United Kingdom.
>> It would be a striking and dramatic gesture in pursuance of these policies to announce our determination to construct a fixed link across the Channel, and to follow this by effective action. But the effectiveness of the Channel

link as a demonstration of our European-mindedness must depend on the speed and the readiness with which Her Majesty's Government reach a favourable decision and the promptitude with which the decision is followed up. Delay will be interpreted, particularly in France, as fresh evidence of British insularity, and may be exploited against us by French propaganda.

On the financial side the civil servants estimated that the tunnel would show a return on capital of between 9 and 11 per cent, much the same as would be expected from new investment by nationalized industries. Allowing for the capital being divided equally with the French, the cost was estimated at £75 million at 1962 prices spread over six years, which would add one per cent to public investment. It was a tragedy that the scheme was not proceeded with at this juncture, when prices were relatively low – before the galloping inflation of the succeeding decades. It is notable, too, that a Conservative Government was willing to consider a nationalized tunnel – a far cry from their attitude to nationalized industries thirty years on. The report continued: 'Room would have to be made for the tunnel in the public sector; expenditure for it would hardly be appropriate to cut private investment; and the only alternative to this course would be to cut private consumption.'

The committee noted that the Channel Study Group proposed a project that would be privately financed but government-assisted in the form of a loan. This proposal, they said, was 'complex and difficult', but significant also in that it called for a decision not only on the venture itself but also on the nature of its ownership. This, they said, might take the form of (a) private enterprise, (b) a hybrid organization, involving both private and governmental capital participation, or (c) a public undertaking. Five arguments were cited in favour of a public undertaking (all would have been anathema to Prime Minister Margaret Thatcher), and it was noted, not surprisingly, that the trade unions wanted full public ownership while British manufacturers wanted it to remain private.

The committee considered that 'a new and uninterrupted link' with the Continent for rail and road vehicles without the need for transhipment 'would bring advantages to all parts of the country and would not conflict with the Government's policy for strengthening the North East and Scotland'.[28] It was expected that the cross-Channel ferries from Dover, which at that time were all operated by Townsend Ferries, 'might even remain in business thereafter, [but] it would have an unsatisfactory financial effect on the short sea liners who included British Railways using ports other than Dover.'

The Economic Steering (General) Committee considered this paper on 20 September 1963 and decided that 'in the end' they would have to recommend to Ministers that the tunnel should go ahead but – they felt with unnecessary caution – that 'a great deal of further study would have to be undertaken, and an inter-departmental committee of under-secretaries under the chairmanship of the Ministry of Transport should pursue the necessary studies as a matter of urgency.' On 8 October Marples told the Cabinet he hoped to be able to submit to the Cabinet all the considerations involved in November. Marples did not meet his deadline.

Patrick Reilly at the Foreign Office remained concerned at continuing French reports that British Ministers did not appear to be at all keen on the project and the impression of French officials that 'we were playing it slow for electoral reasons'; Reilly also pointed out to the Treasury and the Ministry of Transport that a debate in Parliament was impossible before a Cabinet decision had been made. The Foreign Office continued to press for the earliest possible action and to deplore the lack of urgency by Marples and the civil servants at the Ministry of Transport.

Rab Butler, now Foreign Secretary in Alec Home's Government, talked to the French Ambassador on 5 November 1963; French technicians, notably the Ministry of Finance, were against the project, de Courcel said – 'however General de Gaulle was for it; he at Birch Grove had said the lack of a fixed link between England and France was an anachronism.' De Courcel had no doubt that the General's view would prevail, and that the project was psychologically important. Butler assured the Ambassador that he favoured links with France in all fields and closer Anglo-French relations.[29]

When at last the Ministerial Economic Policy Committee of the Cabinet got down to deciding whether or not to recommend the tunnel project to the Cabinet, they showed no prejudice against it being a nationalized undertaking. However Reginald Maudling, Chancellor of the Exchequer, produced a memorandum on the public investment programme, explaining to the committee that all economic sources available for investment, whether private or public, were being 'fast pre-empted; the tunnel was such a big project that unless it coincided with a recession it would call for an increase of taxes if carried out as a nationalized undertaking.' He also emphasized that private investment 'was just beginning to move forward again'; and if the tunnel was proceeded with by private capital there were very few unused resources to draw upon. Overall his view was: 'The risks of overload were considerable and it would not be right to embark upon the tunnel without making room for it in advance.'

Marples stated that his discussions with Jacquet, the French Minister of Transport, showed that the French were enthusiastic and wanted to start work immediately, floating the scheme as a partnership between state finance and private capital including French road haulage interests. The French were now pressing for an early decision, as were the private interests involved in the Channel Study Group, so that the Government were faced with a dilemma: if they decided that Britain could not afford the project both the Study Group and the French Government 'would then declare they could find the whole of the finance on their own'. There was then a distinct possibility that the tunnel might be built with French and American finance excluding the United Kingdom altogether, and the French would 'put all the blame on us'. Marples had experienced great difficulty in preventing Jacquet discussing the French view with the press and 'unless a decision was reached very soon, by January 1964 at the latest, there was a risk of a serious leak to the press.'

In discussion it was agreed that the project was economically sound and that the benefit to trade greater than had been thought; if the French Government undertook the whole project without British participation 'it would be in our economic interest to accept, but there would be serious political objections'. However, summing up, Maudling said that although it was agreed that the tunnel was desirable it was also considered that it should not be undertaken 'if the result would be to overstrain the economy', and therefore there must be a delay before definitive advice was given to the Cabinet.[30]

A decision was thus postponed. We can be sure that if Macmillan had still been in Downing Street the project would have been approved in the autumn of 1963, so keen was he always on plans to expand the economy. Fortunately the 14th Earl of Home did not have the jaundiced views of his forebear the Duke of Wellington, who as Prime Minister in 1830 opposed the railways because they would enable the ordinary classes to move about unnecessarily, and who was particularly opposed to the London–Portsmouth railway on the ground that an invading French army might use it. In January 1964 Home's Cabinet finally approved the tunnel scheme, and on 4 February 1964 Marples and Jacquet issued a historic joint statement: 'The construction of a rail Channel tunnel is technically possible and in economic terms it would represent a sound investment of the two countries' resources. The two governments have therefore decided to go ahead with this project.'[31] Thus Macmillan's sensible approval of the Channel tunnel when he had been Minister of Defence in 1956 finally came to fruition six months after his resignation.

De Gaulle thought that a Channel tunnel financed jointly by France and Britain would go a long way towards repairing the damaged relationship between the two countries caused by his January 1963 veto on Britain entering the EEC, and he co-operated enthusiastically with the British Government, saying roundly '*Je suis tunneliste.*' A further and costly detailed geological survey was financed jointly by Britain and France; it revealed no geological problems but Barbara Castle, Minister of Transport in the Labour Government which had replaced the Conservatives, announced on 29 June 1966 that site work could not begin until 1968 so that the tunnel could not become operational until 1974 at the earliest. No work was started before the Labour Government fell in 1970 and the Heath Government, which superseded the Wilson administration in that year, gave a completion date of 1979.[32]

In September 1973 the Heath Government published a White Paper, *The Channel Tunnel*, and in the afterglow of Britain's accession to the EEC an agreement was signed, amid great publicity, by Heath and the French Prime Minister Georges Pompidou at Lancaster House in which the French and British governments agreed to build and finance the tunnel jointly. Work began with high expectations; however the Heath Government fell in 1974 and the incoming Wilson Government abandoned the project. It was not until after Margaret Thatcher's second election victory with a steamroller majority of 144 in the 1983 General Election that the Wilson Government's 1973 decision was reversed and the tunnel development restarted, to be completed in 1994.

During the 1950s the rapid increase in the number of cars and lorries reduced the volume of railway traffic, and the resulting loss of profit made necessary a reappraisal of the role of the nationalized British Railways. At the start of the decade the railways still showed a profit before interest and other charges, but by 1960 this had degenerated into a working loss of £67.7 million. The figure sagged to £87 million in 1961 and to £104 million in 1962, producing a total loss that year to the British Transport Commission of £143 million although all its activities apart from British Railways and Inland Waterways had been profitable. Meanwhile the number of motor vehicles in Britain between 1953 and 1962 had increased from 3.19 million to 8.2 million.

In 1945 the private railway companies in Britain had emerged from the Second World War exhausted and battered. Passenger timetables had been drastically curtailed, and special military traffic had taxed the equipment and personnel beyond the limit of endurance: not only had endless troop trains and special freight trains to be organized but, because of the U-boat threat, a considerable amount of coastal traffic, mostly coal, had had to be transferred from sea to rail.

Only bare maintenance on track and signals was possible during the war and the rolling stock became seriously run down. The railway companies were inadequately compensated for the damage they suffered from enemy action and were forbidden during the war and immediately afterwards to raise their rates. Thus between the armistice in 1945 and the date they passed into state ownership in 1947 they lacked both the necessary finance and, with expropriation around the corner, the motivation, to repair the war damage; LNER in fact were on the verge of bankruptcy.

When the Labour Government nationalized the railways they did not produce an adequate programme of capital expenditure for renovation and the railways were given a low place in the post-war queue for scarce raw materials. Only a handful of sizeable improvement schemes were authorized at first, and the recently nationalized railways had to renovate on the cheap while a huge output of new motor transport flooded on to the roads to provide cut-throat competition. Neither the Churchill nor the Eden governments showed enthusiasm for putting state capital on a large scale into railways, and rival claims on state resources were given priority.

However under the Churchill Government at the start of 1954 a comprehensive programme of modernization and re-equipment of British Railways was formulated by the British Transport Commission. Unfortunately this was permeated by the belief that redesigning steam engines could prolong the age of steam, and it was assumed automatically that, as one expert, G. R. Allen, put it, the railways had 'a God-given right to passengers and freight', and as long as trains could travel faster the railways would be sure to make a profit provided they were 'lavishly re-equipped with every known device that promised more economical working'. In the Commission's plan there was almost no effort to assess the effects of the explosion in road transport on the railways. In addition the prospect of almost unlimited spending power after years of parsimony made the regional managers over-ambitious.

The Chairman of the British Transport Commission from 1953 to 1961 was General Sir Brian Robertson; he was excessively sympathetic to the trade unions. He also appeared oblivious to the fact that at the end of the fifties the transport of goods by road was increasing far faster than that by rail which had been ousted from a major share of short distance traffic. As chairman, Robertson was responsible for the reappraisal of the Commission's 1954 plan at the end of 1958. With blind optimism the Commission urged a speed-up of modernization as the panacea for trading losses, and predicted that if this was done there would be an annual working surplus by 1963 of £50 million to £100 million. This was based on unrealistic assumptions about both wage and cost stability. Soon after the publication of the plan the Commission's findings were superseded by a prolonged wages dispute and strike threats. These culminated in the Guillebaud Committee set up to investigate railwaymen's pay; they came to the irresistible conclusion that railwaymen's wages must be increased to equal those in other basic industries. The result was a merry-go-round of pay increases which with other cost increases made nonsense of the Commission's forecast of substantial profits by 1963.

The report of the Parliamentary Select Committee on Nationalized Industries published in July 1960 strongly criticized the British Transport Commission's management and performance. Its most important conclusion was that the nation must decide on political grounds whether unprofitable railway activities were to continue as social services, or whether British Railways should be given freedom to act like other commercial undertakings; if the Government wanted for political or social reasons to dictate the railways' commercial policy it must openly subsidize uneconomic services. Otherwise, they argued, British Railways should be allowed to refuse unremunerative traffic, select what it wanted to carry, and be relieved of its obligation to be a 'common carrier'.[33]

Shocked by the Select Committee's report the Government appointed a committee in the spring of 1960 to advise on the future of the railways. Its chairman was Sir Ivan Stedeford, a leading industrialist, Chairman and Managing Director of Tube Investments, Governor of the BBC, and holder of other public appointments. The dominant individual on the Stedeford Committee however was Richard Beeching, a senior ICI executive. An accountant specializing in cost accounting, he had gained a reputation by ruthlessly streamlining ICI's own factories and achieving striking reductions in production costs. By analysing the British Railways accounts he produced arguments showing that there would have to be massive closures of uneconomic stations and branch lines if British Railways was ever to show a profit again. He worked entirely on figures of costs and treated the social need for extensive branch lines as irrelevant.

The Stedeford Report was delivered to Ernest Marples, Minister of Transport, in the late autumn of 1960. Though the report was kept secret it was known to recommend large-scale reductions in passenger and freight services, whilst Dr Beeching of ICI was known to be mainly responsible for its conclusions. Marples informed the Prime Minister that the British Transport Commission had been 'incompetent' both technically and financially, and that Robertson must be superseded as chairman – that is, sacked.

Marples recommended to Macmillan that Beeching should replace Robertson at short notice. At a meeting at Admiralty House on 22 December 1960 between Macmillan, Marples and Lord Mills, the Paymaster-General, Marples stated that he intended to appoint Beeching as Chairman of the British Transport Commission at a salary of £25,000 a year. This shocked the other two; the going rate for chairmen of nationalized industries at that time was around £10,000, and the pay proposed for Beeching was two and a half times Robertson's current salary.

Lord Mills, himself a successful industrialist much relied on by

Macmillan for advice on industrial affairs, questioned whether Beeching
was the right man for the job; he himself, he said, 'did not hold so high
an opinion of Mr Beeching', whilst he feared criticism also from the
railway unions with whom Beeching would be unpopular. Mills recommended that further thought should be given to the appointment, and
particularly to the possibility of finding a railwayman to do the job.
However the Prime Minister and the Minister of Transport had already
decided on Beeching, and Mills was overruled. If a man of the calibre
of Beeching was needed, the Prime Minister said, it seemed unlikely that
one could be obtained at less than £20,000 a year. It was decided to leave
open the question of what reason should be given for going as high as
£20,000 when chairmen's salaries in other nationalized industries were
so much lower.[34]

The Government decided to weather the storm over the inflated salary,
and Beeching was offered the job as Chairman of the Transport
Commission at a salary of £24,000 a year, in succession to Robertson
who was given a peerage. His appointment was received badly by the
rail unions, especially as it was known that he had been the most influential member of the Stedeford Committee and wanted wholesale railway
closures.

It was a disastrous decision, and a tragedy for the nation that Macmillan
paid no heed to Mills. In his memoirs Macmillan describes Mills as 'a
tower of strength' but over the railways the Prime Minister preferred
Marples's advice to that of Mills.[35] Marples had been a great help to
Macmillan as his Under-Secretary when Macmillan was Minister of
Housing in the early days of Churchill's 1951 Government, enabling him
to achieve a target of 300,000 houses a year; Macmillan had an exaggerated opinion of his ability. In his memoirs published eleven years later
Macmillan continued to record a favourable view of Beeching, writing:
'We were fortunate in persuading Dr Beeching, one of the most able
and fertile brains in the industrial and commercial world, not only to
sit upon the [Stedeford] Committee which drew up the scheme but to
become Chairman of the Transport Commission to preside over the
changes.'

Macmillan and Beeching had a meeting à deux on 10 May 1961.
Macmillan asked Beeching about the possibility of selling off railway
property. Like Margaret Thatcher later, the Prime Minister was intent
on any manoeuvre which would reduce the Government's public borrowing requirement so as to make room for tax cuts. Beeching's reply showed
that he had no understanding of the Prime Minister's mind because he
gave the music hall reply: 'The problem was capital gains [on railway
property] were not shown in regional accounts.' This ought to have
shaken Macmillan's faith in Beeching: the latter obviously had no under-

standing that the Government would gladly sell off assets such as railway property to finance modernization.[36]

A Government White Paper, *Reorganization of the Nationalized Transport Undertakings*, had been produced in December 1960 – embodying some of the Stedeford Committee's recommendations but with all references to a smaller railway system and cutting uneconomic services removed by the Prime Minister. The chief proposal of the White Paper was the abolition of the British Transport Commission and its replacement by four separate boards to run the railways, docks, inland waterways and London transport. The 1947 Transport Act of the Attlee Government had given the Commission the difficult job of combining all these tasks under one head.[37]

The proposals expressed in the White Paper were complicated and difficult to incorporate in one bill, so not until August 1962 did the Transport Act 1962 receive the Royal Assent. All assets and liabilities were transferred to the new boards with a vesting date of 1 January 1963. In the intervening period Beeching was put in charge of British Railways, and according to Macmillan 'with remarkable energy carried out most detailed studies of freight and passenger traffic costs by methods [of cost accounting] quite unknown in railway history'.

With hindsight some experts claim that Beeching was a bad cost and management accountant because in his analysis of rail costs he allocated the fixed overhead costs to every branch line and station, ignoring the contribution their earnings made towards total income. Instead he should have worked in the principle of marginal costs, since in closure decisions the only relevant costs were those variable ones of individual branches and stations which would be avoided if closure took place. The actual outcome was that the Board's total income was lower, while all remaining operations each bore a higher burden of unavoidable fixed overheads.*

Soon Beeching was at daggers drawn with the trade unions. In September 1962 he published a scheme for the closure of sizeable sections of the railway workshops where locomotives and rolling stock were built and repaired. With appalling lack of tact neither Beeching nor Marples bothered to consult the unions before announcing their decision to close the workshops. At a meeting on 28 September 1962 at the Ministry of Labour George Woodcock, Secretary-General of the Trades Union Council, told John Hare, Minister of Labour, that the railway unions had been

---

* These sophisticated arguments about total turnover were not considered by either Marples or Macmillan but devastating criticism of Beeching's method of approach was published in the *Guardian* in May 1963 by D. L. Munby, Oxford University Reader in Economics and Organization.

deeply offended by the lack of consultation over the workshops closures. Not only had insufficient time been allowed them at the meetings to consider the detailed plans before being asked to comment on them, but more important on 19 September details of the proposed closures had been released to union members in the workshops at the same time as they were released to union officials. This had put the unions in an impossible position as no union leader could recommend the dismissal of his members at one place of work in preference to those at another.

Lamely Hare excused this lapse by saying it had been done 'for the best of motives. The purpose had been to prevent possible leaks and to alleviate misapprehensions as soon as possible.'

Woodcock replied that leaks would have been unlikely and would not have mattered. 'However,' he said, 'all of this was water under the bridge, and the trade unions were most concerned lest the same objectionable procedure should be followed in regard to the much bigger problem of the proposed redundancies in the operating grades [e.g. redundancies through the closing down of rail services].' He emphasized that it was essential for the unions to be given 'prior knowledge of the detailed plans [of the Beeching closures] and also the opportunity to comment about the size as well as the shape of the redundancy plan'.[38]

Hare tried to pour oil on the troubled waters by telling Woodcock that he would report the talk to Marples and see if Marples would discuss with Beeching a meeting to consider the procedure for future consultation. A note of the Hare–Woodcock talk was sent to Macmillan; he minuted to Marples that he was impressed by what Woodcock had said, which he thought was 'of the utmost importance . . . Beeching is better at making plans than getting them across, so we must all help.'

Marples then invited Beeching and Woodcock to a private lunch in his home, and told the Prime Minister:

> They started frostily but finished splendidly. The conversation was off the record and was free and forceful but courteous.
>
> Woodcock gave his views on the place and functions of the unions; Beeching his on management. I think Woodcock made a real impression on Beeching. As a result I see the possibility of a beneficial modification in his dealing with the railway unions. I am seeing Beeching again today. I will keep you informed.

Three days later Marples reported to the Prime Minister that he had seen Beeching again twice and that Beeching 'remains convinced of the principles underlying Woodcock's arguments', but does not like 'a public image of himself and the BTC always being mean employers who are forced to dispense justice by the skill of the virtuous unions'. However Woodcock in a telephone conversation with Marples had seemed 'very pleased' with the lunch.[39]

On 28 February 1963 Beeching as head of British Railways, with the BTC now disbanded, sent his seventy-page plan, *The Reshaping of British Railways*, to Marples. After reading it Marples minuted to Macmillan:

> The thought underlying all the report is that the railways should meet that part of the total transport requirement of the country for which they offer the best possible means, and that they should cease to do things for which they are ill suited. It gives more costings and information in an intelligible form than ever before.[40]

The Beeching Plan was considered by the Cabinet in March 1963. They were told that 'the list of stations and lines to be closed would cause an outcry', but the personal inconvenience to millions of passengers 'was the price for efficiency'. It was also pointed out that the wholesale contraction of the rail network coincided with the start of the motorway building programme which would give rise to allegations of 'a deliberate policy to run down the railways in favour of promoting private motoring'. The Cabinet was told that Beeching's report

> would involve drastic alterations in the existing system and a substantial curtailment of services especially in the more remote parts of the country . . . nevertheless in spite of the considerable objection which would be raised in the areas affected by the proposals . . . the Board's approach should be accepted as being in accord with government policy.

The Cabinet recorded that the Beeching proposals

> flow from the most massive compilation and systematic analysis of information about the railways ever attempted and offered a firm prospect of a modern railway system suited to the country's future needs. It was agreed the existence at that time of a subsidy of £150 million a year to the railways was a measure of the railway's claim on economic resources which could be used better elsewhere.
>
> The Board's lucid analysis and bold proposals accord with the Government's expectations. The aim, which is wholly consistent with the Government's policy of growth, modernization and redevelopment, is to produce an efficient railway system handling those traffics technically suited to rail. The extensive reshaping of our railways is essential . . . The most controversial part of the plan is the withdrawal of many passenger services, and passengers must be told if better railway services are to be provided to meet the needs of the nation such measures are necessary.

The Beeching Plan called for the initial closure of 5,000 miles of railway lines, and some 2,359 stations deemed 'hopelessly uneconomic'.

The Cabinet was anxious about the trade unions' reaction to the loss of 70,000 jobs called for by Beeching, and recorded that this could be minimized through emphasizing that 'most of this reduction would be effected by normal wastage and control of recruitment. Even so there

will be problems for those displaced'; the Cabinet was also told of plans
for 'confidential briefings' to national newspapers in an effort to portray
the Beeching proposals in the best possible light, with particular
attention being paid to the two London evening newspapers 'whose
treatment of a report often sets a tone which the national dailies
follow'.[41]

Marples was authorized by the Cabinet to prepare a statement for
publication. Macmillan had been alarmed by the Cabinet discussion
and also by Marples's draft statement which made clear that Beeching
proposed to massacre much of the railway system purely on grounds of
profit forecasts while ignoring the social needs and resulting inconvenience to the public. As usual he turned to the ubiquitous Burke Trend
for advice. Trend, now Secretary to the Cabinet, reported that the
average man would say: 'Fewer trains means more buses (and private
motor cars); and more road traffic means, or should mean, more and
better roads. What are the Government doing about this? It is here that
the Minister's memorandum is disappointing.' Marples's statement,
Trend continued, implied that he would wait for somebody else to take
the first step –

> for the Highway Authority to say that the roads are not adequate, or for
> the bus operators to say that they might be able to put on an extra service
> or two.
>   Neither of these faces squarely the duty which many people will regard
> as imposed on the Ministry of Transport by the Beeching proposals – to take
> some positive initiative in re-shaping the roads and road transport services
> of this country by means of a comprehensive plan which will complement
> Beeching's plan for re-shaping the railways.

Trend ended by saying he had a sneaking feeling that the publication
of the Beeching Report might be the right moment for the Government
to follow up and take a second bite 'by commissioning a further complementary study – in effect a second Beeching Report – on the problems
of roads and road transport'. Trend was right, but no survey of roads
and road transport was commissioned by the Macmillan Government or
its successors.[42]

On reading Trend's trenchant minute Macmillan suggested that he
should himself either redraft Marples's statement on the plan or should
offer to make a substantial contribution to a redraft. This was typical
of the detailed effort which Macmillan was ready to put into the work
of his departmental Ministers. Trend advised against such a method of
working because 'so much inter-departmental work had gone into the
existing draft, and if we tried to inject a substantial new passage written
from a different viewpoint and in quite different language the result

might be unfortunate. Nor would the Minister [Marples] feel it was his own statement.' Instead Trend suggested that Macmillan should send Marples a minute indicating the lines on which a redraft might be attempted, and he sent the Prime Minister a draft.

Macmillan immediately wrote a personal minute to Marples saying that he had been thinking further since the Cabinet discussion; he emphasized that in his statement Marples must get across that the Beeching Plan was a first step towards an integrated plan for transport as a whole and that it was intended to supplement it by the end of the year with further studies on the improvement of the roads and road transport services.

> Ought we not to start off by saying that the whole purpose of the Government's transport policy is to produce an efficient transport service for the country as a whole in which all the elements, particularly road and rail, will be properly co-ordinated; that to try and do so without first solving the problem of the railways was to try and fight a battle with one hand tied behind our backs ... Will you consider having another look at the whole statement from this point of view?[43]

On 27 March 1963 the Beeching Plan was made public and put on sale by the Stationery Office. In his statement to Parliament, amended in the light of Macmillan's minute, Marples said:

> The report is a major contribution to the Government's policy of providing an efficient economic and well-balanced transport system for Great Britain as a whole. When the new shape and pattern of the railways are clear we shall have a foundation on which we can create such a system. It is not possible to have effective and efficient co-ordination until we have as a basis a modern twentieth-century railway system.
> In the meantime steps are being taken by the Secretary of State for Scotland and myself to see that any additional demands on our roads will be met.[44]

Alas, the 'additional demands on our roads' were not properly considered by either the Macmillan Government or their successors, thus leaving the Britain of thirty years later with an almost insoluble problem. Nor was Marples's statement more than hot air since no serious scheme had been planned for the roads, for all that this problem worried the Prime Minister if not his Minister of Transport.

Eventually the Beeching axe cut the mileage of the railways from 17,500 in 1963 to 11,000 in 1975 – little more than half the 20,000-mile network at the peak of railway travel in 1914. There was fierce public reaction to the cuts. Informed criticism stressed that the railways should never have been studied in a vacuum; instead the most cost-effective role for all forms of transport in the economy should have been studied in their totality, with special attention being paid to those forms of transport which were receiving covert subsidies that concealed their competitive ability. Another valid criticism was that it was wrong to produce a rail transport plan which ignored the likely expansion of the population in certain conurbations, especially on the south coast, and in the depressed areas which the Government planned to reinvigorate with subsidies. One of Beeching's glaring mistakes was to seek to cut down services to areas where new towns were contemplated. Another was his recommendation that no cross-Channel ferry services could be viable except from the port of Dover: he abolished the three days-a-week cross-Channel ferry from Southampton to Le Havre on the grounds that it could never be made to pay; within a few years foreign firms were operating roll-on car ferries sailing from Southampton several times a day. However the most damning indictment of Beeching in 1963 was that he had callously and completely ignored the social consequences of his measures.

Within a few weeks of publication of the Beeching Plan the Hall Report was published by the Ministry of Transport to study likely inland transport developments over the next twenty years. This diagnosed correctly the future explosion in road transport, but did not present any plan for dealing with the ensuing problems. Unfortunately their terms of reference forced the members of the Hall Committee to consider road transport in isolation without taking into account probable developments in air, rail and sea transport. This made the report nearly valueless.

Within the regions and especially in remoter parts there were howls of indignation at Beeching's proposed closures. The Transport Users Consultative Committee, set up to investigate passengers' complaints after nationalization, held local hearings which were often stormy and received considerable publicity in the provincial press. However grounds of objection to the TUCC were carefully delineated. Complaints could only be made on the ground that lack of a train service would cause personal hardship, and not that Beeching's assessments of losses on particular lines were invalid or that the lines could be run more economically. TUCC advice to the Minister on whether or not to close had to be based solely on the issue of hardship, and was only 'advice' which the Minister was free to accept or reject. Marples in several cases ignored TUCC submissions that social hardship would result from a closure and allowed Beeching to go ahead.

Spurred on by trade union anger at the proposed massive dismissal of railwaymen, Labour's immediate reaction was to indulge in vicious attacks on the Government and threaten that the surgery would be halted when they came to power. However when they gained power in

October 1964 their attitude quickly changed to a reluctant acceptance that Beeching's analysis was unanswerable.

In his 27 March statement to the Commons Marples had stressed:

> The report makes it clear that in the remoter areas of the country there will be special problems. (This applies not only to Scotland and Wales but in some parts of England and to communications with Northern Ireland.) But a widespread network of bus services already exists and I shall see that where necessary adequate alternative means of transport are available before a railway passenger closure takes place.

This raised the awkward question for the Government of subsidies to certain rural bus services. The Jack Committee in March 1961 had recommended subsidies to rural buses partly from the rates and partly from the Exchequer. In September 1963 the Ministry of Transport proposed that county councils should be enabled to subsidize rural bus services and recover a rate deficiency grant from the Treasury on such expenditure, and recommended that the Government should try to devise means of enabling the 'small man' to operate minor services while at the same time stimulating voluntary arrangements for 'lifts' in private cars. The Economic Policy Committee of the Cabinet were divided over these recommendations, considering it might be 'objectionable to introduce yet another subsidized social service'.[45]

The Minister of Housing Keith Joseph urged prior consultation with the County Councils Association before any public announcement was made, and in addition an experiment in some selected areas over a two-year period during which the Ministries of Transport and Housing would co-operate with the local county councils in trying to work out a sensible scheme. There was controversy over whether the 'small man' should be allowed licences to operate bus services, and in Whitehall there was a body of opinion which thought doing so would jeopardize the rural bus network.

As so often Burke Trend summed up the problem succinctly for the Prime Minister in a personal minute on 24 September 1963:

> The Government are in a dilemma – do they intend to rely for the provision of rural bus services on private enterprise (i.e. the small man) or on local management (i.e. the county council) or on Exchequer management? If there are objections to the first two of these possibilities, is it worth considering the third – i.e. the Minister's power under the Transport Act 1962 to require the Railways Board to ensure the provision of substitute bus services when rail passenger services are withdrawn? (Does the Minister hope to keep quiet about it in public? If not, is he wrong?)
>
> The Minister says with some justification that 'we cannot expect the Board to carry indefinite commitments to see that these services go on.'

Perhaps not, but should it not be incumbent on some other parts of the new transport machinery to see that they are maintained – with if necessary Exchequer subsidy? It is difficult to see how otherwise the Government will live up to their claim that they will press forward by all appropriate means . . . the provision of a modern transport system.

By the time this reached Macmillan's desk he was within a few days of his prostate attack, and he did not deal with the grave problem raised in Trend's minute nor did his successors Alec Home and Harold Wilson.[46]

The issue of whether each family should have a measure of public transport available has never been resolved, and the pattern of rural transport has become completely illogical. Chance intervention has given some areas heavily subsidized services while others have scarcely any public transport at all. No Government after Macmillan's had the courage to face this problem although Macmillan's minutes make it likely that he, as Prime Minister, would have tackled it with his customary thoroughness. As a result of Macmillan's sudden departure Beeching's dismantling of the railways must be looked on as one of the major aberrations of the Macmillan Government.

CHAPTER 18

A Bad Year

AFTER THEIR THIRD successive General Election defeat in October 1959, the Labour Party suffered from damaging internal quarrels and in the aftermath the Conservatives, in the first by-election of the new Parliament on 17 March 1960 in the Yorkshire marginal seat of Brighouse and Spenborough, won the seat from Labour with a swing to them of under one per cent. However, following the 1960 Budget which reversed the tax cuts of 1959, the Government lost popularity and a Liberal revival unlike anything since the 1920s occurred, which reached its peak in the early part of 1962.

From 1960 to 1962 Liberal candidates consistently forced Labour into third place in by-elections in Conservative territory; and at Labour-held Paisley in Scotland in April 1961, which they had not fought in the General Election, the Liberals were almost victorious, pushing the Conservative vote down from 43.8 per cent to 13.2 per cent with the popular Scottish figure John Bannerman as their candidate.

This Liberal revival peaked at Orpington on 14 March 1962 where the Liberal candidate, Eric Lubbock, won this hitherto safe Tory seat by 7,855 votes. Orpington is a prosperous suburb in the south-east corner of Greater London and had been won in 1959 by the Conservatives with a majority of 14,760. Polling in by-elections normally takes place on a Thursday, but for technical reasons the by-election in Blackpool North was held on the day before Orpington – Wednesday, 13 March. Here the Liberals who had been in third place in the General Election came second, only 973 votes behind the successful Conservative whose majority was reduced from 15,587. Had Blackpool North polled the day after, instead of the day before Orpington it would have produced another Liberal victory since Liberal credibility would have improved dramatically overnight.

The pay pause, rising prices, together with high and demonstrably inequitable taxation, were the cause of Conservative unpopularity at the time of Orpington. With opinion polls giving Labour no chance in that seat the voters went in for preferential voting on a large scale. In a well-publicized broadcast Eric Lubbock asserted that an important factor in his win was the unpopularity of the Schedule A property tax which the Liberals were campaigning to abolish. This factor has been much overlooked by commentators, and there is no doubt Macmillan blamed Selwyn Lloyd for not abolishing it in the 1962 Budget, as he had urged.*

The Orpington result, *The Times* wrote on 15 March, was 'the most severe blow the Conservatives have suffered since they returned to power in 1951'. On the same day Macmillan turned up unexpectedly at an important Conservative meeting in London and announced: 'What has happened is that Conservative voters have abstained, or voted Liberal as a by-election protest against some things they don't like, some things they don't understand, and some things where perhaps they are not patient enough to look to the end. I do not blame them.' Once again Macmillan was determined to show his 'unflappability'.[1]

His diary however tells a different tale. Fearing that tactical voting, with Labour voters deserting their own candidate for a better placed Liberal, could prove disastrous in traditionally safe Conservative seats, he wrote:

> We have been swept off our feet by the Liberal revival ... I fear the truth is that after ten years of unparalleled prosperity the people are bored ... we have made it possible for people to gratify their exasperation at minor difficulties by voting against the Government. In a word we have made England safe for Liberalism.

In a later entry he noted: 'The Conservative Party gets weaker and the Liberals eat into our position like rats ... They are voting Liberal to give the Government a smack in the eye.'[2]

In the safe Labour seat of Pontefract, where a by-election was held a week after Orpington with no Liberal standing, the Conservative vote remained steady. However at the Stockton-on-Tees by-election on 5 April 1962 the Conservative share of the poll fell from 46.3 per cent to 27.8 per cent, almost entirely as a result of the Liberals taking their votes.

The Liberal upsurge at Orpington in 1962 is largely an unexplained phenomenon. Since then, whenever a Conservative Government is unpopular, a massive protest swing at by-elections from them to the Liberals has become common; but the nearest parallel to Orpington until the 1990s was the spectacular Liberal victory at Conservative Sutton and Cheam during the Heath Government in December 1972 when the Liberal share went up from 14.6 per cent to a staggering 53.6 per cent.

---

* See Chapter 5, pages 81 ff.

In the three months following Orpington Conservatives continued to poll badly at by-elections. At Derby West on 6 June a relatively weak Liberal candidate came within 1,200 votes of winning this safe Conservative seat; the intervention of an Independent probably deprived the Liberals of a win. The Liberals were taking a much higher proportion of votes from the Conservatives than from Labour.

The Leicester North-East by-election on 12 July 1962 had dramatic consequences. In 1959 the Conservatives had been only 1,431 votes behind Labour, but in the 1962 by-election the Conservative vote plummeted from 17,990 to 6,578, putting them in third place with the Liberal candidate a close second to Labour. On Monday, 9 July, already forewarned, Iain Macleod, now Chairman of the Conservative Party, told Macmillan that the Central Office prediction was that the Tory candidate would lose his deposit at Leicester and it was essential to have an urgent Government reshuffle before the recess; Martin Redmayne, the Conservative Chief Whip, confirmed Macleod's alarming advice.

On 21 June Macmillan and Rab Butler had lunched together. Both were agreed, so Macmillan recorded in his diary, that Selwyn Lloyd must be replaced as Chancellor of the Exchequer. Butler was left in no doubt about what was in the Prime Minister's mind, and on 6 July Macmillan confirmed what he was about to do when Butler and Redmayne lunched with him at Admiralty House. Macmillan then asked Butler's opinion on Maudling's succeeding Lloyd as Chancellor. Dismissing Macmillan's doubts about whether he was sufficiently senior, Butler came out in favour of the appointment. However after the sackings Butler was to write that Macmillan had made Lloyd 'into a martyr'.

On 11 July, with his customary lack of discretion, Butler revealed Macmillan's decision to sack Lloyd while lunching at the *Daily Mail* with Lord Rothermere and Walter Terry, the lobby correspondent. On the morning of the 12th the *Daily Mail* had a great scoop, reporting that the Chancellor was likely to go, and that this information came from 'the highest possible source'. The Commons and Lords lunch tables were full of gossip that Butler had leaked the truth. Appalled at the *Daily Mail* story, Macmillan that morning, according to his official biographer, had one of his 'rare losses of nerve', although he had earlier recorded in his diary that he was 'sure it was right to make a change at the Treasury'.[3]

With Conservative MPs restive and the press derisory at the Conservatives' loss of popularity, the Prime Minister felt he must do something dramatic and in what is known as 'the night of long knives' he took desperate action. That day, 12 July, while Leicester was polling, he sacked seven of his Cabinet including the Chancellor of the Exchequer, who was held responsible by the public for Macmillan's own brain-child, the unpopular pay pause, and to whom Macmillan attributed responsibility for Conservative unpopularity for his failure to abolish Schedule A tax in the spring 1962 Budget. The drastic medicine worked, as will be seen; the best comment was that of Jeremy Thorpe, the Liberal MP and later leader, who declared: 'Greater love hath no man than that he lay down his friends for his life.'

Instinctively Macmillan believed that there was a plot to displace him by Conservative MPs who feared that without a new leader the Conservative Party would lose the General Election. He wrote to the Queen:

> I formed the view that there might be a Parliamentary or Party intrigue which might lead to a real danger to the Government. This would be enormously added to by the weekend press and all its speculations. It might therefore well be that unless action were taken rapidly, action would be too late, and that by the early days of next week the Government might be found unable to maintain itself. I therefore decided to get the whole thing done within the day. I cannot conceal from Your Majesty the dangers in our political situation if the present run of opinion continues as exhibited in by-elections.[4]

Macmillan was astray in believing there was a 'plot' against him. There was no conspiracy as such, although after the Orpington débâcle Ministers and MPs had naturally been discussing his departure. This was echoed by the press who predicted that the Conservatives must have a younger leader if they were to win the coming General Election. Macleod was frequently tipped as the front runner. Macmillan found this speculation about his future most aggravating and repeated his assertion that there had been a 'conspiracy' against him at the interview in which he sacked Lloyd on 12 July, and again three weeks later.

The carnage was soon over: 'if it were done when 'tis done, then 'twere well / It were done quickly.' Selwyn Lloyd had no inkling on the morning of 12 July that he was to be sacked. At the Cabinet meeting that morning there was a full economic discussion in which Lloyd took a prominent part, and at the end of the discussion he referred to the report in the *Daily Mail* of his likely demise. Macmillan denied any responsibility for the rumours, and Lloyd then asked him if he would approve Lord Justice Sellers, a Court of Appeal judge, as chairman of the proposed National Incomes Commission. According to Lloyd a 'distrait' Macmillan agreed.

At 4.15 p.m. Tim Bligh, the Prime Minister's principal private secretary, who was a personal friend of Lloyd's, appeared in the Chancellor's room at the Treasury. He was, according to Lloyd's diary, 'ashen pale and stammering more than usual'. Bligh had been told by

Macmillan that Lloyd was to be summarily sacked and not offered another job. Bligh said: 'The PM wants to see you at six this evening. We have always been good friends, and I must warn you it is about the reshuffle.' Lloyd said: 'Does he want me to go?' Bligh said: 'Yes.'

Bligh had been shocked at the news. For five and a half years Lloyd and Macmillan had been the closest of colleagues and on the friendliest of terms. Macmillan frequently lent Chequers to Lloyd for the weekend and they had regular and frank discussions about the vital affairs of state. It seemed impossible that Lloyd could be sacked at a moment's notice, and the Prime Minister's entourage could hardly believe it.

When they met at Admiralty House Macmillan began by asking Lloyd if he wanted to go into the City for 'the final decade of his active life'. Lloyd said 'No.' According to Lloyd's account of the interview at Admiralty House, Macmillan replied:

I am in great difficulty. I could go myself, leaving Butler in charge. He would not last six months. Secondly we could go on as we are, but never has a Government had so low a measure of political support in the country. Thirdly I could reconstruct in a radical fashion, and that is what I propose to do.

Selwyn replied that they had frequently talked of a government reconstruction at some stage, but 'did not this sudden move savour of panic?' Macmillan said that 'the situation was desperate and something had to be done quickly.' Lloyd responded: 'It is wrong psychologically to do it at this moment, and if you intend a radical reconstruction you had much better wait until October.' Macmillan then said 'the situation was too desperate for that. I said "Do you not think they will say it is 'the old man' who ought to go?" He said "Maybe." I asked him when he wanted it announced. He said he wanted it out by 7 p.m. the next day. He referred to press leaks.'

To Macmillan's surprise Lloyd refused the offer of a peerage. Lloyd wrote in his diary:

So we parted after five and a half years of close association . . . he had allowed me to use Chequers, shown sympathy in my domestic troubles [Lloyd's divorce] and had been very thoughtful for the comfort and convenience of myself and my daughter. I thought he was damaging his own position beyond repair.

Here Lloyd was wrong; within a few months of the sackings Macmillan's position was greatly improved. But Macmillan's allegations at their interview that there was a 'conspiracy' against him, and that Lloyd was in some way part of it, were particularly trying to Lloyd one of whose great qualities was loyalty.

Lloyd then talked to his close friends John Hare, Minister of Labour, and Nigel Birch (who had never been offered a Ministerial post since his 1958 resignation in sympathy with Thorneycroft). Birch was bitter against Macmillan and tried to persuade Hare to resign as a protest against Lloyd's dismissal. This would have been an acute embarrassment for Macmillan and might even have put the future of the Government at risk. However Hare was not made of resigning stuff. Still Birch put the knife in, writing to *The Times*:

> Sir,
>   For the second time the Prime Minister has got rid of a Chancellor of the Exchequer who tried to get expenditure under control.
>   Once is more than enough.
>
>   Yours truly,
>   Nigel Birch

Lloyd has recorded in his diary the strangest episode of the 'night of long knives'. Three weeks later, on 1 August, Macmillan to Lloyd's surprise asked him round to Admiralty House for a tête-à-tête. As Bligh, the private secretary, greeted Lloyd at the front door, he said to him: 'He is spending all the time thinking of how to bring you back ... He is depressed about the Common Market.' According to Lloyd's diary, after a silence, with doubt as to who would talk first:

> [Macmillan] said that he had been very sorry about it all. I said that my regret was the damage that it had done to him. I could not understand why he had not discussed it with me beforehand. He said that he had made a mistake. He had been rushed. One day he would tell me the conspiracy against him which had forced his hand. I said that we had talked about everything else together. He had underestimated my loyalty. Did he think that I would lead a revolt against him? He said 'No,' but Butler had been plotting to divide the party on the Common Market, and bring him down.*
> He realized that he had made a mess of it. He had meant to talk to me on 12 July about something which would happen this week or even after the House was up. His only anxiety was Europe. He would fight an election on that, perhaps lose, and then the Party and not the Queen would choose the next leader. That was important to me. I asked when he would do this. He said, 'Next autumn,' I said '62 or 63'? He said 63.

Lloyd wrote of this unsuccessful effort to mend the bridges: 'I am afraid my conclusion was one of his utter ruthlessness and his determination to retain power by the sacrifice of even his closest friends. He was now concerned to conciliate me because I had become a possible danger.'[5]

---

* Macmillan's suggestion that Butler had been plotting to divide the Conservative Party over the Common Market and bring Macmillan down was wild. Butler was not a plotter.

In addition to Lloyd the Ministers sacked were Lord Kilmuir (Lord Chancellor), Harold Watkinson (Defence), Dr Charles Hill (Housing), Lord Mills (Minister without Portfolio), John Maclay (Scotland) and David Eccles (Education). They were replaced by Reginald Maudling, Reginald Manningham-Buller (who became Lord Dilhorne), Peter Thorneycroft, Sir Keith Joseph, William Deedes, Michael Noble and Sir Edward Boyle. Rab Butler left the Home Office and was given the 'nebulous' post of First Secretary of State: a demotion although Macmillan made out that it was the equivalent of Deputy Prime Minister, a post which does not exist under the British constitution although it was used in the official listings. Eccles was offered another Cabinet post but declined, saying he must be Chancellor of the Exchequer or nothing; he was clearly not of this calibre.

Kilmuir, who had some time before told Macmillan he would like to quit in 1963, was bitter. In his memoirs he wrote:

> I got the impression that he was extremely alarmed about his own position, and was determined to eliminate any risk for himself by a massive change of Government. It astonished me that a man who had kept his head under the most severe stresses and strains should lose both nerve and judgement in this way.

Lloyd recorded in his diary that both Kilmuir and his wife were 'extremely angry' when he talked to them at a dinner party. Kilmuir complained to friends that his cook would have been given more notice of dismissal than he had; when Macmillan heard of this he commented that it was easier to get Lord Chancellors than cooks.[6]

Harold Watkinson too was completely unprepared for his dismissal. He has described his interview with Macmillan:

> I found the PM alone, but with Tim Bligh, his Principal Private Secretary, hovering around. Harold Macmillan looked tired and distressed. In emotional terms he told me that the Government was in crisis. He painted a picture of a political situation that was beyond my wildest dreams and his forebodings of Ministerial revolt, centred upon Selwyn Lloyd, did not seem to me to make sense. I did not know at this time that he had already seen Selwyn and removed him from his office as Chancellor of the Exchequer. Nor was I aware of the fact that Selwyn had said that he wished to continue in the Commons to defend his financial policies. Yet even if I had known of the rift between Harold Macmillan and his previous Chancellor I would still have doubted whether the Prime Minister was correct in his judgement of the situation. Selwyn, who was a friend of mine, was not of the stuff of which rebels are made.[7]

By bringing in younger blood in the shape of Keith Joseph, Edward Boyle and William Deedes, and replacing Lloyd by the warmer and obviously more able Reginald Maudling, the purge was to be of major benefit to the Government's image. However the short-term result was a sharp drop in Macmillan's popularity. On 11 July his rating was: Satisfied 47%. Dissatisfied 39%. Don't know 12%. On 20 July, following the purge, it was: Satisfied 26%. Dissatisfied 52%. Don't know 12%. Apart from Selwyn Lloyd none of the usual letters were exchanged between the Prime Minister and the outgoing Ministers and the press emphasized that Macmillan had been 'ruthless'.

Butler's view was that by 'the night of long knives' Macmillan created 'one of the strongest young Cabinets of the century'. Lloyd had delayed unduly in modifying the rigours of deflation; particularly sensitive on this issue, Macmillan had determined to dismiss him largely so that the Treasury brief against rapid expansion could be rewritten.[8]

Butler diagnosed the situation correctly; Selwyn Lloyd with his nonconformist conscience felt that reflation would lead to rapidly rising prices and balance of payments crises which would damage the pound and cause the brakes to be slammed on, and do damage to national prosperity. With his eye on the coming General Election Macmillan was determined to boost Conservative popularity by raising living standards rapidly through reflation. In his new Chancellor, Reginald Maudling, Macmillan had a man without Lloyd's scruples about putting the economy at risk and one who was ready, in conjunction with Macmillan, to seek ways of ensuring expansion without producing runaway inflation which were unorthodox and contrary to Treasury thinking. As we have seen in Chapter 6, the more flexible Maudling was ready to consider devaluation of sterling and import controls as weapons to prevent balance of payments crises if living standards rose too fast in the run-up to the General Election. Neither Macmillan nor Maudling suggested selling off nationalized industries and using the money realized to cut taxes before the election as the Thatcher and Major governments have done.

Macmillan's original biographer, Nigel Fisher, who was a junior Minister at the time, sums it up well:

> Macmillan needed a boom to coincide with an appeal to the country; he had stage-managed this successfully in 1959 and was anxious to repeat the performance. He tried hard to persuade Lloyd to expand the economy, but failed – so the Chancellor who had become a political liability had to go. He had eliminated in Selwyn Lloyd the obstacle to reflation, and had appointed a Chancellor whose views were in tune with his own. It is at least questionable whether these views and their implementation over the following two years were in the national interest. They were certainly in the Conservative interest.

On the whole the sackings of 12 July were well received by

Conservative MPs. On 19 July Macmillan spoke to the 1922 Committee of back-bench Tory MPs; 250 turned up and he had a reasonable reception. He wrote in his diary: 'Feeling is now moving definitely towards me and my action'; letters to him from the public were two to one in favour, and he expected the same ratio to be operating in the postbags of other Conservative MPs.

Regarding the proceedings at the meeting with the 1922 Committee Tom Lindsay, the *Daily Telegraph* chief lobby correspondent who was always reliably informed, wrote: 'Hopes of the reconstruction turning out for the best were more prevalent at the end than at the beginning ... The duration of the meeting was in itself an indication that things had gone pretty well. It lasted only about half an hour.'[9] *The Times* Parliamentary correspondent took a less favourable view, reporting that the 1922 Committee only lasted twenty minutes because Macmillan pleaded another engagement, and 'some were impressed but others suspended judgement waiting for the debate on the Labour censure motion'. Lloyd was reported on the same day as saying: 'I am an expansionist but not on inflation.'

In the censure debate on 26 July the back-bench Conservative Gilbert Longden, amid much Labour laughter, congratulated Macmillan on keeping his head when all around him were losing theirs. Grimond accused the Prime Minister of being an exhausted man trying to regain the voters' favour by doing 'things everyone else had said for years ought to be done'. At no point in the debate, *The Times* claimed, did Macmillan 'get to the heart of the matter'. In the course of it he had produced a gimmick in the shape of the National Incomes Commission which was to replace the Council on Prices, Productivity and Incomes (disbanded the previous year) as a permanent body to investigate incomes in the private and public sector. Its main difference from COPPI was that it would hold its sittings in public, not private. It did not appeal to the Labour Party and the trade unions any more than COPPI:* the trade unions refused to attend sittings and it became a dead letter.

Gaitskell in leading for the Opposition made the mistake of concentrating on personalities not policies. The Government Whips worked hard; there were no Conservative abstentions and the majority was 98, four more than the formal majority. However Macmillan had made powerful enemies who were to come close to doing him down twelve months later.

In their leading article the next morning *The Times* commented that Selwyn Lloyd more courageously than any other Tory Chancellor with the exception of Thorneycroft had grasped the nettle of inflation:

---

* See Chapter 10, pages 204 ff.

If however the change presages a retreat from the central position taken up
by Mr Selwyn Lloyd to precipitate the reflation of the economy with any
thought of buying the Conservative Party out of electoral troubles it will
deserve to be remembered as an act of cowardice ... The general appearance
of the new Ministry is a decided improvement on the old. So root and branch
a reconstruction is the measure of the electoral issues.

Here was the sting and it was echoed by other astute commentators.

In his resignation letter Lloyd had written: 'I realize the policies with
which I have been associated have been unpopular. On the other hand
I believe they have been right and have had a considerable measure of
success.' Macmillan replied tendentiously that they would be continued,
but this was not believed since Maudling was widely expected to be more
lenient over reflation.

The Tory Party Conference went off well, with Macmillan personally
receiving 'a tremendous welcome'; the emphasis was on the EEC, not economic policy. Sensibly Maudling waited until November before reversing
Lloyd's austerity measures in a mini-Budget. Then he cut the tax on
motor cars and reduced bank rate and purchase tax, as has been seen.

The Liberal surge that had brought them close to winning Leicester
North-East, although they had not contested it since 1955, did not burn
itself out for a few more months. In November at Chippenham the
Liberal candidate, Christopher Layton, came within 1,500 votes of
winning this safe Conservative seat. If the Labour vote had polarized,
as at Orpington, he would have won but in this area with many factories
Labour obtained 29 per cent of the vote. In March 1963 in Labour-held
Colne Valley Liberals came a close second to Labour although they had
been in third place in 1959. After that Liberal support tailed away, with
the abolition of Schedule A tax in Maudling's spring 1963 Budget
depriving them of one of their most potent weapons, and voting support
coalesced once again round Conservative and Labour.

De Gaulle's veto in January 1963 on Britain's entering the EEC
completed a bad twelve months for the Macmillan Government. The
coldest winter for two centuries pushed unemployment up to a post-war
peak of 4 per cent and there was a corresponding unexpected downturn
in the economy. In February 1963 Labour were 15 per cent ahead in
the Gallup Poll, with the Liberals slumping badly. It was Labour's largest
lead in seventeen years.

Then the Macmillan Government were involved in two serious
scandals – first Vassall, then Profumo.

John Vassall was a cypher clerk in the British Embassy in Moscow. He
was a homosexual; KGB officers took incriminating photographs of him

and then blackmailed him into acting as a Soviet agent and betraying secrets. His contacts with certain Russians had been known to the British Embassy in Moscow and his homosexuality suspected but ignored by the Foreign Office for seven years. He had been attached to naval intelligence in London in 1956 but his 'vetting' there had not disclosed that his homosexuality made him a security risk.

The discovery that Vassall was a spy had serious repercussions for the Government: he had been employed for a time as private secretary to Tom Galbraith when the latter was Civil Lord of the Admiralty, and Galbraith had since become Under-Secretary at the Scottish Office. Rumours circulated widely that there had been a homosexual relationship between Galbraith and Vassall. Galbraith resigned with Macmillan's approval. No evidence of such an affair could be found, and when letters between them were published as a White Paper Galbraith was completely exonerated.

In the Commons debate on Vassall in early November Thorneycroft, the Minister of Defence, treated the matter flippantly and the Labour Party and the press accused Galbraith and Peter Carrington, First Lord of the Admiralty, of culpable negligence. Macmillan then appointed a tribunal under Lord Radcliffe to examine 250 sensational newspaper reports about Vassall. Reporting in April 1963 Radcliffe reached the conclusion that not one of these allegations could be justified. James Margach, the *Sunday Times* chief lobby correspondent, has commented that the editors and journalists concerned 'had been given every opportunity and offered the protection of privilege to justify their allegations. They failed to do so and the tribunal completely vindicated both Ministers [Galbraith and Carrington].'*

There was an unfortunate sequel. Two journalists refused to disclose the sources of information on which they had based their stories, and in March 1963 these journalists were sentenced each to six months imprisonment 'for contempt of court'. With these two martyrs to press confidentiality, relations between Downing Street and Fleet Street sank to a low ebb at an unfortunate moment, for the Vassall scandal was quickly to be followed by Profumo.

In his autobiography Macmillan admitted to being depressed and worried at the Government's electoral prospects in the early spring of 1963, but by the end of April he felt 'we were now through the worst'. On 27 and 28 April he held a two-day meeting of Ministers at Chequers; Macmillan describes this glowingly. The archives tell a different story.

The conference was first suggested by Martin Redmayne, the Chief

---

* See *Security in the Public Sector* (Cmd 1681, April 1963).

Whip, as a means of restoring Party morale; Macmillan reluctantly agreed, hoping 'it would emphasize the solidarity of the Party'. Bligh minuted to Macmillan that Brooke, Thorneycroft, Sandys and Home would not want to come and the meeting could 'do more harm than good'. However Macmillan persisted and invited his colleagues to dine and sleep at Chequers. The meeting was to discuss 'Britain in the Seventies'.

In a thank-you letter Butler was derogatory about the discussion on social benefits (he thought it got off to 'a bad start') but promised to begin work on a pamphlet 'Britain in Top Gear'. It never saw the light of day. Hailsham in his letter admitted disappointment with the whole affair, and thought spending on higher education was 'more important for the old age of the present generation than higher pensions'. The social discussion, he considered, 'got bogged down', and he did not see why those who drew full wages for twenty to thirty years should not be able to make their own provision for pensions; he did not want to enter into a competition with Labour over higher pensions. Given the gap between Hailsham's reactionary position and that of the young reformers Macleod, Maudling and Heath over social policy, the discussion must have been almost comic. Macleod described it as 'a much publicized and somewhat pointless planning weekend at Chequers on the modernization of Britain'. Home, who was at Chequers on the morning of 27 April, did not even attend.[10]

Meanwhile even as publication of the Radcliffe Report was boosting the Government's stock, disaster struck. Jack Profumo, Secretary of State for War, was the son of an extremely wealthy Italian-born KC, Baron Albert Profumo, who had been an unsuccessful Tory candidate and owned an enormous stake in Provident Life Assurance. Profumo's mother was American and his parents lived at Avon Dassett near Banbury in a beautiful country house. They were charming and hospitable and popular with the neighbourhood. Both his sisters married into the aristocracy. Although his abilities did not fit him for the highest Cabinet posts Profumo was a successful politician; he had been Minister of State at the Foreign Office and performed well both there and in his job as Secretary of State for War. He and his actress wife Valerie Hobson were well known and much liked. Profumo got on well with the army chiefs and with the Labour Opposition. He seemed to have a glittering future and scarcely an enemy in the world, apart from the Labour MP Colonel George Wigg who had taken offence at pointed remarks made by Profumo in a defence debate, on which subject Wigg considered himself a great expert.

Unfortunately Profumo had been strongly attracted to a good-looking model, Christine Keeler, whom he had met when she had been parted

from her bathing costume at Lord Astor's Cliveden swimming pool on
7 July 1961. She was the mistress of Stephen Ward, a talented artist
and osteopath of great charm, who had been given appointments to
sketch the Royal Family; he was popular in the newspaper and political
world and had rented a cottage from his friend Lord Astor at Cliveden.
In the next few days Profumo contrived with Ward to meet Keeler at
Ward's flat and there he slept with her.

Alas, Keeler was concurrently in cahoots with Captain Yegveny
Ivanov, the naval attaché at the Soviet Embassy in London, who was
under police surveillance, and it was reported to MI5 that both Ivanov
and Profumo frequented the flat in which Keeler lived. As a result the
Secretary to the Cabinet, Sir Norman Brook, conveyed a warning to
Profumo on 9 August 1961 that there would be a security risk if he
continued to visit Keeler. Cancelling his next appointment to see her
Profumo wrote this imprudent letter to her:

9.8.61

Darling,
   In great haste and because I can get no reply from your phone.
   Alas something's blown up tomorrow night and I can't therefore make
it. I'm terribly sorry especially as I leave the next day for various trips and
then a holiday so won't be able to see you again until some time in
September. Blast it. Please take great care of yourself and don't run away.

Love J.

P.S. I'm writing this 'cos I know you're off for the day tomorrow and I
want you to know before you go if I still can't reach you by phone.

After 9 August 1961 Profumo hardly saw Keeler again – their liaison
lasted only a brief five weeks – and, although he and his wife had been
on very friendly terms with Ward, they discreetly but rigorously cut
down their social contacts with him. Profumo had also been informed
by the Secretary to the Cabinet that Ivanov had used the good offices
of Sir Godfrey Nicholson, MP, a rich distiller of impeccable character,
who was a patient and admirer of Ward, to try to pass information from
the Foreign Office to the Soviet Embassy on a confidential basis about
both disarmament and the Berlin crisis, and had arranged for Ward to
meet Sir Harold Caccia, the head of the Foreign Office. Caccia declined
an invitation from Ward to meet Ivanov.[11]

Through the report by Lord Denning and the recently released Public
Record Office archives it is now possible to tell the complete story of
the Profumo affair. It reflects discredit on the Macmillan Government
although there was no breach of security of any sort. Denning found
that Stephen Ward's activities, 'although misconceived and misdirected,
were not deliberately mischievous'. Ward was also employed by MI5 to

try to discover from Ivanov intelligence about Soviet activities. Later MI5 disowned Ward when the Prime Minister became alarmed that he might name Ministers once he was charged with living on immoral earnings.

Unluckily for Profumo and the Macmillan Government rumours of the Profumo–Ivanov–Keeler triangle had already reached the press. They surfaced abroad and in an article in the *Queen* magazine in July 1962, and rapidly became widespread in London. In January 1963 Profumo received the disconcerting news that Keeler had signed a contract to sell her story to the *Sunday Pictorial* (the forerunner of the *Sunday Mirror*) for £1,000 and Johnny Edgecombe, a West Indian drug pusher and lover of Keeler, was about to be tried at the Old Bailey on the charge of having shot at Keeler in Ward's flat. Keeler was to be a key witness. Ward, through Lord Astor, communicated the ominous tale to Profumo, and immediately on receiving the news Profumo got on to the head of the Security Service and pleaded with him in vain to get either D notices served or 'something' to stop publication. Ward lunched with Profumo at the Dorchester where Ward revealed that Keeler had also handed over the 'Darling' letter to the *Sunday Pictorial*. In an interview with the police Keeler had also made a voluntary statement revealing her association with Profumo and the fact that Ward had asked her to find out from the Minister the state of play about the release to West Germany of atomic bomb secrets.[12]

On 28 January at 11 in the evening Profumo called on the Attorney-General, Sir John Hobson, revealed his five weeks' association with Keeler and the existence of the 'Darling' letter, but denied vigorously that he had ever been intimate with the girl. Profumo proffered the ingenuous argument, which Hobson surprisingly accepted, that in the show business circles in which Profumo and his wife moved the expression 'darling' was so commonly used that it was meaningless. The gullible Hobson accepted Profumo's version but told the Secretary of State that he must take proceedings if the story was published, and put him in touch with a solicitor, Derek Clogg of Theodore Goddard.*

On 4 February Profumo saw Hobson again: this time the Solicitor-General Peter Rawlinson was also present. Profumo told them that Keeler had suggested he should give her £5,000 to renege on her contract with the *Sunday Pictorial*. The matter was referred to the Director of Public Prosecutions but he declined to intervene. (In his report Denning also expressed himself satisfied that there was no sinister motive in this request for money.) To the law officers Profumo now admitted he had

---

* Later Hobson was to tell Denning that on 28 January 'he retained a reasonable incredulity' regarding Profumo's story which he thought 'odd' and 'suspicious'.

given Keeler presents and asserted vigorously that he would sue for libel if any story was published impugning him. Rawlinson reminded Profumo that in a libel case the defendant might try to prove that Profumo had been guilty of adultery. Profumo told the law officers it would be grossly unfair if he were driven from public life when he was innocent and only a victim of malevolent gossip. The Radcliffe Tribunal was about to report on Vassall, and the Cabinet was apprehensive of further malicious rumours about Ministers such as those which had toppled Galbraith. In his autobiography Rawlinson records that he felt 'uneasy' about the Profumo denial. It would have been better for Profumo if Rawlinson had acted on this 'uneasiness'.[13]

On 1 February Mark Chapman-Walker, General Manager of the *News of the World*, called on John Wyndham, one of the Prime Minister's secretaries, while Macmillan was in Rome for conferences with the Italian Government; he revealed that Profumo 'had compromised himself with a girl who was involved with a Negro now charged with an attempted murder', and that Keeler's story had been sold to the Daily Mirror Group, proprietors of the *Sunday Pictorial*. Chapman-Walker said that the story would include passages 'in which she was involved with Profumo and in which the Russian naval attaché also figured'.

Wyndham wrote the following alarming minute for the Prime Minister:

Top Secret
According to Mr Chapman-Walker Mr Profumo is alleged to have met this girl 'Kolania' through Lord Astor at Cliveden, where they chased her naked round the bathing pool.
According to Mr Chapman-Walker it is also alleged that:
(i) 'Kolania' got into this company through the agency of a Mr Ward, who Mr Chapman-Walker described as a 'psychopathic [*sic*]* specialist' of Wimpole Street;
(ii) Mr Profumo, visiting 'Kolania' in Mr Ward's house, passed in the passage the Russian Naval Attaché on his way out from 'Kolania';
(iii) 'Kolania' has two letters on War Office paper signed 'J' – although it is not suggested that these letters are anything more than ones of assignation.

Macmillan saw the minute as soon as he returned to London. It should have alerted him to the extreme danger into which Profumo was plunging his Government. It did not, and his failure to nip the affair in the bud produced fearful troubles.[14] Alistair Horne writes that the

---

* Ward was an osteopath.

one person who could have alerted Macmillan to the true nature of the affair was John Wyndham whom Macmillan regarded almost as a surrogate son, and who had his ear close 'to the ground in London clubland and society'. Horne continues: 'There is no evidence to suggest that he did; or, if he did, it was in such muted terms as not to be heard by Macmillan.' Wyndham's minute above was a clear and by no means muted warning: Macmillan chose to ignore it.

That same evening Bligh, alerted by Wyndham, interviewed Profumo and told him that he would normally have reported the incident immediately to the Prime Minister but as he was out of the country he was not sure how to proceed. Profumo asked Bligh not to inform the Prime Minister at all; Bligh said he must. As a result Profumo saw Martin Redmayne, the Chief Whip, on 4 February. Profumo outlined his version of the story to Redmayne in the presence of Bligh. Profumo put two questions to Redmayne: Should he tell the Prime Minister? and should he resign? Redmayne replied in the negative to both. On Redmayne, because of this bad advice, falls grave responsibility for what followed. Clearly Profumo should have resigned as Secretary of State. However, so great was the fear of more damage to the Government from disclosures of lax security that the Chief Whip was loath to allow this. At this stage Radcliffe had not yet cleared Galbraith.

Thus the Attorney-General, the Solicitor-General and the Chief Whip accepted Profumo's denial although friends who knew him well would never believe that he had interested himself in an uneducated young girl like Keeler without ulterior sexual motives. Rawlinson in his memoirs claims that Profumo disarmed them by insisting he would sue any publication that repeated the story. On 8 March 1963 the opportunity to sue occurred when the popular and well-informed lobby correspondent Andrew Roth, in his weekly newsletter *Westminster Confidential*, claimed that call-girls, needing money, had revealed Profumo's involvement with Ivanov. He also wrote that Charles Fletcher-Cooke was in contact with a good-looking youth on remand from a Borstal. Fletcher-Cooke was Under-Secretary at the Home Office.

THAT WAS THE GOVERNMENT THAT WAS!

'That is certain to bring down the Government!' a Conservative MP wailed – 'and what will my wife say?'

This combination of tragedy and tragi-comedy came from the effort of this MP to check with a newspaperman on the story which has run like wildfire through Parliament.

The best-authenticated version is this: that two call-girls came into the limelight as a result of the effort of a Negro to kill them for having given him a venereal disease. This notoriety having made their calling difficult, the two girls started selling their stories to the Sunday newspapers, the *Sunday Pictorial* and the *People* in particular.

One of the choicest bits in their stories was a letter, apparently signed 'Jock' on the stationery of the Secretary for War. The allegation by this girl was that not only was this Minister, who has a famous actress as his wife, her client, but also the Soviet military attaché, apparently a Colonel Ivanov. The famous-actress wife, of course, would sue for divorce, the scandal ran. Who was using the call-girl to 'milk' whom of information – the War Secretary or the Soviet military attaché? – ran the minds of those primarily interested in security.

It was probably knowledge about this story as well as the scandal concerning Charles Fletcher-Cooke and his young good-looking car-borrowing friend which led the Chief Whip, Brigadier Redmayne, to tell a correspondent with resignation: 'We have all the luck!'

The Attorney-General and Profumo agreed however that *Westminster Confidential*, though read by nearly all MPs and lobby correspondents, had too small a circulation to justify a libel action. It was a strange decision unless Hobson by now was seriously doubting Profumo's veracity.

The editor of *Westminster Confidential*, Andrew Roth, had a lobby pass as the representative of a French newspaper. Instead of advising Profumo to sue, Redmayne now attempted to take away Roth's pass, writing to Bligh, 'I do not want particularly to take any action about it myself but I value your advice.' Bligh replied that it was 'difficult for us who are clearly members of the executive to nudge the Sergeant at Arms' who was a servant of Parliament. This attempt at revenge by Redmayne was unedifying.[15]

Bligh minuted to the Prime Minister that Roth's 'pamphlet' was definitely libellous but it might be 'a mistake to launch on a libel action in respect of documents which so few people had seen'. (He was ignoring the influential nature of the readership of *Westminster Confidential*.) According to Bligh the damage caused to a Minister's reputation by the 'reporting in the press that would then take place would far outweigh any damage caused by the pamphlet itself'.

Bligh, on behalf of the Prime Minister, also sought the views of the Attorney-General on the smears. On 17 March Hobson replied:

There is no doubt in my mind that the document published by Parliamentary Profiles Services Ltd [the company responsible for *Westminster Confidential*] is defamatory of both Profumo and Fletcher-Cooke.*

I have discussed the position with Profumo and his private legal adviser. Profumo is disinclined at the moment to take any action, and intends for

---

* Fletcher-Cooke denied 'impropriety' but admitted 'error of judgement'. He resigned in order to take legal action. He was knighted in 1981.

the time being to ignore the publication. He understands that this is in accordance with the views of the Prime Minister. His private legal advice is in this sense too.

I ought to let you know that Profumo told me that the press have begun in the last few days to try and get in touch with his wife. While his information is that the *Sunday Pictorial* and the *People* have decided to drop the girl other papers may now begin to get and seem to be getting interested.

The trial in which the girl is concerned starts tomorrow at the Old Bailey and after that and probably next week I suspect myself there is a substantial risk that stories may begin to appear in the national press.

Gossip has also revived today in the smoking room [of the Commons].

I agree that for the moment Profumo can afford to ignore this publication, but I feel it may become increasingly difficult for him to maintain his position much longer.[16]

Profumo's enemy in the Commons, Wigg, had smelt out Profumo's involvement with Keeler, and Keeler's liaison with Ivanov; he thought it the perfect scandal with which to demolish the Government while they were reeling under the impact of Galbraith and Vassall. Harold Wilson and other members of the Shadow Cabinet constantly planted the story off the record with journalists. The author's sister, who worked for *The Times*, was Chairman of the Women's Press Club of London; she was told of it in confidence by Harold Wilson when he was guest of honour at their club dinner.

Late in the evening of Thursday, 21 March, during a Commons debate on the imprisonment of the two journalists for their failure to disclose their sources to the court in reporting on the Vassall–Galbraith affair, Wigg, supported by Barbara Castle, Richard Crossman and Michael Foot, mentioned the mass of rumours surrounding the conduct of a certain Minister; they invited the Government to deny it. Wigg smoothly alleged that he was motivated solely by 'security considerations'.

Profumo, who on his way home from a dinner had called in at the Commons during the debate, was told of Wigg's remarks, but the Chief Whip merely told him he might now have to make a statement. He went home at midnight to find his house surrounded by journalists, but breaking through their cordon he and his wife went to bed soon after midnight, both taking strong sleeping pills.

When the debate ended at 1.30 a.m. Redmayne consulted with Macleod and Hobson; the three thought it was a splendid opportunity for Profumo to deny the allegations without the Minister taking out a libel action. They decided this must be done urgently to prevent the Sunday newspapers exploiting the Government's embarrassment and headlining the unanswered rumours as part of the current press campaign against the Government. William Deedes, Minister without Portfolio, and responsible for government propaganda, was in the House at the end of the debate; he and the Solicitor-General were summoned to Redmayne's room. The five Ministers agreed that Profumo must make a statement that very Friday morning.* However, having taken sleeping pills, the Profumos did not respond to telephone calls so the Chief Whip sent a secretary in his car to their house. With difficulty the Profumos were awakened at 2.45 a.m. Derek Clogg was also summoned.

Arriving at the Commons in the early hours of 22 March Profumo was told that the Government could not afford a repetition of the Galbraith affair, and therefore he must either make a personal statement denying the allegations or resign his office forthwith. In a split second's miscalculation Profumo said the charges were untrue. Immediately Macleod instructed the law officers to draft a statement which Profumo was called on to make to the House later that morning. In haste Rawlinson and Hobson went to a separate room and Rawlinson drafted the statement; Profumo left the wording of it to the law officers. Hobson and Rawlinson worked in a manner reminiscent of Kilmuir at Chequers in 1959 after the Cabinet had decided to reject the Devlin Report. When Profumo read the statement proposed for him he remarked: 'Must I really say I was friendly with her?' The others pointed out that there was no alternative in view of the 'Darling' letter. After consulting Clogg, Profumo agreed the statement and made no further comments.[17]

When the author saw Lord Denning in October 1994 Denning had refreshed his memory from his thirty-year-old papers, and was more fiercely critical of the behaviour of the Chief Whip and the four Ministers who had interviewed Profumo in the early hours of 22 March, than in his 1963 written report. He reiterated to the author several times in strong terms that in his view it was a 'dreadful thing' to bring Profumo out of bed at that hour of the morning when he was 'groggy' from sleeping pills. His view is that it should have been left over the weekend and that Redmayne and the Ministers 'did it for their own protection which was most unfair. I have every sympathy with Profumo for being called out in the middle of the night and forced to sign a statement without being given any opportunity to consider the matter. It is the constitutional duty of the Attorney-General to advise Ministers about personal statements, when asked, and for Ministers to follow that advice.' Denning emphasized that in Profumo's case he did not ask for advice; it was proffered, not sought.

When the official documents relating to the Denning Report were released under the thirty-year rule on 1 January 1994 there was

---

* The Chief Whip is not technically a Minister but as he attends all Cabinet meetings he is frequently referred to as one.

considerable comment on the affair in the national press. On 14 February 1994 Lord Denning sent a note to be added to his archive in the Hampshire Record Office: 'They insisted that Mr Profumo, awakened from a drugged sleep, must make a denial by 11 a.m. which he did. They should have waited until Monday morning to see him with a statement from him in the afternoon.'[18]

On 2 January 1994, the day following the release of the official documents, William (now Lord) Deedes wrote an article in the *Sunday Telegraph* showing that he shared Denning's view; he too was shocked at the way in which the Profumo statement was railroaded through in the early morning of 22 March 1963 by the five Ministers.

> I have felt deep uneasiness about the way some of us handled this business in 1963 and contributed to the disaster. Was it really sensible to convene a meeting of Ministers at 2 a.m. in the Chief Whip's room at the House of Commons and summon Jack Profumo from his home to this Star Chamber instantly to answer 'Yes' or 'No' to charges which Labour MPs had been bandying in the House earlier in the night?

Profumo reached the House in a 'bemused state', Deedes went on, because he had taken a sleeping draught and then been woken up.

> I have often wondered as one present at this extraordinary gathering whether in these circumstances I would instantly have owned up to the truth, the whole truth and nothing but the truth.
>   Later we were accused of being hoodwinked; but I think the charge against us is graver than that. We created circumstances which made the truth extremely hard to tell. If it emerged in court that policemen had been guilty of such procedures I think it likely that a judge would order the accused to be discharged.

Like Denning, Deedes deplores the 'hurry':

> We were moreover in a desperate hurry. This was the early morning of Friday when the House would meet again at 11 a.m. Questions would be asked. A quick answer had to be found.
>   I set out the circumstances in full for the first time so that others may consult their conscience and declare confidently, if they can, that in these circumstances they would unhesitatingly have owned up. It is a difficult test but a crucial one because for three decades the chattering classes, adulterers amongst them, have been pleased to say that it was not the infidelity that mattered but a lie to the House of Commons. Whether the circumstances which led to this lie constitute mitigation or not I leave to others to judge . . . Jack Profumo has elected to serve the full sentence . . . he has done more in the service of other people's lives than anyone I know . . . it may be a good time for this sorry tale to be reviewed.[19]

In his autobiography published in 1989 the Solicitor-General, now

Lord Rawlinson, shows none of Deedes's contrition for his behaviour
in the early hours of that Friday. Instead he quotes a letter he wrote
to the Chief Whip on 14 June after Profumo's admission of deception:
'I of course regret we were so totally deceived but I utterly reject any
suggestion that Profumo's claim was one which could be obviously or
readily rejected'; Profumo told 'not only a wicked series of lies' but it
was also 'a most brazen and convincing performance'. Rawlinson goes
out of his way pointedly to contradict the allegation in the Denning
Report that Profumo was 'groggy' from sleeping pills, writing: 'I did
not gain any impression of drowsiness; his statement and interjections
belied any lack of understanding.'[20]

During this early morning conversation with Profumo it transpired
that Ivanov and Ward had been guests at a party at Macleod's flat – albeit
self-invited – and all five knew that Profumo had given Keeler presents
and been alone with her in the Ward flat more than once. They also
knew of the existence of the 'Darling' letter in the possession of the
Mirror Group although they did not see the text. Later when the
Cabinet were given this information they recorded: 'It might well be
asked why they had not insisted at the time [22 March] on examining
possible implications more deeply.' This question remains unanswered
even today.[21]

If Profumo had admitted publicly that he had slept with Keeler,
in view of Keeler's known liaison with Ivanov he would have had
to resign as Secretary of State, but he could have continued as an MP
with every prospect of being restored to office. Instead he chose to lie
in the Commons; by doing so he broke his career. This was a
spontaneous and tragic error of judgement, and it was unfortunate that
the Chief Whip and his other colleagues should have rushed Profumo
at this crucial moment.

Butler later recorded that early on the morning of 22 March Macmillan
telephoned him, asking him to be in the Chamber to 'hold his hand'
while they listened to Profumo's personal statement. Butler exclaimed,
'Not on a Friday morning, surely?' He told Macmillan that all Profumo
need say (and that in the fullness of time) was that accusations had been
made against him, and that he demanded an enquiry; until it reported
he would withdraw from his Ministerial post. If Butler's advice had been
taken Macmillan would have been spared many tribulations.[22]

The statement had duly been shown to the Prime Minister who made
minor alterations and came to the House to support Profumo. At 12
noon Profumo addressed the Commons; the key words of his speech ran:

Between July and December 1961 I met Miss Keeler on about half a dozen
occasions at Dr Ward's flat when I called to see him and his friends. Miss

Keeler and I were on friendly terms. There was no impropriety whatsoever in my acquaintanceship with Miss Keeler.

Later Profumo was to tell Lord Denning that he had been preoccupied during the preparation of his statement with the breaches of security alleged by Wigg because of the involvement simultaneously of Ivanov with Keeler so that he thought the fact that he had slept with her was 'subsidiary'. This explains his sudden loss of judgement.[23]

There was general derision at first when Profumo made his personal statement in the Commons. The *Daily Herald* made it plain they did not accept his denial, writing 'the statement could not in itself end the uneasiness in the country and in Parliament'; while *The Times* complained of delay in facing up to the rumour and relieving 'the mounting tension'. *Private Eye* printed a cartoon of Profumo sitting on a bed with a balloon saying 'And if Private Eye prints a picture of me on a bed I will sue them.' (In his statement Profumo had emphasized that he would 'not hesitate to issue writs for libel and slander if scandalous allegations were made outside the House'.)

On 27 March Harold Wilson, leader of the Opposition, came to see Macmillan and revealed that he had had correspondence with Stephen Ward in November 1962 about Cuba in which Ward had stated that he knew from the London Soviet Embassy that Khrushchev was hoping for a peaceful settlement at a Summit meeting. Wilson told Macmillan it might or not be a 'red herring'. Macmillan clearly thought it was.

On 1 April Profumo asked Macmillan for permission to issue writs for libel against the French *Paris Match* and the Italian *Tempo Illustrato* and their London distributors. Macmillan did not object, and Profumo went ahead, winning token damages which he gave to an army charity. It seemed unlikely that a Minister could both lie to Parliament and perjure himself in the law courts.

On 5 April Keeler told the police she had been Profumo's mistress; they also knew of her involvement with Ivanov and Ward, who were being watched by the Security Service. According to Lord Denning 'it was not the duty of the police to report 'a moral misbehaviour by a Minister'. (But had there been co-operation between the police and the Security Service, the Government might have been spared the ensuing scandal.)

On 9 April Wilson wrote to the Prime Minister enclosing a letter from Sir Frank Soskice, Shadow Home Secretary, together with a memorandum from Wigg reporting a conversation he had held with Stephen Ward which Soskice had referred to MI5. MI5 reported to the Prime Minister that 'no further action' was required on Wigg's report 'from the security aspect' and that at the time of Profumo's connection with Keeler no information had been given to them by the police.

On receiving the packet from Wilson Bligh wrote to Redmayne: 'The only slightly disturbing point is the suggestion that Mr Profumo wrote more than one letter to Miss Keeler. It is not that this is dangerous in itself but like the clock that strikes thirteen, it is not only unsettling but casts doubts on all that has gone before.' Bligh was beginning to rumble the truth but his master was still dangerously complacent.

On 7 May Stephen Ward asked for an interview with Bligh. This was granted, and Ward was seen by Bligh in the presence of an MI5 Director, Colonel Cumming; Ward alleged that Profumo had lied when he told the Commons he had never been intimate with Keeler.[*] According to Bligh the purpose of Ward's call was to 'blackmail' the Government into calling off police enquiries about him and a likely prosecution, in return for his keeping quiet about Profumo. At the time Ward knew that the police were contemplating prosecuting him for living off the immoral earnings of prostitutes.[24]

In a later memorandum to the Prime Minister Bligh set out the position: 'As this ploy had produced no dividends Stephen Ward wrote on 19 May to the Home Secretary saying that Mr Profumo's statement to the House of Commons was untrue. He wrote in similar terms to his MP (Sir Wavell Wakefield) on 20 May and to Mr Harold Wilson on the same date.'

After reading Ward's letter Wilson asked to see Macmillan and a meeting was arranged for 27 May with Redmayne and the Labour Chief Whip Herbert Bowden present as well as Bligh. The record of the twenty-minute meeting shows that Wilson knew he was on to a good thing and was playing his cards skilfully:

Mr Wilson told the Prime Minister he had been somewhat disturbed to receive the Prime Minister's letter of 14 May in which he appeared to suggest that the Ward case was closed. Mr Wilson went on to say that Ward was a self-confessed Soviet intermediary: indeed he had said so himself in the letter he wrote to Mr Wilson on 1 November 1962, at the time of the Cuba crisis. It was beyond dispute that Ward hob-nobbed with Ivanov. He must be regarded as a tool of Russian Communism. Ministers had frequently met Ward: indeed Mr Profumo said in his statement in the House of Commons that he had been to his flat on half a dozen occasions. Did Ministers know that Ward was a security risk? It would seem from the amount of mingling that had gone on that Ministers had not been told. They could not possibly have known. Mr Wilson went on to say that should the

---

[*] As soon as Ward said this Bligh records that he broke off the conversation and began to take notes.

Security Commission which the Prime Minister had referred to in the course of the debate on the Radcliffe Report on Vassall be set up, he would regard it as an appropriate body to which to refer the material he had forwarded to the Prime Minister. Alternatively the Prime Minister could set up a committee or a judicial enquiry which could sit in private and take evidence in private as might be thought appropriate.

Mr Wilson went on to say that if the Government were not prepared to initiate any action on this he would reserve the right to raise the matter in the House of Commons. He quite understood that the Prime Minister would wish to think the matter over.

The Prime Minister thanked Mr Wilson for having spoken to him before raising the matter publicly. He thought it possible to exaggerate the role which Stephen Ward had played during the Cuban crisis. There had been offers made by a number of well-intentioned people to act as intermediaries in order to bring about the easing of tension between Russia and the United States.

He doubted whether Stephen Ward bore quite the character or role which Mr Wilson had suggested. All the material which Mr Wilson had forwarded to the Prime Minister had been referred to the security authorities who had examined it and were satisfied that there were no unresolved security problems left over. He could understand that Mr Wilson might feel that Mr Profumo had not chosen his friends wisely (Mr Wilson interjected that the Opposition were not concerned with Ministers' private lives) but he was unable to follow the argument about a position detrimental to the security of the state having taken place. He would however ask the security authorities to look again at all the material and advise him on the position.
Copy only to Sir Roger Hollis

Bligh reported to the Prime Minister that he and Redmayne saw Profumo on 'a number of occasions' separately, and told him that allegations were still being made, 'and with increasing strength that he had misled the Commons', but Profumo continued to maintain that his statement was correct.

By now, in spite of his brave words to Wilson, Macmillan was thoroughly perturbed. Accordingly on 29 May he talked to Sir Roger Hollis, head of MI5, and was told what he and his private secretary did not know beforehand (although they should have been so informed):

In a statement which Christine Keeler made to the police in January 1963 she said that on one occasion, when she was going to meet Mr Profumo, Ward had asked her to discover from him the date on which certain atomic secrets were to be handed to West Germany by the Americans. It is understood that Miss Keeler denies having ever put such a question to Mr Profumo ... the evidence would not be likely to support a successful prosecution of Ward under the Official Secrets Act. He is not known to

us to have been in touch with any Russian since Ivanov's departure. The
security risk that Ward now represents seems to be slight.

Alarmed at the possibility that Ward might have asked Keeler to
question Profumo about atomic secrets, Macmillan at once decided to
ask Lord Dilhorne, the Chancellor, to conduct an investigation at high
speed, telling him to interview such people as he liked 'in the family,
that is police, ministers, and civil servants but no one else'. After talking
to Dilhorne and the Chief Whip on 30 May, Macmillan wrote to Wilson
informing him of the nature of Dilhorne's investigation: 'I think it
important that you should be in no doubt about it.'

Once Macmillan had asked Dilhorne to carry out the enquiry he
prepared to embark on his holiday in Scotland; as he was about to leave,
a handwritten minute from Harold Wilson arrived with patronizing
advice: 'I feel you would allay a great deal of anxiety and gossip if you
were to announce direct or on a lobby basis term [non-attributable] that
you have referred the matter to the Lord Chancellor.'[25]

The archives of the Prime Minister's Private Office, which were not
revealed to Denning, show that from 1 February onwards Macmillan
had been well informed about Profumo and Ward, but had taken the
matter too lightly. However his interview with the head of MI5 on 29
May sent him reeling, and in his worry he came close to interfering with
the course of justice although in the event nothing untoward occurred.
Macmillan and his law officers knew that a prosecution of Stephen Ward
for living off immoral earnings was imminent, and they feared that
Profumo would be called as a witness. If they had believed Profumo's
statement to be true there should not have been any worry, but by now
his veracity was being doubted by his colleagues. On 30 May, the same
day that Macmillan asked Dilhorne to conduct the investigation into the
allegations about Profumo's involvement with Ivanov, the Prime Minister instructed Bligh to ask Sir Joseph Simpson, Commissioner of Metropolitan Police, to talk to the Lord Chancellor in six days' time (6 June).
Simpson replied to Bligh that he 'hoped this engagement was not being
fixed on the hopes that nothing would have happened over Ward before
then'.

The Director of Public Prosecutions [Bligh recorded] was now prepared to
proceed against Dr Ward if a certain witness [Christine Keeler] returned
to this country over the weekend. She was expected to do this and to be
prepared to make a statement on Tuesday, 4 June.

The Commissioner said that if the Lord Chancellor wished to see him
before Tuesday he would of course be willing to go along. But he would
know that I recognized the delicacy of the position. The police could not

conduct their actions on the basis of instructions from the Government. I said that I was of course aware of this.

I subsequently reported this to the Lord Chancellor who said that the Thursday meeting with the Commissioner should stand and that the police must go their own way. Neither he nor any other member of the Government would wish to interfere with this.

I rang back the Commissioner and asked him to adhere to the 10.30 meeting on Thursday, 6 June.

The only construction that can be put on this memorandum by Bligh (only released on 1 January 1993 and not given or shown to Denning) is that Macmillan hoped to postpone the arrest of Ward until after Dilhorne's report was received and they had taken action to cushion themselves against the massive publicity about Profumo which was bound to be aroused by Ward's arrest. Otherwise why was it necessary for Bligh to emphasize to Simpson that no member of the Government would wish 'to interfere with the police'? This was a principle known to everyone connected with Government and needed no comment.

Profumo and his wife were holidaying in Venice when they heard that Dilhorne was making a fresh enquiry. Dilhorne was a tough lawyer; he had not endeared himself to his Tory or Labour colleagues in the Commons, and was known by the nickname of Reggie Bullying Manner. Profumo immediately confessed to his wife that he had lied to the Commons and returned to London to be greeted by hordes of journalists.

Bligh recorded: 'On the evening of 3 June, Whit Monday, Mr Profumo rang me up and said there had been a serious development and he wished to speak to the Chief Whip as soon as possible. A meeting was arranged for Tuesday, 4 June and at this meeting Mr Profumo revealed the truth.' Having done so, Profumo resigned.

That day, after Profumo had admitted his guilt to his Cabinet colleagues, Bligh asked Sir Joseph Simpson to call at Admiralty House and said it would be helpful to the Prime Minister to know the timetable of the Ward case and the police enquiries although the Prime Minister would not in any way wish to be involved 'in what the police were doing'. Prima facie Bligh's account of his interview with Simpson on behalf of the Prime Minister appears equally unconstitutional.

> Sir Joseph Simpson called at 2.30 p.m. today at my request. I explained that the Prime Minister was confronted with a certain problem of timing on one aspect of this whole affair, and it would be helpful, although the Prime Minister would not in any way wish to be thought to be involved in what the police were doing, to know what the timetable was likely to be in relation to Dr Ward and the police inquiries.
>
> Sir Joseph Simpson said that Dr Ward had called in at Scotland Yard and

had said that he understood that they were making inquiries about him. He had nothing to hide and would like the police to come to his house and look round, and examine his accounts and books and so on. If they wanted to find out anything he was the best person to tell them. The DPP had decided that the police could not proceed without taking up this offer. There would, therefore, have to be some delay, even at the risk of Mandy [Rice-] Davies [another call-girl involved with Ward and Ivanov] leaving the country. It might be, therefore, that the police would not move against Ward until next week. They would certainly not be doing so before Thursday evening.

We had some more general discussion about the case – whether Mr P would be called as a witness, and so on, but there was nothing of interest that need be recorded.

Sir Joseph Simpson on leaving said that there were some newspaper people outside. I said that if anyone asked him what he had come for he should say that he had been discussing car parking arrangements for the Trooping.[26]

This series of exchanges between the Prime Minister's Office and the Commissioner of Metropolitan Police can at best be described as highly questionable. They are not mentioned in the Denning Report as Denning knew nothing of them: but they would have been dynamite for Harold Wilson if they had seen the light of day then, for Denning's terms of reference were:

To examine, in the light of the circumstances leading to the resignation of the former Secretary of State for War, J. D. Profumo, the operation of the Security Service and the adequacy of their co-operation with the police in matters of security; to investigate any information or material which may come to his attention in this connection, and to consider any evidence there may be for believing that national security has been, or may be, endangered; and to report thereon.

The failure of the Government to show Denning the documents relating to Sir Joseph Simpson is sinister, and confirms the author's suspicion that Macmillan was close to tampering with the course of justice by delaying Ward's arrest. It was also highly irregular for Bligh to ask Sir Joseph Simpson to tell a lie if he was questioned about his presence at Admiralty House, and shows how concerned Bligh was to cover his tracks. Lord Denning has confirmed the author's impression that the documents suggest the Government were trying to interfere with the course of justice. He himself was not properly briefed before he started work on the report: the Prime Minister sent him a personal letter asking him to take it on; he was given one civil servant from the Home Office and one from the Treasury as assistants.[27]

In a confidential note on 5 June Bligh recorded that at 8.30 a.m. he talked to the Prime Minister in Scotland who accepted Profumo's resignation. At 10.30 Redmayne and Bligh saw Profumo who had consulted his lawyer about his draft letter of resignation. The lawyer drew attention to the fact that this contained a libel on Miss Keeler, but according to Bligh 'it was felt that worse things had happened since King Lear.' Profumo checked up on the dates and confirmed that he had first met Keeler at Cliveden on 7 July 1961; Norman Brook had warned him of 'the security risk involved' on 9 August 1961, on which day he had written the letter to her beginning 'Darling' and had never seen her again.

Bligh then took a 'submission' of Profumo's resignation to Butler who signed it on the Prime Minister's behalf, sent it to the Palace at midday, and arranged for a police guard to be put on Profumo's house in Regent's Park. He also told Dilhorne that Macmillan wanted him to go ahead with his enquiry.[28]

On the Prime Minister's return to London he and Wilson met amicably but could not agree on the shape of the public investigation into possible breaches of security arising out of Profumo's resignation. Wilson and Opposition spokesmen pressed for a Parliamentary Select Committee to investigate in particular 'the circumstances in which Mr Profumo's statement denying intimacy with Keeler had been drafted' and the part played in it by the law officers. Obviously such a committee would split on Party lines and Macmillan told the Cabinet that there was no possibility of agreeing the form of the enquiry with the Opposition; he asked them to approve his announcing in the Commons that there would be a judicial enquiry conducted by Lord Denning. Originally Macmillan considered placing the enquiry in the hands of Lord Radcliffe whose report had exculpated Galbraith and the Foreign Office in the Vassall affair. However the law officers pointed out to him that Radcliffe was a Chancery lawyer specializing in tax, and that the Profumo enquiry with its sinister security implications needed a judge who was a criminal expert. Denning's appointment was duly confirmed on 21 June.

Profumo's resignation was discussed in Cabinet on 12 and 13 June, being the sole item on the second day. On the first day there were recriminations the like of which are rarely recorded in Cabinet minutes:

> Mr Profumo had admitted to the Chief Whip as early as 4 February 1963 that a letter he had sent on 9 August 1961 as a result of a warning he had received on that day from Sir Norman Brook had been couched in affectionate terms. He had also admitted that on one occasion he had given her a present and on two occasions been alone with her in Ward's flat. These facts were known to those Ministers who had discussed with Mr Profumo early on 22 March the text of the personal statement which he was to make to the Commons and it might well be asked why they had not insisted at the time on examining their possible implications more deeply particularly

by asking Profumo for a copy of the letter and so judging for themselves whether it conveyed any presumption of an improper association. By accepting Mr Profumo's own account of his relationship with Miss Keeler they could be held to have failed to exercise the degree of judgement required by circumstances in which suspicions should surely have been aroused.

Agonizing over the vulnerability of the Ministers who had advised Profumo to deny the charge of his liaison with Keeler, the Cabinet indulged in a witch hunt. Deedes alleged in a memorandum to Macmillan that there was a 'chilling' resemblance between what happened to Vassall in Moscow and Profumo in London, and this was evidence of a Russian plot to enlist 'spies' and cause 'social demoralization'.

At the second meeting the report begun by Dilhorne on 30 May was available to the Cabinet and Dilhorne announced that 'No further enquiry is necessary from the security angle.' But that had not been good enough for Harold Wilson when he was shown the Dilhorne Report by the Prime Minister.* Macmillan had therefore decided to instruct Dilhorne as Lord Chancellor to hold a second and secret enquiry, the most bizarre result of which was to raise the suspicion of sexual scandal against Selwyn Lloyd although he led the purest of lives.[29]

Lloyd had been introduced to Ward in a letter from Sir Godfrey Nicholson, the Tory MP and distiller; Lloyd had agreed to allow Ward to paint his portrait while he was Chancellor of the Exchequer on 29 March 1961. Dilhorne summoned Lloyd to his room on 7 June 1963 and cross-examined him about this in the presence of Sir George Coldstream, head of the Lord Chancellor's office. Lloyd told Dilhorne that Ward, while he was sketching, spoke 'a great deal about his contacts with people prominent in public life' which resulted in him, Lloyd, taking an instant dislike to Ward because of the over-familiar manner in which he discussed Ministers he knew. Ward told Lloyd he had friends in the Russian Embassy, and expressed the view that the best way to deal with the Iron Curtain countries was to have social contacts with them. Lloyd told Dilhorne that the tone of Ward's remarks alerted him, so he gave his private secretaries instructions to make enquiries through the secret service about Ward.†

On 28 August 1961 Lloyd had asked his principal private secretary David Hubback to send Nicholson's letter of introduction to Sir Norman

---

* Dilhorne was in a certain difficulty because Sir Godfrey Nicholson, Ward's MP friend, was Lady Dilhorne's brother-in-law. It was Nicholson who had introduced Ward to Caccia, the Permanent Head of the Foreign Office, twice.

† According to Lloyd's official biographer Selwyn Lloyd seriously feared he would be accused of 'guilt by association'.

Brook who sent it on to Sir Roger Hollis, the head of MI5. A minute to Macmillan stated: 'It would be better to say nothing further to Mr Lloyd on this subject.' The Prime Minister was concerned lest it should become known to the press that enquiries about Ward had been instituted as early as 1961 and ignored.[30]

The debate on Profumo was scheduled for Monday, 17 June, amid grave adverse publicity for the Government, and especially for Macmillan. The Tory MP for Carlisle, Dr Donald Johnson (who had spent part of his life in a mental hospital), declared that he could not fight his marginal seat at the General Election as long as Mr Macmillan was Prime Minister, and that the Prime Minister had been brought into 'widespread ridicule'.

A solicitor, Michael Eddowes, published a letter which he had sent to 10 Downing Street stating that he had told the Security Service before Profumo's Commons statement that he had heard from Christine Keeler that Ivanov had asked her to find out the date on which nuclear warheads were to be delivered to West Germany. Ward told the press when he was arrested that he had informed the Security Service of Keeler's double liaison with Ivanov and Profumo in 1961. John Hare admitted that he had lent Profumo his car to drive Keeler in Regent's Park.

Other red herrings began to surface. On 11 June the *Daily Mail* published a letter from Boofy Gore, a Harmsworth journalist and socialite who was now the Earl of Arran, to his fellow Scottish earl Lord Home, about his contacts with Stephen Ward and Ivanov during the Cuba crisis. This was comic but unhelpful to the Government, giving publicity to an absurd attempt by Ivanov to organize a Summit meeting in London at the height of the Cuba crisis.

Vitriolic articles directed against Macmillan made out that he was too old, out of touch and incompetent, and that an alert Prime Minister would have found out long before. Several other Ministers were smeared. A photograph of a headless man at a sex orgy was said to be Duncan Sandys, Secretary of State for Commonwealth Relations, who was widely accused of being associated with Ward and Keeler. This was untrue. The Duchess of Argyll's divorce suit was currently achieving lurid headlines with salacious undertones in the reports; rumour had it that she had been associated with Ward and Keeler, and it was known that she had been Sandys's mistress.

At the Cabinet meeting on 19 June Sandys stated that one of the allegations involved him in some difficulty but the rest were completely untrue, and he discussed privately with the Prime Minister whether he ought to resign. Sandys had been involved in some doubtful activities as second secretary at the Berlin Embassy in the early 1930s, after which he had left the diplomatic service: either this or the Argyll divorce could have been the cause of Sandys's discomfort. Whatever the reason, following his discussion with the Prime Minister he decided with Macmillan's concurrence not to resign and instead to request Lord Denning to investigate specific allegations against him.[31]

Press comment following Profumo's resignation had been vociferous. In the *Sunday Telegraph* Peregrine Worsthorne wrote: 'Conservatives can survive bad measures but not bad men and bad measures,' and lobby correspondents recalled how Neville Chamberlain in 1940 had been driven out of 10 Downing Street by a revolt of a number of Conservative MPs on the floor of the Commons. The editor of the *New Statesman* said on television he had known the truth all along but could not publish it because his paper could not afford the libel damages which might follow. The *Sunday Pictorial* published Profumo's 'Darling' letter to Keeler, while the Stock Exchange nosedived. At a dinner Selwyn Lloyd, still smarting from Macmillan's abrupt dismissal of him, talked of the decline of political standards, while even the Tory *Daily Telegraph* wrote: 'At present the Conservative Party is a shambles.'

Worst of all for the Establishment was the moralizing leader in *The Times* of 11 June. Headed 'It is a moral issue', it commented on how fortunate it was for Macmillan that because of the Whitsun recess he had eleven days to work out the answers to the questions which the resignation of Profumo imposed, and to rally his Party behind him:

> For the Conservative Party and it is to be hoped for the nation things can never be the same again ... It remains strange that not a single member of the Government resigned when the affair broke in March and he [Profumo] did not resign. There is no hiding place from the tidal overthrow and disaster.

The Times editor Sir William Haley well deserved Macmillan's nickname for him 'Halier than Thou'; his leader was widely commented upon and reproduced, providing ammunition for a 'sudden rash of attacks' on the Government. On television Hailsham told the interviewer Robert Mackenzie furiously, '*The Times* is an anti-Conservative newspaper with an anti-Conservative editor.' It was alleged by columnists that Enoch Powell was about to resign on grounds of conscience over the moral issues; on the eve of the debate however he stated that he would support the Government.

In the Commons debate on 17 June Harold Wilson was determined to make every ounce of political capital out of the Government's discomfiture. The issue, he said, was not the personal fate of Profumo but whether any other Minister 'connived' at his deception of the Commons; he emphasized that no one on the Labour side had leaked anything to the press but had communicated their whole knowledge in confidence to the Prime Minister, who acknowledged it only 'casually', taking the attitude 'What has this to do with me?' which was a great contrast to Clement Attlee's attitude to the case of Belcher at the Board of Trade.* This was a telling point well made by Wilson. He accused Macmillan of gambling with national security for political reasons:

> We shall never know whether there was a breach of security or not . . . What we were concerned with was clear evidence . . . that there was a long-standing condition of security risk as long as the Secretary of State for War was part of this quadrilateral made up of Miss Keeler, Ward the self-confessed Soviet intermediary, and Ivanov the Soviet military attaché. I do not think Ward to be a spy; he was too unstable for the Soviet authorities who usually make use of better material.

Wilson asked Macmillan why, when he knew the degree of security risk, he did not accept Profumo's resignation? 'Was it offered and refused? If it was not offered why was it not demanded? We cannot escape the conclusion that the answer to the question is that politics and not security come first, and because a born gambler does not operate that way.'

It was a telling speech by an able debater, but Macmillan was equally persuasive in his reply. He said that in January 1963 when Profumo had talked to Redmayne the Chief Whip, Hobson and Rawlinson, he (Profumo) had asked whether he should resign and the other three replied that there was no need to do so if he had not slept with Keeler; in a passage for which he was later much criticized Macmillan stated that he as Prime Minister had not questioned Profumo personally because he thought Profumo would speak more freely to the Chief Whip and the law officers than to him, 'his political chief', and because 'an examination of this kind, in the probing detail necessary, would have made it difficult, if not impossible, for him to feel in future, however innocent he might have been, that he enjoyed my confidence'. If he had demanded his resignation, Macmillan went on, and Profumo had subsequently sued successfully in the courts for libel '– as he did – the feeling would have been that an innocent man had been treated unjustly'. The law officers and the Chief Whip had been made aware that Profumo had written in 1961 a letter to Keeler beginning 'Darling' but they had not seen a copy of it, and Profumo had explained that 'in circles in which he and his wife moved it was a term of no great significance. I believe that might be accepted – I do not live among young people much myself.'

---

* J. W. Belcher had been accused of taking bribes when Under-Secretary to Wilson at the Board of Trade in 1948 and his behaviour was investigated at a public enquiry under Lord Justice Lynskey with great publicity; it ended in ignominy and resignation for Belcher – a railway clerk bewildered by his Ministerial job where he foundered out of his depth.

Then, asking with a rhetorical flourish whether 'I [would] not have been guilty of great harshness if I had demanded his resignation', Macmillan was interrupted by the former Labour Cabinet Minister, Emmanuel Shinwell, who said: 'The Right Hon. Gentleman disclaims any appearance or any intention of harshness in connection with Mr Profumo, but what about the harshness when he dismissed seven Ministers a year ago?' Selwyn Lloyd went scarlet as Macmillan replied:

> I have had the difficult task Prime Ministers have of making changes for what seemed to be improvements in the national service. Of course it is a difficult task. I have not had to do so by telling a Minister that terrible rumours are circulating about him and that I cannot believe his denial. That is of quite a different order.

There were loud cheers from the Tory benches at this, in which Lloyd conspicuously did not join in.

Macmillan had misjudged the mood of the House in saying that, had he interviewed Profumo himself, they could not have continued their relationship of mutual confidence, and in trying to gain sympathy by stating that he was the 'last to hear'. Why he was the 'last' was difficult to explain. Support was not always forthcoming from members of his own side. In the course of the debate Anthony Lambton stated that he had known on 22 March that Jack Profumo was lying, while Nigel Birch, still smarting at not being taken back into the Government after his resignation four years before, advised Macmillan to resign and make way for a younger man:

> We know a deal more now about Profumo than we did at the time of the statement, but we have all known him pretty well for a number of years in this House. I must say that he never struck me as a man at all like a cloistered monk; and Miss Keeler was a professional prostitute.
>
> There seems to me to be a certain basic improbability about the proposition that their relationship was purely platonic. What are whores about? Yet Profumo's word was accepted. It was accepted from a colleague. Would that word have been accepted if Profumo had not been a colleague or even if he had been a political opponent? Everyone must, I think, make his own judgement about that . . .
>
> Profumo on his own admission had been guilty of a very considerable indiscretion, for a Minister at any rate. He was not a particularly successful Minister. He had no great place in this House or in the country. I cannot really see that the Prime Minister was under any obligation whatever to retain his services, nor do I think that getting rid of Mr Profumo would, in fact, have made the political situation any worse than it then was. On the other hand, to retain him entailed a colossal risk and a colossal gamble . . .
>
> What is to happen now? I cannot myself see at all that we can go on

acting as if nothing had happened. We cannot just have business as usual.
I myself feel that the time will come very soon when my Right Hon. Friend
ought to make way for a much younger colleague . . . I hope that the change
will not be too long delayed.

Such effective vitriol has seldom been poured into the ear of a Prime
Minister by one of his own supporters in the Commons. When it finally
came to a vote, there were 27 abstentions and the Government majority
was down to 69.

The next morning, *The Times* lead headline was 'Macmillan unlikely
to be leader in the next Election'; this was the general tone taken by
the press. A meeting of the 1922 Committee was scheduled for 21 June.
Speculation was rife in the newspapers and in Parliament that this
meeting would result in the substitution of Maudling for Macmillan as
Prime Minister. However Derek Walker-Smith, a former Conservative
Minister, checked the 1922 Committee's ardour for a change of leader
by asserting that if Macmillan was driven out the Queen might not send
for an alternative Conservative leader, but for Harold Wilson instead;
it was well known that Wilson would then call for a dissolution. This
was scare-mongering but it did the trick.

In the press reports on the proceedings of the 1922 Committee only
Maudling was suggested as the likely successor; no one else was taken
seriously. Lord Poole, Chairman of the Conservative Party in the Lords,
said that '[Macmillan's] resignation would be suicidal' for the Conservatives. Coming from the Chairman of the Party who was not himself
an MP, this was ill received by the MPs who thought it patronizing;
Maudling continued to be the front runner. Typical was *The Economist*'s
report on 22 June: 'it seemed difficult to doubt that Mr Macmillan must
be ready to retire to an earldom as soon as the Party can definitely
determine his successor'; Maudling, it said, was the favourite to succeed
with 'a swiftly growing body of opinion in the middle of the Party now
seeming to be gathering in his support'.

Harry Boyne, chief political correspondent of the *Daily Telegraph*,
polled 100 Conservative MPs: his results showed 71 members supporting
Maudling, against 9 for Butler, 5 for Hailsham, and one each for Heath
and Powell. The Chairman of the 1922 Committee also made extensive
enquiries into back-bencher preferences, coming up with more or less
the same result as the Boyne poll.[32]

The Economist tipped Butler as second favourite giving Hailsham and
Heath outside chances, while Macleod was considered to be more likely
to win after the Tories had crashed to defeat in the General Election.
The eventual winner, Lord Home, was mentioned but he was thought
not to want the job. However *The Economist*, like most newspaper

commentators, correctly dismissed as 'constitutional nonsense' Walker-Smith's argument that the Queen might dissolve Parliament if Macmillan resigned.

As Chairman of the Party, Macleod became worried by the widespread press comment that Macmillan would have to resign because of bungling the Profumo incident, and on 21 June he sent a phone message via Bligh to the Prime Minister saying that, having spent a lot of time in the Commons during the last forty-eight hours, he had found the general atmosphere much steadier; he therefore hoped Macmillan would say to the Cabinet that morning that

> whatever the results of last Monday's debate the Government had to get on with the job of governing and that was what you proposed to do. Mr Macleod feels that if you indicate in any way that you have been thinking about your own position this will very quickly reach the press. A good firm lead from you on 'business as usual' says Mr Macleod, would stop the activities of all the little king-makers.

This was the advice Macmillan wanted, and it gave him heart.

Macmillan and Home also discussed whether the secret Dilhorne report should be given to the United States to reassure them on the security aspect. Burke Trend and Roger Hollis were consulted, and agreed that a copy should be sent to Ormsby-Gore in Washington so that if necessary some particular point could be explained to senior members of the administration. But when they came to Birch Grove at the end of June, as has been seen,* Kennedy and his advisers believed that with the Profumo affair Macmillan's reign was over.[33]

On 29 June Macmillan told ITN News that he hoped to lead the Conservative Party in the General Election, and had plenty of support from MPs; this was no more than he had told the 1922 Committee on 10 April. Harold Wilson commented that 'the 1922 Committee was like a group of aboriginal savages in a frenzied ritual dance with only one end in view, to obtain the Prime Minister's head as a sacrificial offering', while Lambton said that 'Civil war would break out if he stayed.'

As more and more rumours surfaced about 'headless men' and the involvement of other Cabinet Ministers and well-known personalities with Keeler and Ward, or in sexual capers, the camaraderie of the Commons seemed to yield to light-hearted and humorous gossip between back-bench Labour and Conservative MPs, and as the session ended the tension eased, while everyone waited for the report by Lord Denning.

The successful conclusion of the multilateral test ban treaty in Moscow

---

* See Chapter 15, page 363 ff.

on 25 July 1963 did much to restore Macmillan's prestige, and the agitation for his resignation faltered. A *Daily Mail* opinion poll of 2 August showed a remarkable recovery by the Tories, who had closed the gap behind Labour from nearly 20 per cent to only 6 per cent.

Coming on top of by-election reverses and the strain of sacking his colleagues on the night of long knives, the Profumo scandal had taken a severe toll of Macmillan's health. He always tended to the hypochondriacal, and during the summer of 1963 his colleagues noted that he was tired and depressed. Yet in his diary he recorded on 2 August:

> I feel sure the Party is recovering its senses, and unless we have some some tragic result from Lord Denning my own position in the Parliamentary Party is much improved. In the country at large I feel sure there is a swing towards me personally just out of sympathy and sense of fairness.

Only three weeks before he had written: 'I do not remember ever having been under such a sense of strain. Even Suez was clean about war and politics. This is all dirt and a Titus Oates atmosphere about Ministers.'

Macmillan hoped that the Denning Report would vindicate his actions, but he began to have doubts whether he would lead the Conservatives into the next General Election. He even considered announcing his resignation in October at the Conservative Conference although he was in reasonably good health. Clearly the strain of waiting for the Denning Report was telling on him and as usual he was working very hard.

Before Parliament rose Macmillan held two important meetings with his Parliamentary colleagues. On 18 July he met all the Ministers not in the Cabinet including Ministers of State, under-secretaries and Parliamentary secretaries both in the Lords and the Commons. He said to them:

> We were struck by a sad and tragic event like that of Titus Oates or in my time of Pemberton* who won his election on his black book with its

---

* Noel Pemberton Billing was a rogue Tory MP who had won East Hertford at a by-election in 1916 during the wartime electoral truce. He stood as the champion of air power, and became a hero later in the war when he won a libel case in which he alleged that the Germans possessed a black book containing the names of 47,000 perverts in Britain. Almost the sole survivor of Jingoism he reappeared as a candidate in the Hornsey by-election in May 1941, and stood three times more, unsuccessfully. In the Second World War he stood for the defeat of Germany by bombing alone and for defending Britain by equally spaced upward-pointing lights intended to confuse the enemy and enable the RAF to see the bombers against a background of light. He made some impression using a yellow Rolls-Royce and arguing for a post-war policy of replacing General Elections by a multiplicity of by-elections and proposing an additional assembly of the trades and professions together with a women's parliament. He was a comic, and by 1963 forgotten figure known only to older MPs. Macmillan must have appeared out of date in alluding to him; he also referred to Billing in the debate on the Denning Report when he was no longer Prime Minister in October 1963.

threats of disclosure of traitors and perverts ... [Passage closed for fifty years] ... I do not in the least resent certain movements in the Party and press. There has been most warm response and support from the people outside in the country. If I had yielded to the temptation to go it would have been fatal to the Party and I am sure it would have brought down the country among other nations. They would have said there was much more underneath.

My task is to see the end of the story. If there are difficulties ahead I have to see the end, and that I will do. I hope you know me well enough to know that I want what is best for the Party and the country. The only thing that matters is to win the election if we can and if not, to make the best showing we can. We must choose the best opportunity for having it. We must go into it under the leadership most likely to win, whether it is mine or someone else's. I will take the course that is best for the Party.

In spite of his reference to 'someone else' this was taken as an indication that Macmillan expected to lead the Party into the election unless something untoward cropped up to damage his credibility. According to the Prime Minister's files it was 'a most satisfactory meeting with long and considerable applause'.

A week later Macmillan faced the 1922 Committee and was given, he wrote in his memoirs, 'a triumphant vote of confidence'. He followed the same line as with the junior Ministers, and there was considerable applause when he said again that his sole purpose was 'to serve the Party and the nation and win the General Election'.[34] Macmillan now felt that national opinion was swinging back to the Party and to him personally, and he was 'cheered' by the *Daily Mail* Poll of 2 August.

Despite this showing, Macmillan's diary entries reveal that while awaiting the Denning Report he was acutely apprehensive about its content and consequences – so much so that he more than once contemplated resignation. He even wrote that he did not want to bring his long premiership 'to an ignoble end or look as if I was afraid of facing any difficulties which might still confront us. I did not wish to go down to history as a Prime Minister who had been drowned by filth which had seeped up from the sewers of London.'

Then, as his report was approaching completion Denning drafted a letter to the Prime Minister stating that all the rumours about Ministers were 'mischievous' and 'without the slightest justification except two':

I am sorry to tell you that in relation to Mr [X] and Mr [Y] I cannot confirm the same conclusion. I am satisfied that for a considerable number of years and up to a few years ago Mr [X: a senior Minister] had an association with a prostitute and that, in the course of this association, conduct took place of such a character as would expose Mr [X] to a risk of undue pressure. It is right that I should add that I am satisfied that Mr [X] had not been subjected to such pressure and that national security has not in fact been endangered, but I am also satisfied that the conduct was of such a nature as to constitute a security risk.

Mr [Y: a junior member of government] invited me to enquire into certain rumours about him. I have done so and I regret to inform you that Mr [Y] did three years ago go to a party of a homosexual character and that he there participated in homosexual conduct.[35]

This letter is not in the Prime Minister's files in the Public Record Office but the draft lies in the closed Denning archive in the Hampshire Record Office. The author and publishers have promised Lord Denning they will not identify any Minister from his papers as he feels it would betray the promises of confidentiality he gave to witnesses (including Ministers) when he took their evidence in 1963. It would be entirely unjust to name the second man who is still alive. However his promising political career did not blossom after this damaging information reached the Prime Minister's office.

Macmillan must have been distressed to receive this letter with its ominous undertones for his future, and on 2 August noted in his diary: 'I fear that Lord Denning's Report . . . will condemn one important and one unimportant Minister . . . This will be another great shock and make my position impossible.' On 16 August Denning went to Admiralty House and took evidence from the Prime Minister. In his diary entry on that day Macmillan wrote that from what he could glean from 'the energetic judge' he continued to fear 'there was going to be trouble about two Ministers, but how formidable that will be I do not know.' Macmillan, as has been seen, was already aware from his talk with Sandys during a Cabinet meeting that Sandys was in the clear; thus it is plain that Denning on 16 August mentioned these two Ministers to the Prime Minister in informal conversation.[36]

Anyone who knows this period of political history can be in no doubt that the senior Minister was Ernest Marples, Minister of Transport. Piers Dixon, Sandys's son-in-law who is writing a biography of Sandys, has shown the author a diary entry which makes plain that Sandys was aware of continuous stories about Marples being involved with prostitutes, and various lobby correspondents who were operating at the time have confirmed to the author that these rumours were prevalent and widely believed.

Fortunately for the Conservatives, Denning whose official instructions were 'to consider any evidence there may be for believing the national security has been or will be endangered', decided not to mention anything about the two Ministers in his written report. He told the author that in his view their conduct was 'discreditable' but not 'a threat to security'. However in his published report he wrote in paragraph 294: 'I would normally regard homosexual behaviour or perverted practices with a prostitute as creating a security risk at any rate if it was of recent date.' There is, thus, a strong element of contradiction in his decision to omit any reference to the two Ministers concerned which may cause some, particularly surviving members of the Labour front beach at the time, to dispute his judgement. Ernest Marples continued in office until the dissolution of 1964, and probably the incoming Prime Minister, Lord Home, was never informed by Macmillan of Marples's bad reputation.

Macmillan must have been relieved when he read the Denning Report. Had Denning named the two Ministers and the Under-Secretary and described their 'discreditable conduct' – as he might well have done – this coming so soon after Profumo's resignation and the Galbraith affair would have resulted in the Government being pilloried by the press, and Macmillan would have been at grave risk of being driven from power.

When issued by the Stationery Office on 26 September 1963, the Denning Report became a best seller. But a public hoping to find sala-cious titbits about orgiastic goings-on among the highly placed were disappointed. All they obtained was the information that Stephen Ward procured

mistresses for his influential friends. He did not confine his attention to promiscuity. There is evidence that he was ready to arrange for whipping and other sadistic performances. He kept collections of sadistic photographs. He attended parties where there were sexual orgies of a revolting nature . . .

There is a great deal of evidence which satisfied me that there is a group of people who hold parties in private of a perverted nature. At some of these parties, the man who serves the dinner is nearly naked except for a small square lace apron round his waist such as a waitress might wear. He wears a black mask over his head with slits for eye-holes. He cannot therefore be recognized by any of the guests. Some reports stop there and say that nothing evil takes place. It is done as a comic turn and no more. This may well be so at some of the parties. But at others I am satisfied that it is followed by perverted sex orgies: that the man in the mask is a 'slave' who is whipped: that the guests undress and indulge in sexual intercourse one with the other: and indulge in other sexual activities of a vile and revolting nature.

In an obvious reference to Sandys the report noted that the rumours 'were entirely without foundation. In addition to being accused by rumour mongers of being the headless man at sexual parties, it was said that Sandys had paid money so as not to be cited as a co-respondent in the Duke of Argyll's divorce suit.' Denning recorded that there was no 'evidence' to justify Sandys being cited. However his private papers show that he was in little doubt there had been intimacy between Sandys and the Duchess. Denning wrote in his notes

DS had strong motive for having his name kept out of the divorce suit . . .
It would have been very satisfactory if DS had been able to assure me . . .
that he had *not* committed adultery . . . It is not my province to investigate
whether DS committed adultery with the Duchess of Argyll. I am satisfied
that even if DS committed adultery there is not the slightest reason for
supposing it would have been a security risk.[37]

When the transcript of the Denning Report was sent to the Prime
Minister on 16 September, Macmillan was at first alarmed, and hastily
summoned a group of senior Ministers to a meeting on 18 September.
Although the report had given the Government and the Prime Minister
an almost clean bill of health and disclosed that there had been no security
risk, there was still anxiety at certain charges; one sentence in paragraph
286 was particularly damaging: 'It was the responsibility of the Prime
Minister and his colleagues, and of them only, to deal with the situation
and they did not succeed in doing so.'

Macmillan told his colleagues that Denning was 'satisfactory' apart
from paragraph 286. However Macleod was unduly pessimistic, saying
that 'the report would do the Government an immense amount of harm';
Denning's verdict was 'false' being based on 'wrong legalized reasoning'.
Butler noted that paragraph 341 – 'there had been no lowering of
[security] standards' – was 'very good' but, like Home, he disagreed with
Macleod: political events, he believed, had 'bypassed the Profumo affair'
although paragraph 286 was 'very awkward'. Edward Boyle remarked
of the report that 'Two thirds consists of a historical survey which goes
into far more detail than the terms of reference made either necessary
or desirable . . . Lord Denning was not invited to approach his task in
the spirit of a historian nor to write a brief for the critics of the
Government.'

Much to the annoyance of the Cabinet, Denning showed a certain
sympathy for the Profumos in paragraph 180 of his report, quoting
Valerie Profumo's remarks:

I just simply know that, if it had not been for the extraordinary
concatenation of circumstances of timing that day, and that early morning,
Jack would never have made that statement. I was there and I know about
the sleeping pills and the tiredness, and the fact that we were really groping
round the house, letting in strange people and getting through loads of
reporters still on the doorstep . . . I am sure that, had we had time, as a
husband and wife, instead of . . . with a time gun [*sic*] . . .

The Attorney-General Sir John Hobson took paragraph 286 as a criticism of his own action and sent Macmillan a letter of resignation, stating
that his overriding feeling was that having appointed an independent
umpire who had awarded the point against him they should accept his
findings.

It is in the general interest that I should resign. Not only do I feel that this is the right and honourable thing to do from my own personal point of view (which is unimportant), but that it is the general interest of the country that the consequences and findings should be acted upon, however much public opinion generally may or may not accept them.

It seems to me that the only grounds for not resigning are the following –

(1) the way in which it affects your own position;

(2) that the error was of such a minor nature that it does not call for resignation;

(3) that an attack on the administration of justice is likely to be mounted in the ensuing months and I ought to be there to meet it.

I do not myself believe that my own resignation (which must I think also involve the resignation of the Chief Whip) would place any necessity upon you to do the same. The Denning Report makes it perfectly clear that you were relying on the Chief Whip and myself, as I think you were surely entitled to do, and the failure which has been found was entirely ours. I cannot think that in these circumstances anybody would think that you yourself ought to resign over such an issue, and I am sure that the terms upon which I insisted in resigning could make it plain that you were not sacrificing me for your own benefit – and had not done so – as would be the fact.

As to the second point, while the fault may be small, it nevertheless has been declared, and it is exactly the charge which was made by many speakers in the debate in the House of Commons who have now been supported by the findings of Denning. The Government did not accept the Devlin Commission's findings,* and I am sure it will do the Party very much harm if it is not seen to have acted upon and accepted the Denning conclusions however wrong we may think them to be.

As regards the third point that the coming onslaught on the administration of justice ought to be met by me, I certainly do not think my presence indispensable, though I recognize it would be better if I was available and no doubt I should be accused of running away.

Nevertheless, upon the balance of general convenience both of the country and the Party and forgetting altogether my own personal interests, I do still very strongly feel that the right thing is that I should resign as a result of the Denning Report.

I think I ought to make it clear to you however, as I said yesterday, that I am prepared to do whatever is in the best interests of the country as a whole and I recognize that my resignation cannot be treated apart from the position of the Chief Whip and, possibly, of yourself. I am therefore prepared to act in whatever way you and your colleagues may consider the best although I hope they will accept the view which I put forward.

---

* In 1959 the Government had been under fierce criticism for refusing to accept the Devlin Report (see Chapter 12). The Opposition would have had a field day by coupling the two refusals together if the Government also refused to accept Denning. Hobson was quite right to point this out. Dilhorne too stated that Denning must be accepted.

Macmillan realized at once that it would be a death blow to his position both as Prime Minster and as leader of the Tory Party if Hobson resigned, and he persuaded him to withdraw his resignation, arguing that it would only do damage to the Conservative Party.

Hobson had also told the Chief Whip that he had decided to resign. Redmayne accordingly minuted to Macmillan: 'He was agitated. I could not myself persuade him that he was wrong, so had to tell him to put his case in writing. As I said yesterday in these circumstances it is harder not to resign.' As Hobson's resignation letter and his memorandum made clear, he was of the opinion that Redmayne should resign as well – a fact not known until the papers were released under the thirty-year rule on 1 January 1994.

In his memoirs Lord Rawlinson reveals that he too offered to resign. There is no document relating to this in the archives which are otherwise very complete; he must therefore have made the suggestion orally to the Prime Minister, and may not have expected it to be accepted.

With his resignation letter Hobson sent to the Prime Minister a memorandum highly critical of the Denning Report, showing his anger at its findings and especially at the sympathy shown by Denning to the Profumos:

Memo on Denning Report from the Attorney-General
The rule of the divorce law upon which Lord Denning relies for his conclusion [regarding reliance on reasonable belief in a spouse's misconduct as grounds for divorce] is good sense in circumstances where you believe a wife or colleague has sinned but can't actually prove it. It is right in such an event that a person should be blameless in making the breach without having to justify his condemnation by strict proof.

Denning however has turned the rule inside out and now apparently people, including wives, partners and colleagues, ought to be condemned or at least disposed of if there are reasonable grounds for believing that they have done wrong even if you accept from them that they have not in fact erred. Indeed you are now blameworthy if you do not act upon the basis that they are guilty if there are reasonable grounds to believe that they may be, even if you are satisfied for the time being that they are not. Your confidence and continued trust in your wife or partner and your willingness not to condemn until there is some certainty of guilt ought to be destroyed as soon as 'influential people' would have reasonable ground to believe that a person may have erred without knowing his or her version and without regard to a personal assessment of that person's version of the facts and general truthfulness.

This is bad law and worse morals. Even a policeman who has reasonable grounds to believe that a person has committed a felony is not bound to arrest him or charge him or keep him in custody if he receives an explanation which satisfies. The Denning proposition is odd morality as it means that in the conduct of public and private family affairs, the denials of those whom we trust and ought to trust must go for nothing whenever there are other facts which would give influential people who know of those other facts only (and not of the denial or the character of the person making it) reasonable ground to believe that an error has been committed.

Lord Denning concluded his interview with me by asking whether I agreed that as far as I was concerned, if JP had been speaking the truth, I had done everything correct at each stage and could not be faulted. I told him that I accepted this analysis of the situation (which had not occurred to me) as one I certainly would not dispute. He never asked me whether I had asked myself the question which he now suggests ought to have been asked or gave me the slightest opportunity to deal with that problem upon which he has now criticized me.

As a matter of fact I did consider that exact problem in the JP instance. I had also met with it on a previous occasion with another Minister. Of course if there are reasonable grounds for suspecting a colleague of conduct which disqualifies him from continuing in office and he either does not deny it or his denials are of an evasive, equivocal or otherwise unsatisfactory nature, he must go at once even though there is no immediate final proof. But if the reasonable grounds to suspect are counter-balanced by the strongest denial and by conduct quite inconsistent with guilt, the choice is between dishonouring, even if only temporarily, a man who is innocent [Galbraith] and not immediately condemning a man who may be guilty [Profumo]. One can then only choose on the balance of a personal assessment based on incomplete facts whether he was guilty or innocent or had behaved in a way which made it impossible for him to remain a Minister.

It may be said that I should have made a better assessment of the facts or done more to find them out. This is easy with hindsight. Denning harps on the newspaper photographs which showed that Keeler was a prostitute early in 1963. But JP's whole case was that she was not a prostitute in the summer of 1961 and in any event his acquaintance with her was incidental to his visits to Ward. I cannot accept even now that if by chance in the company of a friend I meet a woman who 18 months later becomes a notorious prostitute therefore my association with her must have been indiscreet if not immoral. It should also be remembered that in January to May 1963, I knew nothing of the sexual activities or reputation of Ward and all I knew was JP's description of him as a rather Bohemian yet cultured, talented and amusing character. The facts revealed in his trial were then wholly unknown to me.

Lord Denning also relies (in para. 181(5)) on JP's phrase 'No one will believe I did not commit adultery with CK' to make a point showing that there were reasonable grounds to believe that he had committed adultery and that therefore the answers to his proposed test were in our possession. But JP used this phrase solely in relation to the admitted use of the word 'Darling' in the letter. This (he said) alone will condemn me among non-theatrical and other people who keep this phrase for special use, yet there are those like myself who use it freely and indiscriminately and without any implication of affection far less indiscretion. With the latter view I agreed and knew at the time it was true of JP.

Lord Denning also criticizes the failure to send for the letter. He mis-states however my reason for not sending for it (para. 181A(6)). I was not representing JP. Clogg represented him. It seemed to me that it was not right to try to use my position as a Minister of the Crown (for I had no powers) to send for a letter when litigation seemed imminent between a fellow Minister and those in possession of the letter in which it might be of importance. It also occurred to me that if I did send for it I might justifiably be accused of attempting to suppress the letter, or at least of trying to use my position as a Minister to help a friend and to get possession of the letter on behalf of JP. Having reconsidered the matter in the light of the report, I am still convinced that it would have been wholly improper for the Attorney-General to send for this letter in those circumstances. Just imagine the headlines if I had done so and the request had been refused. Lord Denning does not advert to the point that since the letter was admitted by JP to exist and to contain the word 'Darling' his denials could only in my view at that time have been maintained on the basis that the letter contained nothing else. If the letter contained more and had been produced as was likely at any moment, he was liable to be utterly confounded by that event, and that he should act and swear as he did when he knew that letter existed seemed to be substantial confirmation of the fact that he had nothing to hide. Indeed it was expected during each week that the letter would be published the following Sunday by the paper.

No doubt if I had taken a more cynical and less charitable view of JP and thought the worst of a colleague from the first, I would not have accepted his version. Perhaps this is how we ought to view our colleagues when they are in difficulty and I am blameworthy for not being tough and having done so. If that is the situation, I have no regrets. What however I do find especially galling is that the deceiver is castigated scarcely at all (and his wife has enlisted Lord Denning's sympathy for the poor fellow and his pills) while those whom he deceived by an utterly selfish calculated and clever piece of persistent lying are told they are to blame and are responsible. It seems upside down to me.[38]

When the author showed this document to Lord Denning the Law Lord was scathing about Hobson's use of the expression 'galling' in relation to Denning's interview with Mrs Profumo, and his statement that Denning's approach was 'upside down'. Denning emphasized that it was his duty to interview Mrs Profumo, who was a most valuable witness to the circumstances in which the incriminating statement was made in the early hours of 22 March after Profumo had taken sleeping pills and been harassed in his house by journalists. Denning also objected to the use of the word 'deceiver', pointing out that Profumo was more a 'victim' than a 'deceiver', because of the awful way in which he was forced to make his personal statement at 3.30 in the morning. Denning expressed considerable sympathy with Profumo and his wife; he stressed that, according to the evidence he was given, the law officers demanded an immediate statement on 22 March when it would have been altogether better to leave the matter over the weekend; and it was wrong for the law officers to go off into a separate room to draft the statement. Denning thinks that Mr Clogg, Profumo's solicitor, was out of his depth; in fact Clogg was a divorce specialist, not a libel lawyer. That Hobson acknowledged some portion of guilt in his letter of resignation was no surprise to Denning: it was Hobson's duty, in Denning's view, to resign as 'architect' of Profumo's incriminating statement.[39]

Dilhorne was always exceptionally self-satisfied and in no way considered that Denning's strictures on the conduct of Ministers amounted to personal criticism of himself. He rounded on Denning's report in a letter to Macmillan:

Denning's criticism of Ministers
This is, I think, wholly unjustified. He makes a strong point of the injustice of acting on anything but evidence. What evidence had the Ministers concerned that Profumo's conduct was 'such as to create amongst an influential section of the people a reasonable belief that he had committed adultery with such a woman in such circumstances as the case discloses'? In my view they had none. While I recognize that a Minister's conduct may be of such a character as to make his resignation inevitable even though it is not established that he has been guilty of misconduct, in this case the Ministers concerned had only Mr Profumo's account – not the information Denning had – and on that information no sensible person would consider his resignation was required even if one accepts the test adopted by Denning in paragraph 181(5).*

I do not think that many people – and certainly not many lawyers – will accept that test.

I do not think any analogy can be drawn between what is a just excuse for a wife leaving her husband and the position of a Minister. It would be opening the door to McCarthyism if Ministers could be hounded from public life because an influential section of the people held a reasonable belief – based on rumour and gossip – that a Minister had misconducted himself.

I certainly do not think we should attack the report or the press but I think we should make it clear that we do not accept as right the test proposed by Denning.

Once the report is published, I think a number of constitutional lawyers will question this test and I would like to stimulate some of them to do so.

If this test is not accepted, the fact remains that Profumo's deception was not discovered. I do not think this is very damaging. I am sure the public will accept that there is rightly a reluctance to refuse to accept the word

---

* The reader will gasp at the phrase 'no sensible person'; the evidence shows that 'any sensible person' would believe that Keeler had been Profumo's mistress. Dilhorne can only have believed that there was no conclusive evidence of an intimate relationship. In paragraph 181(5) Denning pointed out that the crucial point was not whether Profumo had committed adultery, but whether his conduct ('proved or admitted') was such as to lead ordinary people reasonably to believe that he had.

of a colleague and it would be very bad for public life if that reluctance were diminished or destroyed.

Apart from paragraph 286 the report is very satisfactory, and while one should not minimize the effect of this paragraph, it should not lead to the rest of the report being overlooked.

Commenting to the author on Dilhorne's memorandum, Denning observed that the Ministers (apart from Macmillan and Butler) were obviously in a dither when they first read the report.

There was no need for this. I had exculpated them. Dilhorne's memorandum was bad-tempered, and his proposal that once the report was published he would 'stimulate' a number of constitutional lawyers to question whether I was correct in asserting that a wife has just cause for leaving her husband, if she *reasonably believes* he has committed adultery, is ludicrous.

According to Lord Denning, Dilhorne would have found no 'constitutional lawyers' of standing prepared to argue this point against Denning.[40]

The Denning Report turned out to be an anti-climax which dashed the hopes of the Opposition that the Government would be proved guilty of a security lapse. In the trauma of the moment Macmillan and his Ministers were more worried than they need have been. The report acquitted the Government on this score. When Harold Wilson was asked to read the draft at Admiralty House he remarked off the cuff that there was not much in it: 'not much for me', Macmillan supposed he meant. The initial fears of Ministers of its likely damage to the Government were not fulfilled. Macmillan resisted a strong plea from Wilson to recall Parliament for an immediate debate. There could thus be no public inquisition until November by which time, as *The Economist* correctly remarked, the Denning Report would be 'a political dodo'.

After consulting with Harold Wilson Macmillan ordered the immediate publication on 26 September of the full Denning Report with only one minor cut in a paragraph referring to the possibility of Ivanov being recruited as a defector or a double agent. Any outstanding qualms among Ministers were dispelled by its reception in the national press. *The Times* leader commented rather unkindly: 'While [the Prime Minister's] integrity was unchallenged Parliament might wish to consider whether further enquiries might have turned the scales between belief and disbelief in Mr Profumo's words ... The reason for leaving it to his colleagues was unclear.' However the *Spectator* stated categorically that there was no ammunition in Denning with which to attack the Government, and other columnists perhaps reluctantly adopted the same tone. Hailsham finished a television interview in *This Week*, according to *The Times*, 'with another burst of telegenic anger directed against the interviewer Robin Day'.

As Macmillan said on television, 'The trouble is, as we all know, I was deceived.' He had done his best but felt it would be a terrible thing if he had told a man he was a liar and he proved to be telling the truth.

> I would rather carry the burden of having made a mistake and been proved wrong than having had it the other way and destroyed the man's life . . . All this vile and poisonous cloud of slander and lies about our Ministers and others in high places is dissipated altogether.

On 18 June, the day after the Profumo debate, the US Ambassador in London David Bruce had sent a telegram to the White House:

> Macmillan's admission that he did not know what was going on at critical times was in circumstances pitiable and extremely damaging. He did not try to shirk responsibility, but on his own account did not give impression that he knew how to exercise it in unfolding developments of case on which nearly everyone in Parliament appeared to be better informed than the Prime Minister . . .

Bruce thought the debate would not end the affair, and that 'the Macmillan Government was mortally wounded'; in the view of the Embassy there would be no move to replace Macmillan before the President's visit to Birch Grove at the end of June, but he had become an electoral liability and 'his replacement cannot be too long delayed'.[41]

Although knowing nothing of Bruce's June report the Foreign Office were worried that the Denning Report would shake American confidence in the British security system. Happily this did not occur. In comment US editorials took the line that the Denning Report was an 'anti-climax' with nothing sensational or new; the majority spotlighted paragraph 286 with its assertion that 'it was the responsibility of the Prime Minister and his colleagues, and of them only, to deal with the situation'. Although the affair was thought by the American press to have damaged the Conservative Party and made a General Election in 1963 impossible, fortunately no American newspaper took the line that any important information had been gained by Ivanov through his association with Keeler.

Still *Time* magazine on 4 October declared that to many critics the judge's verdict on the security question was 'far from reassuring'. Other newspapers echoed Denning's suggestion that Ivanov 'had succeeded only too well' in weakening United States trust in Britain, but the *Kansas City Times* concluded that 'the high standards of human decency which have contributed to Britain's historic greatness remain as solid as they were before the British public ever heard of Dr Stephen Ward and Miss Keeler and their amoral ways.' Denning was praised for a thoroughgoing and competent piece of work, and as the *Detroit Free Press* put it: 'This is a far and happy cry from our habit of raking up everything as the report [on the McCarthy hearings] accused the McCarthy enquiry of doing.' The Washington Embassy reported to the Foreign Office that American comment tended to regard the Profumo affair as now being 'a closed chapter'.[42]

At the Ministerial meeting of 18 September, two days after he had received Denning's transcript, Macmillan mentioned to Lord Home that he was considering retirement before the General Election; Home replied that this would cause 'complete disunity in the Party and that great troubles will follow'. If Macmillan's memoirs are correct, he conceived the contingency plan of announcing to the Tory Party Conference in October that there would be no election until 1964, and that he would no longer lead the Party then. How serious he was we shall never know. However he had qualms about his position during the three months between this announcement and the election of a new Conservative leader 'during which I am to be PM under sentence of death'. Yet he also wrote in his diary: 'If I announced my determination to go on it would be accepted – and welcomed by a great majority.'

Having in the event been put in the clear by Denning, Macmillan's itch was to 'go on', and he nervously tested Party opinion. On 7 October Oliver Poole, Chairman of the Party in the Lords, came to see him and was of the opinion that Macmillan should resign. Macmillan however told Poole that he had decided to go on because

> (1) I should seem to be deserting and this would especially affect the marginal seats.
> (2) I would seem to have yielded to the group of malcontents who are swayed either by personal or purely reactionary sentiment.
> (3) I should leave the Party in complete disarray with some for Butler, some for Hailsham, some for Maudling.[43]

Macleod had also changed his mind about the damage Denning had done to the Conservatives. As Chairman of the Party he wanted to capitalize on the Conservative sense of relief and the national sense of anticlimax by announcing that there would be no election in 1963. On 24 September he proposed to Macmillan that they need not wait for Macmillan's speech at the Blackpool Conference to 'put an end to the election jitters', and he suggested to the Prime Minister that he (Macleod) should make a press statement on Saturday for all the Sunday papers to carry:

> North, South, East, West in every area in this country and to hundreds of constituencies I have insisted that it is their duty to have their constituency organization ready to go into an election at any time. This advice I repeat to you in my own constituency. But I am also on record on a score of occasions both here and in America as saying that there will be no General

Election this year. I see no reason whatever to alter my opinion. No new
decision has been taken. I am simply repeating to you what I have said many
times on other platforms. The Socialists of course clamour for an early
election. So they did in 1958. But we defeated them decisively when the
election came the following year. And we will do so again.

Macmillan replied to Macleod: 'I agree. This is a very impressing [*sic*]
formula.' Macleod's statement received great publicity and the nation was
given the impression that Macmillan would lead the Tories in a 1964
election.[44]

Then came disaster. During the night of 7/8 October Macmillan was
struck by prostate trouble. His doctor and friend Sir John Richardson
was on holiday in the Lake District. Instead Macmillan was seen by Dr
King-Lewis who did not know him. King-Lewis told the Prime Minister
he had either a 'benign' or a 'malignant' tumour. Macmillan, always
highly nervous about his health, panicked. He convinced himself he had
cancer, and on impulse decided to resign forthwith. He soon regretted
this decision. The tumour was diagnosed as benign. Thus he had nothing
to fear on the health front and could have continued to lead the
Conservatives indefinitely. Sir John (now Lord) Richardson has written
to the author that Macmillan was well within ten days.

During the evening of 8 October Macmillan was taken to the King
Edward VII Hospital for Officers, and the press were informed that he
would have an operation for the removal of the prostate gland. The next
day Home told the Conservative Party Conference in Blackpool that
Macmillan would not continue as Prime Minister and that the procedure
for finding a new Conservative leader must be put into operation.

By coincidence six weeks before, on 31 July 1963, the Peerage Bill
had become law and members of the House of Lords could from then
on disclaim their titles. It was the result of a long and spirited battle
by the Bristol MP Anthony Wedgwood Benn to avoid elevation to the
Upper House on the death of his father Lord Stansgate; it meant that
both Lord Home and Lord Hailsham could now disclaim their titles and
stand for election to the Commons. Both became contenders for the
premiership. Without the Peerage Bill neither Hailsham nor Home could
have been candidates for the leadership.*

As the shock of the end of Macmillan's era as Prime Minister was
digested by the delegates at Blackpool only two names were mentioned
for his successor: Butler and Hailsham. The newspapers declared it was
a contest between the two.

Already, according to Macleod, Macmillan had decided that Butler
would not be the right leader because he lacked 'the steel that makes

---

* Originally the Peerage Bill provided for peers to disclaim their titles on the dissolution of
Parliament but a Lords amendment made the Act operative from the date of Royal Assent.

a Prime Minister and the inspiration a leader needs to pull his Party through a fierce General Election'. Contrarily, Macleod himself has recorded that Butler had 'the priceless quality of being able to do any job better than you think he will, and of attracting to himself wide understanding and support from many people outside the Tory Party'. Macmillan made Hailsham his choice.

Unfortunately for Hailsham he became something of a figure of fun at Blackpool when addressing the Conservative Political Centre on the evening of 10 October. Alistair Horne has written: 'The conference swiftly fell to primeval warfare, with the two rival camps motivated as much by common antipathy for each other as by positive motives. "Stop Rab" and "Stop Quintin" became the cries.' However Hailsham overdid his act by throwing his hat in the ring so soon. In his excitement he became almost incoherent and although he received a hysterical ovation at the conference he went on in a state of great excitement to a Young Conservative dance brandishing his one-year-old child at the cameras and mixing baby foods. In Home's words there followed 'a swift reaction against his candidature'.[45]

Randolph Churchill added to the vulgarity of Hailsham's campaign by distributing American-style lapel badges. Redmayne observed later: 'Alas for Hailsham the cork had popped too soon ... his was a spent force after that night.' Rab Butler described it as being reminiscent of the Nuremberg Rally and Kenneth Young said that the Young Conservatives greeted Hailsham 'with the sort of rapture more often accorded to pop singers than to potential Prime Ministers'.

With Hailsham's over-evident eagerness his bandwagon halted almost as soon as it had begun to roll, and Home and Maudling became the likely candidates to undo Butler.*

It remains a mystery why Maudling, who had been the front runner in June, was no longer so in October: he had evoked the enthusiasm of the younger members of the Party, but his liberal policy towards Africa had alienated some more traditional Conservatives. In a letter to the author Lord Boyd-Carpenter pointed out that Maudling was 'very much both socially and intellectually of the newer type of political leader and basically did not establish any real contact with the older fashioned elements in the Party'. Sir Edward Heath told the author that in his view Maudling with his popular 1963 Budget had seemed the coming man, but that the charisma did not last.

Macleod, also a potential leader, decided that Maudling's chances were better than his own and he helped Maudling with the speech which the

---

* In January 1964 Hailsham wrote to Butler: 'I do not think any of us behaved dishonourably or without dignity (I would not say this for all the other but minor figures).'[46]

latter as Chancellor of the Exchequer would make to the conference. This speech could have made Maudling the front runner again, but he fluffed his opportunity. His lack of enthusiasm and spontaneity in delivering it convinced too many present that he was not the type to 'convert the uncommitted or inspire the faithful' in an election campaign. The *Sunday Express* lobby correspondent Wilfrid Sendall wrote that when he read the embargoed copy of Maudling's speech he thought it

> a cracker ... It was eloquent, moving and wise ... given the delivery it deserved it would have brought the conference to its feet and swept Maudling to the front in the leadership race ... if only the delivery could have matched the words, but alas it fell abysmally below them. Handed to a Churchill or a Macmillan the text would have produced a famous speech. Maudling wrecked it.

Maudling himself wrote, 'My friends told me that it was very important that I should get it right. I am afraid I did not.'[47]

The Times reported:

> on this morning's showing the next Prime Minister would be the fourteenth Earl of Home with the Chancellor well down among the also ran. Mr Maudling it must be recorded had only himself to blame. As the first serious contender for the throne to address the conference since Mr Macmillan's announcement he was confidently expected to close the economic debate by a rousing speech. It did not happen.
>
> With the economic tide flowing the Government's way at last, and with a personal incentive as great as any man could ask for, this was surely a moment for sounding the brass. Mr Maudling had left the mute stuck in his trumpet.
>
> The reactions which followed his speech were amusing, instructive, or depressing, depending on one's personal point of view. The clapping started slowly, grew to a moderate volume, and there it stuck. In an effort to get the bandwagon moving, a few of Mr Maudling's supporters on the platform, and a sparse scattering in the body of the hall, jumped to their feet and cheered. But the bulk of the conference would not be budged. They stuck to their seats and damned the Chancellor with faint praise. One by one, the Maudlingites faltered and sat down.
>
> By contrast, the standing ovation which had been given to Lord Home a short while before was made to look the more remarkable. His speech on foreign affairs had been able and witty, its delivery crisp and assured. In content it contained not a whit more news than that of Mr Maudling, yet it qualified Lord Home for [a] thunderous reception.

Home had spoken shortly before Maudling, replying to the Foreign Affairs debate. He like Maudling said practically nothing new but his delivery was tiptop, and the content, as *The Times* lobby correspondent correctly reported, was able and witty, and confidently delivered. After the speech Home would not give away whether or not he wanted the job, but the next day he charmingly offered a prize to any journalist who could point to a single clue in his speech.

A secret meeting of the 1922 Committee was held in an obscure Blackpool hotel that evening; they were joined most significantly by Redmayne, and the Chief Lords Whip Lord St Aldwyn. Two of those present supported Maudling and two Hailsham but the remainder were for Home; there was virtual unanimity that Home was the candidate most likely to unite the Party at a moment when recent vicissitudes had created sharp divisions. They also agreed that in the selection process Party members in the Commons and Lords should be asked to express not only their first choice but their second preference, and also whether they were particularly opposed to any of the four candidates. They all agreed that Home would do well on second preferences and there would be scarcely any opposition to him. There is strong evidence that John Morrison, MP for Salisbury and Chairman of the 1922 Committee, had spoken to Rab Butler and warned that 'The chaps won't have you' – a warning spoken in all seriousness, not in jest.[48]

With both Maudling and Hailsham dishing their chances at Blackpool, in London on the following Sunday Macmillan saw Butler, Hailsham, Heath, Home, Macleod and Maudling; and on Monday, Boyle, Brooke, Hare, Joseph, Sandys and Soames. The Prime Minister had suddenly switched his support to Home and told all these Ministers so.

From the moment he went into hospital Macmillan did everything he could to keep Rab Butler out of the succession. This is strange. In all moments of genuine difficulty during his premiership he had turned to Rab for help, and Rab had always responded with great loyalty. William Rees-Mogg writing about the succession in the *Sunday Times* (13 March 1982) suggested that 'Macmillan found it difficult to behave well to a man to whom he had once behaved badly.' However it is easier to forgive Macmillan for putting his own claims forward to be Prime Minister in 1957 than for his role in doing Butler down in 1963.

Macmillan wrote in his diary: 'Practically all these Ministers whether Hoggites or Butlerites or Maudlingites agreed that if Lord Home would undertake the task ... the whole Cabinet would cheerfully unite under him.'[49] This assessment must have been wishful thinking. Macmillan also saw Selwyn Lloyd though he was no longer in the Cabinet, and Lloyd agreed enthusiastically that Home should have the succession; he had pressed Home to stand at Blackpool and now became his chief supporter.

According to Macleod, there had been deadlock in the Cabinet regarding the succession at Blackpool, with four for Butler and four for Home, and in his view it was disgraceful that no Cabinet meeting was held to resolve the deadlock. Instead Macmillan from his sick bed (by now he was recovering nicely from his prostate operation) ordered Redmayne to canvass the views of MPs, and Lord St Aldwyn those of the Tory peers; while Lord Dilhorne, Lord St Aldwyn, Lord Poole and John Morrison, Chairman of the 1922 Committee, were to collect the views of the Party. His decision not to hold a meeting of the Cabinet was extraordinary and probably decisive in the selection of his successor.

On 16 October a *Daily Express* poll showed public support for candidates in the following percentages:

	All parties	Tories only
Butler	39½	38
Hailsham	21½	27
Maudling	11	10½
Home	9½	10
Others and undecided	18½	14½

When he left for Blackpool Home was not a declared contender. Not until Blackpool was over did he declare himself or start to organize his eventual victory. It would have been out of keeping with Home's character, if he had already decided to stand, for him to have told the mass meeting at Blackpool: 'We choose our leader not for what he does at a Party conference but because the leader we choose is in every respect the whole man who is fit to lead the nation.'

Both Macleod and Lloyd have left authoritative accounts of the leadership struggle of October 1963 in which they played important roles. Macleod has recorded that he knew on 17 October that only two of the Cabinet favoured Home, and eleven were for other candidates, while he was sure the *Daily Express* poll was accurate. Yet Dilhorne reported to Macmillan that ten Ministers wanted Home, three Butler, four Maudling, and two Hailsham. Dilhorne also told Macmillan that Macleod voted for Home, which discredits Dilhorne's findings.* Macmillan's official biographer, Alistair Horne, interviewed Enoch Powell, Lord Butler, Lord Eccles and Lord Aldington. They all told him Dilhorne was astray. Yet in a letter in 1980 written to Alistair Horne, Dilhorne insisted he was correct. Macleod's widow, when asked by Horne, was adamant that Macleod would never have voted for Home.[50]

Redmayne, according to Macleod, had been 'working hard for a week to secure the maximum support for Home', and so influenced MPs that he was justified in telling Macmillan that a majority of MPs favoured

---

* Apart from their divide over social policy where Macleod was more radical than Home their clash over African independence had embittered their personal relationship.

Home, and Home was marginally ahead on the first count of MPs, and outstandingly so on alternative choices. (There were still four runners: Home, Butler, Maudling, and now as an outsider Hailsham.) Lord St Aldwyn not surprisingly reported that the peers were overwhelmingly for Home. This prompted Macleod later to quote a verse inspired by the death of Tom Harrison, the originator of the Madge opinion polls: '... And he'd not been gone a week when a report arrived for Madge / Heaven's 83.4 per cent pro God.'

During the evening of 17 October Macmillan dictated a letter to the Queen recommending Home; with this letter he enclosed memoranda from Dilhorne, Redmayne and St Aldwyn justifying his advice. He also dictated an official letter of resignation.

However as rumours started to circulate during the afternoon of 17 October that the 'enquiries' had given Home a majority and that Macmillan was recommending him to the Queen as the next Prime Minister, Butler, Maudling, Hailsham, Powell and Macleod went into full revolt. After dinner Lloyd and Dilhorne went to Home's house in Carlton Gardens, the official residence of the Foreign Secretary. The two heard Powell and Macleod telling Home over the phone that they would not serve in a Cabinet under him. Maudling did the same and he, Aldington and Erroll joined Macleod at Powell's home in South Eaton Place in a conclave that came to be known as the 'midnight meeting'. Hailsham also telephoned to Home and declined to serve, but with considerably less courtesy. The pavement in South Eaton Place now became crowded with journalists as the conclave continued.

According to Lloyd, Redmayne joined Home and rang South Eaton Place from Carlton Gardens to tell the dissidents that 'Ten members of the Cabinet had made Home their first choice.' This was received with incredulity at South Eaton Place. Redmayne then said that Home had received the highest number of votes from Conservative MPs. According to Lloyd, Home informed Redmayne that Maudling, Powell and Macleod had all told him 'firmly and positively that they were against his selection'. Hailsham's rude call had come while Redmayne was with Home. Lloyd quotes Home as being so discomforted that when Lady Home said 'It looks rather smelly now' the Foreign Secretary replied: 'I was quite prepared to come forward as the candidate to unify the Party accepted by everyone; but if it is said that my coming forward would split the Party then it is a different proposition.' Dilhorne attempted to console Home, saying he should pay 'no attention' to the dissidents who were just 'a bunch of disappointed and over-ambitious colleagues'.

Lloyd drove Redmayne to Powell's house leaving the Homes unhappy about the turn of events. Lloyd then went home, leaving Redmayne to face the anger of Maudling, Powell, Macleod, Erroll and Aldington, who all insisted that Macmillan must be informed at once 'of their feeling against Home'.

As soon as Lloyd reached his flat he rang Peter Walker who had junior office; Walker said to Lloyd, 'the very people who had stopped Hailsham are now trying to use him to stop Home.' From Powell's house Redmayne sent a message to Macmillan that there was a serious Cabinet revolt against Home. Macmillan became angry; his doctor Sir John Richardson described him as 'in a terrible state; old and grey and furious'. Mollie Butler, Rab's wife, told the author that she received calls that evening from five Ministers – Hailsham, Macleod, Aldington, Erroll and Maudling – as well as from the MP Lord Lambton and the editor of the *Express* John Junor, all stressing that Home must not become Prime Minister.[51]

At 8.30 on the morning of 18 October Redmayne and Bligh arrived at the hospital accompanied by the Ulster Unionist MP Knox Cunningham who was Macmillan's Parliamentary secretary. Butler later commented:

> One presumes and hopes that the Chief Whip informed the Prime Minister, as he was requested to do, that seven or eight members of the Cabinet were opposed to the choice of Home. What is certain is that Macmillan decided to ignore this powerful objection and acted (as he had done in 1962) with utter determination and despatch, making a definite recommendation of Home.[52]

Home himself had telephoned Macmillan at breakfast time saying that he felt aggrieved at having been asked to come forward only as a compromise candidate for the sake of 'unity', and that he now felt like withdrawing. Macmillan urged him to stand firm: 'if we give in to this intrigue, there will be chaos ... go ahead and get on with it.'

With the decision made, Bligh was duly despatched to the Palace with Macmillan's letter of resignation. After a good night's sleep helped by pills, Macmillan had recovered from his earlier vexation and, informed of the Cabinet opposition to Home, he instructed Cunningham to add an addendum to the long report to the Queen, explaining that Redmayne had told him of the 'midnight meeting' – thereby discharging his responsibility but not altering his recommendation for Home. A large white envelope containing all the documents for the Queen was reopened to include the addendum, and given to the Queen at the hospital at 11.30 a.m. by Macmillan seated in a wheelchair. His long reign was over; but the succession was still in doubt.

On her return the Queen immediately summoned Home to the Palace and asked him if he would form a Government. Home, conscious of the opposition of Butler, Macleod, Maudling and Powell, replied that he was doubtful but would try. In order to avoid embarrassment to the Queen in the event of failure, as advised by Macmillan, he did not kiss hands but went to 10 Downing Street. This was an astute move which strengthened his position because the media hailed him as the new Prime Minister with gusto when he reached No. 10, although doubts were raised by some lobby correspondents whether he would succeed in recruiting a strong enough Cabinet. Undoubtedly this move was inspired by Macmillan.

It would certainly have been in Butler's power as Deputy Prime Minister to have instructed the Cabinet Secretary to summon the Cabinet to discuss the succession. Had Home found Butler at work as Deputy Prime Minister when he arrived at No. 10 the situation would have been bizarre. With a Cabinet meeting called, Butler in all likelihood would have emerged as Prime Minister for with his letter of resignation Macmillan no longer exercised any power. The Palace gave the Queen wrong advice in recommending her to summon Home and ask him to form a Government. In British politics there was no precedent for this, whilst the Conservative Party constitution offered no procedure for the election of a new leader.

A Cabinet had met under Butler on the morning of 15 October but Butler, with characteristic lack of guile, did not put the position of the new Prime Minister to a vote. Had he done so he would have had a majority in his favour. The Ministers had no expectation that the choice would be made without another Cabinet meeting; they were completely bypassed.

On his return from the Palace Home asked Butler to call on him at Downing Street. Butler agreed; this was a fatal mistake. He should instead have insisted on a meeting of the Cabinet. According to a memorandum by Butler, Home told him that everything depended on Butler himself and Maudling agreeing to serve. According to Butler:

> I replied that I must reserve my position on two grounds: first, whether it was right for an hereditary peer to succeed at the present time; secondly, whether he could command enough unity in the Cabinet ... matters had been rushed and insufficient consideration given to the difficulties.

Butler then gave Home a list of the names of the Ministers who were unwilling to serve; Home 'took them down and said he would see them'.

At a meeting later in the day in Downing Street Hailsham gave way, agreeing to serve under Home although he stated that he would have preferred Butler. Butler was on the horns of a dilemma; in his memoirs he wrote that Hailsham's defection to Home was an erosion of support, and next morning he accepted the Foreign Office. Explaining his action in his memoirs Butler writes: 'In my talk with him [Home] I had put the need for unity first and it seemed to me that the most unselfish way of achieving unity was to serve with a friend rather than to force the issue the other way.' Dilhorne wrote to Butler:

> You have held the Tory Party together at a very critical time. I do not doubt that if you had refused to serve, Alec would have failed to form a Government and if you had then been sent for, which seems most likely, I think you would have started under very heavy criticism, for it would be hard to justify a refusal to serve on the ground of policy – for there was no difference of policy – and differences of policy are really the only justification for refusing to serve a colleague. Many would have thought that you had refused to serve Alec only to secure your personal advantage and that would certainly have done serious harm to your standing.[53]

Dilhorne was right about 'the very serious criticism', but it was not the view of the national press nor of all Butler's colleagues that there was no difference of policy. Butler had always been a supporter of radical policies whereas Home was right wing. Macleod's verdict was that 'the Tory Party for the first time since Bonar Law' was being led from the right of centre. Home saw both Powell and Macleod separately, trying hard to persuade them to change their minds; he was unsuccessful. They would not serve in the Cabinet under him.

For three weeks between his appointment and his victory in the Kinross and West Perthshire by-election Home was Prime Minister without a seat in the Commons or Lords. However he won the Kinross by-election comfortably.

Media reaction to Home's election was damaging to the Tories. One devastating comment came from Anthony Howard in the *Sunday Times* even before the result was known: 'The Conservatives have ceased to be gentlemen without becoming democratic.' In the same paper William Rees-Mogg, a recent Conservative Parliamentary candidate, wrote of the result that it was 'not fairly conducted' and 'produced, as a compromise, a man who had decisive support only from his predecessor against three candidates each of whom had stronger claims'; this was strong meat from the newspaper which was the most influential Conservative opinion former.

According to the *Observer* the Tories had been forced to 'settle for a second best. It is very doubtful that he has the perception and imagination for effective statesmanship in a rapidly changing world.' *The Times* stated that Home was 'untried on the home front and economics', and that he had won 'after deadlock in the Cabinet at Blackpool with five for Butler and five for Hailsham, with Butler weak on the nuclear deterrent'. Beyond dispute Home became Prime Minister against the majority vote of the Cabinet solely because Macmillan willed it.

It is hard to explain why Macmillan from his hospital sick bed should have plotted continuously to prevent Butler from becoming Prime Minister – especially in view of Butler's consistent loyalty to him over the threatened resignations by Macleod, Maudling and Perth, while Butler's recent success over Central Africa was an enormous relief to the Prime Minister. Butler's widow is bitter about Macmillan, telling the author that he was always 'false', and kept her husband out of the succession because he did not want to be succeeded by a 'better man'. She even suggested that Macmillan had entrusted Butler with responsibility for the Central African Federation knowing that failure would both finish Butler off and divert the blame from Macmillan. She dates Macmillan's antipathy to Butler from the time her husband assumed command of the Conservative Research Department in 1945 after Macmillan had lost his seat in the General Election. There Butler reshaped Conservative policy to meet the post-war challenge, and in doing so recruited the exceptionally talented Powell, Maudling and Macleod for his team. She thinks that Macmillan felt he should have been entrusted with this task.[54]

One undoubted factor which told against Butler was that a number of right-wing Conservative MPs consistently expressed opposition to him because he had been a prominent appeaser before the war as Under-Secretary at the Foreign Office, and rumours circulated, not entirely without foundation, that he had favoured obtaining details of Hitler's peace terms through Stockholm after Dunkirk in 1940. If Butler was tainted, so was Home, who had been Neville Chamberlain's private secretary and accompanied him to meet Hitler at Munich. However Home was younger and then in a less responsible position.

Labour and Liberal spokesmen and much media comment emphasized that with Home the Conservative Party had shifted to the right. How far is this true? Sir Edward Heath who represented the left-of-centre section of the Tory Party, disagrees and insisted to the author that Home was centre of the road on social policy. It is not possible to point to anything specific done by Home as Prime Minister which could be pronounced right wing. Indeed his twelve months in Downing Street produced little action apart from abolition of resale price maintenance.

By refusing to serve in the Home Cabinet Macleod destroyed his chance of becoming the Conservative leader. Home much liked Heath and immediately promised him the Board of Trade; there Heath established a dominance and became poised to take over as Party leader, while Macleod instead became editor of the *Spectator* and in their columns expressed sour criticism of the Party's selection method for its leader and of other government policies, which did not increase his popularity within Party ranks.

Home's main problem was to select the date for the General Election. Maudling, conscious of the mounting balance of payments deficit, argued for a spring election; the less politically astute Hare, Minister of Labour, argued strongly for the autumn. Home, feeling that his popularity was increasing each month, plumped for October.

It is estimated that if 900 people in eight marginal constituencies had voted Conservative instead of Labour in 1964 the Government would have survived. Contrary to public expectation Home showed good judgement as Prime Minister and his charm and obvious sincerity and integrity did much to help the fortunes of the Conservative Party.

In the end Labour won the 1964 General Election with an overall majority of four seats. Considering how the defection of Macleod and Powell had damaged the Conservatives it was a creditable result for Home. However nearly all political observers agree that if Macmillan had remained the leader, which his health in fact would have permitted, or had Butler been Prime Minister, their mastery of politics and debate and their political skills and experience would have given them a marked superiority over the astute but less consistent Harold Wilson, and brought the Tories to power for better or worse for a fourth term of office.

Notes

Initials and numbers refer to papers in the Public Record Office, Kew.

Chapter 1   Mending Bridges with Ike

1. Lamb, *Failure of the Eden Government*, pp. 183–230.
2. Ibid.; FO 800/728.
3. Prem 11/1105.
4. Lamb, op. cit., pp. 261–79.
5. Butler, *The Art of the Possible*, p. 194.
6. Cab 128/30; Lamb, op. cit., p. 287.
7. T 236/4190; Cab 128/30; Lamb, op. cit., pp. 290–3.
8. Prem 11/1107; Lamb, op. cit., pp. 304–5; Rhodes James, *Anthony Eden*, p. 591.
9. Lamb, op. cit., p. 206.
10. Prem 11/1786.
11. FO 371/129331; Clarke, *Nuclear Diplomacy and the Special Relationship*, pp. 43–5.
12. Macmillan, *Pointing the Way*, p. 24; Prem 11/1838; Prem 11/1787; Horne, *Macmillan*, p. 24.
13. Lamb, op. cit., pp. 216–29.
14. Prem 11/1786.
15. Ibid.; Prem 11/1787.
16. Prem 11/1787; Thorpe, *Selwyn Lloyd*, p. 282.
17. Lamb, op. cit., p. 159; Macmillan, *Riding the Storm*, pp. 269–71.
18. Prem 11/2368.
19. Ibid.
20. Ibid.
21. Prem 11/2386; Prem 11/2387.
22. Prem 11/2388.
23. Prem 11/2380; Prem 11/2388; Cab 128/30.
24. Ibid.
25. Ibid.
26. Prem 11/4027; Prem 11/2388.
27. Prem 11/2381.
28. Prem 11/2388; Prem 11/2381.

29. Prem 11/2386.
30. Prem 11/2376.

Chapter 2   Vote-winning Budgets

1. Cairncross, *Robert Hall Diaries*, p. 94.
2. Dow, *Management of the British Economy*, p. 101.
3. T 230/373.
4. Cairncross, op. cit., p. 122; Brittan, *Treasury under the Tories*, p. 189.
5. Prem 11/2973.
6. Cairncross, interview with author.
7. Dow, op. cit., p. 101.
8. Horne, op. cit., p. 70–1.
9. Boyd-Carpenter, *Way of Life*, pp. 137–9.
10. *Spectator*, 24 April 1971; Horne, op. cit., p. 73.
11. Cairncross, op. cit., pp. 145, 153.
12. Prem 11/2305.
13. Dow, op. cit., p. 104.
14. T 171/196.
15. Horne, op. cit., p. 142.
16. Prem 11/2667.
17. Prem 11/2662.
18. Prem 11/2973.
19. Prem 11/2311.
20. Prem 11/2663.

Chapter 3   The 1959 General Election

1. Cook and Ramsden, *By-Elections in British Politics*, pp. 191–7; Butler and Rose, *British General Election of 1959*, pp. 35–41.
2. Davenport-Hines, *The Macmillans*, p. 299.
3. Prem 11/1293.
4. Horne, op. cit., p. 152.

Chapter 4   Economic Policy 1960

1. Brittan, op. cit., p. 205.
2. *The Times*, 9 December 1959.
3. Cairncross, op. cit., p. 221.
4. Prem 11/2962.
5. Cairncross, op. cit., p. 232.
6. Prem 11/3291; Horne, op. cit., p. 143.

Chapter 5   Selwyn Lloyd as Chancellor

1. Cairncross, op. cit., p. 241; Brittan, op. cit., p. 210. Cairncross, unpublished TS, 'The economy in the sixties'.

2. T 171/505.
3. Prem 11/3762; Prem 11/3758; Boyd-Carpenter, letter to author.
4. T 171/503; Prem 11/3758; T 171/520; Cairncross, op. cit., p. 261.
5. Prem 11/3290; Prem 11/3291.
6. Prem 11/3290.
7. Cab 128/135.
8. Prem 11/3290.
9. Cab 128/135.
10. Prem 11/3757.
11. Macmillan diary in Horne Archive, entry for 25 November 1961.
12. Brittan, op. cit., p. 238; *New Outlook*, July 1962.
13. *Growth of the United Kingdom Economy to 1966*; *Conditions Favourable to Faster Growth*, HMSO 1962. Reports of National Economic Development Council.
14. Prem 11/3742; Cairncross, unpublished TS, op. cit.
15. Prem 11/3287.
16. Prem 11/3757.
17. Cairncross, unpublished TS, op. cit.; *Incomes Policy*, HMSO 1962.
18. Macmillan, *End of the Day*, p. 63.
19. Thorpe, op. cit., p. 335.
20. *Spectator*, April 1962.
21. Prem 11/4202.
22. Cab 128/35; Prem 11/3765.
23. Prem 11/3765.
24. Prem 11/3742.
25. Cairncross, unpublished TS, op. cit.

Chapter 6   Macmillan's Last Chancellor

1. Thorpe, op. cit., p. 337.
2. Fisher, *Macmillan*, pp. 279–80; Thorpe, op. cit., p. 339; Macmillan, op. cit., p. 91.
3. Cab 128/35.
4. Thorpe, op. cit., pp. 343–53.
5. Maudling, *Memoirs*, p. 105; *Economist*, 10 November 1962.
6. Cairncross, unpublished TS, op. cit.
7. Prem 11/4195.
8. Prem 11/3742.
9. Prem 11/4192.
10. Ibid.
11. Prem 11/4202.
12. Prem 11/4209; Maudling, op. cit., pp. 102–22.
13. T 121/625; Cairncross, unpublished TS, op. cit.
14. Prem 11/4209.
15. Prem 11/4202.
16. Prem 11/4200.
17. Maudling, op. cit., p. 115.

18. T 230/373.
19. Cab 128/135; Morgan, *The People's Peace*, p. 214.
20. Maudling, op. cit., pp. 116–19.

Chapter 7   EFTA of the Seventeen

1. T 324/183; Lamb, op. cit., pp. 59–102.
2. Cab 128/31; Cab 128/32. Lamb, op. cit., pp. 95–102.
3. FO 371/134488.
4. FO 371/134486.
5. FO 371/134491; FO 371/134495; FO 371/134500.
6. FO 371/134495.
7. Maudling, op. cit., p. 70.
8. FO 371/134499; FO 371/134503.
9. FO 371/134504; FO 371/134498.
10. FO 371/134498.
11. FO 371/134450.
12. FO 371/134504.
13. FO 371/134511.
14. FO 371/134510.
15. FO 371/134511.
16. FO 371/134513.
17. Camps, *Britain and the European Community*, p. 174; FO 371/134520.
18. FO 371/134520; Prem 11/2826.
19. Prem 11/2826.
20. FO 371/134520; FO 371/134514.
21. Cab 134/35; FO 371/134520; Prem 11/2826.

Chapter 8   EFTA of the Seven

1. FO 371/134504.
2. Camps, op. cit., p. 177.
3. Prem 11/2826.
4. Prem 11/2827.
5. FO 371/134514.
6. Prem 11/2827.
7. Cab 128/31.
8. Prem 11/2827.
9. Camps, op. cit., p. 231.
10. Prem 11/2870.
11. FO 371/142504; Prem 11/3132.
12. Prem 11/3132; FO 371/142504.
13. Prem 11/3132.
14. Ibid.
15. Prem 11/3133.
16. Ibid.
17. Cab 128/34.

18. Prem 11/3141.
19. FO 371/158264; FO 371/158171; Macmillan, *Pointing the Way*, p. 327.
20. FO 371/158171.
21. FO 371/158170.
22. FO 371/158175.
23. Prem 11/3556.
24. FO 371/158173.
25. FO 371/158270.
26. FO 371/158264.
27. FO 371/158173.
28. Cab 128/35.
29. Ibid.
30. FO 371/158176; FO 371/158173.
31. FO 371/158177.
32. Prem 11/3556.
33. FO 371/157178.
34. FO 371/158177.
35. Prem 11/3195.
36. Prem 11/3557; Prem 11/3558.
37. Cab 128/35; Prem 11/3557.
38. Prem 11/3558.
39. Cab 128/35.
40. FO 371/158781.
41. Camps, op. cit., p. 41.

Chapter 9   EEC Negotiations

1. Prem 11/3338.
2. FO 371/164778; FO 371/164775.
3. FO 371/164775.
4. FO 371/164778.
5. FO 371/171149.
6. FO 371/164780; FO 371/164781.
7. FO 371/164835.
8. FO 371/164832; Prem 11/3775; FO 371/164789; Horne, op. cit., pp. 328–9; De Gaulle, *Mémoires d'espoir*, II, p. 177.
9. Cab 128/36.
10. Prem 11/3635.
11. Cab 128/36.
12. FO 371/164794.
13. Cab 128/36.
14. FO 371/164801.
15. FO 371/164791.
16. Cab 134/1512; Dixon, *Double Diploma*, pp. 285–8.
17. Cab 128/36.
18. FO 371/164801.

19. FO 371/164791.
20. Cab 134/1512; FO 371/164789; Dixon, op. cit., p. 191.
21. Cab 134/1537; Macmillan, op. cit., p. 117.
22. FO 371/164837; Dixon, op. cit., p. 299.
23. FO 371/164802; Dixon, op. cit., p. 292.
24. Evans, *Downing Street Diary*, p. 211.
25. Cab 134/1536.
26. FO 371/164793.
27. Camps, op. cit., p. 463.
28. Cab 134/1512.
29. Cab 134/1539.
30. Macmillan, op. cit., p. 30. Lady Butler, interview with author.
31. Cab 134/1515.
32. FO 371/164804.
33. FO 371/164812.
34. Cab 134/1512.
35. Sir Michael Franklin, unpublished diary.
36. FO 371/164807.
37. Lord Roll, letter to author. Sir Patrick Reilly, letter to author.
38. FO 371/164808.
39. FO 371/164809.
40. FO 371/164810.
41. Sir Edward Heath, interview with author.
42. FO 371/164812.
43. Prem 11/4230; Macmillan, op. cit., p. 354.
44. Clarke, *Nuclear Diplomacy and the Special Relationship*, p. 418, quoting from a despatch from the US Paris Embassy to Washington, in Kennedy Centre.
45. FO 371/173308.
46. Sir Edward Heath, interview with author.
47. FO 371/173297.
48. FO 371/164811; Cab 128/36.
49. Sir Edward Heath, interview with author. Papers of Sir Pierson Dixon in possession of his son Piers Dixon. Sir Patrick Reilly, letter to author.
50. Dixon, op. cit., pp. 311–12.
51. FO 371/171413; FO 371/171414; FO 371/171416; FO 371/171417.
52. Horne, op. cit., p. 447; FO 371/171414.
53. FO 371/171412.
54. Sir Patrick Reilly, letter to author.
55. FO 371/171441.
56. FO 371/173308.
57. FO 371/171417.
58. Sir Patrick Reilly, letter to author; Nora Beloff, *The General Says No*, p. 16.
59. Macmillan, op. cit., p. 367, 371–2.
60. Cab 128/36; Cab 134/1512.
61. Prem 11/4220.

Chapter 10   After the Veto

1. T 178/17; Cairncross, op. cit., p. 123.
2. Cab 128/37.
3. *Expansion Without Inflation*, New Outlook pamphlet, Liberal Publication Office.
4. Cab 134/1696.
5. Cab 134/1106; Cab 134/1697; Cab 134/1678.
6. Cab 134/1701; Blackaby, *British Economic Policy*, pp. 421–31.
7. Cab 134/1701.
8. Ibid.
9. Campbell, *Heath*, pp. 150–7.
10. Information from Tom Sharpe QC; Neale, *The Anti-Trust Laws of the USA*, p. 531; Blackaby, op. cit., p. 428; Robert Stephens, *New Society*, January 1964; Richard Lamb, articles in *The Times*, 12 May 1964 and 29 August 1966.

Chapter 11   Kenya

1. Prem 11/3413; Blundell, *So Rough a Wind*, p. 291.
2. Prem 11/3413; Blundell, op. cit., pp. 294–5; Fisher, *Macmillan*, p. 150.
3. Ibid.
4. Cab 128/35.
5. Statutory Instrument No. 791 of 1963, 'The Kenya Order in Council'.
6. Horne, op. cit., p. 414.

Chapter 12   Wind of Change

1. Macmillan, op. cit., p. 295.
2. Kirkman, *Unscrambling an Empire*, p. 84.
3. Cab 128/35.
4. Horne, op. cit., pp. 179–80.
5. Welensky, *4,000 Days*, pp. 152–61.
6. Kirkman, op. cit., p. 235.
7. Prem 11/2783.
8. Sir Edgar Williams, letters to author. Kirkman, op. cit., pp. 51 and 113; Rhodes House Archives.
9. Horne, op. cit., p. 181.
10. Macmillan, *Riding the Storm*, pp. 735–8.
11. *Spectator*, July 1969; Welensky, op. cit., pp. 130 and 134. Information from Sir Edgar Williams; Rhodes House Archives.
12. Prem 11/2784.
13. Prem 11/3994.
14. Prem 11/3075; Prem 11/3040.
15. Macmillan, op. cit., p. 161; Prem 11/3075.
16. Prem 11/3085. Information from Sir David Hunt.
17. Prem 11/3075; Prem 11/3076; Macmillan, op. cit., p. 163.
18. Prem 11/3081.

19. Prem 11/3176; Prem 11/3240; Macmillan, op. cit., p. 487; Welensky, op. cit., p. 198; Kirkman, op. cit., p. 39.
20. Prem 11/3077.
21. Prem 11/3486; Prem 11/3485.
22. Prem 11/3485.
23. Prem 11/3485; Prem 11/3486.
24. Kirkman, op. cit., p. 89; Prem 11/3949.
25. Welensky, op. cit., p. 301.
26. Prem 11/3487.
27. Ibid.
28. Kilmuir, *Political Adventure*, p. 315.
29. Prem 11/3486.
30. Kirkman, op. cit., p. 98.
31. Prem 11/3492.
32. Ibid; Welensky, op. cit., p. 307; Prem 11/3486; Cmd 1483.
33. Prem 11/3490; Prem 11/3492; Kilmuir, op. cit., p. 315.
34. Prem 11/3493; Welensky, op. cit., p. 315.
35. Macmillan, *End of the Day*, p. 314; Fisher, *Macleod*, p. 169.
36. Howard, *Rab*, p. 285.

Chapter 13   The End of Federation

1. Maudling, *Memoirs*, pp. 89–99.
2. Prem 11/3494.
3. Maudling, op. cit., pp. 89–99.
4. Prem 11/3494.
5. Prem 11/3491; Prem 11/3492.
6. Prem 11/3492; Maudling, op. cit., p. 99.
7. Prem 11/3485; Macmillan, op. cit., p. 531.
8. Butler, op. cit., p. 210.
9. Welensky, op. cit., pp. 338–40.
10. Prem 11/3944; Butler, op. cit., p. 212.
11. Howard, *Rab*, pp. 292–3.
12. Prem 11/3943; Butler, op. cit., p. 217.
13. Prem 11/4419; FO 371/16134; Wilson, *A Prime Minister on Prime Ministers*, p. 320.
14. Prem 11/4419; FO 371/16134; Butler, op. cit., p. 226.
15. Prem 11/4420; Prem 11/4421.
16. Prem 11/4421; Butler, op. cit., p. 230.

Chapter 14   Defence

1. Prem 11/1326; Lamb, *Eden Government*, pp. 55–6.
2. Prem 11/867; Lamb, op, cit., p. 111.
3. Prem 11/1777; Prem 11/2415.
4. Freedman, *Britain and Nuclear Weapons*, pp. 4–7; Prem 11/1777.
5. FO 371/126683.
6. Air 17/942; Def 5/81.

7. Lamb, *Churchill as War Leader*, London, 1991, pp. 320–1.
8. Air 8/2064; Clarke, op. cit., p. 116.
9. Adm 215/179; Air 19/813.
10. Cab 131/19; Cab 131/23; Watkinson, *Turning Points*, p. 122.
11. Cab 131/23; Prem 11/2940.
12. Ibid.
13. Ibid.
14. Ibid.
15. Ibid.
16. Cab 128/34; Prem 11/2940.
17. Prem 11/2941.
18. Prem 11/2940; Prem 11/2941; FO 371/159651; FO 371/159652.
19. FO 371/159651; FO 371/159652; Prem 11/2940; Prem 11/2941. Clarke, op. cit., p. 272.
20. Watkinson, op. cit., pp. 148–51.
21. Kennedy Library, quoted in Clarke, op. cit., p. 299; Kennedy Library, quoted in ibid., p. 303.
22. Kennedy Library, quoted in ibid., p. 331.
23. Prem 11/3605.
24. Cab 133/244; Cab 131/25; Def 6/70. Statement on Defence 1962, *The Next Five Years*, HMSO.
25. Prem 11/3711; Prem 11/3709; FO 371/166312; Def 3/336; Clarke, op. cit., pp. 335–6.
26. Prem 11/3246.
27. Ibid.
28. Macmillan, *End of the Day*, p. 146.
29. Ibid., pp. 172–9; Prem 11/3719.
30. J. Bayliss, *Anglo-American Defence Relations*, p. 101; Clarke, op. cit., p. 352; Prem 11/3716.
31. Prem 11/3716.
32. Cab 133/245; Clarke, op. cit., pp. 338–421, has given a comprehensive and well-researched account of the Skybolt–Polaris crisis.
33. FO 371/173292.
34. Ibid.
35. Prem 11/4229.
36. Ibid.
37. FO 371/173292; Cab 128/36.
38. Clarke, op. cit., p. 411.
39. Prem 11/4229.
40. Cab 128/37.
41. FO 371/173292.
42. Bundy, *Danger and Survival*, pp. 493–4; De Gaulle, *Discours et messages*, IV, 66–76.
43. Clarke, op. cit., p. 413; Zuckerman, *Monkeys, Men and Missiles*, p. 254.
44. FO 371/173355.
45. The author is indebted to Brian Cathcart, author of *Test of Greatness*, for this

information; *Economist*, 16 December 1963; *Test of Greatness*, p. 21; BBC Radio 4 talk, 'A Bloody Union Jack', 5 May 1986.

Chapter 15   Khrushchev and the West

1. Prem 11/2715.
2. Macmillan, *Riding the Storm*, pp. 575 *et seq*.
3. Prem 11/2715; Prem 11/2720.
4. Prem 11/2720.
5. Eisenhower Library, Abilene, quoted in Horne, op. cit., p. 121; Macmillan, op. cit., p. 583.
6. Prem 11/2716.
7. Ibid.
8. Prem 11/2717.
9. Ibid.
10. Prem 11/2716; Prem 11/2718.
11. Prem 11/3005; Prem 11/3006; Prem 11/2703; Prem 11/2716.
12. Prem 11/2705.
13. Macmillan, op. cit., p. 85.
14. Prem 11/3005.
15. Macmillan, op. cit., p. 195.
16. FO 371/151922.
17. Ibid.; Prem 11/3005.
18. FO 371/151923.
19. Ibid.
20. Prem 11/3005; Horne, op. cit., pp. 230 and 231.
21. FO 371/151923.
22. Horne, op. cit., pp. 300–6.
23. Sorensen, *A Question of Character: Life of John Kennedy*, pp. 294–312; Pierson Dixon's unpublished diary in possession of Piers Dixon; McGeorge Bundy, Oral History interview, in J. F. Kennedy Library.
24. Sorensen, op. cit., p. 558; Clarke, op. cit., p. 13.
25. Dixon, unpublished diary, op. cit., 21 September 1961; Horne, op. cit., p. 312.
26. Clarke, op. cit., p. 214.
27. Prem 11/3804; Prem 11/3805.
28. Prem 11/3804; Prem 11/3805.
29. Prem 11/3804.
30. Ibid.; Prem 11/3805.
31. Prem 11/3805.
32. Prem 11/3804; Prem 11/3805.
33. Macmillan, op. cit., p. 178. Prem 11/3802; Prem 11/3806.
34. Horne, op. cit., p. 362.
35. Prem 11/3689; Sorensen, op. cit., pp. 269–76.
36. Prem 11/3689.
37. Prem 11/3809.

38. Prem 11/3690.
39. *The Times*, 29 October 1962.
40. Prem 11/3691; Macmillan, op. cit., pp. 212–18.
41. McGeorge Bundy, Oral History interview, in J. F. Kennedy Library; Horne, op. cit., pp. 382–3; Booker, *Neophiliacs*, p. 177.
42. Prem 11/3806.
43. Ibid.
44. Prem 11/4262; Prem 11/3806.
45. Prem 11/4262.
46. FO 371/171235.
47. Ibid.; Macmillan, *End of the Day*, p. 463.
48. FO 371/171235; Sorensen, op. cit., p. 722.
49. Prem 11/4586; Sorensen, op. cit., pp. 722–35.
50. FO 371/173294.
51. FO 371/173293.
52. Prem 11/4586; Cab 132/246.
53. Prem 11/4586; White Paper on British Guiana Constitutional Conference, Cmd 2849 (1965).
54. Prem 11/4759.
55. Horne, op. cit., pp. 515, 517. Letter from McGeorge Bundy to author.
56. Prem 11/4586. The cutting from the *Daily Express* is on this Downing Street file.
57. Ibid.
58. Ibid.
59. FO 371/171197; Cab 128/35; Zuckerman, *Monkeys, Men and Missiles*, pp. 118–19.
60. Newhouse, *De Gaulle and the Anglo-Saxons*, p. 246; Freedman, *Britain and Nuclear Weapons*, pp. 86–150.
61. FO 371/173309; FO 371/173310.
62. FO 371/173309.

Chapter 16   The Far East

1. Colville, *Fringes of Power*, pp. 684–6, 131–41; Lamb, *Eden Government*, p. 14.
2. Prem 11/666; Lamb, op. cit., p. 111; Prem 11/687.
3. Prem 11/649.
4. Prem 11/666.
5. Macmillan, *End of the Day*, p. 237; Cab 131/14; Prem 11/867.
6. Toye, *Laos*, p. 142; Macmillan, *Pointing the Way*, pp. 329–36.
7. Lederer, *A Nation of Sheep*, p. 21; Toye, op. cit., p. 127; Sorensen, *Kennedy*, p. 640.
8. Sorensen, op. cit., p. 641.
9. Prem 11/3280.
10. Prem 11/2961.
11. Ibid.
12. Prem 11/3280.

13. Prem 11/3739.
14. Ibid.
15. Prem 11/3280; Prem 11/3281.
16. Prem 11/3739.
17. Ibid.
18. Ibid.; Macmillan, *End of the Day*, p. 243.
19. Prem 11/4180. Toye, op. cit., pp. 128–30.
20. Ibid.
21. Ibid.
22. Macmillan, *End of the Day*, pp. 245–6; Prem 11/4186.
23. Lamb, op. cit., pp. 119–24; *Foreign Relations (United States) 1952–1954*, Vol. XIV, p. 610; Prem 11/867; Prem 11/869.
24. Cab 138/29; FO 371/11504.
25. Prem 11/879; Macmillan, *Riding the Storm*, p. 550.
26. Prem 11/2300.
27. Ibid.
28. Ibid.
29. Prem 11/2300.
30. Ibid.
31. Prem 11/3738; Horne, op. cit., pp. 104–6; Macmillan, *End of the Day*, pp. 236–46; Macmillan, *Pointing the Way*, pp. 329–38.

Chapter 17   Home Affairs

1. Hughes, *Sydney Silverman*, pp. 144–56.
2. Lamb, op. cit., pp. 34–9.
3. Butler, op. cit., p. 201–2. Lady Butler, interview with author.
4. Cab 129/104; Cab 128/35.
5. Prem 11/824.
6. Cab 128/27; Cab 129/72.
7. Ibid.
8. Prem 11/824.
9. Cab 129/73; Cab 128/29; Lamb, op. cit., pp 15–24.
10. Prem 11/824.
11. Ibid.
12. Cab 129/27.
13. Ibid.; Prem 11/824.
14. Cab 128/29; Cab 129/77.
15. Prem 11/2920.
16. Cab 134/1466.
17. Prem 11/2920.
18. Cab 134/1467; Cab 134/1469.
19. Cab 129/105.
20. Horne, op. cit., p. 422.
21. Shepherd, *Macleod*, p. 268.
22. Hunt, *The Story of the Channel Tunnel*, pp. 1–77.

23. Hunt, op. cit., pp. 77–94.
24. Cab 134/1697.
25. Prem 11/5449.
26. FO 371/171102.
27. Ibid.
28. Cab 134/1803.
29. FO 371/171102; FO 371/171103.
30. Cab 134/1803.
31. Hunt, op. cit., pp. 19–20.
32. Hansard, Commons, 4 February 1964.
33. Allen, *British Railways after Beeching*, pp. 1–12; Gourvish, *British Railways*, pp. 9–13.
34. Prem 11/4028.
35. Macmillan, *End of the Day*, p. 53.
36. Prem 11/4028.
37. Cmd 1248 (1960).
38. Prem 11/4578.
39. Ibid.
40. Ibid.
41. Cab 128/37; Cab 129/113.
42. Prem 11/4578.
43. Ibid.
44. Hansard, Commons, 27 March 1962.
45. Prem 11/4550.
46. Ibid.

Chapter 18   A Bad Year

1. Cook and Ramsden, *By-Elections in British Politics*, pp. 214–15.
2. Macmillan, *End of the Day*, pp. 58–9.
3. Butler, op. cit., p. 233; Macmillan, op. cit., p. 91.
4. Macmillan, op. cit., p. 99.
5. Thorpe, *Selwyn Lloyd*, pp. 342–54; Lloyd Papers, Churchill College, Cambridge.
6. Thorpe, op. cit., p. 348; Kilmuir, *Political Adventure*, p. 324; Davenport-Hines, *The Macmillans*, p. 301.
7. Watkinson, *Turning Points*, p. 161.
8. Butler, op. cit., p. 232.
9. Fisher, *Macmillan*, pp. 277–9.
10. Macmillan, op. cit., pp. 407–8; Prem 11/4406; *Spectator*, 17 January 1964.
11. Lord Denning's Report, HMSO, Cmd 2512, September 1963.
12. Ibid.
13. Ibid.; Rawlinson, *A Price Too High*, p. 93.
14. Prem 11/4368.
15. Ibid.
16. Ibid.

17. Denning Report, op. cit.
18. Denning Archives, Hampshire Record Office, Winchester. Lord Denning, interview with author.
19. *Sunday Telegraph*, 2 January 1994.
20. Rawlinson, op. cit., pp. 95–8.
21. Cab 128/36.
22. Howard, op. cit., p. 298.
23. Denning Report, op. cit.
24. Prem 11/4368; Denning Report, op. cit.
25. Prem 11/4369.
26. Ibid.
27. Lord Denning, interview with author.
28. Prem 11/4369.
29. Cab 128/113; Cab 129/114.
30. Prem 11/4371.
31. Ibid.
32. Fisher, op. cit., p. 327; Goodhart, *1922*, p. 191.
33. Prem 11/4371.
34. Prem 4361; Macmillan, op. cit., pp. 486–7; Cook and Ramsden, op. cit., p. 173.
35. Denning Archive, op. cit.
36. Macmillan, op. cit., pp. 488–9.
37. Denning Report, op. cit.
38. Prem 11/4372; Rawlinson, op. cit., p. 101.
39. Lord Denning, interview with author.
40. Prem 11/4372. Lord Denning, interview with author.
41. Horne, op. cit., p. 483, quoting from Kennedy Library, Box 171, Folder 14. The full unexpurgated Denning Report is on Prem 11/4373.
42. FO 953/2111.
43. Macmillan, op. cit., p. 499.
44. Prem 11/4373.
45. Horne, op. cit., p. 547.
46. Butler, op. cit., p. 250; Fisher, *Tory Leaders*, p. 104.
47. Maudling, op. cit., p. 126.
48. Goodhart, op. cit., pp. 193–5.
49. Macmillan, op. cit., p. 573.
50. *Spectator*, 17 January 1964; Thorpe, op. cit., pp. 372–80; Lloyd Papers, op. cit.
51. Thorpe, op. cit., pp. 379–81; Horne, op. cit., pp. 562–5. Lady Butler, interview with author.
52. Butler, op. cit., pp. 247–8.
53. Howard, op. cit., pp. 316–20; Butler, op. cit., p. 249.
54. Interview with Lady Butler.

Bibliography

Allen, G. Freeman, *British Railways After Beeching*, London, 1966

Bartlett, Christopher J., *The Long Retreat*, London, 1972

Bayliss, John, *Anglo-American Defence Relations*, New York, 1981

Beloff, Nora, *The General Says No*, London, 1963

Blackaby, Frank (ed.), *British Economic Policy 1960–1974*, Cambridge, 1978

Blundell, Sir Michael, *So Rough a Wind*, London, 1964

Booker, Christopher, *The Neophiliacs*, London, 1969

Boyd-Carpenter, John, *Way of Life*, London, 1980

Brittan, Samuel, *The Treasury under the Tories 1951–1964*, London, 1964

Bundy, McGeorge, *Danger and Survival*, New York, 1988

Butler, D. E. and Rose, Richard, *The British General Election of 1959*, London, 1960

Butler, D. E. and King, Anthony, *The British General Election of 1964*, London, 1965

Butler, Lord, *The Art of the Possible*, London, 1971

Butler, Mollie, *August and Rab*, London, 1987

Cairncross, Alec, *The Robert Hall Diaries 1954–1961*, London, 1991

Cairncross, Alec and Watts, Nina, *The Economic Section 1939–1961*, London, 1989

Campbell, John, *Edward Heath, A Biography*, London, 1993

Camps, Miriam, *Britain and the European Community*, Oxford, 1964

Cathcart, Brian, *Test of Greatness*, London, 1994

Churchill, Randolph, *Rise and Fall of Sir Anthony Eden*, London, 1959

Clarke, Ian, *Nuclear Diplomacy and the Special Relationship*, Oxford, 1994

Colville, John, *The Fringes of Power*, London, 1985

Cook, Christopher and Ramsden, John, *By-Elections in British Politics*, London, 1973

Crawford, Iain, *The Profumo Affair*, London, 1963

Davenport-Hines, Richard, *The Macmillans*, London, 1992

De Gaulle, Charles, *Mémoires d'espoir*, Paris, 1970

— *Discours et messages*, IV, Paris, 1970

Dixon, Piers, *Double Diploma: The Life of Sir Pierson Dixon*, London, 1968

Dommar, Arthur, *Conflict in Laos*, New York, 1971

Dow, J. C. R., *The Management of the British Economy, 1945–60*, Cambridge, 1964

Drummond, Gordon D., *The German Social Democrats in Opposition, 1949–1960*, Oklahoma, 1982

Evans, Harold, *Downing Street Diary 1957–1963*, London, 1981
Fall, Bernard B., *Street Without Joy*, London, 1981
Fisher, Nigel, *Iain Macleod*, London, 1973
—— *Tory Leaders*, London, 1977
—— *Harold Macmillan*, London, 1982
Franklin, Harry, *Unholy Wedlock*, London, 1963
Freedman, Lawrence, *Britain and Nuclear Weapons*, London, 1980
Goodhart, Philip, *1922: The Story of the 1922 Committee*, London, 1973
Gourvish, T. R., *British Railways, 1948–1973: A Business History*, Cambridge, 1986
Greenwood, Sean, *Britain and European Cooperation since 1945*, Oxford, 1992
Horne, Alistair, *Macmillan 1957–1986*, London, 1989
Howard, Anthony, *Rab – The Life of R. A. Butler*, London, 1987
Hughes, Emrys, *Sydney Silverman, Rebel in Parliament*, London, 1969
Hunt, David, *On the Spot: An Ambassador Remembers*, London, 1975
Hunt, Donald, *The Story of the Tunnel*, Upton-upon-Severn, 1994
Irving, Clive, Hall, Ron and Wallington, Jeremy, *Scandal '63*, London, 1963
Jones, Griff, *Britain and Nyasaland*, London, 1964
Kilmuir, Earl of, *Political Adventure: The Memoirs of the Earl of Kilmuir*, London, 1964
Kirkman, William P., *Unscrambling an Empire*, London, 1966
Lamb, Richard, *The Failure of the Eden Government*, London, 1987
Langer, Paul F. and Zasloff, Joseph J., *North Vietnam and the Pathet Lao*, Cambridge, Mass., 1970
Lederer, William, *A Nation of Sheep*, London, 1961
Macmillan, Harold, *Riding the Storm 1956–1959*, London, 1971
—— *Pointing the Way 1959–1961*, London, 1972
—— *At the End of the Day 1961–1963*, London, 1973
Maudling, Reginald, *Memoirs*, London, 1978
Morgan, Kenneth O., *The People's Peace 1945–1989*, Oxford, 1990
Neale, A. D., *The Anti-Trust Laws of the USA*, Cambridge, 1962
Newhouse, John, *De Gaulle and the Anglo-Saxons*, London, 1970
Panteli, Stavros, *A New History of Cyprus*, London, 1984
Penrose, Edith and E. F., *Iraq: International Relations and National Development*, London, 1978
Pinder, John, *Britain and the Common Market*, London, 1961
Purcell, H. D., *Cyprus*, London, 1969
Rawlinson, Peter, *A Price Too High*, London, 1989
Reeves, Thomas G., *A Question of Character – A Life of John Kennedy*, London, 1991
Rhodes James, Robert, *Anthony Eden*, London, 1986
Rich, Paul B., *Race and Empire in British Politics*, London, 1986
Rose, Saul, *Britain and South-East Asia*, London, 1962
Rowley, Charles K., *The British Monopolies Commission*, London, 1966
Shepherd, Robert, *Iain Macleod*, London, 1994
Sorensen, Theodore C., *Kennedy*, London, 1965
Stephens, R. B. and Yamey, B. S., *The Restrictive Practices Court*, London, 1964

The Times, *House of Commons 1959*, London, 1959

Thorpe, D. R., *Selwyn Lloyd*, London, 1989

Toye, Claude Hugh, *Laos*, London, 1968

Trevelyan, Humphrey, *The Middle East in Revolution*, London, 1970

Watkinson, Harold, *Turning Points*, Salisbury, 1986

Welensky, Roy, *4,000 Days*, London, 1964

Wilson, Harold, *A Prime Minister on Prime Ministers*, London, 1977

Young, Wayland, *The Profumo Affair – Aspects of Conservatism*, London, 1963

Zuckerman, Solly, *Monkeys, Men and Missiles: An Autobiography*, London, 1988

Appendix

Macmillan's First Cabinet
January 1957

The Cabinet

Prime Minister and First Lord of the Treasury	Mr Harold Macmillan
Lord President of the Council	The Marquess of Salisbury
Home Secretary and Lord Privy Seal	Mr R. A. Butler
Lord Chancellor	Viscount Kilmuir
Secretary of State for Foreign Affairs	Mr Selwyn Lloyd
Chancellor of the Exchequer	Mr Peter Thorneycroft
Secretary of State for Commonwealth Relations	The Earl of Home
Secretary of State for the Colonies	Mr Alan Lennox-Boyd
Secretary of State for Scotland	Mr John Maclay
Minister of Defence	Mr Duncan Sandys
President of the Board of Trade	Sir David Eccles
Minister of Agriculture, Fisheries and Food	Mr Derick Heathcoat Amory
Minister of Labour and National Service	Mr Iain Macleod
Minister of Housing and Local Government and Minister for Welsh Affairs	Mr Henry Brooke
Minister of Education	Viscount Hailsham
Minister of Power	Lord Mills
Minister of Transport and Civil Aviation	Mr Harold Watkinson
Chancellor of the Duchy of Lancaster	Dr Charles Hill

Ministers not in the Cabinet

First Lord of the Admiralty	The Earl of Selkirk
Secretary of State for War	Mr John Hare
Secretary of State for Air	Mr George Ward
Minister of Pensions and National Insurance	Mr John Boyd-Carpenter
Minister of Supply	Mr Aubrey Jones
Minister of Health	Mr Dennis Vosper

Minister of Works	Mr Hugh Molson
Postmaster-General	Mr Ernest Marples
Paymaster-General	Mr Reginald Maudling
Minister without Portfolio	The Earl of Munster
Minister of State, Scottish Office	Lord Strathclyde
Minister of State for Foreign Affairs	Commander Allan Noble
Minister of State for Foreign Affairs	Mr David Ormsby-Gore
Minister of State, Board of Trade	Mr Derek Walker-Smith
Minister of State for Colonial Affairs	The Earl of Perth
Attorney-General	Sir Reginald Manningham-Buller
Lord Advocate	Mr W. R. Milligan
Solicitor-General	Sir Harry Hylton-Foster
Solicitor-General for Scotland	Mr William Grant

Macmillan's Cabinet after the resignation of Peter Thorneycroft, Nigel Birch and Enoch Powell, in January 1958

The Cabinet

Prime Minister and First Lord of the Treasury	Mr Harold Macmillan
Home Secretary and Lord Privy Seal	Mr R. A. Butler
Lord Chancellor	Viscount Kilmuir
Secretary of State for Foreign Affairs	Mr Selwyn Lloyd
Chancellor of the Exchequer	Mr Derick Heathcoat Amory
Secretary of State for Commonwealth Relations	The Earl of Home
Secretary of State for the Colonies	Mr Alan Lennox-Boyd
Secretary of State for Scotland	Mr John Maclay
Lord President of the Council	Viscount Hailsham
Minister of Defence	Mr Duncan Sandys
President of the Board of Trade	Sir David Eccles
Minister of Labour and National Service	Mr Iain Macleod
Minister of Housing and Local Government and Minister for Welsh Affairs	Mr Henry Brooke
Minister of Power	Lord Mills
Minister of Transport and Civil Aviation	Mr Harold Watkinson
Minister of Education	Mr Geoffrey Lloyd
Minister of Agriculture, Fisheries and Food	Mr John Hare
Chancellor of the Duchy of Lancaster	Dr Charles Hill
Paymaster-General	Mr Reginald Maudling

Ministers not in the Cabinet

First Lord of the Admiralty	The Earl of Selkirk
Secretary of State for War	Mr Christopher Soames
Secretary of State for Air	Mr George Ward

Minister of Pensions and National Insurance	Mr John Boyd-Carpenter
Minister of Supply	Mr Aubrey Jones
Minister of Health	Mr Derek Walker-Smith
Minister of Works	Mr Hugh Molson
Postmaster-General	Mr Ernest Marples
Minister without Portfolio	Lord Mancroft
Minister of State, Scottish Office	Lord Strathclyde
Minister of State for Foreign Affairs	Commander Allan Noble
Minister of State for Foreign Affairs	Mr David Ormsby-Gore
Minister of State for Colonial Affairs	The Earl of Perth
Minister of State, Board of Trade	Mr J. K. Vaughan-Morgan
Minister of State for Welsh Affairs	Lord Brecon
Attorney-General	Sir Reginald Manningham-Buller
Lord Advocate	Mr W. R. Milligan
Solicitor-General	Sir Harry Hylton-Foster
Solicitor-General for Scotland	Mr William Grant

Macmillan's Cabinet after the October 1959 General Election

The Cabinet

Prime Minister and First Lord of the Treasury	Mr Harold Macmillan
Home Secretary	Mr R. A. Butler
Lord Chancellor	Viscount Kilmuir
Secretary of State for Foreign Affairs	Mr Selwyn Lloyd
Chancellor of the Exchequer	Mr Derick Heathcoat Amory
Lord President of the Council and Secretary of State for Commonwealth Relations	The Earl of Home
Secretary of State for Scotland	Mr John Maclay
Lord Privy Seal (and Minister for Science)	Viscount Hailsham
Minister of Aviation	Mr Duncan Sandys
Secretary of State for the Colonies	Mr Iain Macleod
Minister of Defence	Mr Harold Watkinson
Minister of Housing and Local Government and Minister for Welsh Affairs	Mr Henry Brooke
Minister of Education	Sir David Eccles
Paymaster-General	Lord Mills
President of the Board of Trade	Mr Reginald Maudling
Minister of Agriculture, Fisheries and Food	Mr John Hare
Minister of Labour	Mr Edward Heath*

---

* Promoted to Lord Privy Seal with responsibility for Europe, July 1960

Chancellor of the Duchy of Lancaster	Dr Charles Hill
Minister of Transport	Mr Ernest Marples

Ministers not in the Cabinet

First Lord of the Admiralty	Lord Carrington
Secretary of State for War	Mr Christopher Soames
Secretary of State for Air	Mr George Ward
Minister of Pensions and National Insurance	Mr John Boyd-Carpenter
Minister of Health	Mr Derek Walker-Smith
Minister of Works	Lord John Hope
Postmaster-General	Mr J. R. Bevins
Minister of Power	Mr Richard Wood
Minister without Portfolio	The Earl of Dundee
Minister of State, Scottish Office	Mr J. Nixon Browne
Minister of State for Foreign Affairs	Mr D. Ormsby-Gore
Minister of State for Foreign Affairs	Mr John Profumo
Minister of State for Colonial Affairs	The Earl of Perth
Minister of State, Commonwealth Relations Office	Mr C. J. M. Alport
Minister of State, Board of Trade	Mr F. J. Erroll
Minister of State for Welsh Affairs	Lord Brecon
Attorney-General	Sir Reginald Manningham-Buller
Lord Advocate	Mr W. R. Milligan
Solicitor-General	Sir Jocelyn Simon
Solicitor-General for Scotland	Mr William Grant

The Macmillan Cabinet before the night of long knives, 12 July 1962

The Cabinet

Prime Minister and First Lord of the Treasury	Mr Harold Macmillan
Home Secretary	Mr R. A. Butler
Lord Chancellor	Viscount Kilmuir
Chancellor of the Exchequer	Mr Selwyn Lloyd
Secretary of State for Foreign Affairs	The Earl of Home
Lord President of the Council and Minister for Science	Viscount Hailsham
Chief Secretary to the Treasury and Paymaster-General	Mr Henry Brooke
Secretary of State for Scotland	Mr John Maclay
Secretary of State for Commonwealth Relations	Mr Duncan Sandys
Chancellor of the Duchy of Lancaster	Mr Iain Macleod
Minister of Defence	Mr Harold Watkinson
Minister of Education	Sir David Eccles
Minister of Aviation	Mr Peter Thorneycroft
Minister without Portfolio	Lord Mills

Secretary of State for the Colonies	Mr Reginald Maudling
Minister of Labour	Mr John Hare
Lord Privy Seal	Mr Edward Heath
Minister of Housing and Local Government and Minister for Welsh Affairs	Dr Charles Hill
Minister of Transport	Mr Ernest Marples
Minister of Agriculture, Fisheries and Food	Mr Christopher Soames
President of the Board of Trade	Mr F. J. Erroll

Ministers not in the Cabinet

First Lord of the Admiralty	Lord Carrington
Secretary of State for War	Mr John Profumo
Secretary of State for Air	Mr Julian Amery
Minister of Pensions and National Insurance	Mr John Boyd-Carpenter
Minister of Health	Mr Enoch Powell
Minister of Power	Mr Richard Wood
Minister of Works	Lord John Hope
Postmaster-General	Mr Reginald Bevins
Secretary for Technical Co-operation	Mr Dennis Vosper
Minister of State for Foreign Affairs	The Earl of Dundee
Minister of State for Colonial Affairs	The Earl of Perth
Minister of State for Welsh Affairs	Lord Brecon
Minister of State, Scottish Office	Lord Craigton
Minister of State for Foreign Affairs	Mr J. B. Godber
Minister of State, Home Office	Mr David Renton
Minister of State, Board of Trade	Sir Keith Joseph
Attorney-General	Sir Reginald Manningham-Buller
Lord Advocate	Mr William Grant
Solicitor-General	Sir Jocelyn Simon
Solicitor-General for Scotland	Mr D. C. Anderson

In the night of long knives, 12/13 July 1962, the Prime Minister sacked seven full members of the Cabinet – Selwyn Lloyd, Viscount Kilmuir, Lord Mills, John Maclay, Harold Watkinson, David Eccles and Charles Hill, together with four junior Ministers – Lord John Hope, the Earl of Perth, Sir Jocelyn Simon and David Renton. The new Cabinet thereafter was:

The Cabinet

Prime Minister and First Lord of the Treasury	Mr Harold Macmillan
First Secretary of State	Mr R. A. Butler
Secretary of State for Foreign Affairs	The Earl of Home
Lord President of the Council and Minister for Science	Viscount Hailsham
Lord Chancellor	Lord Dilhorne

Chancellor of the Exchequer	Mr Reginald Maudling
Home Secretary	Mr Henry Brooke
Secretary of State for Commonwealth Relations and Secretary of State for the Colonies	Mr Duncan Sandys
Chancellor of the Duchy of Lancaster	Mr Iain Macleod
Minister of Defence	Mr Peter Thorneycroft
Minister of Labour	Mr John Hare
Lord Privy Seal	Mr Edward Heath
Minister of Transport	Mr Ernest Marples
Minister of Agriculture, Fisheries and Food	Mr Christopher Soames
President of the Board of Trade	Mr F. J. Erroll
Chief Secretary to the Treasury and Paymaster-General	Mr John Boyd-Carpenter
Secretary of State for Scotland	Mr Michael Noble
Minister of Health	Mr Enoch Powell
Minister of Education	Sir Edward Boyle
Minister of Housing and Local Government and Minister for Welsh Affairs	Sir Keith Joseph
Minister without Portfolio	Mr W. F. Deedes

Ministers not in the Cabinet

First Lord of the Admiralty	Lord Carrington
Secretary of State for War	Mr John Profumo
Minister of Aviation	Mr Julian Amery
Secretary of State for Air	Mr Hugh Fraser
Minister of Power	Mr Richard Wood
Minister of Pensions and National Insurance	Mr Niall Macpherson
Minister of Public Building and Works	Mr Geoffrey Rippon
Postmaster-General	Mr Reginald Bevins
Secretary for Technical Co-operation	Mr Dennis Vosper
Minister of State for Foreign Affairs	The Earl of Dundee
Minister of State for Welsh Affairs	Lord Brecon
Minister of State, Scottish Office	Lord Craigton
Minister of State for Foreign Affairs	Mr J. B. Godber
Minister of State for Colonial Affairs	The Marquess of Lansdowne
Minister of State, Home Office	Earl Jellicoe
Minister of State, Board of Trade	Mr Alan Green
Attorney-General	Sir John Hobson
Lord Advocate	Mr William Grant
Solicitor-General	Sir Peter Rawlinson
Solicitor-General for Scotland	Mr D. C. Anderson

Index

Index

Acheson, Dean, 300
Addington, Henry, 421
Adenauer, Konrad, 164; and EFTA, 114–15, 117–18, 122, 129, 134; and Britain's EEC negotiations, 139, 172, 177; relations with de Gaulle, 172, 197; de Gaulle vetoes Britain's EEC membership, 197; and Berlin, 323–8, 331n., 335, 336, 345; failed Paris Summit (1960), 337, 338
Admiralty, 286, 422
Africa: West African independence, 221–2; HM tours, 242, 244–7; 'Wind of Change' speech, 11, 246; see also individual countries
African National Congress (ANC), 246, 256
Agricultural Act (1957), 167n.
Air Ministry, 284
Aldington, Lord, 495, 496–7
Algeria, 11, 18, 20, 118, 327 and n.
Allen, G.R., 432
Allied Control Commission, 322
Alsop, Joseph, 326–7, 331
Amery, Julian, 29, 239, 240, 242, 310
Amory, Derick Heathcoat: as Chancellor, 9, 51–6, 69, 95; 1958 Budget, 53; 1959 Budget, 53–4, 56–7; 1959 General Election, 64; calls for price stability, 64–5; 1960 Budget, 65–7; and Plan G, 108; and EFTA of the Seven, 128, 129; and acceleration of Treaty of Rome, 135; considers applying for EEC membership, 138; opposes Blue Streak, 286; and Polaris submarines, 289; retirement, 68, 69, 139
Anderson, Colin, 29 and n.
ANZUS, 397
apartheid, 246
Aqaba, Gulf of, 26
Arab League, 30, 31
Arabs, 19, 331
Argyll, Duchess of, 472–3, 481–2
Argyll, Duke of, 481

Armed Services Committee, 371
Armitage, Sir Robert, 232, 234, 235, 236, 239, 240, 242, 247, 248, 250
Armstrong, Sir William, 72, 79, 94–5, 187–8, 194, 395, 426
Aron, Raymond, 298
Arran, Earl of, 472
Asquith, Herbert, 59, 422
Astor, John, 239
Astor, Lord, 455, 456, 457
Aswan Dam, 17, 28
atom bombs see nuclear weapons
Atomic Energy Act (1958), 286
Atomic Energy Committee, 371
Attlee, Clement, 104, 474; nuclear weapons policy, 3, 321; rejects Schuman Plan, 102, 139; opposition to membership of EEC, 156–7; establishes Monopolies Commission, 206–7; Korean War, 282; immigration problem, 411; Transport Act, 435
Australia, 273, 401; EFTA negotiations, 119; and Britain's EEC negotiations, 153, 159, 169, 174, 178–9; and nuclear tests on Christmas Island, 307–8; South-East Asia Defence Treaty, 382; and Laos, 388, 390, 393; Quemoy crisis, 402
Austria, 7, 111, 118, 122, 128, 129, 130, 134, 135, 153

Baghdad, 32
Baghdad Pact, 31–2, 38, 39, 40, 41, 113
Bahamas, 311
balance of payments crises, 69, 72–4, 91–2, 96, 100–1
Baldwin, Stanley, 412
Balewa, Sir Abubakar, 221
Ball, George, 316
Banda, Dr Hastings, 11, 234, 240, 245, 246–52, 266, 268–9, 273–5, 278
Bandung Conference (1955), 383
Bank of England, 54, 98; and reopening of Suez Canal, 29; 1957 sterling crisis,

46, 47; special deposits, 66n.; 1961
sterling crisis, 73, 75; 1962 Budget,
81
Bannerman, John, 443
Barber, Anthony, 54
Barclay, Sir Roderick, 113, 141, 142, 143,
145, 148–9, 162, 169
Baring, Sir Evelyn, 238, 240 and n., 242
Batista, Fulgencio, 351
Bay of Pigs invasion (1960), 5, 351–2
Beaumarchais, Jacques de, 192–3
Beaverbrook, Lord, 159, 183, 227, 317
Bedell Smith, Walter, 380, 381
Beeching, Dr Richard, 433–7
Beeching Plan, 14, 437–41, 442
Beerbohm, Max, 65
Belcher, J.W., 474n.
Belgian Congo, 11, 222, 251, 254
Belgium, 104, 148
Bell, Sir Raymond, 173, 198
Beloff, Nora, 201
Ben-Gurion, David, 18–19, 37, 40
Benelux countries, 104, 111, 135, 136
Benn, Anthony Wedgwood, 491
Bentley, Derek, 409, 410
Berlin, 74, 161; Britain and America hold
talks on, 299, 300, 301; under Allied
Control Commission, 322; airlift,
322; Khrushchev threatens, 323–37,
342, 343–6, 347–50, 359–60; failed
Paris Summit (1960), 5, 339; Berlin
Wall, 5, 343, 344, 345, 350; and
the Cuban missiles crisis, 353, 354,
357–8
Bevan, Aneurin, 22, 60, 337
Bevin, Ernest, 282, 320
Beyen, Johan, 105–6
Bidault, Georges, 378, 380
Bikini atoll, 304n.
Billing, Noel Pemberton, 478 and n.
Birch, Nigel, 9, 45, 51, 448, 475–6
Birch Grove, 6, 363, 364, 367
Bishop, Sir Frederick, 30–1, 136, 419
Blackpool North by-election (1962), 443
Bligh, Sir Timothy, 52, 257n., 310, 497;
role as adviser, 1, 293; 1960 Budget,
65; balance of payments crisis, 72;
and the 'night of long knives', 89,
446–7, 448, 449; critical of Harrod,
92; proposes import controls, 97;
and Laos, 388; Chequers conference,
454; Profumo scandal, 12, 13, 458,
459, 465 and n., 466, 467–70
Blue Steel, 302 and n.
Blue Streak, 284, 286–7
Blundell, Michael, 225, 226
Board of Trade, 74, 96, 152, 161, 206–7,
209, 211–12, 213, 216–17, 352, 422
Bohlen, Charles, 375
Bonham-Carter, Mark, 58–9, 63

Bonham-Carter, Violet, 59
Booker, Christopher, 356
Boothby, Robert, 1
Bowden, Herbert, 465
Boyd-Carpenter, John, 49–50, 70–1, 423, 492
Boyle, Dermot, 319
Boyle, Sir Edward, 54, 108, 449, 482, 494
Boyne, Harry, 476
Brandon, Henry, 318n.
Bremerhaven, 288, 289
Bretherton, Russell, 104n., 112–13, 118, 120
Briggs, Captain, 225
Brighouse and Spenborough by-election
(1960), 443
British Channel Tunnel Company, 422, 423
British Farmer, 167n.
British Guiana, 6, 364–7, 368, 369
British Petroleum, 97, 98
British Railways, 428, 431–41
British Transport Commission (BTC), 431,
432–7
Brittan, Samuel, 69, 205
Brixton, 411
Broadbent, Ewen, 286
Brook, Sir Norman, 73, 84, 235, 236–7,
267, 276, 283, 305, 306–7, 308,
412, 454, 455, 470, 471–2
Brooke, Henry, 276, 410n., 494
Brown, Professor Arthur, 275
Brown, George, 37, 354
Bruce, David, 348, 353, 360, 364, 367,
488–9
Brunel, Isambard Kingdom, 422
Brunet, Jean-Pierre, 144
Brussels Treaty (1948), 289 and n.
Budget Committee, 70
Budgets: *1955*, 56; *1956*, 45; *1957*, 46;
1958, 53; *1959*, 9, 53–5, 56–7, 59,
64, 68, 87; *1960*, 64, 65–8, 443;
1961, 69–72; *1961 emergency*, 75, 76,
87; *1962*, 81–3, 85, 87, 444, 446;
1963, 83, 87, 92–6, 452, 492; *1964*,
92, 101
Bundy, McGeorge, 298, 299 and n., 316,
318n., 341, 342–3, 356, 367–8, 369,
374
Burma, 401
Burnham, Forbes, 364, 366, 369
Burrows, Sir Bernard, 320
Butler, Sir Michael, 192
Butler, Mollie, 179n., 265, 276, 409, 497,
500
Butler, R.A.: as possible successor to Eden,
24–5; Suez crisis, 20–1, 22–3, 24;
1955 Budget, 56; 1957 sterling crisis,
49; soothes Boyd-Carpenter, 71; and
economic policy, 88; 'night of long
knives', 88, 276, 445, 448 and n., 449,
450; attitude to EEC membership,
105–6, 146, 158, 179 and n., 183;
and EFTA of the Seven, 129; EEC

negotiations, 154, 166, 168n., 171, 179; and the Central African Federation, 11–12, 231, 272–81; loses Chairmanship of Conservative Party, 265; loses Home Office, 276; and Northern Rhodesia franchise, 269–71; and nuclear policy, 315; and Laos, 385; and capital punishment, 409–10; immigration problem, 417–21; and the Channel tunnel, 429; HM's opposition to as his successor, 14, 447, 494, 500; Chequers conference, 454; and the Profumo scandal, 12, 463, 470; and choice of HM's successor, 476, 490, 491–2, 494–6, 498–9; and the Denning Report, 482

Cabinet Africa Committee, 231, 250
Cabinet Common Market Negotiating Committee, 166, 171, 177, 179, 182, 203
Cabinet Defence Committee, 287
Cabinet Economic Policy Committee, 10, 106, 204, 208–9, 211, 212–13, 214, 216, 218, 219, 414, 425
Cabinet Sub-Committee on Monopolies, 209, 211–15, 216
Caccia, Sir Harold, 341, 397; Suez crisis, 21, 22; 1958 Middle East crisis, 34; and EFTA, 125, 128; EEC negotiations, 169, 187, 188; nuclear weapons policy, 285, 290, 293–4, 295, 374; and size of Britain's conventional forces, 298; Berlin crisis, 326–7, 329–30; and British Guiana, 367; Quemoy crisis, 404; meets Stephen Ward, 455
Cairncross, Sir Alec, 9, 47, 51, 69, 73, 76n., 79–80, 81, 85, 90, 92
Callaghan, James, 99, 233, 240, 244
Cambodia, 4, 377, 381, 382, 392, 396, 401
Cambridge, Duke of, 422
Campaign for Nuclear Disarmament (CND), 306, 372
Camps, Miriam, 127, 177n.
Canada, 132, 349; and Britain's EEC negotiations, 143 and n., 159, 169, 178; on International Supervisory Commission, 381, 382; and Laos, 389, 395; Quemoy crisis, 401
Cape Town, 246–7
capital gains tax, 81, 82
Capital Issues Committee, 48 and n.
capital punishment, 407–10
Cardiff, 411
Carli, Guido, 115–16
Carli plan, 115–16, 118, 120, 121, 130
Carmarthen by-election (1957), 58
Carrington, Peter, 453
Castle, Barbara, 430–1, 460
Castro, Fidel, 351, 352, 353, 357, 361

Cattani, Attilio, 162
Central African Federation, 11–12, 51, 153, 231–65, 266–81, 500; *see also* Nyasaland; Northern Rhodesia; Southern Rhodesia
Central African Office, 273
Central Council of Conservative Associations, 413
Ceylon, 153, 160, 401, 415
Challe, General Maurice, 18
Chamberlain, Joseph, 422
Chamberlain, Neville, 25, 56, 306, 412, 473, 500
Chamoun, Camille, 32, 33, 34, 41
Champs, Château de, 166–7
Channel Study Group, 423, 424, 425, 428, 430
Channel tunnel, 421–31
The Channel Tunnel (White Paper), 431
Chapman-Walker, Mark, 457
Chauvel, Jean, 141
Chebab, General Fuad, 34, 41, 42
Chequers, 271, 447, 453–4
Chiang Kai-shek, 3–4, 396–8, 400, 403–5
China, 341; Quemoy crisis, 3–4, 396–406; test ban treaty negotiations, 361, 370, 371, 373; Vietnam war, 377; and Laos, 382, 384, 389, 392, 394; Bandung Conference, 383
Chippenham by-election (1962), 452
Chou En-lai, 3, 81, 379, 382, 383, 396, 397, 399–400, 406
Christmas Island, 303–9, 347
Churchill, Randolph, 25, 61, 492
Churchill, Winston, 25, 207; style as Prime Minister, 1; Quemoy crisis, 3, 398–9, 402, 404, 406; attitude to Schuman Plan, 102–3; calls for creation of European army, 103–4; creates Central African Federation, 231; nuclear weapons, 282, 285; and the Vietnam war, 378–81; immigration problem, 410–11, 413, 416; railway policy, 432
CIA, 5
Clappier, Bernard, 120, 174–5, 184
Clarke, Ashley, 148, 162
Clarke, Ian, 297
Clarke, R.W., 113
Clemenceau, Georges, 350
Cliveden, 455, 457, 470
Clogg, Derek, 456, 461, 486, 487
Clyde, Polaris base, 3, 287–92, 294, 296, 312
coal mining, 78
Cobbold, Lord, 46, 72
Cohen, Lord Justice, 204, 205
Cohen Committee *see* Council on Prices, Productivity and Incomes
Coldstream, Sir George, 471
Coleraine, Lord, 241
Colne Valley by-election (1963), 452

Colombo, Emilio, 161, 166, 180, 185, 196, 197, 198
Colonial Office: ignores African independence movements, 222; Hola Camp incident, 223, 238, 239; and the Devlin Report, 235, 241; Nyasaland emergency, 239; and the Central African Federation, 243, 250; Nyasaland Conference, 252; Northern Rhodesia franchise, 261, 266, 267; immigration problem, 411
Colonial Policy Committee, 269
Colville, John, 378
Committee of Imperial Defence, 422–3
Common Market *see* European Economic Community
Commonwealth: Britain considers applying for EEC membership, 8, 104, 105, 106, 107, 108–9, 111, 139, 140, 141, 142–3, 146, 148–9, 151, 152–4, 156, 157; and EFTA negotiations, 111–12, 114–21, 129, 131; import duties, 137 and n.; and Britain's EEC negotiations, 159, 160, 162, 163, 166–78, 189, 194, 201; and Southern Rhodesian independence, 279–80; and Quemoy crisis, 401; immigration problem, 410–21
Commonwealth Immigrants Bill, 420–1
Commonwealth Immigrants Committee, 419–20
Commonwealth Prime Ministers' Conference (1962), 178–9, 180, 186, 187, 202
Commonwealth Relations Office, 139, 231, 250, 252, 255, 267, 268
Communism: and Baghdad Pact, 31–2; British Guiana, 364–7; China, 3–4; Cuba, 351; Laos, 387; Middle East, 3, 43; Quemoy crisis, 396–406; Vietnam, 4, 377, 396
Competition Act (1980), 219
Compton, Sir Edmund, 99
Concorde, 426
Conditions Favourable to Faster Growth (NEDC), 78
Conservative Central Office, 155n., 445
Conservative Newsletter, 155n.
Conservative Parliamentary Party, Commonwealth Affairs Committee, 412
Conservative Party: attitude to EEC, 7, 183; Suez crisis, 22, 23, 24; and Eden's successor, 25; by-election losses, 58–9, 81, 88, 443–5; 1959 General Election, 59–63, 154, 158, 167n.; Profumo scandal, 95; 1964 General Election, 101, 501; and Britain's application to join EEC, 157, 158; and Kenyan independence, 225; and the Central African Federation, 232, 254–5, 280, 281;

and White Paper on Northern Rhodesia, 259; and capital punishment, 407–8, 410; immigration problem, 412; HM suspicious of conspiracy against himself, 446; reactions to 'night of long knives', 450–1; under Home's leadership, 500–1
Conservative Party Conferences: *1956*, 408; *1958*, 222, 419; *1961*, 421; *1962*, 179, 182, 186, 202, 452; *1963*, 478, 489, 490–1, 492–4
Conservative Political Centre, 492
Conservative Research Department, 500
Cook, Don, 326
Cornish, William, 413
Corporal ballistic missile, 26
Council of Europe, 103
Council on Prices, Productivity and Incomes (COPPI), 91 and n., 204–6, 209, 451
County Councils Association, 441
Courcel, Martine de, 429
Cousins, Frank, 60
Couve de Murville, Maurice, 331; becomes French Foreign Minister, 118–19 and n.; opposition to EFTA, 121, 122–3; Britain's EEC negotiations, 162, 165, 169, 170, 172, 174, 175, 181–2, 184; de Gaulle vetoes British membership of EEC, 192, 196, 197, 200
Craig, Christopher, 409
Crawford and Balcarres, Earl of, 413
Cripps, Sir Stafford, 83, 321
Cromer, Lord, 79, 97–8
Crossman, Richard, 460
Cuba: Bay of Pigs invasion, 5, 351–2; missiles crisis (1962), 6, 351, 352–9, 361, 364, 464, 472
Cumming, Colonel, 465
Cunningham, Knox, 497
Cyprus, 10, 33, 153
Czechoslovakia, 328

Daily Express, 60, 61, 159, 240, 248, 317, 368–9, 495, 497
Daily Herald, 317, 464
Daily Mail, 57, 88, 240, 295, 445, 446, 472, 478, 479
Daily Mirror, 240, 405
Daily Mirror Group, 457, 463
Daily Telegraph, 189, 240, 317, 451, 473, 476
Dalhousie, Earl of, 249–50 and n., 255, 266
Dalton, Hugh, 321
Davenport, Nicholas, 82, 95
Davies, Clement, 58
Day, Robin, 488
De Gaulle, Charles, 114, 246; opposition to Britain's membership of EEC, 7–9, 15, 90, 94n., 99, 144–7, 149, 155, 157; and EFTA of the Seventeen,

118–22, 123–4, 125; reduces tariffs
to OEEC, 127; and EFTA of the
Seven, 134; acceleration of Treaty of
Rome, 135–6; Britain considers
applying for EEC membership, 140,
141, 142; and Britain's EEC
negotiations, 161, 165–7, 175,
176–8, 184, 189–94; desire to
become nuclear power, 165, 167,
192–3, 196, 301, 372; meetings with
Macmillan, 166–7, 189–94; relations
with Adenauer, 172, 197;
referendum on his presidency, 184,
189; vetoes Britain's EEC membership,
192–3, 195, 196–203, 318, 319, 452;
and European defence, 297; USA offers
France Polaris missiles, 319; and Berlin,
326, 329, 332, 336; failed Paris Summit
(1960), 337, 338, 340; Kennedy visits,
341–2, 368; test ban negotiations,
368, 371–2, 373–5; and the Channel
tunnel, 425, 426, 429, 430
de Gran (French engineer), 422
Debré, Michel, 144
Deedes, William, 12, 449, 460–1, 462–3, 471
Defence White Paper (1962), 300–1, 310, 316
Defence Department (US), 26, 327
Deloncle, Habid, 376
Democratic Party (USA), 297, 373
Denmark, 7, 111, 122, 128, 130, 134, 191
Denning, Lord, 12, 13, 455, 456, 461–2,
464, 467, 468, 469, 470, 473, 486
Denning Report, 13, 461–2, 463, 469, 477,
478, 479–89, 490
Department of Trade, 218, 219
Derby North by-election (1962), 88
Derby West by-election (1962), 88, 445
D'Erlanger, Leo, 425
Detroit Free Press, 489
Devlin, Christopher, 237n.
Devlin, Lord, 11, 234, 235–6, 237, 241
Devlin Commission, 11, 60, 232, 234–7,
238–9, 240–2, 244, 461, 483 and n.
Diefenbaker, John, 178, 349
Dien Bien Phu, 4, 378–80, 382
Dilhorne, Lord (Reginald Manningham-
Buller): and the Devlin Report, 239,
240; and the 'night of long knives',
449; and the Profumo scandal, 467,
468, 469, 470, 471 and n., 477; and
the Denning Report, 483n., 487–8;
and choice of HM's successor, 495,
496, 499
Dillon, Douglas, 128, 131–2, 134, 135
Director of Fair Trading, 218
Director of Public Prosecutions, 456
Dixon, Piers, 480
Dixon, Sir Pierson: Suez crisis, 19, 22, 24;
1958 Middle East crisis, 41–2; EEC
negotiations, 141, 146, 147–8, 161,
162, 164, 165–6, 171, 173–7, 191,

194–6, 202, 374; de Gaulle vetoes
Britain's EEC membership, 8, 9,
198; USA offers France Polaris
missiles, 319; and the Channel
tunnel, 426
Dominion Party (Central African
Federation), 232
Dorman Long, 424
Dover, 422, 426, 428, 440
Drummond, Sir Eric (later 16th Earl of
Perth), 147n.
Du Cann, Edward, 212
Duff, Peggy, 372–3
Dulles, John Foster, 132, 284, 341; Suez
crisis, 17, 18, 19; reopening of Suez
Canal, 27, 29; attempted Communist
take-over of Syria, 30–1; and Baghdad
Pact, 31; 1958 Middle East crisis, 34,
36–41, 42; and creation of EEC, 123,
125, 132; Berlin crisis, 327, 328; and
the Vietnam war, 377–81; South-East
Asia Defence Treaty, 382; Quemoy
crisis, 3–4, 396–405; resignation and
death, 133, 330

East Africa Federation, 363
East Germany, 323–8, 330, 331, 333,
334–7, 343–5, 349, 360
Eccles, Sir David, 75, 82, 122–3, 331, 449,
495
Economic Advisory Council, 423
Economic Steering Committee (Civil
Servants), 427–9
Economic Survey, 76
The Economist, 47, 90, 368, 426, 476–7, 488
Edden, A.J., 112–14, 119
Eddowes, Michael, 472
Eden, Sir Anthony: Quemoy crisis, 3–4,
396–400, 404, 406; opposition to
EEC, 6, 102, 103, 104–6, 111, 126;
Suez crisis, 17–24, 29, 45, 61;
resignation, 24–5, 62; Baghdad Pact,
31; elevation to House of Lords, 58;
1959 General Election, 60; and
Britain's application to join EEC,
159; style as Prime Minister, 231;
opposes defence cuts, 282; and the
Vietnam war, 378–81; and capital
punishment, 407, 408; immigration
problem, 412, 413, 415–17
Edgecombe, John, 456
EFTA *see* European Free Trade Area
Egypt, 423; Suez crisis, 17–24; reopening
of Suez Canal, 27–30; 1958 crisis,
41–2
Eisenhower, Dwight David, 299, 301;
Anglo-American relations, 2–4, 25–6,
132–3; Cold War, 5; Suez crisis, 17,
19, 20; 1958 Middle East crisis,
34–7, 39–40, 42–3; visits London,
59–60; 1959 Western summit

meeting, 134; offers Thor missiles to HM, 284, 285; and Britain's nuclear independence, 285, 286; allows Britain to purchase Skybolt, 287, 296; and Polaris, 287–93, 294, 315; Berlin crisis, 326–30, 332–3, 335–6; Khrushchev visits USA, 333–5, 337; meets HM, 337; nuclear tests, 337, 373; failed Paris Summit (1960), 338–9, 340; Khrushchev's hostility towards, 338–9, 341; U-2 spy plane shot down, 338, 339–40; and Cuba, 351, 352; and the Vietnam war, 377–81, 396; and Laos, 384–5, 386; Quemoy crisis, 396–400, 403, 405–6

Elizabeth, The Queen Mother, 203

Elizabeth II, Queen, 2, 13, 50, 62, 261, 265, 446, 448, 476, 477, 496, 497–8

Ellis, Ruth, 409, 410

Ellis-Rees, Sir Hugh, 106

Eniwetok atoll, 303–4 and n., 307

Erhard, Dr Ludwig, 114, 118, 141, 143, 197, 200

Erroll, Fred, 79, 183, 208–9, 211–12, 215, 217, 352, 496–7

European Commission, 190–1, 200

European Committee, 150

European Economic Community (EEC), 26, 81; NEDC reports, 78; Britain's attitude to, 102–11; Messina conference, 104–5; and Plan G, 108–10; Treaty of Rome, 110, 111; and EFTA of the Seventeen, 111–25, 126–8; and EFTA of the Seven, 128–32; acceleration of Treaty of Rome, 131, 134, 135; common agricultural policy, 131, 141n., 142, 144, 149, 159, 160–1, 199; Lee Report, 136–8; Britain considers applying for membership, 138–57; Britain's negotiations to join, 6–9, 111, 158–203; de Gaulle's veto, 7–9, 15, 90, 94n., 99, 192–3, 195, 196–203, 204, 318, 319, 452; Common External Tariff, 210; GATT negotiations, 211; Competition Court, 219; and the Channel tunnel, 425, 426

European Economic Relations Committee, 427

European Free Trade Area (EFTA), 7; EFTA of the Seventeen, 110–25, 126–8, 131; EFTA of the Seven, 99, 111, 128–32, 134, 135, 136–9, 142, 143, 145, 155, 157, 203

European Fund, 189

Evans, Harold, 176, 248

Evans, Timothy, 409, 410

Evening Standard, 159

Expansion Without Inflation (Liberal pamphlet), 207–8

exports: trade gap, 64, 69; balance of payments crises, 69, 72–4, 91–2, 96, 100–1

Fair Trading Act (1973), 218

Fairlie, Henry, 57

Fanfani, Emilio, 180

Far East, 363, 377–406

Faure, Edgar, 104, 112, 113, 117, 118

Faure plan, 117, 120

Fawzi, Dr Mohamed, 18, 24, 27, 41–2

Fayat, Henri, 196, 198

Federal Review Conference, 253

Federation of British Industries, 116–17, 331

Feisal, King of Iraq, 32

Felt, Admiral Harry, 389

Field, Winston, 277, 279, 280, 281

Figgures, Sir Frank, 115, 144, 145, 163

First World War, 422–3

Fisher, Nigel, 264, 450

The Fixed Channel Link (White Paper), 427

Fletcher-Cook, Charles, 458, 459 and n.

floating exchange rates, 46–7

Foot, Dingle, 251

Foot, Michael, 240, 373, 460

Foreign Office: Anglo-American relations, 6, 133; reopening of Suez Canal, 29; attitude to EEC, 107; and EFTA of the Seventeen, 114, 116, 120, 124; and EFTA of the Seven, 128; Britain considers applying for EEC membership, 142–4, 147, 150, 155; EEC negotiations, 186–7; and Polaris submarines, 293; Berlin crisis, 324, 325–6, 330, 333, 345, 348; Cuban missiles crisis, 357; and British Guiana, 364; and NATO/Warsaw Pact non-aggression pact, 371; test ban treaty negotiations, 372; and Laos, 391, 395; Quemoy crisis, 399; and the Channel tunnel, 425–6, 429; Vassall case, 453; and the Profumo scandal, 455; and the Denning Report, 489

Formosa, 4, 396–404, 406

Fort William, 291

Foster, William C., 361

Fouchet Plan, 190–1 and n.

Fox, Charles James, 421–2

France: desire to become nuclear power, 7–8, 164–5, 167, 192–3, 196, 301, 372; opposition to Britain's membership of EEC, 7–9, 15, 90, 94n., 99, 144–50, 155, 163–4; Suez crisis, 18–24, 61; reopening of Suez Canal, 28; Schuman Plan, 102; and EFTA of the Seventeen, 111–12, 113–25, 126–8; and acceleration of Treaty of Rome, 135–6; Britain considers applying for EEC

membership, 140–2, 143–4; and
Britain's EEC negotiations, 161,
163–8, 172–8, 180–2, 184, 189–94,
199–202; de Gaulle's referendum,
184, 189; de Gaulle vetoes Britain's
EEC membership, 192–3, 195,
196–203, 204, 319; Polaris missiles,
319; Berlin crisis, 326, 331, 332;
Kennedy visits, 341–2, 368; test ban
negotiations, 361, 370, 371–2,
373–6; refuses to co-operate with
NATO, 368, 376; Vietnam war,
377–82, 396; South-East Asia
Defence Treaty, 382; and Laos, 384;
Channel tunnel, 421–31
France, Sir Arnold, 176, 198
Franklin, Sir Michael, 185n.
Franks, Lord, 77
Fraser, Hugh, 270
Freese-Pennefather, H.W.A., 148
French Channel Tunnel Company, 422, 423
Fylingdales, 312

Gaillard, Félix, 118
Gainsborough by-election (1956), 58
Gaitskell, Hugh, 47, 179, 335; Suez crisis,
29; 1958 Middle East crisis, 33; 1959
General Election, 60; and Britain's
EEC negotiations, 169; opposition to
EEC, 183, 198; and the Central
African Federation, 233; meets
Khrushchev, 337; and the atom
bomb tests, 347; Cuban missiles
crisis, 354, 356; Quemoy crisis,
404–5; immigration debate, 421; and
the 'night of long knives', 451
Galbraith, Tom, 453, 457, 458, 460, 461,
470, 481, 485
Gallup polls, 59, 95, 189, 343, 452
Gareloch, 287, 288–9, 291, 292, 297
Gates, Thomas, 288, 290, 297
GATT, 10, 92, 120, 126, 209, 210, 211
Gaza Strip, 26
Gazier, Albert, 18
General Elections: May 1955, 413; October
1959, 2, 6, 9, 45, 56, 57, 58–63,
64, 125, 146, 154, 167n., 333, 419,
443; October 1964, 10, 14, 62, 96,
101, 216, 241, 410, 489–91, 501;
April 1966, 62; June 1970, 218;
February 1974, 62; October 1974,
62; June 1983, 431
Geneva: Vietnam war conference (1954), 4,
378–81, 385, 387; Foreign Ministers'
conference (1959), 59, 330, 331–2,
333; disarmament conference, 309,
344, 346; test ban negotiations, 337,
339, 340, 343, 350, 360–2; Laos
conference (1961–2), 387–9, 391,
392, 393; Foreign Ministers' meeting
(1962), 346–7

Germany *see* East Germany; West Germany
Ghana, 221, 222, 244, 401
Giap, General Vo, 377
Gilmour, Ian, 241
Gladwyn, Lord (Gladwyn Jebb), 29, 113,
119, 121, 123, 125, 127, 140, 147,
423–4, 425
Glasgow, 290–1
Gold Coast Colony, 221
Gordon Walker, Patrick, 48
Gore-Booth, Paul, 125, 127
Göring, Hermann, 350
Gouldie, W.H., 224n., 238
Greece, 113, 363
Green Shield stamps, 215 and n.
Greenfield, Julius, 255 and n.
Grimond, Jo, 62–3, 154, 211–12, 321, 451
Gromyko, Andrei, 328, 331, 332, 333,
344–5, 346–7, 349–50
Grooters, Dr, 173–4
*Growth of the United Kingdom Economy to
1966* (NEDC), 78
Guardian see Manchester Guardian
Guillebaud Committee, 432

H-bombs *see* nuclear weapons
Habbaniya, 32
Hailsham, Lord: 1957 sterling crisis, 49,
50; and the 1959 Budget, 54; 1959
General Election, 61; 1962 Budget,
82; opposition to EEC membership,
158, 183; EEC negotiations, 168n.;
and nuclear policy, 317; test ban
negotiations, 363, 369, 370, 371,
373; Chequers conference, 454; and
the Profumo scandal, 473, 488; and
choice of HM's successor, 476, 490,
491–2, 494–8
Haley, Sir William, 90–1n., 421, 473
Halifax, Lord, 25
Hall, Sir Robert, 9, 45, 46, 47, 49, 51,
53, 55, 64 5, 67, 69, 70, 73, 79,
98–100, 204–5
Hall Report, 440
Hallstein, Walter, 114, 117, 122, 126, 128,
170, 186, 197
Hammarskjöld, Dag, 3, 24, 27, 34, 36,
41–2
Hankey, Sir Maurice, 423
Harding, Field Marshal Sir John, 378
Hare, John, 153, 435, 436, 448, 472, 494,
501
Harriman, Averell, 362, 363, 370, 371,
388, 392, 394–6
Harrison, Tom, 496
Harrod, Roy, 9, 47, 52, 53, 54, 55 and
n., 64, 67, 79–80, 85, 91–2
Hartington, Lady, 363–4
Hashemite Union, 32
Healey, Denis, 29
Heath, Sir Edward: in favour of British

membership of EEC, 139–40, 141, 158; Britain considers applying for EEC membership, 143–4, 146–7, 150; EEC negotiations, 7–9, 126, 151, 157, 159–77, 179–82, 185, 188–9, 194–6, 198–203; de Gaulle vetoes Britain's EEC membership, 193, 195, 196–7, 200–3; and tariff cuts, 209; and resale price maintenance, 215–16 and n.; test ban negotiations, 369; immigration problem, 420; and the Channel tunnel, 425–6, 431; Chequers conference, 454; and choice of HM's successor, 476; on Maudling, 492; on Home, 500
Hereford by-election (1956), 58
Herter, Christian, 133 and n., 294, 329 and n., 330–1, 332, 333, 338 and n., 341
Heyworth, Lord, 205
Hill, Dr Charles, 449
Hitler, Adolf, 25, 105, 322, 500
Ho Chi Minh, 377
Hobson, Sir John, 12, 456 and n., 459–60, 461, 469, 474, 482–3, 484–7
Hola Camp, 60, 223–4, 237–40, 241–2, 244
Hollis, Christopher, 241
Hollis, Sir Roger, 466, 472, 477
Holloway, Admiral James L. (US), 33
Holy Alliance, 324 and n.
Holy Loch, 295, 296–7, 311
Holyoake, Keith, 153, 178, 307–8
Home, Lady, 496
Home, Earl of, 6, 25n., 203; EEC entry negotiations, 8; and colonial independence, 11; becomes Foreign Secretary, 69, 139, 266; 1961 sterling crisis, 74; 1964 General Election, 101, 501; Britain considers applying for EEC membership, 143, 156; nuclear weapons policy, 196, 295–6, 306n., 308, 314, 315, 321; and Kenyatta's release, 226–7; and the Central African Federation, 233, 252, 273, 277, 279; and the Devlin Report, 235, 236; and Banda's release, 247–8, 248–50; Northern Rhodesia Conference, 255–7; and White Paper on Northern Rhodesia, 257–9; Northern Rhodesia franchise, 260, 261; Berlin crisis, 345, 348, 349–50, 359–60; Foreign Ministers' meeting, 346–7; and Bay of Pigs invasion, 352; Cuban missiles crisis, 357, 359; test ban negotiations, 361, 369–70, 374–6; and British Guiana, 364, 366; and Laos, 388–92, 394–5; and capital punishment, 410n.; immigration problem, 413, 415, 418; and the Channel tunnel, 430; transport policy, 442; Chequers conference, 454; and the Profumo

scandal, 472, 477, 481; and choice of HM's successor, 476, 491, 492, 493–7; and the Denning Report, 482; HM considers retirement, 490; becomes Prime Minister, 10, 14, 89, 100, 214, 215, 497–501
Home Office, 265, 409, 411
Homicide Act (1957), 408–10
Hone, Sir Evelyn, 259
Hone, General Ralph, 275
Hong Kong, 4, 399, 401
Hood, Lord, 36–7
Hoogwater, Dr, 172
Hornby, Richard, 58, 408
Horne, Alistair, 1, 13, 167n., 183, 202, 356, 368, 457–8, 492, 495
Hound Dog missile, 312
House of Commons: Suez crisis, 22, 23, 24, 29; 1958 Middle East crisis, 37; 1957 sterling crisis, 48; EEC debate (1960), 138; EEC negotiations, 154–5, 171; Macleod's ability in, 224; and Kenyan independence, 227–8; Hola Camp debate, 238–40, 244; debates Devlin Report, 240–1, 244; and the Central African Federation, 254; cancellation of Blue Streak, 287; and control of Polaris, 295; and the atom bomb tests, 347; Cuban missiles crisis, 356; test ban treaty, 373; debates capital punishment, 407–8, 409, 410; immigration debate, 421; debates Channel tunnel, 423; Vassall debates, 453, 460; Profumo scandal, 12–13, 460–4, 465, 466, 470, 472, 473–7, 483
House of Commons Estimates Committee, 217
House of Lords: and Kenyan independence, 228; and the Central African Federation, 254; debates capital punishment, 407–8; Peerage Act, 491
Howard, Anthony, 499
Howard, Professor Michael, 320
Howard League for Penal Reform, 407, 410
Howitt, Sir Harold, 204
Hoyer Millar, Sir Frederick, 38, 39
Hubback, David, 471–2
Hughes, Emrys, 29
Hull, General John, 397
Human Rights Commission (UN), 245
Humphrey, Senator George, 21, 22
Hungary, 328, 335, 336
Hunt, Sir David, 242n., 246–7, 248
Hunt, Sir John, 162–3
Hussein, King of Jordan, 32–3, 36, 37, 38, 41–2, 43
Hutton, Graham, 90–1 and n.

Ibn Saud, King of Saudi Arabia, 31
Iceland, 113
ICI, 433

immigration, 410–21
Import Duties Act (1932), 109, 220
imports: import controls, 91–2, 96–7; trade
    gap, 64, 69; balance of payments
    crises, 69, 72–4, 91–2, 96, 100–1
income tax, 56
incomes policy, 76–7, 79, 80, 84–6, 87–8,
    89–90, 204–5
Incomes Policy – the Next Step (Treasury
    White Paper), 80
Independent, 99
India, 153, 252, 341; Harrod proposes aid
    to, 80; and Britain's EEC
    negotiations, 160; independence, 221;
    and Vietnam war, 381; Quemoy crisis,
    401; immigrants, 415, 416, 417
Indo-China, 377–82, 396
Indonesia, 341, 401
inflation, 45, 52, 55–7, 77, 88, 90, 93,
    450, 451–2
Inland Revenue, 71
International Control Commission (ICC)
    (Laos), 381, 382, 383, 385, 395
International Monetary Fund (IMF), 22, 45,
    80, 85, 93, 98
Iran, 31
Iraq, 3, 30, 31, 32, 35, 38–9, 41, 44
Ireland, 113, 191, 411, 412, 414, 416,
    420–1
Israel, 18–20, 23, 24, 26, 29, 37, 61
Italy, 98, 143, 148, 161, 172, 180, 273, 368
ITN News, 477
Ivanov, Captain Yevgeny, 13, 455–6, 458,
    459, 460, 463, 464, 465, 467, 469,
    472, 474, 488, 489

Jack Committee, 441
Jackling, Roger, 163
Jacquet, Marc, 425, 429, 430
Jagan, Cheddi, 364–8
Jamaica, 411, 418
Japan, 304n., 396, 399, 401
Jay, Douglas, 159, 217
Jebb, Gladwyn *see* Gladwyn, Lord
Johnson, Dr Donald, 472
Jones, Aubrey, 217
Jones, Glyn, 273, 274
Jordan, 3, 30, 32–3, 36, 37–8, 39–43, 59
Joseph, Keith, 441, 449, 494
Junor, John, 497

KADU, 226, 227, 229–30
Kansas City Times, 489
KANU, 226, 227, 228, 229–30
Katay, Don, 382–3, 384
Kaunda, Kenneth, 256, 259, 260, 261–2,
    263 and n., 264, 268, 271, 277,
    278–9
Keeler, Christine, 12, 13, 454–60, 463–7,
    470–5, 477, 485, 489
Kelvingrove by-election (1958), 58

Kennedy, Jackie, 341–2
Kennedy, John, 73, 331n., 477; becomes
    President, 341; and Laos, 4, 385–7,
    392, 394–6; nuclear tests, 5–6, 304–9,
    344; meets HM, 6, 299–300,
    311–17, 342–3, 348–9, 359, 363–71,
    386; Anglo-American relations, 26;
    refuses to be exploited in 1963
    General Election, 59; and British
    membership of EEC, 145–6, 150,
    151, 155; and Polaris, 192, 193, 197,
    295–6, 312–16, 319; tries to persuade
    Britain to give up nuclear weapons,
    297–9; and size of Britain's
    conventional forces, 300–2, 316; and
    Skybolt, 310–12, 317–18; visits France,
    341–2, 368; meets Khrushchev, 342;
    Berlin crisis, 344–6, 349, 350, 360;
    Bay of Pigs invasion, 5, 351–2;
    Cuban missiles crisis, 6, 351, 352–9,
    361; test ban negotiations, 360–3,
    371–6
Kennedy, Ludovic, 58
Kennedy, Robert (Bobby), 362
Kenya, 10–11, 221–30, 237–40, 241–2, 245,
    256, 264 and n.
Kenya Conference, London (1960), 224–5,
    226
Kenyatta, Jomo, 10–11, 223, 225, 226–30
Key Industries Duties, 109
Key West, 385, 386–7
KGB, 452
Khrushchev, Nikita, 5, 40, 59, 299, 301;
    and attempted Communist take-over
    of Syria, 31; nuclear tests, 309, 344;
    Berlin crisis, 323–37, 343, 349,
    359–60; meets HM, 327–9, 330,
    337, 338; visits USA, 333–5, 337;
    failed Paris Summit (1960), 337,
    338–41; hostility towards Eisenhower,
    338–9, 341; U-2 spy plane shot down,
    338, 339–40; meets Kennedy, 342;
    test ban negotiations, 350, 360–3,
    369, 371; Cuban missiles crisis, 6,
    351, 352–9, 464; and Laos, 387,
    389, 392, 395; Quemoy crisis, 406
Kikuyu tribe, 223, 227
Kilmuir, Lord (David Maxwell-Fyfe), 50;
    and the Central African Federation,
    11, 262; and choice of Eden's
    successor, 24; and the Devlin
    Report, 237, 239, 461; and
    Northern Rhodesia White Paper,
    257, 258, 269–70; and capital
    punishment, 408; immigration
    problem, 411, 416–21; 'night of long
    knives', 449
King Edward VII Hospital for Officers, 491
King-Lewis, Dr, 491
Kinross and West Perthshire by-election
    (1963), 499

Kirkman, William, 231, 237, 260
Kirkpatrick, Sir Ivone, 24, 38, 423
Kissinger, Henry, 200
Koniev, Marshal, 347
Korea, 401
Korean War, 282, 378, 386
Kroll, Dr, 345
Kuwait, 30, 39, 44, 46
Kuznetsov, Vasily, 355

Labour Party: 1958 Middle East crisis, 37;
    by-election successes, 58, 183; 1959
    General Election, 60–2; 1964 General
    Election, 101, 501; and Britain's
    EEC negotiations, 156–7, 158, 171,
    189, 195; competition policy, 216,
    217, 218; and the Central African
    Federation, 231, 232, 233–4; and the
    Monckton Commission, 233, 244;
    Hola Camp debate, 240; and nuclear
    tests, 305; nuclear weapons policy,
    320; abolition of capital punishment,
    410; immigration debate, 421;
    nationalization of railways, 432; and
    the Beeching Plan, 440–1; internal
    quarrels, 443; popularity, 452;
    Vassall case, 453; and the Profumo
    scandal, 460
Lae, Captain Kong, 384
Lahr, Dr Rolf, 170, 198
Lambton, Anthony, 239, 475, 477, 497
Laniel, Joseph, 381
Laos, 4–5, 363, 377, 381, 382–96, 401
Law, Andrew Bonar, 423, 499
Layton, Christopher, 452
Le Havre, 440
League of Empire Loyalists, 228
Lebanon, 3, 32–8, 40, 41, 42–3
Lee, Sir Frank, 65, 70, 71, 77, 80, 131,
    136–8, 141–2, 146, 163, 165
Lee Report, 136–8, 155
Leicester North-East by-election (1962),
    445, 452
Lennox-Boyd, Alan, 11, 108, 232, 273; and
    Kenyan independence, 222; Hola
    Camp incident, 223–4, 237, 238–40;
    and the Nyasaland emergency, 234,
    236, 239, 240, 241, 242; immigration
    problem, 412, 413, 415–18; Nyasaland
    leaves Central African Federation, 278
Levin, Bernard, 82, 241
Lewisham by-election (1957), 58
Liberal Party: 1929 Yellow Book, 90 and
    n.; 1958 Middle East crisis, 37;
    by-election successes, 58, 59, 71–2,
    81, 88, 167n., 443–5, 452; 1959
    General Election, 62–3; Britain
    applies for EEC membership, 154;
    attitude to EEC, 183; critical of
    monopolies, 207–8, 211–12; and the
    Central African Federation, 232

Liddell Hart, Basil, 343
Liesner, Hans, 219
Limassol, 10
Lindsay, Tom, 451
Lindsay Keir, Sir David, 413
Linnhe, Loch, 288n., 291, 292
Liverpool, 411
Lloyd, Selwyn, 3, 26; Anglo-American
    relations, 2, 133; as Chancellor,
    9–10, 95, 139, 451–2; Suez crisis,
    17, 18, 22, 45, 61; reopening of
    Suez Canal, 27–8, 29; and attempted
    Communist take-over of Syria, 30–1;
    1958 Middle East crisis, 34, 36,
    38–41; 1961 Budget, 69–72; 1961
    sterling crisis, 72–6; 1961 emergency
    Budget, 75, 76, 87; incomes policy,
    76–7, 84, 86, 87–8; NEDC, 77–9;
    1962 Budget, 81–3, 85, 444, 446;
    'night of long knives', 10, 88–9,
    445–50, 451–2; 1963 Budget, 83, 87;
    and Plan G, 108; and EFTA of the
    Seventeen, 119, 121, 123, 127; as
    Foreign Secretary, 266; and Polaris
    submarines, 289; Berlin crisis, 328–9,
    331–3; and Laos, 390n.; Quemoy
    crisis, 400, 403–4, 405–6; and the
    Profumo scandal, 471–2, 473, 475;
    and choice of HM's successor, 494,
    496–7
Lloyd George, David, 90, 350, 423
Lloyd George, Gwilym, 411, 413, 415–16
Lloyd George, Lady Megan, 58
LNER, 432
London: immigrants, 411, 413, 414, 418;
    race riots, 418
Long, Dr, 371
Longden, Gilbert, 451
Louw, E.H., 246
Lubbock, Eric, 443–4
Luce, Admiral John, 389
Luns, Dr Joseph, 119, 161, 180–1, 196
Luxemburg, 104, 148, 170, 172
Lynskey, Lord Justice, 474n.
Lyttelton, Oliver (Lord Chandos), 278

Maastricht Treaty, 191n.
MacArthur, General Douglas, 386
McCarthy, John G., 125
McColl, René, 317, 368–9
MacDonald, Ramsay, 423
McEwen, John, 174, 175, 178
Mackenzie, Robert, 473
Maclay, John, 449
Maclean, Fitzroy, 29
Macleod, Iain, 50, 88, 500; and colonial
    independence, 11; threatens
    resignation over cuts in public
    spending, 80; and the Orpington
    by-election, 81; EEC negotiations,
    182–3; and Kenyan independence,

224–9, 230; and Nyasaland, 245; and Banda's release, 247, 249–51; Nyasaland Conference, 251–2; and the Monckton Report, 253–4; Northern Rhodesia Conference, 254–7; White Paper on Northern Rhodesia, 257–9; Northern Rhodesia franchise, 260–4, 267, 268–71; character, 262, 267; becomes Chairman of Conservative Party, 264–5, 266; opposes Southern Rhodesia's independence, 279; immigration problem, 420, 421; by-election losses, 445; and choice of HM's successor, 446, 476, 492–3, 495–7, 499; Chequers conference, 454; and the Profumo scandal, 12, 461, 463, 477; and the Denning Report, 482, 490; and timing of 1964 General Election, 490–1; refuses to serve in Home's Cabinet, 252n., 500, 501

McMahon Act, 374

Macmillan, Lady Dorothy, 1, 369

Macmillan, Harold:
  in Eden government: Suez crisis, 18, 19–24, 45, 61; 1956 Budget, 45; attitude to EEC, 103, 104–8; Plan G, 108–10
  as Prime Minister: becomes Prime Minister, 24–5, 45; policy advisers, 1; style as Prime Minister, 1–2; achievements, 14–15; 1959 General Election, 58–63, 333; indecisiveness, 272–3; by-election losses, 443–5; 'night of long knives', 10, 88–9, 445–52; suspicions of conspiracy against, 446, 447, 448; popularity, 450; and calls for his resignation, 476–9; choice of successor, 14, 476, 491–7, 499–500; ill-health, 478; considers retirement, 490–1; and timing of 1964 General Election, 96, 490–1; prostate trouble, 13–14, 491, 495; opposition to Butler as his successor, 13–14, 494, 500; resignation, 14, 491, 496, 497
  home affairs: capital punishment, 410; immigration problem, 412, 417–21; and the Channel tunnel, 423–30; and the Beeching Plan, 433–40; Vassall case, 452–3; Profumo scandal, 12–13, 454–78; and the Denning Report, 479–89
  economic policy, 9–10, 15, 45–57; 1957 Budget, 46; 1957 sterling crisis, 46–51; 1960 Budget, 64–8; 1961 Budget, 69–72; 1961 sterling crisis, 72–6; incomes policy, 76–7, 80, 84–6, 87–8, 89–90, 204–5; NEDC, 77–9; Harrod advises, 79–80; 1962 Budget, 81–3; 1963 Budget, 83, 87,

92–6; reflation, 88; proposes import controls, 91–2, 96–7; tries to prevent sterling crisis, 96, 100–1; proposes selling dollar portfolio, 97–8; floating pound, 98–100; monopolies, 206–8, 211–14; overhaul of competitive policy, 206–20
  European policy: EFTA of the Seventeen, 110–25, 126–7; EFTA of the Seven, 128–32; considers applying for EEC membership, 138–57; and acceleration of Treaty of Rome, 135–6; EEC negotiations, 6–9, 111, 158–203; meetings with de Gaulle, 166–7, 189–94; de Gaulle vetoes Britain's EEC membership, 192–3, 195, 196–203, 204
  foreign policy: Anglo-American relations, 2–6, 25–7, 31, 43, 125, 132–5, 158, 303; fears Communism in Middle East, 3; and Laos, 4–5, 384–96; Quemoy crisis, 4, 400–6; Berlin crisis, 5, 323–37, 343–6, 347–50, 359–60; meets Kennedy, 6, 299–300, 311–17, 342–3, 348–9, 359, 363–71, 386; colonial problems, 10–12; 'Wind of Change' speech, 11, 246; reopening of Suez Canal, 27–30; Baghdad Pact, 31–2; 1958 Middle East crisis, 33–44; Kenyan independence, 222–30; Central African Federation, 231–65, 266–81; Nyasaland, 231–7, 240–2, 246–52; Hola Camp incident, 237–40, 241–2; African tour, 242, 244–7; and White Paper on Northern Rhodesia, 257–60; Northern Rhodesia franchise, 260–4; meets Khrushchev, 327–9, 330, 337, 338; failed Paris Summit (1960), 337, 338–40; meets Eisenhower, 337; and Bay of Pigs invasion, 352; Cuban missiles crisis, 6, 351, 352–9; British Guiana, 364–7, 368, 369
  defence policy, 282–321; Polaris submarines, 2–3, 8, 192–3, 196, 287–97, 310–11, 312–16, 318–20; nuclear tests, 5–6, 303–9, 347; Thor missiles, 26, 284–5; determination to be independent nuclear power, 196, 283–7; cuts expenditure, 282–3; Blue Streak, 284, 286–7; Skybolt, 287, 288, 290, 296–7, 305, 310–14, 317–18; USA tries to persuade Britain to give up nuclear weapons, 297–9, 302–3; size of conventional forces, 298–9, 300–2, 316; NATO multilateral force proposals, 311–12, 315, 320; test ban negotiations, 360–3, 369–76, 477–8

McNamara, Robert, 289n., 297–8, 301, 302–3, 310–11, 316, 317

Macpherson, Mr (Jamaican Minister of Labour), 411
Makarios, Archbishop, 10, 11, 51
Makins, Sir Roger (Lord Sherfield), 51, 65, 99–100, 106–7, 304, 397
Malawi, 11–12, 281; *see also* Nyasaland
Malaya, 153, 377, 399, 401, 404
Malaysia, 363
Malinowsky, R.Y., 290
Malvern, Lord, 278
Manchester Guardian, 65, 228, 240, 317, 363, 372–3
Mandela, Nelson, 246
Manley, Norman, 418
Manningham-Buller, Reginald *see* Dilhorne, Lord
Mansholt, Sicco, 170, 175, 182, 188
Mansholt Plan, 159
Margach, James, 453
Margaret, Princess, 203
Margolin, Robert, 128, 161, 167
Marjoribanks, James, 147
Marples, Ernest: and the Channel tunnel, 425, 426, 429–30; Beeching Plan, 14, 433–41; Denning Report, 13, 480–1
Marshall, John, 176
Marshall Islands, 304n.
Marshall Plan, 105
Mason, Sir Paul, 360–1
Massigli, René, 423
Matsos, 3–4, 329n., 396–406
Matthieu, Albert, 422
Mattingly, Garrett, 248n.
Mau Mau, 11, 222–4, 226, 228, 230, 237–8, 245, 264n.
Maude, Evan, 53
Maudling, Reginald, 52, 77, 500; as Chancellor, 10, 89, 452; and colonial independence, 11; 1957 sterling crisis, 50; incomes policy, 86, 89–90; 1963 Budget, 92–5, 452, 492; and import controls, 92, 96; tries to prevent sterling crisis, 96, 100–1; opposes sale of dollar portfolio, 97–8; and floating pound, 100; 1964 Budget, 101; and EFTA of the Seventeen, 110, 112–22, 124, 125, 126–8; and EFTA of the Seven, 128–9; Anglo-American relations, 134–5; opposition to EEC membership, 138, 149–50, 152, 157, 158, 183; EEC negotiations, 139; and tariff cuts, 211; and price fixing, 214; and Kenyan independence, 229, 230; becomes Colonial Secretary, 265, 266–8; and Northern Rhodesia franchise, 267–72; and the Channel tunnel, 429, 430; 'night of long knives', 445, 449, 450; Chequers conference, 454; and choice of HM's

successor, 13, 476, 490, 492–7; 1964 General Election, 501
Maxwell-Fyfe, David *see* Kilmuir, Lord
Mboya, Tom, 225, 226
Meade, Professor James, 99 and n.
Mekong valley, 392
Melton by-election (1956), 58
Mendès-France, Pierre, 104, 381
Menzies, Robert, 178, 279–80, 307–8
Merchant, Livingstone, 133
Messina Conference (1956), 26, 104–5, 117
Messina Plan, 106
MI5, 455–6, 464–5, 472
Middle East, 331; Suez crisis, 17–20; attempted Communist take-over of Syria, 30–1; Baghdad Pact, 31–2; *see also individual countries*
Middlesbrough by-election (1962), 88
Middleton, Sir George, 33, 34, 37
Midlands, immigrants, 413, 414
'midnight meeting', 496, 497
Millard, Sir Guy, 25
Mills, Lord, 433–4, 449
Ministerial Economic Policy Committee, 429
Ministry of Agriculture, 161, 163, 167n., 185–6
Ministry of Defence, 286, 293, 297, 372, 392, 404
Ministry of Housing, 441
Ministry of Labour, 418, 420
Ministry of Transport, 429, 440, 441
Moch, Jules, 423–4, 425
Moffat, Sir John, 256, 260, 262, 264, 269
Mollet, Guy, 18, 20, 28, 29–30, 114
Molotov, Vyacheslav, 378, 379, 381
Monckton, Sir Walter, 233
Monckton Commission, 233–4, 243, 245, 247, 249, 251, 253–4, 272–3
monetarism, 15, 47, 48
Monnet, Jean, 146–7, 189, 196, 200
Monopolies Act (1948), 218
Monopolies and Mergers Act (1965), 216, 218
Monopolies Commission, 206–8, 211–13, 215, 216–19
Monopolies, Mergers and Restrictive Practices (White Paper), 216
Montgomery, Field Marshal Lord, 343
Morocco, 18
Morrison, John, 494, 495
Morrow, Ed, 63
Moscow, 327–9, 452–3
Mosley, Sir Oswald, Bt, 90n., 419
Mountbatten, Lord, 286, 289 and n.
Munby, D.L., 435n.
Murphy, Robert, 37, 327
Muscat and Oman, 30

Nam Than, 392
Napoleon I, Emperor, 421–2
Napoleon III, Emperor, 422

Nash, Walter, 402
Nassau, 8, 359
Nassau agreement (1962), 311–20
Nasser, Gamal Abdel, 17, 18, 20, 21, 23, 27–30, 31–2, 33–4, 37, 39, 40–2, 45
National Assistance, 414
National Board on Prices and Incomes (NBPI), 217–18
National Campaign for the Abolition of Capital Punishment, 410
National Economic Development Council (NEDC), 77–9, 84, 85, 87, 206
National Farmers Union (NFU), 145, 146, 157, 158–9, 163, 167n., 185–6
National Incomes Commission (NIC), 86, 87, 91, 95, 206, 446, 451
National Institute of Economic and Social Research, 94
National Insurance, 70, 72
National Security Council (US), 298, 397
NATO, 74, 113, 124, 193, 202, 203, 345; and British independent nuclear weapons, 282, 285, 298; and Polaris, 286, 297, 311, 313–15, 318; MRBM programme, 288–9, 291, 292, 293, 311; conventional forces, 300–2, 316; multilateral force proposals, 311–12, 315, 320, 367; Berlin crisis, 348, 349, 350; and Bay of Pigs invasion, 352; Cuban missiles crisis, 354, 355; France refuses to co-operate with, 368, 376; proposed non-aggression pact with Warsaw Pact, 371
Navarre, General Henri, 378
Nazis, 7, 126, 155, 322
Neale, Alan, 219
Netherlands, 104, 119, 143, 148, 161, 172
Nevada, nuclear tests, 303, 304, 306, 307
New Kenyan Party, 225, 226
New Statesman, 408, 473
New York Herald Tribune, 331
New Zealand, 401; EFTA negotiations, 119, 147, 153; and Britain's EEC negotiations, 159, 169, 171, 178; and nuclear tests on Christmas Island, 307–8; South-East Asia Defence Treaty, 382; and Laos, 388, 390, 393; Quemoy crisis, 397, 402
News Chronicle, 240, 248
News of the World, 457
Ngala, Ronald, 226, 229, 230
Nicholls, Sir John, 148
Nicholson, Sir Godfrey, 455, 471–2 and n.
Nigeria, 153, 221, 222
'night of long knives' (1962), 10, 88–9, 266, 445–52
1922 Committee, 13, 24, 421, 451, 476, 477, 479, 494
Nitze, Paul, 301
Nixon, Richard, 297, 334 and n.
Nkrumah, Dr Kwame, 221

Nkumbula, Harry, 277
Noble, Andrew, 148
Noble, Sir Michael, 449
Norstad, General Lauris, 298, 347, 354
North Cornwall, 1959 General Election, 63
North Devon, 1959 General Election, 63
North Vietnam, 4, 377, 382, 383–4, 387, 392, 394, 396
Northern Rhodesia: membership of Central African Federation, 231–2, 242–3, 244; independence movement, 222, 233, 252, 253, 254; Monckton Commission, 233–4, 253–4; HM visits, 245; Colonial Office responsible for, 250; Northern Rhodesia Conference, 253, 254–7; Macleod's White Paper, 257–60; franchise proposals, 260–4, 267–8, 269–71; passive resistance campaign, 262; secession from Central African Federation, 11–12, 269, 275–7, 278–9, 280, 281; Butler visits, 278
Norway, 7, 25, 111, 128, 129, 130, 191
Norway Gap, 348
nuclear weapons, 14–15, 282–3; Skybolt missiles, 2, 287, 288, 290, 296–7, 305, 310–14, 317–18, 319; Polaris submarines, 2–3, 8, 60, 192–3, 196, 286, 287–97, 310–11, 312–16, 318–20; Thor missiles, 2, 26, 284–5, 286, 294, 295; tests, 5–6, 303–9, 337, 343, 344, 346, 347; French desire to become nuclear power, 7–8, 164–5, 167, 192–3, 196, 301, 372; Britain's independence, 196, 283–7; Blue Streak, 284, 286–7, 294; USA tries to persuade Britain to give up, 297–9, 302–3; Blue Steel missile, 302 and n.; tests suspended, 333; Geneva test ban conference, 337, 339, 340, 343; disarmament conference, 344, 346, test ban negotiations, 347, 350, 358, 360–3, 369–76, 477–8; Eisenhower threatens to use in Korea, 378, 386; and Laotian civil war, 385; Quemoy crisis, 397–406
Nuri-es-Said, 32
Nutting, Anthony, 58
Nyasaland: independence movement, 222, 243; emergency, 224, 226, 232–3, 234–7, 239, 240–1, 245; membership of Central African Federation, 231–2, 242, 243, 244–5; Monckton Commission, 233–4, 254; Devlin Report, 234–7, 239, 240–1; Banda's release, 247–51; Nyasaland Conference, 251–2, 277; secession from Central African Federation, 11–12, 269, 273, 274–8, 281
Nyasaland Congress Party, 234–5
Nyerere, Julius, 279

Obote, Milton, 279
Observer, 201, 358, 499
Ockrent, Roger, 117, 118
Ockrent Report, 118, 119–20, 121
Official Secrets Act, 466
Oman, 30
Organization for European Economic
    Co-operation (OEEC), 105–6, 108,
    110, 112, 116, 117, 119, 122–4,
    126, 127, 130
Orkneys, 348
Ormsby-Gore, David, 369, 404; nuclear
    weapons policy, 302–3, 310, 311,
    317–18 and n.; and Christmas Island
    nuclear tests, 304; friendship with
    Kennedy, 341; Berlin crisis, 345,
    347, 348; Cuban missiles crisis,
    352–3, 354, 355, 356, 357; test ban
    treaty negotiations, 361, 362, 375;
    and British Guiana, 364–5; and the
    Profumo scandal, 477
Orpington by-election (1962), 81, 167n.,
    443–4, 446, 452
Orsini, Felice, 422
Osborne, Cyril, 412
Ottawa, 349
Ottawa Agreement, 158

Paish, Professor Frank, 93, 95
Paisley by-election (1961), 443
Pakistan, 31, 153, 160, 363, 382, 401, 415,
    416, 417
Palazzo Chigi, Rome, 180
Pan-African Congress (PAC), 246
Paris Match, 464
Parker, Lord Justice, 49
Pathet Lao, 382–4, 386, 387, 389, 390,
    392–3, 394, 395, 396
pay pause, 76–7, 79, 80, 85–6
pay roll tax, 70–1, 72
Peerage Act (1963), 491 and n.
Penney, Sir William, 308
Pentagon, 294, 297, 311, 329, 385, 392
People, 459, 460
Perth, 17th Earl of, 11, 270, 271; on de
    Gaulle's views on British membership
    of EEC, 146–7; and EFTA
    negotiations, 153; and Central
    African Federation, 233, 266, 269,
    270; and Devlin Report, 235, 236,
    237, 242; and Northern Rhodesia
    Conference, 259; resignation, 269–71
Pescadores, 396, 397, 400
Peyrefitte, Roger, 426
Phelps Brown, Professor Henry, 78, 205
Philippines, 382, 401
Phoumi, General, 384–5, 387, 389, 392
Pinay, Antoine, 127
Pincher, Chapman, 295
Pineau, Christian, 18, 20, 28, 113, 114
Plain of Jars, 383, 384, 385, 394

Plan G, 108–10
Plowden, Lord, 70, 137 and n., 155, 156
    and n.
Poland, 335, 381, 382, 395
Polaris submarines, 2–3, 8, 60, 192–3, 196,
    286, 287–97, 310–11, 312–16,
    318–20
Pompidou, Georges, 181, 184, 431
Pontefract by-election (1962), 444
Poole, Lord, 49, 476, 490, 495
Port Said, 19, 20, 21, 22
Portugal, 7, 111, 113, 118, 122, 128, 129,
    130, 191
Potsdam Agreement (1945), 342, 344
Powell, Enoch, 9, 252n., 476, 500;
    resignation, 2, 51, 501; Financial
    Secretary to the Treasury, 45;
    monetarism, 47, 49; Hola Camp
    debate, 239; immigration debate,
    421; and the Profumo scandal, 473;
    and choice of HM's successor, 495,
    496–7; refuses to serve in Home's
    Cabinet, 499
Powell, Sir Richard, 152–3, 286
Powers, Captain Gary, 337–8
Poynton, Sir Hylton, 365
Pravda, 373
Press Association, 19
price controls, 205–6
Primrose, Sir J. Ure, 234 and n., 235–6
Private Eye, 464
Profumo, Baron Albert, 454
Profumo, Jack, 6, 12–13, 95, 281, 336 and
    n., 363, 454–77, 490; Denning
    Report, 479–89
Profumo, Valerie, 454, 455, 468, 482, 486
Public Accounts Committee, 217
Public Record Office, 1, 10, 12, 356, 455
public spending, 49–51, 73, 75
Public Sector Borrowing Requirement
    (PSBR), 54n.

Qasim, General, 32, 39, 41, 43, 44
Queen magazine, 456
Quemoy, 3–4, 329n., 396–406

Radcliffe, Lord, 413, 453, 470
Radcliffe Report, 453, 454, 457, 466
railways, 431–41
Rambouillet, 189
Ramsbotham, Hon. Sir Peter, 192–3 and n.
Ravanel, Jacques, 425
Rawlinson, Peter, 12, 456–7, 458, 462–3,
    469, 474, 484
Redmayne, Martin, 72, 269; Profumo
    scandal, 12; Macleod threatens to
    resign, 80, 257; and the 'night of
    long knives', 88; nuclear weapons
    policy, 315–16, 318; by-election
    defeats, 445; Chequers conference,
    453–4; and the Profumo scandal,

458, 459, 460–1, 465, 466, 470, 474, 483–4; and choice of HM's successor, 492, 494, 495–6, 497
Rees-Mogg, William, 494, 499
Registrar of Restrictive Trading Agreements, 207
Reilly, Sir Patrick, 8–9, 163, 175–6, 185, 186, 188, 195, 199, 201, 326, 339, 426–7, 429
Renison, Sir Patrick, 222, 226, 227
Rent Act (1958), 61
Reorganization of the Nationalized Transport Undertaking (White Paper), 435
Republican Party (USA), 297, 373
Resale Price Maintenance Act (1964), 214–15, 216
The Reshaping of British Railways (Beeching Plan), 437
Restrictive Practices Act (1956), 207–8, 212, 213–14
Restrictive Practices Court, 207, 216, 218–19
Restrictive Trade Practices Act (1968), 218
Retail Price Index, 56–7, 70, 76, 77
Reuter, Ernst, 322
A Review of Restrictive Trade Practices Policy (White Paper), 219
Rhee, Syngman, 403
Ribbentrop, Joachim von, 25
Rice-Davies, Mandy, 469
Richardson, Sir John, 491, 497
Rickett, Sir Denis, 46, 98
road transport, 431, 432, 437, 438, 439, 440, 441
Robbins, Lord, 46, 47, 70, 95, 137 and n.
Roberts, Sir Frank, 349, 357, 361
Robertson, General Sir Brian, 432, 433, 434
Robertson, Sir Dennis, 204
Robinson, John, 200
Rochdale, 63
Rochdale by-election (1958), 58
Roll, Eric (Lord Roll), 144, 148, 161, 165, 167, 176, 186, 187, 198
Rome, Treaty of, 6, 7, 8, 110, 111, 122, 123, 126, 127, 131, 133, 134, 137, 138, 139, 142, 155, 158, 160, 202
Roth, Andrew, 96, 458–9
Rothermere, Lord, 88, 445
Rothschild, Robert, 106
Rountree, William, 39, 40, 43, 44
Rowan, Sir Leslie, 107
Royal Air Force (RAF), 30, 32, 282, 283–4, 296
Royal Commission on Capital Punishment, 407
Royal Navy, 33, 286, 425
Rumbold, Sir Anthony, Bt, 141, 176–7, 193, 331, 333
Rusk, Dean, 299, 311, 316, 331n.; and Britain's EEC negotiations, 177;

background, 341; Berlin crisis, 345, 349; test ban negotiations, 346–7, 361, 369–70, 374; and British Guiana, 364, 365–6; and Laos, 388, 390, 391, 392

St Aldwyn, Lord, 494, 495, 496
Salisbury, Lord, 2, 108; Suez crisis, 23; and choice of Eden's successor, 24; resignation, 1–2, 51; opposition to EEC, 156, 183; and Kenyan independence, 225; support for Central African Federation, 232; and the Monckton Report, 254; and White Paper on Northern Rhodesia, 259; and Northern Rhodesia franchise, 269, 272, 277; immigration problem, 416
Sananikone, Phou, 383, 384
Sandys, Duncan: and colonial independence, 11; support for EEC membership, 138–9, 153–4, 158; praises Kenyatta, 226; and Kenyan independence, 229, 230; and the Central African Federation, 252–3, 274; Northern Rhodesia Conference, 255–7; and White Paper on Northern Rhodesia, 257–9; Northern Rhodesia franchise, 260–3, 267–70; moves to Commonwealth Relations Office, 266; defence cuts, 282–3; nuclear weapons policy, 283–4, 286, 287, 315; and British Guiana, 364, 365–7, 368; and the Duchess of Argyll's divorce case, 472–3, 481–2; and the Profumo scandal, 472–3, 480, 481
Sangatte, 422
Saturday Evening Post, 347
Saudi Arabia, 30, 31
Savanhu, Jasper, 232
Schaus, Eugène, 170, 172, 198
Schedule A tax, 52 and n., 71–2, 81–2, 83, 93, 444, 446, 452
Schroeder, Gerhard, 198
Schuman, Robert, 104, 174–5
Schuman Plan, 102–3, 117, 139
Scottish Office, 453
Seaborg, Glenn T., 304
Second World War, 220, 285, 431, 478n.
Select Committee on Nationalized Industries, 433
Sellers, Lord Justice, 446
Sendall, Wilfrid, 493
Serpell, Sir David, 425
Sèvres, Treaty of (1956), 19, 23
Sharpeville massacre (1960), 246
Shawcross, Sir Hartley, 244–5
Shearer, Moira, 58
Shell, 351
Shinwell, Emmanuel, 295, 475

Sich, Rupert, 207–8
Sierra Leone, 153, 221
Silverman, Sydney, 407–8, 409
Simon, Lord, 29 and n.
Simpson, Sir Joseph, 13, 467–9
Sinai Peninsula, 18, 26
Singapore, 404
Skybolt missile, 2, 287, 288, 290, 296–7,
    305, 310–14, 317–18, 319
Slessor, Sir John, 319–20
Smith, Ian, 281
Soames, Christopher, 74, 144–5, 150–1,
    154, 158, 167 and n., 185–6, 494
es Solh, Sami, 33
Sorensen, T.C., 342, 384–6
Soskice, Sir Frank, 238, 464
Soustelle, Jacques, 122, 126
South Africa, 242, 246–7, 249
South-East Asia Collective Defence Treaty,
    382
South-East Asia Treaty organization
    (SEATO), 382, 385, 386, 387, 389,
    390, 391, 392–3, 404
South Vietnam, 4, 382, 387, 392, 396, 401
Southampton, 440
Southern Rhodesia, 250, 365, 366;
    independence movement, 222, 252,
    254, 279–80, 281; membership of
    Central African Federation, 231–2,
    242, 244; British restraints on, 247
    and n., 248; likelihood of unilateral
    declaration of independence, 248–9;
    and dissolution of Central African
    Federation, 11–12, 245, 258, 274,
    276–7
Souvannaphouma, Prince, 383, 384, 392,
    393, 394
Souvanouvong, Prince, 383, 394
Soviet Union: nuclear weapons, 5, 287;
    arms sales to Egypt, 17; Suez crisis,
    19, 20; attempted Communist
    take-over of Syria, 30–1; and
    Baghdad Pact, 31–2; 1958 Middle
    East crisis, 39; influence in Iraq, 44;
    EEC attitude to, 164; Sputnik,
    285–6, 298; Berlin crisis, 299,
    322–37, 339, 343–6, 347–50, 359–60;
    nuclear tests, 304, 305, 309, 337,
    343, 344, 346; HM meets
    Khrushchev, 327–9, 330, 337, 338;
    Khrushchev visits USA, 333–5, 337;
    failed Paris Summit (1960), 337,
    338–41; shoots down U-2 spy plane,
    337–8, 339–40; Kennedy meets
    Khrushchev, 342; proposed peace
    treaty with East Germany, 349–50;
    test ban negotiations, 350, 360–3,
    370–4, 477–8; Cuban missiles crisis,
    6, 351, 352–9, 361; and Laos,
    384–5, 387–9, 392, 394, 395–6;
    Quemoy crisis, 398, 402–3; Vassall

case, 452–3; and the Profumo
    scandal, 455–6, 471, 474
Spaak, Paul-Henri, 104, 105, 106, 107,
    109–10, 115, 165, 169, 170, 196,
    200, 203
Spaak Report, 105, 107, 108
Spain, 191
Sparrow, John, 413
Spectator, 51, 82, 95, 178–9, 241, 488, 500
Sputnik, 285–6, 298
Stalin, Joseph, 378
Stansgate, Lord, 491
State Department (US): nuclear weapons,
    26; Middle East policy, 3, 30, 38;
    and attempted Communist take-over
    of Syria, 31; and creation of EEC,
    125; NATO multilateral force
    proposals, 311; Berlin crisis, 325,
    327, 330, 345; test ban negotiations,
    362, 374; and Laos, 385
Stationery Office, 235, 439
Stedeford, Sir Ivan, 433
Stedeford Committee, 433, 434
Steel, Christopher, 116, 141, 148, 197
Stephens, Robert, 219
sterling crises, 46–51, 72–5, 96
Stevens, Sir Roger, 43, 275
Stock Exchange, 49, 57, 61, 81, 82 and n.,
    423, 473
Stockholm Convention (1959), 130–1
Stockton-on-Tees by-election (1962), 88,
    444
Stonehouse, John, 215
Strauss, Franz-Josef, 350
Suez Canal, 17, 26–30, 40
Suez Canal Authority, 28
Suez Canal Company, 97, 98, 423
Suez Canal Users Association (SCUA),
    17–18, 27, 29
Suez crisis (1956), 2, 17–24, 25–6, 45–6,
    60, 61, 98
Suez Group, 29
Sunday Express, 159, 493
Sunday Pictorial, 456, 457, 459, 460, 473
Sunday Telegraph, 12, 462, 473
Sunday Times, 318n., 343, 358, 368, 453,
    494, 499
'Sunrise', Operation, 234
Super-Octopus, 305–6
Sutton and Cheam by-election (1972), 444
Sweden, 7, 25, 111, 122, 126, 128, 129–30
Swinton, Lord, 226–7, 412
Switzerland, 7, 111, 118, 122, 128, 129,
    130, 135
Syria, 20, 30–1, 39

Tachen, 396
Taiwan *see* Formosa
Tandy, Sir Arthur, 172
Tanganyika, 223, 279
taxation: Schedule A, 52 and n., 71–2,

81–2, 83, 93, 444, 446, 452; 1958
Budget, 52–3; 1959 Budget, 56;
1959 General Election, 61; 1960
Budget, 66, 67; pay roll tax, 70–1,
72; regulators, 70–1, 72; 1961
Budgets, 71, 75; capital gains tax,
81, 82; 1963 Budget, 94–5

Tempo Illustrato, 464
Tennant, Mark, 275
Terry, Walter, 445
Thailand, 377, 382, 386, 387, 388, 390,
391, 392–3, 396, 401
Thant, U, 354, 355
Thatcher, Margaret, 62, 198, 219, 220,
428, 431, 434
Thatcherism, 48
This Week, 488
Thomas, George, 240
Thompson, Llewellyn, 334 and n., 344,
345, 347, 360
Thor missiles, 2, 26, 284–5, 286,
295
Thorneycroft, Peter, 29, 448, 454; as
Chancellor, 9, 45, 95, 451; 1957
Budget, 46; 1957 sterling crisis,
47–50; resignation, 2, 51; Britain
considers applying for EEC
membership, 153; incomes policy,
204–5; and nuclear weapons policy,
298, 310, 311, 312, 313–14, 315,
319; 'night of long knives', 449;
Vassall case, 453
Thorpe, Jeremy, 63, 446
Thorpe, Richard, 89
Tiger Bay, Cardiff, 411
Time magazine, 409
The Times, 29, 57, 64, 90, 122, 128, 134,
171, 176, 178, 229, 237, 239, 240,
338, 358, 366, 373, 421, 427, 444,
448, 451–2, 460, 464, 473, 476,
488, 493, 499
Tomkins, Sir Edward, 144
Tonbridge by-election (1956), 58
Torquay by-election (1956), 58
Torrington by-election (1958), 58–9, 63
The Tory Swindle (Labour election leaflet),
60–1
Townsend Ferries, 428
trade unions: and incomes policy, 76, 83,
95, 451; attitude to EEC
membership, 159; wage increases,
206, 220; and the Channel tunnel,
428; and the Beeching Plan, 434,
435–6, 437–8
Trades Union Council (TUC), 60, 77, 85,
435
transport: railways, 431–41; roads, 431,
432, 437, 438, 439, 440; rural buses,
441–2
Transport Act (1947), 435
Transport Act (1962), 435, 441

Transport Users Consultative Committee
(TUCC), 440
Treasury: Suez crisis, 18, 22; 1957 sterling
crisis, 46, 47, 49; 1959 Budget, 54;
1960 Budget, 65–6; economic
arguments with HM, 65; tax
regulators, 70; 1961 sterling crisis,
72, 73, 75–6; pay pause, 77; 1962
Budget, 81, 85; 1963 Budget, 87,
94–5; worried about inflation, 88;
and import controls, 96–7; and sale
of dollar portfolio, 97–8; 1964
Budget, 101; attitude to EEC, 107;
and EFTA of the Seven, 128–9; EEC
negotiations, 156, 161; opposition to
financial aid for Laos, 395; and the
Channel tunnel, 426, 429
Trend, Sir Burke, 1, 14, 55, 242–4, 257n.,
262, 267, 275, 278, 417, 438–9,
441–2, 477
Trevelyan, Sir Humphrey, 361–2, 397
Trinidad, 385
Truman, Harry, 282
Tunisia, 11, 160
Turkey, 10, 31, 38–9, 113, 340, 355–6, 416
Turton, Robin, 179, 227

U-2 spy plane, 337–8, 339–40
Uganda, 223, 279
UK Initiatives in Europe [Plan G], 108–9
Ulbricht, Walter, 349, 350, 359
unemployment, 51–2, 54–5, 57, 64, 418,
452
Union Routière, 424
Uniscan Free Trade Area Plan, 122, 127,
128–32
United Arab Republic, 32, 33, 37, 38
United Federal Party (Nyasaland), 250, 254,
259
United Nations (UN): Suez crisis, 18–24;
reopening of Suez Canal, 27; Muscat
rebellion, 30; and attempted
Communist take-over of Syria, 31;
1958 Middle East crisis, 40, 41–2;
and dissolution of Central African
Federation, 277; Berlin crisis, 344;
Cuban missiles crisis, 354, 358;
Quemoy crisis, 397–8
United Nations Committee on Colonialism,
273
United States of America: Anglo American
relations, 2–6, 25–7, 31, 43, 125,
132–5, 158, 303; Suez crisis, 19–23;
refuses to sell oil to Britain, 20, 22;
Thor missiles, 26, 284, 285;
reopening of Suez Canal, 29; Middle
East policy, 30; and attempted
Communist take-over of Syria, 30–1;
and Baghdad Pact, 31; 1958 Middle
East crisis, 33–44; import controls,
92; and sale of dollar portfolio,

97–9; and creation of EEC, 125, 131–2; and EFTA, 128, 145; and British application for membership of EEC, 135, 138, 142, 151, 155, 177; price leadership, 207; and Blue Streak, 284; and Britain's nuclear independence, 284–6; Polaris submarines, 287–97, 310–11, 312–16, 318–20; Skybolt missile, 287, 288, 290, 296–7, 305, 310–14, 317–18; tries to persuade Britain to give up nuclear weapons, 297–9, 302–3; and size of Britain's conventional forces, 298–9, 300–2, 316; Kennedy meets HM, 6, 299–300, 311–17, 342–3, 348–9, 359, 363–71, 386; nuclear tests, 303–9, 337, 344, 347; NATO multilateral force proposals, 311–12, 315; Berlin crisis, 325, 326–7, 329–36, 344–6, 347–9, 359–60; Khrushchev visits USA, 333–5, 337; Eisenhower meets HM, 337; failed Paris Summit (1960), 337, 338–41; U-2 spy plane shot down, 337–8, 339–40; Kennedy presidency, 341; Kennedy meets Khrushchev, 342; test ban negotiations, 350, 360–3, 369–76; Bay of Pigs invasion, 351–2; Cuban missiles crisis, 6, 351, 352–9, 361; and British Guiana, 364–7, 368, 369; Vietnam War, 377–82, 396; Korean War, 378, 386; and Laos, 382, 383, 384–96; South-East Asia Defence Treaty, 382; Quemoy crisis, 396–406; and the Profumo scandal, 477, 488–9

United States Air Force, 384
United States Atomic Energy Acts, 285
United States Navy, 384, 397

V bombers, 284, 287, 301, 312, 314
Vassall, John, 354, 452–3, 457, 460, 466, 470, 471, 480
Venice Conference (1956), 107–8
Versailles Treaty (1919), 304n., 350
Verwoerd, Hendrik, 242n., 246
Victoria Falls Conference (1963), 280, 281
Vienna, 342
Vientiane, 383, 384
Viet Cong, 384
Vietminh, 377, 382, 393–4
Vietnam *see* North Vietnam; South Vietnam
Vietnam war, 377–82, 396

wage restraint *see* incomes policy
Wakefield, Sir Wavell, 465
Walker, Peter, 497
Walker-Smith, Sir Derek, 13, 156, 179, 476, 477
War Office, 286, 422
Warburgs, 98

Ward, George, 283–4
Ward, Stephen, 13, 455–6, 457 and n., 463–9, 471–2, 474, 477, 481, 485, 489
Warsaw Pact, 335, 345, 371
Warwick by-election (1957), 58
Washington Post, 326
Watkinson, Harold: nuclear weapons policy, 286–7, 288–9, 290, 295, 296–7, 300, 301; nuclear tests, 308; and Laos, 387, 388, 390, 392, 393; Quemoy crisis, 404; 'night of long knives', 449
Watson, Duncan, 275
Watson, General Albert A., 348
Weekend Telegraph, 224
Welensky, Sir Roy, 242–3, 244–5, 267; creation of Central African Federation, 231, 232; and the Monckton Commission, 233–4, 244, 253–4; and the Devlin Report, 235, 236n., 241; meets HM, 245; and Banda's release, 247–8; Nyasaland Conference, 251–2; Northern Rhodesia Conference, 254–7; and Macleod's White Paper, 257–60; Northern Rhodesia franchise, 260–4, 267–70, 271–2; meets Butler, 273, 275; dissolution of Central African Federation, 11, 275–80
Wellington, Duke of, 430
West Bank, 40
West Germany: Schuman Plan, 102; and EFTA of the Seventeen, 116; EEC membership, 125, 148; and acceleration of Treaty of Rome, 135, 136; and Britain's EEC negotiations, 143, 172, 177, 198; Brussels Treaty, 289 and n.; NATO multilateral force proposals, 311; Berlin crisis, 322–37, 339, 343–6, 347–50, 359–60; East German refugees, 343; *Gastarbeiter* scheme, 416
West Indies, 153, 411, 413, 414, 415, 417, 418, 419–20
West Lothian by-election (1962), 88
Western European Union (WEU), 106, 141
Westminster Confidential, 458–60
Whitehead, Sir Edgar, 244, 245, 247, 248, 249, 255, 256, 258, 259, 269, 274, 277, 279
Wigg, Colonel George, 454, 460, 464–5
Williams, Sir Edgar, 234 and n., 235–6, 241, 242
Willis, Robert, 367
Wilson, Harold, 25, 198, 501; EEC negotiations, 9, 189; 1957 sterling crisis, 48–9; 1959 Budget, 56; 1959 General Election, 61, 62; attacks 1960 Budget, 67–8; 1961 Budget, 72; and the NEDC, 78; competition policy, 216; Cuban missiles crisis,

354, 356; immigration problem, 421; and the Channel tunnel, 431; transport policy, 442; and the Profumo scandal, 460, 464, 465–6, 467, 469, 470, 471, 473–4, 476, 477; and the Denning Report, 488; 1964 General Election, 101; as Prime Minister, 97, 98
Wilson, Sir Horace, 306
'Wind of Change' speech, 11, 246
Windscale, 320–1
Winnifrith, Sir John, 185–6 and n., 188
Wolseley, General Garnet, 422
Women's Press Club of London, 460
Wood, Richard, 77
Woodcock, George, 76n., 85, 435–6
Woolley, Harold, 146, 167n.
Wormser, Olivier, 120, 141, 142, 143, 144–5, 146, 147, 148–9, 152 and n., 155, 166, 169, 181, 198

Worsthorne, Peregrine, 473
Wright, Sir Michael, 32, 38, 39
Wright, Roy, 369
Wyn Harris, Sir P., 234 and n., 235–6
Wyndham, John, 12, 405, 457, 458

Yemen, 363
Young, Kenneth, 492
Young Conservatives, 492

Zambia, 11–12, 281; *see also* Northern Rhodesia
Zimbabwe *see* Southern Rhodesia
Zuckerman, Sir Solly, 297, 299, 308–9, 371
Zulueta, Philip de, 1, 6, 43–4, 123–4, 135, 151, 176, 189, 192, 203, 289, 291–2, 293, 296, 299, 303, 311, 318n., 336, 340, 347, 348, 364, 369, 391